P9-DGL-675

THE FEMALE WORLD

THE FEMALE WORLD

Jessie Bernard

THE FREE PRESS
A Division of Macmillan Publishing Co., Inc.
NEW YORK

Collier Macmillan Publishers
LONDON

The Free Press
A Division of Macmillan Publishing Co., Inc.
866 Third Avenue, New York, N.Y. 10022

Collier Macmillan Canada, Ltd.

Library of Congress Catalog Card Number: 80-69880

Printed in the United States of America

printing number

2 3 4 5 6 7 8 9 10

Library of Congress Cataloging in Publication Data

Bernard, Jessie Shirley
The female world.

Bibliography: p.
Includes indexes.
1. Women—Psychology. 2. Women—Social conditions.
I. Title.
HQ1206.B374 305.4'2 80-69880
ISBN 0-02-903000-5 AACR2

"... women possess a world of their own which is not comparable with the world of men."

Georg Simmel

"To be born a woman means to inhabit, from early infancy to the last day of life, a psychological world which differs from the world of the man."

Mirra Komarovsky

"Women live in such a different economic, cultural, and social world from men that their reactions cannot be understood from a master model developed in male society."

Berit Ås

"Because of our social circumstances, male and female are really two cultures and their life experiences are utterly different."

Kate Millett

Contents

Preface and Acknowledgments

A QUESTION AUTHORS are sometimes asked is, how long did it take you to write this book? The answer is, of course, it all depends. This particular book seems to have had a long gestation period (Lipman-Blumen, 1980). The need for it had been gnawing at me for some time. A skeletal version of Chapter 2—written in the early 1970s—appeared in 1978 (Bernard, 291-340), and finally the whole book wrote itself.

I am not at all sure that it is a good book—I am fully aware that I have spread myself too thin—but I am quite certain that it is, nevertheless, an important one. The next author, profiting by the mistakes made in this book, will do much better. I hope any errors of detail that may have escaped the eagle eye of my editor, Ms. Gladys Topkis, will not blunt the overall thrust of the book, which I see as twofold. The manifest, perhaps too manifest, sociology-of-knowledge theme attempts to overcome some of the inadequacies of current male-created knowledge. The second, more latent, theme has to do with providing women themselves with a view of their world from their own perspective. I hope such a view has a liberating effect on them by raising their self-evaluation, helping them to recognize the validity of their own experiences and the importance of their own part in the total societal structure. Writing it has had such an influence on me.

My indebtednesses are obvious. They are especially great to all the dedicated researchers—in history, literary criticism, economics, political science, psychology, and sociology—who have created the corpus of feminist scholarship on which I have leaned so heavily. I include all those who have sent me drafts of their as yet unpublished work. I could not possibly list them all and it would be invidious to single out specific names. I hope they will all feel at least partly rewarded by this anonymous thank you. I would like them to know how fruitfully they have contributed to my thinking.

PART I

Concepts and Collage

The premise of this book, stated in Chapter 1 and elaborated in Chapter 2, is that we all live in single-sex worlds and that most of what we know—from history, the humanities, the social and behavioral sciences—deals with the male world. What we do know about the female world from male research is how it impinges on the male world. This book assumes that the female world is worthy of study in and of itself, quite apart from its impact on the male world.

As a counterfoil to this more or less abstract discussion, Chapter 3 presents a collage of descriptive illustrations or examples of at least some aspects of the female world in operation. The search for complete or adequate illustrations proved a wild goose chase. For an adequate sample one would need to know the demographic structure for each example (age, status, class, group), as well as the networks, the coalitions, the issues, the boundary-maintenance devices (if any), the culture, the values, and so on.

As it is, only some of these items showed up in several of the examples located, and none showed up in all of them. But there were some interesting illustrations of different lifestyles among women-on-their-own and different ways in which women have lived together without men. Rather than discard them because of incompleteness, I have included them here on the assumption that if they were interesting to me, they might also be interesting to others.

1

Premise and Apologia

> By focusing on women and by addressing facts that have conventionally been ignored or taken for granted, we hope to reappraise old theories and pave the way for future thought. . . . Our conception of human social life will be broadened when they [theorists] address women's lives and strategies along with those of men. . . . We must integrate an interest in women into a general theory of society and culture. [Rosaldo and Lamphere, 1974, vi]

This statement by two anthropologists expresses the general perspective of this book; it seeks to broaden "our conception of human social life" by addressing "women's lives and strategies," but not—for reasons presented below—"along with those of men." The idea is to deal with the female world in and of itself, as an entity in its own right, not as a byproduct of the male world. The underlying premise is that most human beings live in single-sex worlds, women in a female world and men in a male world, and that the two are different from one another in a myriad of ways, both subjectively and objectively. R. D. Laing tells us that "insofar as we experience the world differently, in a sense we live in different worlds" (1971, 157). A major theme here is not only that women and men do indeed experience the world differently but also that the world women experience is demonstrably different from the world men experience. One primatologist, in fact, goes so far as to say that men and women constitute two different species (Hrdy, 1977), a statement that uses exaggeration for effect, no doubt, but nevertheless a quite supportable figure of speech.

All the data undergirding the premise of two single-sex worlds obviously cannot be presented here; that is the burden of the whole book. But a few minor cues can offer illustrations, if not "proof." At school, for example, at church, at work, at play, boys and girls and men and women are governed by different norms, rules of behavior, and expectations; they are subject to different eligibility rules for rewards and different vulnerability to punishments. Sometimes the differences are as great as the differences, if not between species, at least between countries.

The history of art provides an imaginary but nonetheless fact-based illustration. Imagine one country in which there are art schools and academies to teach and train artists, master artists to whom they can be apprenticed, salons in which to exhibit work, ways to cut down on expenses by sharing the cost of models, a student life where theories and ideas and news can be discussed. There are competitions and prizes for good work. There are common experiences and common understandings. Now imagine another country where there are no schools and academies, no apprenticeships, no salons in which to exhibit work, no ways to share expenses for models, no competitions for prizes, no shared student experiences, no opportunities to hear about theories, no exposure to current artistic ideas, no knowledge of the news in the art world. The world women lived in during the sixteenth century, which was, in fact, lacking in these amenities, was clearly a different world from that of their male contemporaries, which supplied them. This deprived female world is imaginary only in the sense that it was not geographically distant from the contemporary, resource-rich male world. It did not have to be geographically remote to be different. And if one extends this analogy to other areas—laboratories and scientific equipment, or coaching and athletic equipment—the extent of the differences between the two worlds becomes even more visible. Even in our own society today.

We recognize the two worlds in the behavior all around us. We know, for example, that both men and women behave differently in same-sex and mixed-sex groups and that the sex ratio in mixed sex groups also makes a difference (Ruble and Higgins, 1976); that in Iraq "a man's [mere] presence is enough to terminate a miming event among women" (Farrer, 1975, x); that in some cultures, including our own, certain expressive forms are sex-specific; that in some, certain tools are used by only one sex (Farrer, 1975, x); that almost universally, little conversation is reported between the sexes; that in Morocco, "men are ignorant of a body of women's folklore that comes into play only when women are together" (Farrer, 1975, x). Sometimes the two worlds are spatially separate, as, for example, in the case of purdah, or of Muslim seclusion of women. Sometimes, though not spatially separate, they are sociologically separate, each with its own symbolic system for maintaining boundaries between them.

Even when men and women are together, they elicit different responses. A woman is not responded to by a man in the same way that a man is responded to. This alone makes the situation different for the man and the woman being responded to. Nor do men and women see one another in the same way. The research literature by men (and by women who have been trained by men) portrays women as basically passive and dependent. This protrayal does in fact reflect the way women tend to behave vis-à-vis men or in the presence of men, so the passive-dependent image seems entirely valid from the perspective of the male world. That is the type of female behavior men see, deal with, interact with; it is taken for granted in the male world. Actually, of course, if women *were* passive and dependent they could hardly survive. In the female world on their own, they are active, aggressive if necessary, not dependent, at least not more so than anyone normally is. But this is not the scene the male world sees them in.[1]

Nor is the existence of these two worlds of recent origin; some of the data on which the two-world premise rests come from observational studies of subhuman primates and early hominids.

The Female World among Sub-Human Primates

Jane Lancaster, a primatologist, notes that although male primates "constitute only a small percentage of a primate society, they often receive more than their share of attention" (1973, 5). They are large and their behavior is conspicuous. So we know quite a bit about aggressiveness, dominance, and territoriality in the male primate world, but until the women researchers began to study it, "the social-political behavior of females and nonadults rarely was mentioned, let alone seriously studied." It is only recently that we have begun to learn about the intense, busy, active life in the female primate world. Although there is admittedly no way to reconstruct human social evolution nor any way to understand human social life today in terms of prehuman life, it is still interesting to remind ourselves how primordial the female world has always been.

The variety of ways in which animal social life has been organized is astonishing. One formal schema that brings some order into this diversity among primates takes this form (Scott, 1968, 344):

	Male	*Female*	*Young*
Male	male-male(s) (1)	female(s)-male (2)	young-male(s) (3)
Female	male-female(s) (4)	female-female(s) (5)	young-female(s) (6)
Young	male(s)-young (7)	female(s)-young (8)	young-young (9)

Since it is common for young males—"juveniles"—to leave the female-young grouping (cell 8) as soon as they are able, female-young groupings may be viewed as essentially all-female (cell 5) as far as adult females are concerned. And since multi-female, one-male groups (cell 4) preclude extensive interaction among males while encouraging it among females, they may be viewed as socially close to an all-female group.

The relative frequency of the several forms is difficult to determine. Still, in terms of frequency of occurrence and numbers involved, the female world has probably overshadowed the male world since before the emergence of homo sapiens. Thus, "except for solitary or monogamous mammals, the social systems of most mammals living in cohesive social groups have as a permanent core several related females and offspring" (Kleiman, 1977, 494). Kummer concludes that "the only pervading type of subgroup consists of a mother, her infant, and quite often its older siblings" (1971, 32). DeVore also notes that "females with immature offspring may form separate bands of their own" (1968, 353). Sometimes the females in a harem will go off by themselves to give birth and remain apart until the offspring can survive on their own. And among the chimpanzee, "a mother and her offspring form long-term social bonds. Female offspring remain with their mothers longer than males. The young of the same mother associate; long-term sibling ties develop and are maintained even after the mother's death" (Zihlman, 1978, 40). The lives of females in their world are lively, active, and intense. They cooperate, they help one another, they support one another. Little of what they do would seem strange, I feel sure, to modern women anywhere.

The nonhuman female primate—like her human counterpart—sometimes finds giving birth and having to take care of an infant a "surprising and baffling" experience (McGinnis and McGinnis, 1978, 28). She sometimes needs and gets help from others, especially from juvenile and adult females that happen to be without infants of their own at the time.

> Attracted to the infant, they frequently visit with the mother to watch and sniff the baby. When they find it away from its mother, they pick it up, play with it, or attempt to groom it. Whether the mother tolerates these interactions depends very much on the species. . . . In a captive colony of anubis baboons . . . nearly every mother finally allowed one female to hold and

> groom her baby. This role . . . usually fell to the mother's closest grooming companion. . . . Among the chimpanzees, the infant's older sisters are especially eager to handle it.[2] [Kummer, 80]

Although the female world tends to be stable, occupied with the daily business of living and undisturbed by the comings and goings of the males, its members can organize to protect themselves and their young against male misbehavior if necessary. Sometimes, for example, they join together in "coalitions" in "dominance encounters" against annoying or disturbing males (Lancaster, 1973, 7). Lancaster describes such a coalition in action among vervets against males monopolizing a favorite food resource or frightening an infant. "Even females from the lowest genealogies chased away males who made one of their infants scream" (7). Or annoyed another female. Thus, for example, "when a female screamed and solicited aid by glancing rapidly back and forth between the male and the females whose support she sought," the females' joint attack was fast and furious. They attacked, "running and usually screaming at the male," who would "turn and run as fast as he could until he reached the nearest tree or rock" (8). These protective females continued to threaten him for a while and then returned to their infants. If the male returned, it was "on their terms, not his." So "institutionalized" was this scenario that several times Lancaster saw "all the nearby adult males leave the vicinity, even though they were innocent of frightening the youngster" (8). From the perspective of the female primate world the males do not look all that impressive.

Understandably, primate society is matrifocal almost by definition. A matrifocal form of social organization has been found whenever field study has extended over a long enough period of time to establish the actual bond between specific, individual mothers and their offspring. There are usually several such subgroups in a troop. They include both males and females, although none of the males is the father of the offspring. Sometimes these units become large enough to include several generations, and the oldest female assumes a kind of matriarchal position. Although females seldom leave their native home range as males frequently do, their offspring will follow them if they do. Thus, if or when females migrate, the oldest one, with longer experience, is a kind of storehouse of knowledge, and, according to one observer, may therefore supply the background for important leadership decisions with respect to travel arrangements (Lancaster, 1973, 7). "Both field and captive studies suggest that it is the matrifocal core that provides a primate group with stability and continuity" (6). Observers who return after several years can still identify groups by the adult females; the males, on the other hand, have wandered away and become dispersed. "In one forest-living population of annubis baboons in Uganda . . .

groups can be defined only by their stable female membership" (Kummer, 1971, 12).

Because the male world, especially among primates, has received so much research attention, it does not seem necessary to give it "equal time," but at least a nod in its direction is warranted. In contrast to the seemingly warm and affectionate ambience of the female primate world, that of the male primate world seems less "sociable," even though males associate with other males more than females associate with either sex (Zihlman, 1978, 402). The quality, if not the quantity, of the social life seems different in the two worlds. Males who are left out of one-male groups "can either lead a solitary life . . . or they can join forces and form so-called all-male groups. . . . All-male groups are typical of open-country species, whereas solitary males are typical of the forest" (Kummer, 68). In an artist's rendition of a mountain gorilla troop, the dominant male stands alone, another male lies in a supine position all by himself, and "a solitary male . . . watches from afar" (Wilson, 1975, 540-541). Among one baboon group, a subadult male "sits near the group, separated from it by a few feet. . . . An old adult male may sit or groom with a big subadult male. Other adult males simply sit alone. About 20 percent of the adult males in the troop are singles that have no females of their own" (Kummer, 20, 22). A subtle kind of interaction is constantly operating among the males, including shifting, scratching, and moving about, as well as the usual grooming activity.

Even when the males are not expelled from the female world for gluttony or disorderly behavior, as noted above, they sometimes want to escape it. Thus Lawick-Goodall has noted that male chimpanzees, like their human counterparts today, take leave of the female world for all-male companionship from time to time. They often "travel about and feed in all-male groups and are more likely to groom each other than they are to groom females or youngsters" (1971, 186). A similar "escape" from the female world is reported among annubis baboons. "Some adult males occasionally leave their group to live solitarily or with another group for days or months" (Kummer, 1971, 12).

Escapism and Exclusivity of the Human Male World

After this brief excursus into the primate world, then, back to human beings. Hunting did make a difference among humans, but it probably exaggerated the two-world pattern of prehuman life. Lionel Tiger tells us that "males derive important satisfactions from male bonds and male interactions which they cannot derive from male-female bonds and interactions" (1970, 128). The initiation ceremony among preliterate societies serves, he says, as a symbolic break from the female world (172-73), a break that we noted also in the prehuman female world, from which young male juveniles either were excluded or escaped. And, as Lawick-Goodall has noted, the all-male city clubs, country clubs, faculty clubs, bars, pubs, and taverns that characterize the current scene in our society have strikingly similar analogues in the chimpanzee world; even today, millennia away from the hunting stage, men and women still spend most of their lives with other members of their own sex rather than with one another, whether at work or at play.

Because of the way in which work is divided and organized, women in the labor force associate mostly with women during the work day, as men do with men. So, too, with the housewife. Most of her time that is not devoted to her relationships with her children—and some of that too—is spent in relationships with other women, as is true of many subhuman females described above, and no doubt was true of primitive human females also.

A great deal of the leisure as well as work time of both men and women is spent with members of the same sex. A well-known study of Bethnal Green, a British community, reported, for example, that "for many men the bar in the pub was as much a part of their living space as the room in their home, with the difference that one was more or less reserved for members of their own sex while the other was not" (Young and Willmott, 1962). It was in this all-male environment that men found "conversation, warmth, and merriment." Thorne and Henley (1975, 265-266) cite another British study, of the miner's all male world (J. Klein, 1965, in Thorne and Henley, 1975). "Within the culture of miners, there is strong segregation between the sexes. The woman's place is in the home; the man's place is outside it, in his world of work, and with male friends at the club, the pub, the corner, the sports ground. 'It is with other men that they are at their most relaxed, at ease and emotionally expansive'; the bond between men is so deep that in some ways they form a secret society." LeMasters reports a similar situation in taverns in the United States (1975). Even the social life organized on a couple basis tends to fall apart, with the women congregating at one end of the room and the men at the other. Aside from the playful flirtation that is often permitted, what do the men and women have in common? What is there for them to talk about? And anyway, how much time is actually spent in even this couple-organized leisure-time activity?[3]

The dependency relationship of a wife to her husband in our society may determine almost every other relationship between them, but the total amount of time the husband spends each day interacting with her is small. Anthropologist Ray Birdwhistell reportedly found that the average married couple in the United States spends only about twenty minutes a week in direct conversation with each other (R. Bell, 1975). In a review of research on working class wives, Samuels found that they have "little expectation of friendship or companionship" from their husbands. They seek these kinds of relationships from other women. "The most intimate communication is almost exclusively feminine, with daily contact between the blue-collar woman and her mother or sisters." (1975, 8)

"Togetherness" is not the same for males and females. Because women have been the child carers and homekeepers, they have had a shorter tether than men; in most marriages they could safely be taken for granted. Even if a peripatetic husband was not present or, if present, was not talking or even interacting, the wife was still "there" serving as a stabilizer of his life. In another context, Lofland (1976) speaks of this idea of the "thereness of women." The amount of psychological time a husband spends with his wife is not necessarily the same as the amount of psychological time his wife is "spending" with him. Her round-the-clock "thereness" can amount to more time than the time he spends in her presence. He can go about his business secure in the knowledge that she is there to listen, to respond, to interact when or if he needs her. She cannot be so sure about his "thereness."

Nor does sex provide much "togetherness." It is reported that intercourse takes an average of only about two minutes, with three to ten seconds of this time occupied by the male orgasm (McCarthy, 1978). Participants in a conference dealing with the subject estimated that couples in their thirties spend an average of only thirty to forty hours per year in sexual activity (Ojai Conference, 1977).

Not only do men distance themselves regularly or sporadically[4] from the female world, retreating into their own, but they also positively exclude women from their world. A fast-growing research and expository corpus is now documenting and illustrating in detail and on a wide scale the many exclusionary techniques—explicit and implicit, blatant and subtle—used today to keep women off male turf or to discourage them from remaining if they do enter (Bernard, 1976c). The resulting one-sex world has been documented extensively in ethnic and working-class studies (Gans, 1962, chapter 11); it exists also in the country-club set.[5]

Some of the countless exclusionary patterns whose function is to preserve the male turf from the incursion of females are literally segregative in the spatial sense, such as male hangouts like those referred to above, where women are not even permitted to enter.[6] Some are not spatial in the physical sense but are segregative in the psychological or symbolic sense.[7] Language, for example, is a nonspatial way to keep the two worlds at least conceptually distanced from one another, since anything that has the effect of hampering or barring communication can serve as a segregating mechanism. Language is, in fact, one of the most powerful devices used by the miners in the study cited earlier for "deliberately excluding women, children, and strangers, partly through 'pit-talk' or swear-words used familiarly within the group, and offensively to those outside" (J. Klein, 1965, 265-266). Curse words, swearing, profanity, and obscenity have been permitted to men, forbidden to women. The control power inherent in language is one of the basic components in the male world (see Chapter 16).

Sometimes the separation of the worlds becomes even more definitive—permanent rather than temporary or occasional. Leslie Fiedler has commented on the fact that in the American novel the archetypical hero from Rip Van Winkle down has been a man fleeing from the female world into his own escapist world (1960, xx-xxi). The fleeing male has also been reported in the history of the West as well as in urban history. He showed up in the middle of the nineteenth century as the "tramp" (Demos, 1974). He is well known in the social work literature as well, in the guise of the "homeless man" (Bernard, 1981).

Sometimes discussed among feminists are the pros and cons of separatism as a deliberate policy. Actually, the separatism is there, whether it is deliberately sought or rejected on ideological principles. The basic issue is not whether to encourage it but how best to use it.

Misogyny of the Male World

The male world is not only segregative and exclusionary vis-à-vis the female world but is even, in varying degrees, positively hostile to it. It is quite easy for observers, even scientific observers, to read human emotions into the behavior of the animals they observe, as did for example, Konrad Lorenz. Pairs of penguins and birds and ducks can look like loving spouses, but how the males feel toward females outside these pair-bonds is not easy to observe. Among human beings, though, there is clear evidence that although individual men may love individual women with great depth and devotion, the male world as a whole does not.[8] Terms like "hatred" or "hostility" may be too strong to describe this response, so the term "misogyny" has been invented. As long as women know their place and keep in it, misogyny need not rear its ugly head. Women are "dears" and "lovelies." But when they intrude on the male world, they become "damfool women." Not many men except *entre nous* are as candid about their dislike for the company of women as the one who wrote in the July, 1966 issue of the *Yale Alumni Magazine:* "Gentlemen—Let's face it—charming as women are—they get to be a drag if you are forced to associate with them each and every day" (6). And also among working-class men: "it is difficult to talk with the men and women who frequent The Oasis [bar] without feeling that somehow these two groups of people are not very compatible. The men prefer the company of other men. . . . This blue-collar man . . . prefers men as a species to women; except for sexual purposes, he finds women dull and uninteresting" (LeMasters, 1975, 102).

This male misogyny is expressed in numerous ways including verbal putdowns, insults, and disparaging remarks. The English language itself is denigrating to women (see Chapter 16). There are, for example, more pejorative terms for women than for men, as well as more derogatory animal terms applicable to women than to men (Eble, 1972). A survey of insults among males in a hundred languages found more addressed to females or involving females than males (Gregerson, 1977). A woman may love an individual man and derive happiness from his emotional reciprocation but she derives little happiness from the male world as such (Chapters 2, 6).

Although its separatism, exclusionism and misogyny may help us understand the male world, to elaborate further on them would be to succumb to the temptation to deflect the discussion to the male world—as so much discussion of the female world tends to do—instead of hewing to the female line. This goal is harder to achieve than one might suppose because so much of human knowledge comes to us through a "prism of sex" (Sherman and Beck, 1979; Snyder, 1979).[9] As a result of this male bias in human learning, it is almost impossible even to conceive of a female world as an entity in and of itself, with its own character, its own validity, its own legitimacy.[10] It is invisible (Ås, n.d. 145; 1979, draft).[11]

Righting an Intellectual Balance

Some readers will find the deliberate omission of the male world glaring, in and of itself a form of misanthropy. I recognize the logic of such an argument. No misanthropy is intended. The intent is, rather, to achieve an intellectual balance. It is the male world that has been the major focus of practically all research in literature, history, and the social sciences from Plato and Aristotle through Hobbes and Adam Smith right down to modern academic social scientists. An almost inexhaustible corpus of descriptions, analyses, interpretations, and explanations of the male world has resulted. Since virtually all of human knowledge is thus a male creation, such knowledge deals only with a world seen through male eyes.[12] It would, therefore, only be carrying coals to Newcastle to include the "lives and strategies of men" in a discussion of the female world.

Some will object that, according to the old cliché, "it takes two to tango," the two sexes live in worlds so inextricably intertwined that one cannot be examined without reference to the other. True. Still, the male world has been observed, studied, researched, analyzed, and interpreted with a minimum recognition of the female world, with in fact hardly a glance in its direction. It has, so to speak, intellectually tangoed by itself.

There are negative consequences of the neglect of the female world. It limits our intellectual horizons. Arlene Daniels illustrates how the criteria used in selecting the objects of research attention bias the picture: "The exclusion of women from the 'real' or 'important' world of sociological investigation arises because of the more general belief that what women do is trivial and not worthy of scientific enterprise. Those experiences that make [the world of] women different from [that of] men and that might provide them with unique or unusual approaches to the problems presented within this enterprise are excluded from attention" (1975, 346). Robert Hefner reminds us of another "cost" of the uneven balance. He notes that although topics such as discrimination, oppression, segregation, class, caste, and the like have attracted a considerable amount of attention from male students, the application has not included their impact on women: "Apparently, the consciousness of social scientists on matters of sex discrimination, sexism and feminism has simply not yet reached a level where these concerns become manifest in most of their work" (1975, draft).

Whether due to lack of challenge, to intellectual misogyny, or simply to unraised consciousness, the result has been the same: inadequate attention to and therefore ignorance of the female world.[13] It has remained terra incognita. With restrictive consequences for the corpus of human knowledge. Even when there has been research dealing with women, it has tended to be about the male world, about the relationship of women to men in marriage, or the place of women in the male work world. Whether carried out by men or by women, it has tended to reflect the male point of view. It has often missed or ignored what did not interest men, who could not see women except in relation to themselves, at home or in the work force. From where they stood, all they could see was how women fit into their world. From any other perspective women were ciphers or, in any event, uninteresting as subjects of study. Much of what is known is therefore fairly superficial. For "surface structure may express the male view of the world," as anthropologist Edwin Ardener tells us, "obscuring the existence at deeper levels of an autonomous female view" (Farrer, 1975, xi).

There is one more "balance" to be righted, this time involving a corollary to the "ignore-ance" of the female world by male researchers. Since they were not interested in the female world, it did not occur to them to ask whether their findings about the male world also applied to the female world. They seem to have assumed implicitly a kind of sexual symmetry, that is, that whatever existed in the male world also existed in the female. The discussions here do not attempt to determine whether or not the phenomena described occur in both worlds and no assumption is made either way, that they do or that they do not. It makes little difference in studying the female world that it is either unique or the same as the male world. It is important in its own right. The female world is seen here not as the "other" but as autonomous and worthy of study in and of itself without regard to the male world.

But why did not women fill in the lacunae in the corpus of knowledge? Because, like their fellow students, they were trained by men transmitting male-created knowledge. As a result of the screening-out practices referred to above in the creation of knowledge, until recently academic curricula reflected the same biases. What training women scholars received was training in the male canon. A major paradigm shift was required to overcome this defect in their training. It is only recently, therefore, that women scholars have undertaken serious research specifically on the female world with the attitude that it is worthy of consideration in and of itself. Thus, only now is there emerging among women researchers in a variety of disciplines a no longer negligible concern with new conceptualizations dealing with the world women live in. Women anthropologists challenge the assumptions of conventional research in their discipline that women are scientifically uninteresting and they emphasize the theoretical importance of studies of women for our general understanding of human social life (Rosaldo and Lamphere, 1974, vi). There is a groping in the other social sciences also toward a way of seeing women as more than an aggregate of individuals who differ from men in crucial ways, or as mere sex-role performers, or as persons who occupy a status in the male world. These researchers seek a way to think about women in terms of the relationships among women *qua* women. In brief, no longer simply as the "other."[14] For the present, therefore, a kind of intellectual "affirmative action" seems to be called for; that is, until we have caught up in our knowledge of the female world, it seems justifiable for us to imitate this particular male mistake and concentrate exclusively on the female world to the extent that this is feasible.[15]

So much, then, for the fundamental premise of this book: namely, that there does exist a female world separate and distinct from the male world, intellectually neglected, and worthy of study in its own right. But to recognize the existence of such a female world and to grant the validity of studying it does not mean that one can follow through with a clear-cut typology and adequate formulation of its exact nature—its operation, for example, or its dynamic, its structure, its characteristic processes, its boundaries—or of the way it interweaves with the male world, or of how it has changed and is changing. Nor even, in fact, does it mean that there is an adequate conceptual tool kit available for studying it. In Chapter 2 we make an attempt to deal with this task.

Notes

1. An analogue in the other direction is the view women have of men. The times when they have the full and interested attention of men is when the men are "horny," sexually interested if not actually aroused. Or when they are in need of nurturing (hungry, sick, depressed). This is the way men present themselves to women, so this is the picture women have of them. Women do not see men in the locker room or during all those hours when they are not sexually turned on, when they are absorbed in their work or in one another. Thus whole areas of the male personality are not perceived by women.
2. Such interest in infants does not seem to be limited to females. Adult males may also show keen interest in infants and may even adopt them. Such interest may not, however, be disinterested, for adopting young females is one way to start a harem of one's own (Kummer, 1971, 82). The possessiveness of the mother in some species vis-a-vis their infants resembles the possessiveness of dominant males vis-à-vis their females.
3. Weisberger, reviewing the LeMasters book, notes that skilled well-paid workers, not assembly-line robots, "go straight from the job to the bar with their pals, return home as late as possible to hunker down before the TV set, and spend restless Sundays visiting or tinkering. Their favorite recreations are hunting and fishing on a strictly stag basis" (*Washington Post,* May 28, 1975). He calls this behavior "matchless examples of male bonding."
4. Sometimes the segregation is partial, so that "one does not so much deal with segregation as with segregative punctuation of the day's round, thus ensuring that subcultural differences can be reaffirmed and reestablished in the face of contact between the sexes. It is as if the joining of the sexes were tolerable providing periodic escape is possible; it is as if equality and sameness were a masquerade that was to be periodically dropped. And all of this is done in the name of nicety, of civilization, of the respect owed females, or of the 'natural' need of men to be by themselves" (Goffman, 1977, 316).
5. Item: "At Burning Tree—the 'Club of Presidents' . . .—women in 1975 are still as welcome as tourists at the Central Intelligence Agency. 'Women distinguish Burning Tree by their absence,' declares *The History of Burning Tree,* a recounting of the 53-year-old club's growth into one of the most famous golf clubs in the world. . . . Several club members make it clear they intend to keep Burning Tree as one of the last eight to ten all-male golf clubs in the country and the only one in the Washington area. . . . More

than one decision of the board has been motivated in large part by the grim determination to prevent any breach in the dike keeping the lovelies out" (Bredemeier, 1975). A woman cabinet member, Oveta Culp Hobby, and Lady Astor were refused permission to play. The horror of the presence of women traces back to a time more than fifty years ago when a "foursome of males had to endure a bunch of damfool women playing in front of them."

6. In the Klein study of miners, "a woman going into the office [of a bookie] is subjected to jokes and language which in a more neutral locality would lead to a fight" (1965, 265).
7. In the European shtetl an elaborate avoidance system prevailed to prevent any violation of the separating rules: "Separation of the sexes is obligatory. . . . Most men . . . learn to glance sideways with a look that sees and does not see. . . . If a difficult social situation forces a very orthodox man to shake hands with a woman, he deftly slips his caftan over his hand to avoid contact" (Zborowski and Herzog, 1952, 137).
8. Item: "A wife may call her husband [via the Citizen's Band] out beyond the inshore lobster pots, and complain: 'I don't care whether those fish are biting or not. Supper's on the table, and you'd better get back here fast!' To which he may reply, to the delight of all male eavesdroppers, 'Honey, if it was not for sex, men would kill every woman in the world within forty-eight hours!'" ("No Comment," Ms. Magazine, May, 1978, 105).
9. A classic example is a statement by W. S. Laughlin: "Hunting is the master behavior pattern of the human species. It is the organizing activity which integrated the morphological, physiological, genetic and intellectual aspects of the individual human organism and of the populations who compose our single species. Hunting is a way of life, not simply a 'subsistence technique,' which importantly involves commitments, correlates, and consequences spanning the entire bio-behavioral continuum of the individual and of the entire species of which he is a member. Man evolved as a hunter, he spent over 99 percent of his species' history as a hunter, and he spread over the entire habitable area of the world as a hunter" (quoted in Tiger, 1970, 122-123). Where were the women? What were they doing? How did hunting integrate the morphological, physiological, genetic, and intellectual aspects of *their* organism?
10. I once sat next to an insurance salesman on a plane trip. After the usual pleasantries, he asked about my trip, and I told him I was going to a meeting at which the topic was to be mothers and daughters. That intrigued him—I suppose they are the beneficiaries of much of the insurance he sells—but what interested me was his reply: "I have one of each." He could not see women except as related to him.
11. An examination of the course offerings in any department of sociology, for example, shows a plethora of courses on how the male component of the social structure operates, courses about occupations, mobility, power, aggression, achievement, stratification, competition, conflict, economic inequality, minorities—in brief, primarily about the world of men. Women appeared in these curricula in discussions of either their status in the male world or of marriage and the family. The first tends to deal with women in

the labor force but it is still about the male world. The second, sometimes called the "female intellectual ghetto," is often also from a male perspective. Essentially the same or similar points can be made about other disciplines.

12. Since a disproportionate amount of that knowledge in recent times has been created by white men in the West, especially the United States, it is even more restricted in its perspective. What we know most about, therefore, is the male world in western society since the end of the eighteenth century. What we know outside this focus is usually in terms of how it impinges on that particular male world.
13. Indeed, such "ignore-ance" of the female world is one of the major grievances of feminist scholarship. From the point of view of women, one of the most painful manifestations of misogyny has been the male contempt for feminist scholarship, the refusal to grant it validity or worth, its often patronizing brushoff. In the nineteenth century, Americans were offended by "a certain condescension in foreigners"; thus James Russell Lowell (1869) quoted Carlyle's contemptuous question, "Who reads an American book?" The male world sometimes shows the same kind of condescension and asks in effect: "Who reads a book written by a woman?" Other products of the female world—of its artists, painters, sculptors, musicians—are also disparaged because they do not necessarily conform to male conceptions and the parochialism of the male world often prevents it from even attempting to understand the female perspective (Bernard, 1980a). Daniel G. Freedman gives a sociobiological interpretation: "It is apparently imperative for the male to feel superior to the female—or at least unafraid—for continuously successful copulations, and it may well be for this reason that males everywhere tend to demean women, belittle their accomplishments, and, in the vernacular . . . 'put them down.' I have not heard of a culture in which the males do not engage in this chauvinistic sport" (1979, 61).
14. Some years ago, when I published *Marriage and Family among Negroes* (1966), I did not view black institutions merely as deviations from those of whites. I viewed them as autonomous, worthy of study in and of themselves without regard to how they compared with the white world. The approach here with respect to sex is analoguous to that one with respect to race.
15. Still, sometimes the male world has to be referred to if only as a control. And, as we shall note, the basic parameters defining the female world are often the relative degree and kind of its isolation or separation from the male world and the relative degree of its autonomy and independence from that world.

2

Conceptualizing the Female World

The Concept of "World"

What do you *mean,* "female world"? Even if one accepts the premise that this world exists, though no satisfactory typology for dealing with it has yet emerged, one must still have some kind of handle for conceptualizing it. The characterization "female" is not too problematic—although our growing knowledge about transsexualism makes it more so now than it may have been in our self-assured past—but what about "world"?

Admittedly, the term is inadequate. But, even lacking as it does the scientific credentials for carrying the weight of detailed sociological analysis, it is nevertheless well-enough understood for everyday communication and, in the present context, useful as a starting point. We usually know what is being referred to when someone speaks of the theatrical world, the sports world, the dance world, the music world, the world of fashion, the world of finance, the scientific world, the suburban world, the business world, the gambling world, the academic, publishing, literary, even the chess world, the world of born-again Christians, of the jet set or beautiful people. A complex society like ours literally encompasses scores of such worlds. We might be hard put to define these worlds, but that there is something real involved hardly anyone would deny. All have their heroes and heroines, their lores, their myths, their language and vocabulary, their beliefs, codes, styles and structures. The female and male worlds are only more comprehensive and more complex. It would be hard to find another term that would encompass the same meaning. "Community" is not quite right. Nor "group." Nor "set." Nor "coterie." Nor any other word at all. What else could we call the Christian world? the political world? the racing world? the fantasy world? the world of make believe? the gambling world? the sailing world? the upper-class world? the world of the slum?

The abridged *Oxford English Dictionary* devotes two columns to definitions of the word "world." I select for use here a definition dating back to 1673: "a group or system of things or beings associated with some common characteristics (denoted by a qualifying word or phrase), or considered as constituting a unity." The "common characteristics" here are those of the female sex. The unity in the definition does not, of course, imply "consciousness of kind," solidarity, undifferentiated homogeneity, or perpetual sweetness and light. Sometimes, as the definition implies, the unity is imputed.

Conceptualizing the Female World

There are several ways to conceptualize the female world, and which one we use makes a difference in our thinking. The easiest and most naive way is simply on the basis of biology, as a collectivity or aggregate of individuals with clear-cut and unequivocal anatomical characteristics. To be sure, as noted above, research on transsexuality has made the boundaries of such a world more and more equivocal;[1] but male-female is still the simplest way to view the two worlds, that is, the male world as identical with the male sex and the female, with the female sex. Simple. But it is inadequate because a collectivity or an aggregate as a paradigm for a sociological world washes out its essential qualities, its structure, its culture, its "style." Other conceptualizations that have been used are in terms of "place," of occupation, of culture, of ethnic group, and of "sphere."

Conceptualization in terms of *place* has been perhaps the commonest—place, that is, in the male world. This conceptualization has tended to serve as a weapon in conflict in the hands of militant feminists. They have used male intellectual tools against male stereotypes. Some have appropriated Marxist analyses and seen women as a class, a proletariat vis-à-vis the male bourgeoisie. Or as a caste. Or as a minority group. Or as a marginal group. Or, by analogy with blacks, as "niggers." Simone de Beauvoir—invoking half a dozen sociological categories—has conceptualized the female world as an encapsulated enclave in the male world:

> Sometimes the "feminine world" is contrasted with the masculine universe, but we must insist . . . that women have never constituted a closed and independent society; they form an integral part of the group, which is governed by males and in which they have a subordinate place. They are united only in a mechanical solidarity from the mere fact of their similarity, but they lack that organic solidarity on which every unified community is based; they are always compelled— . . . in clubs, salons, social-service institutes—to band together in order to establish a counter-universe, but they always set it up within the frame of the masculine universe. Hence the paradox of their situation: they belong at one and the same time to the male world and to a sphere in which that world is challenged; shut up in their world, surrounded by the other, they can settle down nowhere in peace. [53, 562][2]

It is, of course, legitimate, even essential, to study women's place in the male world, but such legitimacy does not preclude the necessity for studying women's world in its own right. Furthermore, the "place" conceptualization implies a misconception, namely that the male world is the "real" world, coterminous with society as a whole. The male world is not the whole social system, not the whole of society, nor, as is sometimes implied, even the "mainstream." It takes both the female and the male world to add up to the "real" world. The female world is as much a part of society and even of the "mainstream," as the male. The "place" conceptualization of the female world tells us more about the male world than it does about the female. The concept of an autonomous female world does not imply complete isolation from the male world any more than it implies that it is only a "place" in the male world.

It is, of course, true, as Beauvoir states, that the female world is not closed and independent. It is equally true that it is integrated with the male world. Just as, of course, it is true that the male world is integrated with the female world. But the female, like the male, world is also a separate entity, more than simply a class or caste or enclave or mere appendage to the male world. And we do indeed have "to clarify the paradoxes of women's position, both isolated and integrated" (Faragher and Stansell, 1975, 162).

Related to, but not identical with, the "place" conceptualization, however "place" itself is conceptualized—as class, caste, minority group, enclave—is one in terms of occupation. The female world is viewed as analogous to, say, the organization man's world (Whyte, 1956), the railroader's world (Cottrell, 1940), the lawyer's world (Smigel, 1970), or the blue-collar worker's world (Shostak and Gomberg, 1964). The analogous occupational world of women would thus be the world reflected in women's pages, women's magazines, with their strong emphasis on child care, nutrition, food processing, homemaking skills, consumership in general and, increasingly, voluntary community work. Not exactly the Kinder, Küche, Kirche concept, but not too far beyond it (Tuchman, Daniels, and Benet, 1978). Analyses of the nineteenth-century cult of domesticity, the home economics movement, the current discussions of the homemaker's role, and the growing number of studies of the media version of women contribute to our knowledge of this occupational conceptualization of the female world. But they do not encompass all the parameters of that world.

Quite different from either the "place" conceptualization, with its conflict orientation, or the occupational conceptualization is another that has a different connotation—namely, one in terms of culture, with its essentially benign implications. Although the concept of culture has exerted enormous influence on our thinking, at least since the publication of Ruth Benedict's *Patterns of Culture* in 1934, consensus as to its precise definition has not yet been achieved. Indeed, in one approach to the study of women, they are, as representations of Nature, excluded from culture altogether (Ortner, 1974, 67-68). Still, the concept of a female culture has found proponents.

Faragher and Stansell tell us that in the nineteenth century "a distinctly female sub-culture emerged from 'women's sphere' " (1975, 152). They define subculture as the " 'habit of living'. . . of a minority group which is self-consciously distinct from the dominant activities, expectations, and values of a society" (152). In the case of the women they were studying—participants in the great westward movement of the nineteenth century—child-rearing, religious activity, education, home life, associationism, and female communality were the constituents of a female subculture. Profound female friendships constituted the actual social bonds among its members (152-153). The authors admit that the concept is hazy and ill defined but, for want of a better, they consider it useful.

E. E. LeMasters also accepts the culture conceptualization of the female world. He considers it important to distinguish male and female cultures in preparing young people for marriage. If they know how different the two cultures are, he argues, young people would be less bewildered when they have to adjust to them in marriage (1957, chaps. 22, 23). His analysis of the two cultures was admittedly superficial, but he hoped it would be adequate to soften contacts between members of "alien" (Smith-Rosenberg's term [1975, 28]) worlds.

More recently, Patrick C. Lee and Nancy B. Gropper have proposed a conceptualization of culture around sex roles, so that instead of viewing sex roles as an aspect of culture, female culture is viewed as a product of the female role and male culture of the male role. They see the components of such cultures as "rituals, roles, dress customs, gestures," communication patterns, reference groups, and artifacts of sex role—that is, the "visible properties and practices of sex role as it is reflected in everyday life" (1974, 371). In a related way, Ås sees female culture as "a complex, comprehensive, and potent system of values which are shared by most women" (n. d., 145).

Some of the more militant feminists deny both the existence of a female culture and the value or necessity of creating one. "Women," says one such critic, "neither have an independent culture, nor participate freely in male culture. Now, to lack a culture is a hideous thing. Because it is to some extent supportive, and provides a retreat from fear, its participants value it" (Battle-Sister, 1971, 419). She notes that some women are therefore trying to create a female culture, "complete with counter-institutions . . . [including] day-care centers, communes, female literary magazines and journals, apprentice training programs, and women's institutes" (419). But, argues this author, if such a female culture is to be merely a placebo, a comforting cacoon, a retreat from the male world, it will be futile, "easily neutralized, easily co-opted, and [will] essentially change nothing." It might even be counterproductive. For "culture is a political phenomenon, dependent upon and reinforcing the social structure in which it is located. Counter-culture, stripped of a power base, is politically meaningless" (420). Battle-Sister believes, in fact, that the very absence of a female culture may turn out to be an advantage.

Berit Ås, a Norwegian sociologist who has been studying the concept of female culture for almost a decade, combines both the conflict and the support emphasis in her approach, which serves, in effect, as a rebuttal to Battle-Sister. Her concern is mainly to correct the "false and insufficient picture of women" that neglect of female culture fosters; a second concern is "to offer a therapeutic tool to support self-reliance and cultural consciousness in women"; and finally, a third is "to politicize certain problems common to women" (1979). Although a suitable conceptualization of the female world has to be more than a stick for use in attacking the male world,[3] recognizing the existence of a female culture as part of the female world, quite independent of its relations to the male world or male culture, has, I believe, great benefits for female understanding.

Quite aside from pro or con ideological arguments, there is a legitimate basis for viewing the female world in cultural terms if cultures are conceptualized as encompassing systems of institutions. The institutions women participate in are not the same as those men participate in (Bernard, 1975, 265). We know, for example, that the labor market in which women participate is not the same as that in which men participate, that occupational segregation by sex is the rule (Blaxall and Reagan, eds., 1976). The marriages of wives are different from those of husbands in terms of the rules that govern them (Bernard, 1972, chap. 1). Women do, indeed, live in a "culture" with rules or norms—whether legislated or crescive in nature—that are different from those governing men. It would not, therefore, be too fanciful to speak of separate cultures in this sense.

Related to all three of these conceptualizations—place, occupation, culture—is one that sees the female world as analogous to ethnic groups (Hefner, 1975, draft). Hefner notes that this analogy brings into possible use broad areas of research that have been cultivated in other contexts but not applied to women, such as the psychology of prejudice, the sociology of segregation, of solidarity, pluralism, assimilation, melting pot, and the like. He does not deny that the unique sexual bond between individual men and women negates the conceptual validity in its application to much of the thinking dealing with ethnic groups. Still, he thinks the ethnic analogy is worth exploring, for it is true that both ethnic groups and the female world have structures, that both have characteristic cultures—customs, traditions, mores—"consciousness of kind," and other attributes of a sociological world. But the uniqueness of a one-sex world sets it off from any standard sociological model. And the ethnic-group conceptualization is no more successful than the culture conceptualization in communicating the dynamism called for; like the cultural conceptualization, it is too static.

A conceptualization of the female world in terms of women's separate *sphere* enjoyed great favor in the nineteenth century and well into the twentieth. It was one of the few conceptualizations with a self-conscious ideological basis, one that saw the female world as autonomous though functionally integrated with the male world. Although it was primarily a male construct, there were women—like Catharine Beecher—among its proponents (Sklar, 1973).[4] We defer attention to this important conceptualization to Chapters 4 and 5 below.

Our conceptualization of the female world is mainly in terms of the admittedly inadequate dictionary definition of a system of beings with some common characteristic that is considered as constituting a unity. The term "system" implies structure. The female world in this view is a sociological entity with a characteristic demographic structure (age, marital status, education, income, occupation), a status and class structure, and a group structure, a sociological entity with a characteristic culture. A sociological entity with its own boundary-maintenance system, but also with faultlines. On the optimistic assumption that this general conceptualization of the female world is accepted, we proceed on much thinner ice to the problem of trying to characterize it. The approach is roundabout, in terms of a series of polarities that have challenged social theorists for almost two hundred years and which, I hope to show, have relevance here.[5]

An Indirect Approach to Characterizing the Female World: Polarities

Half a century ago, F. Scott Fitzgerald pointed out that if a sleeping student in a given college course were called upon, all he had to do on waking up was to say "supply and demand" and the professor would consider his answer correct. In another course today he might say "industrialization and urbanization." The phenomena subsumed under these rubrics do indeed explain a great deal about modern life, including the current female world. And the contrast between the preurban, preindustrial world of small solidary kin- and locale-based groups on one side and the urban, industrial, impersonal world on the other was a major preoccupation of social thinkers in the nineteenth century and remains so in the twentieth. All kinds of relationships changed in this transition. A variety of conceptualizations—not based on sex differences, be it noted right off—were offered to describe and to interpret the changes. Most of the theorists were men, and gender was not attached to any of the concepts they derived.

Among the polarities was one proposed by a British jurist, Sir Henry Maine (1861). He contrasted societies in which relationships were based on status with those in which they were based on contract. In a status-based society, duties, obligations, and privileges adhered to certain positions in society. In a society operating on a contractual basis, duties, obligations, and privileges were specified and limited to those agreed upon by the involved parties themselves; beyond these agreed-upon specifications there were no legitimate demands or obligations. The theory was used to explain the changes in human relationships then in process as the West became industrialized.

A German sociologist, Ferdinand Tönnies (1887), saw the change in terms of a contrast between *Gemeinschaft* and *Gesellschaft*, terms which—though a French sociologist, Emile Durkheim, did not consider them susceptible to precise translation—are commonly interpreted to mean community—in the social or psychological sense rather than limited to the physical sense,[6]—and capitalism. Some writers saw the new capitalist world of *Gesellschaft* as lethal to the human spirit, signalling an enormous human loss, that resulted in widespread alienation, leaving modern human beings in a futile "quest for community."

Another set of contrasting systems or polarities was propounded by Pitirim Kropotkin (1903), a Russian thinker, on one side and Herbert Spencer (1862), an English social philosopher, on the other. Kropotkin taught that mutual aid was a major factor in the survival of the species by natural selection, and he looked to its expansion in the future: "The current of mutual aid and support . . . flows still even now, and it seeks to find out a new expression which . . . would . . . be superior [to that of the past] in its wider and more deeply humane conception" (1975, 207). Spencer, on the other hand, exalted the more "rugged-individualistic" factors in his theory of the struggle for existence and the survival of the fittest individuals. Throughout the latter part of the nineteenth century, advocates of mutual aid fought for the solidary vision and classical economists for the competitive (not conflict or Marxist) version. Reformulated, this polarity resonates among the sociobiologists today in their conceptions of individual versus group selection.[7]

In more recent times there have been other polarities. Sociologist C. H. Cooley, for example, contrasted the world of primary-group relationships with the more abstract, impersonal, often brutalizing world of institutions: "We are . . . led to create a kind of institution which . . . may brutalize or ossify the individual, so that primary idealism in him is almost obliterated" (1909, 53). Ruth Benedict, borrowing the terms from Nietzsche with some modification, emphasized styles, particularly "Apollonian" and "Dionysian" cultures (1934, 72ff.). The Apollonian Pueblos, for example, distrusted individualism: "institutions that would give individuals a free hand [were] outlawed." Common tradition was the true guide. The Dionysian Indians, on the other hand, "valued all violent experience" and sought to "break through the usual sensory routine."

Still more recently the polarities have taken a somewhat different slant. The late Talcott Parsons conjured up a set of so-called pattern variables, consisting of five contrasting characteristics: ascription-achievement; specificity-universalism; affective-affect neutral; diffuse-particularistic; and collectivity-individual orientation (1951, 335). Mancur Olson, Jr. contrasts the world studied by the sociologist (represented by Parsons) with the world studied by the economist. In the former, Olson says, rationality is almost a cultural peculiarity; in the world studied by the economist, human beings are assumed to be rational. Stability is a major preoccupation in the world of the sociologist and is viewed as a product of common processes of socialization; a sense of belonging, avoidance of alienation, and group identity are felt to be important. In the economist's world, efficiency and optimality are valued. Olson concluded that "the economic and sociological ideals . . .

[are] not only different, but polar opposites: if either one were attained, the society would be a nightmare in terms of the other" (1968, 114). He viewed them as truly incompatible "expressions of the most fundamental alternatives human societies face" (114).[8]

One final model of differences, again not propounded as sex-based, is Kenneth Boulding's contrast between the "integry" and the economy. We know a great deal about the dynamic of the economy. Indeed, a long line of thinkers from Mandeville, Hobbes, Smith, Spencer, and Marx down to Keynes and his followers have been dealing with it. Essentially, it is a world in which monetary exchange mediates a large part of human relationships. The folk cliché tells us that "money makes the mare run." The economy, according to the classical model, is highly competitive, impersonal, rational, calculating, and motivated by self-interest. It was seen by its nineteenth-century advocates as just, fair, the best way to organize production; by its opponents, as a harsh jungle, inhumane, cruel. Even today, "making it," whatever the cost, is exalted. Humans relate to one another on a monetary or "cash nexus" basis. Goods and services are exchanged on the basis of equivalent units and, according to Adam Smith, both sides gain by the transaction. Although exchange could be quite personal—as in shops, bazaars, and the like—it could also be extremely impersonal, requiring little human interaction. Indeed, the so-called silent trade among preliterate peoples did not involve any personal contact at all. The stock exchange today—as contrasted, for example, with the Florentine rialto where Shylock was to exact payment for his contracted loan—is perhaps the most impersonal of institutions. Few people who buy on it have any contact with the sellers. Indeed, probably most exchanges today are almost abstractly symbolic, a transfer of entries in a book or a computer printout.

In marked contrast to the dynamic of the economy is the dynamic of the integry, which Kenneth Boulding defines as "that part of the total social system which deals with such concepts and relationships as status, identity, community, legitimacy, loyalty, love, trust, and so on" (1969, 3). It is a world—to use another sociologist's terms—of "attraction, loyalty, identification, association" (Mayhew, 1971, 74-75). Boulding sees it as "a distinct segment of the social system with a dynamic of its own" (1969, 3), a dynamic which I have characterized as one of love-and/or-duty (Bernard, 1971). Here the rule is not the exchange of money or the symbols of money but "grants" of goods and services. We know far less about the integry and how it operates than we know about the economy. We are, in fact, only now "barely beginning to understand the processes by which a community is built up or destroyed; by which unions or schisms take place; by which loyalty is created, legitimacy accepted, and love fostered" (Boulding, 1973, 5). In other words, about the integry.[9]

Gender of the Polarities

The foregoing polarities have been introduced to show that recognition of contrasting modes of thinking, feeling, and interacting long predates the concept of the female world. None of them rests on any theory of intrinsic sex differences.[10] Not one of the theorists saw the polarities in terms of male and female worlds. These contrasting worlds were conceptualized by men, propounded by men, agitated for by men, fought against by men. Their approach was not at all gender-related. Both sexes could—and presumably did—participate in any or all of the conceptualized worlds.

Although the polarities mentioned above were not identified as sex-based by their proponents, the first term in each may be viewed as characterizing the female world and the second, as characterizing the male world. To use Maine's conception, the female world has indeed been a status-organized world and the male, a more contract-organized one. The female world has indeed been a more kin- and locale-based one, reflecting the "Blut-und-Bod" (blood and soil) character of the Gemeinschaft; the Gesellschaft or capitalistic world has indeed been an exchange world, peopled primarily be men. Benedict's characterization of the Apollonian and the Dionysian is indeed consonant with the conceptualization of the female world as conservative and tradition-bound and the male world as violent. Kropotkin's mutual aid may indeed be viewed as representing the ethos of the female world and Spencer's survival of the fittest as illustrative of the rugged individualism characteristic of the male world. The female world can indeed be characterized by Parsons' ascription, diffuseness, particularism, collectivity-orientation, and high affectivity and the male world, by achievement, specificity, individualism, muted affect, and universalism. Olson's analysis of the sociologist's world fits the conceptualization of a female world quite well and the economist's, of a male world. And finally, although Boulding does not specify the integry as a female world, a good case can be made for the conception that historically the integry has indeed been a woman's world or rather, perhaps, that it has been "manned" by women.[11] It has, that is, performed the integrating function of holding the whole system together.[12]

Although the theorists did not themselves state their points in terms of male and female worlds, they were not wholly unaware of the gender-related aspects of their conceptualizations. In the nineteenth century, the world of industry and politics was seen in male terms, as representative of male values and virtues, as one of harsh striving, of conflict and competition, and the female world was seen as a necessary counterpart, a world of love and support (Chapter 4).

Characterizing the Female World

Out of this welter of characterizing aspects of the polarities two have served as the organizing linch-pins of the present book, namely the kin- and locale-based or Gemeinschaft nature of its structure and the love- and/or-duty ethos of its culture.

The conceptualization of the female world as Gemeinschaft in nature is neither new nor original. Tönnies himself identified the Gemeinschaft with the female world in a highly sentimental manner: "the realm of life and work in Gemeinschaft is particularly befitting to women; indeed, it is even necessary for them" (1957, 162).[13] And at the turn of the century, Veblen was already pointing out that women "live under a regime of status handed down from an earlier stage of industrial development and thereby they preserve a frame of mind, and habits of thought, which incline them to an archaic view of things generally. At the same time, they stand in no such direct organic relation to the industrial process at large as would tend strongly to break down those habits of thought which, for the modern industrial purpose, are obsolete" (1917, 323-324).[14] More recently, Scheppele makes the same point:

> The transition from Gemeinschaft largely missed women. In fact, in the move from farms to cities, women lost many of the productive duties they had generally performed on the farms. Although many tended urban gardens and still produced much of the food for the family, the active working partnership between husbands and wives was replaced by a division of labor where the wife tended the home and family and the husband went out into the world of work. Women's immediate worlds changed much less than men's did. Women did not form ties outside the home and immediate community. Women did not change their mode of social relations. Women did not expand their social circles and interact with groups of people who were not likely to know each other. In short, women still lived primarily in Gemeinschaft. [1977, draft]

The characterization of the female world in the present context as Gemeinschaft in nature does not rest on sentimental or patronizing or largely negative perspectives[15] but rather on the evidence from a respectable research literature which documents the fact that the world of women has indeed been a kin- and locale-based world—a world of "Blut-and-Bod"—performing an integrating function.[16]

Women, for example, have been, par excellence, the persons who have maintained relationships with relatives (Adams, 1971), even when they were "too close for comfort" (Glick, 1975, 13). A study of a Mexican family found "centralizing" women to be pivotal in kinship systems; they were "keepers of the family tradition," fulfilling "an important integrating role in channeling, switching, and storing information pertaining to the entire kinship network" (Lomnitz and Lizaur, 1978, 399) A study of brothers also found that contacts between and among them were mediated by sisters and mothers (Arkin, 1979). Women, in brief, have been, and many remain, the mainstay of the kin- and locale-based ties that constitute the underpinnings of Gemeinschaft. I do not regard this integrating function as archaic or obsolete, as Veblen, viewing it only in an industrial context, seemed to do. Nor as, in effect, a kind of social retardation, as Scheppele, again viewing it in an industrial context, seemed to do. Nor as, in effect, Tönnies seemed to do, in a sentimental vein, for Gemeinschaft can be mean as well as generous, hurtful as well as gentle, cruel as well as kind, crippling as well as supportive. Men, the folk cliché reminds us, can hate like brothers. Gemeinschaft can be racist, sexist, bigoted, and provincial as well as protective. I view the female world as an integrating system with as much conceptual validity as, say, the economy or the polity.

On the culture side, the female world is characterized by its love-and/or-duty ethos. In his own studies of altruistic love, Sorokin found that in our society the integry was in fact inhabited by women:

> Non-institutionalized kindness and unselfishness . . . seem to be stimulated mainly in women. If boys show these tendencies (considered "feminine" by our culture), the traits are discouraged in early childhood as being "sissified." In the adult life of our highly competitive world, men would have difficulty in supporting their families and in successfully rising from the status of office boy to bank or corporation president if they were highly unselfish, altruistic, and self-sacrificing. In girls and women, on the other hand, these tendencies, in a moderate and conventional form, are encouraged and stimulated. They begin to practice them early in the home, with neighbors and members of the family; and they continue to do so in various forms during their adult age. [1950, 21]

And a generation later, Victoria Samuels, reviewing the literature on working-class women, found that they were still the products of a world of "strongly conditioned values of . . . duty, sacrifice, repression, denial of self-interest . . ." (Samuels, 1975, 9). A recent study of the moral development of women corroborates the "strongly conditioned values of . . . duty [and] sacrifice." It found that to these female subjects morality meant "obligation and sacrifice" and that these far outweighed "the ideal of equality" (Gilligan, 1977, 485) (Chapter 21). It was on the basis of this kind of evidence that several years ago I characterized the female world as one with a love-and/or-duty ethos (1971).

The Greeks distinguished three kinds of love: erotic, philanthropic, and "agape," or humanitarian. The first, in the form of romantic love, has been and remains a major value in the female world (Chapter 20). Loving friendships and philanthropic activities have also constituted a major component in the female world (Chapters 5, 11). And agape—humanitarianism—has long characterized the female world (Chapter 20).

It should be noted that when we say that the female world "is characterized by" or "does" something or other, we mean that the norms—legal, conventional, moral, whatever—prescribe, permit, or at least tolerate this behavior. When we say, as we did earlier, that the male world does not like women, we mean that its norms permit, encourage, even prescribe behavior that is hostile to women.[17] Nor is the female world immune to nonconformity. Not all members of any specific world live up to every item that composes it. Thus we have unconventionality, immorality, criminality, delinquency, and other forms of nonconformity in the female, as well as in the male, world. Some nonconformity even takes the form of attacks on the status quo, as in the long tradition of women reformers, participants in the women's rights movements, feminists of all kinds, abolitionists, and the like. Some takes the form of crime, though to be sure, to a large extent it is limited to crimes available in a restricted setting.

So much, then, for the conceptualization and the characterization of the female world. They were not imposed on a body of systematic data but grew out of a wide seining of the research literature. In the absence of relevant data in so many areas, it might have been easier to write a book on Greek or Afghan or South African or Japanese society from the traditional male perspective than it is to write this one about the female world even in my own society. In those undertakings the data available would have come in standard chunks, with conventional conceptualizations suitable for the purpose. In the present book they have had to be mined out of somewhat intractable male-oriented research. Except, of course, in the case of the invaluable feminist research now entering the mainstream of scholarship.

Final Comments

Since there is not as yet enough scholarship or scientific knowledge from which to draw a complete and coherent picture of the female world as here conceptualized and characterized, the approach is eclectic, drawing on materials wherever available, from whatever source. All are accepted as grist for the mill, for the sociology of the female world is still at a stage where broad brush strokes are legitimate. It is not anywhere near the stage of traditional sociology where refinement of concepts and perfection of techniques and elaboration of old ideas are as important as fresh new insights and perspectives. Although this eclectic approach is interdisciplinary, the result is not intended as an encyclopedic "new synthesis," but rather as an integration. Since not all researchers in any one discipline necessarily agree on either the nature of the phenomena they describe or the interpretations they make, a choice between or among disparate conclusions is often called for. Inevitably my own biases show. I hope they are as defensible as their counterparts.

There is disagreement not only on conclusions but also on emphases. A major issue among female researchers is the relative importance to be assigned to the oppression and to the power of women, to the negative and to the positive aspects of their lives (Lougee, 1977, 631). My bias is in the direction of an appreciative point of view vis-à-vis women and their world. An extensive literature documents their oppression in detail. An enormous amount of feminist time, energy, thought, and research has been directed to this goal. It seems to me that we are now at a point of diminishing returns in this effort. Not that I think we should abandon it but only that the expected scientific returns are becoming less and less crucial. I take the misogyny of the male world as a given, as part of the environment of the female world. It has to be recognized and dealt with. But exclusive emphasis on the victimization perspective, on the negative aspects of the female world, seems to me to have a deleterious effect on female self-image and self-esteem as well as on knowledge. There is more to the female world than oppression.

One final introductory statement. Many women whose opinions I greatly respect oppose the very concept of a female world, fearing that it can be used against women or that it inevitably glorifies the female world, placating women and reconciling them to a subordinate position vis-à-vis the male world. I do not agree. I feel that research devoted to understanding the nature of the female world—its structure, its culture, its functioning—can counteract the tendency to see the female component in societies as somehow deficient, deviant versions of the male world. It may raise consciousness about the strengths of the female world available for dealing with male misogyny and oppression.

There is, of course, no intention to imply that the female world described here is the same as all the female worlds of the past or of the future. The female world has changed. It is changing. It is not set in concrete, not rigid. It is different today from the way it used to be and from the way it is becoming. It changes according to its own tempo, its own style, its own logic (Bernard, 1976). But change does not mean that it was more like the male world in the past or that it is becoming more like the male world now or moving in that direction for the future. The male world is not the necessary model for the female world. Convergence may or may not be in process. I believe the two worlds were different in preindustrial times and will probably remain different in postindustrial times, but different in different ways. That pleases me.

I hope, finally, that I do not come through as an observer from another planet, notebook in hand, commenting sardonically on the strange antics of the inhabitants of the female world. I profess no "what-fools-these-mortals-be" objectivity. I write, I hope, as a concerned member of the human family. This tentative exploration of the nature of the female world has been one of the most challenging and illuminating in my own intellectual history.[18]

General Plan of the Book

The backbone of this book rests on the concepts of structure (Chapters 6-15) and culture (Chapters 16-22). But our conceptual tool kit is no more adequate with respect to these two concepts than with respect to "world."[19]

There is, for example, no consensus with respect to the referent for the term "social structure." "The concept 'social structure' is, paradoxically, so fundamental to social science as to render its uncontested definition virtually impossible" (Udy, 1968, 489).[20] With so much leeway in conceptualization I cannot be faulted for defining social structure to suit my convenience rather than seeking an uncontested definition. So, following the by-now hallowed precedent established by Humpty Dumpty behind the mirror, "social structure" here means just what I want it to mean, namely: "stations" and "spheres" in Part II, demographic composition—including age, marital status, and class—in Part III, and group composition in Part IV.

In addition to a structure, a world must also have a culture. The lack of conceptual consensus with respect to culture here becomes almost ludicrous.[21] For the sake of expedience, only four of the many consensually accepted components of culture—language, technology, aesthetic values, and ethical values—are selected for discussion in Part V.

However conceived, both social structure and culture usually imply relative stability, though change is not precluded. Some people, usually the more radical, think change comes too slowly; they despair of achieving the reforms they seek. Some think change comes too fast; they deplore the collapse of institutions. Whatever anyone thinks or wants, change is an inevitable fact of life. Change is an underlying theme throughout our discussions, especially the changes incurred by the activities of the current women's movement.

Notes

1. On the other hand, transsexuals help illuminate the difference between the two worlds. Thus Jan Morris, once a male, contrasts the female and male worlds from the perspective of a person who has inhabited both, and finds the differences great. She could well understand "what Kipling had in mind, about sisters under the skin" (1974, 178). The style of interaction among the women of the town she lived in was warmer, closer, more comfortable than that of the male world she had formerly lived in and rejected.
2. Beauvoir implies that separation and integration are inconsistent or incompatible. Still, we know—from the disintegrating effect the loss of slaves had on the antebellum economy of the South—how well integrated into that society the segregated blacks had been. After the Civil War a well-understood code of racial behavior maintained separation between the still-integrated races. Separation and integration are not incompatible. Nor are separation and independence identical concepts. Conceptualizing a distinct female world does not imply "a closed and independent society." It is, of course, true that "women have never constituted a closed and independent society." For even the convents and the beguinages had to operate in a society that included men. And, of course, women "form an integral part" of any society. The sexes are inextricably bound to one another no matter what form the relationship takes. Even in the "lesbian nation" envisioned by some radical women, women would still need men for impregnation (Johnson, 1973, 278). There are, to be sure, degrees of both integration and independence.
3. The fact that the female world and the male world are different and, as we shall note presently, operate on different principles, producing and resulting in asymmetry, does not itself imply conflict. Some of the differences may be viewed as integrative, not divisive, as Durkheim taught us in his discussion of organic solidarity. Boulding's concept of the integry recognizes this integrating kind of difference. In general, Lionel Tiger notes, "so long as the male bond is not actively threatened . . . it is possible to maintain a view of the harmony rather than conflict of 'the two spheres' " (1970, 117).
4. Artemis March suggests a fivefold classification of conceptualizations of the female world: as relatively autonomous but interdependent with the male world; as actively antipatriarchal; as a female elaboration of dominant cultural institutions; as support networks among women to sustain them so that they can sustain men; and as a world of friendship and religious sorality as revealed in the work of women historians of the nineteenth century, especially Smith-Rosenberg and Cott (1978, draft).
5. Polarities—"on the one hand, on the other hand"—seem to be built into the human mentality on the basis of the bilateral symmetry of the human body. The placement of the organs of sight, smell, and taste on the ventral side of the body leads also to the polarity of front and back, forward and backward. The limited movement of the neck muscles suggests the polarity up and down. And so on. A habit of mind tuned to polarities might well tend to see the world in these terms: left and right, up and down, forward

and backward. And also, by analogy, light and dark, hot and cold, beautiful and ugly, good and bad. The projection of these polarities onto the sexes is only a stone's throw away from ascribing gender to them, rendering light masculine and darkness feminine and so on. In any event, gender polarities have been imposed on male and female bodies from time immemorial on the basis of their common biological traits quite independent of their individual differences.

6. Community in the physical settlement sense was *Gemeinde*.
7. In its current formulation it deals with an "altruistic" gene and a "selfish" gene, the first undergirding a theory of group survival, the second, of individual survival (Dawkins, 1978). In the present context, the "altruistic gene" or group-selection theory corresponds to the Kropotkin mutual aid approach and the "selfish gene" or individual selection theory, to the Darwinian.
8. An economist, Arthur M. Okun, pointed out: "In establishing a capitalistic democracy, the United States has built a society on two differing foundations. The capitalistic foundation attaches top priority to efficiency—operating through market incentives for getting the economic job done in the way that obtains the most useful output from our labor, capital, and natural resources. The democratic foundation, in contrast, emphasizes egalitarian and humanitarian values of cooperation, compassion, and fraternity." (*Washington Post*, Nov. 25, 1978)
9. Boulding later abandoned the term "integry" and substituted the concept of the "grants economy," including the economy of fear as well as of love (1973). Decisions in the grants economy are not made on exchange principles but on such bases as community or threat. The rules of the economy say that if a firm cannot compete in the market with foreign firms it should be eliminated. But nations do not follow that rule. They switch to the grants economy; they grant a subsidy in the form of a tariff to keep foreign competition out, to protect "our" side. If the economy were allowed to operate only according to the market principle and competition were the only process governing it, the game would soon be over; the smartest or fastest or whatever would win all the marbles and take over the whole system. This is not permitted. The principles of what Boulding originally called the integry are invoked. Transfer payments of one kind or another are made. Subsidies are granted. "Our" side—read: nation—is protected against other nations. Boulding recognized that there were other, less benign ways to violate the exchange market canons of the economy also, by threat and terrorist extortion.
10. One ancient polarity that has been sex-identified is the Oriental yin-yang polarity, basic principles in the universe representing the male and the female, the male associated with light, warmth, the sun, and the female, with darkness, coldness, the moon. Although there is a considerable corpus of writing on this polarity, its relevance here is not compelling.
11. Although Boulding's transformation of the concept of the integry into a concept of a grants economy expanded the basic premise, I believe—absence of overwhelming research documentation precludes more than this—that the integry as Boulding originally conceptualized and analyzed

it, or as an economy of love, as he later analyzed it, is a legitimate model for the female world. The world of women conceptualized as the integry is seen as part of the infrastructure which performs a supportive and integrative function in modern societies. The integry can also be contrasted with the polity, also operating essentially as part of the male world, performing according to a male perspective. When women participate in either the economy or the polity they do so under the specifications laid down by the male world. They do not, however, thereby surrender the female world. The problems that arise in thus participating in the male world of the economy and the polity are looked at in later chapters. For the present, the integry is viewed as a female world, the economy and the polity as parts of a male world. Since my original appropriation of Boulding's concept of the integry-economy, Mina Gaulfield has made an analogous Marxist statement in terms of the concepts of use-value and monetary-exchange value (1977, 60-77). Her statement about production for use-value corresponds also to the Gemeinschaft world and production for monetary-exchange-value to the Gesellschaft. The first, in the present context, corresponds to the female world, the second, to the male world. Devotees of the dialectical approach to sociological analysis may see the polarities here discussed as another kind of dialectic, namely, "dialectical genderism." As a matter of fact, proponents of androgyny seem to imply a kind of Hegelian dialectic in which male qualities—thesis—and female qualities—antithesis—finally arrive at a kind of synthesis in the form of androgyny.

12. It is because of the dependence of the total society on the integrating function of the female world that any threat to this stabilizing role arouses so much anxiety. "Most Americans today are familar . . . with the kinds of anxieties that can be generated by the changing roles of women in our society. The very stuff of everyday life—the personal relations of marriage, child-rearing, work and love—have been transformed, and the transformation has brought men and women . . . crises of doubt, hostility, guilt and insecurity. . . . Any threat to the strength of family ties . . . raises anxieties at many levels" (Teter, 1978).

13. For women, the home and not the market, their own or friend's dwelling and not the street, is the natural seat of their activity. In the village the household is independent and strong, also in the town the household is preserved and has a certain beauty; only in the city does the household become sterile, narrow, empty, and debased to fit the conception of a mere living place which can be obtained everywhere in equal form for money. As such it is nothing but shelter for those on a journey through the world. Staying at home is as natural for the women as traveling, according to the traditional attitudes of the people, is unbecoming to them. . . . All the woman's activity is more inward than outward. The end of this activity lies in itself and not in some outside aim. Therefore, personal services belong by nature to the realm of the woman because they reach their perfection in their very existence and do not even show a good or product as a result. Also, many tasks in agriculture befit the woman and in the soundest cultures, have been put on her shoulders, often, however, to the point of excess; for farming is labor unconscious of itself, drawing

strength from the heavenly breezes. Farming can be conceived as a service to nature, close to the household and immediately bearing fruit. [1957, 162-163]

See Chapter 3 for a description of African cultures in which it is the men who are kin- and locale-based and the women who conduct trade in distant markets.

14. As late as midcentury, Jaffe and Stewart (1951) did not even consider women to be part of the modern industrial order, that is, of the Gesellschaft.
15. The locale-based lives of women, especially working-class women, have been described, almost contemptuously, as "claustrophobic" (Rainwater, Coleman, and Handel, 1959). The neurosis known as agoraphobia is sometimes designated as "housewives' syndrome" because practically all cases are women.
16. Marx taught that capitalism, or the Gesellschaft, would ultimately destroy itself by its own contradictions. The integry—family, church, charity—which operates on opposite principles to those of the economy, is what holds it together. Although the polarities were viewed as characteristically opposites, they were not necessarily conceived of as in conflict with one another. Indeed, Adam Smith recognized the validity of both. In his day he was as well known for his book on the moral sentiments as for his book on the wealth of nations. Even the most convinced political economists in the nineteenth century recognized the need for violating the classic rules of the economy from time to time. They later even extended their discipline to accommodate the welfare state. Otherwise the economy, operating according to its (male) logic would self-destruct.
17. Sociobiologist Daniel Freedman thinks this hostility to women is in the male genes.
18. Jean Lipman-Blumen, reviewing the corpus of my work, finds that a good deal of my intellectual history seems to have been in the direction of defining the female world (1980).
19. Merton and Lazarsfeld cite C. S. Peirce to the effect that "no study can become scientific . . . until it provides itself with a suitable technical nomenclature, whose every item has a simple definite meaning universally accepted among students of the subject" (1954, 274). With this strict test to pass, it will be a long time before a scientific treatise on the female world is forthcoming. In the meanwhile, only a "first approximation" is feasible.
20. For example, Leach defines social structure as "the web of mutual positions and inter-relations in terms of which the interdependence of the component parts may be described" (1968, 482). Hiller also emphasizes the status approach but adds the rules that govern their relationships: "The structure or organization of a society consists of statuses, such as occupations, offices, classes, age and sex distinctions, and other circumstance-occasioned reciprocities and rules of conduct" (1974, 330). The British, Leach tells us, emphasize the rules; they "make their descriptions of social structure in terms of sets of rules defining the interdependent rights and obligations attaching to sets of offices" (Leach, 1968, 488). Stinchcombe, on the other hand, underplays the rule component; he interprets social structure

as including "groups, institutions, laws, population characteristics, and sets of social relations" (1965, 142). The 1974 program of the American Sociological Association had "social structure" for its theme. It noted that "everything in social life can be viewed with a focus on social structure as well as from a socio-psychological perspective" (Blau, 1975, 2). The lack of consensus revealed in the papers presented at these meetings was interpreted by Merton as a sign of vitality rather than of inadequacy (in Blau, 1975).

21. Milton Singer, for example, includes "social structure as a theory of culture" (1968, 530). But Talcott Parsons sees culture as determining social structure (Blau, 1975, 17). Blau thus characterizes him as a "cultural determinist rather than a social determinist" (1975, 17). Parsons sees cultural systems as beyond social systems. They consist of " 'patterns' of meaning, that is, of values, of norms, of organized knowledge and beliefs, of expressive 'form' " (cited by Blau, 17). It becomes a toss-up therefore whether culture should be viewed as an aspect of structure or structure as an aspect of culture.

3

A Collage

SINCE MOST HISTORY has been written by men and has dealt only with events and people of interest to them, women who were living independently of or separate from men, for whatever reason, have escaped notice or have been dismissed as uninteresting. The proportion of such women at any given moment in time has varied historically, but it has always been considerable. Elise Boulding has estimated it as anywhere between a fifth and a half (1976, 102-103). E. A. Wrigley gives the even higher estimate of 40 to 60 percent (1969, 90). Such an independent life might result from any one of a number of contingencies—widowhood, desertion, divorce, polygyny, spinsterhood, or just late marriage. Many other women have lived not independently of men but still widely separated from them psychologically and socially, as in places where purdah has prevailed, a system which results "in a sharp separation between the worlds of men and women, even for those who do not observe seclusion in their own families" (Papanek, 1973, 866). And some women have lived independently as a matter of deliberate choice.

Choice is, of course, an equivocal concept. How voluntary, for example, was convent life for a young woman whose parents could not or would not dower her adequately? How voluntary, for that matter, is purdah for countless women today? How voluntary have been the lives of women left alone by such vagaries of fate as war, or of women in fishing villages during the long absences of their husbands?

How and where have all these women lived? The work of feminist scholarship has just begun, so there is still a great deal to be learned before we can truly understand their varied lifestyles. In lieu of well-rounded, in-depth studies covering the gamut of female life styles over time and place the following examples and illustrations—fragmented and incomplete as most of them are—are offered as at least a starting point. And since most of the data that we do have were generated by research in our own country or in the Western world in the past century or two, at least a glance at other times and climes seems a proper introductory gesture to make, no more than good manners require. These examples are presented in part also as a counterfoil to the rest of the book, which deals primarily with female lifestyles—all too often middle-class lifestyles—in Western society.

There is no particular rhyme or reason for the selection of the examples presented. They do not by any stretch of the imagination constitute a scientific sample of the ways women have lived, worked, and played together, of the many kinds of relationships they have evolved among themselves, of the kinds of structures they have built for themselves, of the kinds of interactions that have characterized their lives together. They constitute only a convenience "sample," and there is no way to generalize the picture they present nor even to judge how representative this "sample"—or rather, perhaps, this potpourri of networks, collectives, associations, spheres, what-have-you—is of the ways most women have lived. They tell us little, if anything, about the lore, the beliefs, the culture these women inherited or created for themselves. Or about rebels. We catch only bits and pieces, small swatches of the sanctions that governed their lives. With all its inadequacies, this collage is offered in a most tentative way, as illustrative rather than as paradigmatic. For these reasons there is no typology, no theorizing, no generalizing.

Nevertheless, some classification of the cases is necessary to avoid utter incoherence. A historical or chronological presentation would have had some advantages except that it might have implied a kind of intrinsic historical sequence or even, perhaps, a sort of evolution toward some specific form, and no such trend is claimed here. Possible paradigmatic parameters are suggested at the end of the chapter, but at this point we note only that occupational and ideological criteria of classification seem to encompass most of the examples. They tend to blur at the edges, however, for what begins as occupational may easily become ideological with time. Nevertheless, occupation is an interesting criterion. Such an approach is a counterpoise to the customary perspective that tends to see women primarily in their family context (that is in their relationships with men), thus giving only a truncated image of women in their own right. The amount of space devoted to examples of any one category is in no way meant, of course, as an index of the importance to be attached to it in terms of either precedence or numbers of women involved.

Although degree of choice involved is not always an applicable criterion for classifying the examples, in one case, according to Elise Boulding's reading of the evidence, there did sometimes seem to be choice; in the case, for example, of the female vagabonds of the Middle Ages.

Vagabonds

For whatever reason, there were women in the Middle Ages who found vagabondage a congenial life style. Boulding pictures them as "hearty, hard-working, fun-loving women who move[d] partnerless through the Middle Ages able to pick up the pennies they need[ed] at a fair or celebration of some kind" (1976, p. 109). In towns they were entertainers and ran soup kitchens; during wars, including the Crusades, they ran first-aid stations. When needed, they could be good fighters. Free-floating, mobile, autonomous, freewheeling, they were, Boulding reminds us, "a social category we have no labels for today" (109). They were their own women. It would be interesting to know if they grouped together. Did they move about in partnerships? Did they follow some kind of circuit? Was territoriality involved? Did each have her own turf? If so, how did she protect it?

Entrepreneurs

Not as the peripatetic jacquelines-of-all-trades that the vagabonds may have been but as stable entrepreneurs, doing business apparently on their own, were the small businesswomen of Athens. Many were inn- and café- and shopkeepers. In the marketplace they seem "to have had, if not a monopoly, at least a privileged position," selling "all kinds of comestibles" (Lacey, 1968, p. 32). After the standard and unflattering descriptions of women in classical history (not those in classical drama) it would be interesting to learn more about these entrepreneurs. Such a woman could not have been secluded in the gynaeceum "if peddling vegetables in the marketplace was her only source of livelihood" (Slater, 1968, 5). Were they married or were they women without men? Did they help and support one another? They probably did. We are, for example, told that poor women "found pleasure in the company of other women, for they gossiped while fetching water, washing clothes, and borrowing utensils" (Pomeroy, 1975, 80).

From a surprising nonliterary source, Amy Swerdlow "reads" some interesting answers. Rather than draw on Xenophon and other male commentators, she consulted Attic vases for her appealing interpretation of the work life of Greek women. Unlike the picture of the gynaeceum-confined life of a housewife painted by Xenophon's manual on domestic duties, she finds evidence of women working together, preparing and spinning wool, from vases in which their pleasure in one another's company is clearly shown. Granted that there is idealization, Swerdlow says, "The communal nature of the work and the serenity and dignity of the women cannot be denied" (1978, 273). She also finds scenes of companionship among young women at the baths. If the wealthier women did not go to the baths, at least middle-class women did. Thus, although neither history nor literature deigns to mention it, "scenes of women in close companionship with each other abound in Greek vase painting" (273). And, Swerdlow argues, if female affection had not been an important part of a woman's life, it would not have appeared so frequently in vase painting. She concludes that numerous sixth- and fifth-century paintings of female religious rites give us the strongest clue to the fact that the "Athenian matron did, indeed, have a culture of her own, perhaps a 'subculture' from which men were excluded" (277). The evidence of the vase paintings shows these women as strong, active, and free. Swerdlow believes that since women were the purchasers of these vases, the paintings were probably designed to show them as they wished to see themselves (282). If middle-class women thus worked together, there is no reason to suppose that the businesswomen did not also.

In Rome as in Athens, freedwomen comprised a large proportion of the shopkeepers, selling such luxury items as dye and perfumes and also more earthy goods such as beans, nails, pipes, and bricks. Some were butchers (Pomeroy, 1975, 200).

I would like also to know more about the "sylk women" of London in the fourteenth and fifteenth centuries. The silk industry "was almost entirely in the hands of women, and wives of the better-class citizens of London specialised in it." They took apprentices and registered their indentures "in the usual way" (Power, 1975, 61). Were they autonomous women? "They were sufficiently conscious of common interests to petition the Crown in 1368 and again in 1455 against the competition of alien men, Lombards in particular" (61). Although the silk women did not seem to have a gild, there appears to have been some kind of organization among "websters," or women in the wool industry. "The only instance of anything remotely approaching a gild of women workers . . . is orders issued in Southampton in 1503 for the regulation of packing of wool for loading onto ships, which seems to have been done by women. Women were to choose two of their number annually to be wardens of their company, vacancies . . . to be filled by nomination of Mayor and Corporation, and women were to 'work with balons and pokes with their own hands and not to bawl or scold one with another' " (01). What, one wonders, were they bawling and scolding one with another *about*?

For all these enterprising women, I would like to know what their group life was like on the inside. Its age structure, for example. Its internal organization. Its culture. Were all these businesswomen married or were they women without men, widows perhaps? How did they live? Did they support one another psychologically? Were they autonomous? What kind of ideology underlay their life style? Did they enjoy camaraderie among themselves? It would be interesting to know the answers.

Managers

A society like that of Sparta took the separation of warriors and women for granted. There the Dorian tradition of a "communal social structure and separation of the sexes" prevailed (Lacey, 1975, 42), allowing a considerable amount of independence to women. They married late and the separatist-communal life style exempted them from the traditional isolated work of women. At Gortyn the free men lived in all-male groups and the women managed the home and property (39). A similar situation prevailed in Rome. "Absence of men, . . . an abiding feature of history as Rome conquered and governed distant territories, encouraged independence among women and unstable marriage" (Pomeroy, 1975, 181). The Punic Wars left a large part of the business of the city in the hands of women. They managed.

Similarly, many a medieval estate was left in the hands of chatelaines during the Crusades, as were Southern plantations left in the hands of the Southern Lady during our own Civil War. In our own country, the New England men who spent a good deal of time at sea or who went on the overland trails to the West left behind them communities of women who, like other women without men, created their own special life style. Michelle Clark, commenting on Mary Wilkin Freeman's work, notes that these New England women lived "in a world in which women's primary relationships . . . were to each other rather than to men. Wilkin's women are fiercely protective and respectful of other women in their communities. They are dependent on each other economically as well as emotionally. This dependence, of course, leads to hostility as well as affection. These women fight, envy, disagree, compete, bicker, and manipulate. But underlying the hostility are loyalty and intense involvement with each other" (1974, 195). Wives of men in military service presumably live in this kind of relationship today.

African Female Worlds

Women anthropologists point out that male researchers in their discipline were at a disadvantage in studying the lives of women because they had not had access to female informants (Paulme, 1971, 1); the male informants did not know much about the female component of their own cultures, so they told the researchers what they were expected to tell. (One amusing female informant replied to an inquiring anthropologist: "What do [men] know about what their women do?" Implying a considerable distance between the nale and female aspects of this culture. Even more, it might be added, between male anthropologists and the women of the cultures they study.) Only recently has there been serious, intensive anthropological work beamed precisely at delineating women's worlds.

As in the European examples presented so far, the basis for the organized work life of African women lies in the sexual division of labor. In Nigeria, for example, according to informants reflecting a past generation—that is, "old wives"—women often formed "small collectives with their personal friends, and hoe[d] each others' lands in turn, either for safety or to keep each other company, singing together as they work[ed]. They did not grumble about this heavy labour in the sun-drenched and steaming fields; indeed, their self-respect depend[ed] upon it, and one of the chief complaints of husbands was that ambitious wives neglect[ed] the home for the farm" (Andrewski, 1971, 17-18). In this society, women had their own court system, and if an uncircumcised woman insulted a member of an organization of circumcised women, the offended woman "had the right to sue the offender in the court of the women's society. The offender, if proved guilty, was punished" (36).

Among the Sande women of tropical Africa, there is "an initiation group that bears entire responsibility for education and for general behavior" (Paulme, 112). The Njayai and Humoi societies among the Mende, also of tropical Africa, "are formed to look after the mentally sick and to ensure the fertility of the soil by adopting the appropriate procedures, and they are at the service of every community" (112). What is especially intriguing is the fact that "these women have techniques both for promoting the development of the personality and for encouraging self-confidence" (112-113). In other African communities "village women run their own associations and institutions, and often have their own cults, complementary to those of the men, so essential for group solidarity" (5).

The assignment of trade to women in some African societies expands their horizon and can tend in the direction of female solidarity over wide areas.[1] "Almost all housewives [among the Dogon, Kissi, coastal Baga, and Bete] are obliged to carry on some form of trade . . . and attendance at the markets, which are held on fixed days in the surrounding countryside, necessitates journeys—often long ones" (Paulme, 7). Because of the importance of women in commerce and agriculture in southern Nigeria, groups formed "for the purpose of carrying out their various activities . . . have become powerful organizations" (113).

Patrilocal customs also play a part in expanding the horizon of women and laying the groundwork for expanded solidarity. Thus, whereas men among the Dogon, Kissi, coastal Baga, and Bete all spend their lives in their native villages,

> a married woman always has two homes and owes a dual allegiance. . . . The effect of this is that throughout her life she will often be fighting a lonely battle in defense of her own interests: her home and her children; and even there she has to relinquish her sons at an early age. On the other hand, whereas men never seem to conceive of ties other than those of kinship linked with common residence (so that acceptance of a stranger in their midst requires recourse to the fiction of making him a "brother" or an affine), among women the mere fact of belonging to the same sex is enough to establish an active solidarity. An appeal addressed by a woman to other women will reach far beyond the boundaries of a single village, and a movement of revolt among women will always be a serious matter, even if its immediate cause be of minor importance. [Paulme, 6-7]

The mere existence of such female bonding constitutes a valuable resource. It can, for example, generate a considerable amount of power. Here is an Asian (Taiwanese) illustration:

> Every woman valued her standing within the women's circles because at some time in her life she might also need their support. The concept of "face" has immediacy for men in village society, and their "face" was in danger when unfavorable aspects of their behavior were being talked about. If a woman brought her complaints against a brother-in-law or son to the women's community, each woman would bring the topic up at home, and before long it was also being discussed by the men with considerable loss of face for the culprit. In the Taiwanese village I know best, some women were very skilled at forming and directing village opinion toward matters as apparently disparate as domestic conflicts and temple organization. The women who had the most influence on village affairs were those who worked through the women's community. [Wolf, 1974, 162]

The examples of female association based on common work so far presented have had little to say about their "local habitation," separate "turf," or spatial location. But even in nomadic societies, Elise Boulding points out, women work—preparing food and making clothes and containers of wool and skins—in close company with other women in their own space, separate from men's, thus constituting a strongly knit community (1976, 289). The examples that follow attempt, however minimally, to include this spatial dimension. Without some knowledge of it, female communal life seems unanchored and it is difficult to picture the processes involved in it. We begin with the courtyard.

The Courtyard

Elise Boulding has called attention to the significance of the life organized by women around the courtyard, where from time immemorial, and even today, women in many parts of the world spend most of their lives. A 1978 French film, for example, shows a present-day Chinese courtyard shared by thirty-eight members of seven families, half an hour from Peking. The older women take care of the small children while mothers and fathers go off to their separate jobs. Such courtyards are modern relics of an archetypical female life style.

Anthropologists have described groups of women washing clothes together at the river or meeting at the well, where they go to fetch water, or chatting amiably in the courtyard. They bring back films of women in preliterate villages who look not too different from "courtyard" women in present-day societies. Today, as millennia ago, for many a woman "the courtyard is the master-integrator of all other [activities]. The courtyard is her administrative base as well as the scene of most of her productive activity. Here is where the older women organize work routines for the community and teach or organize the teaching of the girls, and of the boys under ten years of age" (E. Boulding, 1976, 133).

Boulding divides the activities of women in Neolithic times into three spheres, the hearth, the courtyard, and the fields. The first included the care and feeding of infants and the last, gathering, planting, cultivating, and the care of animals, among other activities. The courtyard included both production and social organization. Production involved processing food, practicing crafts, and building. But social organization involved village administration. These women transmitted their lore—genealogies, songs, herbal medicine—and tribal dances and rituals. They worked in groups, not only in their crafts but also in other creative activities, inventing new songs and dances for ceremonial occasions. The courtyard was a kind of staging platform for leadership. It tended to provide practice in exercising control over members of the village. Thus, "if and when women celebrate jointly with men at religious ceremonies and games, they perform as an independent unit with their own leaders" (Drinker, 1948, 9). Although the courtyard seems better adapted to nonurban than to urban settlements, it has persisted to some extent for the lower classes, even with urbanization. But there was "successive cramping and contraction of living space for the poor in the newly walled town and cities" (Boulding, 1976, 191) which tended to restrict the physical dimensions of female space and, as a consequence, the psychological and social dimensions also.

The "Lowell Girls"

A far cry from the archetypical courtyard in every way—time, place, age structure—were the lives and spatial dimensions of the factory workers who operated the mills in early nineteenth-century America; yet theirs was still an occupationally based life style with its own allotted space.

The young women who worked in the textile mills of New England in the 1830s[2] lived in boarding houses provided by the mill owners. The "girls" were recruited by the mills from all over New England. Most were between fifteen and thirty years of age (Dublin, 1975), but in Rhode Island 40 percent were under twelve (Foner, 1979). In 1836 they constituted three-fourths of the work force in one plant, and all but 4 percent were native-born. About three-fourths of them lived in the company-provided boarding houses—with accommodations for twenty-five young women, four to six in a room—and only slightly more than a tenth lived at home. They lived an all-female life, having little contact with men either at work or in the boarding house (Dublin, 31). Here is how one historian has described their life style:

> The female operatives in Lowell in the mid-1830s formed a community based on bonds of mutual dependence. Their experiences in Lowell were not simply similar or parallel to one another; they were inextricably intertwined. Women worked together in the mills with experienced operatives teaching newcomers work skills; in addition they lived together in company-owned boarding houses adjacent to the mills. Furthermore, the women were conscious of the existence of community and articulated this consciousness in their writings. Community was both an objective and a subjective reality in the lives of female operatives. . . .
>
> The boarding-house was . . . the center for the social life of operatives. . . . In this setting they ate meals, rested, talked, sewed, wrote letters, and read books and magazines. From within this circle, they found friends who accompanied them to shops, to evening lectures, or to church events. On Sundays or holidays they often went out together for walks along the canals or into the nearby countryside. The community of operatives, in sum, developed in a setting in which women worked and lived together 24 hours a day.
>
> The boarding house provided the social context in which newcomers to Lowell made their first adjustment to urban, industrial life. Women . . . usually . . . came because they knew someone—an older sister, cousin, or friend—who worked in Lowell. A newcomer was usually directed to a specific address, and her first contact with fellow operatives generally came in the boarding house, not in the mill.

> From her arrival at the company boarding house, a newcomer felt the influence of the community of operatives. [They socialized her into the community by changing her language, accent, clothes.] It was an unusual and strong-willed individual who could work and live among her fellow operatives and not conform, at least outwardly, to the customs and values of this larger community. [Dublin, 1975, 32]

In addition to the pressure to conform to group patterns of speech and dress, the women enforced an unwritten code of moral conduct. Dublin quotes a contemporary minister's account. "A girl suspected of immoralities, or serious improprieties, at once loses caste. Her fellow boarders will at once leave the house, if the keeper does not dismiss the offender. In self-protection, therefore, the patron is obliged to put the offender away. Nor will her former companions walk with her, or work with her, till at length, finding herself everywhere talked about, and pointed at, and shunned, she is obliged to relieve her fellow-operatives of a presence which they feel brings disgrace" (Dublin, 1975, 32; Miles, 1845, 144-145).

What kind of life style these young women might ultimately have built for themselves we do not know. They did not remain "Lowell girls" for very long. They were in the eye of an industrial storm. They were not protected from the conflicts of early industrialization. In time the owners no longer had to win the approval of the agricultural community; they could lower wages—and did; they could increase productivity by requiring longer hours—and did; they could worsen working conditions—and did. Many of the original "Lowell girls" participated in "turnouts" or strikes in 1834 and 1836. It would have been hard for them to go to work when their roommates were marching about town and attending strike rallies (Dublin, 1975, 32). They also helped in the ten-hour petition campaign of 1840.[3] But there were other young women living at home,[4] not subject to the influence of the boarding-house solidarity, able and willing to take the places of the original "Lowell girls," and they did.

So much, then, for examples of occupationally defined female life styles and their settings. They vary as widely as the societies in which they were imbedded. Perhaps in time we will be able to ferret out more details that will help us find common elements among them or clear-cut differences that will help define typologies. We leave it at that here and turn to ideologically defined female life styles and settings.

Ideologically Defined Communities

It is not always easy to distinguish occupational and ideological bases for communities. Once a pattern of relationships has become firmly established in a society—whatever its origin—it takes on an ideological rationale. Thus, if a particular division of labor arises in a society it soon seems the "natural" if not divinely revealed way to allocate tasks. Most of the examples presented here are ideological in the religious—Christian or Moslem—sense. In addition there are others that are ideological in the counterculture sense.

To say that convents were ideologically based is not to deny that they served an important practical function. They offered a safe haven to women for whom no other part of the societal structure made provision. The sex ratio of the middle ages is a perplexing puzzle. On one side we have records of communities in which the exaggerated surpluses of males seems to show almost conclusively that female infanticide was practiced (deMause, 1976, 528); on the other hand there was all that fighting, which may have killed off a lot of men.[5] Perhaps the slaughter of the female infants could not keep up with the mutual slaughter of young men. Then, too, there were all those religious orders taking men out of the marital or family picture. In any event, during the first millennium and a half there seems to have been a surplus of women without men and no place for them in the social structure. The convent was one solution.

Convents: The First Millennium and a Half

Convents began to spring up in the third and fourth centuries. By the tenth century, there were convents all over England, France, Germany, and Ireland, and they continued to flourish through the first half of the second millennium. They varied greatly over time and place. Putnam makes a special point of the changes in the twelfth century that transformed the early convent, an aristocratic institution based on feudal principles, to the poverty-bound orders of "poor Clares" that later substituted asceticism and silence for comfort and scholarship (1910, 103).

The early aristocratic convents were cultural establishments of a high order, with great libraries and traditions of scholarship which enabled a talented woman to pursue a learned career under auspicious circumstances. These convents were part of both the feudal system and the Church, so both worldly prizes and spiritual rewards "were within [a woman's] grasp" (Putnam, 71).[6] Although the roots of the great convents were in an earlier, prefeudal system, they were strengthened rather than weakened by the rise of feudalism. "Being always a landlord and sometimes a very great one, she [the great abbess] shared the prestige of the landlord class" (83). She might be summoned to parliament; she presided at her own courts. In Europe she had control of her own armed knights; in some cases, she struck her own coins; she was active politically (84). Nor was she denied recognition as a scholar. "She was treated as an equal by the men of her class, as witnessed by letters we still have from popes and emperors to abbesses. She had the stimulus of competition with men in executive capacity, in scholarship, and in artistic production, since her work was freely set before the general public. . . . In the cloister of the great days, as on a small scale in the college for women today, women were judged by each other, as men are everywhere judged by each other, for sterling qualities of head and heart and character" (72).

On the more mundane side, the women in the convents were best known for their artistic weaving and needlework. But others wrote disquisitions, poetry, or drama, or dabbled in natural science. One of them, Hrotsvith, was "the first of the humanists" (Putnam, 93). No wonder, Putnam concludes, that "no institution in Europe has ever won for the lady the freedom of development that she enjoyed in the convent of the early days. The modern college for women only feebly reproduces it" (71). True, but—with members not bound by vows nor distinguished by a habit, with no special residential requirements, allowed to indulge freely in artistic and intellectual activities—one wonders just how such a system operated.

The convents seem to have been well administered: "The daily business was in the hands of a number of officials called obedientiaries chosen among the most experienced inmates. The most important of them were the Sacristan, who had the charge of the church fabrics and lighting of the house, the Chambresses who looked after the nuns' clothes, and the Cellaress who looked after food and servants, saw to repairs and superintended the home-farm" (Power, 1975, 93). The farm provided bread, meat, beer, vegetables, dairy products. Fish, salt, spices had to be bought outside. "The household staff varied with the size of the nunnery. Wages were paid to a priest, or a chaplain, and a bailiff, the latter an invaluable factotum and general manager. The larger convents employed a male cook, a brewer, a baker, a dairywoman, a laundress, a porter and one or more maidservants" (Power, 94). Required domestic work was discarded by the thirteenth century. "In some of the larger houses individual nuns even had private servants" (96). We must, indeed, as Putnam warns us, "divest our minds of the conventional picture of the nun" when we think about the women in the great early convents (83).[7] Until the twelfth century, abbeys were "centers where the daughters of nobles might live a pleasant life and receive such education as the times afforded" (84). For many women, no doubt, the convent provided "a sense of fulfillment and freedom of action in the world they could never otherwise have had" (E. Boulding, 1976, 366). And for some—especially the great administrators and scholars—creative careers. But there was another, more frivolous side as well.

Putnam draws an analogy between these convents and the modern women's college. From the glimpses Power gives us, the early nuns seem more like boarding-school girls, hard to keep in line, almost impossible to discipline.[8] Bishops, for example, fought in vain to eliminate contact between the nuns and secular women. No way. Some of the convents, always hard up for cash, took in boarders or accepted wives and daughters during the absences of husbands or fathers, and some of these temporary inmates even brought companions and maids with them. The bishops "greatly disapproved of boarders and were always trying to turn them out, but never succeeded"(Power, 1975, 91). Nor did they succeed in their continual attempts to keep the nuns shut up (99). In the *Bull Periculoso* of 1300, Pope Boniface sternly ordered nuns never to leave the convent and never to have outside visitors. What happened? "At one nunnery in the diocese of Lincoln, when the bishop came to read the Bull and deposited a copy in the house, the nuns pursued him to the gate when he was riding away and threw the Bull at his head. More practical bishops soon stopped trying to enforce the Bull as it stood" and just tried to enforce a modified form. "But nuns went out just the same" (99).

Nor did the bishops succeed any better in their battle against female vanities. "Perennially recurring was the question of fashionable dresses. . . . For more than six centuries the bishops waged holy war against fashion in the cloister and waged it in vain. . . . Synods sat, archbishops and bishops shook their heads over golden hairpins, and silver belts, jewelled rings, laced shoes, slashed tunics, low-necked dresses, long trains, gay colours, costly materials and furs" (Power, 98). To no avail. The boarders still came with fine clothing and the nuns went on imitating them (91).

Nor did the bishops have better success with pets. "Bishops . . . for century after century tried to turn animals out of convents without the least success. Nuns just waited till the bishop went and whistled the dogs back again. Dogs were easily the favourite pets, but nuns also kept monkeys, squirrels, rabbits, and birds. They sometimes took animals to church with them" (98).

Intellectual standards and moral conditions began to decline in the later Middle Ages. So did internal discipline. "But the most common fault was to gabble through the services as quickly as possible" (96-97). Chaucer's portrait of Madame Eglentyne in *The Canterbury Tales* represents the increasing frivolity and worldliness. "The bishops were especially shocked to find nuns still retaining the vanities of their sex. The three D's (dances, dresses, dogs) drew special condemnation" (Power, 98). Expense accounts showed expenditures for wassail on holidays, bonfire nights, and harpers and players for Christmas, despite the bishops' banning of "all manner of ministrelcy, interludes, dancing and revelling" (98).

Nevertheless, despite all the evidence of frivolity, "nunneries were a boon for women of the Middle Ages" (99). To the unmarried, they offered a scope for their abilities, assured self-respect and the respect of society. They offered training in organization, in government, and in the management of great households and estates. They provided a good education. "Even if they suffered decay, and sheltered the idle with the industrious, and black sheep with white, the nunneries still represented an honourable profession and fulfilled a useful function for gentlewomen of the Middle Ages"[9] (99). But by the time the feudal ideas of the Norman Conquest had become dominant, the heyday of the great abbeys in Europe was already over; prioresses, less important than abbesses, took over the convents.

Three forces were at work in Europe in the later Middle Ages that were to transform the aristocratic institution the early convents had been—a place for great ladies—into an institution of "poor Clares": the rediscovery of Christianity, which gave rise to the mendicant orders; increasing recognition of what had been submerged in social philosophy; and the rise in literature of mysticism and romance (Putnam, 96). None of these forces had been operating when the great abbeys were founded in the third and fourth centuries. Now their day was about over. The great abbesses were replaced by the "Little Sisters of the Poor." The nunnery became a quite different kind of world, with a different orientation, a different population.

> The great monastic expansion of the twelfth century took a long step toward democracy in the cloister. The problem of the unattached woman of the lower class had become a menace to society. The great orders of Fontevraud and Prêmontré as well as many less famous were organized in the interest of the helpless of all classes and particularly of the lost woman. Of Fontevraud we are told that "the poor were received, the feeble were not refused, nor [even] women of evil life, nor sinners, neither lepers nor the helpless." Thousands of women entered these orders. From a bull of 1344 it is to be inferred that there were at that time about four hundred settlements of Prêmonstrant nuns. All the women in these settlements were professed, and their lives were spent in constant labour, which ultimately brought worldly as well as moral profit. These orders spread rapidly and widely. They were in harmony with the general tendency of the age, both ideally and practically; for while they gave ease to the rising social conscience of the upper classes, they also helped the growth of skilled labour and trade organisation among the lower. [Putnam, 1910, 100]

Under the influence of these trends, even great ladies, often convent bred, renounced their privileged positions to serve the poor and sick.

The world of the mendicant orders was in direct contrast to that of the old aristocratic abbeys with their vested interests. The Poor Clares lived in huts and, using Putnam's comparison, were like the Salvation Army workers today vis-à-vis charitable millionaires (103). The life of the Poor Clares was one of strict asceticism, hierarchical control, and self-obliteration. They had no time for culture or the arts. They were precursors and, in part, preparers for the Protestant Reformation (103), which bode no good for women or their world, least of all for the Lady. Putnam tells us "Luther had a thoroughly Mohammedan notion of woman's status—only as a wife and mother had she a right to exist. Her education became a matter of no importance and virtually ceased" (104).

The Counter Reformation brought an end to the relaxed life in convents, but efforts to impose greater discipline on the recalcitrant women were not always successful, especially among the wealthy or aristocratic. Some houses in northern Italy sent legal representatives to Rome to get their local bishop or the Papal visitor's new rules overturned or mollified. "Sometimes they resorted to direct action, fleeing the convent *en masse* in protest, beating up the visitor or locking him in the cellar" (Liebowitz, 1978). Some, by scaring them with reminders of the additional marriage dowries that would be needed if they left the convent, had their families pressure the Church to mitigate the reforms. The success of their efforts varied, depending on the determination of the local bishop, religious superior or visitor, the nuns' own organizational and financial ability, and the degree to which they could rally family or public support.

The degree of community also varied widely among these convents. In some there was "peace and harmony," as, for example, in a Concettione house in Siena. There, "the abbess said that she was satisfied and that the nuns were obedient, and no one else in the community had any complaints to make" (Liebowitz, 1978). Other houses in Siena also seemed to have a fair degree of harmony. Galileo's daughter received a great deal of moral support from her sister nuns during her father's trial, for which she was grateful. But such harmony was not universal. As the houses became larger—some had over 200 members—and more crowded, "there was a loss of the cohesiveness and personal community possible in a small convent." Personalities clashed. The nuns accused one another of being troublemakers and "complained about arrogant *converse* [lay sisters]." Inequalities bred resentments. Like sororities on a university campus, such "groupings could develop into cliques or opposing factions, with jealousies about who held the offices in the house" (Liebowitz, 1978). Nor did poverty and poor food help.

By the end of the sixteenth century—along with traditional convents for women from established and noble families who became nuns and poor girls who became lay sisters, as well as boarders—there were special convents, called *convertite*, established for repentant or converted prostitutes. Most had entered between the ages of ten and twenty anywhere from a fifth to a third involuntarily. And those who entered "voluntarily" did so to avoid a life of prostitution. These establishments became "catch-all holding institutions for women," a kind of dumping ground for "women who had committed crimes" as well as for repentant and unrepentant prostitutes. Understandably, therefore, many—especially those who had been forced into these houses—found the life "very difficult." In these gerrymandered *convertite* "one can see all these institutional problems [poor food, poverty, inequality, favoritism] writ large, resulting in the breakdown of any sense of community" (Liebowitz, 1978). In Milan the women complained of favoritism, backbiting, and reprisals among the governing body of nuns. Some of the 141 members tried to escape, even, in some cases, by suicide. No wonder the older nuns looked back nostalgically to the time before their house had become, in effect, something halfway between a house of detention and a house of refuge. Nor were conditions much better in Siena, where three-fourths of the twenty-five women were discontented and unwilling to remain even though the convent was relatively uncrowded. Here, too, there was resentment of favoritism. Being sent out on the street to beg was a welcome escape.

For all the difficulties confronting the convents, they survived with remarkable tenacity until well into the twentieth century. The current crisis in the convent is looked at below.

The Beguinages

A special and exceptionally interesting female life style in the thirteenth and fourteenth centuries was the lay analogue to the convent: the beguinage or *Samenung* or *Gotteshaus* or urban female commune, designed originally for rural female migrants to the city. The beguinages had all the advantages of convents at that time but few of the disadvantages, for they were free from church control. At the peak of the movement, in the thirteenth century, there were some two to three hundred beguines in Strasbourg, out of a total population of 20,000. By 1330, there were thirty houses with places for 300 women. After 1330, fifty more arose. They comprised a whole quarter of the town, constituting the nucleus of a well-defined neighborhood of unattached women. There were 2,000 beguines in fourteenth-century Cologne and 20,000 in all of Germany (Phillips, 1941, 227).

The houses—each accommodating about seven women—varied in wealth, in the kinds of activities in which their members engaged, in house rules, and in degree of religious emphasis, thus offering a wide choice of living conditions to interested women. Some were known for their spiritual enthusiasm and austerity, others, for the independence and respectability they offered. Those sponsored by the Franciscans seemed to cater to the poor; their approach was mainly spiritual and impersonal. Those sponsored by the Dominicans seemed to cater to wealthier women; their approach was more direct and more personal (Phillips, 224-225). In all, however, the members performed for one another the functions ordinarily supplied by families. I can easily imagine a young rural-reared beguine in fourteenth-century Strasbourg learning from her sister beguines how to behave in her new urban setting very much as the New England country girl learned from her sisters in the boarding houses how to behave in the industrial setting of Lowell in the nineteenth century.

Despite the beguine's sponsorship by the Franciscans and Dominicans, Phillips makes a strong case for the relatively minor part played by religion per se in the beguine movement. The women, though they followed religious practices, were not motivated primarily by religious devotion, he believes, but by economic concerns and, Power adds, by general discontent with their lot (1975, 30). In effect, the houses constituted social security systems.[10] Women bought into them very much the way elderly people today buy into retirement homes. For the poorer women endowments of one kind or another from the wealthy or from other sources supplied the resources. Members could inherit wealth, but their estates went to the beguinage upon their death. In addition, they could earn money on their own. They supplied a variety of occupational services to the community such as nursing, wool processing, sewing, baking, spinning, running hospitals and schools. "Carrying only a spindle, a beguine could settle anywhere and immediately have work" (G. Clark, 1975, 77).

One of the rules of all the beguinages—and central to the whole life style—was that men were not allowed into the houses. The women wore a habit that proclaimed to everyone that they wanted no part of male sexuality, or even of male companionship. They may not have wanted to dedicate themselves to the Church as the members of the religious orders did (ostensibly, at least); they may have wanted only to pursue the ordinary activities of the workaday world on their own, but not under male hegemony. Perpetual virginity must have seemed a small price to pay to be protected from the harshness of the male world. So, in return for the freedom and chance for self-development, the beguines dedicated themselves to lifelong virginity or, if they had formerly been married, to lifelong chastity. It was doubtless a good trade-off for most of them.

Historians are now telling us that the centuries which male historians have labelled the Dark Ages were not all that dark for women but that the centuries of the first half of the second millennium—which ushered in what male historians have called the Renaissance—were bad for women (Schulenburg, 1979, 33-54). It was in this period—the thirteenth and fourteenth centuries—that the beguinages had their heyday. For many women they were refuges, analogous though by no means identical to the houses we are now beginning to provide for abused women, except that they were primarily for unmarried women.

The beguines were extraordinarily successful. They were so well organized that by the middle of the thirteenth century they had formed guildlike corporations which they used in bargaining with the city, the Church, or overlord for privileges (G. Clark, 75-77), for tax relief, or for the right to practice certain occupations without joining the guilds. Their success was, in fact, their undoing. Both the Church and the guilds came in time to see them as threats. The Church began to impose regulations on them, a move that had the effect of isolating them and, finally, of transforming them into a mere status group concerned primarily with defending their privileges. Persecution by the guilds was the *coup de grace.* By the end of the fourteenth century this female regimen had all but disappeared.

Religious or Economic Ideology?

As in the case of the beguines, a blurring of the religious and economic motif took place, but on a spectacularly grand scale, in convents in Mexico City in the seventeenth and eighteenth centuries. It is, in fact, perhaps farfetched to classify these late-blooming convents under the rubric of ideology at all. From the records of their activities some, like La Concepción, La Encompación, and Jesus Maria, seem to have been more financial than religious in their operation. They were, in fact, great banking institutions, making profitable investments wherever they could, including slum property as well as great haciendas. Although some of the members in one of these were musicians, it was the accountants who seem to have taken over; they managed its business affairs, showing remarkable skill and talent in the process. They did much better, in fact, than their majordomos had done (Lavrin, 1976, 259). They extended mortgages and loans "to property-owners, since the latter suffered from chronic shortage of capital funds. These loans and mortgages paid a 5 percent interest to the convent, and provided a significant percentage of their income" (262).

Among the borrowers, in addition to landowners, were officers, knighted gentlemen, members of governmental bureaucracies, merchants, silver dealers, and even a small number of women, widows of rich men for the most part, or women with houses or land, or women from rich families (263). These borrowers "formed a closely knit group of entrepreneurs who supported each other as bondsmen and requested loans when their friends returned money" (263), thus keeping the convent's money in constant use. "The economic association of the merchants and the nuns was a loyal and a long-lasting one, stretching from the last decade of the seventeenth century to the first decade of the nineteenth century" (265).

In the eighteenth century, real estate became a favorite form of investment. The convent thus came to own houses of all classes from the richest nobles to the poorest (269). The nuns were, in fact, "slumlords." About a third of the tenants in the low-income houses were women heads of households, either widows or spinsters (269).

> As financial units, the nunneries reflected the trends of the economy in general. Throughout the seventeenth century they experienced the same administrative difficulties as other clerical, lay corporations and economic units, such as haciendas. Nunneries adjusted to the character of the times by changing the nature of their investments and blossomed in the eighteenth century. . . . But the feminine orders did more than simply reflect the economy; they influenced it by offering credit to the entrepreneurial classes of society. Thus, they were not only expressions of the social order but they [also] reinforced it from an economic point of view. In addition, the bulk and value of their property made them as important as some of the most powerful of the masculine orders, and an element of great economic significance in the life of the colonial city. [270]

A Diversion: A Dual-Sex Ideological Community

The freedom from sexual bonds which women had sought in convents and beguinages was combined with cooperative and loving ties to men, but especially to women, in an almost unique kind of female world—that is, among the Shakers in our own country in the nineteenth century. In these communities, women of child-bearing age, twenty to forty-five, outnumbered the men by two to one or even, in some cases, by three or five to one (Campbell, 1978, 28). For the most part these women came from large families that had been broken up by death, seeking security and surrogate kinship ties, and, perhaps, escape from marriage. Diaries and letters show how strong were the bonds between and among these women. A kind of life which is lacking in published accounts comes through in these personal documents. A great deal of "human warmth and exchange of information" was generated by visits of women among the several Shaker settlements and "must have substantially strengthened the Shaker network and . . . helped the separate settlements maintain a unity of human affection and purpose" (31). Not only was Shaker doctrine theoretically egalitarian, but equality was actually practiced in their communities. Affection did grow up between men and women, but the love of the women for one another seemed especially warm.

> Diaries of Shaker women were filled with . . . [loving] sentiments for their fellow women within each settlement and for women in other settlements. Visits as well as correspondence were recorded as frequent and rewarding. In one sister's record of a week's visitation schedule, "Sister Harriet comes here, Elder Sister Hannah goes to the second order. . . . Four sisters and brothers go to New York. . . . Sisters Ann, Prudence, and Florinda and three girls call here and then go to the other families. . . . Sisters Caroline and Marcia came down to help weave carpets." Women corresponded with their new friends, exchanging such comments as "I was so excited to have visited with you," or "thank you so much on behalf of all your Hancock sisters." They also exchanged presents and cherished their attachments. Some visits were remembered for decades—at least one visit for over fifty years—by both the surviving hosts and guests. [30-31]

So much then, for the female world that was based, directly or indirectly, on Christian ideology. But before leaving the subject altogether, a word on the current crisis in modern convents.

Update on Convents

The present time, like the twelfth century, may be viewed as a watershed in the history of the convent. The old "order" has been visibly crumbling. Until Vatican II, the religious orders had followed the rules that they had themselves evolved on the basis of their own experience. The general outcome of these rules was "death-to-self," the elimination of all traits we now—pejoratively—call "feminine" in walk, taste, and dress, and the exaggeration of those we—approvingly—call womanly, such as self-loss, obedience, and service to others (Ebaugh, 1977).

Without training in historical research or even access to the necessary documents there is no way for me to discuss the interpersonal lives of either the aristocratic convent members or those of the Poor Clares, or of the beguines. But by the middle of the twentieth century the world of the women within convent walls had deteriorated to a level that many were finding intolerable. In a time and place that rendered the custom- and tradition-bound routines[11] a handicap rather than a facilitator of the work they wanted to do, many women were opting out. And in their accounts of their experience we get a glimpse of what this particular female life style had become.

Surprisingly, many convents did not constitute psychological communities at all. "Such diminution of personality, combined with the strict rule, had the effect of making many nuns feel remote from each other. 'We felt deprived of relationships,' confesses an elderly woman, 'lonely for sheer companionship' " (Bernstein, 1976, 240). And for love.[12] "The rules warned time and again against a deep friendship between sisters, a partial friendship that 'always tends to have unhappy effects.' There it was, right in the rule book. But where did human tenderness come in? Why was there no provision in the system for Christ's commandment of love, his second after 'Thou shalt love thy God above all'; 'Thou shalt love thy neighbor as thyself'? And the teaching of St. Paul? That charity is greater than law? . . . What was ununderstandable was the rule that did not recognize that one of the prime reasons I was able to continue doing God's work as long as I did was because of the goodness and counsel of [women] such as Mother Eucharia . . . and Sister Corita. Both women felt that it was not wrong to love one's sister. It was not wrong to smile, to touch, to compliment" (Turk, 1971, 105). This nun was removed from a position for which she was well suited because of too-close ties with a sister. They loved each other, and she felt that "a rule that forbade the latter [relationship] was not only a rule that went against Christ's teaching, it was a rule of fear' " (106).

If the nuns were isolated from one another within the community, different orders were also isolated from one another. They were as little known among themselves as foreign countries. "Nuns in convents down the road didn't have anything to do with each other. It's only in the last five years that I've met members of any community other than my own" (Bernstein, 1976, 240).

Only now are we learning what had been happening in this particular kind of female life style. Thus one woman, Midge Turk, entered a religious order after a conflicted novitiate only to find that acquiring the discipline, product of centuries, was often traumatic for modern women. Not the least traumatic aspect was learning to live with other women: "Perhaps the most difficult thing I had to learn during those days was how to live uncritically in such extremely close contact with so many women, many of whom I probably would not have associated with in the outside world. It has been said that the real penance, the real agony of any religious order is the community life itself"[13] (Turk, 1971, 56-57). Only after strenuous effort did she finally achieve sisterhood: "As my novitiate drew to an end I keenly felt that [as Sister Agnes Marie] I was part of a very special group of mostly bright women who were dedicated to working for others. I had learned to share everything, to put the well-being of others before my own, to care unselfishly, . . . to be as true a Christian as possible" (57).

In the 1960s, new winds were stirring. The nuns "spent many hours examining the problem of living and working with the same group of women day in and day out. And it *was* a problem, agreed to by all the superiors present. We lived much too close, but a normal expression of human warmth was regulated by rule. We did not compliment each other. We took no time to enjoy the results of a job well done, for it was a sign of pride. On the whole we practiced greater charity and greater concern for those outside our community than for those within" (Turk, 152).

The women and the orders that were amenable to the new trends in the outside world came to emphasize communication, outside as well as inside the convent (Ebaugh, 1977, 33). They still valued the rewards of membership in their order and continued to share intense commitment and feeling of belonging to a dedicated group of élite status in the Church (47). But mingling in the outside world led some to a knowledge of themselves as women that had been eliminated by the old regimen. It raised doubts (48). The rewards of their life style seemed reduced in magnitude, the costs greater (49).

There was by no means a consensus in many of the orders with respect to the future. What kind of life style did they want to adopt? Many appreciated the old, strictly regulated life. The pains of freedom seemed greater than the rewards. A generation gap appeared. Some younger sisters felt exploited by the older ones. Some of the older sisters resented the fact that they had had to go through stricter times (Turk, 82). The outcome in most cases was a great relaxation of rules. One of the most symbolically significant was modification of the habit or even dispensing with it altogether. One of the most practically significant was retiring from the convent but not from the work they had cut out for themselves. Thus women in some orders came to live lives of service with no other identification than a symbol worn around their neck or pinned to their clothes. Case in point: In the Immaculate Heart of Mary convent, fifty women remained; thirty-five received dispensation from their vows but did not join the new community which 280 of the original members had formed to continue doing the same kind of work they had been doing, but now outside the Church.

Perhaps the most far-out religious women are those who do not even depend on priests for the celebration of communion: "I belong to a very small community of nuns," explained Sister J. "When we have our chapter meetings . . . we grow very close to each other. It seems a shame to have to bring in a priest from outside for the eucharist" (Hyer, 1978). They minister not only to one another but also to women outside. "We have a shortage of priests and I was taking the eucharist to people in the parish. . . . One lady, a shut-in, said she couldn't receive communion because she had committed a sin. She told me her sin, and I told her, 'In the name of the church and in my name, your sins are forgiven,' and she received communion" (Hyer, 1978). One day the learned male hierarchy, debating learnedly on the subject of ordaining women priests, will turn from their scholarly tomes and find female religious performing priestly functions very well, thank you, and there is no collapse of the social order.

For the women the question is: Can they be in but not of the world? The answer to this question as well as a solution to the problems of the convent in this day and age is still in process (Ebaugh, 1977).

Diverse as all these many life styles are, they are not too hard to understand. Perhaps because—except for the Africans—all share a common Western heritage they do not seem utterly strange to us. They might not be congenial to live in, but they do not seem out of bounds. Not so the life shaped by the ideology of purdah.

Muslim Ideology and Female Life Styles

Even women who are not living independently from men, even women closely related to men, married to them, in fact, may live their own separate lives with life styles of their own, in our own society as well as in those that separate women institutionally. It is only more extreme in some societies, notably in Muslim societies, than in others.

It is difficult to trace purdah historically, for, as Elise Boulding points out, no society in this century is proud of it. Thus "historians writing about the period before and after the start of the Christian era are apt to blame some *other* culture for initiating a practice of the seclusion of women from public life. . . . So the Christians blame the Moslems, and the Moslems the Persians. But . . . when the Persians conquered the Greeks, Persian women had nothing but contempt for gynaeceum-bound Athenian women" (1976, 343). Boulding herself suggests that the practice of female seclusion arose among the Greek and Hebrew trading communities around the Mediterranean beginning about 200 B.C. She cites George Tavard's study of women in Christian tradition to the effect that wealthy Jewish merchants, drawing on their own traditions and also on that of the Greek *gynaeceum*, may have entered into "Veblenian" competition with one another to show how expensively excluded they kept their wives (345). Still, as Boulding reminds us, the more we learn about female exclusionism, the less certain we are about it.

Although the Koran did not authorize the seclusion of women, tribal custom among the Muslim did (Fernea and Bezirgan, 1977, xxv). The veil began as a symbol of privilege rather than as an ideological imperative. Whatever the origin, the result was the creation of two different "societies": "The long practice of veiling, seclusion, and general social segregation of the sexes have helped to create and maintain two quite different societies; the world of men and the world of women" (xxv). The women's world developed its "own cultural values, its own definitions of status and prestige, whether the settings have been urban, rural, or nomadic" (xxi). It is interesting to note—as illustrative of the bias in our research—that old as this secluded world is, it has been so inadequately studied that there is "much . . . yet to be learned about these separate worlds, their expression in verbal, emotional, and social terms, their interactions and juxtapositions in all aspects of life" (xxv). Only recently has it begun to be studied by women, to "perceive the complex network of relationships and power bases that emanate from it" (xxv).[14]

Hanna Papanek has analyzed the subtle ramifications of this female life style in its modern form, including those ramifications that deal with the division of labor. For one of the interesting concomitants of segregation by purdah is the existence of a set of parallel systems. In one, the female, women can acquire competence and high status in the prestigious professions, for there must be physicians and professors to cater to the separate needs of women (Papanek, 1971, 524-526). On a lower level the work of women has been weaving, sewing, embroidering, home piecework from factories, cooking, child care; raising chickens, sheep, goats, vegetables; processing milk, yogurt; and fortune-telling (Fernea and Bezirgan, xxvi). The system of seclusion, in brief, produced both privilege and exploitation. Women in some classes enjoyed a pleasant life while women in others endured demeaning isolation. "The upperclass women's world 'behind the veil' had its full share of ceremonies, comforts, friendships, enjoyments and household servants. But the life of poor women in a Bengali village . . . justly fits the description provided by the rural reformer Akhtar Hameed Khan—'our women are like frogs down a deep well' " (Papanek, 1973, 300).

One of the most interesting processes in the Arab world today is the unraveling of the old system of female segregation. It happens at different rates in different countries, even—at however slow a rate—in the most conservative of all, Saudi Arabia (Harwood, 1978).

Lesbian Communities: Counterculture Ideology

So much for female life styles based on religious ideology. The final examples are of a kind of female community based, in a way, on political ideology, namely lesbian communities. The beguines had mingled in the life of the outside world protected by their habit which proclaimed to all and sundry that they were not interested in male relationships. Analogous to the beguines in their rejection of male relationships but by no means identical with them are the women who establish lesbian communities for themselves in modern settings. These communities also consist of households of varying size whose members keep in touch with one another by way of an active network. The members of the several households share recreational facilities and activities; some earn their living in female-operated enterprises, such as bookstores or gas stations.

Most of the information about female worlds discussed so far has to be pieced together from fragmentary—largely historical—data. In the case of present-day lesbian communities we have the advantage of the insights of sophisticated participants and academic researchers. One academic study describes a community of between two thousand and five thousand women in San Francisco in the mid-1970s (Wolf, 1979). Like the beguines, these women lived in certain areas of the city, usually "ethnically mixed, older, working-class areas" which "bound each other and have in common a quality of neighborhood life, low-rent housing, and the possibility of maintaining a kind of anonymity" (98). The households varied in composition from single individuals living alone to couples sharing a household, to mothers and their children all living together, to collectives or "houses" sharing political activisim, to mixed groups such as a lesbian living with gay men or with a heterosexual mother and her children (100-101). Propinquity facilitated a considerable amount of socializing and visiting, an important part of the social life of the community.

There was heterogeneity among the members. There were older gays socialized in a frightening ambience and younger, more militant and aggressive gays. There were upper-class professional women and working-class women, married and nonmarried, political activists and nonactivists, separatists and nonseparatists, bar-oriented and home-oriented members. Some thought of themselves as cultural feminists, some as lesbian feminist socialists. There was factionalism, even conflict. But there were recognized ways for dealing with it. When divisive differences threatened, "mutual friends may try to mediate, or the women in question may meet to work through the differences between them. If a resolution is not possible, those who are in disagreement may simply agree to disagree" (31). In this event, the women were released from their friendship or pair relationship and freed to seek another partner or realign themselves in a different social unit (81).

In the present context it is of interest to note that lesbian friendships, "the core of their personal support group," are taken most seriously; they serve the function of kin (97-98). Still, it is the pair relationship that is the building block of the community (88). It is above all egalitarian in nature. Most of the women say they seek mates who will be their partners not only sexually but also emotionally and intellectually. But since such relationships are hard to find—in this or in any other human community—the most typical pattern is one of "serial monogamy," that is, of fidelity as long as the relationship lasts but not necessarily permanent commitment (93).

The basic values of the community are mutual support and sisterhood. "These women are there when you need them!" Ideologically committed to egalitarianism, it seeks to function without any formal structure. What structure there is takes the form of "a series of overlapping social networks in which friendship groups focus around pair relationships or special interests" (80). The more activist women became more widely known than the less activist women, but there was a determined effort to prevent the rise of personal power or leaders. Actually, some women tend to have more influence than others on the basis of personality characteristics, "but there is a self-conscious effort at maintaining group process in decision making" (80). As a result of such repudiation of formal structure, there is great fluidity in group configuration, members moving in and out of groups with great freedom (80). There is not necessarily interaction between or among all members of the community, but all recognize one another and know where they fit into the overall structure (80).

Among the community facilities are seven bars, two coffee shops, and several bookstores (103). There are dances, benefits, classes (80). Social life tends to consist of entertaining in the home.

Wolf summarizes some of the outcomes of life in this community for its members. One is a new conception of women's history; another is a reaffirmation of the intuitive aspects of life to counterbalance the consequences of a competitive social system. Especially important is the sense of self-worth, often a casualty of the social condemnation of lesbianism. Among the unconscious assumptions of such groups, Wolf lists the following: women can overcome the bad effects of their socialization in a misogynist male society; a world governed by people with female characteristics would make it possible for all to develop their potential and live cooperative and caring lives; children are less experienced than adults but no less deserving of respect; the nuclear family stifles children; relationships between and among women must be egalitarian; theology has been male-oriented and must be restructured to center on or, at least, include females.

Another study describes a lesbian community in Oregon from the perspective of a participant. This research, by Barnhart (1975), was designed to study family relationships, not community structure, but it did include some background information on the community. In fact, commitment to the couple relationship was considered as less important than commitment to the community. When or if a couple relationship came to take precedence over the community, members were ostracized. In a conflict of loyalties—partner or community—the first gave way to the second. Pair relationships were less stable, more uncertain, less permanent. When or if the pair relationship was felt to be more permanent than the community relationship, the women left (112-113).

The community functioned much like a family. Barnhart quotes Melford Spiro's study of relationships in the kibbutz in the 1950s: "The kibbutz can function without the family because it functions as if it, itself, were a family; and it can so function because its members perceive each other as kin, in the psychological implications of that term. . . . [The members] view each other as . . . comrades, who comprise a group in which each is intimately related to each other, and in which the welfare of the one is bound up with the welfare of the other" (92). She also quotes Robert Redfield, an anthropologist, to illustrate the folk nature of the community: "As in a folk society, the members have a strong sense of belonging together. The group . . . see their own resemblances and feel correspondingly united. Communicating intimately with each other has a strong claim on the sympathies of the others."

A sexual preference for women is only the least of the three commitments required for membership in a lesbian community. Most important is "identifying with the counterculture youth movement and advocating its ideas." Next is "devoting the major portion of time and energy to the Community, placing primary value on Community activities, and having as an ideal, commitment to the Community." And only finally, being a lesbian (Barnhart, 93). Indeed, if one leaves out one phrase, "to form pair relationships," the functions of the lesbian community do not sound too different from those of a beguinage, namely: "the primary function of the Community is to provide the members with a psychological kin group. Secondary to this main function, and because of it, the individual is able to achieve economic stability, to be instructed on behavior and values of Community membership. . . . A feeling of esprit de corps appears to give the member a feeling of security, identity, and ego enhancement" (92). The community, then, organizes the lives of its members, enforcing rules for their behavior. It exercises its control "through a characteristic life style, exclusive membership, a system of values and ideals, beliefs, and folklore" (93). It provides living arrangements, leisure-time activities and, for some, work. A core member "lives in a communal Community household, . . . works in a Community job, and . . . relaxes by participating in Community leisure activities" (93). Thus, in return for their commitment, members receive support, friendship, and love (103).

It is not hard for me to imagine a young nun or beguine torn between a lover and her convent or beguinage. Not a likely occurrence, to be sure, but at least imaginable. Just so may a young lesbian be torn between her love for another member of the community and loyalty to the community itself. If a pair relationship thus comes to take precedence over the community, there may ensue a "basic conflict between the individual's involvement in a pair and her involvement in the Community. Because of the values of the Community, the member lives in a quandary. She must choose between the Community and her pair relationship. For most, the Community and its values are chosen" (111-112).

Barnhart summarizes her findings:

> Belief in the counterculture ideals, even if not realized, pulls women into the Community. . . . What distinguishes the Community . . . is the amount of social and ideological integration which forms a cohesive bond within the Community, giving the group a social structure and organization not found in nonresidential urban groups. . . . Like a Kibbutz . . . it shows strong signs of psychological kinship. . . . [It] involves a belief and value system based upon the women's movement and counterculture and lesbianism. . . . Demonstrable and recognized social values . . . define the norms . . . for the group to follow. There is a sanction system that regulates the participants' actions and behavior, encouraging them to behave according to acceptable norms. In the Community, as in the Kibbutz [as, indeed, in a convent or beguinage or Lowell boarding house], a member who violates accepted norms experiences pressure from the [other] members. [112-113]

Different as they are in almost every way, both occupationally and ideologically based female life styles have something in common. The women are together because they are engaged in common or related tasks or because they share common beliefs. But these two parameters do not include all kinds of female communities. Arlie Hochschild, for example, tells us about her discovery of "an unexpected community" in a housing project in San Francisco (1973). There has to be room in any collage of female life styles for such "accidental," or fortuitous or adventitious communities. Hochschild's happened to be a cheerful one; others—prisons, mental hospitals, concentration camps—are not.

Adventitious Female Worlds

The idea of the "merry widow" is a modern conception, applying—when or if it ever does—only to financially well-endowed women. In societies which assume the economic dependence of women on men, the death of a male support, in the absence of surrogate family support, can be calamitous. Thus widows and orphans have been charges on the conscience and resources of communities from time immemorial.[15] But if a woman has independent means or is self-supporting, though she may not be merry, yet with other women around her, she can still be content. As they were, for example, in Merrill Court, the "unexpected community" Hochschild tells us about.

It was adventitious in the sense that no one had planned or even anticipated it. It just evolved. It consisted of forty-three old people, mainly women, most of them—thirty-five—widowed. "The social arrangements that took root early in the history of Merrill Court later assumed a life of their own. They were designed, as if on purpose, to assure an *on-going* community. If we were to visually diagram the community, it would look like a social circle on which there are centripetal and centrifugal pressures. The formal role system, centered in the circle, pulled people toward it by giving them work and rewards, and this process went on mainly 'downstairs.' At the same time, informal loyalty networks fluctuated toward and away from the circle. They became clear mainly 'upstairs.' Relatives and outsiders pulled the individual away from the circle downstairs and networks [pulled them] upstairs although they were occasionally pulled inside both" (1973, 47). "Upstairs" relationships were closer than "downstairs" relationships. One stopped in for a cup of coffee in "upstairs" relationships; inviting a person to lunch was more serious. Information was relayed by way of friendships and neighboring activities, serving thereby as a form of social control. The women took care of one another: those in good health looked after those in poor health; those who could easily go down for mail brought up mail for those who could not; a friend would take care of another's plants during her absence, or lend kitchen utensils, or take phone messages, or even write letters for those who could not write well enough (53). Still, much as these women enjoyed their friendships with one another, they retained warm relationships with their children, especially daughters. Both kinds of relationships—family and friends—were warm and affectionate, though different in quality.[16]

Adventitious in a wholly different way is the female community of the prison. Here one of the most interesting aspects is the style of organization the women and girls create for themselves, namely a familial pattern. Current research on female prisons reports a complex of family roles, male as well as female, all performed by the women. Both adult women and girls tend to form families which include husbands, lovers, and brothers as well as wives, sisters, and mothers. One informant in an institution for delinquent girls reports: "That's all everybody talks about. Who's going with who. Who's getting married" (Giallombardo, 1974, 244).

In contrast to the male inmate community, which tends to be violent, power-oriented, and engaged in illicit activities, the female inmate community organizes itself according to the sex roles of outside society:

> The way in which roles are defined in the external world influences the definitions made within the prison. General features of the cultural definitions and content of male and female roles in American society are brought into the prison setting, and they function to determine the directional focus of the inmate cultural system. . . . The family group in female prisons is singularly suited to meet the inmates' internalized cultural expectations of the female role; it serves the social, psychological, and physiological needs of

> the adult female inmate. Together, the prison homosexual marriage and the larger kinship network provide structure wherein the female inmate may express herself during incarceration. [2-4]

Some of the sexual relations between and among the women are unstable, but there are also large networks of "loosely structured nuclear families, matricentric families of varying sizes, and other kinship dyadic configurations or family fragments" (2). All this, of course, is quite outside the formal prison structure imposed on the women.

We are offered a glimpse into yet another kind of female "community" in another kind of prison, this time an insane "asylum." Here the patients represent every shade of mental illness, of background, of education. There is hardly any common basis even for friendship. The formal structure is feudal, with a hierarchy of personnel in positions of power over the women ranging in qualifications and sympathy from some night nurses, quite untrained for the chores they must perform and not incapable of real cruelty, to psychiatrists, some, but not all, of whom show sympathy and understanding. Within this structure the women learn to help one another, to mitigate some of the worst suffering. One perceptive patient, assuming the role of observer, writes in her notebook addressed to "Shakespeare":

> It is odd what living here with these people does to you. There can be little companionship motivated by any common interest in a specific subject. There is no common meeting ground for conversation or exchange of opinions—and yet, there is something that flows between us, I think, greater and more sympathetic than if we were able to converse intelligently with each other.
>
> We know each other better than most people in other places ever learn to know one another. Our understanding is greater than any explanation that could be contained in words. I do not know what it is, because I have no understanding of it—and yet I have felt it keenly when it was in operation; an invisible current of communication which brought very close to my own soul things others were feeling. And more than once there has been evidence of keen understanding and sympathy in the hearts of those others towards me, flowing out in mysterious channels, so hidden, so subtle as it flowed through the turmoil of their raving that I do not wonder at the fact that some folk miss it completely.
>
> People who are sane know little of the things communicated by other means than the clumsy speech organs. Though there is little communication in the accepted sense of the word between these people here, I think I must be very demented myself for thinking the understanding between us is greater than other people have.
>
> All the small things which are the grip of sanity have fallen away and we are all run together and mingle as one in the great brotherhood of dementia. We share as one person the things each experiences individually. . . . [Jefferson, 1975, 133-134]

Illustrative of another adventitious female "community," this time not in an ordinary prison but in a Nazi concentration camp, is one woman's account of her experiences at Ravensbruck:

> The fact that I survived Ravensbruck I owe first—and most definitely—to chance, then to anger and the motivation to reveal the crimes I had witnessed, and finally to a union of friendship, since I had lost the instinctive and physical desire to live. This tenuous web of friendship was, in a way, almost submerged by the stark brutality of selfishness and the struggle for survival, but somehow everyone in the camp was invisibly woven into it. It bound together surrogate "families": two, three, or four women from the same town who had been arrested in the same "affair," or perhaps a group formed within a prison cell or in a railroad car at the time of their deportation—all of them later clinging to one another to keep from being engulfed in the horrors of the prison camps. The major dividing line—more than nationality, political party, or religion—was language. But there were networks of mutual aid which functioned above these sometimes artifical divisions. [Tillion, 1975, xxii]

Does It Add Up?

With such a kaleidescopic range of social forms—from banking establishments to scholarly retreats, from industrial lobbying groups to bawling websters, from prison "families" to cloistered schoolgirls—it will be understandable why I promised no theory, no typology, no generalization at the beginning of this chapter. Without standardized data for all of the examples, not even comparison is feasible. Beyond the cliché that the specialization of function between the sexes which leads to a sexual division of labor[17] and the consequent sharing of tasks and functions may explain the existence of a female world, there is no simple theory that explains the special forms it takes in any particular time or place. Have they depended on the ecological environment? economic organization? technological development? ownership of the means of production? adventitious forces? all or none of the above? Must we invoke a unique explanation for each form, or can we find commonalities among them? Are there common threads running through the variegated forms? Does a twentieth-century lesbian community, for example, have anything in common with, say, a beguinage?

Even for descriptive purposes, what are the essential parameters? Size, of course, and demographic structure, including age, education, and class, both within the community and vis-à-vis the outside world. But these social forms are more than a sum of variables. What degree—extreme or moderate—and what kind of separation or segregation—spatial, ideological, symbolic, physical, all of the above—were involved? Did the women live in closely delineated spatial boundaries or in scattered habitations? What kinds of boundary-maintenance techniques were used? physical or symbolic or ideological or all of these? How autonomous were the women as individuals or as communities? How independent of the male world? What was the degree of choice involved in participation in the first place? What kinds of formal organization characterized them? Informal? Were there social networks? What were their extent and nature? What kinds of alternatives were there? And beyond description there are other questions. What kinds of systems made for close bonding among the women? What kinds discouraged it? What kinds were centrifugal, which centripetal? And so on.

Interesting and important as these questions are, both substantively and theoretically, they are not pursued further here. Instead we turn to the story of a female world that we know considerably more about: our own. We begin our discussion, then, with a brief historical overview of the American scene.

Notes

1. The importance of marketing or trade in the lives of women is highlighted by the work of anthropologists, especially in Africa. Among the Belgian Congolese, about half of the traders were women in 1959; some were hawkers, but most traded in the market (cited by Paulme, 1971, 268). In Togoland, petty trade was the most important of the three traditional occupations (the other two being agriculture and dressmaking), and the "middlemen" were practically all women (270). Paulme also refers to the economic independence of African women resulting from their aptitude for trade, "which enables them to accumulate possessions quite separate from those of their husband" (270). She refers also to Ghana, where women show the same aptitude for trade and by 1959 were beginning to organize themselves (271). Especially interesting is the part played by women as illicit traders in beer. Paulme, citing E. Hillman, tells us that "this trade is changing the status of women, for they are acquiring independence and control of their own lives. (Widows and women who have been abandoned prefer to make their own living by this trade rather than return to their own families.) The trade has given rise to an association of the nature of a mutual aid society or a savings bank. These data, collected in Johannesburg in 1933-34, are still valid, and for other urban centres as well" (281).

   Whether or not women in other parts of the world who engaged in trade resembled the African women there is no way of knowing. Still, the African experience is suggestive. As an afterthought, it is interesting that when women increased their personal resources they spent their earnings differently from the way men did. "Instead of buying traditional titles to prestige, as the men continue to do, they prefer to spend it on material improvements and on sending their children to school" (Paulme, citing Ottenberg on the Afikpo Ibo, 285).

2. Their story lends itself to so many contexts that it seems constricting to use it merely to illustrate a special kind of female life style. It is important for the light it casts on early industrial capitalism, on the impact of women's family roles on labor organization, on the public-relations use made of the young women, on attitudes toward women in the labor force, on the mettle of the young women themselves as they engaged in spontaneous explosions or "turnouts" when their working conditions deteriorated and their wages declined, on their attempts to organize a union or Factory Girls' Association (Josephson, 1949, 226-227), on the process of succession whereby one ethnic group—in this case the Irish—followed another—in this case, daughters of New Englanders—in the lower echelons of industry. So much history and sociology are reflected in this short span of time—the 1830s—that any one facet extracted from the situation dwarfs the total picture. Still, for present purposes only one aspect is selected, namely the kind of lives these young women lived among themselves in the mill-provided boarding houses.
3. The "Lowell girls" did not have good leadership. When, for example, Orestes Brownson, thinking he was championing the cause of labor, referred to the moral hazards of young women living alone, Harriet Farley, editor of the *Lowell Offering*, the operatives' magazine, did not see that he was dealing with the basic issue of labor conditions, and fell upon what she interpreted as an aspersion on the moral character of the young women. She thus became an apologist for the owners—accused, in fact, of toadying to them—rather than a champion of the women (Josephson, 1949). She emphasized the ladylike behavior of the operatives, who would not become the tools of aristocrats or demagogues or surround City Hall in a mob; they would find more acceptable ways to redress their wrongs. She had lost touch with the young women; not many of them subscribed to her magazine anyway. Before long she was herself replaced by another woman—Sarah G. Bagley—and her magazine was replaced by *The Voice of Industry*, more representative of the operatives' point of view.
4. Most of the "Lowell girls" were still closely tied to their families even when they were not living at home. They planned to marry after a few years.
5. The sex ratio in Frankfurt in 1382 was 1,100 women for every 1,000 men; in Nuremberg in 1449, 1,207; in Basel in 1454, 1,246 (Power, 1975, 55).
6. Emily Jones Putnam, relying on the research of Eckenstein's *Woman under Monasticism*, sketches the process by which the Church took over native holy personages and practices and redefined them as Christian. In this process "the old status of woman was abundantly reflected. A purely patriarchal religion would not serve; the Virgin and the female saints became more and more necessary to bridge the chasm. It is not by accident that the festivals of the Virgin so often coincide with those of heathen deities" (1970, 74-75).
7. Nunneries were variously supported. Many of the wealthy early ones were, in effect, great feudal estates with incomes from extensive land holdings. Some were beneficiaries of endowments or of wills. Many of the women brought doweries with them and the boarders, of course, no doubt paid their way. Later on many were frugally run by religious orders vowed to

poverty. Some were great financial institutions.

8. For example:

> Except for certain periods of relaxation, strict silence had to be observed, and if nuns had to communicate with each other they had to do this by a sort of deaf and dumb language. The persons who drew up the signs in use seem to have combined preternatural ingenuity with a very exiguous sense of humour; the speechless pandemonium which went on at convent dinner must have been more mirth provoking than speech. A sister who wanted fish would "wag her hands . . . in the manner of a fish tail"; if she wanted to say "pass the milk" she would "draw her little finger in the manner of milking"; a guilty sacristan struck by the thought that she had not provided incense for mass would "put her two fingers into her nostrils." [Power, 1975, 93]

9. Gaye Tuchman sees some of these convents as, in effect, "preparatory schools" for the seventeenth- and eighteenth-century salons (1975, 181).

10. In the foundation documents, these women agreed upon eleven articles for the organization of each house. These dealt almost exclusively with protecting the common property and guaranteeing to each a continued income. The only provisions of a religious or moral nature were simply the obligations of the beguine life. Any unchastity was to result in the expulsion of the guilty person; no man was to be brought into the house at night; and deference was to be shown for the religious counsels of the Dominican adviser. Future members were to adopt a religious dress similar to that of the others already there. "Habitum nostrum susceptura" was the phrase used to describe the step of entering the house. For the rest, the predominant interest seems to have been the maintenance of the common property. No one was to disturb the others in the house. Obedience was to be promised to the mistress of the house, but since the statutes provided for no regimen of religious discipline there is no reason to suppose that the original authority of the mistress extended beyond the administration of property and the material life of the group. . . . At a ceremony in which the statutes were to be read within a year after the entry of the newcomer into the house, she was to promise to obey the rules. . . . The peculiar thing about these houses was not their monastic character but the fact that they arose through the mutual agreement of women who, on their own initiative, gave an impersonal institutional character to the property and houses owned by themselves or their families. [Phillips, 1941, 166-167]

11. Helen Ebaugh notes that until Vatican II, the religious orders were in effect following the rules delineated by Robert Jay Lifton in his study of *Thought Reform and the Psychology of Totalism*. (1977, 197).

12. There is little, if any, serious research dealing with sexual relationships in convents, beguinages, or factory life. From Boccaccio we learn that there was a considerable amount of sex play in the monasteries and convents, but there is little genuine documentation of it. There is in the lesbian culture a bit of—humorous—lore about women in convents. One story, for ex-

ample, has to do with a sister in charge of novices who always had a long queue of young novices waiting to talk to her. The bottom line was that when the young women came in she encouraged them to nurse from her breast. Midge Turk comments that "all those eighteenth-century European works about nuns being raped and loving it certainly haven't helped matters" (1971, 55). In her own American experience of eighteen years she knew "of no overt sexual relationships between nuns and real-world men or between nuns and priests. There were a few relationships between nuns. . . . This is not to imply that there didn't exist neurotic unconsummated attachments. There did. But they were the exceptions" (56). Sisters were forbidden even to visit each other in their rooms (108).

13. Turk tells of her own experience in coming to terms with other women. Required to examine herself for faults, she found that one of her worst was her critical attitude toward women she did not like. "It was a tremendous step forward when one day I found that I was actually happy that someone I didn't really like at all had succeeded in doing well something that I couldn't do at all. This was so new to me, so exciting, really. The sense of brotherhood [sic] I felt was surprising and absolutely true" (56-57). A considerable amount of emotional weight was imposed by the enforced rules of behavior. Even disagreements had to be extremely low-key. "It was at St. Joseph's that I witnessed my first nun argument. Some point was being hotly contested, but the exchange was almost whispered, softly and calmly. 'Sister, I would like to disagree with you about that.' 'Oh, of course, Sister, if you disapprove.' Nuns did not yell. I remember thinking that it took a lot to be angry in that manner" (67).

14. To say that there have been few studies of seclusion does not mean that there was no writing at all on the subject. An occasional woman writer did pierce the walls of a hareem or of female quarters and report on what she saw. Harriet Martineau was one such reporter. After describing the extreme grief shown by one of the women in an Egyptian hareem, Martineau, in 1848, notes that

> it was not a child of her own that she was mourning, but that of a white girl in the hareem; and that the wife's illness was wholly from grief for the loss of this baby; a curious illustration of the feelings and manners of the place! The children born in large hareems are extremely few; and they are usually idolised, and sometimes murdered. It is known that in the houses at homes which morally most resemble these hareems (though little enough externally) when the rare event of the birth of a child happens, a passionate joy extends over the wretched household; jars are quieted, drunkenness is moderated, and there is no self-denial which the poor creatures will not undergo during this gratification of their feminine instincts. They will nurse the child all night in illness, and pamper it all day with sweetmeats and toys; they will fight for the possession of it, and be almost heartbroken at its loss; and lose it they must; for the child always dies—killed with kindness, even if born healthy. This natural outbreak of feminine instinct takes place in the too populous hareem, when a child is given to any one of the many who are longing for the gift; and if it

dies naturally, it is mourned as we saw through a wonderful conquest of personal jealousy by this general instinct. But when the jealousy is uppermost—what happens then?—why, the strangling the innocent in its sleep—or the letting it slip from the window into the river below—or the mixing poison with its food; the mother and the murderess, always rivals and now fiends, being shut up together for life. If the child lives, what then? If a girl, she sees before her from the beginning the nothingness of external life, and the chaos of interior existence, in which she is to dwell for life. If a boy, he remains among the women till ten years old, seeing things when the eunuchs come in to romp, and hearing things among the chatter of the ignorant women which brutalise him for life. . . .

We saw, I think, about 20 more women—some slaves—most or all young. . . . The girls went out and came in, but, for the most part, stood in a half circle. . . . Some went to play in the neighbouring apartments. . . . Everywhere they pitied us European women heartily, that we had to go about travelling, and appearing in the streets without being properly taken care of—that is, watched. They think us strangely neglected in being left so free, and boast of their spy systems and imprisonment as tokens of the value in which they are held." [Martineau, 1848, present citation from Goulianos, 1973, 202-204]

For a more scholarly study of the Egyptian women's secluded life style in the late nineteenth and early twentieth centuries, see Margot Badran, "Huda Shacrawi: Memoirs of an Egyptian Nationalist and Feminist" (Paper read at the Fourth Berkshire Conference, Mt. Holyoke College, August 1978). By this time upper-class women had learned that Islam did not require separation; new networks with European, especially French, women stimulated new ideas; French novels, plays, and operas showed life in an integrated society; salons for women gave them opportunities to talk among themselves; the European women who served as nurses and teachers had an important impact on children and girls. In time these women were permitted to travel. Unveiled in Europe, they found it harder to resume the veil at home. The recent work of Hanna Papanek carries on the story from there.

15. Serving as professional mourners was a common occupation for widows in classical times. There were 1,500 members of an Order of Widows in Rome early in the second century, and 3,000 in Antioch (Boulding, 1976, 359).
16. Gerde Wekerle reports a similar solidary group of older women in Carl Sandburg Village, a high-rise development in Chicago (1975). Older women in ethnic enclaves also preserve vestiges of these solidary worlds (Schoenberg, 1976, draft).
17. For a sketch of women's share in the division of labor, see E. Boulding, (1976, 95-117).

PART II

Stations and Spheres

Now that the Victorian age has receded far enough behind us so that we can see it in perspective, and now that historians are uncovering so much of its structure and operation, their work becomes a major source for understanding the world of women that was such an interesting part of that age.

We begin in Chapter 4 with a brief statement of the way the female world looked to many people at the end of the eighteenth century and how a "fixed station" or status conceptualization gave way to a "sphere" conceptualization (which, it may be noted in passing, resembled in many ways Boulding's concept of the integry, discussed above in Chapter 2). In the nineteenth century, the concept of women's sphere was a powerful ideological tool to explain and justify the increasing separation between the worlds of women and of men which accompanied industrialization and urbanization. It did not wholly supplant the earlier station concept—spheres themselves contained statuses—but it did give the older view greater scope. Chapter 4 recounts how women's sphere arose as an ideological construct and functioned to reconcile women to a subordinate relationship with men.

Chapter 5 deals with the way women's sphere looked from the inside, with the actual behavior of women—including the friendships they formed and the support they derived from them—rather than with ideology. It also briefly considers the ideology of women's sphere, the "philogyny" or homosociality it fostered, and its long survival into the twentieth century.

4

Stations and Spheres

An Old Idea: Stations

> The rich man in his castle,
> The poor man at the gate.
> God made them, high or lowly
> And ordered their estate.
> Sunday school song sung in 18th and 19th centuries

At the end of the eighteenth century, European society consisted of a system of "positions" or "places" or "stations" or statuses, and people knew their own precise location in it. Those in lower positions "knew their place" vis-à-vis their "betters" and did not "presume." A whole array of boundary-maintaining devices—etiquette, clothes, language, vocal intonations, posture, body carriage, facial expressions—kept the several levels clearly distinguished. All, obviously, prescribed by God and necessary for social order.

The world view of most people was still physiocratic, oriented toward the land. The landed gentry held a high position, ascribed on the basis of inheritance; one did not have to earn position. At the same time, though, there were tough, enterprising, astute men who were learning how to organize production in factories, how to expand markets, how to create and manage capital and credit, how to bank. In

1776, Adam Smith had taught them and the government that land was only one of the factors producing national wealth. Labor and capital were also fundamentally involved as well as the talent for putting them all together. These entrepreneurs had low status, along with people "in trade." They did not appear prominently in the literature of the age. Indeed, inherited wealth was far more honorific than earned wealth. To the landed gentry, the signs of the new system were appalling, including railroads which contaminated the rural scene, and towns which blemished the landscape. Less visible to the naked eye but no less devastating to the old order was the tearing up of old class and sex-role structures, and, in the process, the reorganizing of work, as hundreds of thousands of men and women were uprooted from the farms and deposited in towns. The impact on women was epochal.

Although this ancient régime, this old structure, was caving in by the end of the eighteenth century, not everyone noticed. It takes a long time to see what is actually happening to a society. When people did notice, however, many fought the changes they saw creeping up on them, in both the class and the sex-role structure. Among these who resisted change was Hannah More, an influential British writer, near-contemporary of Mary Wollstonecraft. In one of More's innumerable tracts and disquisitions, *Coelebs*, she laid down the pattern for a lady. It became, in America as well as in Great Britain, the model of feminine behavior, the hallmark for the Victorian gentlewoman—modest, pious, charitable, pleasing in both appearance and manner, and above all, proper. Propriety was, according to More, the first, second, and third requisite of the female role (Jones, 1968, 195).

More was an ardent, prolific, and widely acclaimed protector of the status quo. It was clear to her that although some places in society were humbler than others, all were honorable and respectable. The occupants of every station had responsibilities toward those of every other. In More's version of the principles people should live by, "People were rigidly classified and their duties laid down. The gentry were under obligation to look after the laborers on their estates and expected, but not compelled, to distribute part of their riches among their dependents. If the rich evaded this duty they could look forward to punishment in the next world, while if the poor suffered over much, it would be made up to them in Heaven" (Hopkins, 1947, 7).

This mind-set with respect to the class structure of society was echoed with respect to the sex-role structure. For just as peasants had their place, carpenters theirs, the gentry theirs, the clergy theirs, so also did women have their position in the scheme of things. The natural order applied to the sexes as well as to the classes. And, more to the point, it was wrong to try to tinker with it or attempt to change it seriously (as Wollstonecraft's execrable "Vindication of the Rights of

Women" so obviously did). Most people probably agreed with More that any "questioning of church, government, social distinctions, was ... sacrilegious and theories looking toward governmental changes ... [were] treasonable" (Hopkins, 222). Neither More nor Wollstonecraft could of course have known how fundamental were the changes already in the process of restructuring their society.

More did, however, believe that she could see the implications for the social order of changes in the sex-role structure as well as in the class structure of society. They would be harmful to women. "They little understand the true interests of woman who would lift her from the important duties of her allotted station, to fill with fantastic[1] dignity a loftier but less appropriate niche" (1799, 21). It was better all around for women to know their place and stay in it:

> Is it not ... more wise as well as more honorable to move contentedly in the plain path that Providence has obviously marked out to the sex, and in which custom has for the most part rationally confirmed them, than to stray awkwardly, unbecomingly, unsuccessfully, in a forbidden road? Is it not desirable to be the lawful possessors of a lesser domestic territory, rather than the turbulent usurpers of a wider foreign empire? to be good originals, rather than bad imitators? to be the best thing of one's own kind, rather than an inferior thing even if it were of a higher kind? to be excellent women rather than indifferent men? [21-23]

Hannah More, of course, was writing about the "place" of middle- or upper-class women, of "gentlewomen," of "ladies." Not all women had the kind of place she prescribed for them. And although Mary Wollstonecraft was aware of the problems of working women, they were primarily the problems of genteel working women. The "place" of a considerable number of women was not mentioned. The place of the earliest industrial working women, for example, the women who were crawling in the mines for coal, or who were in the "workhouses" with locked doors, farmed out with their children by their straw-boss husbands. Or the luckier ones, in New England mills. That these women existed did not blemish the image of women's "station"; More's tracts went through numerous editions throughout the nineteenth century. Nor was she a voice crying out in the wilderness. There were countless other writers, preachers, and polemicists carrying the same message.

In time the affluent Victorian lady More had written for and of became more and more fragile, delicate, clinging, helpless physically—though not morally or spiritually—weak, dependent, modest, pure.[2] We know that relatively few Victorian women were really like this. No society could afford such a model for half its population. Certainly American society could not. The frontier called for just the opposite, as did the settled farms and even the mills and factories, not to mention the households of working-class families. The Victorian lady was a luxury that only affluent families could afford,[3] and probably not every woman, even the affluent, wanted to be such a lady.

Resistance, however, eloquent though it might be, was impotent in the face of the changes then taking place. The end of the eighteenth century and the beginning of the nineteenth marked a transition, a point at which local markets were beginning to give way to more complex markets and more and more work was beginning to move out of the home, separating, even segregating, the work of women from that of men. A new doctrine, a doctrine of sexual spheres, thus arose to facilitate, explain, rationalize, and justify this growing separation of women in the home from men in outside work. The new situation that had to be explained and justified was described by Tocqueville when it had crystalized in 1840 as follows:

> In no country has such constant care been taken as in America to train two clearly distinct lines of action for the two sexes, and to make them keep pace one with the other, but in two pathways which are always different. American women never manage the outward concerns of the family, or conduct a business, or take a part in political life; nor are they, on the other hand, ever compelled to perform the rough labor of the fields, or to make any of those laborious exertions which demand the exertion of physical strength. No families are so poor as to form an exception to this rule. [1840, 225]

A New Idea: Spheres

I have not made a purposive search of the literature to find the first usage of the term "women's sphere." According to the Oxford Dictionary, the term "sphere" was first used in other than astronomical or geometrical contexts in the early years of the seventeenth century, so there may well have been some application of the concept to women long before the late eighteenth century. Wollstonecraft (1792) used both the station and the sphere conceptualizations. She spoke, for example, of the duties of a woman's station as well as of the male station (142), of rank (147), of respectable station (148), but also of the female world (174) and of women's sphere (177). Whatever the date when the concept of women's sphere was introduced, it colored people's thinking about women for well over a century. In contrast to the "station" concept, which implied an integrated system in which all positions were in well-defined and fixed status relationships with one another, the "sphere" concept denoted a separatist system. Equal in value, its apologists insisted, but nevertheless separate.

For a long time almost all of the thinking dealing with women implied, wittingly or unwittingly, that there was something archetypical about women's sphere, something traceable to Adam and Eve. "Etiquette books, advice books on child rearing, religious sermons, guides to young men and women, medical texts, and school curricula all suggest that late eighteenth- and most nineteenth-century Americans assumed the existence of a world composed of distinctly male and female spheres, spheres determined by the immutable laws of God and nature" (Cott, 1977, 9). Many still did, until yesterday.

Actually, as Kraditor notes, the restrictive concept of sphere did not seem so appropriate for the male world (1968). For the female world it was quite suitable. There is something cosy, protected, safe about the concept of a sphere. A sphere is enclosed and hence fits Erikson's conceptualization of the essence of what is female, "inner space" (1965, 239). It is also round and hence conforms to the curves of the female body. It has clear-cut boundaries. It might, in fact, well have served Peter the Pumpkin Eater.

Ideological Validation of Women's Sphere: The Problem of Equality and Subordination

The symbolism of the sphere was, I think, significant. It conveyed the idea of a clearly bounded entity with psychological and sociological "territoriality," a kind of female "turf," with a modicum of autonomy if not complete independence. There was a hint of this in More's figure of speech describing proper women as "lawful possessors of a lesser domestic territory, rather than the turbulent usurpers of a wider foreign empire." But more importantly, it helped to deal with the psychological problem of female inferiority and subordination.

Problems of equality troubled the female world not only with respect to slavery but also with respect to their own domestic servants (Chapter 11). Such inequality conflicted with the American democratic ideal (Beecher, 1841). It troubled them with respect to their own world vis-à-vis the male world as well. In the male world the solution came finally to be that if opportunities were equal, positions would be distributed on the basis of achievement and no one could be faulted for the inequality of the results. (Any boy could rise to become president of the United States. . . .) But this solution could not be applied to women.

Until late in the eighteenth century, Cott tells us, women had no consciousness of inferiority, although they were conscious of subjection. But both More and Wollstonecraft painted a horrendous picture of many women as indeed inferior in the sense of being frivolous, tyrannical, vain, trivial in their interests, childish, devious, trained only to please men. In the late eighteenth century questions began to be raised: Was this female weakness vis-à-vis men natural or artificial? Biological or cultural? Was such female inferiority the basis for female subordination and submission? Was the subordination of women a cause or a result of inferiority? Both More and Wollstonecraft came down hard on the artificial or cultural side; both faulted female education (read socialization). More writes:

> Till Women shall be more reasonably educated, and till the native growth of their mind shall cease to be stinted and cramped, we have no juster ground for pronouncing that their understanding has already reached its highest attainable point than the Chinese would have for affirming that their women have attained to the greatest possible perfection in walking, while the first care is, during their infancy, to cripple their feet. At least, till the female sex are more carefully instructed, this question will always remain as undecided as to the degree of difference between the masculine and feminine understanding, as the question between the understandings of blacks and whites; for until Africans and Europeans are put more nearly on a par in the cultivation of their minds, the shades of distinction, if any there be, between their native powers can never be fairly ascertained. (1799, 30-31)[4]

Even if women were inferior to men in certain respects, this in no way impugned them, for "the true value of woman is not diminished by the imputation of inferiority" (25). Nor did More believe that every woman was inferior to every man. Women had to insist on their own abilities because if they admitted any inferiority at all, "the weakest man instantly lays hold on the concession; and on the mere ground of sex, plumes himself on his own individual superiority; inferring that the silliest man is superior to the first-rate woman" (28-29). To the extent that women were inferior, then, this could be explained in terms of their socialization.[5] Proper education could go a long way toward surmounting it. And since innate inferiority was not imputed to women, their subordination had to be accounted for on other grounds. Catharine Beecher supplied such grounds.

A Functional Validation of Women's Sphere

Catharine Beecher (1800-1878) was the great theoretician and apologist for the separate-but-functionally-equal nature of women's sphere. Much of her apologia, with its frank recognition and acceptance of women's subordinate position, was based on her reading of Tocqueville, who had clearly distinguished equality from identity. Beecher substituted the division between the sexes for the division Tocqueville drew between classes. Trying to make men and women identical was preposterous; as he said, the attempt would result only in "weak men and disorderly women" (1840, 224). She had no illusions about equality. Nor did she, like More or Wollstonecraft, with their feudal historical backgrounds, view subordination as necessarily natural. It was, rather, a necessary political expedient for the maintenance of democracy. Although she exaggerated and emphasized gender differences, at the same time she sought to reconcile the political inequality of women with the ideology of democracy by emphasizing the importance of women's sphere.[6] The equality was in the functional contribution of women's sphere. Their work gave women a consciousness of the importance of their separate world for the national well being.

By accentuating sex differences, Beecher's conception thus circumvented the whole issue of inferiority. Women were performing a great national service, no less important than the service performed by men—that of providing religious morality and child nurture (Cott, 1977, 200). Success in the national experiment, indeed, rested largely on the success of women in their sphere. "A cultural halo ringing the significance of home and family—doubly brilliant because both religious and secular energies gave rise to it—reconnected woman's 'separate' sphere with the well-being of society" (199).

Still, it could not be taken for granted that women would accept their subordinate position freely without indoctrination. Different as they were, both More and Wollstonecraft believed that education should be designed to reconcile women to their subordinate position as well as to prepare them for it. In keeping with her principles, More established schools for the poor, "to convince them that God demanded of them contentment with their lowly station, long hours of work, low wages, coarse food, and plain living. Any laborer in the field or factory with exceptional ability was expected to use his good brain in making the most of what he had, not in obtaining more" (Hopkins, 1947, 7). The same logic applied to women. More wanted female education improved in order to make women better satisfied with their station in life. "The more a woman's understanding is improved, the more obviously she will discern that there can be no happiness in any society where there is a perpetual struggle for power; and the more her judgment is rectified, the more accurate views will she take of the station she herself was born to fill, and the more readily will she accommodate herself to it" (15).

Strangely enough, Wollstonecraft, who also saw the inferiority of women as a result of socialization and wanted their education improved so that they could take care of themselves should the occasion arise, agreed with More. Though she thought that "the female world [was] oppressed," she still saw education as better fitting women for it. She hoped the benign changes in the female world as a result of improved education would spread, and she looked forward to "general diffusion of that sublime contentment which only morality can diffuse" (1794, 174). One of her most telling arguments in behalf of female education was that it would make women better mothers. "So forcibly does this truth strike me," she wrote, "that I would rest the whole tendency of my reasoning upon it, for whatever tends to incapacitate the maternal character, takes woman out of her sphere" (177).

But despite their similarities (both, as Cott notes, deplored the way women were dealt with as sex objects and drudges, both advocated better education for women, and both upheld the mother's responsibility toward children [1977, 202]), More and Wollstonecraft were basically different in their orientation. Wollstonecraft's injection of the women's rights issue into the ongoing discussions of women's sphere immediately put the two ideologies in an adversary position. The concept of women's rights, said More, excited in women's hearts "an impious discontent with the post which God had assigned them in the world" (1799, 22). Nevertheless, Wollstonecraft's argument, Cott tells us, served to help women work out their own views; it gave them something to think against.

It was religion, however, that turned the balance. A religious movement known as the Second Great Awakening swept America in the late eighteenth and early nineteenth centuries and produced a different kind of sisterhood, one based on conversion (Cott, 1975). The "awakened" women "thought of themselves as one in their allegiance to the Savior and . . . shared their anxieties and exultations of faith" (Melder, 1977, 31). This Second Great Awakening, according to Cott, settled the issue with respect to egalitarianism, ensuring that the concept of the women's sphere would be one of subordination. The functions that made the female sphere equal to the male sphere in importance, if not in position, were emotional support, moral hegemony, and homemaking.

Women's Sphere as Realm of the Heart

> [Women's eyes] are the books, the arts, the academes,
> That show, contain, and nourish all the world. . . .
>
> Shakespeare, *Love's Labor Lost*,
> IV, iii, 351-353

The sphere of women reflected the love-and/or-duty dynamic. It was a realm of the heart and it was duty-bound to raise the moral level of society. Just as the instrumental role of women's sphere was to be taken seriously, so also and especially was its supportive, positive, expressive role. Women's sphere came to resemble Boulding's conception of the integry, as "that part of the total social system which deals with such concepts and relationships as . . . loyalty, love, trust, and so on" (1969, 3). It was a realm of the heart, whose "ruling purpose was to express affection, sympathies, consideration and tenderness toward others—in short, to love" (Cott, 1977, 164). Sex-role distinctions, Cott tells us, were already universal by the late eighteenth century, and "heart" was distinctly female (163).

The importance of this supportive, expressive function, or "heart," was highlighted as the brutality of the new economic system—the Gesellschaft—began to make itself increasingly felt. The home came to be seen as a protection against the harshness of the outside world. Aileen Kraditor has summarized the classic statement of the function of women's sphere as it appeared in this country: "Certain recurrent themes . . . portray the business and political world as one of strife, and the home as a peaceful refuge, where the higher values are nourished. The ugly features of the outside world are accepted as necessary for progress, but progress would be futile unless balanced and ennobled by the conservative influence of the home. Destruction of the home means destruction of the delicate balance between progress and stability, between warfare and peace, between a certain necessary brutality and an equally necessary refinement. . . . The home was the bulwark against social disorder, and woman was the creator of the home" (1968, 13).

One of the major functions of women's sphere, therefore, was "to define an oasis of non-commercial values in an otherwise acquisitive society" (Sklar, 1973, 161). It supplied the balm needed to heal the wounds inflicted by the outside world. It made life in the male world tolerable. Women were required, as Sklar notes, to "perform a kind of penance for the sins of a society they were not fully allowed to enter" (162). Although they could not participate actively in the outside world, they were indispensable to its functioning. The sphere of women undergirded both the economy and the polity. "The Queen of the Household . . . occupied a desperately necessary place as symbol and center of the one institution that prevented society from flying apart" (Kraditor, 1968, 13). It was literally an integry, and integrating force holding the whole social system together.

It might be argued that it was only because the cult of domesticity protected women's sphere from the harsh new Gesellschaft that women's sphere was able to retain "heart," that if it, too, had had to struggle in the economy it would have lost its characteristic nurturing quality. I am not so sure. Even the women who went into the factories took the "heart" specification of their world with them.

Looking at the situation from the other end of the telescope suggests another possibility. If it had been possible for women as self-conscious members of their sphere—a kind of female lobby, with practice in participation in the polity—to make themselves felt, they might conceivably have brought "heart" to it and had some say in the way both the economy and the polity developed.

The Moral Function of Women's Sphere

Lydia Maria Child (1802-1880) was one among many writers who emphasized the moral obligations of women's sphere. She saw women as inherently noble and good and therefore responsible for the moral level of society. But such an assignment called for an expansion of the sphere of women and greater equality between the sexes. No more were women to regard themselves "as household conveniences, or gilded toys" or to "consider it feminine and pretty to abjure all such use of their faculties as would make them coworkers with man in the advancement of those great principles on which the progress of society depends" (1829, 235-236). As men became more like women—more modest, pious, and affectionate—under the influence of women, there would be a corresponding moral improvement in society. This would be possible because women had greater piety, emotional sensitivity—or "sensibility"—and capacity for nurturing. They had special responsibility to be the moral guardians of men.

Child wrote stories, novels, and didactic works addressed primarily to middle-class women to disseminate her ideology of the moral responsibility of women's sphere. Jeffrey notes that Child's success implies "that by the 1830s middle-class women possessed a set of values and priorities that were in some respects distinct from those of middle-class men. It suggests, further, that proposals aimed at enhancing the status and power of women . . . were perceived at the time . . . as steps that would enable women to exert their moral leadership more adequately and thereby keep American society from further moral degeneration. . . . As keepers of the home they came to be identified as a new élite of 'gentle rulers' who could replace the declining élites of the colonial and Federalist eras and, through their moral influence on men and children, preserve the public virtue without which America's experiment in republicanism would surely fail" (1975 124-125).

The virtues of women as taught in women's sphere were those of submission: "Meekness, humility, gentleness, love, purity, self-renunciation, subjection of will" (Coxe, 1842, 29). To the extent that this model was subscribed to it resulted in a character easy to live with but quite incompetent for participation in the world outside the home. The extensive body of research on women in recent decades suggests that the character deformities it bred have lingered long after the demise of the ideology of women's sphere itself. The picture of women painted by this research shows them to be passive, dependent, fearful of success, unaggressive, unassertive (Mandle, 1979, chap. 3). Granted that the tests and the interpretations of the results are often from a male perspective, still they do show what a long shadow the women's-sphere ideology cast.

The Bottom Line: The Cult of Domesticity

There was an instrumental as well as an expressive aspect to women's sphere, namely household management. Catharine Beecher paid a great deal of attention to it. Her classic work, *A Treatise on Domestic Economy*, first published in 1841 and reprinted every year until 1856, had an enormous influence among women in this country, not only on their thinking about the practice of household management but also on their thinking about women. It covered every aspect of women's sphere: planning a house, running a household, rearing children. Women, said Beecher, should take this aspect of their role seriously; they should prepare for their contribution to the national enterprise as men approached their vocations.[7] This lesson was part of the separate-but-equal theory of women's sphere. But it was already becoming ominous.

"If on the one hand," Tocqueville wrote in 1840, "an American woman cannot escape from the quiet circle of domestic employments, on the other hand she is never forced to go beyond it" (1840, 225). The operative words are "cannot escape."

Although the female world had existed in prototypical if not in archetypical form since even before human beings appeared on the scene (Chapter 1), it was not until the eighteenth century that, in the form of women's sphere, it became the object of a cult. Almost apotheosized theologically, the belief in it became practically a tenet of religious faith, encapsulated later in the dogma that woman's place was in the home, and that, conversely, home was her place, her world (Cott, 1977, 74).

The cult of domesticity strengthened and validated the idea of women's sphere. In time almost everyone came to assume that this separate sphere was the natural—if not necessarily the divine—way of organizing society. This conceptualization of the social order became part of the received wisdom, surviving into our own day among some segments of the population—the older, ethnic, rural enclaves—and remaining as a nostalgic image in the minds of many others.

Before the eighteenth century most women were so busy contributing to the family's subsistence income that they could not be restricted to the household. They had to go wherever their work took them. The Book of Proverbs (31, 10-27), for example, describes the formidable amount and variety of work a good woman did in those days while her husband sat at the gates, in learned disquisition, perhaps, with his cronies. A virtuous woman was almost an industrial conglomerate in and by herself. She not only cooked, spun, wove, sewed, and made candles in the household, but also planted and harvested in the field. She was active in the marketplace; she shopped for wool and flax; kept her eye on the real estate market, looked for available land, manufactured clothing and other items and sold them and fine linen to the merchants. In addition, she was wise, kind, and charitable. Nor were the generations of women who followed her any less industrious. We noted in Chapter 3 some of the many places women have had in addition to the home since biblical times. So the dogma that restricted women to the home was actually rather novel.

From a slightly different angle, it could be said not only that women had a lot of places as well as the home but also that almost everyone's place had been in the home when that was where most production of goods took place. Indeed, instead of thinking of work being taken out of the home with industrialization, it might just as well be said that the home was removed from the work site and became a relatively new phenomenon—a place increasingly specialized for consumption. For everyone, it might be added, except the women who managed it:

> In the old days the home was in the shop or factory. The important things were the looms or the workbench and tools; the home itself was incidental. It was as though everyone lived in a little factory, for when the home was the industrial unit it was as much a small factory as a home. Most people prior to the Industrial Revolution did not have homes, in reality they lived in little workshops. The removal of its industrial functions to larger factories with power machinery meant that more of the home could be devoted to family living. The emergence of homes specialized for family life alone rather than for industrial purposes is a new phenomenon in our history, to which we are not accustomed even yet. . . . Thus instead of thinking that industrial functions have been taken out of the home, it may be equally legitimate to think of the home as splitting off from industry. . . . The home as we know it—a place where families live but do not work—is relatively new in human history (Bernard, 1942, 1973, 518-519).[8]

A considerable amount of services continued to be supplied in the home for a long time, but even this form of work began to suffer attrition late in the nineteenth century and especially in the twentieth (Ogburn and Nimkoff, 1955). Even then the belief that woman's place is in the home persisted, now meaning primarily that her place was not in the work force.

It was not until local markets—where women, like the woman described in Proverbs, sold produce and textiles and handicrafts—gave way to more complex and distant markets and more and more work came to move out of the home, that the spheres of men and women began drastically to separate, even to segregate. In American colonial times, family members had worked as a production unit, with, to be sure, a clear-cut division of labor but not an equally clear-cut separation of "spheres." By the end of the eighteenth century, however, the domestic sphere was becoming conceptually separate (Cott, 1977, 199). At least "the shift of production and exchange away from the household, and a general tightening of functional 'spheres' [specialization] in the economy and society at large, made it seem 'separate' " (Cott, 199). That was new.

Lydia Maria Child's book on *The American Frugal Housewife* (1830), for example, assumed that men and women worked together in the household, but only eleven years later Beecher was addressing a self-consciously female constituency (Sklar, 1973, vi-vii). Grandmothers of Beecher's readers early in the century could "as married women engage in income-producing work at home and meet child-care responsibilities at the same time" (ix.). That was going to become more and more difficult with time.

The apologists for domesticity—Catharine Beecher, Lydia Sigourney, Sarah Josepha Hale, Lydia Maria Child—were often themselves professional women; *they* did not assume that the home was the *only* sphere for women (Jeffrey, 1975). Or, better, perhaps they saw more than homemaking as part of women's sphere. Teaching, writing, and moral reform were also appropriate activities for women because they, in effect, performed the same kind of moralizing function as women's domestic work. And, as we shall note in Chapter 13, women did participate widely in such activities.

Even Hannah More had conceded that philanthropy was consonant with women's place. The breakdown of the old order was leaving enormous poverty in its wake, so More saw the care of the poorer classes as a charge on women. Jones notes that by including benevolence in the role-script of women she was "unwittingly inserting the thin edge of the wedge into masculine premises" (1968, 195).

For most women, however, the identification of women's sphere with domesticity shrank their world, deflated it, rendered it impotent. It was, again in Tocqueville's words, like a cloister. "In the United States," he said, "the inexorable opinion of the public carefully circumscribes woman within the narrow circle of domestic interests and duties, and forbids her to step beyond it" (1840, 212). To the extent that inexorable public opinion did restrict women to such a sphere the consequences could be severely negative. If women's sphere had room only for domesticity its boundaries would be seriously restricted. A sphere thus cut off from the outer world would tend to become parochial. The moral perspective could be narrowed, become intolerant, even limited to sexual sins. Cut off from the vital issues of the day, it could make personal gossip a major preoccupation. A large number of women could, in effect, be ciphered out of the polity. Women's sphere could thus easily become a prison or a gilded cage or a doll's house. Indeed, as time went on the concept became more and more destructive especially for the affluent, as it deprived them of work as well as of independence. The frivolity, triviality, and irresponsibility attributed to women were to a large extent a result of restrictions imposed by women's sphere.

Many women in the sphere were not happy. An enormous literature of sermons and polemics was required to keep them reconciled to the restrictions to which they were subject. Their poetry was filled with unexplained weeping. Although they were supposed to be the moral guardians of society, they were kept ignorant of moral evil, victims of "benign blindness" (Stimpson, 1979).[9] Such topics as prostitution and homosexuality and sexual "perversions" were kept under wraps. Women's sphere might recognize the existence of fallen or lewd women; they might have run across the term "whore" in the Bible. But they were not provided with a vocabulary to talk about the world of sexuality (E.C. Parsons, 1913). Ignorance was defined as innocence. They knew about abortion, of course, but it was among the subjects spoken of only in whispers. If there were to be violations of the mores of women's sphere, they wanted to be spared the need to face them (Bernard, 1949, chap. 24). They—and everyone else—wanted women's sphere to reflect a law-abiding, God-fearing, morally pure image. Men might violate the rules of women's sphere, but the women in it preferred not to have to deal with all that. They wanted to be protected from it.[10]

So the darker side of women's sphere was rarely known. For example, for decades, perhaps centuries, many—usually poor—women had defined physical abuse as part of the female role. They assumed that all women were in the same situation. Abuse was a fixture of their lives.

Among middle-class women, whose sphere did not define abuse as part of the female role, the solution to abuse when it could not be eliminated was secrecy. They felt unique, alone. The "skeletons in the closet" so often referred to might be relatives or ancestors who had strayed and become "family secrets." The secrets might be wife-beating, infidelity, alcoholism, all kinds of breaches of the moral code of women's sphere. The contents of such closets might be the topic of whispered rumors and gossip, but—in a world where propriety was all important—not of open discussion. As recently as the mid-1970s it was possible for a woman in the audience of a television talk show to cite as evidence of moral decay that now, in contradistinction to the past, women openly *discussed* abortion; it was no longer a hush-hush subject. A woman might even say that she would not favor prosecution of lesbians if only they would stay in the closet.

Reprise: Ideological Tenets of Women's Sphere

Women's sphere was an ideological construct for explaining and rationalizing the sexually separatist system that had by now crystallized in the United States. The ideology had several components: (1) a belief that although women were not intrinsically inferior to men, their sphere still had to be subordinated to that of men in the interest of national welfare; (2) a belief that women's sphere had its own contribution to make in the form of running the household competently and taking care of all its members, a female profession to be prepared for and taken as seriously as any other; (3) a belief that women's sphere was a place for emotional sustenance and for healing the hurt inflicted by the outside world; (4) a belief that women's sphere had a duty and responsibility to uphold and transmit the moral standards of society; and (5) a belief that the home, extended to include related moral and charitable activities, was the natural, normal, and only concern of women's sphere.

Ideology, however, was one thing; living it was something else again. Human relations were not ready-made ideological artifacts. Ideology made women's sphere a realm of the heart. It was up to the women themselves to forge the "bonds of womanhood," the sisterhood, the support systems that were its essence and made it bearable in a world not always congenial or supportive to women. Excluded from partnership in the management of the economy or the polity, cut off from shared companionship with men, they sought emotional sustenance from others in their sphere, and supplied it to them in turn.

Notes

1. "Fantastic" as a product of "fantasy."
2. The incredible tenacity of social forms is illustrated by the fact that this stereotype of femininity was echoing down to even the present time. Thus Erving Goffman, discussing "the arrangement between the sexes," noted as recently as the late 1970s that

> in terms of what interpersonal rituals convey, the belief [in Western society] is that women are precious, ornamental, and fragile, uninstructed in, and ill suited for, anything requiring muscular exercise or mechanical or electrical training or physical risk; further, that they are mostly subject to contamination and defilement and to blanching when faced with harsh

> words and cruel facts, being labile as well as delicate. It follows, then, that males will have the obligation of stepping in and helping (or protecting) whenever it appears that a female is threatened or taxed in any way, shielding her from gory, grisly sights, from squeamish-making things like spiders and worms, from noise, and from rain, wind, cold, and other inclemencies. [1977, 311]

3. Veblen was to document her situation at the end of the nineteenth century.
4. More disapproved of the girls' academies that were beginning to spring up in the seventeenth and eighteenth centuries. Some were of moderately high standard.

> But in general the education of girls was then, except in the charity schools, lamentably neglected. Some gentlemen's daughters received instruction at home from their parents or from their brothers' tutors, some, when so rare a bird could be found, from an educated family governess. Some few attended the more select of the schools in existence, but the majority had no education at all and, according to Richard Steele, were not ashamed of their illiteracy. Dean Swift, expressing in 1723 his usual contempt for the "generality of women," alleged that "not one gentlemen's daughter in a thousand could read or understand her own natural tongue." . . . And it might be asserted without fear of contradiction that the daughters of the comfortable middling classes, precluded by law or custom from attending the grammar schools, and by fear of loss of caste from attending the endowed or subscription charity schools for the poor, were in no better case. Yet, half a century later, Dr. Johnson could assert, "All our ladies now read." [Jones, 1968, 6]

In the nineteenth-century United States, girls' schools became the basis for close and often lasting relationships. "As young women moved away from their homes to be instructed at female academies and seminaries, they formed close connections with classmates which often developed into permanent intimate friendships" and thus became the basis for "sisterhood" (Melder, 1977, 31).

5. Both More and Wollstonecraft looked to education for improvement, however differently they conceived of it. More had been active in the antislavery movement and though her concern for the working classes was not targeted on women, as Wollstonecraft's was, she nevertheless included girls in her schools for the poor.
6. Beecher's view of women's sphere changed with time. As new opportunities for women opened up, women could establish homes of their own, even adopt children, and live fairly independent lives. Women's sphere could become more autonomous and distance itself from the male world. "Between 1841 and 1869 Catharine Beecher not only witnessed the development of an industrial society, but she also committed herself to the creation of a more autonomous [female] culture" (Sklar, 1973, 167).
7. Patricia Branca, on the basis of British data, has conceptualized the Victorian housewife as the first modernizing woman. A spate of activities new to the domestic scene now had to be mastered, such as budgeting, procurement, technology. See Chapter 17 below.

8. A contrasting point of view is expressed by Walter E. Houghton in his analysis of the Victorian frame of mind: "In the eighteenth century the coffee house had often been the center of man's social life. There he smoked, dined, wrote letters, discussed politics and literature, and got drunk. A manual for gentlemen, written in 1778, urged them to beware of 'thinking domestic pleasures, cares, and duties, beneath their notice. . . .' " (1957, 341-342). Houghton attributes this change from communal to domestic social life to a great religious revival movement and, concomitantly, to large families (342). Houghton is discussing the English situation, not the American.
9. Stimpson used the term to refer to intellectual rather than moral blindness.
10. The suppression of public recognition of sex and sexuality by the Victorian ethos resulted in an enormous preoccupation, not to say fascination, with the subject, as well as hostility toward it.

5

Inside Women's Sphere

The Replenishment of Heart in Women's Sphere

The very conditions that made healing by the female world necessary in the outside world precluded replenishment of the emotional resources of the female world itself. Men, striving in a harsh society, were not likely to reciprocate in the area of heart. They "could not be expected to respond in kind to women's feelings" (Cott, 1977, 168). Only women could.

Toqueville had noted early in the nineteenth century that men in America did not have much time for love. The severe division of labor, further, kept the sexes apart, and the standards of business discouraged intimacy. "Almost all men in democracies," he said, "are engaged in public or professional life; and . . . the limited extent of common incomes obliges a wife to confine herself to the house, in order to watch in person and very closely over the details of domestic economy. All these distinct and compulsory occupations are so many natural barriers, which, by keeping the two sexes asunder, render the solicitations of the one less frequent and less ardent—the resistance of the other more easy. . . . The tumultuous and constantly harassed life which equality makes men lead, not only distracts them from the passion of love, by denying them time to indulge in it, but it diverts them from it by another more certain road.[1] All men who live in democratic ages more or less contract the ways of thinking of the manufacturing and trading classes; . . . they are apt to relinquish the ideal" (1840, 221). Much abnegation was thus demanded of the woman by Americans, he continued, and "a constant sacrifice of her pleasures to her duties" (212). Furthermore, "affairs of gallantry" were out of the question (217).[2] Indeed, the ideology of women's sphere rejected the very idea of male gallantry as "merely the flimsy veil which foppery throws over sensuality, to conceal its grossness" (Child, 1829, 235-236).

Idealized as female "heart" may have been in the ideology of the sphere of women, in reality "the identification of women with 'the heart' was a gloss on the inequality of the sexes" (Cott, 1977, 167), deriving not from women's intrinsic virtue but "from their dependent status." They had little choice; there were few if any alternatives to their sphere, however unequal the emotional returns.

The resulting "relational deficit" (Bernard, 1976) in the lives of women might have been even more serious than it was were it not for warm and supporting relationships among women. Female friendships were, in fact, what made many marriages bearable. Cott tells us, for example, that "wives who had female friends or relatives living with them seemed the most contented of women" (1977, 193). Thus, although not encompassed in the theory of women's sphere, the function "heart" performed among women themselves in the form of supportive friendships was just as important as its supportive function for men, if not more so. For, "although it was intended to stress the complementary nature of the two sexes while keeping women subordinate, the identification of women with the heart also implied that they would find truly reciprocal interpersonal relationships only with other women. They would find answering sensibilities only among their own sex" (Cott, 168). Implicit rather than explicit in the ideology of women's sphere, these "bonds of womanhood," to use Cott's poetic phrase, constituted the actual—as distinguished from the ideological—vital core of women's sphere in the nineteenth century.

Women's Sphere as Realm of Sisterhood

"Who but a woman can know the heart of a woman?" Daniel Dana asked in 1804. And, says Cott, "in their actual friendships women answered him: no one" (1977, 168). Women alone could know the heart of a woman.

A number of factors undergirded and stimulated female friendships or female "homosociality," a term used by Carroll Smith-Rosenberg in her account of women's world of love and ritual among the affluent in the nineteenth century (1975). Whatever else might split the female world, there were many "bonds of womanhood" among them, certain biological experiences that all shared. Smith-Rosenberg plays up this biology-based form of bonding as the underpinning of female relationships in the nineteenth century.

There was, first, the experience of motherhood not only as a social and political role (as Catharine Beecher, not herself a mother, had seen it), which defined them as a class with expectations and prescriptions refracted through that role (Cott, 1977, 189), but also as a widely shared personal experience serving to create and strengthen the bonds of womanhood. As Smith-Rosenberg put it: "The biological realities of frequent pregnancies, childbirth, nursing, and menopause bound woman together in physical and emotional intimacy" (1975, 41). On the basis of such common biological experience, a social framework was set up in which "a specifically female world did indeed develop, a world built around a generic and unself-conscious pattern of single-sex or homosocial networks." These intimate networks became "institutionalized in social conventions or rituals which accompanied virtually every important event in a woman's life from birth to death" (41), following the biological ebb and flow of women's lives from childhood on through old age. Thus the physical and psychic trauma involved in "marriage and pregnancy, childbirth and weaning, sickness and death" were made easier to bear by the existence of friends who offered "each other aid and sympathy and shared such stressful moments" (24). Physical proximity was not necessarily involved; the very fact that this world is revealed to us in part by letters shows that the women were often physically separated from one another. It was the "intense bonds of love and intimacy" that bound them together "in emotional proximity to each other," whether physically together or apart.

The moral superiority that was inflicted on women's sphere also came to serve as a bond of womanhood. Women experienced a common revulsion against male carnality. Lydia Maria Child saw the "immensity" of men's sexual aggressiveness and stood "still, puzzled and frightened" by it; she expressed hostility toward men "as the disrupters of family life" but she did not "see a safe remedy" (quoted in Jeffrey, 1975, 123). Other women looked to one another for help, if not for remedy, since women's moral nature freed them from carnality. Thus sisterhood "drew on . . . concerns for sexual and individual defense and integrity" (Cott, 1977, 172). Such moral superiority "created proud solidarity among women, and encouraged them to view their own friendships as more honorable than heterosexual relationships because they excluded carnality" (189). Though as intense as heterosexual love, the love women bore one another was assumed to be not carnal but innocent. Fears of homosexuality were not then expressed, as they later came to be, to darken the picture.

Margaret Fuller, for example, emphasized the angelic qualities that made the love of women for one another similar to love between the sexes. "It is so true that a woman may be in love with a woman and a man with a man. It is pleasant to be sure of it, because it is undoubtedly the same love that we shall feel when we are angels. . . . It is regulated by the same laws as that of love between persons of different sexes, only it is purely intellectual and spiritual, unprofaned by any mixture of lower instincts. . . . Its law is the desire of the spirit to realize a whole, which makes it seek in another being that which it finds not in itself" (quoted in Melder, 1977, 31). In this passage, Melder notes, Margaret Fuller showed the "profound emotional significance which middle-class women attributed to their friendships. In a romantic age, when sensitivity and emotion were invested with great power, interpersonal ties of sisterhood had intense value" (31).

Allied with the moral superiority of women was their religious role. And here, too, was a prop for women's world. Sex segregation in religious activities as well as other forms of association accentuated women's consciousness of differentiation and "of their own sisterhood" (Cott, 1977, 180), as did academies and seminaries for the education of girls and young women, which increased contacts and thus facilitated friendships among women (Melder, 1977). "As young women moved away from their homes to be instructed at female academies and seminaries, they formed close connections with classmates which often developed into permanent intimate friendships" and thus became the basis for "sisterhood" (31).

Another emerging trend also contributed to the creation and strengthening of the bonds of womanhood in women's sphere. Participation in the voluntary associations then becoming so important in the new republic was providing women with the heady experience of equality among peers outside the strictly domestic realm. These voluntary associations emphasized equality and thus eroded the old hierarchical "station" mentality that had marked the old regime. "Women's reliance on each other to confirm their values embodied a new kind of group consciousness" (Cott, 1977, 194).

Although there were status inequalities in the female world (see Chapter 11), egalitarianism as an ideal was still valued and, as an experience, cherished. At the beginning of the nineteenth century "female friendships assumed a new value in women's lives . . . because relations between *equals*—'peer relationships'—were superseding *hierarchical* relationships as the desired norms of human interaction. In the seventeenth century an ideal of orderly, reciprocal relations between acknowledged superiors and inferiors had guided politics, vocations, and family roles (though perhaps imperfectly). During the eighteenth century this ideal was increasingly eroded. By the post-Revolutionary years the moral justification behind apprentices' services to masters, the people's deference to governors—even children's obedience to parents—was undermined by newer ideals of individual achievement, equal representation, and popular rights. . . . Myriad voluntary associations in the young republic reaffirmed the decline of deference and its replacement by an activist conception of a polity of peers" (Cott, 1977, 187). Female homosociality expressed in friendship was such a peer relationship. Since men were not their peers, "women . . . sought and valued peer relationships where they could find them: other women" (188). These relationships did not call for subordination on the part of anyone or for "disparagement of women's capacities" (173). Between and among themselves women did not experience the uncomfortable psychological distance that sex-role typing placed between them and men. In the "secure and empathic world" their friendships provided, women could share sorrows, anxieties, joys, with the certain knowledge that other women had experienced them also (Smith-Rosenberg, 1975, 42) and would not regard them as evidence of inferiority.

Here was a world to which men had little access and of which they had little understanding, in which they were, in fact, "aliens" (Smith-Rosenberg, 1975, 28), a world held together not only by the shaping forces outside but also by strong bonds cultivated from the inside. In brief, a world in which "female friendships, by upholding such attributes as 'heart' as positive qualities, asserted that women were different from but not lesser than—perhaps [even] better than—men" (Cott, 1977, 190). It was a loving, supportive world. The women who lived in it in its ideal form did not think of themselves as oppressed or deprived.

Not all women, however, shared this world. Women's sphere was not the same everywhere. There were other women's worlds, each following its own orbit, not only different class worlds but also different regional ones: on the Eastern seaboard, for example; or north, south, and frontier; or forest clearings, oceanlike plains, western seacoasts. The female world of New England could have been centuries away from a prairie woman's world.

Although the cult of domesticity might serve as a bond of womanhood—"women practicing the domestic vocation perceived it as an experience that united them with other women" (Cott, 1977, 189)—not everyone could afford it. The women who had to enter the labor force could not always afford it. Nor could widowed mothers, nor the very poor. It tended to flourish in the affluent urban centers, especially in the northeast, where most of the population was still rural. "Clearly, women could keep house better, literally and metaphorically, in 'civilized' parts, where churches, kinfolk, and women friends supported them" (Stansell, 1976, 90). They had a harder time on the trails to the

West and on the barren prairies. Both the bonds of womanhood and the cult of domesticity were often casualties in those hostile settings.

Cases in Point

In the diaries and memoirs of women on the Overland Trail, 1842-1867, we can get a feeling for what the women's sphere with its cult of domesticity was all about. From the costs its loss incurred we get an intimate picture of what support the female networks provided women, what comfort the accoutrements of domesticity supplied. All too often both the "heart" and the "domesticity" of women's sphere were casualties of the westward movement, and women mourned their loss.

By and large, the trek to the West was a male idea: "The man usually initiated a plan to emigrate, made the final decision, and to a greater or lesser degree imposed it on his family" (Stansell, 1976, 90). Some women acquiesced; some resisted; some even mutinied. Some became reconciled; some never did. More than one woman, out of sight and sound of the wagon, threw herself onto the "unfriendly desert" and gave way to sobs, like a child, wishing herself "back home with [her] friends" (Faragher and Stansell, 1975, 156).

During the first part of the great journey, a semblance of the old division of labor between men and women could be maintained. The cult of domesticity could be preserved, albeit in a modified form. But as the going became rougher the women had to do more and more of the hard labor. Nevertheless, against great odds, they worked to preserve what the cult of domesticity had trained them to value; they tried "to maintain the standards of cleanliness and order that had prevailed in their homes back East" (Faragher and Stansell, 1975, 157). They cared for sanitation; they watched over food preparation, preventing both waste and illness, and, above all, they did what they could to support and comfort one another by preserving against almost overwhelming odds the world of the amenities, of gentleness, that constituted women's sphere (148).

At night, women often clustered together, chatting, working, or commiserating, instead of joining the men: "High teas were not popular, but tatting, knitting, crocheting, exchanging recipes for cooking beans or dried apples or swapping food for the sake of variety kept us in practice of feminine occupations and diversions." Besides using the domestic concerns of the Trail to reconstruct a female sphere, women also consciously invoked fantasy: "Mrs. Fox and her daughter are with us and everything is so still and quiet we can almost imagine ourselves at home again. We took out our Daguerrotypes and tried to live over again some of the happy days of Auld Lang Syne." Sisterly contact kept "feminine occupations" from withering away from disuse: "In the evening the young ladies came over to our house [sic] and we had a concert with both guitars. Indeed it seemed almost like a pleasant evening at home. We could none of us realize that we were almost at the summit of the Rocky Mountains." The hostess added with somewhat strained sanguinity that her young daughter seemed "just as happy sitting on the ground playing her guitar as she was at home, although she does not love it as much as her piano." Although a guitar was no substitute for the more refined instrument, it at least kept the girl "in practice with feminine occupations and diversions; . . . no big whip would tempt her to unwomanly pleasure in the power to 'set things going'" (Faragher and Stansell, 158).

But, much as the women tried to preserve their world, to practice the domestic skills and talents, when wagon loads had to be lightened, it was the part of the load representing their sphere that had to be sacrificed.

> Books, furniture, knick-knacks, china, the daguerrotypes . . . the guitars of young musicians—the "various articles of ornament and convenience"—were among the first things discarded on the epic trash heap which trailed over the mountains. On long uphill grades and over sandy deserts, the wagons had to be lightened; any materials not essential to survival were fair game for disposal. Such commodities of woman's sphere, although functionally useless, [had] provided women with a psychological life-line to their abandoned homes and communities, as well as to elements of their [very] identities which the westward journey threatened to mutilate or entirely extinguish. Losing homely treasures and memorabilia was yet another defeat within an accelerated process of dispossession. (158).

And when the going got really rough, the last vestiges of the female world—the support women gave one another—had to be sacrificed.

Wagon trains sometimes had to break up into smaller units, so that women found themselves isolated, alone, cut off entirely from the support of other women. "Female companionship, so valued by nineteenth-century women, was unavailable to the solitary wife in a party of hired men, husband, and children that had broken away from a larger train." The women viewed their separation from other women rightly as, in effect, a death sentence (159).

Although both men and women suffered on the Overland Trail, the suffering was of a different order for the women. It occurred in a male world. The work was hard for both men and women, but it was unaccustomed work for the women, unfeminine work, a violation of their domestic role, which had been so cultivated "back home." On the trail a woman's very identity, which depended on association with others in her sphere, was dissolved. "Civilization was far more to these women than law, books, and municipal government; it was pianos, church societies, daguerrotypes, mirrors—in short, their homes" (161). And, most of all, supporting networks. All sacrificed on the trail.[3]

Not all of the westward movement was by way of the trails. Some of the pioneers came by ship. The women were thus spared a great many hardships. They did not have to deal with Indians. They did not lose the company of women. They did not have to do hard, male-type work. Their belongings were not jettisoned. They could retain the amenities. Their husbands were business and professional men who could afford decent housing. Still, they had had to part with family and friends. And although—perhaps because—they arrived in San Francisco still "stereotypically sex-role defined" (Saxton, 1978), they were unhappy "in this masculine paradise." And, expectably, they "seldom saw their husbands." True to the kin-orientation of the female world, these women "served as family correspondents" (Saxton).[4]

The Faragher-Stansell documents cover the years 1842 to 1867. In those years the great western plains were bypassed as too barren for cultivation; the West Coast was the destination. But in time the intervening spaces also came to be settled. And the story told in books and documents dealing with prairie settlements in the years 1865 to 1890 is even more depressing than the story of the Overland Trail. The costs to women were appalling. Life on the prairies was lethal for them, as Stansell makes painfully clear in her study of the impact on women of "this masculine imperium" (1976, 89). "The West in the years after 1840 still appeared to be masculine terrain . . . a man's country" (88). Her research shows that the severity of the cultural disruption which homesteading the Great Plains inflicted on women was unparalleled in the history of nineteenth-century frontiers.

For the first six or seven years they lived not in houses, in which the domestic amenities—even such basic amenities as cleanliness—could be enjoyed, but in sod huts, tarpaper shacks, or dugouts which rain could reduce to a sea of mud and dry weather to a depository of dust and straw. There was no way a woman could make a home of such quarters. In winter the water froze; in summer the air stifled. "Housekeeping as a profession in the sense that Catharine Beecher promulgated it was impossible under such circumstances (Stansell, 91). When, after drought, grasshoppers, unseasonable rains, debt payments, mortgage installments, there was any profit, it went for seed, stock, farm machinery and tools. Not for labor-saving appliances for the wife. Although some farms in the 1880s had washing and sewing machines, "for the most part . . . the machine age did not greatly help woman. She continued to operate the churn, carry water, and run the washing machine—if she were fortunate enough to have one—and do her other work without the aid of horse power which her more fortunate husband began to apply in his harvesting, threshing, and planting" (92) (see Chapter 17).

Nor were there churches to supply solace and companionship. Apathy and even hostility toward religion were common. "Few families read the Bible, sang hymns, or prayed together" (Stansell, 92). Except among the immigrant communities, churches and the activities that revolved around them were lacking. The observance of religious rites and activities was makeshift or absent.

Most serious of all was the deprivation these women suffered because of the lack of "the network of female friendships which had been an accustomed and sustaining part of daily life 'back home' " (92). The men could escape to the saloon in town, but not the women. There was no transportation to spare, and neighbors were too far away for walking. A young woman in Nebraska wrote in her diary: "If the country would only fill up, if there were only schools or churches or even some society. We do not see women at all. All men, single or bachelors, and one gets tired of them" (quoted in Stansell, 94).

Women were farmhands first and homemakers or mothers after. And no more than the men Tocqueville described were the farming pioneers emotionally expressive. In one case "three wives fled before [Jules Sandoz] found a woman who resigned herself to the emotionless regimen of his farm" (93). The writer Hamlin Garland, himself a son of the middle border, referred to his people as "a Spartan lot . . . who did not believe in letting our wives and children know they were an important part of our contentment" (quoted by Stansell, 94).

The prairie women were troubled by the peripheral nature of their maternal role and missed the cultural support they needed for rearing their children. "Without help from the old networks of kin and institutions, a mother could not be assured of success" (quoted in Stansell, 95). With the loss of the support of her female world, she suffered "a general attenuation of the womanliness which had been central to her own identity and sense of importance in the world" (95). Young girls, however, who had not been exposed to the old cult of domesticity and its accompanying cult of true womanhood, were better able to cope. They learned how to help their fathers, how to do male chores. They were comfortable in men's clothes. As long as "we do not degenerate mentally," said one of these girls, "it is all right" (Stansell, 94). They did not degenerate mentally. "A second generation came to maturity; some were daughters like the strong farm women of Willa Cather's novels, who managed to reclaim the land that had crushed their mothers" (96).

The price had been great. Fear, depression, mental breakdown, insanity, suicide, murder haunted that first generation of prairie women. Their lives revealed what the loss of support from their sphere had cost them.

There can be little doubt that for a great many women, east, west, north, and south, the "bonds of womanhood" were supportive and the resulting sisterhood a real, genuine basis for building their lives around. Granted that some of the evidence from letters might be mere literary conventions, the evidence from diaries and other personal documents leaves no doubt that deeply experienced "homosociality"—even, perhaps, in some cases, homosexuality—did exist as a fundamental component of women's sphere. Women who were deprived of it suffered grievously.

The Fate of the Female World of Love

The story of the near demise of this nineteenth-century pattern of female friendships has yet to be worked out in detail by the historians. What is already available from their work, however, clearly points to some of the forces that attacked it.

The blighting effect of geographic mobility on female friendships was already being noted by the middle of the nineteenth century. The cases of the women on the Overland Trail and on the prairies exemplified the destructive effect such movements could have on relationships among women. Although these ties could, Melder believes, withstand the strain of migration—"the sisterhood of family members, existing through generations of mother, daughters, sisters, and cousins, persisted despite frequent separations due to migrations" (31)—still, for women not in family relationships, migration doubtless severed many ties. One of the most poignant glimpses of what migration meant for female kin and friendship networks is supplied by Lavinia Porter, who left for the west on the Overland Trail in 1860:

> I never recall that sad parting from my dear sister on the plains of Kansas without the tears flowing fast and free. . . . We were the eldest of a large family, and the bond of affection and love that existed between us was strong indeed. . . . As she with the other friends turned to leave me for the ferry which was to take them back to home and civilization, I stood alone on that wild prairie. Looking westward I saw my husband driving slowly over the plain; turning my face once more to the east, my dear sister's footsteps were fast widening the distance between us. For the time I knew not which way to go, nor whom to follow. But in a few moments I rallied my forces . . . and soon overtook the slowly moving oxen who were bearing my husband and child over the green prairie. . . . The unbidden tears would flow in spite of my brave resolve to be the courageous and valiant frontierswoman. [Quoted in Faragher and Stansell, 153]

We have seen how dismal the outlook was for a supportive network of friends in her new setting. On a relatively minor scale, the same disruptive effect on female networks is reported in current research on women when the move is only from the city to the suburbs, or when women must pull up roots to follow husbands transferred from one city to another. Although even today supportive networks and friendships can and do develop in the new neighborhoods—a well-organized neighborhood, in fact, seems "to be a particularly valuable resource for the stressed blue-collar female" (Warren, 1975)—still, all too often they lack the permanence and stability that characterized them in slower, less mobile times. In a sense those that do remain—often in waning ethnic enclaves—seem to represent only the lingering echoes of the Gemeinschaft female world, a relatively stable kin- and place-anchored world. We pick this thread up again in Chapter 12.

Important also was the twofold impact of psychiatry in changing the homosocial norms of the female world. Without specifying their precise nature, Smith-Rosenberg notes that "a number of cultural taboos evolved" (1975, 27) in the twentieth century under the aegis of psychiatric writings on homosexuality. First, the strong bonds of affection permitted, even encouraged, among women in the nineteenth century fell under a pall of sexual suspicion under Freudian influence. The young girl was now discouraged from homosocial relationships and encouraged at an early age to form relationships with boys. It is true, as Smith-Rosenberg notes, that nineteenth-century women used the same conventions in their letters as those that heterosexual lovers might use. The letters reflected intimacies that would be frowned upon among women today. Smith-Rosenberg reminds us, however, that whether or not there was actual physical lovemaking is beside the point. There was an accepted cultural pattern that permitted such intense relationships. The letters may simply have reflected the general romanticism of the age, stylistic conventions of the times. Many of these relationships may not even have been personal in the sense of involving close proximity. Even making allowances for these other interpretations, Smith-Rosenberg believes that, though not necessarily sexual, they were real, not merely conventional, relationships. Still the psychiatric interpretation may have had a considerable muting effect.

The other negative impact emanating from psychiatry was its discouragement of talking to friends about personal problems. As a result, in twentieth-century Western culture, we were told by a psychiatrist in 1964, there is "a general absence of the kind of friendship that could readily provide the relationship required for therapeutic conversation." He protested the idea that only experts are suited for such "therapeutic conversation" and rejected the trend toward having to "purchase friendship" in the form of psychiatric sessions (Schofield, 1964, 161), as many others were to do a decade later (Chapter 12).

The feminist movement may also have played a part in the demise of the intense relationships between women characteristic of the nineteenth century. Nancy Sahli, who has made a detailed study of these relationships and their sudden ending at the turn of the century, thinks it did. "As women began to be perceived by themselves and others as being capable of rational, intellectual thought, it seems evident that they would want to use this ability rather than their emotions to make decisions advancing their position vis-à-vis the male world and, in their search for equality with men, that they would perceive this capacity as being on a higher status scale than that of the emotions" (Sahli, 1978, 26). Sahli comments also that as long as female friendships remained nonthreatening, they could be ignored. But autonomous feminists did constitute a threat to the established order. One of the most powerful weapons against them was to label them abnormal and thus to condemn them and discredit their cause (27).

Ann Seiden and Pauline Bart do not accept the idea that female friendships have actually declined. What did decline at the turn of the century, they argue, was the valuation placed on them. They believe that discouragement, even denigration, of female friendships served the function of increasing the emotional dependence of women on men (Chapter 12).

It may even be that we are talking here of the whole process of attenuation of Gemeinschaft, which came somewhat later in the female world than in the male world, about the alienation that Marx was analyzing in the middle of the nineteenth century. But whatever caused it, or whatever its nature, the loss of the nineteenth-century type of friendship left women in a peculiarly vulnerable position since the male world did not offer the same emotional support that women friends had supplied in the past.

There were doubtless other processes at work to undermine the strong and loving support system embodied in these relationships. In any event, for whatever reasons, the old passionate relationships lost their legitimacy. The old "secure and empathic world" in which women shared their sorrows, anxieties, and joys "with the certain knowledge that other women had also experienced them" all but disappeared (Smith-Rosenberg, 1975, 14). The very concept of female friendship became downgraded.

Interpretations of Women's Sphere

How should we evaluate the ideology of women's sphere in terms of its impact on women themselves? Modern scholars differ in their judgments of it (Cott, 1977, 197-205). On the negative side, some, basing their judgments on the didactic literature which rationalized the existence of women's sphere, see it as imposed on women to serve the male view of social utility and order and see women as victimized by it, imprisoned (Cott, 198). Although it did open some avenues to women outside the home, "it barricaded all others" (Cott, 203). For many, therefore, it constituted a source of strain. Also, by depriving women and men of common ground it opened the door to antifeminism and misogynist philosophies (196).

In writing about the women who could not share the benefits of women's sphere, Foner shows how its ideology was deliberately put to exploitative use by both employers and unions (1979). Lower pay, for example, was justified on the ground that women's earnings were secondary to the family economy, used mainly for "pin money," since they were supported by men. Women's natural interests were in home and family, and they could not, therefore, be regarded as full-fledged participants in the labor force. They were unorganizable for the same reason, said the unions. Rather, they needed protective legislation, which had the effect of depriving them of high-paying jobs. Since labor force participation was not viewed as part of the female role nor the work site as a legitimate part of women's sphere, the needs and rights of female workers were not taken seriously by employers, by unions, or even by the women workers themselves. They were prime targets for exploitation by employers, who, as one might expect, rarely missed the mark.

On the more favorable side, still according to Cott (198), is the view of some modern feminists based on the published works of women writers themselves which sees women as refining and exploiting the ideology of women's sphere for their own purposes, using it as justification to advance educational opportunities, to gain influence and satisfactions, and even to express hostility toward men. The women's sphere ideology "articulated a social power based on their special female qualities rather than on general human rights. For women who previously held no particular avenue of power of their own—no unique defense of their integrity and dignity—this represented an advance." In any event, these scholars concede that this ideology constituted "a necessary stage in the process of shattering the hierarchy of sex and, more directly, in softening the hierarchical relationship of marriage" (Cott, 1977, 200).

Even more favorable is the view of others (Cott, Sklar, Smith-Rosenberg, Farragher and Stansell, Daniel Smith) based on the private documents of nonfamous women, that the women's sphere ideology was the foundation for a subculture that supplied a source of strength and identity and supportive sisterly relations; this view implies that the ideology's tenacity owed as much to women's motives as to the imposition of men's or "society's" wishes (Cott, 200-201). Cott notes that the more reliance the researcher places on private documents, the more favorable seems to be the evaluation of women's sphere. My own predilections lie in this direction. My major criticism of women's sphere is that its physical, social, and intellectual boundaries were too narrowly defined, too narrowly restricted, too limiting.

Not all women accepted the boundaries laid out for women's sphere even in the nineteenth century. "The internal dynamics of woman's sphere, by encouraging women to claim a social role according to their sex and to share both social and sexual solidarity, provoked a minority of women to see and protest those boundaries" (Cott, 1977, 204). And even to demand their extension. Without the consciousness created by the women's sphere, "no minority of women would have created the issue of 'women's rights.'" Nevertheless, although women's sphere ideology did "contain within itself the preconditions for organized feminism, by allotting a 'separate' sphere for women, and engendering sisterhood within that sphere, it can in no way be interpreted as 'proto-feminist' "(201). Certainly not feminist in the current sense. Indeed, nineteenth-century feminism may be seen as sparked by the minority referred to above who felt oppressed by women's sphere, who created the issues of women's rights, a minority who came to see the status of women in the male world as a more cogent basis for ideology than the separatism for which the ideology of women's separate sphere had been designed. "The ideology of woman's sphere," however well it served the sisterhood of those who could afford it, "had inherently limited utility to reform woman's lot" (195). The constraints it imposed became more and more glaring as "feminist eyes sharpened" (205), culminating finally in the great explosion of the 1960s which left not one tenet of that ideology intact.

The Fate of the Ideology of Women's Sphere

Whether positive or negative, good or bad, favorable for women or unfavorable, the ideology of women's sphere lingered on far longer than did the reality it had been called upon to explain or rationalize. Its longevity is, in fact, quite astonishing. "Where the claims of a theory prove to be unfounded but, nevertheless, are still widely accepted, one may speak of restraining myths" (Hamilton, 1975, 9). In this sense, the ideology of women's sphere may be said to have constituted a "restraining myth" until well into the twentieth century. It persisted, as we shall presently see, long after the facts of life ceased to fit the world for which it had originally been created. With inhibiting impact on women's world. In the introduction to a book that does not even list "women" in its index or have anything at all to say specifically about women (Hamilton, 1975), Harlan Hahn makes a suggestion that has peculiar relevance for them: "Instead of emphasizing the supposed talents of political elites and alleged limitations on the capabilities of the public, researchers might consider the possibility of theoretical developments which stress efforts to maximize rather than to restrict the abilities of all segments of the population. Political scientists and sociologists may be required to correct the severe injustices that have been committed by imposing unnecessary restraints upon human potential, Perhaps most important, attention might be devoted to plans for restructuring social and political institutions to permit the attainment of this potential" (2-3). Such "severe injustices" were "committed by imposing unnecessary restraints upon human potential" in the case of women by the women's sphere ideology. The "severe injustices" took the form, as Cott has noted (1977), of job discrimination, lower pay, and character aspersions growing directly out of the women's sphere ideology. It was to take a long time before this "restraining myth" began to be corrected and "plans for restructuring social and political institutions" began to be rendered practicable.

Women's sphere ideology met with increasing challenge as we entered the twentieth century. It began to wane first among the affluent classes, especially among the most educated. College women longed for "causes." They sought serious careers. Their colleges became, in Calvin Coolidge's words, "hotbeds of radicalism" (Bernard, 1964, 33). They did not accept or even recognize the differences on which women's sphere ideology rested. Or they rejected, if not the existence of differences, their relevance. They resented the patronizing condescension men showed them.

At the same time, while this affluent class of women was striking at the walls of women's sphere, working-class women were eagerly welcoming it. They were more than willing to enjoy the separate, secure life of women's sphere if their husbands could afford it; they had no interest in "causes" or careers. Women's sphere gave them as long a tether as they wanted. They entered the labor force if they had to, but reluctantly. And their husbands felt as they did. So, as a small, affluent class of women protested women's sphere ideology, working-class women earnestly bolstered it. The conditions of life in the twentieth century ensured that the number of women who rejected the ideology of women's sphere would grow and the number who cherished it would decline. The "tipping point" in these trends seems to have come in the 1960s, precipitating one of the most remarkable paradigmatic crises in many decades.

It is difficult to pinpoint historical events like the end of the women's sphere ideology. But Cott lists some of the forces making it more and more anachronistic: urbanization, technological advances, the declining birth rate, the increased complexity of a multiethnic society, the suffrage debates, the higher education of women and the rise of the individualistic, restless "new woman." In addition, the range of women's sphere was expanding; in the last quarter of the century there was a proliferation of associations and clubs dealing with wide community problems such as public health, social welfare, working conditions of women, child labor. This breach of women's sphere accustomed women to serious participation outside its walls. So long as such activity "was consciously seen and justified as an extension of woman's traditional role as moral and physical nurturer" it was acceptable (Cott, 1977, 26). But it had unintended consequences for the ideology of women's sphere.

Restraining Myths versus Reality

That aspect of the "restraining myth" dealing with women's participation in the labor force was perhaps especially anomalous. As we have noted, even in its heyday, women's sphere ideology was a luxury which only the affluent, primarily urban, could implement. There were many who could not. True, if women had to earn their own living they did so at home, if possible, where the cult of domesticity could be maintained—laundering, sewing, baking, taking in roomers and boarders, or doing piecework—or they worked in someone else's home (Smuts, 1959, 14-18). But even if they went to work in factories or stores or offices the myth was perpetuated. Even as paid workers they lived a different kind of life in a different kind of world from that of the men. They still identified with women's sphere, followed its standards. They still lived at home or, where possible, under carefully supervised conditions—as in the case of the "Lowell girls"—and saw their sojourn in the outside world as temporary. They expected to return to the home when they married. They continued to believe that women's sphere was their destiny and that they were only transient participants in the labor force. Their real place was in the home, well into the twentieth century.

But the myths on which the ideology of women's sphere rested became harder and harder to sustain as the twentieth century wore on.[5] Labor-force participation by women increased phenomenally after 1940, rising from 29.9 to almost 60 percent (59.6) in 1978 and projected to be 68.3 percent by 1990 (Smith, ed., 1979, 14). Further, more and more years of women's lives were spent in the labor force, from around eleven years at the turn of the century (National Commission for Manpower Policy, 1957, 10) to 45.3 years for single women, 34.9 years for childless women, and 20 years even for mothers of three children by 1960 (Garfinkle, 1969). The situation was a "travesty" (Cott, 21) of the ideological model. But since many, especially the married, were doing it for the family's sake they could be seen as still holding down the fort, however different the site.

Another restraining myth that did not jibe with reality had to do with the changing structure of the family. Women's sphere ideology implied a family in which the father was the breadwinner and the wife remained at home to take care of the children, the now traditional "nuclear family." As the supply of young unmarried "working girls" declined in the twentieth century with increased years of schooling and early marriage (Carlson, 1979, draft), the demand for the services of women in the labor force continued to increase. Thus, finally, against all the weight of women's sphere ideology, against all the weight of the belief that "woman's place is in the home," even married women were sucked into the labor force. The proportion of employed married women, husband present, more than doubled between 1947 and 1977, from 20.0 to 54.0 percent (R. E. Smith, 1979, 76). The two world wars added their influence, and by the second half of the century the demand for the services of women in the labor force was so compelling that not only married women but even mothers of young, even preschool, children were being "conscripted." In 1974 the proportion of mothers of school-age children (six to seventeen) who were in the work force passed the halfway mark. It reached 57.9 percent in 1978 and was projected to reach 70.1 percent in 1990. When the proportion of employed mothers of even preschoolers rose from 10.8 percent in 1948 to 41.6 percent in 1978, the myths became impossible to support. And the projections for 1990 suggest a continuation of these trends. By that time, it is estimated, 66.7 percent of employed women will be married with husband present, and 55.3 percent of employed women will have preschool children (R. E. Smith, 1979, 76).

As a matter of fact, in 1975 only a relatively small proportion of husband-wife households (29.4 percent) fit the definition of the nuclear family. There were, among husband-wife households, more in which the wife contributed to family income (35.3 percent) than those in which she did not (29.4 percent). (See Table 5-1.)

TABLE 5-1 Husband-Wife Families by Number of Children and Earner Status of Spouses

Number of Children	*Husband Only Earner*	*Both Spouses Earners*
None	10.1%	15.3%
One	5.9	8.0
Two	7.3	7.2
Three	3.8	3.1
Four	1.5	1.0
Five or more	.8	.1
Total	29.4	35.3

Source: Department of Labor Press Release, March 8, 1977, Table 4.

In one-child husband-wife households there were a third more in which the wife was an earner (8.0 percent) than in which she was not (5.9 percent). In two-children husband-wife households, the proportions in which the wife was and was not an earner were virtually equal. Only when the family had three or more children were there proportionately fewer households in which the wife was an earner than in which she was not.

Thus the kind of household for which the women's sphere ideology was designed was clearly on its way out. The women who had "staked their major claim to social power on their [domestic] 'vocation' " (Cott, 1977, 205) now saw it slipping away. "Women's sphere" was being bled by the flow of women into the labor force.

Despite the startling trends in female employment outside the home and in family structure, the restraining myths persisted. The "women's place is in the home" cliché was still given at least verbal obeisance. Thus, in a sample of 149 husbands in 1927, only 7.8 percent accepted the idea of married women working outside the home; six years later only 11.0 percent of the same sample accepted it. In the late 1930s, the *Ladies' Home Journal* surveyed both men and women and found only 12 percent of the women and 10 percent of the men in favor. Even a large sample of youth—13,528—assented only to the extent of 16.8 percent in 1937 (Bernard, 1942, 180-181).

Not until 1972 did a majority of male college freshmen—presumably an avant garde—reject the idea that a woman's activities were best restricted to the home, and then by only a relatively small margin.[6] By the mid-1970s even the presumably conservative blue-collar women workers had discarded the women's place ideology. A study of 120 such women found them in no way conforming to it; almost nine out of ten of them (86.1 percent) disagreed with the statement that "except in special cases, the wife should do the cooking and house-cleaning and the husband should provide the family with money" (Walshok, 1977). More than two-thirds (69.4 percent) did not believe that "there is nothing more fulfilling to a woman than the raising of her children." In the face of the fact that these women saw "paid employment as an integral aspect of the adult role, not merely an option or an extension of homemaking roles" (1977), the persistence of the women's place ideology in popular thinking seems even more remarkable.[7]

In the post-World War II decade there was a brief efflorescence of the women's sphere ideology, a decade of "togetherness" and large families. Still, Betty Friedan, talking to suburban housewives—the beneficiaries par excellence of the women's sphere ideology—found that despite their earnest efforts to live up to the so-called feminine mystique, a kind of refurbished version of the ideology of women's sphere, they were depressed. And young radical women in the peace and civil rights movements were learning that even among their avant garde and idealistic male colleagues they were relegated to a "women's sphere," subordinated, expected to do the menial work and to supply emotional support, the whole women's sphere routine. They were enraged to find such views in a presumably avant garde setting.

Coup de Grâce

In an amazing éclat these young women began almost to vie with one another to see who could most perceptively articulate all the relics of the women's sphere ideology—the innumerable habits, practices, customs, traditions, conventions, norms of all kinds that hemmed them in—all the subtle, and not so subtle, ways in which they were taken advantage of by the male world.[8] All of a sudden, so it seemed, they refused to conform. They rejected and unmasked all of the restraining myths. They refused to accept the male definition of anything. They insisted on the right to validate their own experiences, to interpret their own world from their own perspective. They refused to endorse male prerogatives by deference. They ceased to endow men with taken-for-granted superiority. In an astonishing burst of underground mimeographed papers and newsletters they created a wholly new view of both the male and the female worlds. They demolished the tenets of the women's sphere ideology point by point. They rejected the whole idea of subordination; the marital vow calling for obedience had long since been rejected and now the idea was rejected in all areas of life. They rejected the idea that homemaking was an exclusively female responsibility. They saw the healing role of the home as, in effect, subsidization of a destructive industrial system, a way of making it tolerable. They rejected the moral-redemption function. They saw no "natural" or "normal" restriction of women's activities.

For the most part, this paradigmatic revolution at first reached only a relatively small part of even the female world, mainly the avant garde intellectuals in the arts and academia. Only slowly did it seep into other segments of the female world. As it did, it showed itself in the coming out of the closet of battered wives, in the greater willingness of women to leave destructive marriages, or choosing not to marry in the first place, in demands for greater sharing of family responsibilities—in brief, for "restructuring social and political institutions to permit the attainment of [human, in this case, female] potential" (Hamilton, 1975, 2-3).

There were, however, others still living happily in women's sphere who were horrified, shocked, traumatized. Here were *women* acting in unbelievable ways, saying incredible things, using forbidden words, expressing heretical thoughts, violating the basic code of propriety of women's sphere. They shrank from the picture these radical women were painting of their world. They were still fighting a rearguard battle in the 1980s. The traditional family was still their cause.[9]

Why So Slow a Demise?

Why did it take so long for the misfit between ideology and historical trends to be recognized? It is striking to note how applicable some of the points made by feminists over a century ago still are today. Why did it take so long for them to be heard? Much depended on how large an audience found their message relevant. When the talk of rights or grievances touched only a small number of women it had little chance to be widely heard. As long as most women lived in the separatist women's sphere, the question of rights would tend to be about their rights within that sphere, as wives or as widows. As the number of women exposed to the conditions of industrial life increased, the audience that could understand the issues grew. The "severe injustices" became increasingly clear and, for some, increasingly galling. Not until the 1960s, though, were there enough women in a position to find the issues relevant to produce the ideological explosion (Bernard, 1976).

Even within a public that is ready for a message there are different kinds of readiness. In a given population there is, for example, a small group of innovators who are ready to accept the message; somewhat slower are the "early accepters"; more reluctant are the "early majority"; then the "late majority." Finally, last to come around are the "laggards" (Bernard, 1976, 213). In brief, a growth curve. The 1960s and 1970s apparently marked a time when only the laggards—usually the older women, the rural, the less educated—were resisting. The innovators or avant garde, meanwhile, were seeking to rethink, reconceptualize, revamp the female world to adapt it to "modern times."

Not, as yet, with complete success. Although the old ideology of women's sphere does not fit into the current scene, we have not as yet evolved a consensually acceptable ideology that does, despite an enormous amount of research and thinking devoted to the question.[10] So there is still a condition of "normlessness" (Carlson, 1979). The new reality into which we seem to be settling is one in which women will continue to enter the labor force soon after they complete their schooling, whether or not they marry, and remain for many years continuously or with breaks, whether or not they have children. But the appropriate ideology for this reality has not yet been achieved. The "women's-two-roles" ideology presented by Myrdal and Klein in the 1950s has boomeranged. It undermined the old "woman's place is in the home" ideology and legitimized the participation of women in the labor force, but as yet the supports called for by the new ideology have not been forthcoming. As a result, overload is a major hazard for many women today.[11] In the meanwhile, there remains a lag—narrowing, it is hoped, but still glaring—between a suitable ideology and current reality. An ideology suitable for this day and age must wait until consensus is reached in our society about what "use" we wish to make of women.[12]

After this long historical running jump, we turn in Part III to a discussion of the contemporary female world as current research portrays it. Not that we have left history entirely behind, for from time to time we need a backdrop for perspective on the present. But for the most part it is the structure of the female world today that engages our attention from here on.

Notes

1. Tocqueville's observation received validation almost a century and a half later: "The time factor . . . makes Steve Rubell a victim of the late 70s malaise. The 33-year-old co-owner of Studio 54 slouches on one of those couches shaped like a giant condom at his disco emporium and says of asexuality . . . 'It's peculiar to people who are involved in work and can't put all their energy into too many sources. If I'm here 16 hours a day, I can't run out and think of fucking' " (A. Bell, 1978, 21).
2. The gap between the lives of women before and after marriage was often commented on, especially by foreign observers. Sklar notes that mothers at weddings wept for their daughters (1975, xiii)—understandably, for marriage for many was not so desirable a status. In a letter to her friend Laura Lovell, written on July 27, 1820, Eliza Chaplin expressed her opinion on marriage:

   > While we may think 'there is a *magic* in that little word "home," there are many within my knowledge, who are never so happy as when exiled from thence. . . . *Many,* I believe, submit to the chains of hymen, and verbally acknowledge them *silken,* but their conduct tells another tale. The society of *entire* strangers and those perhaps not possessing half the merit or attractions of their companions is constantly courted, while the presence of the husband, or wife, awakens no sensations of pleasure. Well, perhaps if it were *only* this. But feelings of disgust—nay—even of *contempt,* are sometimes visible in the countenances of the married pair, when subjected to an interview. Whose heart would not revolt at such a state?" [Quoted in Cott, 1977, 76]

   The choice not to marry became a serious alternative at the end of the nineteenth century (see Chapter 7 below). "Its last decades witnessed the highest proportion of women never-marrying in all of American history. Toward the turn of the twentieth century, when the frequency of divorce rose, the proportion of women marrying returned to more typical levels" (Cott, 1977, 83).

3. It should be noted that for men as well as for women conditions did not seem auspicious for friendship.

   In the twentieth century there is a general absence of the kind of friendship that could readily provide the relationship required for therapeutic conversation. . . . We have bowling friends, golfing friends, hunting and fishing friends, and drinking friends. Shared interests, cultural or political, athletic or aesthetic, provide the medium of friendship rather than the interdependencies that fostered the close, sharing friendships of older, less urbanized communities. [Schofield, 1964, 161].

4. Much of the correspondence was, understandably, about health and illness: "By December, Margaret is meditating on life and death and tells how much she misses her family." Death was particularly frightening when one was "separated from all family and from the church graveyards which have been familiar since childhood." A woman writes home expressing her grief at the death of her sister. Wishes she could stop in for tea with her family. Her husband, like all the other men, spends all his time making money. Has no time for a wife. She spends much time without speaking a word, suggesting deep depression. She has no friends, no life of her own (Saxton, 1978, draft).
5. All told, the women's sphere version of the female world as a fully functioning reality—as contrasted with its ideology—even for the affluent, lasted perhaps not much longer than a century. There are, however, little ossified relics of it even today. Lynne Dobrofosky has described one of them among officers' wives in the military, as codified in a *vade mecum* by N. Shea (revised in 1966 by A.P. Smith). Here women's sphere remains almost intact in pristine form. It says in an only slightly different way what dozens of etiquette books and polemics in the early nineteenth century had said: the wife must make a congenial home, rear a family the husband can be proud of, and support him emotionally. Her life should revolve around him first, the children next, and a happy home third. Wives should not work outside the home, unless extra money is absolutely essential. They must be brilliant generals as homemakers, financial geniuses, culinary experts, top interior decorators, perfect hostesses, devoted wives and mothers, social successes. Whether the next revision of this code will change these specifications is an interesting question. It is alleged that there is a considerable amount of alcoholism and sexual promiscuity on any military base. Perhaps the next revision will address this problem. An interesting study of Air Force wives covering two decades gives some insight into the processes involved in the final demise of the code among them. The number of children of squadron wives declined from an average of 3.7 in 1966-68 to 1.1 in 1977-78. The proportion working outside the home increased in the same time span from zero to almost 40 percent (Watkins, 1978, draft). Watkins attributes the changes to increased education and to the women's movement.
6. The proportion varied among different kinds of institutions. Most liberal were men in private universities, only 34.6 percent of whom accepted women's place ideology. Most conservative were men in private two-year

colleges, among whom 55.9 percent still endorsed it in 1972. In 1971 the comparable figures were 35.8 percent and 64.3 percent. Overall the 1972 proportion was 46.7 compared with 51.9 percent in 1971.

7. Another myth that has been quite restraining has to do with the personality of women. The research produced by men and by women trained by men reproduces the stereotyped image of women in the ideology of women's sphere almost item by item: passive, dependent, weak, lacking in self-concept, lacking in self-confidence, in ego strength, in almost every male virtue. This was the kind of woman her sphere called for. And from the male point of view this was the kind of woman she was. Vis-à-vis the male world she may have been. But in her own world—as I read about her and as I remember her from my own childhood—she stood tall. The male view of her is analogous to the American's view of immigrants; they were dumb. Or to the white man's view of blacks: they were dumb. Anyone who did not fit into their own world must, by that very fact, be dumb. Women today show up poorly on almost all the tests set up by men, or by women trained by men, which are conceptualized and structured to show how different women are from men on male values and in the male world.
8. Some of this work was assembled by Robin Morgan in *Sisterhood Is Powerful, An Anthology of Writings from the Women's Liberation Movement* (New York: Vantage, 1970). Another early statement was by Shulamith Firestone in *The Dialectic of Sex* (New York: Morrow, 1970), with the subtitle "The Case for Feminist Revolution."
9. Although fewer than a third (29.4 percent) of all husband-wife households conformed to the traditional pattern of husband-earner, wife-nonearner, "the" family became a rallying cry of a strong so-called profamily movement, almost a crusade, in the late 1970s. The New Right coopted the traditional family—exclusively defined as "persons who are related by blood, marriage, or adoption"—which, under its aegis, became the centerpiece of a coalition of those who were opposed to unionism, right-to-work laws, ERA, abortion, contraception, sex education in the schools, public-supported child-care centers, rights of homosexuals, and labor-force participation by married women and in favor of public support of Christian schools, prayer in the schools, and censorship. The three White House Conferences on Families in 1980 became battlegrounds for assaults on any plan, proposal, or suggestion that did not buttress the nostalgic image of the traditional family.
10. At mid-century, Alva Myrdal and Viola Klein wrote a book on *Women's Two Roles* for the International Federation of University Women, surveying "the needs for social reforms if women are to be put into a position to reconcile family and professional life" (1956, xiii). It described measures called for in order thus to integrate the lives of modern women, including part-time work, extended maternity leave, training for reemployment of women returning to the labor force after time out for childrearing, employment for older women, location of employment to make it available for women, housing built with the needs of working women in mind, better shopping facilities, "rationalizing housework," "public services to relieve the domestic work load," "canteen services" at work and school, day nur-

series and nursery schools, modern organization of domestic service (Chapter 9). And when President Kennedy established a Commission on the Status of Women in 1961, he included "recommendations for services which will enable women to continue their role as wives and mothers while making a maximum contribution to the world around them." Arriving at an ideology to implement this recommendation is proving far harder then originally anticipated.

11. A survey of 82,638 employed women by the National Commission of Working Women reported in June, 1979, that 70 percent of married women workers found the "burden of the job combined with the family" a problem and about the same proportion—67 percent—would like more help at home. Almost three-fifths (59 percent) had no time for leisure. Only fourth on the list of problems, surprisingly, was low pay, a problem reported by fewer than half (47 percent) of the married women (1979, 2).
12. The experience of the Soviet Union illustrates how ideologies—and the policies they support—vary according to the way national needs are defined. When policymakers become concerned about the birth rate, policies to encourage motherhood are promulgated; when they become concerned about the labor force, policies encouraging labor-force participation are favored (Bernard, 1971).

PART III

The Social Structure of the Female World

If women's sphere may be viewed as an ideological construct that rationalized and justified a status quo, the female world which constitutes the subject of Part III may be viewed as an empirical construct that describes a status quo. The discussion here is concerned with the demographic structure of the female population, its descriptive features (Chapters 6 and 7), and with the stratification or class patterns of the female world built on this demographic skeleton (Chapters 8-11).

The individual human beings who constitute the population of any society do not live in miscellaneous or random relationships with one another. Children do not relate to one another in the ways they relate to older people; married people do not relate to others in the ways single people do. Demographic characteristics are the bricks out of which sociological worlds are constructed. Although age is one of the most purely biological of the demographic variables, even it receives social and cultural modification; it is, in fact, basic in any sociological world. It is related to fertility, which in turn calls for a widely ramifying system of marital statuses. Chapters 6 and 7 explore these demographic variables, briefly fleshed out with sociological data. They are based on pedestrian, matter-of-fact, documentable data, with few if any surprises. There is little attempt to offer paradigms or theoretical models to explain them.

Chapter 6 thus begins with an overview of the age structure of the female population and then somewhat expands the description of the subworlds or "sequence of statuses" (Zelditch, 1968, 250) through which females pass seriatim on their way to adulthood, namely: the "pink world" of those up to five years of age; the elementary-school world of the six- to-thirteen-year-olds; the world of adolescent society; and the "prime time" between eighteen and mid-twenties. Chapter 7 then picks up the story, looking at the marital-status structure of the female world, including the worlds of the never married, the married, mothers, and the formerly married, both divorced and widowed. The emphasis is not on individual psychological developmental stages but on the outside forces or expectations impinging on girls and women as they reach and pass through certain ages, regardless of where they may be in their own individual development. Although the distinction between the structure of the female subworlds and the individual female human beings who pass through them is thus maintained, there is recognition of the fact that the two—structure and human being—are not always synchronized, that, in fact, asynchrony is common.

Human relationships are structured in other ways also. The last four chapters in Part III deal with the vertical dimension of the female world—that is, with social stratification. Social stratification is one of the major preoccupations of students of societies; few topics in sociology have elicited more research and analysis. The number of books, monographs, and papers on the subject runs perhaps into the thousands. And if we include all the research using stratification variables, even thousands more.[1] Relatively little of all this work deals with social stratification in the female world. The "status" of women in the male world or in the societal stratification system has, to be sure, been an almost compulsive concern of women researchers (Chapter 2), but not the stratification system within the female world itself. Although it is profoundly influenced by its relations with the male world, it has a character of its own that deserves attention.

Chapters 8 and 9 are introductory to, and Chapter 11 illustrative of, the social-class structure of the female world described in Chapter 10, which is the central concern of much stratification research. Chapter 8 wrestles with the rock-bottom status or vertical dimension of social class. This status dimension is an evaluational aspect of social class, often expressed in terms of "high" and "low." Chapter 8 also pays some attention to social mobility, individual and societal. Chapter 9 addresses the "colder," less invidious dimension of social class, namely "socioeconomic status" as operationalized in terms of education, income, and occupation. After these introductory comments, the hardest task of all is attempted in Chapter 10, a synthetic "mix" of status, education, income, and occupation to arrive at a possible picture of the social-class structure of the female world.[2] Chapter 11 departs from the systematic approach to social stratification and looks at two concrete cases in point, namely social class in the household as revealed in the history of domestic service in this country and in the elite career women's structure in the world of community voluntary service.

Notes

1. In the *International Encyclopedia of the Social Sciences* there are forty-nine pages on "Social Stratification," twenty of them on social class. Under "Social Change" there are also 110 references to social class. The article on "Sociology" has only fifty-three pages. In addition there are eight pages each on "Class Consciousness" and "Class Struggle." "Social Status" has seven pages devoted to it. Under "Lower Class" there are ten subheadings; under "Proletariat," 5; under "Middle Class," 24 items; "Bourgeoisie," 6; "Working Class," 16, "Élites," 53 items.
2. Power and life chances are other "objective" dimensions. Barber also includes religious and moral purity, ethnicity and family, and local-community status (1968, 292-294).

6

Age and the Subworlds of Children and Girls

THE FEMALE WORLD may be viewed as a series of age-bounded, sequential subworlds, each consisting of a different set of rules, norms, expectations, and values. The resulting age structure is only one component of the female world, but it is especially crucial.

Some Elementary Demographic Facts

Females are born into the world with numerically minority status: they constitute only about 49 percent of all infants at birth. It is estimated that only about two-thirds as many females as males are conceived but that the greater viability of females increases their proportion from conception throughout life. Overall, females were a minority of the total population of the coterminous United States until 1940, when for the first time they were almost though not quite equal in number to men (65,608,000 to 66,061,000). A decade later, they had become a clear majority (75,864,000 to 74,833,000). In 1950 there were 101.4 females for each 100 males in the United States. And by 1976, there were 105.5 females for every 100 males. Since then the ratio of women to men has steadily increased; today, among adults twenty-one years of age or over females constitute about 53 percent of the population. By the year 2000, projections vary from 104.8 females for every 100 males to 106.3, according to the assumptions made about birth, death, and immigration rates, and by 2025, it is estimated that there will be 107 females to every 100 males (Table 6-1).

The numerical inequality between the sexes varies, then, by age. When childbearing was a hazardous undertaking and when male immigration exceeded female,[1] females remained in deficit, especially during the child-bearing years. At the turn of the century, for example, women aged between twenty-five and forty-five were in serious deficit. The deficit was even greater in the 45-to-55 age bracket, when years of overwork made them easy victims to such diseases as tuberculosis.[2] Rita Mae Kelly and Mary Boutilier have summarized some of the research dealing with the health care of women in the nineteenth century in an attempt to account for the deficit:

> Until the twentieth century there was an extreme paucity of knowledge about medicine in general and female sexuality and gynecology in particular. This ignorance had serious consequences for women's health. . . . The topic of female invalidism was prevalent throughout the century. . . . Lower-class women often did not have the luxury of invalidism. If a woman worked, it was a minimum of ten hours a day with at best a half hour off for meals. Once her work day was finished, she could go home to clean, wash, cook, to be mother and wife. [1978, 19]

TABLE 6-1 Number of Females per 100 Males*

Year	Females per 100 Males
1820	96.8
1830	97.0
1840	96.5
1850	95.9
1860	95.5
1870	97.8
1880	96.5
1890	96.5
1900	95.8
1910	94.3
1920	96.1
1930	97.6
1940	99.3
1950	101.4
1960	103.1
1970	105.4
1976	105.5
2000	104.8, 105.6, 106.3 (according to assumptions)
2025	107.0 (according to assumptions)

*Source: Bureau of the Census, Statistical Abstract of the United States, 1977, 25, 6. Figures to 1950 are for coterminous United States; thereafter, for all states.

These were the conditions in the female world reflected in the turn-of-the-century data. With improved health care, especially control of tuberculosis, and improved obstetrical care, the greater viability of females has resulted in a "creeping" majority of women in all age brackets beyond the early twenties. In 1976 the "breakeven" point—the age at which the number of women first equals that of men—came at about 22-24 (Statistical Abstract, 1977, 6). In that year there were 101.2 women for every 100 men in the 22-to-24-year-old bracket.

The greater viability[3] of females thus allows them to lessen the disparity in numbers between the sexes at conception and to equal the number of males in the early twenties. Although the female edge over males in life expectancy was growing—from 1.0 year in 1920 to 7.7 years in 1976, when it was 69.0 years for males and 76.7 for females (National Center for Health Statistics, March, 1978, 2)—there was some evidence that the growth in this difference was moderating. Thus, from 1975 to 1976, for example, life expectancy had improved somewhat more for males (0.4 percent) than for females (0.3 percent).[4] Still, the greater viability of women means that the female world has an age structure with a relatively large proportion of older members. Thus the female world today is about two-and-a-half years older than the male world. In 1970 the average age in the female world was 29.3 compared with 26.8 for the male world, in 1976 the figures were 30.2 and 27.9.

The age structure of the female world as of 1976 is shown in Figure 6-1. At that particular historical moment, young women aged fifteen

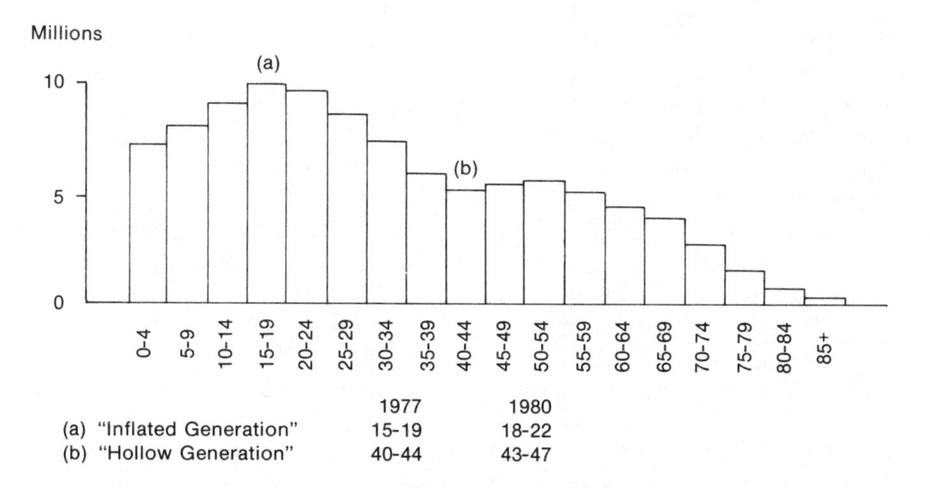

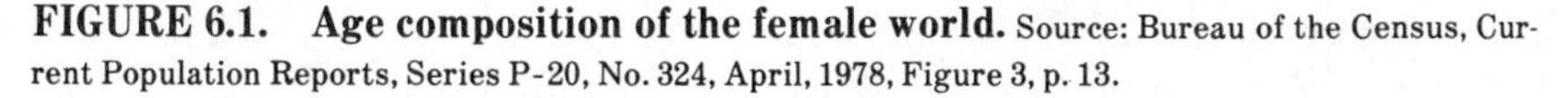

FIGURE 6.1. Age composition of the female world. Source: Bureau of the Census, Current Population Reports, Series P-20, No. 324, April, 1978, Figure 3, p. 13.

to twenty—part of the baby boom of 1954-1959—constituted the largest age component of the female population,[5] and women in their early forties—part of the depression cohort—a comparatively small one. The latter group, we note in passing, constitutes a kind of "swing generation" in the female world today. We shall have more to say about them presently.

Age in Historical Context

Age is far more than a biological or strictly chronological phenomenon. It means different things at different times. It means one thing when marriage customarily occurs at sixteen, as it did in the time of Romeo and Juliet; another, when it occurs at twenty-six. Or if, for example, one is born into a world in which, as in Jane Austen's day, no woman over twenty-three could ever hope for romantic love. When Balzac wrote about a woman of thirty, a woman's age meant something else again. And when a woman of fifty could be the heroine of a love story by Noel Coward in a popular women's magazine in 1965, age again meant something different. Adolescent girls in "women's sphere" in the nineteenth century lived in a world quite different from "adolescent society" today. Age is one thing when entrance into the labor force occurs customarily at twelve or thirteen; another, when it occurs at eighteen or twenty. It means one thing if a last child is expected to be born when the mother is under thirty; another, if it is expected when she is over forty. It is one thing when women are rendered invisible as sexual beings at the age of, say, thirty; another, when they are, to use Farber's term, permanently available. The accepted behavior, the expected behavior, the sanctioned behavior were different in all these worlds. In brief, being twenty—or any other age—a hundred years ago was not the same as being twenty—or any other age—at the present time.[6] Expectations, norms, customs, attitudes change. Worlds, in a word, change. And age has different significance in such changed worlds.

The concept of political or social generation was introduced by French and German sociologists to refer to people subjected to common historical events which they share because of when they were born. Wars, depressions, strikes, reforms, crises of many kinds leave indelible imprints on those growing up when these events happen. Glen Elder, for example, has shown how the great depression of the 1930s influenced women who were growing up at that time (1974), and Paul Glick has shown how it affected the age at marriage and even the fertility of these women (1975). One's world is different, we repeat, according to when one is born, when one grows up, when one marries, bears children, loses a husband, or becomes widowed. The term "cohort" is used by demographers to refer to people born at about the same historical moment.

A population profile may therefore be viewed as a kind of archaeological dig, each age-cohort representing a past "culture" level— or, in the present context, "world"—that obtained during its early years of socialization.[7] The further up one goes in age the farther back one goes in history. Thus an eighty-year-old woman tells the oral historian what her world was like at the turn of the century; her memories are like retrieved artifacts. Such "archaeological" differences by age tend to show up in most polls or surveys. Older women reflect a world of the past. We expect them to be living in a more conservative world than younger women. Predictably, therefore, in polls and surveys it is usually the older women who reject the premises and conclusions of the feminist movement (Bernard, 1975, chap. 8). They were reared in a different world and they cling to it.

The profile of the female world shown in Figure 6-1 reveals two age brackets of special interest: a "hollow" generation of women roughly thirty-five to fifty years of age in 1977, and an "inflated" generation of females fifteen to twenty-five years of age in 1977. The first is, of course, a result of the low birth rate in the 1930s, and the second, of the high birth rate in the 1950s and early 1960s. What we have may be essentially a bimodal distribution in the female world in the mid-1970s.

If we characterize every cohort not by the year of birth but by the years of early socialization—say, ages five to fifteen—it is interesting to compare and contrast the ambiences in which they spent their childhood. The women at the bottom of the hollow generation—say, forty to forty-five in 1977—were children, five to ten, in the years 1937 to 1942; the women of the most inflated generation—fifteen to twenty in 1977—were five to ten in the years 1962 to 1967. The first group were late depression and wartime children; the second, the "antiestablishment" generation of the 1970s.

Glen Elder has made a detailed study of women who were born in 1920-1921 and hence are somewhat older than the actual hollow generation, but near enough in age to warrant careful attention (1974). He found these women to be different from women born either before or after, a conclusion confirmed in polls and surveys. In one study this "swing generation" lined up with younger women on one item—"It is much better for everyone involved if the man is the achiever outside the home and the woman takes care of the home and family"—but with older women on another—" It is more important for a wife to help her husband than to have a career of her own" (Bernard, 1975, 166). They tend to have greater attachment to home and family values (Elder), but they also show interesting and, until now, unique trends. Many, for example, are so-called returnees, women returning to school now that their children are in school.

The inflated generation as a whole is still too young to have demonstrated lifelong characterizing behavior, but we do know that those in their early twenties are going to college in larger numbers than previous cohorts, that they are delaying marriage, that they plan to have fewer children, and that they are in the labor force in larger numbers.

Developmental Stages versus Serial Worlds

Just as the meaning of age differs according to the historical world it occurs in, so also does one's world at any historical moment differ according to one's age. A girl in any given historical period is in a different world at the age of ten than she is in at the age of twenty, and is in a still different world at age fifty. It is as if she is on an escalator moving from one floor to another in a building that is also moving. The world the members of any one cohort inhabit changes, literally, as they grow older. The infant does not live in the same world she will live in when she goes to school or gets a job or marries or has her first child. For, along with the others in her cohort, she passes through a series of worlds as she grows older, the boundaries of which are fixed by law or culture or bureaucratic regulations. Ready or not, she is welcomed or catapulted into them. Sometimes there are rites of passage that mark the transition from one world to another; sometimes there are none. She is simply not permitted into some worlds until a certain age; she is unwillingly or reluctantly forced into others.[8]

The concept of serial or sequential worlds is not the same as that of developmental stages. When age is approached as a developmental variable we get a series of stages, and a wide variety of such stages has been delineated (Havighurst and Chickering, 1980), most of them until recently dealing primarily with the lives of men. But the approach by way of serial worlds is somewhat different. It is concerned not with the developmental stages through which girls and women pass but with the worlds— of expectations, norms, values—in which their development takes place. The several female worlds are, in fact, thought of as a series of nested worlds organized on an age basis. Nothing in the biological or psychological development of the individual infant, girl, or young woman accounts for the several worlds she passes through in her development. All these worlds exist before she enters them; she makes relatively little impact on them.

Although the successive-worlds approach parallels the developmental or stages approach, the focus and emphasis are different. Now not the individual female but the web of rules—legal, customary, moral, traditional, conventional—to which she is exposed in the developmental calendar is the center of concern. The psychological processes by which these rules are absorbed by the infant and child—for the understanding of which we owe so much to the social psychologists—are not the subject of discussion; they are taken for granted. The reality emphasized in the serial-world approach is the objective existence and relative stability of the structures in which this socialization takes place. These worlds do change, to be sure, but not so rapidly as those who pass through them. The small child passes through what is here called the "pink world," reacts to it, is acted upon by it in idiosyncratic ways, and then passes on to the next world. The "pink world" remains.

Ordinarily, for most people serial worlds and developmental stages are synchronized inasmuch as the worlds themselves have evolved to deal with the several developmental stages. But not always and not for everyone. Sometimes we are thrown into a world for which we are not developmentally prepared, and sometimes we are developmentally prepared for a world into which we are not permitted to enter. In both cases a phenomenon known as "asynchrony" results.

Asynchrony

Although there is a rough synchrony between individual development and the worlds in which it takes place, some individuals, as Elder, Rockwell, and Ross have found, are "out of phase" (1978).[9] These researchers distinguish several forms of such asynchrony. One that has been studied fairly intensively has to do with young women who enter the world of marriage "out of phase," especially before the age usually specified for entrance into this world, before they are developmentally ready for it.

Asynchrony is especially important in the female world since the life calendar of women is so often "out of sync" with the life calendar of men, especially in the work world, which is based on the male life calendar. The late teenage years and early twenties are a time of preparation for and introduction to professional careers; often in the case of women they are years for bearing and rearing children. This asynchrony means that women are often seven or eight years behind men in career positions, with effects on occupational mobility as well as on pension and retirement benefits.

Serial worlds, then, may or may not parallel the individual female's development. She may be catapulted into a world for which she is in no way developmentally prepared. A high-school teacher once tried to prepare her female students for the shock they would experience when the airport porter first addressed them as "ma'am." A young woman with a minority background commented on her resistance to the interest shown by her female relatives, aunts and great-aunts, in her physical development. She was not ready to join their adult female world. "I hated it. They watched my body develop, felt my breasts to see how they were growing and, in general, seemed to be flaunting their superiority in a realm I only vaguely sensed. I knew so much more than they did about the modern scene. Yet here they were more knowledgeable than I. I became angry with the whole body thing" (personal interview). Conversely, there are some who feel that they are ready for an older world long before they are admitted to it. Age per se in its developmental aspects remains a major component of the female world—age at menarche, at sexual initiation, at marriage, at birth of first child, at menopause—but the several worlds are different from the development that takes place in them.

Both the demographic (cohort) structure and the several female subworlds through which the cohorts pass are real, but they are real in different ways. One can, for example, imagine assembling all the members of a given cohort—say, all the five- to thirteen-year-olds—in a given space. The demographic cohort can thus be easily pictured. But the set of rules, norms, expectations that constitutes the world they live in is harder to "see." It is no less real for that.

An Unpreferred Sex

The little girl is born into a world in which she is probably a disappointment, especially to her father. We know that historically infanticide or neglect has had more female victims than male,[10] resulting in some times and places in extremely high ratios of males to females (de Mause, 1976, 16-22).

Results of research with respect to sex preferences for children vary. Thus, "the preference for sons over daughters found so commonly in many parts of the world is generally believed to have been replaced in the United States by a preference for a balanced family composition, or at least one child of each sex" (Coombs, 1977, 259). And a survey by Philip Shaver of 80,000 readers of *Redbook* magazine found the traditional preference for sons to be on the wane. Almost three-fifths—58 percent—of the respondents expressed no preference; 21 percent said they preferred a daughter; 19 percent, a son (*Washington Post*, April 21, 1978). Shaver explained this by "profound changes in the way women think about themselves—and about the opportunities that might be open to their daughters."

But other studies do not corroborate this finding. One of them queried 1,500 young married women and 375 of their husbands. The women preferred sons two to one; the men, three or four to one (*Ms.*, May, 1978, 20). Far from thinking in terms of the opportunities open to their daughters, the reasons the women gave for wanting daughters included "because it was fun to dress them and fuss with their hair, and also because girls were not as mean as boys." Nor does the most authoritative study corroborate the trends reported by the *Redbook* study. Data from the 1973 U.S. National Survey of Family Growth (NSFG), employing a new measure designed to probe underlying sex preferences, indicate that "about one-half of married women have an underlying preference for sons, one-third prefer daughters and only one-fifth have a clear preference for balance. The son preference evidenced by the frequent choice of a male for the first birth is usually thought to be counterbalanced by a preference for an equal number of each sex as family building proceeds. The findings from this study, however, indicate that son preference is quite pervasive in the American culture; and while son preference in the United States is less extreme than in many countries, daughter preference is less prevalent than in some others" (Coombs, 1977, 259).

Intriguing was the finding that more older women (over thirty) than younger women preferred daughters (35 to 28 percent). The author suggests that this results from their having had the experience of having daughters. Women with only an elementary school education, but also those with some college, tended to show more son preference than other women, but "the chief influence of education [was] a reduction of the proportions in the extreme categories . . . , particularly among women with college education." Although higher incomes were associated with a moderating of the boy preference, still income, usually associated with education, was not, overall, a strong influence. The major conclusion the author draws with respect to stratification and sex preference is that "educational, economic, regional and urban-rural variations in sex preference are quite moderate" (263). So also is the effect of labor-force participation by women. There seems to be remarkable agreement across the board in favor of sons.

One interesting "deviation" deserves attention. "In the United States, being Catholic contributes to a somewhat greater girl preference, if both husband and wife are Catholic" (263). Thus 38 percent of Catholic women married to Catholic men have a bias in favor of daughters compared to 30 percent of other women. This influence does not seem to be related to a Spanish cultural background, which also favors daughters. "Spanish origin either of husband . . . or of wife reduces the proportion in the boy-preference end of the scale and not only increases the proportion with a girl preference but makes that preference more extreme. Forty percent of the wives of Spanish origin have a girl preference, about equal to the proportion that have an underlying boy preference" (263). The several ethnic groups with Spanish background differ among themselves, boy preference being more marked among Puerto Ricans than other groups of Hispanic origin, and girl preference—54 percent—being more marked among the Cubans (263). The relatively strong preference for daughters among

Spanish-background women cannot be explained on the basis of their religion. Nor, as a matter of fact, by family size or education. The author does not feel there are yet data to explain these interesting findings (264).

Nor does she feel the overall findings can explain the son preference. "Sex preferences for boys are often explained by their value as adults (to carry on the family name or for support in old age, for example); and preferences for girls by their value in childhood (companionship and help around the house). Does this imply that women who have strong son preferences are more future-oriented, while those with daughter preferences are concerned with more immediate needs? There is no evidence on this point. The value of children's work is frequently cited and care of smaller children and help with household tasks are pointed out as reasons for wanting girls. Yet girls perform these function in Taiwanese households with no evidence of resulting daughter preference. We suspect that sex preferences are more deeply rooted in the culture and reflect a constellation of cultural attitudes about sex roles and values" (265). In the absence of definitive evidence to explain son preference in the female world, anyone's insights may be as relevant as anyone else's. Including the hypothesis that these women wanted to please their husbands, who, they assumed, wanted sons as validation of their maleness.

In interesting contrast to this well-documented evidence on sex preference for own children is the finding that people who adopt children show an overwhelming preference for girls (1964, Benet, 1976) presumably reflecting a residue of the feeling that only a natural child should carry the family name (and carry on the family line). A spot check on four adopting agencies in the District of Columbia found three that could see no clear-cut sex preference shown and one that did find a slight preference for girls. The usual pattern was to prefer a child of a sex different from the sex of a child already in the family. If the children were beyond infancy, the sex preferred was usually determined by the sleeping facilities available in the home.

Preferred or not, many a little girl is born to women who have a strong underlying preference for sons, although the chances are good that in most cases the child's intrinsic appeal will soon win welcome and considerable affection and attention. Though a mother may have preferred a son, she and her daughter soon establish a complex relationship that is probably going to be the closest they will ever have, one of the most long-lasting and powerful dyadic relationships in the female world, a relationship which we are only now beginning to research in all its ramifications (Rich, 1976; Chodorow, 1978; Friday, 1978; Bernard, 1978). Yet, it is hard to ignore de Mause's comment that the pervasive son preference cannot help but have disquieting effects on little girls (1976, 5-6).

The Pink World

The female infant is born into a "pink" world, so called here because pink is the traditional feminine color, announcing by the infant's clothes and blankets that she is a girl. This world has been heavily researched by social psychologists and students of human development for clues to a variety of questions, especially with respect to sex differences in child-rearing practices. Is the little girl treated differently by her parents from the way the little boy is by his? The research results are not unequivocal. Nor, according to Jeanne Block, well conceptualized (1976, 283-304). One survey of almost 200 studies of socialization reported "surprisingly little differentiation in parent behavior according to the sex of the child" but still found that there were "some areas where differential 'shaping' does appear to occur" (Maccoby and Jacklin, 1974, 338-339). Parents, for example, tended to "shape" boys and girls differently in terms of dressing them differently, encouraging sex-typed interests, assigning sex-differentiated chores, and supplying different kinds of toys. One critique of this survey concludes that even more differences would be uncovered if more fathers had been included in the research and if theoretical aspects were better articulated (Block, 1978). Actually, the pink world is a female world. Fathers have little to do with it or say about it. Bronfenbrenner in 1973, for example, cited research reporting that fathers spent on an average less than a minute to twenty minutes a day with infants of either sex (1974, 151).

Whatever the adequacies or inadequacies of the research on the pink world, we do know that so well has the five-year curriculum succeeded in shaping the little girl for her future that by the time she enters kindergarten, in her last year in the pink world, she has a well-established identity as a girl, fixed usually no later than the age of three and perhaps earlier. And along with her firm identity as a girl she has acquired clear-cut knowledge of her feminine role. Everyone in her world has been transmitting this knowledge to her in the form of dress, hair, toys, games, and chores since literally the moment she was born. She comes to kindergarten thoroughly primed for the feminine role. She is helpful, nurturant, supportive, loving (Best, forthcoming).

The kindergarten pink world is different from home, but not too different, for the 31 percent of all three- to four-year-olds and the 80 percent of all five-year-olds (as of 1976) who attend. The world of the kindergarten is still a female world and, for the little girl, still oriented toward the mother or her surrogate. There is a teacher instead of a mother and a lot more children to play with. But the curriculum is just the same. Thus, one researcher notes, "The girls were encouraged to spend time in the doll corner, while . . . wheeled toys and small building equipment like large blocks were routinely assigned to boys, as were erector sets" (Best). It was not that the wheeled toys and large blocks were denied to the little girl; she could choose to play with them if she wanted to. But "they were not automatically assigned to girls."

Still, this was a world the little girl was comfortable in. It was the only world she knew anything about. It was *the* world. She was not a passive creature in it. She was competent and more than held her own vis-à-vis the boys, who had not yet discovered the male world either. Sometimes the boys had to appeal to their teacher for protection against the little girls' aggressiveness. Females in this world were the bosses. The little girl, like the teacher, was a female. She was entitled to boss. And she did (Best).

Cases in Point

"Michelle, David, and Andrew had been assigned to work with the large building blocks in the classroom. The boys had decided to work together while Michelle . . . chose to work alone. It soon became evident that the boys had carried most of the building blocks to their working area, leaving Michelle with only a few blocks with which to build her house. She quickly solved her problem. Ignoring the blocks the boys had piled on the floor around them, she pulled blocks from their house and carried them to her own. Soon she had taken so many blocks from the boys' house that hers was bigger and taller than theirs." The boys appealed to the teacher but in vain; she refused to intervene. So "the boys endured her [Michelle's] assault on their house without counter-attack" (Best, forthcoming).

Diane lorded it over the sandbox. On this particular day "she decided who should have sand and who should not." When a little boy complained to the teacher and began to retrieve his sand, Diane warned, "'Don't you dare knock over these things.' . . . Intimidated by the implied threat in her words and discouraged by his teacher's apparent lack of support, he quickly moved his hand away. 'I don't like sand, anyway' " (Best, forthcoming).

The Schoolgirl's World

Practically all six-year-olds are in school. It is a world somewhat different from either home or kindergarten but so far as the little girl in the primary grades (first through third) is concerned, it is still a world she can understand, a female world, still the whole world. In spontaneous games she has the best—and bossiest—lines. She helps the teacher, and it is real help, like washing the blackboards, clapping erasers, keeping closets, bookcases, and coat racks neatly in order. She also helps classmates. She performs the classic female nurturant role for crying boys, rejected boys, reckless boys. She is also the complete martinet who enforces the imperatives of this world with complete conviction. On little boys as well as on little girls.

Only gradually does the little girl learn that there may be other worlds. Only gradually does she learn, for example, of the exclusivity and misogyny of the boys' world. In the preschool pink world, where adults counted for more with her than peers, there had been no occasion for the little girl to learn about the male world's contempt for girls.[11] The first grade introduces her to it. Girls are told by boys that ball games are for boys only because "girls aren't hardly made" for ball games. In the second grade they learn more about male exclusivity as the boys begin to distance themselves more and more from the girls and to take over the patterns of the male world.[12]

At the time of Best's study—the mid-1970s—dolls constituted a serious issue in the small schoolgirl's world. Although in the first, second, and third grades the girls said they were going to be wives, mothers, teachers, or nurses, they fiercely denied that they liked to play with dolls. Dolls were in fact a sensitive point, with the girls defending themselves against male misogyny. Dolls were used by the boys to put them down. They were among the tools used to show male contempt. "No other putdown by boys carried quite the same invidious meaning as their taunt that girls must be babies because they played with baby dolls, a toy for babies. Girls were quick to catch the inference of inferiority and they resented it" (Best). From grade one through grade three, the girls defended themselves: they did *not* care for dolls; they did *not* play with them. Thus, from a first-grader: "I don't play with dolls. I like to play ball and do all the things boys do outside." And another: she NEVER! played with dolls; she played Cowboys and Indians. Though some second-graders admitted, reluctantly, that they did play with dolls, most were uncomfortable with the subject. A third-grader: "Dolls are stupidious" (Best).

The challenge from the boys put the girls on the defensive. They had lived until now in a world which had been sedulously preparing them for a future of marriage and motherhood. They had taken the female world to be the only authentic world. The misbehavior of boys in that world was not just a violation of the norms of the female world but conformity to the rules of a different world, a world that judged them differently, that in effect made fun of them for conforming to the standards of the female world.

Learning about the male world was to be one of the main courses in the latent curriculum of junior high school. And the importance of beauty in relating to it, of senior high school. Until high school the male world had seemed deviant, different from the real—that is, the female—world. At the onset of adolescence the fact was becoming clear to the girl that the male world was not merely a deviant female world but a world in its own right, with its own autonomy, different from the female world she had assumed until now to be the only one. It was a world that was hard to articulate with. Boys seemed either to love you or to have contempt for you (Best). And it was important to be pretty if you wanted them to do one rather than the other.

No Rites of Passage

In some societies a great deal is made of menarche (Delaney, Lupton and Toth, 1976). There are elaborate rites; it becomes perfectly clear to the girl that she is moving from one world to another, that a new set of rules is henceforth to be followed. Whatever or however she may feel, she has become a woman. Even, in some societies, ready for marriage and childbirth. And students of anthropology have amassed a widespread lore—fears and superstitions—on the subject of menstruation, including male practices to protect themselves from it.

In our own society menarche is made little of. There are no widespread rites of passage to mark it. Some ethnic groups may retain symbolic rites but they seem to mean little to the girls themselves, whatever they may mean to the adult women who carry them out.[13]

Starting in about the fifth grade, schools have to be prepared for the onset of menstruation among the girls. The news spreads. In some schools to be first is status-conferring, in others, embarrassing; to be last is anxiety-generating. It is often difficult for mothers to discuss anything about the female body with their daughters. so preparation for menarche is strained by both the reluctance of the mother and resistance by the girl. American industry has taken over a good deal of the responsibility for teaching girls about menarche.[14] From the mother's point of view a major concern is how, if not to protect virginity, at least to prevent conception.

The Female World in Adolescent Society

Although fourteen- to seventeen-year-old girls constitute only 7.5 percent of the total female population, they attract a disproportionate amount of the public's attention. In the high-school world or "adolescent society" they come to share a teenage culture, become members of a consuming public that is extremely lucrative to a number of industries—among others, clothes, cosmetics, sports, entertainment, records—a world in which clothes are designed for them, cosmetics created for them, music recorded for them, magazines edited for them. An image is created of and for this young woman. Her complexion, hair, figure, posture, breath, teeth, and diet command pages and hours of medical attention. And as far as physical beauty is concerned it must be conceded that the product created by that world is successful. Girls of this age are by and large extraordinarily attractive. One rarely if ever sees defective teeth, faces blemished by infant or childhood diseases, rachitic bones. Even when, as in the 1960s, there was a revulsion among some of them against the oppression of that beguiling world, the young women came through as attractive, despite dishevelled hair and ill-fitting, even ragged jeans.

The little girl had learned early the importance of beauty for physical attractiveness. In the pink world she had already been smiled at, called adorable, her eyes and hair made much of, her hair beribboned. In kindergarten she could hardly fail to notice that some children were preferred to others, and it did not take long in the primary grades to notice differences in appearance, to notice that some children were made fun of because of their clothes or looks. Even her own preference, in fact, was for the girl who was pretty over the girl who was plain.[15]

But in the adolescent society of high school the big lesson hits home, as James Coleman has so convincingly shown. In fact, in the 1950s, when he made his study of adolescent society as it functioned at that time, the importance of physical attractiveness was almost the most salient lesson taught in the underground curriculum. And although the study was made long ago, most women who are in their thirties or older today probably entered the adult female world under circumstances not very different from those Coleman reported.

Popularity and beauty or attractiveness were major values in that world; academic success was far from a top priority. Although there were, expectably, class differences, they did not override the general importance attached to attractiveness: "The [class] variation among schools in . . . scholastic achievement is not nearly so striking as the fact that in all of them, academic achievement did not 'count' for as much as did other activities in the school. Many other attributes were more important" (Coleman 1961, 264). It was the attractive girls, not the top-ranking students, who were the models others patterned themselves after. "The girls who were named best dressed, and those named as most popular with boys, were in every school far more often mentioned as being in the leading crowd and as someone to be like, than were the girls named as best students" (265).

Of some interest was the fact that the years in which popularity and beauty were most highly valued were the middle—sophomore and junior—high-school years. By the time the girls were seniors there was a slight downward turn in the proportion who gave priority to popularity and beauty: "Apparently, there is a period in the sophomore and junior years when good grades among girls are particularly devalued. It seems likely that this is related to the beginning of regular dating and the consequent importance of attractiveness.... It is the sophomore and junior year when . . . good looks and popularity with boys are most important, and the senior year that they are least important" (Coleman, 169-170). Coleman relates this trend to the process of separation from the parents' world. The freshman girl still lives in a world under the control of her parents and reflects the value they place on academic success. As a sophomore and junior she is "rebelling" against parental values and taking on the coloration of her peers. By the time she is a senior this "rebellion" has lost its novelty. She still remains closer to her peers and more distant from her parents than she had been as a freshman but less markedly so.

In view of the importance assigned to beauty and clothes in adolescent society, it is understandable that a powerful media apparatus exists to cater to the young girl as a consumer of cosmetics and clothes. Some periodicals—for example, *Seventeen*, *Glamour*, *Mademoiselle*—at least make a pretense of being more than advertising media. But some unabashedly and openly sell ploys. One, for example, called *Once*, consists of 38 pages of advertising and 32 pages of editorial material. Published by "13-21 Corporation," it is "basic for certain kinds of advertising to teen-age girls" (Rossman, 1978). The advertisements are for personal care products such as lotions, shampoos, acne treatments, and perfumes. The editorial material deals with what to wear, things to do, personal care. It is free for the asking. It can reach two-thirds of the girls in this country.

Coleman was extremely critical of school systems that permitted "the relations between boys and girls . . . to increase the importance of physical attractiveness, cars and clothes, and to decrease the importance of achievement in school activities" (Coleman, 50). He felt there might be ways "that schools themselves could so shape these relations to have a *positive* effect, rather than a negative one, on the school's goals" (50). There was some evidence that this was possible, for, in a university laboratory, school popularity and good looks were found to be far less important than in the public schools, especially beyond the freshman year (56). Coleman does concede that these values—beauty and clothes—are permissible as long as they do not monopolize the total environment of the school, "so long as there are *other* ways a girl can become popular and successful in the eyes of her peers" (52). And that there are such other ways is evidenced by the emphasis on "a nice personality." Still, he feels that "in adolescent culture these superficial, external attributes of clothes and good looks do pervade the atmosphere to the extent that girls come to feel that this is the only basis or the most important basis on which to excel" (52).[16]

Although there has been no replication of the Coleman study of adolescent society there has been another study which throws light on certain aspects of life among adolescents in 1977.[17] And it has the added value of being a kind of third "replication" of a study of a famous community, "Middletown," first studied in 1924 by Robert and Helen Lynd. Since the Lynds had compared their 1924 findings with what they could glean from newspaper and historical reports of the 1890s, their report was a kind of first "replication." They revisited Middletown in the 1930s for a second "replication." Then in 1977 another study of the community was made, designed to be as nearly as possible a genuine replication of the 1924 study. Of the several aspects of this replication, Harold Bahr's analysis of the responses of high-school students is the most relevant here. Among the findings reported, one of the most interesting so far as the female world is concerned is that there appears to be a kind of convergence in process with respect to the customs governing the behavior of boys and girls.

With respect, for example, to evenings spent away from home, the restraints in 1924 were more rigorous for girls than for boys. "By 1977, this difference had disappeared, so that both boys and girls were spending evenings away from the home at about the same frequency as had boys [in 1924]. In 1924 males were almost four times as apt to be away from home every evening of the week as were female students (19 percent as compared to 5 percent); by 1977 the males still had a slight edge in proportion away from home every night (24 percent versus 18 percent for the girls) but the females were more apt than the males to be away from home five or six nights a week (28 percent versus 23 percent for the males) and the proportions of students home most of the time (5 to 7 nights a week) was the same for both sexes (25 percent for males and 25 percent for females)" (Bahr, 1978).

Equally relevant, if not more so, as an index of convergence between the male and female worlds of adolescence were changes in sources of spending money. There was not much change in the male world but a considerable change in the female world. "The 1977 females were much less apt to receive money from their families, and more than four times as likely to be earning their own spending money. Thus, as with the evenings-at-home question, the comparisons reveal a situation where male students in 1977 seem comparable to the male students in 1924, but the two sets of female students differ markedly. . . . In 1924 the females were strikingly different from the males, being much more apt to receive their spending money from parents in the form of fixed allowances or on a demand basis. . . . By 1977 . . . there was no difference in sources of spending money between high school boys and girls in Middletown." The world of young women was offering a taste of at least partial independence and supplying some experience in paid work.

There was evidence of convergence of the two worlds also in sources of information about sex. In both worlds, parents as a source had declined about half, still remaining more frequent among girls than among boys (23 percent versus 20 percent), but friends had increased as sources in the female world. "The drastic change occurs among the female students, for whom parents were the main source of sex information in 1924. The 1977 results show friends as important a source as parents (both 35 percent) followed by schoolteachers and books or films (both 9 percent). The [data] . . . also reveal the pattern . . . noted previously of female students becoming more like the males. By 1977 the proportion of females identifying friends as the primary source of sex knowledge was almost the same as for males, and in the other categories their distribution was much closer to that for males than was the case in 1924."[18]

An analysis of sources of conflict with parents shows clearly the astonishing changes in the female world in the last half century and the tendency toward convergence with the male world. "In 1924 going to unchaperoned parties was a greater source of conflict for females than for males; in 1977 the reported rates are the same. Compared to the males, female students in 1924 were more apt to report disagreements about home duties and less apt to report disagreement about school grades; in 1977 the male-female differences for both these sources of disagreement had decreased."

Interesting, not as evidence of convergence between the male and female worlds of adolescence but as an index of changing values with respect to parenthood in both worlds, were the qualities held most desirable in parents. "In 1977 students were less likely to rate cooking and housekeeping skills, active church participation, and 'never nagging' as important qualities in a mother. Whereas in 1924 both males and females had rated being a good cook and housekeeper as the single most important quality for mothers, by 1977 this characteristic had dropped to third position. Much more important in 1977, particularly in the ratings by female students, were spending time with children and respecting the children's opinions, the same two qualities that had been ranked as most desirable in fathers. In other words, the parental traits deemed most desirable by Middletown students in 1977 were the same for both mothers and fathers: that they spend time with their children and respect their opinions."

Much that was so distressing to Coleman in adolescent society can be interpreted in terms of the importance ascribed to marriage in the female world. The emphasis on beauty, on dating, on popularity in adolescent society can be explained as presocialization for getting commitments in the "prime time" between eighteen and, say, twenty-five, following high school.

Prime Time in the Female World

Researchers ask women a great many questions about their personal lives but they rarely ask why they get married. Except for a small and decreasing number of religious, few women make a deliberate or conscious decision never to marry, if, in fact, one can even call entering marriage a decision when one considers all the pressures bearing down on young women to marry. It is so taken for granted that they will marry that almost everything in their world is based on that outcome. The young women liberationists in the late 1960s stated it succinctly; the rule prescribed was: "Better dead than unwed." The Milton Abbas Rhyme from Dorset put it in equally urgent terms: "St. Catherine, St. Catherine, oh lend me thine aid,/And grant that I never may die an old maid!/A husband, St. Catherine!/A good one, St. Catherine!/But anyone better than no one, St. Catherine!/A husband, St. Catherine!/Handsome, St. Catherine! Rich, St. Catherine! Young, St. Catherine!/Soon, St. Catherine!" In a time when there was no place in the social structure for women outside of the family, the pressure to get young women married was understandable. Though somewhat modified, it remains today. We are only now beginning to find a pleasant, congenial place for the nonmarried. So it is understandable that the world in which young women live between the late teens and the mid-twenties is highly marriage-oriented, a world in which the latent if not manifest commandment is: whether you want to or not, find a suitable mate.

The concept of "prime time" is, of course, widely applicable. Time can be prime for a lot of different purposes. For beginning ballet lessons, for example, or for having children, or for participating in Olympic games, or for learning a manual trade or a professional skill. The concept has thus been appropriated for different states in the life cycle. Thus Bernice and Morton Hunt (1975) apply it to the forties, once viewed, especially for women, as "over the hill"; the Gray Panthers apply it to the years sixty-five and beyond, once viewed as practically dead. Assuming again the privilege of Humpty Dumpty, I use the concept to apply to the world in which women live in their late teens and early twenties.

Time may be prime not only for different purposes but also from different perspectives, from the point of view of the young women themselves or from the point of view of others toward them. From a subjective point of view, midlife may, indeed, be prime time. A woman has completed her child-rearing role and is now free to expand her activities. But it is from the outsiders' point of view that the late teens and early twenties are judged prime time here, from the point of view of prospective employers, for example, or of men seeking mates. Several reasons have been given by employers for preferring to hire young women: "For one thing, it was argued that very young clerical workers—those under 22 years of age, for example—were more easily trained and more inclined to accept the company's way of doing things. Second, it was thought that young women were more mentally alert, stronger, more attractive and ornamental than older women. It was also argued that young workers could be started at lower wages" (Oppenheimer, 1970, 135). In this span of years a young woman is also at the peak of physical sexual attractiveness for most men; she is in the most available years for entering marriage.

The years of late teens and early twenties are certainly prime for advertisers. As C. W. Mills noted in the 1950s, "Among those whom Americans honor, none is so ubiquitous as the young girl. It is as if Americans had undertaken to paint a continuing national portrait of the girl as Queen. Everywhere one looks there is this glossy little animal, sometimes quite young and sometimes a little older, but always imagined, always pictured, as The Girl. She sells beer and she sells books, cigarettes, and clothes; every night she is on the TV screen, and every week on every other page of the magazines, and at the movies too, there she is" (1959, 82). And as long ago as 1891, Bryce was pointing out that "in no country are . . . young women so much made of. The world is at their feet. Society seems organized for the purpose of providing enjoyment for them" (608).[19]

Actually, from the point of view of the young themselves, the world of prime time can be rough. It is probably less miserable than the world of adolescence, but it hardly offers the serenity and self-confidence possible in later worlds. There are countless uncertainties and contingencies. Decisions have to be made that can shape their lives for decades.

The options open to them include postsecondary vocational training, college, labor-force participation, marriage, living with male partners outside of marriage, and a host of miscellaneous activities. Very little time is spent, on the average, in occupational training (Spitze, 1978, 475). One study found that most young women enter the labor force some time or other during prime time (Carlson, forthcoming), but according to another study (Spitze, 1978, 475), only about a fifth of all prime time was actually spent in labor-force participation. Although the time spent in college averaged more than was spent in full-time work, it dropped off in each successive year as the young women married and/or left college (475). In 1976, 25.4 percent of young women sixteen to twenty-four years of age were in the labor force, 21.3 percent were in school, 11.9 percent were married. There may, of course, have been some overlap, for some may have been married, in the labor force, *and* in school. Actually, serious consideration of a career is almost impossible for a woman in the prime-time world. Regardless of her interests and concerns, the prime-time world is organized to propel her on to marriage. The norms are like cilia, moving her in that direction. If almost no one takes her seriously and if almost everyone takes it for granted that marriage and motherhood are the first order of the day, it becomes all but impossible to do anything different.

The prime-time world is truncated in the case of working-class young women, for they tend to marry fairly early (Table 6-2). In 1975, about an eighth (11.5 percent) of all 18- and 19-year olds got married. A 1978 study of women in their fifties who had been "early marriers" found that most of them (84 percent) had tended to end their schooling by the age of 19, as compared with only 39 percent among "on-time marriers" (those who had married in their early twenties) (Elder, Rockwell, and Ross, 1978). Most (69 percent) of the early marriers had entered the labor force by age 19 as compared with only two-fifths (43 percent) of the on-time marriers. From these two pieces of information it is evident that more of the early marriers had working-class backgrounds than had the on-time marriers" (58 percent vs. 33 percent). More early-marriers than on-time marriers married men who had not completed high school (55 percent versus 20 percent) and who were manual workers (30 percent versus 13 percent) (Elder, Rockwell, and Ross, 1978). More (53 percent) of the early-marriers than of the on-time marriers (5 percent) had begun childbearing before the age of twenty.

A study of young women just entering the prime-time world in 1978 corroborates the presence of class differences, but also of cross-class similarities. Girls in both the middle class and the blue-collar cliques had jobs. Lynette, the middle-class girl, worked because she wanted to buy her own car. Janet, in the "low-rider clique, was also thinking of finding a job and having a car. Terry, in a rural school, was planning to get a job as good as her boyfriend's" (Johnston, 1978, 78). The middle-class girl was giving more thought to her future than the blue-collar class girl was. "Lynette tells me . . . that she's decided to put off getting serious about a boy until later—until after she's gotten a job, gone to school, and lived alone in her own apartment. She thinks her mother was right about the dangers of getting attached to a boy too early but still, she thinks about relationships all the time" (60). She

TABLE 6-2 Median Age at First Marriage 1890–1974: End of "Prime Time"*

Year	*Median Age at Marriage*
1890	22.0
1900	21.9
1910	21.6
1920	21.2
1930	21.3
1940	21.5
1950	20.3
1955	20.2
1960	20.3
1965	20.6
1970	20.8
1974	21.1
1977	21.1

*Source: Figures for 1890 to 1950, decennial censuses; for 1950 to 1974, Current Population Survey Data; for 1977, Vital Statistics Report, National Center for Health Statistics, July 20, 1979.

is independent, ambitious, but doesn't know what to study in junior college. The author concludes that "The girls I talked to . . . are busy mastering the more traditional feminine techniques: the emotional knowledge necessary to ride out avalanches of private turmoil. . . . If these young women could have any wish they wanted, it would be the wish that most of their mothers would make: to have a wonderful, loving husband, happy children, and a comfortable, well-kept and stable home. Anything more, they say, is frosting on the cake" (58). But the middle-class girls were probably expecting more frosting.[20] One black girl, for example, was "ready to burst into stardom" (62). No job in a motel or coffee shop for her; she was going to be a singer (62).

Prime time is thus telescoped in the case of young women with working-class backgrounds. Nor does it offer much to them. The kinds of work opportunities available to them are not always appealing. Family ties may seem oppressive but escape from them, especially in ethnic areas, is difficult except by way of marriage. They feel as Ruth Carter Stapleton remembers her own prime-time world as reported in an interview: "I had the idealistic view that marriage was the end to all problems. . . . When school began to be pretty rough . . . I became more interested in marriage. If you can't cope with life where you are, then get married and live happily ever after" (*Washington Post Magazine*, Oct. 8, 1978). So the world of prime time is primarily an affluent one.

The world of prime time is unique among all the serial worlds a girl and young woman passes through in that it is a time when her contacts with men, but not the male world, are at a maximum in her lifetime. Fe-

male friends now come to take second place. "Traditi
adolescence . . . a girl has an inseparable best friend
hangs out, talks to on the phone for hours, shares the h
confusions of growing up" (U. West, 1975, 37). But durin
the world of prime time, "the girls may become 'cruising p
ideal [female] partner is not markedly better-looking or w
than you, but is a different type, so you don't always find ... self attracting—and being attracted to—the same men. There is a rudimentary hands-off code in regard to the other's dates. But such a relationship tends to last only as long as both women remain uninvolved with men" (37).

Young women in the prime-time world have lived almost exclusively in a female world. They have had little contact with the male world, for their relationships with males have been as individuals, one by one, so to speak. The misogyny and the exclusivity of the male world are temporarily in abeyance in the world of prime time. Young women are sought after, courted, wooed. They feel loved and protected and assume that the male world is like these individual men—friendly.

The prime-time world is a relatively unstructured one. From the time of Tocqueville on, foreign observers have commented on the relatively great amount of freedom granted to unmarried young women in America. It is today a world of the singles life style, of cohabitation, of communal sharing, of "households of unrelated individuals," of entering into and exiting from love affairs (Hill and Associates, 1977). In Erikson's words, the young woman is granted a "moratorium" between the time she is under parental control and the time she passes into the control of the man she selects to be the father of her children (1968).

Not all young women are developmentally ready. They are conflicted. They are uncertain about what they really want. A job, to be sure. Perhaps a career. They experience a great deal of backing and filling during their four years of college (Angrist and Almquist, 1975). Always the certainty of marriage but always the problem of integrating it into their total life. At a time when career decisions have to be made they are hamstrung because all is contingent on the man they marry.

"When you are young you are loved for your youth; when you are older you are loved for what you are" is an old folk saying. In prime time young women scarcely know what they are. Their world has not tested them. It is hard for many people to take them seriously. Little has been expected of them except that they be charming, attractive, appealing. They are vulnerable, both in their search for a mate and—lacking experience with the male world of careers and carreerism—in their search for work.

But, beautiful or not, almost all the women in any cohort do get married. (And those who do not are not demonstrably less attractive than those who do.) They pass from the world of prime time into the world of marriage, with, in some cases—especially among the affluent—an elaborate set of rites to mark the passage.

Rites of Passage

High school graduation does not so much mark entrance into the world of prime time as exit from adolescent society. But the entrance into the world of prime time in some communities—after a period of social revolt in the 1960s—is once more being marked by debutante balls and parties and cotilions, ostensibly designed to "introduce" the young women to "society" (Gregory, 1979). When she leaves the world of prime time she marks her engagement, again with numerous rites. There are engagement announcements, parties, showers, events of a variety of kinds.

Even more widespread and less class-bound is the wedding, with its rich and symbolic ritual, including folk elaboration, for weddings are important in the female world. Whole industries cater to the affluent; friends and relatives to the less affluent. The "wedding industry amounts to an annual seven-billion-dollar total, including flowers, food, drinks, hall rental, gifts, clothes, jewelry. A bridal dress in 1978 cost between $200 and $475; and bridesmaids' dresses, $40 to $65. It took no less than four to six months to mount a good conventional marriage" ("Her-rah," television program, WRC-TV, Washington, D.C., June 25, 1978).[21] Ideas, plans, fears are shared with relatives and friends, and advice is freely dispensed. For the avant garde the wedding may take an exotic form, in the woods, in the orchard, in the fields. Whatever form it takes, the wedding is a central rite in the female world. Understandably so. It is the bride's show. She is the heroine. She is the star. And with this rite she "passes" into an altogether different world.

Before we leave the subject of the world of prime time, a comment on an interesting phenomenon that has been noted over a long period of time. Although young women in polls and surveys tend, as noted above, to be more liberal than older women on many issues, still young women in prime time are not necessarily feminists. As long ago as 1927, Lorine Pruette, an early feminist, described young women who were bored with "all that feminist pother," and Elaine Showalter notes that by the end of the 1920s, young women, "egged on by advertising which doubled in volume during the 1920s and by the fashion and cosmetics industries, . . . began to praise the old-fashioned 'privileges' of femininity and the joys of 'spending the day in strictly feminine pursuits" (Showalter, 1979, 70, 72). And again in 1978 girls just entering the prime-time world felt that the women's liberation movement came between the sexes (T. Johnston, 61).

The reasons are quite understandable. In the world of prime time women know men only individually, men who seek to please them, who admire them, are attracted to them. "I rather like my position in this male-oriented world, and I am not willing to give it up. . . . I have found no difficulties in asserting myself or realizing my potential in this male-oriented sphere." All around us beautiful young women are being paid tribute in advertisements, television shows, moving pictures. Youth and beauty win a lot of rewards. But even the young woman just quoted concedes that she has "not yet had the chance to get out into the 'real world.' " Because they lack experience with the misogyny of the male world, it is often hard for such young women to see why any woman can object to anything about it. They like men. Isn't the male world the same as the nice men they know? It may take several years before they learn that it is not.[22]

The subworlds described so far correspond roughly to the standard statistical categories for the age structure of a population in our society. Young people may be said to "pass through" them on their way to following worlds seriatim. But the same cannot be said of the subworlds of marriage, of motherhood, of the formerly married, of the never-married, though age is important in all of them.

Notes

1. The average ratio of men to women in the immigrant population in the century beginning in 1820 was 150:100. It declined after 1920 owing to the changing composition of immigration and the the aging of the population (Hutchison, 1956, 18). In 1920 male immigrants outnumbered female immigrants by more than 20 percent; in 1950, by only 2 percent.
2. Besides childbirth, the only cause of death more common among females than among males was diabetes mellitus.
3. Sheila Ryan Johansson believes that the decline in female mortality is due not to the decline in maternal fatalities but mainly to a decline in deaths from tuberculosis (1977, 164). Nor does she accept the concept of biologically based greater viability: "a strictly biological approach to understanding the emergence or existence of a female mortality advantage has serious limitations. Social and economic factors were important as well, and today they are making it more and more deadly to be male" (181).

   Kingsley Davis leans toward a biological explanation of the greater viability of women: "The advantage of females in mortality appears at all ages, both before and after the working ages; it is not wholly explicable in terms of temporary differences in habits such as smoking, diet, and exercise. Perhaps women are biologically more capable of resisting the environmental poisons and stresses of industrial society, especially since women are now freed from a high rate of childbearing. If so, the mortality gap may continue to increase, giving rise to sex ratios still more distorted than those observed today" (1979, 57).

A study in Framingham, Mass., published in the Feb., 1980, issue of the *American Journal of Public Health*, found that mere labor-force participation did not lower the survival advantage of women over men. Women who work have no more heart disease, on the average, than women who stay home, despite the often-voiced fear that as women work more, they will be unhealthier and lead shorter lives (Haynes and Feinleib, 1980). But women in low-level jobs who also had children were at a disadvantage, especially if they had blue-collar husbands. For a discussion of the sociological significance of the greater viability among females, see Peter N. Stearns, "Old Women: Some Historical Observations," *Journal of Family History* 5 (Spring, 1980): 44-57.

4. The years devoted to childbearing and childrearing may be said figuratively to be added on to women's lives in later life, thus making up for "time out," albeit at a time when energy resources are somewhat attenuated.
5. "The major demographic impact during the next several decades will continue to be the aging of the baby boom population. The people born during the peak of that boom—the late 1950s and the early 1960s—will continue to be the largest population group throughout most of their lives" (House Committee on Population, 1978).
6. The age boundaries of the several worlds through which a girl passes on her way to maturity have shifted downward in the past half-century. The age of menarche had been dropping at the rate of about four months per decade at least since 1850, and social patterns began to catch up in the twentieth century. Dating began at an earlier age; the age for getting a driver's license declined; the use of cosmetics began sooner, as did the wearing of brassieres. "By 1970 these activities often began for girls at 12 or 13 rather than at 15 or 16" (Kett, 1977, 265). The bobbysoxers who worshipped Frank Sinatra were between fifteen and eighteen; in the 1960s the teenyboppers were twelve to fifteen. The record industry distinguished only two age groups: subteens, ten to thirteen, and adults, fourteen and over (Kett, 265). Clothes designers distinguished three: nine to thirteen, thirteen to fifteen, and sixteen and over.
7. Cohort analysis sheds light on the changing nature of the phenomena we study. We have become used to being characterized as in an age of anxiety, or alienation, or involvement, or withdrawal, and the like. Sometimes such varying characteristics can be documented by research. In the case of self-concept, for example, researchers tell us that when an instrument was first introduced some twenty years ago, most of the responses were in the "social" category; nowadays they tend to fall in the "reflective" category. There seems to have been, that is, a change in self-concept among the subjects studied (Zurcher, 1977). We know also from Elder's study of children

of the Great Depression that different cohorts have differing attitudes; the women who had been deprived at that time tend to be more family-oriented than other women.

8. A story is told of a popular musician who played the piano at stage rehearsals. One day he struck up a tune that had been popular when he was young. No one knew it. "They're always the same age on Broadway," was his amazed conclusion as it struck him that he was not in the same world they were in. Or, perhaps more relevantly, they were not in the same world he had been in at their age.
9. Making fun of women for reluctance to disclose their age is almost an acceptable convention. If age were entirely a matter of biology, such resistance to it would be logical. But the world a woman is consigned to live in may or may not be suitable to her psychological age. It is designed for an old stereotype, a stereotype based on the lives of women of the past. If a woman tells people she is forty years old, they will deal with her in a way that does not fit the—more youthful—way she feels. She does not feel herself to be the stereotyped "older" person of this world.
10. Hilarion, to his wife, Alis, about 1 B.C.: "If, as may well happen, you give birth to a child, if it is a boy let it live; if it is a girl, expose it." An interesting aspect of the female world in need of further study is the demographic history of women. Female infanticide, for example, by its effect on the sex ratio, may have important sociological ramifications. A considerable corpus of research is already available. See the appendix on filicide in de Mause, 1976, 16-22.
11. An exception was the three-year-old little girl who, with some trepidation, reported that she didn't like the little boys at nursery school because they said "yuck" to the girls.
12. Intrinsic to this process was the separate toilet facilities provided for the boys and girls. The boys and girls made quite different use of their respective facilities. The boys used the toilet room as a quasi-clubhouse for planning their activities and also as a stage for competition, as, for example, seeing who could pee highest on the wall (Best, forthcoming).
13. One young woman tells of being "slapped across the room," although the significance of this symbolic act was never explained to her.
14. American skill and ingenuity have done a great deal to mediate the coping involved. Sanitary napkins, tampons, protection scaled to need have done much to mitigate the uncertainty, risk, discomfort.
15. Jane Lawick-Goodall has reported similar differences in preferences for females by males even among chimpanzees. Flo, for example, was sought by numerous males, Olly by few (1971, chap. 7).
16. Although Coleman felt that adolescent society was preparing young women for somewhat shady careers, as it turned out, even the most popular girls ended up in run-of-the-mill life styles. Thus, Mary Jane Lewis, who was the most popular girl in her class about a third of a century ago (1945), went to college, became a social reporter on her hometown paper, married and had two children, following separation worked in a bank, telephone company, and real estate agency, remarried after divorce and now lives on a farm. Another most popular girl of about a quarter of a century ago

(1952) went to college and entered promotional, public relations, and advertising work, married and took off about nine years to raise three children, and then returned to work with her husband in a public relations firm. Betty Brom was homecoming queen about fifteen years ago (1964). After graduation she began to work in a rubber company, married and worked as a secretary until she became pregnant; she has two children and keeps books for her husband's business. Sara Hoopengardner was homecoming queen almost a fifth of a century ago (1961). She became a nurse, married a civil engineer and followed him to several jobs; now, with three children, they have settled down to a life of farming in order to "have more of a family life" (59) (Perlez, 1978). The less beautiful and less popular girls probably followed lifestyles not very different from these.

17. A similar analysis to Coleman's had been made a generation earlier by Talcott Parsons with respect to mature women in his discussion of the "glamor pattern." This was a pattern that had filtered in between respectable women and those "no better than they should be" (1942). The emphasis in the glamor pattern was "on a specifically feminine form of attractiveness which on occasion involves directly sexual patterns of appeal." Female emancipation at that time meant "primarily emancipation from traditional and conventional restrictions on the free expression of sexual attraction and impulses." The net effect was to dissociate the sexual component from the total personality and thus "to emphasize the segregation of sex roles."

18. The contents of information about sex, whatever its source, have changed remarkably in the past generation. As an example of the trend, a book designed for public schools in Sweden in 1977 "attempts . . . to tackle controversial sexual issues openly instead of blindly ignoring the realities of the world in which today's young people live" (Linner, 1978). In contrast to the past, in which "sex education . . . had as its basic objective to give people information about an important aspect of life that was formerly taboo . . . the emphasis in the 1977 handbook lies elsewhere" (7). Now the goal—defined by Parliament!—is the promotion of "equality between men and women—in the family, on the labor market and in the life of the community at large" (8). Controversial values are not to be avoided. These include: abortion, contraceptives, premarital sexual relations, living together without marriage, sexual activities among teenagers. In all cases recognition should be accorded to conflicting attitudes in the public, "without any taking of sides on the part of the teacher" (4). The student is to be free to make choices, but always to allow responsibility, consideration and concern. The student should "develop an awareness of the complex nature of sexuality and have a chance to adopt a personal position on issues involving intimate relationships" (8). This is far beyond acceptable contents for sex education in the United States.

19. The world of prime time could, as a matter of fact, be quite miserable. Schlesinger described it in the last decades of the nineteenth century: "Allowed to be her natural self until seventeen or twenty, the young lady then made her *debut* at an elaborate party. . . . Thereafter, if she and her parents were determinedly *au fait*, she entered a sort of servitude under the surveillance of a chaperon. She must not receive men in her home alone. . . .

She was not permitted to make formal calls alone, or go unchaperoned to dinners, receptions, balls, concerts, or the theater. . . . Under the watchful eye of the chaperon courtship proved . . . difficult but it was argued in compensation that the maiden's desirability . . . was correspondingly enhanced" (1946, 44-46).

20. The problems of the girls in a black school were reported as somewhat different. Sex dominated the scene. " 'If a dude is good in bed,' I was told, 'pretty soon he'll start asking his girl to pay for it.' Presents first, then clothes, and finally hard cash" (61). But not all the girls interviewed, of course, conformed to this custom.
21. In 1952, 81.0 percent of first-marrying couples had had showers; 69.7 percent had formal weddings; 81.3 percent had church weddings; 87.8 percent had receptions; 94.5 percent took wedding trips. The cost of the marriage was $948; the value of the gifts amounted to $1,505 (Hollingshead, "Marital Status and Wedding Behavior," *Mar. and Family Living*, Nov., 1952, 311).
22. Because they have a good relationship with one man—husband or lover—even many older women think they have a good relationship with the male world. They feel safe. Not until the relationship is broken by death, desertion, or divorce do they find that their relationship with the male world was not all that good after all. They are not protected by it. They find themselves vulnerable to all kinds of exploitation. Law, custom, convention offer them little in the way of generous treatment. In many cases it is only then that a woman who always prided herself on not being a "women's libber" understands what the rejected message of the "women's libbers" had been all about.

7

The Marital-Status Structure of the Female World

"Any Age": A One-Sex World

A British study of the covers of women's magazines distinguished three age levels of readers to whom the magazines were directed: the teens, the twenties, and women of "any age" (Ferguson, 1978). The first two categories are fairly clear-cut. We have glanced at them in Chapter 6. The third is ambiguous, referring to those who are not "young" readers but "just" readers. The "just" readers were still interested in youth and beauty, but magazines addressed to them took "a marginally more realistic approach to demography and admitted the existence of a non-youthful (but never old) female population" (111). Most of the discussion in the remaining chapters of this book deals with the world inhabited by women in this "any age" category—say, roughly twenty-five years of age and over. In 1976, this group constituted about three-fifths (58.3 percent) of the female population. They are, of course, far from a homogeneous population. Most of them were married and mothers, but they differ among themselves in all the ways in which demographers categorize people—by age, race, ethnicity, income, education, residence, occupation, marital status, what have you. They have in common the fact that their world tends to be a one-sex world.

Just as every female in our society lives the first five or six years of her life in a practically all-female world, so also do most of those who live long enough—certainly beyond sixty-five—and the proportion increases with every age bracket thereafter. About three-fifths of the sixty-five-and-over population are women. Between the female world of the young and the female world of the old there is a complex, variegated set of female worlds that also have a one-sex composition, whose members have only relatively superficial interaction with men other than their husbands. The world of the affluent may be one of matinées or golf, tennis, lunch at the country club, or of garden club activities, or of voluntary services in the community. The world of the less affluent married may have less expensive counterparts. Most of the employed, married or single, live in a world with other women in a segregated work site.

In the excitement and challenge of the early years of marriage women may not notice the one-sex nature of their world or even necessarily think of themselves as part of a female world. That comes later. But, in any event, women of "any age" eventually find themselves in an all-female world. The decline in contacts with men begins, of course, with marriage. Marriage as a status in our society has called not only for legal monogamy but also for sexual exclusivity within marriage. As an extension of this rule, outside of the family, few contacts between married women and men are permitted beyond the trivial, superficial, matter-of-fact, socially or at the shopping mall or at the office. Even social life tends to be segregated.

The Marital-Status Structure of the Female World

The marital-status structure of the female world may be viewed as a set of "ideal types" which lay down the specifications for the behavior of women as wives, wife-mothers, widows, and, increasingly, divorcées. The structure itself has little to do with the women who occupy it. Willingly or not, whoever they may be, women are required to conform to the structure, to abide by its specifications for the several marital statuses. These do change, to be sure, but slowly. A considerable amount of time is needed to change the minds of legislators, judges, employers, religious mentors, and others who enforce the role-defining norms that constitute the structure.

As Table 7-1 indicates, census data recognize only four marital statuses—single, married, divorced, and widowed—and these only as of the moment the census is taken. They tell us the marital status the women were living in at a given point of time. That is, they deal only with the prevalence, not the incidence, of each one. When we speak of

TABLE 7-1 Changing Marital-Status Structure of the Female World*

	1890	*1940*	*1950*	*1960*	*1970*	*1976*	*1976 (unstandardized)*
Single	34.1%	24.2%	20.0%	19.0%	12.1%	12.6%	15.0%
Married	54.8	59.3	63.9	65.6	70.8	68.9	66.2
Divorced	0.4	14.8	14.0	12.8	13.0	12.4	13.1
Widowed	10.6	1.6	2.1	2.6	4.1	6.1	5.7

*Source: Figures for 1890 from Donald J. Bogue, *The Population of the United States*, 1959, 215; figures for 1940 and later, Statistical Abstract of the United States, 1977, 38, Up to 1960, the base is all females fourteen years of age and over; since then, eighteen years of age and over. The figures are standardized on the basis of 1960.

"married," therefore, we speak of women currently married and living with their spouses, not of women who have never been married or of women currently in the status of divorce, not of women ever divorced. Not included in the table are those who are separated unless they have a legal separation and then they are often combined with the divorced. The cohabiting—those in a marital status just beginning to take on legal shape—are also not included. And among some of those in the standard statistical categories, there are some, perhaps less than 2 percent, who are living in alternative life styles such as communes, "group marriages," ménages-à-trois, and the like.

Also missing in census data is the status of mistress, "an enviable position," according to one study of the subject (Orth, 1972). "A mistress is a single woman, divorced, widowed, or never married, who is having an enduring affair with a married man who may support her but who today more frequently subsidizes her or merely improves her standard of living. The three essential ingredients of a lover-mistress relationship are that it lasts, that marriage is not realistically expected, and that the man assumes some financial responsibility" (3). Since little is known about this relationship or the relative size of the population involved in it, and since it must be kept *sub rosa*, and since it does not seem to have evolved a culture of its own, it is not included in our discussion of the marital-status structure of the female world.

Marriage Rates

The female world is primarily a world of married women, but the proportion of females fourteen years of age and older in the status of marriage has varied markedly in the last century, from a low of only 54.8 percent in 1890 (Bogue, 1959, 215) to a high of 70.8 percent in 1970 (Statistical Year Book, 1977, 38). In 1976, about two-thirds (68.9 percent) of adult females—eighteen years of age and over—were in the status of marriage; that is, living with a spouse (Table 7-1).

It is not surprising to learn that the marriage rate has been closely related to economic factors; we know that from the history of the business cycle in our own country. Marriage rates fluctuate with depressions and prosperity as well as with wars. But even in the seventeenth century a study of three French parishes found that "changes in the price of wheat correspond very closely with the changes in the number of... marriages.... When the price of wheat was high the number of... marriages ... fell abruptly" (Wrigley, 1969, 66). Religion, the condition of the labor market, legal prescriptions, property rights, and a host of other factors affect the pattern of marriage in any time and place.

Table 7-2 presents the crude marriage rate in our country from 1870 to 1958—that is, the percentage of the total population who married in a given year. This rate is crude indeed because it does not take into account the age and sex composition of the denominator. But it is good enough to give an approximate picture of general trends. It will be noted that the rate was apparently rather low in the last three decades of the nineteenth century. Only in the late 1960s did it return to such a low level, with the exception of the Great Depression year, 1932.

For the years since 1920 the data are somewhat more refined, based on the unmarried (never-married, divorced, widowed) female population (Table 7-3). We can also see, in Table 7-4, the first-marriage rates for women by age, an important datum for understanding the female world. Overall, the first-marriage rate among women fourteen years of age and over declined markedly between 1960 and 1975. In the most-marrying age brackets—eighteen to nineteen and twenty to twenty-four—the rates fell drastically, from 208.4 to 115.0 per thousand and 263.9 to 143.8 per thousand, respectively. The remarriage rate, on the other hand, rose from 327 in 1960 to 401 in 1976 (Statistical Abstract, 1977, 74).

TABLE 7-2 Crude Marriage Rate, 1870-1965*

Year	*Rate*
1870	8.8
1880	9.0
1890	9.0
1900	9.3
1910	10.3
1920	12.0
1930	9.2
1940	12.1
1950	11.1
1960	8.5
1965	9.2

*Source: Donald Bogue, *The Population of the United States* (New York: Free Press, 1959), 238-239, for 1870-1920; Hugh Carter and Paul Glick, *Marriage and Divorce* (Cambridge, Mass.: Harvard University Press, 1970), 41, for 1930-1965.

TABLE 7-3 Marriage Rates per 1,000 Unmarried Women Fifteen Years and Over*

Year	*Rate*
1920	92.0
1930	67.6
1940	82.8
1950	90.2
1960	73.5
1970	76.5
1976	65.2
1977	63.6

*Sources: Vital Statistics Report, Advance Report, *Final Marriage Statistics*, 1977, Vol. 28, Number 4, Supplement, July 20, 1979 for years 1950 to 1977; Hugh Carter and Paul Glick, *Marriage and Divorce: A Social and Economic Study* (Cambridge, Mass.: Harvard University Press, 1970), 41, for years 1920 to 1950.

TABLE 7-4 First-Marriage Rate of Women by Age, 1960-1975*

	Number of Marriages per 1,000 Population			
Age	*1960*	*1965*	*1970*	*1975*
14 years of age and over	87.5	84.4	82.9	68.1
18-19	208.4	166.9	151.4	115.0
20-24	263.9	237.3	220.1	143.8
25-44	—	96.4	82.4	81.7
45-64	—	9.0	8.8	9.2

*Source: Statistical Abstract of the United States, 1977, p. 74.

In the mid-1970s, the overall marriage rate seemed to be waffling, down in some months and up in others. Young women seemed uncertain of what they wanted. Perhaps because the costs and disadvantages of marriage were becoming more visible. Perhaps because there were other options available to them. In any event, the increase in the number of young women who were not living in the status of marriage was startling. Between 1960 and 1976 the overall proportion of never-married women in the female world rose from 11.9 to 15.0 percent, a 26 percent increase. Most remarkable was the 50 percent increase in singlehood among women in the twenty-to-twenty-four age bracket, from 28.4 to 42.6 percent (Statistical Abstract, 1977, 40).

Non-Marriage in the Female World

One would suppose that any institution as fundamental as marriage would be relatively uniform in prevalence over time and place. It is, instead, surprisingly variable. "In some societies it is almost unknown for a woman not to marry, and marry moreover at or soon after the onset of puberty; in others large numbers of women remain single for life (in Ireland in 1901, 22 percent of all women in the age-group 45-54 were still single" (Wrigley, 1969, 10). Nor is marriage unrelated to time and place. The preindustrial "European" marriage pattern differed from the present pattern in America but also from the patterns in other parts of the preindustrial world—for example, India. Outside Europe, Wrigley tells us, marriage for women "was almost universal and came at a very young age" (90). But as early as the sixteenth century in Europe—even earlier in some parts of the continent—there was a pattern in which "between two-fifths and three-fifths of the women of child-bearing age 15-44 were unmarried" (Wrigley, 90).

Although the overall pattern is one in which almost all women get married, early or late, as the case may be, the examples in Chapter 3 of the freewheeling vagabonds, the convent and the beguinage, and of other women who could manage on their own show that marriage was not always the only career open to women. Although for most women there have been few alternatives to marriage—since the home was the only place where, as sister, daughter, or aunt, they could earn their keep even if not married—when alternatives existed there have been those who selected them over marriage.

Even in our own much-married society, marriage has faced competition. We know, for example, that age for age women who have well-paying jobs show lower marriage rates than other women and that divorced or widowed women with economic resources are less likely to remarry than are those without such resources (Bernard, 1956).

The nonmarried status of women in the female world has ramifying implications. If a large proportion of women do not marry the impact will depend on whether they choose not to marry or remain single for extraneous reasons. They may prefer nonlegalized relationships. Or temporary liaisons. Or, even celibacy. Julia Rux, for example, has analyzed celibacy as "an alternative to sex-typed dyadic relationships" and concluded that it can sometimes be a welcome response "to oppression by religious, political, and social institutions" (draft, 1977). It may, in fact, emerge once more as a legitimate option in the female world. "A contemporary movement toward celibacy would represent a rejection of exploitation by political, religious, economic, and social institutions as they impinge on intimate personal relationships. The withdrawal from the dyadic power-relationship model of human interaction would release energy for spiritual and intellectual pursuits [as it had, indeed, in the case of nuns]. New celibates might explore unity-building patterns of emotional support not based on sexuality or dyads. Another function the celibacy option could serve would be the rejection of the compulsive female sexuality of popular culture and the [concomitant] definition of woman as corollary to men." Celibacy is, of course, not the same as nonmarriage but it would be a widely ramifying alternative.

As long as never-married women could earn their keep, their status was respectable. Before industrialization took spinning and weaving out of the home, the term "spinster" was not a put-down; it might even have been a compliment to a woman's industriousness. With industrialization, however, "unmarried women were no longer positive economic assets to the household because there was less need for their labor in spinning, weaving, and other economic tasks; as a result many unmarried women were faced with the unpleasant choice between working for very low wages, or becoming largely superfluous dependents on someone else" (Watt, 1957. Present citation Coser, 1966, 274). The term "spinster" did not enter the English language, according to the *Oxford English Dictionary*, until 1719,[2] when it was defined nonpejoratively as "an unmarried woman beyond the age for marriage." Since the ususal age of marriage could vary, the status of spinsterhood might range from a fairly young age to a fairly late one.

How to deal with the situation was not altogether clear. A system that makes no room in it for women unless they are married or at least protectively embedded in a household[3] will be at a loss as to what to do with them if they have neither husbands nor families. In 1694, Mary Astell suggested the establishment of "monestary or religious retirement" to perform the functions convents had once performed throughout Europe and still did in Catholic countries. Lady Mary Wortley Montagu (1689-1762) also approved of such Protestant nunneries—or rather perhaps beguinages, since they seemed to resemble them in structure—as proposed by Sir Charles Grandison, in Samuel Richardson's novel (1753-54) of the same name. According to Sir Charles, "numbers of young women, joining their small fortunes, might . . . maintain themselves genteelly on their own income; though each singly in the world would be distressed" (quoted by Watt, 275). A modernized form of the beguinage.

Unlike the United States, in which the sex ratio favored women in the sense that there were more men than women until well into the twentieth century, England has had a sex ratio unfavorable to women for many years. "After the census of 1851, England seemed indeed to be suffering a serious outbreak of spinsterdom" (Showalter, 1975, 12). On the basis of the greater survival rate of female infants, only 1 to 5 percent of the female population should have been doomed to "natural celibacy." Actually almost a third of the women over twenty were unmarried. Another 13 percent were widowed. The reasons for this alarming and abnormal and unwholesome social state, according to W. R. Greg, a social philosopher, were the emigration of men, the rising cost of a genteel establishment, and male profligacy. He had little confidence that preaching to men would be an efficacious means of dealing with it; women must take matters into their own hands. Without unseemly or unwomanly independence they should pursue husbands by shipping out to the colonies. Well chaperoned, of course, and quite ladylike. A Female Emigration Society did, in fact, arise to carry out this kind of project (Showalter, 1975). An option between a denigrated status of dependency at home and deportation abroad was a Hobson's choice (i.e., an apparently free choice when there is no real alternative).

In the United States, the proportion of single women was only half as great in 1970 as it was in 1940 (Table 7-1), and about three-fifths as great in 1976. And their status was by no means denigrated. They were doing all right (Bernard, 1972; Radloff, 1979; Kanter, 1978). One study of fifty young (twenty-four to thirty-four years of age), and medium-socioeconomic level, never-married women living alone in an urban area found that they were "not relatively isolated", they had networks of individuals who had "a deep and genuine concern for their well-being," and they "were involved in intimate relations with others." They had created homes for themselves with a comfortable and nurturing atmosphere which pleased them. Their homes also gave them a sense of ownership (Kanter, 1978). Although this small, educated sample cannot be generalized to all never-married women, it nevertheless demonstrates that at least for some the world of the never-married, independent woman is far from bleak and is probably becoming less so all the time.

In the past the female world offered women only two respectable marital statuses, celibacy or traditional marriage. At the present time a wide array of options is becoming increasingly available. Nonmarriage may include cohabiting relationships, and even marriage itself is offering a number of possibilities. In one study of college undergraduates, for example, a dozen possibilities from which students could choose were listed: egalitarian marriage, five-year evaluation and renewal of marriage, long-term cohabitation, traditional marriage, child-free marriage with role reversal, rural commune with shared sex, consensual extramarital sex, serial monogamy, spouse swapping, group marriage (Strong, 1978, 493-503). Even in a world that offered such a variety, the most preferred type of relationship was the egalitarian marriage, far outstripping even its nearest competitor, the five-year evaluation-and-renewal form.[4]

The Changing World of Marriage

The world a young woman enters at marriage is in such flux at the present time that it is difficult to describe it. The pace of change is so fast that, as some students have pointed out, the world reported in research of more than a decade and a half ago seems to be from a different era. As recently as a dozen years ago it might have been fairly easy to delineate the expectations marriage included. The ground rules—specified in custom, tradition, convention, the common law, legislation, in court decisions, in religious, moral, and ethical prescriptions—were fairly clear-cut and although there was a good deal of talk about alternative forms of marriage and conspicuous violations, still, the old rules seemed to prevail.

The public picture of marriage is a romantic one, showing marriage as based on love, never as primarily a means to the kind of life the woman wants, a life of homemaking and motherhood, Whatever doubts or hesitations young women may feel, they know they must hide them. Until yesterday the bride took her husband's name as a matter of course. She gave up her job to become a full-time homemaker. She accepted the rule that the husband was head of the household, had children at decent intervals, dedicated her life to their care and the care of her husband, expected little if any help in either routine household chores or child care, expected little if any recognition for her services in the home, took it for granted that her marriage would last as long as they both lived, and that when he died she would live a quiet but still-helping life. Just listing some of the major items in this marital-status structure suggests how much change is in process.

In the past fifteen years or so almost every ground rule of the world into which marriage ushers women has been challenged. Legal, economic, social—they all seem to be in flux.

Legal Norms of Marriage

The world a woman enters when she marries is usually one that she has only a dim knowledge of. She may learn about it only when some unexpected incident reveals it. She usually understands well that in this world her relationships with men change drastically, but only in recent years is she likely to have learned how her legal—and consequently economic—status will also change. She is legally defined as a dependent, a status that has a host of consequences (Cowan, 1978, draft). It deprives her of control of her economic life. She must, until recently at least, check "married" on documents to notify anyone she might want to deal with—stores, banks, employers, whoever—that she is a "dependent" and must therefore have the signature of her husband. Until recently she might even be denied credit, no matter how creditworthy she might be in her own right. Pensions, disability, insurance, social security may all be affected by the dependency status legally assumed to be inherent in being a married woman. The legal doctrine of "interspousal immunity" means that a wife cannot sue her husband unless she is willing to leave him. As long as they remain under the same roof, her husband is presumed to represent her. Her right to support is therefore no right at all since it is all but unenforceable. She has no right to compensation for her service in the home; legally, that is "gratuitous service." There is a large body of partnership law, but it does not apply to marriage; there is a large body of contract law, but it does not apply to marriage; so also is there a body of law dealing with battery, but it is not applicable in marriage. Under the principle of "conjugal rights" there was until recently no such concept as marital rape.[5]

But the world of marriage is changing, the legal "ground rules" with respect to almost every aspect of its structure are different from what they were even a decade or two ago. Still "the legal structure of marriage has remained stagnant and is consequently a rigid and outmoded vestige of the old social system. The increase in egalitarian family patterns challenges the traditional marriage contract and points to the need for a more flexible legal model, a model which is more suited to the nuclear family unit and to the diverse roles modern husbands and wives must assume" (A. Miller, 1976, 196). In the meanwhile, women themselves are not waiting; they are trying to restructure it by their own efforts.

Customary Norms of Marriage: Labor-Force Participation

Until recently, in line with the ideology of women's sphere, custom prescribed that if a woman had a job, she must give it up at marriage. She changed her occupation from whatever she was engaged in to that of housekeeper when she married. It was taken for granted that she would leave the labor force. She was to devote all her time and energy to her household. In 1973, as we have noted, for the first time the proportion of married women twenty-two to twenty-four years of age and living with their husbands who were in the labor force was more than half (52.9 percent). This new pattern meant that entrance into the world of marriage, as distinct from the world of motherhood, did not now change a woman's life as drastically as it had in the past, especially if she continued in the labor force. Her social life at work might now continue with the same friends. In a modern marriage, also, the household responsibilities may be shared. Thus the difference between the world of the young married woman and that of her unmarried friends, once profound, has become smaller with time, though it does, to be sure, remain to some degree.

Relations with Men

Marriage changes not only a woman's legal status and sometimes her occupation, but also her relations with men. Once a woman is married her contacts with men other than her husband will be severely curtailed. Even in our relatively free society today, a traditional web of rules and regulations restricts her relations with men. Despite a spate of alternatives to the restrictiveness of marriage—open marriage, swinging, group relationships, communal arrangements— the vast majority of women continue to live in a world which limits their contacts with men.

Although social life is organized on a couple basis and although a certain amount of flirting is tolerated in some circles, even so, at social gatherings the worlds of women and of men separate. Unless the hostess makes a special effort to prevent it, the women tend to congregate at one end of the room and the men at the other (Bernard, 1968).

Herbert Gans caught the segregating process of marriage in an ethnic enclave, but he felt it was probably the same—less extreme, perhaps, but similar—in other groups also. Although the hold of the one-sex peer group is "broken briefly at marriage," shortly thereafter, especially with the arrival of the first child, "each of the marriage partners is pulled *centrifugally* toward his or her peers" (1962, 39). Social gatherings break up into male and female subgroups. "The women sit together in one room, the men in another" (48). Consequently, a one-sex peer group of family and friends continues for the rest of the woman's life.

It is in many ways a serious deprivation to be cut off from the company of men, to miss the stimulation of interchange of perspective and viewpoint that is possible. The hunger for male contacts is forced into sexual channels in the form of flirtatious byplay between men and women and coquetry, which are permitted under restricted conditions. Nothing serious, in public at least. Affairs must be conducted discreetly. The kind of interchange that characterized the French salons is rare. Canby, writing in the last years of the nineteenth century, described how serious its lack could be:

> We, in our early middle age, talked to middle-aged women as if they were cinders—agreeable, yes, admirable often, interesting often, yet cinders, good for home walks and garden beds, but long emptied of fire—and like cinders they responded. And hence that subtle interpretation of the special knowledge of each which can make an idea glow between a man and a woman was frozen at the source of its rays. Women suffered most, for the male intellect in an age busy with things had plenty of satisfying facts to talk about. Women past their twenties or married suffered dumbly from an imagination that made them sexless, because they did not know what was

> wrong and would not have admitted the truth if it had been told to them. But men suffered too by a kind of vivacious dullness which was the note of the period. . . . An element, not necessarily the most important, was excluded from the daily diet of our relationships, with the result that society grew anemic as it grew older. Unrest or boredom hovered in the corners under the potted palms of ballrooms, the friendship was real but the gaiety forced, and even with fine people had a note of the trivial and the commonplace. Only a few old tomcats who had kept the convention, if not the fact, of gallantry from an earlier generation could talk, in our town, to a woman of thirty or forty as if she were more than a domestic variety of man [Canby, 1934, 176-177].

Marriage thus draws women back into the one-sex world of their earlier years.

Even more than in "social life" does the daily life of women take place in a female world. Relationships with women come to assume greater salience. "Once you are safely married, with children, it becomes possible to form ties with women again. The friend is usually a neighbor, the wife of the husband's business associate, or the mother of your child's playmate. Hubby has his beer-drinking buddies, and wifey has her girlfriends for gossip and shopping" (V. West, 1975, 37). Married women live in an almost completely female world of kaffee klatches, bridge clubs, baby-airing sessions in the park, book clubs, church groups, whatever. If a woman does not have contacts with other women she is not likely to have many contacts at all.

Nor have women enjoyed a great deal of intimacy with their husbands. Most of the intimate, personal contacts of women are with other women. In Chapter 5, we noted Toqueville's observation that American men were not emotionally attentive to their wives; they were so busy tending to their business that they had little time for affection, and the business habit of mind discouraged the expression of fondness. In 1943 a book on the manners and morals of marriage in America was still echoing Toqueville's point: there was a lack of intimacy in marriage (Cohn, 1943, 26-33). And more recent studies have shown that the same situation still exists, resulting in a "relational deficit," to use Robert Weiss' term (Bernard, 1976b). When a woman has good news to report, her husband is the first to hear; when she is depressed, he will be protected—she will share this news with other women (Belle and others, 1979, 133). Companionship with one's husband is minimal in many marriages. In working-class families, the wife's life tends to run parallel to that of her husband's with relatively little interaction; in middle-class families there is at least an ideology of interaction, though the extent to which it has been practiced is doubtful.

It is not wholly inconceivable that now that young women have more options available to them aside from traditional marriage, they may be in a position to specify the conditions they consider desirable in the marital relationship, including more expressions of affection, and to insist on them. They are already beginning to change the legal, customary, traditional, and moral nature of marriage. Some men find the changes traumatic. Others, especially the younger men, find—sometimes to their own surprise—that they like the newly evolving form marriage is taking. In either case, it makes a difference in the female world.

The World of Mothers

Although motherhood is not in itself a marital status, it is part of the status of marriage for practically everyone since almost every married person has at least one child (Table 7-5). And because reproduction is so basic, a large part of both the infrastructure and the superstructure of any society is devoted to its control. Because the mother is always present when an infant is born, a large part of that corpus of control impacts on her and her world. Mothers and their children are, indeed, viewed as the prototype of human society.

A great deal of the shaping of female character is related to the role of mother. The love-and/or-duty ethos rests solidly on it (Chapter 22). If the mother does not nurture the child, no one else can be depended on to do it. If she does not nurture the child because she loves it she will be made to do so because it is her duty. An almost inexhaustible body of norms—law, custom, tradition, lore, magic, mores, beliefs, attitudes—surrounds the whole reproductive enterprise. Such control is a major preoccupation in the male as well as in the female world; it may also become a major issue between the two worlds.

In addition to this enormous, almost all-encompassing normative structure, there is an equally extensive and no less compelling culture built around the world of mothers. The folk culture, for example, is re-

TABLE 7-5 Fertility Rates, 1950–1978* (per 1,000 women, 15–44)

Year	*Fertility Rate*
1950	106.2
1955	118.3
1960	118.0
1965	96.6
1970	87.9
1975	66.7
1978	66.6

*Source: Statistical Abstract, 1978, p. 60; for 1978, National Center for Health Statistics, Vol. 29, no. 1 (April 28, 1980).

plete with good mothers, bad mothers, stepmothers, fairy godmothers, goddess mothers, witches. A literary—poetic, dramatic, fictional—and musical culture exalts or condemns mothers. The madonna glorified at least one image of the mother.

Since the female contribution to the reproductive process is so much greater than the male contribution in terms of time and vital energy invested in it, reproduction comes to be viewed exclusively as a female function. And, as a corollary, as *the* female function.[6] Women come to be seen almost exclusively in their reproductive function. Their world is shaped with this perspective in mind. In the nineteenth century, for example, the protection of the female reproductive system was used as an argument against higher education for women, as it was later used to "protect" women from well-paying jobs.[7] Everything in a girl's socialization and training has been designed, explicitly or implicitly, in the expectation that she will become a mother. And the chances are great that she will. Although the proportion of young women who say they plan to have no children is increasing, it is still small. Most are going to have at least one child. When we talk about the female world we are talking about a world in which most adult members have children.

The willingness or unwillingness of women to become mothers has become a political issue; programs to increase their willingness have been countered with programs to decrease it. There is scarcely any aspect of any social system that is not involved in the ramifications of the reproductive function and hence in creating normative structures in the female world. The amount of space devoted here to this aspect of the female world is in reverse proportion to its importance. It is so ramifying that adequate discussion would require volumes rather than just pages. Here, therefore, we limit the picture of motherhood to the narrow perspective of the woman herself as she enters this enormously complex aspect of the female world.

If marriage spells greater involvement in the female world, the first child deepens and seals it. Pregnancy and childbirth constitute a uniquely female core of the female world. Few rites in anthropological accounts of preliterate cultures attract more attention than those related to childbirth. The first birth ushers a woman into this special world and, suddenly inundated with advertisements and samples of a whole cornucopia of products and services, a whole new literature of child care and childrearing, she wonders where this has been all her life. This is a world in which she is center stage.

The age at which a woman enters the world of mothers—the birth of her first child—is almost determinative of all the rest of her life. If she enters it as a teenager, the prospect is bleak. The chances are that her schooling will be cut short, that she will bear a large number of children, that they will come earlier than her peers' offspring, and that her marriage will be unstable. Her disadvantaged opportunities in the labor market will mean lifelong poverty (Moore et al. 1979; Furstenberg, 1976). One team of researchers asks, "Would the lives of the early childbearers be better now if they had postponed their first births?" and replies with a clear affirmative. "We are persuaded by the data that they would be better off. All in all, early child-bearers seem to have experienced more difficulties and endured more unhappiness and as a group have ended up less well-off than people who delayed child-bearing. Moreover, although we have not looked at the consequences from a child's point of view, we think that their children would have had easier lives if their parents had been older at the beginning of parenthood and marriage. Because their parents tried or were forced to enter adult roles before many of them were economically or emotionally ready, these children have experienced more poverty, welfare dependency, and marital disruption. Would things have been different . . . if the mother had been, say, 22 instead of 16 when her first child was born? . . . We feel that the woman's age per se does make a difference" (Moore et al., 1979, 45).[8]

Even if the young woman is in sync with the institutional timing for entrance into the world of mothers—early twenties—she may not be prepared. Although it has been taken for granted from her birth, by the girl herself as well as others, that she will become a mother and although she has been surrounded by books, pamphlets, articles, old wives' tales and lore, she is, as Alice Rossi pointed out some time ago (1968), quite unprepared for it.[9] She can prepare her body for childbirth, but how can she prepare it for the sleepless nights, the fatigue, the anxieties, the feelings of helplessness in the face of a crying infant that cannot communicate its pain? for the nameless fears? the unlimited responsibilities? the endless duties and obligations? the pervasive guilt?

In the serial subworld of mothers, the scheduled time for having a first child is in the early twenties and, at the present time, the last child in the early thirties. But the schedule varies by cohort (Table 7-6) and age of mother. In the early 1950s the birth rate among women in all age groups was going up but it began to decline soon thereafter (Table 7-7). There was a slight upward tilt again in the mid-1970s, especially among women in their early thirties. These births may represent the babies delayed by young career women busy until now with their education and professional training (Fabe and Wikler, 1979).

For the most part women have entered the female subworld of mothers not only unprepared but even unaware of the great normative structure they were becoming part of. Women have created, as Smith-Rosenberg has pointed out, a female world of their own. But a growing

TABLE 7–6 Age of Mother at Birth of First and Last Child*

	Period of Birth of Mother							
Parity	1950-1959	1940-1949	1930-1939	1920-1929	1910-1919	1900-1909	1890-1889	1880-1889
First child	22.7	21.8	21.4	22.7	23.5	22.8	22.9	23.0
Last child	29.6	30.1	31.2	31.5	32.0	31.0	32.0	32.9

*Source: Bureau of the Census, *Perspectives on American Fertility, Special Studies*, Series P-23, No. 70 (July, 1978), Table 2-5, p. 20. Authors of this report, Maurice J. Moore and Martin O'Connell.

TABLE 7–7 Birth Rates per Thousand Females by Age of Mother, 1940–1976*

	Age of Mother							
Year	*15-44*	*15-19*	*20-24*	*25-29*	*30-34*	*35-39*	*40-44*	*45-49*
1978	66.6	†	112.3	112.0	59.1	18.9	3.9	0.2
1977	67.8	53.7	115.2	114.2	57.5	19.2	4.2	0.2
1976	65.8	53.5	112.1	108.8	54.5	19.0	4.3	0.2
1970	87.9	68.3	167.8	145.1	73.3	31.7	8.1	0.5
1965	96.3	70.5	195.3	161.6	94.4	46.2	12.8	0.8
1960	118.0	89.1	258.1	197.4	112.7	56.2	15.5	0.9
1955	118.3	90.3	241.6	190.2	116.0	58.6	16.1	1.0
1950	106.2	81.6	196.6	166.1	103.7	52.9	15.1	1.2
1945	85.9	51.1	138.9	132.2	100.2	56.9	16.6	1.6
1940	79.9	54.1	135.6	122.8	83.4	46.3	15.6	1.9

*Source: Public Health Service, *Facts of Life and Death*, Nov., 1978. Department of Health, Education and Welfare Publication No. (PHS) 79-1222, Table 4, p. 4; data for 1978, Final Natality Statistics, 1978, National Center for Health Statistics, Vol. 29, No. 1, Supplement (April 28, 1980), pp. 12-13.

†In 1978 the rate for 15-17-year-old women was 32.9, for 18-19-year-old women, 81.0.

literature by indignant women protests the process by which the female subworld of mothers has been "stolen away" from them, the intimate old female way of dealing with motherhood transformed into a male-dominated world of child experts and medical professionals. They want to retrieve childbirth for women. A movement to restore the midwife is now in process (Wertz and Wertz, 1977), as well as a redefinition of the whole female world of motherhood.

I have pointed out elsewhere that the way motherhood is institutionalized in our society is almost the worst possible way to do it, not good for infants, for women, for men (Bernard, 1974). And now women are beginning to examine their own experiences as mothers from the time of giving birth to the time their sons and daughters are adults (Boston Women's Health Book Collective, 1978), to reinterpret it in terms of life as it is lived in this day and age. Readers are invited to consider an invitation "that parents don't often hear" (3). The ten women who wrote *Our Selves and Our Children* (1978) "found that talking about our own lives and needs as parents . . . [was] a first step to looking more critically at institutions and attitudes in our society which unfairly distort the lives of parents and children today. For we discovered that parenthood *can* be different from our culture's 'institutionalized' version of it. In other words, certain structures of our society generated by sexism, racism or a preoccupation with technological production and profits create an 'institution' of parenthood which violates the potential of parenting experience. In this book we . . . suggest changes in parental role and in social structure which can help us to reclaim our parenthood as an integrated, nourishing enterprise" (5). The world of mothers will never be the same again. The volumes of research—tables dealing with labor-force participation, with child care, with fertility, with the conflicting roles of women, and the equally voluminous body of "multivarite analyses" of variables that grow out of them—are here given flesh and blood. We see the world mothers inhabit from the inside. It is going to make a difference.

At the present time, then, women are attempting to rewrite the "constitution" of the subworld of mothers. They want, first of all, to gain control over the use of their bodies for reproduction in the first place. They want more control over the whole birthing process. They want to have the care of small children more evenly distributed.

An Emerging Female Subworld: "Women of a Certain Age"

A generation ago I wrote that the age of thirty-five seemed an important watershed in the lives of women. It was at that moment that women achieved release from their bonds with their mothers and a certain degree of independence from their husbands. At this age, Eleanor Roosevelt was finally able to free herself from the domination of her mother-in-law; Elizabeth Barrett was free enough of her father to elope with Robert Browning (Bernard, 1956, 278). If a woman was ever to achieve selfhood this was the time; if she did not do it at thirty-five, she probably never would. These observations were made without any systematic research to support them. Twenty years later Gail Sheehy, on the basis of long interviews with women, confirmed them. She found the mid- to late-thirties to be a time when the career woman achieved a kind of independence from her mentor (1976, 324-325). She called thirty-five a "crossroads for women" (377). The last child is now in school; more and more mothers enter or reenter the labor force; if divorced, this is the time the woman remarries (378-383); if married, she may begin to look for a lover, or even, in many cases, leave home. These are interesting developmental events. But our interest here has to do more with the world the woman finds herself in. It is a world not wholly structured as yet. It is still a female world; indeed, it is a female world in which the woman of "a certain age" is likely to find an anchor.

One of the most perceptive insights into the world of "women of a certain age" is presented by Lillian Rubin in her book bearing that title (1979). As in the case of so many changes related to the women's movement, the researcher's investigation of the world women lived in at midlife had the effect of reminding them that they were not alone, that their fears and doubts were not their own "fault," that there were options and choices still available to them, that doors were still open, that the empty nest was an opportunity for a new life, not the seal of an old one. Rubin showed them that whatever choice they made, it should be "based in clear knowledge about how much really is our individual choice, how much was defined for us [by our female world] long ago, on the day we were born girls. For without that knowledge, we suffer in isolation, as if the issues were ours alone; without it, we blame ourselves, each of us thinking this is our unique and personal deficiency; without it, we have no basis even for a fantasy about what changes are necessary in the structure of our social world, so that not only we, but our men as well, can live more fully" (1979, 211-212). They could actually change their world.

In a study of women returning to academia—whose average age was thirty-six—one-fourth gave as one of the changes resulting from their experience an "increased liking and respect for other women" (Astin, 1976, 85). And from interviews with these women, Katz found "women getting together, raising their consciousness, gaining strength and enjoyment from each other, developing a previously denied sense of what it can mean to be a woman" (1976, 93). By the age of forty, Sheehy reports, women have really "found themselves" (1976, 418-422). The nest that has preoccupied so much of a woman's time and energies is now empty and she is free to fly if she wants to. This is a new "prime-time" world, this time prime from the point of view of the woman herself.

What form this new female subworld will take remains to be seen. We have here a population of still young, energetic women whose obligations as mothers are becoming attenuated, who are increasingly engaged in educational activities, political work, and the like, and increasingly subjected by consciousness-raising experiences to a perspective on their world which may reorient their view of themselves as well as of their world.

Sometimes women of a certain age choose divorce; sometimes it is forced on them. The point is sometimes made that permanence in marriage meant one thing when life expectancy did not extend much beyond the child-bearing years. Remaining married for twenty-five years was different from remaining married for half a century. Since life expoctancy increases more rapidly than age at marriage, the proportion of adult years spent in marriage has at least potentially greatly increased. Thus in 1940, the average woman spent just over half (55.5 percent) of her adult years living with a spouse; in 1964, well over three-fifths (61.5 percent) (Carter and Glick, 1970, 63). And undoubtedly the percentage is even higher today.

But so also do a great many women spend a considerable number of years in the world of divorce.

The World of the Formerly Married

A fairly constant proportion of the female world—around 13 percent (Table 7-1)—consists of the "formerly married" that is, of women currently living in the status of divorce, and a much smaller, though growing, proportion (6.1 percent) living in the status of widowhood. These ratios were once reversed. Widows have lived in structured worlds from time immemorial, but the world of the divorceé is relatively recent.

Until well into the twentieth century divorce was so frowned upon that those who were in the status of divorce were sanctioned, especially women. The situation has drastically changed since then. Edith Wharton marked the time when the change occurred in the upper

TABLE 7-8 Divorce Rates per 1,000 Married Women Fourteen to Forty-four Years Old, 1921-1974*

Period	*Divorce Rate*
1921-1923	10
1924-1926	11
1927-1929	12
1930-1932	10
1933-1935	11
1936-1938	13
1939-1941	14
1942-1944	17
1945-1947	24
1948-1950	17
1951-1953	16
1954-1956	15
1957-1959	15
1960-1962	16
1963-1965	17
1966-1968	20
1969-1971	26
1972-1974	32

*Source: Arthur J. Norton and Paul C. Glick, "Marital Instability: Past, Present, and Future," in Oliver Moles and George Levinger, eds., *Divorce and Separation* (New York: Basic Books, 1979).

TABLE 7-9 Crude Divorce Rates, 1940–1978*

Year	Rate
1940	2.0
1945	3.5
1950	2.6
1955	2.3
1960	2.2
1965	2.5
1970	3.5
1975	4.8
1978	5.2

*Source: Statistical Abstract, 1978, p. 60. For 1978, National Center for Health Statistics, Vol. 29, No. 4, Supplement, July 31, 1980.

classes in the early years of the century. But the etiquette books until well into the 1930s and 1940s were still disapproving. Emily Post told us in 1928 that men and women divorced from one another met socially as perfect strangers.

As the number of people in the status of divorce increases, however, they are building their own world, a "world of the formerly married" (Hunt, 1966). They have a subculture of their own—that is, "a private and special set of norms that guide them in their interactions with each other, and from which they derive their own customs, moral values, rules of fair play, and devices for coping with the problems special to their condition. Many of their daily experiences, and many of the feelings they have about each other, their married friends, and themselves, are distinctly different from those of the inhabitants of the larger world around them" (5). Hunt describes the process by which the formerly married discover this subculture and how they are then socialized into it: "Nearly every newly separated person soon senses that some kind of consensual alliance exists among FMs [formerly marrieds]. Feeling at first like an ignorant novice, he [*sic*] strives to learn the unwritten rules that he [*sic*] gathers must exist, soon begins to perceive the subtle bonds of common understanding and fellowship among the separated and divorced, and starts to recognize their special and often unspoken means of communicating with each other" (5-6). Among the "unpublished body of rules of behavior" in this world of the FM are rules dealing with such questions as: "How should a woman behave in front of her own children when a date comes to call? After how long may an FM man make a pass at an FM woman? And since she is surely no virgin, on what grounds can she refuse (if she wants to refuse) without looking silly or offending his pride?" (7). Although there are no categorical answers, there are answers that fall into recognizable patterns. But "there is also much that remains formless and ambiguous" (8). This world is as yet too new to be fully evolved, and its members cover too wide a spectrum to accept single standards (8).

One of the first things novices do learn, however, is that "the society of the Formerly Married does indeed have a busy, varied, and sometimes frenzied traffic in sexual liaisons" (142). The knowledge is, however, misleading. What the novice sees are those who are actively involved in the "marketplace." But many Formerly Marrieds remain isolated and sexually inactive (143). Hunt concludes that there is a wide range of norms, from total celibacy to compulsive promiscuity. Among men, practically all have had some sexual experiences; among women, four-fifths (144).[10]

Hunt's "anthropological" study of *The World of the Formerly Married* was published in 1966, and although it included women, the major perspective was that of the male. From the point of view of the formerly married woman, the world of the "displaced homemaker" is more relevant.

Divorce is often the occasion for the woman's first contact with the male world, as distinguished from individual men. Protected—at least in her own mind—from contact with the outside world, as a married woman she knew men primarily as individuals, many of them friendly and pleasant. With divorce she encounters the legal framework of marriage and finds to her dismay that her rights are few if any and that the contributions she has made to her husband's career or to the household are not considered to have given her a vested right in his estate. Alimony is not usually granted: "Although it is a common belief that alimony awards are a component of most divorces, that belief is simply unfounded. In fact, alimony is awarded in less than 10 percent of all divorces, and, because alimony is deductible from the husband's income and includable in the wife's, payments which are actually for the support of children are often labeled 'alimony' to lower the husband's income tax" (A. Miller, 1976, 120). Child-support payments, even when allotted, are rarely enforced. "The record of child support payments actually made by husbands is a dismal one, as demonstrated by the following statistics: 62 percent [of husbands] fail to comply fully with court-ordered [child support] payments in the first year after the order, and 42 percent do not even make a single payment. By the tenth year, 79 percent are in total noncompliance" (Weitzman, 1974, 1195). Until recently the divorced woman was also denied social security benefits accumulated by her husband during the marriage unless the marriage had lasted for twenty years; this has now been reduced to ten years. It was the increasing occurrence of such situations that led women to create an institutional setting for dealing with them.

Case in Point

The Oakland Displaced Homemakers Center opened its doors in April 1976 with a $180,000 two-year State grant, the first in the country. The center is

> located on the campus of Mills College, a small private women's college, which provides office space at below-market rent, lends office furniture and equipment, gives technical assistance in writing proposals and leading workshops, and allows participants to use a lecture hall and some campus buildings.
>
> Free of charge, the Center provides job counseling, job training and workshops, as well as information and referrals for existing local programs. Workshops have been offered on resumé writing, skills assessment, assertiveness training, job focus, money management, health care and aging, widowhood and stress in mid-life. . . .
>
> One of the major concerns of the Center is its daily calls from individuals who are desperately in need of assistance in the following areas: respite care for mothers of mentally retarded or developmentally disabled children, attendant care for the handicapped, home/health care for the elderly, various levels of assistance at half-way houses for people returning to the community from mental hospitals and all levels of assistance in nursing homes and residential care homes for the elderly. . . . The Center . . . [has solved the problem of supplying these services—traditionally provided by older family members] by developing the 'volunteer contract,' which provides an alternative method of on-the-job training as well as the recent work experience so many employers demand, but not, at least so far, accepted by them as work. [Jessie, draft, 1978].

This interesting structuring of a situation relatively new in our society has social-psychological as well as practical benefits. "The most important aspect of the Center is the growing network of women developed through mutual support that displaced homemakers give to one another. In the first 18 months it dealt with over 1,200 women. These women join groups where they talk about themselves, re-assess their abilities and gain self-esteem. One crucial step is a change in attitude about a woman's place in the world. The State law that created the Center directs it to 'provide programs . . . designed to make the displaced homemaker gainfully employed, healthy, and independent.' These women had bought the dependency aspect of the role of housewife and mother; developing independence is a difficult thing but with strong support networks of other women it can be done" (Jessie, 1978, draft).

Beyond "A Certain Age"[11]

With respect to relationships with the male world, age follows an interesting course. "The process of aging . . . brings about a shift in the basis of solidarity between husband and wife, who move into a more equalitarian relationship with each other and with the world around them" (Talmon, 1968, Vol. 1, 188). The relationship may, in fact, reverse itself. Thus, for example, in ten cultures around the world, it has been reported that in the older age brackets "females tend to be outspoken and more assertive," whereas males tend to become "more passive and giving with age" (D. Freedman, 1979, 62). As Ellen Goodman commented in her description of older women at a recital: "Middle age was a world ruled by the powerful men, but old age was a world inhabited by its surviving women" (1979). She encapsulates the flavor of this world of "surviving" women: "Slowly, the elderly audience walked into the room. There were women helping each other, arm in arm. Women rearranging bridge chairs for each other. Women greeting each other. . . ." This was a world in which they—a considerable number of them widowed—could operate in their own style. A comfortable world.

The World of the Widowed

Helena Lopata has studied the world of the widowed, noting that "urbanization, industrialization, and increasing complexity of social structure have removed the foundations of traditional roles [in the female world] without introducing relevant re-education or necessary modification in the socialization of existing members. Nor have the societies developed adequate means for preserving the self-identity and dignity of those members who are made obsolete by the changes. People quite capable of living in the society in which they were born and socialized are often unable to function in the society in which they are now located" (1973, 264).

Lopata found four ways in which these widowed women come to terms with their new marital status. One adjusts relatively easily and flexibly. Another duplicates the Gemeinschaft or village-type life style into which she was socialized;[12] thus "immersed in kin relations, a very close peer group, or a network of neighbors, such a woman may continue many of her involvements with little modification. . . . This is particularly true of the lower-class urbanite" (265-266). A third is a social isolate, unable to engage in new relationships as old ones disappear; she tends to be passive and hostile (266-268). The last, just the opposite to the isolate, is the socially active woman with high frequency of social contact. The major differentiating factor between these last two women is education (268).

Within the last few years the growth in self-help groups, based on the original theory and experience of Alcoholics Anonymous, for dealing with a variety of crises and difficulties in the lives of women has come to include self-help groups among widows (Silverman, 1975). They constitute vehicles whereby the women in Lopata's third category—the social isolates—can have available to them the social and emotional resources of the other three groups.

Even at best, the status of widowhood has its own legal disabilities for women. The law specifies their rights of inheritance. In some cases they suffer serious injustice. They must, for example, pay an inheritance tax on property which they have helped their husbands accumulate; the husband does not have to do so when his wife dies. Efforts are being made to change this situation.

So much, then, for the age- and marital-status structure of the female world. In the next four chapters we look at a different aspect of that world; its class structure.

Notes

1. The 1970s constituted a time of crisis for marriage in our society, as shown not only in the drastic decline in the first-marriage rate and in the high divorce rate (which doubled between the mid-1960s and the mid-1970s), but also in attitudes expressed in surveys (Bernard, 1980). Elizabeth Douvan, comparing surveys in 1957 and 1976, found, for example, that the proportion of married women who found marriage "all burdens and restrictions" increased from 47 to 57 percent and the proportion of single women with this attitude rose from 36 to 72 percent (1978, draft). Married men showed an increase from 42 to 57 percent, and single men, from 63 to 68 percent. Similar increases were reported for attitudes toward children as "all burdens and restrictions": 33 to 45 percent among married women; 31 to 60 percent among single women; 28 to 45 percent among married men; and 43 to 47 percent among single men (Douvan). In the late 1970s, the crisis seemed to be abating. The marriage rate was increasing and the divorce rate moderating (Bernard, 1981).
2. According to Ian Watt, the transition from the patriarchal system to greater individualism in the seventeenth century brought a crisis in marriage somewhat different from that of the 1970s. The earlier crisis, according to Watt, lowered the status of the unmarried woman. The 1970s crisis did not. "The idea that the 'old maid' was a ridiculous if not obnoxious type seems to have arisen in the late seventeenth century. In 1673 Richard Allestree stated . . . that 'an old maid is now thought such a curse as no poetic Fury can exceed . . . [and as] the most calamitous creature in Nature' " (in Coser, 1964, 274). This interpretation in terms of individualism differs somewhat from that presented in the text. It seems less persuasive than one based on economic dependence.
3. According to one theory of the origin of marriage, women entered into it to be protected against the sexual aggression of men other than their mate (Brownmiller, 1975). Protection may take the form of exclusion or, in Judith Blake's terminology, "interment" (1974, 139). The woman may wear a symbol of her status—a ring, a hat, etc.—to ward off advances from men.
4. This is in line with the general conservatism of élite high-school students noted in Chapter 6.

5. Early in 1979 a case in which a woman charged her husband with rape was tried in Salem, Oregon, one of four states that had legislation covering the charge; Iowa, Delaware, and New Jersey were the other three. The husband was not convicted, and the consensus seemed to be that no legal protection against marital rape had been established.
6. The identification of women with reproduction has led the male world to wipe women of fifty years of age or older out of existence or deprive them of identity as women. Here, for example, is how the author of a best seller, David Reuben, has put it: "Once the ovaries stop, the very essence of being a woman stops. . . . Without estrogen, the quality of being female gradually disappears. . . . Actually, it is a little worse than that. . . . As the estrogen is shut off, a woman comes as close as she can to being a man. . . . Not really a man but no longer a functional woman, these individuals live in the world of inter-sex. . . . To many women the menopause marks the end of their useful life. . . . They may be right. Having outlived their ovaries, they may have outlived their usefulness as human beings. The remaining years may be just marking time until they follow their glands into oblivion" (Myers, 1979).
7. In 1978 women workers at American Cyanamid Corporation charged that the company demanded that they become sterilized or lose their jobs, which exposed them to substances medically harmful to fetuses (Richards, 1/1/79).
8. If the birth is out of wedlock, the consequences for both mother and child are exacerbated. "The girl who has an illegitimate child at the age of 16 suddenly has 90 percent of her life's script written for her. She will probably drop out of school; even if someone else in her family helps to take care of the baby, she will probably not be able to find a steady job that pays enough to provide for herself and her child; she may feel impelled to marry someone she might not otherwise have chosen. Her life choices are few, and most of them are bad. Had she been able to delay the first child, her prospects might have been quite different, assuming that she would have had opportunities to continue her education, improve her vocational skills, find a job, marry someone she wanted to marry, and have a child when she and her husband were ready for it. Also, the child would have been born under quite different circumstances and might have grown up in a stable family environment" (Campbell, 1968, 238).
9. Like the young primiparous female among the chimpanzees described in Chapter 1 above.
10. Although our concern is with worlds, not with personality, it is interesting to look at the way Johnson and Terman described the divorced woman of 1935. "The divorced woman . . . is characterized by greater conative intensity; is more self-assertive, more ambitious, and less docile. She attends energetically and enthusiastically to her own goals and evinces toward others chiefly an amiable tolerance. She is an individualist, little moved by sympathy and little interested in schemes to enhance social welfare. She tends to be intellectual and unmercenary. Her personality lacks the element of sweet femininity but commands respect for its rugged strength, self-sufficiency, and detached tolerance" (1935, 310). In 1978 a similar vig-

nette could well be drawn. Elder, Rockwell, and Ross, for example, comparing women for whom they had both adolescent and mature research data, found that women who had been divorced, tended to be somewhat different from those in stable marriages. As adolescents, women who later divorced had had a narrower breadth of perspective, less skill in impulse-management, and somewhat less coping capability than women who did not divorce. They had greater heterosexual interests. In adolescence the divorced women had been less thin-skinned and uncomfortable with uncertainty, more poised socially, more satisfied with themselves, more tolerant. And, like Terman's divorcées, they tended to be noncomforming or rebellious. As adults, however, the "divorced women are more insightful and introspective, not less, than are women in stable marriages" (14). The divorced women had changed more than the other women. The authors admit they do not know whether divorce was the source or the consequence of personality change. But they do think that "one could . . . readily fit these observations into a model in which the strains of a failing marriage, the experience of divorce and resulting forced independence, and the search for a new mate and remarriage are transformational experiences in the maturation of these women. For the young brides in particular, divorce may be both a time of trauma and a time of growth" (14). Displaced homemakers, according to a professional psychologist coordinator of a Center for Displaced Homemakers, were "incredibly adaptable and flexible" (Jessie, 1978).

11. For a sociological history of "old"—post-menopausal—women, see Peter N. Stearns, "Old Women: Some Historical Observations." *Journal of Family History* 5 (Spring, 1980); 44-57.
12. People today who are in their late fifties or early sixties were born into a society where more than half of the population lived in rural areas. Their work habits were different. And the women especially were closely tied into their Gemeinschaft world. "Yet urban populations have had a preponderance of women since 1920" (Bogue, 1959, 158) and in some cases earlier. Thus, for example, as early as 1830, the proportion of females aged fifteen to nineteen in nine Massachusetts villages ranged from 3.0 to 5.1 percent; in three urban areas the proportions were 5.5, 10.9, and 12.7 percent (Kett, 1977, 96). In New Hampshire, the three largest towns had 7.2, 7.9, and 9 percent females in this age group, much higher than the state as a whole. Kett quotes a rural journal to the effect that "the most intelligent and most enterprising of the farmer's daughters become schoolteachers, or tenders of shops, or factory girls. They condemn the calling of their father, and will nine times in ten marry a mechanic in preference to a farmer" (96). They left home earlier than the boys (247). Still, until well into the twentieth century, most people—male and female—were rural in background.

8

The Status Dimension of Social Class

THE AGE AND MARITAL STATUS STRUCTURES of the female world pose no special conceptual problems. One can apply to them standard demographic categories which fit the female world as well as they do the male world, however much the actual substantive contents may differ. But when we turn to the vertical structure of the female world, the difficulties mount. After so many complaints about the inadequacy of the standard conceptual toolkit for studying the female world, it will come as no surprise that the suitability of still another concept—social status—falls short also.

If one were approaching the social structure of the female world fresh, with no ready-made concepts to use, a better picture of its nature would probably be possible. But having to use a conceptual apparatus designed for the male world by males with a certain set of preoccupations means that the fit is not good. We have already commented on the fascination shown by male primatologists with the whole dominance system, with the "lordly" alpha male, with hierarchical position. And further down in the animal kingdom, with "pecking order." There is no way of knowing how females would have conceptualized the status structure of their world if they had started from scratch. On the assumption that order itself implies structure—however it is arrived at or whatever it is based on—and differentiation, such a conceptualization might have started with mother-child relationships and built on them. Relationships between and among wives, sisters, the old and the young might or might not have been conceptualized in vertical status terms. As it was, of course, females have seen the status structure of their world primarily within a male framework.

Social Status

The term "status," defined as "the legal standing or position of a person as determined by his membership in some class of persons legally enjoying certain rights or subject to certain limitations," entered the English language in 1791. By 1820 it had come to have a less restricted definition: "position or standing in society, a profession, and the like." But until 1920 it was still used primarily in the sense of legally defined rights and restrictions. In 1936 it entered the social-science vocabulary as "any position in a social system," in the work of Ralph Linton (Zelditch, 1968, 251). Without more qualification, this definition leaves out an essential characteristic of social status as it has come to be thought of: namely, its evaluative nature. In actual life, social status is frequently invidious—"offensively discriminating" (*Oxford English Dictionary*)—implying that one status is not only higher than another but also that it is therefore worthier, better somehow or other. Social status is, in brief, inherently an evaluative term. The existence of "high" or "low" statuses precludes equality. This invidious nature of social status means that it can breed an enormous amount of emotion—envy, resentment, feelings of injustice.

Social status is one of the subtlest of all stratification dimensions. Not itself a demographic variable, it is nevertheless related to all of the demographic variables, though not necessarily on a one-to-one basis. The highly educated do not automatically enjoy high social status; nor do the wealthy. "Old" wealth has tended to be accorded higher status than what might now be called "middle-aged" wealth; and the "newest" money—from crime, for example—may have quite low social status. Some kinds of income also have higher social status than others. Occupations are fairly closely related to social status but not one to one. The demographic variables of education, income, and occupation, as we shall see in Chapter 9, are the raw materials for social status, but the way they are combined makes a difference in the values they contribute to social status.

Lipset distinguishes two kinds of evaluative processes involved in status stratification; both are exceptionally important in the female world. One is "accorded" status and the other is "subjective," the first referring to the entity—individual or group or class—as the object on which status is conferred by others and the second, to the entity's evaluation of itself vis-à-vis others in its reference group.

The first meaning, "accorded" status, is "the one most sociologists ... refer to when they use the term 'social class' " (1968, 311). Status may be "accorded" by the common law, by legislation, by judicial precedent, by court decisions, and similar means, which specify the rights and obligations of certain individuals and groups. Licenses grant certain kinds of rights and obligations. Registered nurses, for example, are accorded a certain status. The legal structure in our own country aims for "equality under the law,"[1] so that all who have the status of American citizenship are presumed to have such equality, whatever the actual situation may be.[2] There is, of course, one major and yawning exception: the legal status of men is still higher than that of women in the sense that the law grants them more privileges and prerogatives than the legal status of women has granted them. Only slowly are these legal inequalities being eliminated.[3] Status is "accorded" not only by formal protocol but also—equally important, though not necessarily ever written down—by custom, tradition, convention, attitudes, values. These informal sanctions of social status may have an impact which, though subtle, is no less pervasive than the impact of legally defined sanctions in specifying the prerogatives of certain positions and the behavior due those who occupy them. The rules of etiquette or protocol can be as coercive as those of law in defining the prerogatives of status.[4]

But, as Lipset reminds us, "The location of individuals or groups in the status system depends on the opinion of the individuals who go to make up the system rather than the opinion of the sociologist who observes it" (1968, 311). Even without legal directives or etiquette books, individuals "feel" themselves to be "higher" or "lower" than others.

Two more points before we proceed further. As in the case of female age-related subworlds and individual psychological developmental stages, so also in the case of status, a distinction is made between status as a structural unit and the individual person or persons who may occupy it. The status itself is fairly stable in any ongoing society but the people who occupy it may come and go. Still, it is sometimes useful to think of status as a property of individuals as well as a unit of structure (Zelditch, 252). Thus, the individuals who occupy statuses share the highness or lowliness of the status itself. The monarch *is* "his Highness."

The phenomena, finally, with which the term "social status" deals should be distinguished from the cognate phenomena with which social psychologists deal, such as dominance or ascendance and submissiveness; these are individual personality characteristics, not components of a social system. This distinction is especially relevant in the female world, where personality characteristics such as beauty and sex appeal can often—we hypothesize here—subvert social-status, even power, structures.

Which Way Is Up?

We learn quite early that some people are "higher" than others, that we are to "look up" to them. No one has to tell us. There are plenty of behavioral clues. We have only to see how these people are treated. It is quite easy to learn from the way people act which way is up.

If a visitor to a strange country notices, for example, that there are some people who are always given the right of way, to whom everyone bows, who may or may not acknowledge others, who are always given the best fruit or goody, who never have to do anything for themselves, who are warm when others are cold, the visitor would conclude that they had "higher" positions or status than the others. The others may not have any concept of a status structure in their heads. They do not need one. All they need to know is that there are some people who are entitled—for whatever reason—to privileges and prerogatives. The theoretical structure may be in their heads; the evidence is in the actual behavior of people.

The emoluments of high status may be either practical and matter of fact such as money, wealth, opportunity, access to power, privileges, or they may be symbolic,—a plaque to hang on the wall, a certificate, an award, an appreciative article in the paper—or emotional. Sometimes the symbolic emoluments have quite practical concomitants, such as the use of the executive dining room or lavatory, location near the top man, or carpets or windows in one's office. Indeed, such status symbols may become a major preoccupation in the male or female rat race. Some of the behavioral, as distinguished from the physical or material, clues to status may also be either material or symbolic or both. One is bowed to, for example, or curtsied to, given precedence in line, waited for, shown deference, listened to, shown signs of respect. One receives more Christmas cards than one sends. These kinds of behavior may be ritualized, so taken for granted as to go unnoticed much of the time. Hochschild calls our attention to the fact that emotions are also built into the status structure. Friendly and appreciative emotions go up and hostile emotions, down. Thus one of the most important emoluments of high status is a friendly ambience (1975, 296-297).

Or Down?

The penalties of low status are the converse of these emoluments; one is ignored, put at the end of the line, even insulted with impunity or laughed at. In extreme form, "there may be . . . servility, obsequiousness, groveling, abjection, fawning, or catering on the part of the inferior. The complementary behavior for the high-status person may include arrogance, hauteur, or contempt. Or the pattern may be one of adulation on one level and condescension or patronization on the other; or respectful admiration, even a reverential attitude, on one side and patronization on the other" (Bernard, 1957, 58-59).

These objective behaviorial clues to status do not necessarily correspond with the accompanying subjective or feeling aspects. "The subjective attitudes which accompany status may be marked by either friendly or unfriendly feeling tone. The high-status person may feel appreciation and satisfaction or contempt and resentment; he may feel affection and *noblesse oblige* or arrogance and hauteur. The low-status person for his [or her] part may feel respect, affection, and loyalty, or anger, hostility, and envy. If the basis for the status is spontaneous, the subjective concomitant is likely to be affectionate on the part of the low-status individuals. If it is enforced by law the concomitant may become very great hostility" (62).

"High to Whom?" "Low to Whom?" Social Status, Locale, and Reference Groups

Social status shows itself most clearly in personal interactions. This means that it has a strong locale base. It is in the local community that people go through the motions of deferring, giving precedence, and showing other signs of recognizing social status. In this quasi-Gemeinschaft way social status is an important aspect of the female world. Even the smallest cities have their own "social registers" presided over by anonymous editors who decide on the basis of local community criteria who is "in" and who is "out."

Reference groups also play a large part in social status. "High" and "low" have different significance in different circumstances. In face-to-face or personal situations, where symbolic behavior is directly felt, seen, or heard, where one can be "put down" or "built up" in a concrete, personal way, they are one thing. But in an abstract setting where there is little personal experience of status differences, they can be vague or general, with little immediate impact, so that they cease to have much subjective meaning. The factory operative may know that out there wealthy women spend afternoons at the country club, celebrities lunch at expensive restaurants, college professors hold forth at the podium, but none of this impinges on her directly. Social status in her life has to do with the women in her immediate reference group, women who are considered the best bowlers, cheesecake bakers, or what-have-you. "High" or "low" is hard to conceptualize in a context where there is little interaction among people who have different reference groups. Since most people associate primarily with others of their own status level, they tend to think of themselves as middle class. They live lives that do not necessarily intermesh or give rise to the usual behavioral clues to status.

Unlike imposed scalar dimensions such as schooling, income, or even occupational prestige (Chapter 9), the behavioral criteria are harder to judge "high" or "low." At a social-status level that social scientists label "lower middle class," a woman might know vaguely that there are women who are richer than she or more travelled than she, but whether she necessarily therefore "looks up" to them is debatable. It may depend on whose turf they are on or by which criteria she is judging them. On strictly moral grounds, she may even "look down" on them. She may, if she is an ethnic woman, live in a certain segment of the social structure much as in an enclave. She knows that other women may dress differently, decorate their homes differently, spend their time differently. But if she had more money she still might not dress as they dress, decorate her home as they do, or spend her time as they do. They are not in her reference group, her social orbit, so she has little occasion to compare herself to them or to be subjected to the penalties of inferior social status. Only if she is thrown into contact with these other women, by, say, a sudden rise in the occupation and income of her husband, does her reference group change and the status differences become palpable to her. Now confronting the differences she learns a new mode of dressing, home decor, entertaining. Now she sees the social-class system from a different perspective. Children of immigrants often experience this change in reference group and hence perspective.

Social Status and Self Concept

Since others deal with us according to the social status we are assigned, the objective and subjective behaviors associated with status have an especially important and relevant effect on our self-concept. We tend to judge ourselves in terms of the way others treat us. Self-evaluation reflects the evaluation of ourselves by others (Zelditch, 253). If others "look down" on us, engage in patronizing, condescending, down-putting behavior, we come in time to have a low opinion of ourselves. Few people can maintain a good opinion of themselves if no one else has such an opinion.[5] The cry for "respect" becomes the desperate signature of a popular comedian; the "general public's lack of respect for and recognition of their work" is one of the disagreeable aspects of their occupation mentioned by beauticians (L. Howe, 1977, 239) and countless others. Since social status is always a relative matter, one's reference group is important: "if one has less [than others] in the way of privilege or reward, one feels relatively deprived, whatever the absolute level of advantage" (Zelditch, 1968, 254).

Esteem as a Mitigating Factor

Without the possibility of access to compensatory or mitigating processes, people in low-status parts of the social structure would be subject to unrelievedly low self-concept. Fortunately there is a complementary system that allows for the recognition of merit at whatever social-status level. Hannah More had taught the legitimacy and validity of all "stations," high or low. But she had also insisted that none was basically better than any other. Superiors were, to be sure, to be looked up to, but individuals in all "stations" who performed the obligations of their position well were equally worthy of esteem. A good carpenter was as estimable in his way as a gentleman was in his. A good servant was as estimable as her mistress. As Kingsley Davis has noted, "We attach an invidious value to the status or office as such, independently of who occupies it or how its requirements are carried out. At the same time we attach another kind of value to the individual according to how well or ill he [she] fulfills the duties of whatever status he [she] happens to be in. . . . This evaluation we call *esteem*" (1949, 93-94).

There may be numerous channels for earning esteem. Within given professions there are some who are "musicians' musicians," "dancers' dancers," or "actresses' actresses." They are uniquely good in their work, so good that only their sister professionals are able to appreciate them. They may have no better training, no better jobs, and no more income than their peers, nor any higher status than others, but they are "looked up to," esteemed.

Such esteem may become a formal status if it is formally recognized. Thus there is a status of "beauty queen," defined as the woman who wins an award in a contest; the status of Pulitzer, or any other honorary, prizewinner or Olympic champion. There are doubtless many more purely honorary positions in the male than in the female world.

Status Charade

Since up to now women have not had access to many of the high-status positions in most societies, this deprivation was compensated for in some societies by a separate status system in which men went through the ritual of according superior status to them—bowing, tipping the hat, showing deference—and the outward signs of respect, such as opening doors or giving precedence. But its phoniness was easily exposed if or when a woman asked for equal access to the prerogatives of male status positions. Nor was the chivalrous character ever played out with women of lower status levels. Sojourner Truth, the black nineteenth-century leader, called attention to this discrepancy by asking, at a time when Southern gentlemen were limiting their chivalric courtesies to the class of women who were ladies, "Ain't I a woman?" If women *qua* women were due chivalrous homage, why did she, a woman, not receive it? And even the chivalrous male "women and children first" rule did not prevail over class differences on the Titanic: "the rate of loss of children in the third class was higher than that of men in the first class" (Bernard, 1957, 68, citing Lord, 1955). Indeed, Henley has mapped a wide area of body politics which describes and illustrates the host of nonverbal acts and gestures that implement the status—in her perspective, power—relationship between the sexes (Henley, 1977). Space, time, language, demeanor, touch, posture, gesture, body movement, eye contact, facial expression are all part of this relationship. By means of all of them men are accorded higher status than women (Chapter 16).

As attention is called to these status differentials they come increasingly under control. In the traditional status system women were socialized to accord men status higher than their own by their own behavior. They "looked up" to men. They built men up, showed appreciation, smiled supportively. But today many women are exercising a kind of veto power. They are withholding deference, and rejecting many of the ploys of body politics. They are no longer endowing men with superior status, no longer supplying clothes and crown to the naked emperor (Chapter 22).

Social Stability and Mobility

When status is considered from the old "station," "place," or "position" point of view, the social structure is seen as an essentially fixed and static system of interrelated and intermeshing parts reflecting a division of labor or specialization of function. Each status or station may, according to some, constitute a separate status "culture." Hannah More represented such a perspective, as did Catharine Beecher in this country. Those in less privileged statuses or places were to be reconciled to their position and persuaded not to rebel against it. Social mobility was out of the question.

Still, growing in the eighteenth century was another, more dynamic point of view which saw a person's status not as fixed but as subject to change, especially in the United States. The very concept of *status* (which has the same root as *station* or *stable*) came to be central in thinking about social mobility. The first thing that struck Tocqueville about this country was, in fact, its social mobility, "the innumerable multitude of those who seek to throw off their original condition" (1840, 253). But the second thing that struck him was "the rarity of lofty ambition . . . in the midst of the universally ambitious stir of society. No Americans are devoid of a yearning desire to rise; but hardly any appear to entertain hopes of great magnitude, or to drive at very lofty aims. All are constantly seeking to acquire property, power, and reputation—few contemplate these things upon a great scale" (258). Tocqueville spoke a bit prematurely. A quarter-century later, great industrialists were entertaining hopes of great magnitude, if not lofty aims, and upward mobility for almost everyone was coming to be taken for granted. Social mobility has matched stratification in the almost obsessive attention it has attracted among male researchers. Such mobility has in many cases been the story of their own lives and they seem to be engrossed by it.

A high position may be attained in a variety of ways. One may be born into it, buy it, or marry into it,[6] earn one's way into it, climb into it, finagle one's way into it. The processes are not necessarily the same in the female as in the male world.[7] Although there are some high-status positions in the female world that women achieve on the basis of their own merits—presidents of colleges, positions on important boards, offices in female organizations, awards for community services, leadership in volunteer agencies—there are others that are accorded or ascribed to them as wives rather than achieved by them,[8] sometimes on the basis of law or legislation but sometimes by almost equally compelling formal fiat or protocol. Thus, for example, at an important state or diplomatic function where people are given status according to the importance of their country or to seniority or whatever, the wife of a high-level official outranks the woman whose own rank is only slightly lower than that of the male official. The president's wife outranks the most distinguished scientist, author, artist, what-have-you present. The women most admired in the female world as polled by women's magazines have often been the wives of achieving men. Only recently have achieving women begun to receive recognition in their own right. Sometimes the same achievement garners higher status for men than for women; a woman doing the same work as a man will be given a different title in order to give her a lower status in the system.

Even among researchers it has been taken for granted that the status of a woman was that of her husband. Only recently has that assumption been challenged (Acker, 1973; Oppenheimer, 1977). But women still derive their status from their husbands.

Since upward social mobility has often been less a matter of what a woman has done than of whom she has married, the status reflected in living in a household with high status as measured by income is, in the female world, not necessarily related to achievement.[9] Thus, for example, it will be noted that in all high-income brackets there are relatively more nonearning wives than there are single women with personal incomes (Figure 8-1). Thus almost two-fifths (37.8 percent) of the nonearning wives of husband-wife households lived in high-status households as measured by income ($10,000 or over as of 1970). Less than 3 percent of the single women with personal incomes had incomes in this range. Even in the age bracket with highest incomes (forty-five to fifty-four), only 12.6 percent of the single women had achieved incomes of

Figure 8.1 Income of single women 45–54 years of age and nonearning wives, 1969. Source: 1970 Census, Marital Status, Table 7 and Sources and Structure of Family Income, Table 1.

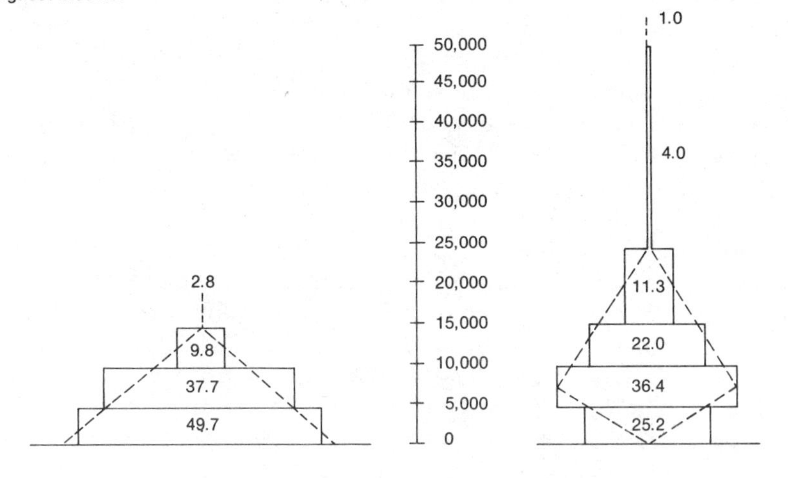

$10,000 or more. If we assume that most personal income comes from earnings and that few wives have unearned incomes, the contrast between achieved and ascribed status in the female world becomes clear. To the extent, further, that a married woman took over the social status associated with the occupation as well as of the income of her husband, she was one-and-a-half times more likely than a single woman who achieved her own occupational status (27.5 percent vs. 19.4 percent) to have the high status accorded a managerial or professional occupation. There were 7.9 times as many wives of managerial and professional men as there were single managerial and professional women.[10] A divorced woman in some circles may derive more social status even from her ex-husband than from her own achievements.

Although a small proportion of men inherit money, for most men high socioeconomic status is presumed to be achieved. Since in the female world high socioeconomic status is ascribed to women on the basis of their husband's status, it is still true, as the cliche has it, that for women marriage is often a better ticket to high status than personal achievement.[11]

It is especially more auspicious for upward mobility among working-class women than, say, education or training. The search for high-status husbands therefore constitutes one of the commonly pursued paths for upward mobility. Elder has analyzed the factors making for success in this process (1969, 519-532). On the basis of a longitudinal study of women from middle- and working-class families born in the early 1920s, he found that "intelligence and academic aptitude were not directly predictive of marriage mobility, although both factors influenced the adult status of the women through their educational attainment. Among women from the working class, physical attractiveness was more predictive of marriage to a high-status man than educational attainment, while the relative effects of these factors were reversed among women of middle-class origin. Social ascent from the working class was also related to sexual restraint and a well-groomed appearance" (519). The findings reported for the late 1950s in adolescent society by Coleman corroborated the relatively greater importance of physical attractiveness as compared to intellectual ability (Chapter 6).

It is understandable, then, in the light of these findings, that in the female world considerable attention and emphasis are placed on beauty. Nor is this a recent phenomenon. There are many precedents for the upward mobility possible by way of charm and beauty, a classical example being Nell Gwynne. The striving for beauty in the female world is thus analogous to the emphasis on achievement in the male world (Parsons, 1942). Although physical build and even athletic prowess are sometimes referred to as factors making for upward mobility in the male world, and although connections and pull are not ignored, they do not receive the attention given to education, class background, and related factors. Nor is "marrying the boss's daughter" given more than humorous attention in male mobility studies; in general relatively more women than men tend to marry "up."

Downward mobility can also occur in the female world, as in the male. In the nineteenth century there was an aphorism, "shirt-sleeve to shirt-sleeve in three generations," suggesting that family position could fall as well as rise. In the female world such downward mobility could happen instantaneously; a single "mis-step" could do it. High moral character would not guarantee high social status, but low moral character could render it out of the question, for personal morality played a considerable part in according social status. A study of a coal-mining town in the 1950s, for example, found both upper- and middle-class women emphasizing conventional middle-class standards. "We do not let women of low moral character into these organizations. I think heavy drinking would keep a person out of these women's clubs. . . . We are very careful in the persons we ask" (Lantz, 1958, 224). Women who violated the moral or sexual canons were once, in fact, called "fallen" women. They were so low on the status ladder as to be ostracized from the women's world altogether. Or they were "déclassée," classless, no longer "received" in proper homes. Edith Wharton described such a case in a short story, "Autre Temps," about a woman whose mere divorce had had this effect (1916).

It is interesting to note in passing that entering the labor force at the turn of the century did not imply downward social mobility for women. Such a woman did not become déclassée; she did not lose status "except in a few ultra-fashionable communities" (Harland and Van de Waters, 1905). "The social position of a woman in business is not affected unhappily by her work. Provided she has the qualities requisite for social recognition and consideration, her business is no detriment. She has the same general opportunities for social recreation that offer themselves to a man of business, and it often happens that her work gives a zest to the enjoyment of such opportunities, unknown to women of idler habits" (446). So much for the old idea that a woman had to remain at home to protect the reputation of her father or husband.

So far the discussion of social mobility has dealt with individual upward or downward movement. But there seem to be times when whole social systems loosen up and large numbers of people can rise. The late eighteenth century seems to have been such a time in France. Strong, successful, talented men were making their way up the economic ladder. But it was the *salonières* who socialized them into their new roles, seeing to it that their social status corresponded to their new economic status.

The Female World and Societal Upgrading: The Salon as a Case in Point

Arlene Daniels refers to wealthy women in a large West Coast city as a "power élite" (Chapter 11). Whether they are or not, the women who ran the French salons were, in fact, such a power élite. Montesquieu is quoted as saying that "they form a kind of republic whose members always actively aid one another. It is a new state within a state; and whoever observes the action of those in power, if he does not know the women who govern them, is like a man who sees the action of a machine but does not know its secret springs" (Badek, 1976, 186). This female-run "state withing a state" played an important part in the upward mobility then in process in that society. Like so much of women's "work," it performed a socializing function. It socialized the upwardly mobile bourgeoisie into the life styles of their new position.

As families achieved "ennoblement on the basis of their economic success," Lougee tells us, "many still retained their lower-class manners" (1976, 212). They had to be shown how to live up to their newly achieved status. They learned by participating in the salons. There they could observe and take over the life style of the nobility.

The salonières were not naive. They saw themselves as implementing a sociological theory. They believed in an open society.[12] They "stressed the fundamental equality of all men" (Lougee, 42). Although they believed money to be the "sole basis of status" (49), they nevertheless "propagated a vision of an expanded aristocracy, open to those who acquired any of numerous forms of prominence." They believed in the "superiority of acquired nobility over inherited nobility" (41). They saw to it that the criteria for admission into the noble class were "sufficiently broad to ensure that upward economic mobility would be rewarded with upward social mobility" (212). And they saw it as women's function to implement this point of view. They saw women "as a social force which promoted the integration of new individuals into the élite" (41). Under the tutelage of women the new rich learned the social graces and were covered with "*le parfum de l'aristocratie*" (53). Teaching men how to become gentlemen "was the social mission of women in eighteenth-century France" (54). The salons were not themselves democratic; they were, in effect a kind of meritocracy, a way of recognizing those with enough ability to make it to the top. And of socializing them to be comfortable in their new social ambience.[13] It might be added in passing that individual mobility was also promoted by the salonières by their sanctioning of interclass marriage as another way to integrate the new social order.

In the nineteenth century an analogous situation developed in the United States. The great post-Civil War spurt in affluence, the age of the robber barons, of the great entrepreneurs who were establishing huge industrial empires and inventing corporations for running them, amassing enormous fortunes, created a new kind of female leisure class. It, in turn, established "society," which, like the salons, socialized the new industrial tycoons into aristocratic European lifestyles (Schlesinger, 1946). "Society" was under the hegemony of the female world and the implementation of its protocol was a fundamental responsibility of women. One student of social class even today finds the women's pages of the newspaper which report on "society" a fertile source for studying the social-status structure (Domhoff, 1978).[14]

Upward social mobility was not limited to the top echelons, to the tycoons. A great many other families were also moving up in American society. Dozens of etiquette books were written to guide them on the path. Women were especially hungry for help. "Thousands of letters" were received, the authors of one such etiquette book wrote in their dedication, letters "asking for just such information as we have written down here" (Harland and Van de Water, 1905). The people who were writing for such help, "anxious to learn the by-laws of polite society, and to order their manners in accordance with what we long ago elected to call the 'Gospel of Conventionality,' " they said, "were not the illiterate and vulgar." Some were men, but it was women in particular who wrote. Changed, presumably improved circumstances had moved some "from secluded homes to fashionable neighborhoods," and this "involved the necessity of altered habits of social intercourse." Other writers were "girls whose parents were content to live and move in the deep ruts in which they and their forebears were born" but who wanted better for themselves, or "people of humble and rude bringing up, who yet have longings and tastes for gentlehood and for the harmony and beauty that go with really good breeding." These were the readers they were writing for, and every page of their manual "was written with a thought of them in our minds."

Women of all classes seemed bound to improve the social manners of their men. A long-running and successful comic strip satirized the efforts invested by a pretentious shrew in "bringing up father." The protesting Jiggs became a male cult hero.

Women as Status Symbols

At the turn of the century, Veblen was calling attention to an interesting course of events transpiring at the top of the status structure. In the past, he noted, men exploited others to do the hard work of the world, and as evidence of their success they themselves could engage in conspicuous leisure and fill it with conspicuous consumption. Leisure and extravagant consumption—palaces and regalia—thus became symbols of high status. Now, however, in the new industrial order, the great exploits were too time-consuming to allow for male conspicuous consumption. So these functions were turned over to women. They became status symbols for men. Instead of themselves having to take time off for conspicuous leisure to engage in conspicuous consumption, the amassers of the great fortunes turned the job over to their wives and daughters, who performed these functions for them vicariously. In Veblen's words:

> It has in the course of economic development become the office of the woman to consume vicariously for the head of the household; and her apparel is contrived with this object in view. It has come about that obviously productive labour is in a peculiar degree derogatory to respectable women, and therefore special pains should be taken in the construction of women's dress, to impress upon the beholder the fact (often indeed a fiction) that the wearer does not and can not habitually engage in useful work. Propriety requires respectable women to abstain more consistently from useful effort and to make more of a show of leisure than the men of the same social class. It grates painfully on our nerves to contemplate the necessity of any well-bred woman's earning a living by useful work. It is not "woman's sphere." Her sphere is within the household, which she should "beautify," and of which she should be the "chief ornament." . . . Our social system thus makes it the woman's function in an especial degree to put in evidence her household's ability to pay. According to the modern civilised scheme of life, the good name of the household to which she belongs should be the special care of the woman; and the system of honorific expenditures and conspicuous leisure by which this good name is chiefly sustained is therefore the woman's sphere. In the ideal scheme, as it tends to realize itself in the life of the higher pecuniary classes, this attention to conspicuous waste of substance and effort should normally be the sole economic function of the woman. . . . The more expensive and the more obviously unproductive the women of the household are, the more creditable and more effective for the purpose of the reputability of the household or its head will their life be. [Veblen, 1899, 179-181][15]

It has been noted that what women gained in this kind of leisure-class status they lost in genuine status by their increased dependency. This "fall" of women may be viewed as a cameo analogue of the "fall" of Rome. No one heard Rome "fall." There was no single moment when one could see it happen. Similarly, one could not see or hear the "fall" of women when the hard-working equal partner in household enterprise became the parasite Veblen described and C. P. Gilman compared to a prostitute. There was no deliberate strategy but, as in the history of the Chinese, women were "subjugated" by being relieved of productive work. The deteriorating effect of this gilded cage on women in affluent families did not escape perceptive observers. A large body of research beginning early in the century identified a "cultural personality type" characterized by relative lack of self-esteem, "feelings of inadequacy, inferiority, low self-regard, dependency, passivity, and the like" (Mandle, 1979, Ch. 3).

In time the leisure-class model seeped down the class structure until even working-class women adopted it. Thus women's sphere, which, in the earlier years of the century, as Beecher had so persuasively argued, had been a productive one, contributing equally with men's to the national well-being, had become a sphere of consumption, even wasteful consumption. Until yesterday, working-class women who could stay home and not enter the labor force were viewed as especially fortunate; they were also demonstrating their husbands' success as a breadwinner.

Other Aspects of the Vertical Dimension of the Female World

There is a considerable research literature on another vertical aspect of social systems, namely authority and power. Practically all of it is based on the way they operate in the male world.[16] It could be omitted here without leaving a serious lacuna except that this particular aspect of social structure, especially power, has become a salient issue in the female world.[17]

Positions of power are positions where decisions are made and policies determined. They are high in the social system because their occupants have resources available for making their will prevail, such as money or votes. Positions of authority are positions that implement decisions or carry out policy. Their occupants are "authorized" to execute specified functions and are usually ranked in terms of their propinquity to the power positions. Authority is generally conceptualized as resting on consensus; one has authority only so long as it is accepted.

Some students tend to discount the very concept of power as "too broad and too vague" (Wolin, 1968, 314). They argue it involves too great a variety of both means and purposes to be useful as an analytical tool. It can, for example, include such seemingly unrelated resources as force, threat, beauty, charisma, prominence in sports or the arts; even hostility and altruism may give one power.

Some theorists, while not calling it an aspect of stratification, would not necessarily discard power altogether. Thus Lipset sees it "as the dynamic resultant of the forces brought into play in different types of social situations" (1968, 311). In keeping with this conceptualization, the most relevant way to look at power in the present context seems to be in terms of the nature of these "social situations" in the Gemeinschaft kin- and locale-based female world.

Power in a Gemeinschaft World

The "social situations" that result in power in a Gemeinschaft world tend to be personal, face to face; they operate within fairly restricted spatial limits. On the kinship side, the institutional or formal aspect of power tends to be patriarchal, that is, concentrated by religious and legal norms in the hands of the father or husband. Some feminists consider the power of males in the home as a more serious handicap in the female world than any other. "Patriarchy" to them is synonymous with sexism, with female oppression.

Paradoxically, the Gemeinschaft world is commonly believed to be a province where female power is great. Samuel Johnson is quoted as saying, no doubt tongue in cheek, that it is a wise provision of the law that it grants so little power to women because God has given them so much.[18] In a small Gemeinschaft circle it is fairly easy to subvert formal power relationships. Thus a strong or clever woman can exercise considerable power in a patriarchal system even without formal institutional resources. There is, for example, the stereotypical mother who has such control over her children that even as adults they cower before her and may not achieve liberation except by fleeing from her. Mike Nichols' skit of the grown man, a prominent space scientist, wilting in a telephone booth as mother berates him for not calling more often is a case in point. The media are full of this image of a powerful mother intimidating her family. It is also encapsulated in the old but obviously untrue cliché, "The hand that rocks the cradle rules the world."

The joker is that this kind of Gemeinschaft power is fragmented and limited. However much power a woman might have within her own little bailiwick, it has no leverage. It doesn't add up. The mother may coerce her sons and daughters in their relations with her but she does not have impact on other men and women, certainly not on her own peers in the female world nor on the sons of other women in state or national legislatures, courts, or other depositories of power in the male world. Power results from weight multiplied by distance. A great concentration of power with a short lever is not really all that powerful. With a long enough lever one can move the universe. But the lever in a Gemeinschaft world is short. Enormous power in the home may move members of the household, but unless it is reinforced by the similar power of other women the strength amounts to little outside the household. And in any event it has little effect on the status structure of the female world.

The locale component of Gemeinschaft allots more power to women than does the kin component, at least potentially. Indeed, women organizing in their neighborhoods are learning how to accumulate a considerable amount of power and to use it at city hall. Thus, for example, when Betty Deacon's Baltimore neighborhood was going down fast and no one was doing anything about it, she began to talk to her neighbors. Soon they "formed a neighborhood organization and started working on neighborhood issues together" (Fahey, n.d., 24), and before long they were exercising a modicum of power. Wekerle has shown that so far as female participation in the community is concerned there is a pyramidal structure; the lower down, the greater the proportion of women involved (draft, 1978). We will comment further on the exercise of power by women in the neighborhood in Chapter 13.

There are few positions of power in the female world. No matter how high the status a woman may reach in the female world, she will not have access to great power. In contrast to this situation in the female world is the fact that there are many positions at nodal points in the male world where power accumulates, positions whose occupants have access to long levers capable of moving mountains. Many of these mountains are in the male world—in the economy and the polity—but this does not mean that the power is irrelevant for the female world. A great deal of this power in the male world relates to the female world, prescribing, for example, its legal structure. The enormous reservoir of power in the legal system has not been available to women until recently. Only in the last decade, for example, has legislation gradually opened the gates to give women access to this power resource, even at the local level, let alone at higher levels. Even contacts with the police might be unavailable to many women. Until recently, for example, when women needed protection against abusive husbands in their own homes, the police were not always willing to supply it; the courts would not back up such use of power as long as the woman continued to live with her husband. Nor was recourse to the power of the courts always accessible. Too often it was expensive and frighteningly intimidating. The legal structure for dealing with working conditions, health care, pregnancy and maternity as related to employment, abortion, and the like was "imported" from, and imposed by, the male world.

Female Power in the Male World

In Chapter 11 we shall describe women who have been labelled a "power élite." These are women who exert a considerable influence in the cultural life of the community. But it is not at all the kind of influence exerted by the salonières. Or even by the suffragists and the prohibitionists. Or by outraged housewives at the checkout counter of the supermarket. Or the kind of influence the women in the antipornography movement hope to exert.

In contrast to such collective efforts are those of individual women who, in the absence of positions with power resources in the status structure of the female world, have sought access to such positions in the male world, defining the female world as, in effect, a "colony" of the male world, suffering from "taxation without representation." Relatively few women have actually breached the walls.

There are a few, very few, wealthy women who can exert the "power of the purse." They command resources in the male world and may control boards and agencies by threatening to withdraw support or by promising to add support. There are also the legendary women credited as being, in the female tradition, the "power behind the throne"; Queen Esther would be an archetype here. But their numbers are small.

Still, some individual women do sometimes break through the barriers into the male power world and, using its channels, rise to high positions in it. But not many, not even proportionately. Such positions in the Gesellschaft are so avidly sought by men that allowing women to enter competition for them, and thus adding to the intensity of the struggle, is negatively sanctioned by all the big guns in the male world, psychological as well as legal, conventional, customary, moral, and a host of other kinds of norms. And when women are granted access to such positions—as by royal succession or inheritance—they are usually surrounded by male constraints. The male power world is not hospitable to women.

An individual reared as women are in a world with a love-and/or-duty ethos is not, as we shall have occasion to discuss in more detail later on (Chapter 22), well qualified to operate successfully in a Gesellschaft system.[19] She is not socialized for success in that milieu. She has not been comfortable with power even in her own world. We shall note in Chapter 11, for example, the moral dilemma in which housewives found themselves in trying to reconcile their power relationships to their domestics with the American democratic ideology. They were uneasy with it. A more sophisticated statement of the same dilemma—this time the incompatibility of power relationships among women—recurred among early feminists in the 1960s. They rejected the notion of women hiring other women to do their "shitwork." Power seems to subvert the love-and/or-duty ethos of the female world; they seem almost antithetical to one another as models for human relations.

Although the female world is beginning to come to terms with power—how to achieve it and how to use it—not only within their own world but also in the male world, it is still far from achieving consensus, for "there are conflicting forces among women" (J. B. Miller, 1976, 117). At one extreme are many women who disclaim any concern with power outside their Gemeinschaft world. They want no part of it. They feel protected; they do not need power vis-à-vis the male world. Or they invoke the principle of "you get more with honey than with vinegar," preferring manipulative power to the up-front exercise of power. But among a growing number of women the issue of power is an increasing concern. They seek the achievement of power in the male occupational and political structure or the mobilization of the female world against the male world as a whole.

"The issues of power have to be faced," a psychiatrist reminds women (J.B. Miller, 117). Unlike men, however, she reassures them, women "do not need to . . . maintain a non-existent structure of dominance; therefore women do not need to take on the destructive attributes engendered by that structure. Women need the power to advance their own development, but they do not 'need' the power to limit the development of others" (117).

Because social status—whether related to power or not—is such a subtle, complex and emotion-generating dimension of social class, researchers have made it a "cooler" and more manageable variable by operationalizing it as "socioeconomic status," in which education contributes the "socio" component, income, the "economic," and occupation, both. We turn in Chapter 9 to a discussion of this conception of status.

Notes

1. Being entitled to specified rights does not necessarily guarantee that one will be able to enjoy them. Because they can afford to engage expensive legal help, wealthy people can enforce their rights more easily than can poor people.
2. "There are no privileged classes in the United States in the sense of official ranks or status; but there are privileged classes in terms of unofficially or crescively enforced rights and obligations" (Bernard, 1957, 61). In a certain sense, though, age defines an important "class of persons" legally enjoying rights, for example, such as driving a car, or drinking, or being tried in a juvenile court or having to attend school, or getting married, or being licensed for any number of activities; one becomes a "senior citizen" with certain retirement rights at a certain age; and so on. For some age-related rights the age specified is different for females. Usually women may marry at a younger age than men, and retirement and pension rights for women have been less than those for men. At the present time there is a

movement to improve the legal rights of children to protect them from, for example, commitment to institutions. In the past, one's status improved with age. Older people were looked up to for their wisdom and experience. Young people were respectful. In our society, especially in the female world, it is youth who "will be served."

3. A great deal of the thinking among women activists has to do with improving the legal status of women regardless of age or marital status. Sometimes this involves drastic rethinking on the part of supporters of the status quo. Legislation is being called for not to secure new rights but to prevent deprivation of taken-for-granted rights, such as access to jobs, schooling, or professional training and, more recently, to athletic and sports programs in schools. For a discussion of the impact of legal status on the female world, see Babcock, Freedman, Norton, and Ross, 1975.
4. After the American Civil War, writers of books on etiquette feared that the old prewar egalitarianism would destroy all sense of the "relative duties of superior and subordinate" (quoted by Schlesinger, 1946, 34). It was up to them to forestall such an unseemly situation.
5. There are anomalies. King George VIII of England was, for example, allegedly the victim of feelings of inferiority. Such feelings may occur in any situation in which one feels unable to deal adequately with contingencies. A person of high status may make another feel inferior by flaunting her own savoir faire in a social situation. The privilege of meeting the world on turf of one's own choosing and no other is one of the major prerogatives of high social status.
6. Bryce, for example, tells us how it was in his country at the end of the nineteenth century: "In England great wealth can, by using the appropriate methods, practically buy rank from those who bestow it" (1891, 620). A man might be vulgar, uneducated, but this would "not prevent him from becoming a baronet, or possibly a peer, and thereby acquiring a position of assured dignity which he can transmit to his offspring" (620). American heiresses in the nineteenth century sometimes also "bought into" the British status structure by way of marriage. They brought wealth into the marriage; their husbands brought titles.
7. Interesting support comes from the work of McClelland, an outstanding psychologist on achievement motivation. When his premises were tried out on women, they did not operate as expected; women had to be dropped from the study. Some years later Rosabeth Moss Kanter, studying the behavior of men and women in the corporation setting, offered explanations for women's apparent lack of the male-type achievement drive. There were built-in structural constraints on women's achievement; the opportunity structure was different (1977). Actually, women do show achievement motivation, but it is often in behalf of others, in line with the love-and/or-duty ethos of their world. Thus, black mothers ever since Reconstruction have worked hard to provide opportunities for upward mobility for their children (Bernard, 1966). Women as both wives and mothers help others—their husbands and children—in upward mobility. There is a considerable body of research demonstrating that corporation wives have been charged with the task of helping their husbands achieve and maintain advantageous connections with their superiors (Whyte, 1956). Psychologist Matina

Horner also found explanations for women's apparently lower achievement orientation in a fear that success would jeopardize other values in their lives (1974).

8. Women might derive high status by way of their children also. The mother of a popular debutante may bask in her daughter's glory.
9. The usual assumption is made here that the wife's social status is that of her husband. In a consumption rather than in a status sense it can be argued that the nonearning wife must share the income with others. But so also must single women who have dependents, as many of them do. The process by which women achieve privileges—including high social status—by way of men is referrd to by lesbians as mediated by the "institutions of heterosexuality" (Chapter 15). The actual money income of wives in many of these high-income households may be quite problematical (Chapter 9).
10. In general, any profession or occupation engaged in predominantly by women tends to have lower social status than those engaged in by men. Thus when the social-work profession wished to upgrade its status it encouraged men to enter it. In time, however, the men tended to take over the administrative and prestigious positions. When men entered the teaching profession they also tended to take over the administrative and prestigious positions.
11. Men in certain times and places have also achieved upward mobility by way of marriage. In seventeenth-century France, for example, we are told that *misalliance* or interclass marriage was well recognized, even advocated, as a legitimate way for a man of *esprit* to improve his economic position. He could bring status, she, money (Lougee, 1976, 49). In nineteenth-century America, as noted above, wealthy heiresses were being married to British peers in a similar way.
12. It is interesting to note that antifeminist women at that time who were more at home in male literary circles than in salons taught that women's place was in the home, that work was a moral imperative, that one's station in life was determined by birth. "Not only a person's vocation but also his lifestyle, his dress, his behavior, and whom he could marry were prescribed by his station. In other words, behavior was a variable of status" (Lougee, 94). In their view, the salonières "perpetuated the disastrous extension to large numbers of lower-ranking individuals of behavior appropriate only to a few personages of eminent rank" (98).
13. The demise of the salon and the eclipse of its ideology have been related to the broad economic forces operating to restructure societies in the nineteenth century. Silver notes that the "rise of commercial society in the nineteenth century demoted women from the highest reaches of cultural creativity and participation as key sponsors of culture. . . . Conservative ideologists elaborated a social philosophy which defined the domestic, nuclear family as a major element of social stability" (1973, 836-851). Thus, as Gaye Tuchman notes, "a doctrine of male authority had evolved" and "the salons lost their ability to absorb all who demanded entry" (1975, 182). Mills notes that there never were salonières in the United States (1959, 78-79), not even among Washington hostesses.
14. Sections of the newspaper that used to report "Society" news later

became "women's news" sections and, more recently, more general items like "living" or "style."

15. The prototype of this new high-status woman had appeared a century earlier. "By the middle of the eighteenth century, urban middle-class women styled themselves after ladies of England and participated in the development of a distinct class-linked femininity. . . . New ideas came first through imported and reprinted English essays, novels, and prescriptive books" (Gordon and Buhle, 1976, 278).
16. The subject of power has greatly preoccupied male researchers. More pages (9) are devoted to the subject of power in the International Encyclopedia of the Social Sciences than to the subject of social status (7).
17. Phenomena cognate to the vertical dimensions discussed in this chapter are those related to leadership and influence. There is a rich literature on women who have served as leaders in the female world and the styles of leadership they engaged in. Indeed, a large part of the research on women deals with such leaders, the battles they fought, their defeats, their victories. But leadership does not imply high status; it is not built into the status structure. Many of the leaders of the nineteenth century were not in high status positions nor does occupancy of a high-status position necessarily confer leadership. Instead of high or low status as related to leadership, we speak of avant garde and rearguard or reactionary. A kind of horizontal process rather than vertical status seems to be implied. In the last decade old-fashioned styles of leadership have been criticized by some of the more avant-garde feminists who do conceive of leadership in status terms. They have decried the "star" system which modern mass media cultivate, thus conferring status on leaders. A cult of "structurelessness" has arisen (Freeman, 1975, 119-129, 142-146).

    Influence is another phenomenon related to temporal priority, though not to leadership. The women's liberation movement has exerted a considerable amount of influence on the female world, though it has no particularly high position in it. We note in passing that the women's liberation movement has also exerted influence in the male world. A growing number of men are beginning to challenge sex-role stereotypes that they find oppressive. Many acknowledge the influence of the women's liberation movement on their own thinking about themselves.
18. Female power in this realm of discourse has been a long-time fear in the male world. Female bodies were supposed to harbor strange powers; menstrual blood was blighting to living things; on occasion witches could wreak enormous harm. The shrew was a stock symbol of female pretensions to power and "taming" her or putting her in her place has been a popular male fancy from Petruchio to Lytton-Strachey's story of Queen Victoria to popular moving picture and television stories of strong he-men conquering pretentious career women. The "castrating" woman remains a popular myth.
19. The "social situations" which bring into play the forces that result in power (Lipset, 311) are altogether different in the male Gesellschaft world than in the female Gemeinschaft world. We have already noted the enormous preoccupation of male primatologists and cultural anthropologists

with dominance, hierarchy, the alpha male; until recently, history was his story; political science has been all about him, as indeed, was economics, with its model of economic man. Whatever the validity of the power-hungry conceptualization of the male world, power retains its fascination as an idea in the male world. A recent bestseller claims to help the reader "find some room at the top" with helpful "tips on making it" (Korda, 1975, jacket flap). Another bestseller by Robert Ringer teaches its readers how to win by intimidation. Korda finds an "instinct for power . . . basic to men and women" (7). The whole world "is a challenge and a game, and . . . a sense of power . . . is at the core of it. All life is a game of power" (4). The rugged individualist is king: "No matter who you are, the basic truth is that your interests are nobody else's concern, your gain is inevitability someone else's loss, your failure someone else's victory" (4). We must all learn to play the power game in self defense (5). "Power . . . pays off" (17). Women can play this game as well as men: "Women should have their share of it [power], and experience tells me they will use it in much the same ways men do" (16). If one enters the power game, one has to play according to its rules.

9

Socioeconomic Status in the Female World

Introduction

In a certain sense, the concept of "socioeconomic status" is a cop-out. It saves one from having to come to terms with the raw status component of social class, with the invidious implications of the term "lower classes," for example. Most Americans, with their egalitarian ideology, find it difficult to speak of the "lower classes." It goes against the grain somehow or other. It sounds snobbish, élitist. Because the very concept of class has so many adhesions connected with it, many students prefer to jettison it altogether. They speak instead of "socioeconomic status" or SES, which is a cold, non-guilt-generating term compared with "class." Socioeconomic status or SES becomes a "variable" "out there," merely descriptive, nonjudgmental, like age or sex or ethnicity or race.[1]

The kind of status referred to as SES differs from the evaluative status discussed in Chapter 8 in that it is "scalar," more susceptible to quantification. We can say that one person has more or fewer years of schooling than another, a higher or lower income, a more or less prestigious occupation as measured on an instrument. In this sense SES is more "objective," "cooler," than "high" or "low" status.

Bernard Barber specifies several "dimensions of social stratification" such as education and knowledge, income or wealth, occupational prestige, religious and ritual purity, family and ethnicity, and power (1968, 292). The first three of these correspond to what Lipset calls the objective aspect of stratification (1968, 310) because they are amenable to measurement or scaling, and they are the ones usually used for operationalizing SES.

The unsuitability of SES as a variable for understanding the female world becomes evident when one considers that many women have no monetary income at all and that only about half of them have occupations that are recognized in the research literature. Most women, whatever other occupation they engage in, are housewives. Only the education dimension of SES includes all women.

The use of SES as a research variable is practically standard, but a host of questions remain. Although the three "dimensions" are related to one another, they do not necessarily coincide, and a large apparatus of conceptual finagling is required to take care of the "status inconsistency" that results when a person is high on one dimension, low on another. High, for example, in education but low in income. Especially in the case of women, whose SES may be high as the wives of distinguished men but low on the basis of years of schooling. In this chapter we report on the distribution of these three standard variables or "dimensions" of SES in the female world, however defective they may be.

Education in the Female World

Although the work and functions assigned to women have always called for at least some training, they have not called for a high level of literacy, let alone formal education; provision for female education was therefore rarely built into the social system. Throughout most of human history, the female population has not been a literate one, nor, worldwide, is it very literate even today. Even in civilized societies, much culture has been created and transmitted orally and its skills passed on by example. Thus today two-thirds of the 800,000 illiterates in the world are female, still depending on imitation of those around them or on oral tradition for whatever education and training they receive. And when educational and training programs are brought into developing countries today, they are often preferentially targeted on males (Boserup, 1970). It is hard for people who depend heavily on print to realize how crippling illiteracy can be, how restricting it can be, how drastically it can shrink the dimensions of one's own personality, especially in a literate society.[2]

Education makes an enormous difference in any society at both ends of the scale. Literacy itself can break the first great barrier of the mind. Its potential was illustrated when the laity were permitted to read scripture. College and university education can be equally explosive. We are only now beginning to see the impact of this force in the female world on a wide scale.

Especially important for the female world has been the rise in the number of college-educated women, for exposure to college makes an enormous difference. It stimulates them to read and think and challenge. Women in the colleges early in the century were already leading the movement to reconceptualize the female world. They were fighting the first battles against the restraints of their Gemeinschaft, kin- and locale-oriented world, just beginning to challenge the "family claim" of the love-and/or-duty ethos. College-educated women have supplied an élite who have been pioneers shaping the course of the female world for over a century. They were the ones who first examined the changing conditions that made the ideology of the women's sphere an inadequate conceptualization. They were the first to see the necessity for expanding the love-and/or-duty ethos of the female world. They were the first to challenge the "selflessness" prescribed in that ethos. They were the first to wrestle with the marriage-versus-career issue. And in the 1970s and 1980s they have been the avant garde who have done the thinking, analyzing, and researching for the whole female world.

There have always, to be sure, been some women who could read. There have even been learned ladies and scholars, from antiquity down. But it was not until about the eighteenth century that the importance of literacy came to be widely recognized and became a value in the female, as well as in the male, world. Both Hannah More and Mary Wollstonecraft were among those who argued persuasively for the education of girls, albeit their ideas of the purpose and contents of such education differed.[3] The education of girls as well as of boys in America became important in colonial times because it was often the mother who was depended upon to teach the children reading, writing, and arithmetic. So at least until well into the nineteenth century, formal education, as distinguished from "finishing," was not a highly differentiating dimension of stratification in the female population. Nor, in fact, is high school graduation any longer a mark of differentiation, as more and more girls reach that level.

Overall, the female population in the United States shows up well so far as the number of years of schooling is concerned (Table 9-1). In 1977, the median number of years of schooling was beyond high school graduation, 12.3. (For white women in 1976, it was 12.4 and for blacks just a year less, 11.4.) But for reasons just suggested, the most significant trend seems to be the increase in women exposed to college. From a small trickle—11,126 resident college students in 1869-1870—to al-

TABLE 9-1 Years of School Completed by Females, 1977*

Years of Schooling	*Percent of Females over Fourteen Years of Age*
0	.7
1-4	2.0
5-8	16.0
9-12	57.9
13-16	20.2
17 or more	3.2

*Source: Bureau of the Census, Educational Attainment in the United States: March 1977 and 1976. Series P-20, no. 314, issued Dec. 1977, Table 1, p. 7.

most a million and a half (1,467,000) in the fall of 1961—the growth in numbers was consistent (Bernard, 1964, 69-70). By 1953, 40 percent of all women between twenty-five and thirty had had at least a year of college (Census Bureau, P-20, 314, 1). The number of women fourteen to thirty-four years of age who were enrolled in college rose almost threefold (278 percent) between 1960 and 1976 (Statistical Abstract, 1977, 154).[4] The number of women enrolled for degrees rose 306 percent in the same period, while total enrollment rose 207 percent. At the turn of the century, about a third of the college population consisted of women. By 1968, about two-fifths (39 percent) of all college students aged fourteen to thirty-four were women; in 1978, about half were, many of them women returning to school after time out for children. Two-thirds of college students over thirty-four were women (Rich, 1979). As we shall suggest later (Chapter 14), a kind of educational homogenization seems to be in process in the female world.

In the context of education as a dimension of socioeconomic status, the increase in the number of women in junior and community colleges—64.8 percent between 1960 and 1976—is of extraordinary significance. This figure reflects one of the most interesting trends reshaping the female world: the movement of women from even the lower socioeconomic levels into colleges. For a considerable part of the student body in these schools is contributed by women from just such socioeconomic levels. Continuing education programs in community colleges as well as in standard institutions make it possible for rapidly increasing numbers of women to be exposed to higher education. Wherever they can get in, whenever the hours are scheduled for their convenience and the tuition is tailored to their resources, they eagerly flock to the colleges. They are asking community colleges to make available to them their resources of faculty, library, and other learning facilities (Astin, 1976). Even the staid old conventional institutions are being asked to provide opportunities to "returnees" or "resumers," women in their thirties and older and hence out of "sync" with the male-scheduled educational system. Especially noteworthy is the growth of programs of women's studies, so called, offering a channel for disseminating the remarkable corpus of feminist scholarship which is discovering, exploring, interpreting, and analyzing the female world itself. Education, including self-education, is in the process of expanding the horizons of the female population, adding notably to its intellectual resources.

Although number of years of schooling is becoming less and less a differentiating factor in the female population, education as distinguished from schooling remains an important social-class dimension. Years of schooling per se constitute only a small part of education as a dimension of social class. Women at the highest socioeconomic levels do not always have strong educational motivation; they do not go to college or university as a matter of course, or if they do, they do not necessarily remain to graduate (Antler, 1978, draft). Nor, among the lower socioeconomic classes, does college erase all the stigmata of social class, as Rita Mae Brown, among others, has shown (Chapter 10). It is primarily in the upper middle classes that higher education for women is taken for granted. And, as we shall see in Chapter 10, these college-educated women constitute a kind of élite in the female world.

Nor is it mere attendance at college that has social-class implications. Which college one attends makes a difference. It makes a difference whether it is vocationally oriented or oriented toward the liberal or fine arts, for vocational schooling has less social-status value than training in the humanities or in the professions or arts. At least some knowledge of the liberal arts, for example, is almost a sine qua non for acceptance in the upper middle class. One need not spell well, but one should have a nodding acquaintance with, or at least have heard of, let us say, John Donne or Restoration comedy.

The nineteenth-century female world was at odds with itself with respect to what the education of women should be, and there was a social-class factor involved. On one side there were the women of the middle and upper-middle classes who wanted exactly the same education that men received. They favored colleges for women modeled on the élite men's colleges and with an identical curriculum. And in time they got them. They also redefined the love-and/or-duty ethos. From time to time there might be a slight nod in the direction of family life, as when Vassar inaugurated a course on "euthenics," but for the most part these colleges hewed strictly to the prestigious classical lines of male liberal arts education. In the 1960s some—like their male counterparts—became coeducational.

On the other side were the land-grant coeducational colleges with a more modest social-class clientele (Chapter 17). Here were the colleges of home economics, planned to train women to take to the farmer's wife the results of scientific research, as her male counterpart, the county agent, was taking them to the farmer (Bernard, 1964). The social-class aura persisted for many decades, the women's colleges—especially the so-called Seven Sisters—producing one kind of female élite, the land-grant universities another, more vocationally oriented, and—in the case of the home-economics colleges—a home and family and community Gemeinschaft orientation, as well as a professional one.

Whatever uncertainties women may have felt with respect to education, men claimed to have known fairly well what was suitable for women. Attitude toward female education, as a matter of fact, constitutes a touchstone to one's conceptualization of women and their world. Benjamin Rush (1746-1813), an outstanding champion of higher education for women, for example, had a clear idea of what women should be trained for, and not a demeaning one. He saw women as having three major responsibilities that required specialized training. The first called for knowledge of accounts, so that women could help their husbands and serve as stewards and guardians of their husbands' property. The second called for the ability to rear children without their husbands' help, including the ability "to instruct their sons in the principles of liberty and government" (Gordon and Buhle, 1976, 282). And, of course, women should know how to manage their servants, who, in this country, did not know their place. In the nineteenth century the upper-middle class added ornamental accomplishments or "finishing" to enhance the pleasures of the home. Their modern counterparts still persist.

At the present time it would seem that the educational opportunities of the female population are similar if not identical to those of the male population. Actually, of course, the schools girls attend are not the same as the schools boys attend, as the description of the "pink world" in Chapter 6 suggests (Bernard, 1975). In high school they study different subjects, have had, until recently, different athletic and sports programs, are exposed to different counseling advice, pursue different majors in college, prepare for different careers, acquire different kinds of knowledge. Education has different impacts, therefore, on women and men. Thus, for example, the income of a college-educated woman in 1976 was less than that of a male high-school dropout (Statistical Abstract, 1977, 452) while professionally or technically trained women received about the same income as male operatives (Table 9-2).

Wealth and Income in the Female Population

Ownership of the means of production has declined as a dimension of class since the time of Marx and especially since the control of the means of production has been separated from ownership. In any event,

TABLE 9-2 Median Annual Earnings by Sex and Occupation, 1976*

Occupation	*Females*	*Males*
Professional, technical, kindred	11,072	16,939
Managers, Administrators, except farm	9,804	16.674
Sales	6,272	14,586
Clerical, kindred	8,128	12,843
Craft, kindred	7,765	13,638
Operatives	6,649	11,688
Laborers, except farm	7,613	10,104
Service workers, except household	5,840	10,036

*Source: Statistical Abstract, 1977, 411.

it has never been suitable for application to women. There is, to be sure, a myth that women own most of the wealth of the country in the form of stocks and bonds. It is not true. There is not much "power of the purse" in the female world. In 1970 women constituted only 30 percent of all shareholders and owned ony 25 percent of all shares held by individuals and 16 percent of all shares (Women's Bureau, 1975, 179). And even the portion of the wealth registered in the name of women is often controlled by trustees, husbands, or other male guardians. The basis for the idea that women own most of the wealth of the country may inhere in the interesting fact that among the few female heads of families in the high-income brackets—$25,000 and over—women—probably the rich widows we hear so much about—receive almost twice as much income ($10,031) as male heads of husband-wife households ($5,123) on the average from dividends, pensions, and other regular payments (1970 Census, Sources and Structure of Family Income, Table 5). It remains true, however, that within the female world, where wealth exists it is associated with social class, indirectly by means of influence, if not directly by way of power.

No more than wealth is income a wholly suitable dimension of social class in the female world. Not all women have incomes of their own (Table 9-3) and among those who have, most are in the lowest income brackets (Table 9-4). Clearly the husband's income must be taken into account. In Figure 8-1 the assumption was made that the social status of a wife was that of her husband, which, in turn, was measured by his income. But being in a household with high social status as measured by income does not mean that the housewife herself has a high monetary income. Much of her "income" is in the form of maintenance or support. The monetary part may be in the form of allowances from her husband, determined by either bargaining or whim.

A great many people work under conditions that they view as demeaning. But many nonemployed housewives at all income levels have felt especially degraded by the unilateral control of their monetary resources. There is a whole body of female lore dealing with the whee-

TABLE 9-3 Income of Adult Females, 1976*

Income	*Percent*
No income	26.7
Less than $2,000	22.1
$2,000-3,999	17.3
$4,000-6,999	15.3
$7,000-9,000	9.5
$10,000-14,999	6.6
$15,000 +	2.5
	100.0

*Source: Statistical Abstract of the United States, 1977, 451.

TABLE 9-4 Persons Fourteen Years of Age and over with Incomes*

Income	*Females*	*Males*
Less than $2,000	30.1	12.3
$2,000-$3,999	23.6	11.3
$4,000-$6,999	20.8	15.2
$7,000-$9,999	13.0	13.7
$10,000-$14,999	9.0	20.6
$15,000 and over	3.4	27.0

*Source: Statistical Abstract, 1977, 451.

dling women must engage in to get money—when is the best time to ask for money; how to finagle bills and charge accounts to disguise expenditures; how to save secretly out of household allowances. Desire for escape from such humiliating conditions was found, in fact, to be a major motive or reward among blue-collar and service workers for entering the labor force. "I've never been good for asking my husband for anything. I don't want to have to ask anybody for anything. And I don't have to say 'Well, honey, can I have this or can I spend that?' [Working] gives me more money, even though what I'm making now isn't that much more. I feel a lot more independent" (Walshok, 1977, 16). And, "the first plus is having money of your own, which makes a hell of a difference." And, "I'm a very independent person. . . . it's my income you know, and I lose by dependence on other people." Understandably, with few exceptions, "none of the women indicated they would stop working even if they did not need the money. . . . The benefits of paid employment outweigh the benefits of homemaking."

Since, as Table 9-3 shows, over a fourth (26.7 percent) of adult women have no income of their own (Statistical Abstract, 1977, 451), a considerable amount of the income, as noted above, is in the form of maintenance or support. Some may also take the form of gifts, a source that has no exact counterpart in the male world. There was a time when diamonds— symbol for all kinds of lavish gifts—were a girl's best friend in the sense that they constituted her best source of security. Whether or not this custom of making extravagant gifts to specific women still prevails, it is probably less acceptable now than in the past (Orth, 1972). In any event, it is viewed by many as analogous to income from high-level prostitution, more or less outside the female world, in the "demi-monde," or half-world. Some of this kind of income is no doubt blanketed into the "no-income" category in Table 9-3.

It is not only the amount of monetary income in the female world that invites attention but also its composition. Unfortunately there are only fragments of data available for understanding it. The census distinguishes several sources of monetary income: "earnings," which include wages, salaries, commissions, bonuses, and the proceeds from own nonfarm business, professional practice, partnerships, and farm self-employment; Social Security payments; public assistance payments; and such other regular payments as interest, dividends, pensions, and the like. But the available data on the structure of monetary income refer only to families. We can, however, compare the sources of income for husband-wife families and female-headed families (Table 9-5). Since we are dealing here with averages, it is difficult to make meaningful comparisons, but the general trends may be delineated.

For a variety of reasons determined by norms of the male world—kinds of work engaged in, hours worked, interrupted work histories, unemployment, and especially discriminatory practices—and for reasons determined by behavior prescribed by the female world itself, earnings in the female population are strikingly lower than earnings in the male population in the same occupational categories (Table 9-2). But in both male-and female-headed families, earnings in 1969 contributed by far the largest proportion of monetary income, though comparatively more in the male-headed families (80.9 percent versus 71.0 percent).

TABLE 9-5 Composition of Family Income of Male- and Female-Headed Families*

	Mean Total Income	*Mean Wage-Salary Income*	*Mean Social Security Income*	*Mean Public Assistance Income*	*Mean Other Income (Interest, Dividends, Pensions)*
Husband-Wife Families (44,002,058)	$11,598	$9,380	$288	$36	$739
Female-Headed Families (5,515,016)	6,219	4,414	521	316	750

*Source: 1970 Census, Sources and Structure of Family Income, Table 5.

Average Social Security payments were relatively higher in the female-headed families, no doubt reflecting the income of surviving widows. Public assistance payments were trivial in male-headed families but averaged 5.1 percent of mean income in the female-headed families. Interest, dividends, and pensions, although they averaged about the same amount in both male- and female-headed families, constituted a much larger proportion of total income in the female-headed families (12.1 percent versus 6.4 percent). In all income brackets, $5000 and over, the income from these sources was higher for the female-headed families, and in some case—reflecting incomes of wealthy widows—remarkably higher.[5] There were, of course, relatively few female-headed families in these high-income brackets.

Whatever its source, size of income has widely ramifying implications. It influences life chances, determines access to prerogatives and amenities, to different kinds of life styles, and thus, indirectly, leads to differentiated social status. Although earned income in the female population is low, it is in a large number of cases enough to provide a woman with a modicum of economic independence if she wants it. And such potential economic independence makes a difference in both the female and the male world. We know, for example, that the marriage rate, age for age, is lower for women who are employed, for, as noted in Chapter 7, jobs or careers constitute notable competition for marriage, especially if women find partners to live with and supply companionship and love. And if suitable job opportunities are available, divorce rates also rise (Moles and Levinger, 1979).

It is hard to emphasize too strongly how this income dimension of socioeconomic status impacts on women. The lack of money can influence the whole worldview of those suffering from it. There has to be pinching, scraping, saving. It is harder to be generous. Public services are often less graciously supplied, if they are forthcoming at all. A world in which so large a proportion does not have money of its own is bound to be different from one in which there are relatively few in this category. In any monetary exchange situation—characeristic of Gesellschaft—the odds are against the person with fewer monetary resources. The power of the purse is overwhelming.

A generation ago the term "culture of poverty" was coined to interpret the seemingly self-destructive behavior of the poor, most of whom are women. Although it has fallen into disuse, in a nonpsychological sense it is true that cultures differ by income, if for no other reason than that the costs of certain cultural values are high. Styles in home decor, in entertaining, in value placed on education, especially for girls, are only a few of the many class-related cultural differences related to income levels.

Why, it may well be asked, do women accept these income inequalities? Some theorists (the functionalist school) ask how systems of stratification hold together and find the answer in socialization to conformity to a status quo, no matter how poorly rewarded. Some, on the other hand, study the way inequalities frustrate people and urge them to reject the status quo, even rebel against it (Lipset, 1968, 298). In the female world most attention so far has been paid to the functionalist approach. Only recently have women paid serious attention to ways of undermining the unequal status quo. Merton has noted that rebellion by an exploited group may be looked at as an adaptive response called for when the existing status quo is seen as an obstacle to the achievement of legitimate ends (1957, 191-192). In the 1970s a considerable segment of the female population was beginning to accept this perspective. It was beginning to reverberate throughout the female world. Even women who proudly denied that they were "women's libbers" were beginning to qualify their position with "but I do believe in equal pay for work of equal value."

The ramifications of the income dimension of socioeconomic status go far beyond social class. They extend into the whole cash-nexus basis of the Gesellschaft and the whole ethos that regulates it. Where human relationships are mediated by monetary exchanges, the love-and/or-duty ethos is a serious handicap. The logic justifying payment for all kinds of services freely supplied by women in the past is almost irrefutable. Why should they not be paid for household services? For emotional support? For tender loving care and all the other services built into the love-and/or-duty ethos? It is hard to see why not on strictly Gesellschaft grounds. Still, a great many women are troubled by this logic, which forces them to accept the Gesellschaft mode of thought. There may be a social-class dimension here but the whole issue is still in process of resolution and the knowledge needed for achieving such a resolution is not yet available (Chapter 22).

Income is, of course, related to occupation, and we know that whatever they are called, the occupations assigned to women in the male world tend to be poorly paid. Even white-collar jobs such as teaching do not have the pay which the preparation called for would seem to warrant.

A Seriously Flawed Conceptualization

The inappropriateness of current models of socioeconomic status becomes clear when we apply the occupational dimension of socioeconomic status to the female world. Housewife, the most important occupation in the female world—in terms of the number engaged in it as well as of sociological importance—is not even included. Most women, whether or not they are in the labor force, are housewives at least part-time and about half of all adult women—those not in the labor force—are full-time housewives. There is, to be sure, an enormous corpus of research dealing with the household, especially by home economists, and a long history dealing with the cult of domesticity in the nineteenth century, as we have already seen. And we shall have more to say of the housewife in later chapters. But what is relevant here is that as an occupation, housewifery[6] does not appear in any of the research on occupation as a dimension of socioeconomic status; it is not even viewed as within the economy because it is not operated on a cash-nexus basis. "It would serve no purpose . . . to include housewives in a count of a country's working force," we are told, because including them "would have no relevance for the significant economic problems of our times" (Jaffe and Stewart, 1951, 14, 18). This occupation is outside the Gesellschaft and therefore outside the male world's concern.

The importance of the household as a strictly demographic unit has long been recognized. But it is also a fundamental social structural unit in our society. It is analogous to the individual plant in the economy, a unit supplying a fundamental service to the total system, as Catharine Beecher never ceased to remind her readers. Even the enormous contribution which women make to business and industry as participants in the labor force pales in significance when compared to the contribution made by all the women managing households. It is precisely the magnitude of this contribution that renders it almost invisible. It is almost too big to be seen. It is taken for granted like any other big fixture in the landscape.

The importance of "occupation housewife" becomes even more salient when we consider the individuals who do not live in a household, who are not provided with its services. In Chapter 10 we see them in a class by themselves, as "outcasts." "Homeless men" have long been a community concern. We have not yet devised an adequate surrogate for the household.

Because "occupation housewife" is not included in the standard research on occupations, when we speak of the occupational dimension of the female world we are speaking only of that half of adult women—51.1 percent—who have jobs in the labor force. In Table 9-6, a column in which all the percentages are halved has been added to portray the fact that housewives are omitted, and another occupational category, "housewife," has been added containing the (roughly) half of adult women who are probably full-time housewives. We leave for Chapter 10 comments on the ambivalent status dimension of "occupation housewife."

TABLE 9-6 Women by Major Occupation, 1977*

Major Occupation	*Proportion of Employed Women*	*Proportion of All Women*†
Professional and Technical	16.1	8
Managers and Administrators	5.7	3
Sales Workers	6.7	3
Clerical Workers	35.1	18
Craft and Kindred Workers	1.6	.8
Operatives	11.7	6
Nonfarm Laborers	.1	.05
Service Workers	20.8	11
Farm Workers	.1	.05
		Housewives 50
	100.0	

*Source: Bureau of the Census. Statistical Abstract of the United States, 1977, p. 406.

†In 1977, when this table was prepared, fewer than half of all women (47.4 percent) were in the labor force, but the relative numbers in various occupations are roughly approximate. The proportion of women in the labor force was 51.1 percent in June 1979 (Bureau of Labor Statistics, 1979, Table 3A) and was projected to reach 54.8 percent in 1990 (Smith, ed., 1979, 14).

Because the discussion of the occupational dimension refers to only half of adult women, we do not speak of the occupational structure of the female world—which the research data do not provide—but rather of the occupational distribution of the half of adult women who are in the labor force, quite a different thing.

As an aside, it may be noted that the relations of women in "occupation housewife" vis-à-vis the male world are different from those of women employed in the male world. They are not in a competitive but in an adversary relationship. The housewife has to fight the male world as a consumer in her "procurement" function. She has to protect herself against the constantly renewed assaults of the advertisers. She can, nevertheless, exert considerable clout at the checkout counter.

The Occupational Distribution of Women in the Labor Force

The increasing participation of women in the labor force is one of the best documented and most salient trends in the female world as well as in the male world. It reverses the old ideological tenet with respect to women's sphere. In the nineteenth century female labor-force participation was hailed by avant-garde women as a counter to the restrictive and deteriorating women's sphere ideology; in the twentieth, as an ethical obligation (Myrdal and Klein, 1956). Actually women, then as now, have entered the labor force because they were needed there:[7] the economy could not have developed as it did without them. Women were in great demand; when unmarried "working girls" came to be in short supply, married women were recruited; and when there were not enough even of them, mothers were recruited, even mothers of preschool children (Oppenheimer, 1970, 1972). These trends have relevance in a variety of contexts, but at this point we look mainly at their impact on occupational distribution.

In 1900 "women had monopolized several clerical and professional occupations that were numerically small in 1900, but which grew very rapidly in the next sixty years" (Oppenheimer, 1970, 151). Oppenheimer attributes two-thirds of this expansion to occupation-specific growth. The jobs in which women had a monopoly multiplied at a rapid rate whereas the supply of young women to fill them actually declined relatively. Carlson has traced the demographic trends involved: "Women between ages 15 and 30 are the base population from which working girls traditionally were drawn, and a clear trend can be observed in the absolute size of cohorts passing through these ages during the last century. In the late nineteenth century and through the first three decades of the twentieth, the total female population between ages 15 and 30 grew by more than two million women every ten years. However, during the next three decades . . . there was practically no growth in the female population age 15 to 30, . . . a gain of [only] one million in three decades, compared to the earlier growth of twice that many women every ten years" (Carlson, draft, 1979). This shrinkage resulted from reduced fertility and declining immigration. Of this shrinking number, more young women remained in school, further cutting into labor-force participation. Early marriage also withdrew young women from the labor force when the norms of the female world called for such withdrawal. "With two such powerful trends in supply and demand pulling against each other, eventually something had to give." The norm against married women working relaxed. The demand for women in the clerical occupations continued and promises to remain high. But the demand is not exclusively for clerical workers.

The occupational distribution of the half of all adult women in the labor force is quite different from that of men. A far larger proportion are in service and so-called helping kinds of work, reflecting the traditional love-and/or-duty ethos of female culture. "As the focus for female aspirations the three 'k's' of an earlier generation—Kinder, Küche, Kirche [children, kitchen and church]—have been replaced by the three 'h's'—healing, helping, and home management. The professions now open to women are in the main in the service sector, calling for 'warm hearts' and 'beautiful bodies' " (Schork, 1978, p. 33).[8]

There are important concomitants to the occupational distribution of women quite apart from the income aspect, for work itself has ramifying influences on personality. Almost fifty years ago, sociologist Pitirim Sorokin reminded us how our work influenced all aspects of our personality, from the physical to the ideological. "Occupation," he said, "marks a whole organism and shapes it, making it conform to its nature. . . . [Occupation] stigmatizes the movement and habitual posture of the body. . . . Still greater is the occupational influence on the processes and on the character of one's evaluations, beliefs, and practical judgments, opinions, ethics, and whole ideology" (1927, 320-321). A considerable literature has commented on the negative impact of housekeeping on the mind (Coolidge, 1912), on neuroticism (Myerson, 1929), on mental health (Bernard, 1942), on occupational dissatisfaction (Oakley, 1974). An equally extensive literature on trends in the occupation of domestic service as related to the female world has illuminated aspects of our society which we shall have occasion to note when we discuss "servanthood" below (Chapter 11). Although women are said to have little aspiration for upward occupational mobility,[9] in connection with the influence of work on behavior, it is interesting to note that men and women in the same work situation[10] seem to respond in similar ways. That the kind of work engaged in has similar impact on psychological functioning for women and for men was shown in a study by Joanne Miller and her associates (1978, draft). And another study, this time of managers, found male and female managers psychologically very much alike. It reported no difference in "critical thinking, temperament, values, intelligence, verbal abilities or leadership style" (Quinn, 1978).

The joker is, however, that men and women are rarely in the same position. The *ceteris paribus* fallacy is involved. Thus Miller and her associates are careful to note that "women's job conditions differ from men's. Our data indicate that, compared to men, women are significantly more closely supervised and significantly less likely to be owners, to occupy a high position in a supervisory hierarchy, to do complex work with data, things, or people, to work under time pressure, to work long hours, to do heavy work, to be held responsible for things outside their control, and to expect dramatic changes in their job circumstances" (draft, 1978).

In general, the occupations that tend to be assigned to women rate low on prestige scales. The index of occupational prestige or status used here (Table 9-7) is the score—coarsely related to years of schooling—accorded them by the U.S. Civil Rights Commission (1978) on the basis of work by Lloyd V. Temme (178, 94). The highest score on this scale is 88. To help interpret this table, the prestige scores of several illustrative occupations are presented here: maids, servants, private household workers, 11; cooks, private household, 17; retail trade workers, 31; lay midwives, 33; typists, 38; health trainees, 39; practical nurses, 43; nurses, 47; social workers, 52; librarians, 64; authors, 68; sociology professors, 72; judges, 78; physicians, 88. The most striking as-

TABLE 9-7 Occupational Prestige Scores of 23,746,639 Employed Women on Temme Scale, 1970*

Score	*Percent*
1-14	4.1
15-29	17.3
30-44	41.8
45-59	23.9
60-74	12.7
75-89	.3
	100.0

*Source: 1970 Census of Occupations, Table 1. Not included, 6,788,019 women in offbeat occupations. Total number of women in labor force, 30,534,658.

pect of this structure is the overwhelming salience of occupations below the midpoint (44) of the scale. The median score for a sample of women from the 1970 Census was below this point, 37.5.

The data used in Table 9-7 are not to be taken as a technically flawless sample. Not all occupations are assigned scores in the Civil Rights Commission study. Only 23,746,639 women are accounted for out of the 30,534,658 women in the labor force in 1970. The 6,788,019 omitted women were in the more offbeat kinds of work, such as packers and wrappers (351,976), sewers and stitchers (883,678), miscellaneous operators (210,147), and the like, largely in the low-prestige occupations.[11]

Not exactly cognate to prestige, a positive quality for an occupation, but probably related to it is the degree of depression associated with those who engage in various occupations. Lenore Radloff has derived depression scores as measured on a twenty-item instrument for a sample of 2,515 white males and females in two communities as of 1971-1973 (forthcoming). On the basis of her findings, it appears that overall, professional occupations, especially the high-level ones, are associated with low depression scores and manual occupations, with high depression scores. Housewives seem to hover near the average. Both high prestige and low depression seem to be related to professional occupations. Income no doubt plays a considerable part in these relationships.

Occupation is far more than a component of socioeconomic status. Labor-force participation itself, regardless of specific occupation, has important reverberations in the female world.

Are Female Labor-Force Participants in the Male World?

The capitalist-industrial economy was overwhelmingly a male creation, operating on principles established by men and therefore reflecting a male style of relationship. But increasingly a place had to be made in it for women, not only in the United States but elsewhere as well, because they were needed there. Whether they wanted to or not, they would have had to be inducted into it, so that today between 40 and 50 percent of the labor force in industrialized countries all over the world (except Japan) consists of women.

A common objection to the concept of a female world argues that since women constitute so large a part of the labor force they are therefore *in* the male world.[12] But the point of view proposed here is that women participants in the labor force are not really "in" the male world, or better, perhaps, they are not really "of" the male world. To use an analogy: an Englishman may work in France, but that does not mean that he is a Frenchman or that England and France are the same. The millions of Italian, Spanish, Greek, and Turkish workers who man the economies of northern and western European countries are not German, French, or Scandinavian. Similarly, a woman may work in the male world but that does not mean that she is a man or that the female and male worlds are the same.

For women bring their own world with them when they enter the work scene. Or, better, it follows them in. They remain within its boundaries. The behavior it has called for until recently is reflected in the etiquette books prepared for employed women. They codify the rules of the female world as they have applied on the work site, and they remained almost unchanged until yesterday:

> In 1935 the etiquette books were advising the office girl to be a model of tact. She was not to point out her employer's mistakes or, if she did, she was to do it indirectly, in a memorandum, for example, rather than verbally in a face-to-face confrontation; she was never to be blunt; she was never to gloat; she was to make it appear that he had found the mistake himself. She was never to puncture his vanity. She was not to argue. She was, in brief, to be a model of the morale-booster, the male-ego builder-upper, a specialist in stroking. In 1956 she was told to "adapt herself to her employer's unexplained silences or other idiosyncrasies without taking them as a personal affront." In 1965 she was to be helpful, admiring, to "let him know you think he's destined to soar to the top"; she was to be smart but never to "allow him to find out you're brighter than he is." In 1967, she was still to "hide her light under a bushel of modesty," and "not win the battle and lose the war" [Bernard, 1968, 284].

As codes of prescribed female behavior these etiquette books did not differ essentially from the long train of forerunners that had characterized the female world of the nineteenth century.

The Scenario according to the "Immigrant" Analogy

James March, an economist, has noted that women enter the male world as, in effect, "immigrants." This is a vivid figure of speech with interesting implications.[13] A classic study of European immigrants to the United States more than half a century ago, for example, described the many ways immigrants, most of them peasants with rural—Gemeinschaft—backgrounds, had had to change in order to cope with their new—usually urban, Gesellschaft—world (Park and Miller, 1921). The analogy may not be close, but in some ways it is suggestive. Like European immigrants to the United States, women bring with them "old country" ways from the female world when they "immigrate" to the male world.[14] As the Lowell girls did. Or as the secretary does when she functions as a "wife." In fact, for many women, labor-force participation constitutes simply a change of site for performing their traditional function of serving their families. To pay for home improvements, for example, or for the children's college education. Such employment does not lead to independence from authority of the husband or demands of the children (Cowan, 1974, 250). Nor departure from the female world. Their work is just a part of their service to the family. And since the kind of work they do is so often in jobs that are subservient, even passive, they do not violate the prescribed role patterns of the female world. They carry their female world with them into the labor force. The male world remains the same.

Like immigrants, to pursue March's figure of speech, working women have been segregated into enclaves. And although a process analogous to "Americanization" does take place among them, as it did among immigrants in the early years of this century, they tend to remain segregated in their own world, operating according to its principles, thus retarding their "Americanization." Like immigrants in a new country, March further notes, women start at the bottom and work their way up as they learn the rules of the game. And a great deal of what we know about immigrants to the United States does, at least figuratively, throw light on what happens to women as they try to enter the male world. They too are vulnerable; they too have to learn to speak and read a new language, to figure out the meaning of all the gestures, nuances, understandings that natives take for granted. Some never do. After a hundred years, the immigrant's "homeland" or "mother" country and the United States change, become different from what they were. So does the female world change. Italy, the Ukraine, and China today are no longer the same as the Italy, Ukraine, or China from which the immigrants came. Nor is the female world the same as it used to be. The Italians, the Ukrainians, the Chinese in this country have become distributed differentially across the American socioeconomic—income, occupational, and educational—structure. According to this scenario, only a faded female "ethnicity" will finally survive as women in the labor force become "Americanized," that is, "assimilated" into the male world.

But even when women have not been segregated into enclaves on the work scene, they have nevertheless lived in a different work world from that of men. Working with men in the same shop or on the same assembly line or in the same office does not mean living in the same world. Even when they are not spatially separated from the male work world, women are socially and psychologically separated. Rosabeth Moss Kanter has shown, for example, that in one of the corporations she observed women were given less encouragment from their superiors to improve and less encouragement to advance; the company was less aware of their contributions (1977, 125). They were not as likely as men to be seen as material for promotion. Thus, a sample of management men predicted no promotion for about a fifth of the women, contrasted with only 6 percent of the men (143). It was a self-fulfilling prophecy. Fewer opportunities for advancement were offered; less advancement was achieved. Even those who overcome the obstacles put in their paths—wittingly or unwittingly—by the work setting find their world more difficult. "It's just that there are so many more things I have to deal with than a man does" (Kanter and Stein, eds., 1979, 137). Or there is, simply, the "raunchy storytelling that can be part of male culture" (136) that has to be dealt with. And, unless protested, "feminine" services are still taken for granted; a smiling face is almost obligatory.

There are different hazards in the work site for women. Sexual harassment, for example, is rare in the male work world; it is a common, everyday hazard in the female (Farley, 1978). The work site does not homogenize the female and the male worlds, nor does it "Americanize" or "masculinize" the female world.

Women are increasingly knocking at the doors of traditionally all-male kinds of skilled blue-collar jobs because they pay better. But even the women who succeed do not thereby enter the male world. In fact, Mary Wolshak has found that their lives are very much like those of other women in even the most segregated female jobs. True, "many describe their husbands as ambivalent or nonsupportive and some of their male coworkers are downright hostile to their new careers"; still, "most report that they carry the full burden of household tasks in addition to their physical labors on the job" (in Fisher, 1978, 33). The norms of the female world still control their behavior, whether at the work site or at home.

Because the economic rewards are so much greater in the male world than in the female world, some women in the labor force reject the female world; they see it as an encumbrance to their own success in the male world; they want none of it. They want to discard their "old country" ways, as successful immigrants did, and take on those of the "new country." They want to be "assimilated." Thus a considerable spate of books began to appear in the 1970s to teach women the rules of the game as played in the male world so that they would know how it operated and learn how to deal with it. The authors of one such book were, in fact, called "missionaries to a female population that wants to be converted" (Berman, 1977, 22). Seminars and workshops have been organized by women's groups on such topics as "Women in the Corporate World," which include lectures on "what it means to be in an alien culture" and "gender differences regarding the issues of power and success," and which help the participants "identify the corporate and individual self-interest necessary for change toward authentic organizations" (flyer for one such conference, 1978). Still, no more than immigrants were they melted down to an undifferentiated homogeneity (Moynihan and Glazer, 1963).

A small, but indeterminate, number of women may, indeed, succeed in "cracking" the male world, in truly becoming "one of the boys." They may indeed have a male identity, feel like men, enjoy the male style of sociality. The most extreme examples of such women are three women who "pass" as men, described by Stoller: "one is an expert machine tool operator, another an engineering draftsman, another a research chemist. Their jobs are quiet, steady, and unspectacular; their work records as men are excellent. They are sociable, not recluses, and have friendships with both men and women. Neither their friends nor their colleagues at work know they are biologically female. They are not clinically psychotic" (1968, 196), Admittedly, these are extreme cases. More likely to occur, but still rare, are the women who, though not in a closet, live the lives of men and who, for one reason or another—their voice, body, manners—are so accepted by men that they are dealt with as men in practically all respects. Or, perhaps better, they are not treated as women.

A somewhat larger number of women may think they live in the male world until something happens that shows how wide the chasm really is. One such woman, for example, could pub-crawl with men, romp with them, even attend burlesque shows with them. But when one evening ended in a visit to a brothel?[15] Women may become "rolewise." They may, in fact, think like men, act like men, live by the rules of the male world. They may reject identification with other women and certainly with the female world. For all intents and purposes they are "men." But they are almost never truly "in." Almost never completely accepted. Nor does their presence change the nature, structure, or functioning of the male world.[16] Though they are in the male world in the sense that they participate in it, they are not truly "of" it. And that is the bottom line.

In terms of practical procedures, women will no doubt continue to be in though not of the male world. But the growth in recognition and understanding of the female world by both women and men will have its impact on both sexes in the work force. With the support that comes from knowledge and understanding of the female world, women will feel stronger, less defensive, supported by the legitimacy of their perspective. The overwhelming male consensus will begin to show cracks.

Entrepreneurial Occupations

Some women earn their incomes outside the corporate structure of the male world. We noted in Chapter 3 that many women throughout history have been self-employed. In Athens, for example, they seem to have run the inns and to have marketed food; in Rome they seemed to have pursued a variety of trades and, during the Punic Wars, to have managed large business establishments. The beguines, the vagabonds, and the sylk women all seemed to have been self-employed. At the turn of the century, women in our own society engaged in work they could combine with home responsibilities; they ran boarding houses, ran dressmaking or millinery establishments, and sold their handiwork (Smuts, 1959, 14-16). They did piecework in "sweat shops." Today there are still women running boutiques, beauty parlors, and other small, highly individualized shops. Increasingly, well-trained women are breaking into the consultant industry, selling their professional expertise on a business basis. The fate of small enterprises in our economy, however, whether run by men or by women, is not bright. There is a high rate of bankruptcy among them. Still, many women are finding a great deal of comfort and satisfaction working in conditions controlled by women and conformable to their style and pace.

Crime as an Occupation

Except for prostitution, successful careers in crime are not usually available to women in either their own or the male world. There are—except, again, in the case of prostitution—no training schools in the form of street gangs, no career ladders for them in organized crime. They can be successful gun-molls, get-away drivers, assistants in fencing operations, in line with the love-and/or-duty ethos of the female world. But the Gemeinschaft nature of the female world influences and limits the kind of crime that is feasible. Most so-called crimes of passion have people who are near or dear to the perpetrators as their victims. Infanticide, for example, is a feasible crime for women; killing lovers or husbands is another (Pollak, 1950). But there are few if any "hit women" who make a career of killing. The male media enjoy the image of "cat fights," of women fighting women in violent confrontations, biting, hair-pulling, kicking one another, and the like. There is little research reported to document how extensive such activity is.

The female world does not offer a rich field for property crimes; it is not rich enough. A maid may be able to pilfer or steal from her employer. But there is not much return on such low-level crime. The prostitute who rolls her customer is a standard stereotype. A common form of crime in which women may be successful is shoplifting. It is in line with the shopping which is one of the functions of their world. But big-time property crime is not characteristic of the female world. There are more profitable areas of crime in the male world; but most women are not well-enough placed in the male work world to be in a position where profitable white-collar crime can be committed. Under supervision, a Patty Hearst may rob a bank; but there are not many female bank robbers. As more and more women enter the labor force the opportunities for more profitable property crimes may increase.

Because the study of victimology is so new, it is difficult to document the validity or invalidity of the statement that women have been more likely to be victims than perpetrators of crime. Most crime is unreported, especially crimes within the household, and it is here that women have been especially vulnerable. Indeed, for many women, physical assault has not even been viewed as exceptional; they had been reared to expect it. It was expected that husbands would beat up their wives. The female world was not immune to crime because of its privacy.

In recent years there has been considerable interest in the possible effect of the women's movement on female crime. F. Adler sees increased female crime as an aspect of "the rising tide of female assertiveness. . . . The female criminal knows too much to pretend, or return to her former role as a second-rate criminal confined to 'feminine' crimes such as shoplifting and prostitution" (1975, 1, 15). Other students challenge the assumption of increased female crime. Norland and Shover concluded that "no clear-cut pattern of change . . . can be observed" (1977, 95). And Rita Simon concurs: "The proportion of female arrest for violent crimes has changed hardly at all over the past two decades"; some violent crimes have actually declined. But at the same time property crimes have increased (1975, 38-39). Most of the increase found in another study was related to the use of alcohol and marijuana (Gold and Reimer, 1974). Balkan and Berger, reviewing the whole corpus of research and applying new—1960-1975—data on females under eighteen years of age, found that they resembled data for adults and that in both, "the highest increases occurred in the nonviolent property offenses of larceny, fraud and embezzlement, and forgery and counterfeiting" (1979, 220). For adult women there were exceptions in the case of violent crimes like murder, manslaughter, and aggravated and other assaults. They interpret their findings not as validation of the theory that trends in female criminality are related to the women's liberation movement but as an indictment of the women's movement for lack of concern for the conditions that foster female crime:

> While the women's movement has provided middle-class females with an understanding of sexual oppression, it has not addressed the particular circumstances of working- and lower-class females, who are involved in the majority of female crimes and delinquent activities. . . . The women's movement needs to view sexual oppression not as an isolated event but in its relationship to a female's class position. [1979, 224]

There is, however, one kind of crime that has potential for highly lucrative returns to entrepreneurs if not to the women themselves, namely prostitution. (Even here, though, other ways of making money are becoming available. Two teenage bank robbers told interviewers that there was "more money in [robbing banks] than prostitution and it takes less time" [Balkan and Berger, 223].) Prostitution has been called the oldest profession. Such a statement would be hard to document; much would depend on the definition of a profession.

Prostitution as an Occupation

Prostitution violates one of the fundamental tenets of the female world—the love-and/or-duty ethos. The prostitute does not engage in sexual relations with her customer out of love for him, nor does she have any duty toward him. It is a cash-nexus relationship of a unique kind, determined almost wholly by the Gesellschaft contract ethos, not conforming to the ethos of the female world.

The organization of this occupation varies over time and place. Much of the research and discussion of its control and most of the ideological rationalization for it have been by men from a male point of view. In the nineteenth century respectable women were assured that prostitution would protect them from unbridled male sexuality (Lecky, 1869). But instead of expressing gratitude for this service, "good" women were supposed to shun the prostitute, look down on her, exclude her from their world. She was to be viewed as fallen, not fit for the company of decent women. And the female world, deprived of knowledge about the sexual world of men, accepted the male definition. They did not complain that they had not asked for such protection. Or necessarily even wanted it.

On their own, women in the early associations in the United States did try to serve the fallen woman (Chapter 13). And at the end of the century women's groups were organized against the international white-slave traffic in women and girls. Jane Addams herself was a leading figure in this movement; Jewish women's organizations—in both the United States and Germany—fought the traffic and offered sympathetic help to both actual and potential victims (Hyman, 1978, 17).[17]

There were other women, both in the West and in eastern cities, who became important entrepreneurs, establishing and running high-class houses where attractive women lived in safety and comfort—often, indeed, in luxury—enjoying the company of distinguished patrons (Adler, 1953). These were female worlds in which the disagreeable aspects of the profession or business—getting customers, arranging for payment, specifying the contractual obligations, and the like—were handled by a businesswise madame who supplied emotional support to her "girls." Here are advertisements from *The Gentleman's Directory* for three such New York houses in 1870:

> Temples of Love
>
> The house at No. 79 Marion street is of the first class, and frequented by the elites of the city. It contains six boarders.
>
> The house No. 53 West Houston street is kept by Mrs. Mayer who furnishes the best accommodations for ladies and gentlemen. This house is kept in a very quiet and orderly manner.
>
> The next house, No. 55, is kept by Miss Ada Blashfield, the dashing brunette, who has eight or ten boarders, both blondes and brunettes. These are a pretty lot.

Left to their own devices prostitutes have a harder time of it. They have to learn the business part of their transaction as well as the service aspect. Gagnon describes what is involved in the prostitute's "apprenticeship":

> The learning experience involves more tasks than simply that of getting over the experience of exchanging money for coitus, although this is the informing and central dilemma of the prostitute. It also involves learning ways of approaching males, setting the price, collecting the fee, managing the sexual contract, and letting the customer go. . . . During this apprenticeship period she must learn a specialized argot not only about sexual behavior but also about the naming of others in the environment: customers, steerers, the police, and other prostitutes. The argot is highly value-laden and in and of itself constrains the neophyte into patterns of action and belief. [1968, 594]

Sometimes the neophyte learns these skills and the vocabulary from a more experienced prostitute. But sometimes she is inducted by a male pimp.

The misogyny of the male world is hard on the prostitute. Without the protection of the madams of the old establishments they often find themselves in competition with one another, so "the relationships with other prostitutes . . . carry with them a fair amount of mutual dislike and mutual exploitation" (Gagnon, 595). Still, cut off from the conventional world, they are thrown back on one another. There is a movement afoot, however, especially in England, to make it possible for prostitutes to create a support system for themselves. A member of Parliament, Maureen Colquhoun, has introduced legislation that would take away the stigma of the "brothel" and make it possible for women to live together to protect and support one another, freeing them from organized crime and dependence on pimps. In the United States the feminist movement has also expressed support for self-organization among prostitutes in protection against exploitation. If there is to be prostitution, they argue, it should be controlled by women.

So much, then, for status, the "vertical" evaluative component of the structure of the female world, and for "socioeconomic status" or SES, the "objective" or at least scalar aspect. Because status is itself a complex mixture of a variety of components—legal, formal, informal, ascribed, achieved, accorded, symbolic—and because the three conventional indexes of socioeconomic status—schooling, income, and occupation—are not adequate for the female world (since, except for schooling, they rely almost completely on data from only women in the labor force or at least women who have incomes), it is difficult to combine them into any meaningful comprehensive conceptualization of the social-class structure of the female world as a whole. Whether it is even possible to arrive at such an inclusive, holistic picture may well be challenged. But it is at least worth a try. The attempt is made in Chapter 10.

Notes

1. The variable "SES" gives the illusion that the researcher is outside the system. The researcher and the analyst are looking at it in a purely disinterested way. If they find, as is often the case, that low SES is associated with crime, immorality, antisocial deviance of many kinds, they can report this without implying the distaste they experience or the contempt they feel. They themselves are above all that. Such an approach is presumed to be "value-free."
2. In a study of illiterate males, Freeman and Kassebaum found that they, in effect, develop a culture of their own, with their own symbols of prestige and disgrace, their own idiom (1956).
3. Hannah More believed that schooling should be designed to help people perform the duties of their station in the best possible way; Wollstonecraft, to help women support themselves if they ever needed to. Education of young women in the nineteenth century was designed to help them fulfill their status role; among affluent families, it took place in finishing schools with currricula designed to make them "accomplished" wives. In

an analogous way, "most Negro colleges were regarded by whites as training grounds for janitors and maids" (Lee, 1978).

4. A Gallup poll in 1978 found proportionately more girls (78 percent) than boys (71 percent) planning to attend college (*Parade*, Dec. 24, 1978, 15).
5. For example, the "other" income in female-headed families was 1.12 times greater than in husband-wife families in the $5,000-5,999 bracket; 1.46 times in the $6,000-6,999 one; 1.95 times in the $7,000-7,999 one; 3.38 times in the $8,000-9,999 one; 2.89 times in the $10,000-14,999 one; 2.78 times in the $15,000-24,999 bracket; and, as noted in the text, 1.96 times in the income bracket $25,000 and over.
6. I am amused by the *Oxford English Dictionary* definitions of the housewife, including, in addition to a woman who manages a household ("with skill and thrift"), "domestic economist" but also, as a second definition "a light, worthless, or pert woman or girl," that is "hussy." By 1824 one of the meanings of "hussy" was housewife.
7. As they enter the military today for the same reason. "The Defense Department . . . is having trouble recruiting enough well-qualified males to fill all the jobs in combat units, and it has a surplus of well-qualified female volunteers. Unless women can be assigned to a much broader range of military jobs, the department says, it will be forced either to leave slots in combat units unfilled or to fill them with less qualified men. That is a powerful argument. It says, in effect, that we can have a first-rate military force if women are used to their full capabilities and a second-rate one if they aren't" (*Washington Post* editorial, March 11, 1978).
8. Even in the 1970s women remained predominantly in the "female intensive" industries. Thus between 1970 and 1975, the number of managers and administrators rose from 19 to 23 percent in "female-intensive" industries, but only from 5 to 6 percent in male-intensive industries. Female professional and technical workers in female-intensive industries rose from 21 to 25 percent; in male-intensive industries, from 8 to 10 percent. There was scarcely any increase of women in craft industries, which are primarily male-intensive (Conference Board, 1979). There is no reason to suppose that a large proportion of women could not fill many of the positions now reserved for men. Individual women prove all the time that they can step into spots in the male world and carry on without missing a beat. They have taken over originally male occupations—like secretary and school teaching—and blanketed them into the female world. But they have transformed them in the process. It is doubtful if women could take over either the polity or the economy as they now operate, and run them as they are now run. At some point they would become different kinds of systems.
9. Rosabeth Moss Kanter has explained why in terms of the opportunity structure in the bureaucracy (1977).
10. Work was judged similar or different not in terms of specific occupations such as nurse, teacher, or secretary, but in terms of "structural imperatives." These were: (1) occupational self-direction (closeness of supervision, routinization of work, substantive complexity); (2) position in the organizational structure (ownership/nonownership, level of bureaucratization, place in the supervisory hierarchy); (3) job pressures (time pressure, heavi-

ness and dirtiness of the work); and (4) job uncertainty (risk of losing job, the possibility of being held responsible for things outside one's control or of a sudden and dramatic change in income, reputation, or position). Intellectual functioning, revealed by interviews, included: leisure-time activities and social orientation, and self-conception (authoritarianism-conservatism, criteria of morality, receptivity to change, self-confidence, self-depreciation, fatalism, anxiety).

11. In the 1920s, George S. Counts derived a scale to measure the prestige of occupations, a scale later improved upon in 1943 by North and Hatt. In the 1960s a new series of studies showed that there had been a considerable amount of stability in the evaluation placed on occupations over forty years (Barber, 1968, 291). In all, the occupations tending to be assigned to women rated low.
12. One man challenged the one-sex-world premise by stating that he had worked at a lathe next to a woman; didn't that prove they were in the same world? For an excellent and explicit description of the differentiation between male and female worlds in archetypical form, see Spradley and Mann, (1975). For efforts to keep business and professional women out of even nonwork situations, see efforts of Jaycees to sanction chapters that admitted them (Jolna, 1978).
13. The immigrant issue included such figures of speech as "invading hordes," "yellow peril," "rising tide of color," implying the sinister consequences that would ensue if these inferior masses were allowed in. The language used with respect to women is not quite so dramatic, but the message is often the same: "Allowing women in is dangerous" (Tiger, 1970, 259).
14. A study of four "pink-collar" occupations—beautician, sales worker, waitress, and office worker—showed, for example, that although these workers recognized and resented the low status accorded their work, they nevertheless minded most the absence of "people-centered"—that is, "feminine"—personnel practices and supervision style (Howe, 1977, 242ff).
15. Dorothy E. Smith calls my attention to Sheila Rowbotham's *Women's Consciousness, Man's World* (London: Penguin, 1973, p. 41), in which a woman suddenly realizes she is seeing herself as a "womanthing" through male eyes. She had been watching a Beatles coach trip on television, identifying with them until they entered a strip-tease joint. "I had caught myself going to watch another woman as if I were a man. I was experiencing the situation of another woman stripping through men's eyes. I was being asked to desire myself by a film made by men."
16. From the male point of view these women may be seen primarily as amenities, pleasant ornaments for the enjoyment of men. Thus, Erving Goffman has this to say about the "arrangements between the sexes" in the male world: "the world that men are in is a social construct, drawing them daily from their conjugal milieu to what appear to be all-male settings; but these environments turn out to be strategically stocked with relatively attractive females, there to serve in a specialized way as passing targets for sexually allusive banter and for diffuse considerateness extended in both directions. The principle is that of less for more, the effect is that of establishing the world beyond the household as a faintly red-light

district where men can easily find and safely enjoy interactional favors. Observe that the more a male contents himself with gender pleasantries—systematically available yet intermittent and brief—the more widely can a preferential category of females be shared by males in general" (1977, 318). Since this was written women have begun to protest sexual harassment on the job both by way of publicity and by recourse in the courts. The "gender pleasantries" were not always so pleasant for the woman involved.

17. There is a fairly long history of concern in the female world for the prostitute. For an engrossing story of a prostitute's relationship with an upper-class woman, see Rosen and Davidson's *The Mamie Papers* (1977). An international organization at the turn of the century was attempting to protect women from the white-slave traffic. Roby and Kerr have traced the efforts of the female world to deal with prostitution in New York City (1972).

10

The Social-Class Structure of the Female World

ALTHOUGH SOCIAL CLASS in the male world has preoccupied social scientists almost obsessively at least since Karl Marx, there is not—any more than in the case of social structure itself—a clear-cut consensus on its definition or on the criteria to be used in conceptualizing it. Or even on what the criteria mean (Gans, 1962, 242-243). Still, some recognition of social class is essential for any discussion of social structure.

The *Oxford English Dictionary* gives the oldest known use of the term "class" as "each of the six orders into which Servius Tullius divided the Roman people for purposes of taxation," obviously a conceptualization based on wealth as the criterion. In the English language the oldest definition of class given in the *Oxford Dictionary*—characterized as now "the leading one"—dates back to 1664 and refers to "a number of individuals (persons or things) possessing common attributes, and grouped together under a general or 'class' name; a kind, sort, division." The criteria for grouping the entities are not specified. Nor is status mentioned. Perhaps most influential has been the conceptualization by Marx, in which ownership of the means of production is the criterion for "classification." It yields capitalists and workers, bourgeoisie and proletariat. Power is the operative criterion in some conceptualizations; it yields the concept of the power élite or ruling class. Status is implied rather than elaborated. A functionalist approach emphasizes values; sometimes the term "class culture" is thrown in.

The characterization of class as social implies that it refers to human beings rather than things. Since at least 1694 there has also been a status or rank dimension in some of the definitions. The fifth *Oxford* definition, traced to that date, is "a division of things according to grade or quality, as *high or low, first, second, third*." Not until 1772, however, were both the human and the status components of social class included in the definition. Thus the second *Oxford* definition is "a division of society according to status." This conceptualization yields upper, middle, and lower social classes, or as many more as one wishes to distinguish, from upper-upper to lower-lower. And since status is likely to be locale-based, at the present time residence is sometimes added as a criterion. We commonly assume that everyone knows what we mean by upper, middle, or lower social class; but when we come down to specific families we are often at a loss. Almost everyone replies "middle class" to questions about his or her own class position.

Although the status aspect of social class was recognized as early as 1772, van Beyme believes that in most of the eighteenth century it was still used as analogous with class in the biological rather than in the current evaluative or hierachical sense. It was not, he thinks, a stratification concept, for "even in the nineteenth century class and status were still not sharply differentiated" (1972, 1). The social-class concept, he believes, originated with the French Revolution, "when for the first time wide social strata became aware of class differences" (1). Class came then to refer to "groups whose members are united on the basis of similar economic and social status and common interests" (1).[1] The implied importance of assigning status to the several classes lies in the implied importance accorded to stratification.[2]

Whatever the history of the concept of social class, in the sociological literature at the present time, classes are usually conceptualized in status terms, as levels or strata, some higher than others as measured on various criteria, whether power, wealth, prestige, or some other. If the terms high and low, upper and lower, were not implied, the several classes might well be viewed simply as different kinds of subworlds.[3]

Little of the thinking on social class has been relevant for the female world. "From the late medieval period onward, 'classes' are primarily about men's relations with other men. The subsumption of women into classes distorts social organization generally, and stratification specifically. An adequate account of women and class has yet to be developed, and requires a much greater understanding of gender relations than we now have. In other words, the question of women and class is in many ways premature, and the ellision of women into male classes has the effect of perpetuating female invisibility" (March, 1978). Granted the prematurity and hence inadequacy of analyzing the social-class structure of the female world, it seems preferable nevertheless to ignoring it and hence "perpetuating female invisibility."

Despite the cliché that Judy O'Grady and the colonel's lady are sisters under the skin—a way to render women invisible by sweeping them all into a homogeneous, undifferentiated mass—there have been social-class distinctions among women at least for centuries if not millennia. In our own country, for example, there were mistresses and maids or, even in more egalitarian households, as we shall note in Chapter 11, housewives and "hired girls" or "hired help." There were ladies but also washerwomen. There were Ladies Bountiful who brought food baskets and warm clothing to poor families, especially to "widows and orphans," that is, to poor "female heads of families." There was "friendly visiting" among the poor, which was the precursor of social casework. There were do-good women who searched out the weak, the sick, the handicapped, to succor or rehabilitate them. The social-status rewards were, in fact, not an inconsiderable part of the benevolent work that women undertook in the nineteenth century (Chapter 13). Charitable activities gave a "patina" to a woman's class position (Lasser, 1978). Thus, for example, the Salem Female Charitable Society was a socially exclusive organization that not just anyone could belong to (Lasser). The work of the Boston Female Asylum, also early in the nineteenth century, was plagued by class problems because of its policy of indenturing its young wards to families. We shall have occasion later to mention social-status levels in voluntary groups today (Chapter 11).

Although the social-class structure of the female world has attracted relatively little attention from serious researchers, it has received pervasive notice in novels and plays. The intersection of social class and family by way of marriage has been a nodal point in the female world and stock in trade for fiction by both male and female authors. The stenographer who falls in love with her boss's son or the heiress who marries the family chauffeur (or her bodyguard) thus loom larger in our imagination than the class separatism we see around us. There are, therefore, few data to support a thorough examination of the social-class structure of the female world.

"Classification" versus "Stratification"

Assigning people to classes is one of the commonest mental tasks we perform. We tend to dichotomize them: conservative/radical, religious/irreligious, and so on. Among women, traditional/modern, family-oriented/career-oriented and again so on. But it is more complicated to allocate women to social classes. If we rely wholly on the standard dimensions of socioeconomic status we lose a great many women. As we saw in Chapter 9, although number of years of schooling applies to all women, income and occupation apply only to women in the labor force, omitting nonemployed women and nonincome recipients—clearly, therefore, inadequate for portraying the social-class structure of the female world as a whole. Where are the welfare recipients? The outcasts? A conception of the class structure of the female world has to make room for all women; we cannot limit it to those who fall neatly into establishment categories. In this first attempt to delineate class structure in the female world, a somewhat different, admittedly more subjective, approach is used, one less easily operationalized than socioeconomic status and therefore more vulnerable to challenge. For status allocation relies on qualitative as well as quantitative characteristics, and the status assigned is more inferential than objectively demonstrable, and not even necessarily on a single continuum.

The allocation of socioeconomic status on the three dimensions presented in Chapter 9 was based on research by social scientists. But as noted above, if one directly asks people what social class they are in, they tend to say "middle class," no matter where the researcher locates them. Actually, the very concept of a social-class structure is itself a middle-class one and the several social classes see it from different perspectives (Schatzman and Strauss, 1955). Much, as we saw in Chapter 8, depends on their "reference groups."

Criteria

Despite Lipset's caveat—that "the location of individuals or groups in the status system depends on the opinion of the individuals who go to make up the system rather than the opinion of the sociologist who observes it" (1968, 311)—the following tentative model of the social-class structure of the female world is offered on the basis primarily of a composite of the standard objective demographic variables used to operationalize socioeconomic status—schooling, income, occupation—but also, where these are not applicable, on such subjective behavioral criteria of status as "social climbing," influence, modeling—that is, who wants to be like whom, or who envies whom, and the like. Income of husbands is also taken into consideration.

The classes thus arrived at are taken to be; Society; media-created Celebrities; Intellectuals; white-collar and pink-collar workers; nonemployed housewives; blue-collar and service workers; welfare recipients; and demoralized, broken, homeless, outcast women. The criteria for this categorization or "class-ification" are fairly straightforward and obvious. In the case of Society, for example, money or income of self or husband is a major criterion, as is "family." The celebrity class has an occupational base but it may in some cases rest on adventitious events. Education and—derivatively—occupation are the prime characterizations of the élite of academic, scholarly, learned women. Occupation is clearly the criterion for the white- and pink- and blue collar working-class and service workers. "Housewife" is a kind of catch-all or residual category based on occupation only indirectly, in the negative sense of nonparticipation in the labor force. Welfare recipients have a legally defined status and classifying them is straightforward. The category "outcast" is invoked to include all women who have no moorings, no place—psychologically or sociologically—to go, a status especially vulnerable in a kin- and locale-oriented Gemeinschaft world. Their family ties are tenuous or vanished. And in a world that relies on such ties, such a position is especially deprived. They may be "warehoused" in institutions; they may be the "bag ladies" on the streets of large cities; they may be the panhandlers; they may be runaway girls; they may be in shelters of one kind or another, including jails. They are women who don't count; they are unimportant; they are expendable. But they belong to the female world; they are as much a part of it as, let us say, university or college professors. We cannot ignore them in conceptualizing the female world. That concept has to be all-inclusive. However low on any status hierarchy they are, they may legitimately ask, as Sojourner Truth asked of men, "Ain't I a woman?" And now, as then, the answer from women as from men must be yes, they are, and however unimportant they are or however low their status, they must therefore be included in the female world along with film stars and college professors.

Classifying women is one thing; assigning them status—"stratifying" them from their own point of view—is something else again.

"Stratifying" the Classes

How does one go about assigning social status or position to these several classes? Should they even be conceptualized as "high" or "low"? If so, on what basis? Which way is "up"? or "down"? Since they all lead such different lives, have such different reference groups, wouldn't it be more realistic to speak of them simply as disparate female subworlds? For some purposes, yes. But in the present context, where the basic idea is to see the female world holistically, as an integrated entity, as a variegated whole, as a unitary though not necessarily united structure, the stratification approach is useful.

In his study of Yankee City, W. Lloyd Warner found six levels or "strata": upper-upper; lower-upper; upper-middle; lower-middle; upper-lower; lower-lower (1941). If we apply this schema, we would classify old, family-based Society as upper-upper; newer, upwardly mobile Society as lower-upper; the élite college-educated women as upper-middle; the blue- pink- and white-collar workers as lower-middle, or "working-class"; welfare recipients as upper-lower; and the outcasts, as lower-lower. (Warner made no provision for a middle-middle class.) The status of media-created Celebrities is somewhat equivocal. Cleveland Amory, a social commentator, was of the opinion that they had just about usurped the place of Society, and C. Wright Mills, a sociologist, seemed to concur. Since they may be talented people and sometimes marry into Society, they might well be assigned the status of lower-upper in the Warner schema.

In deference to Lipset's caveat, and in the absence of any serious attempt to test the validity of the status assignment, we attempt to explain in each case why we place it at a specific status level—why, for example, we think of Society as having higher social status than, let us say, the educated élite, or of welfare recipients as having lower social status than white-collar workers. Where possible, the criteria are in behavioral terms.

One more caveat. In each class there may be a range of levels on different criteria. Thus, for example, there may be a range of income and education in Society; a range of income and education among the Celebrities; a range of income and occupations among the highly educated class of women; there is a range of income and schooling in the several occupational categories at the middle level and among nonemployed housewives; there is also a range of income and schooling among service workers. Schooling and occupation may vary among welfare recipients; some are college graduates. Varying levels of education may be represented among the outcast women. Clear-cut objectivity has been sacrificed for a more intuitive—though still, I hope, behavioral—approach.

Society

C. Wright Mills distinguished a number of high-status male élites in our society: local society, metropolitan society, Celebrities, the very rich, top executives, the corporate rich, military leaders, and political leaders (1959). Of these, few have direct relevance for the female world. Society is one that does have relevance, for it is par excellence in the female bailiwick. In Warner's Yankee City, it will be recalled, the upper-upper class consisted predominantly (58 percent) of women

(1942, 102). And although the sex ratio must be kept roughly equal, the arbiters of who should be admitted and who expelled have tended to be mostly women.

Top status is here accorded to Society not only on the basis of Mills' and Warner's precedent but also on the basis of the desire of so many people to be admitted. They show by their very behavior that they want in. The history of Society is in fact one of social climbing, of perennial attempts by outsiders to be allowed admittance. Its story is one of an in-group constantly—and in the long run, futilely—trying to keep the barbarians at the gate, out of the sacred precincts. The fact that so many wanted in is the evidence used to conclude that this was, indeed, a high status.[4]

In the early days of the Republic, the emphasis was egalitarian. With the affluence of the postwar expansion a new kind of Society developed, one that patterned itself on European models. The structure remained but new families kept invading and transforming it. It was a relatively small social entity that had little impact on other aspects of the female world. Society women might engage in philanthropic efforts, but for the most part they had only peripheral contacts with women of other social classes except, of course, servants.

This Society was parochial and unique. But the story reflected in its efforts to keep out social climbers is the story of interesting historical trends. After the Civil War the movement away from the old egalitarianism accelerated. Writers of books on etiquette and other arbiters of social form "saw their mission . . . [as instilling] a more aristocratic style of behavior, one consonant with the improving fortunes of the middle class" (Schlesinger, 1946, 34). Society as an entity with its own norms, codes, manners, standards, values, boundary-maintenance patterns—all extremely expensive—emerged. And, as before, the "ins" bemoaned the invasion of new pretenders lacking all the necessary qualifications except money.[5]

Edith Wharton, who was herself born into Society and therefore had an inside view, described it as of the 1870s. At the bottom of the social pyramid were the "plain people," respectable but obscure, "raised above their level by marriage with one of the ruling class" since people were not as "particular as they used to be" (quoted by Amory, 1960, 26). Catherine Spicer ruled one end of Fifth Avenue and Julius Beaufort the other, so "you couldn't expect the old traditions to last much longer" (26). In 1887, *Town Topics* was tracing the rise and fall of famous Society families. "Where," it asked, "were the Vanderbilts, socially, even five years ago?" (Amory, 25). In 1913, again the sad refrain: "In New York Society the older families never allowed the turmoil of outside life to enter their social scheme. The best houses were absolutely restful, and the present generation will never know the charm and tranquility which was manifest whenever people like Mrs. Schermerhorn, Mrs. William Astor, Mrs. John Jacob Astor, Mrs. Belmont and Mrs. Paran Stevens entertained their friends" (23-24).

In 1924, once more, "the qualifications for admission [to Society] have broken down or been altered. Society is no longer a unified entity" (22). Five years later, the *nouveaux riches* were taking over everyplace; the moneyed intruders were at the very gates of Newport. "Undesirables are penetrating everywhere" (21). In 1945: "There is no longer any real Society" (20); one didn't even need money any more, just clothes. Emily Post reported in 1950 that "the walls that used to enclose the world that was fashionable are all down. Even the car tracks that divided cities into smart and non-smart sections are torn up. . . . There is nowhere to go to see Best Society on Parade" (19). In the 1960s, one Grande Dame was of the opinion that "the past was lousy," and her picture of it confirms this judgment:

> In the old days it was Mrs. Astor and Mrs. Vanderbilt and Mrs. Belmont and there you were. It was all well defined. When Mrs. Belmont gave a dinner and Mrs. Oelrichs came, they weren't speaking and after dinner, the two coteries went into separate rooms. And, if Mrs. Clews hadn't been "taken up" by Mrs. Belmont, she would have been nothing. But she was—and so everything was all right. It was boring, a lot of it, and it may seem rather silly now.

She adds, however, "Just the same there was style. They were the Old Guard and now there just ain't no such thing" (11-12).

There is still some version of Society in communities everywhere, as Warner's studies of the 1930s illustrate. There are still about a dozen individual city volumes of the Social Register, down from twenty-one in 1925 (Amory, 7). "Society" women still live a unique kind of life and there are still people who covet invitations to their dinner parties, who want to belong to their clubs. But more and more women who have access to this lifestyle are building careers—or quasi-careers of their own—Gloria Vanderbilt in design, for example, Jinx Falkenberg in couture, Jacqueline Onassis in publishing. It is still true, as always, that Society is not what it used to be.

Celebrities

By mid-century the category of Celebrity was in process of usurping Society's place as the highest social status. Mills believed it already had. Certainly in terms of adulation it had. One had a longer history; the other, access to a wider public. Society women coveted celebrity status as much as, if not more than, the other way round. So it was still a toss-up which one was higher than the other.[6]

Early in the century the Celebrity was already beginning to catch up with Society. In 1908, for example, an article on "The Dinner Party" advised that "if one wishes to invite the Van Aspics in order to impress another guest, one must first find someone to impress the Van Aspics. One must find them a celebrity" (Amory, 113). Indeed, Amory finds no difference between Society and celebrity status (144), and Mills coined the terms "celebrated socialites" and "society-minded celebrities" for a kind of hybridization (1956, 78). And he believed that the Celebrities had "stolen the show" (75).

The lecture circuit, Chautauqua, the theater, the opera, had all produced famous women before but hardly enough to constitute a class. Only with the advent of motion pictures, radio, and television did this class win high and broad visibility. Mills traces its history to the emergence of the curious social-class phenomenon known as Cafe Society in the 1920s, "when socialities became really bored with Newport, and began to look to Broadway, then to Hollywood, for livelier playmates and wittier companions" (73).[7] Cafe Society, shaped to a large extent by Prohibition, had its local habitat in restaurants and night clubs (72). Since that time it has become the Jet Set, consisting of the Beautiful People, and within a short time it will have some other name.

Mills distinguished three major categories of women among Celebrities: the society lady, the debutante, and the All-American Girl, the queen who "sets the images of appearance and conduct which are imitated down the national hierarchy of glamour, to the girls carefully trained and selected for the commercial display of erotic promise, as well as to the young housewife in the kitchen" (81). The All-American Girl may be debutante, fashion model, or entertainer; in fact, she is an almost interchangeable, all-purpose commodity (82). She is the model Coleman was protesting in his study of adolescent society. She is the young woman in prime time, most delectable for advertisers, media, and all those who need photogenic subjects.

Whichever is viewed as higher, Society and Celebrity status differ markedly in several important ways. "Society" was based on family. That was crucial. It emphasized the importance of women. Courtship itself called for a great deal of supervision and a considerable amount of Society's time was engaged in it. Chaperonage was a serious institution. The début, or "coming out," was a central ritual. Marriage had enormous significance, for it related whole families and even fortunes. Celebrities as a class are quite different. They may or may not have families of independent prestige, but they are in celebrity status as individuals. Families may even have to be sacrificed for the career which produces the celebrity status. There is a considerable amount of talk among film stars, for example, as to whether family life is even possible among Celebrities, and the high divorce rate among them is sometimes explained in terms of competing career and family demands. Most celebrity-status women are par excellence career women. Society, furthermore, tried to maintain in-group exclusiveness. There is no way that Celebrities could do so. Women move in and out of celebrity status quite independently of anyone's permission.

In terms of impact on the female world there is, again, no contest. There are few if any women in Society who serve as models for girls and women in other classes. Popular female stars—Mills' All-American Girl especially—may become models for millions of girls and women. A certain hairdo, makeup, lotion sponsored by a Celebrity on television or in a popular magazine advertisement can become the hairdo, the makeup, and the lotion of an untold number of girls and women. Few Society women have such clout.

I cannot forbear at this point from introducing, parenthetically, one of the most amusing differences between Society and Celebrity status, based this time on sociobiology. Freedman has traced in an evolutionary context, from subhuman primates to human beings, what he calls the gazing phenomenon as related to status. According to this body of research, one can determine the relative status in a dyad or larger group in terms of who watches, looks at, or gazes at whom (1979). In the present context it is interesting to note that traditionally a Society woman's name appeared in the media only three times in her life: when she was born, when she married, and when she died. Publicity, on the other hand, is the sine qua non of the celebrity class. Indeed, Amory thought that "Publiciety" would be a better name than Celebrity for this class. There is, in fact, a curious kind of symbiotic relationship between it and the media. Celebrities often have public-relations experts and the media are both exploitative of and exploited by the Celebrities. Compare this, for example, with the efforts of Jackie Onassis to avoid publicity.

In the quarter-century since Mills wrote and even the fifth of a century since Amory wrote, the nature of celebrity status has changed. And even since Lowenthal made his analysis in 1961, the composition of the entertainers in it has changed. Not only had the proportion of Celebrities from the field of entertainment and sports more than doubled, from 26 to 55 percent, in the twentieth century, but even more striking was their caliber: "While at the beginning of the century three quarters of the entertainers were serious artists and writers, we find that this class of people is reduced by half twenty years later and tends to disappear almost completely at present" (Lowenthal, 1961, 111-112). The mass media—from movies, radio, and television, to popular journals—have accelerated the speed with which one both enters and leaves celebrity status. Personalities are chewed up and devoured. We almost have a celebrity-for-a-day class and may be on our way to what Andy Warhol predicts, a fifteen-minute universal celebrity class (*Washington Post*, April 25, 1979). To ward off the threat of a shortage, the media have created the "professional personality," that is, a personality with no other role than that of providing them with fodder, someone for us to "gaze" at.

Freedman throws an amusing sociobiological light on the celebrity class. He tells us, for example, that "most of our attention, most of our talk and gossip, is directed to and about dominants in our lives. . . . The popularity of gossip columns involves the same principle. About whom do we read? The mighty, the rich, the beautiful, the acclaimed, and the powerful. And which of us can resist at least a glance at these personal tidbits, particularly when they take the hero or heroine down a notch or two. . . . All of us simply pay more attention to and know more about those at the top" (1979, 56-57).

As in other social classes, of course, there is great heterogeneity in the celebrity class. Some members belong definitely in the Establishment; others are not far from the streets. Some were born with silver spoons in their mouths. Others have clawed their way up. They have different publics. Some become or strive to become household words. Some are known only by the haute monde, and prefer it that way.

Different as Celebrities may be among themselves, they do seem to perform one common function. They create a kind of common ground among widely different social classes. A popular Celebrity—like Lucille Ball, for instance—can hold fifty million people enthralled for years. People in every class know who you mean when you speak of Edith Bunker. For a long time Mary Tyler Moore's version of Mary Richards was everyone's ideal of a successful career woman.

We have used influence as one criterion in assessing where to place women in the female status structure and found it especially great in the two highest classes. But both of these classes can exert influence in the male world as well as in the female. They can help in the upward mobility of political and industrial élites. Celebrities can aid political candidates, lend their names to reform causes or sell their names to advertisers. Often all a Society woman has to do is lend her name for a fund-raising committee's letterhead.

We come now to a class that, though missing from Amory's history and Mills' analysis, exerts influence in the female world of a totally different kind from that of either the Society woman or the Celebrity. Its members are viewed here as constituting a genuine élite even though they are outside of the institutional channels in which Mills located his élites. They are the women who do the thinking, make the analyses, supply the new paradigms, do the research, and write the books, reports, and briefs that can change the minds of millions of people. Including sometimes even the minds of legislators, judges, and others in positions of power in the male world.

The Intellectual Class

It is impossible to understand the female world today without understanding the paradoxical, controversial class denominated in standard sociological analyses as "Intellectuals" or as the "intelligentsia," to which these women belong.[8] Although a considerable and increasing amount of research has been dedicated to the study of great women contributors to the arts and sciences, they have usually been viewed as individuals in a given historical context. Such work is, of course, invaluable and indispensable. But in the present context it is not as talented individuals but as members of a sociologically defined class that they invite out attention.

In our country, the term "intelligentsia" has a somewhat pejorative connotation. It was borrowed from the Russian in 1920 and therefore suffers under its Marxist association. But the *Oxford English Dictionary* gives it an objective definition: "the class consisting of the educated portion of the population and regarded as capable of forming public opinion." The more congenial term, "intellectuals," refers to persons who create, discuss, argue, propagate, and criticize ideas.

We are unaccustomed to thinking of women as members of a class of Intellectuals or as part of the intelligentsia. The relevant research has focussed on them primarily as individuals rather than viewing them as a class. One of the best studies of the "intelligentsia" in the female world is that of Rossi in her editorial work for *The Feminist Papers* (1973). But only recently are we beginning to look at women sociological, economic, and political researchers, historians, psychologists, and literary critics in their role as members of an intellectual class performing the classic function of such a class: creating, critiquing, arguing, debating, defending ideas. So for the most part we have to rely on the thinking about Intellectuals as it has developed in the male world. To what extent analyses of the intellectual class in the male world apply to the female world is hard as yet to determine. The subject itself is not wholly unequivocal. Indeed, an early book on the subject—de Huszar's *The Intellectuals* (1960)—has for its subtitle, "A Controversial Portrait." Male scholars do not necessarily agree on either the conceptualization or the function of an intellectual class.

Karl Mannheim sees Intellectuals as, in effect, *sui generis*, detached from any specific class: "One of the most impressive facts about modern life is that . . . intellectual activity is not carried on exclusively by a socially rigidly defined class . . . but rather by a social stratum which is to a large degree unattached to any social class and which is recruited from an increasingly inclusive area of social life" (1960, 63). He adds that "although situated between classes it does not form a middle class" (63). Schumpeter makes a similar point. "Intellectuals are not a social class. . . . [T]hey hail from all the corners of the social world" (1960, 69). But both Mannheim and Schumpeter agree that intellectuals act as though they were a social class. They have in common "education which binds them together in a striking way. Participation in a common educational heritage progressively tends to suppress differences of birth, status, profession, and wealth, and to unite the individual educated people on the basis of the education they have received" (Mannheim, 62). Schumpeter concurs: "they develop group attitudes and group interests sufficiently strong to make large numbers of them behave in the way that is usually associated with the concept of social classes" (70). But to define them simply as an aggregate of all those who have had higher education[9] would be fallacious, for "that would obliterate the most important features of the type . . . , the fact that their minds are all similarly furnished facilitates understanding between them and constitutes a bond" (70).

The common bond does not mean that there is consensus among them on all issues, for there is not. "A great part of their activities consists in fighting each other and in forming the spearheads of class interests not their own" (Schumpeter, 69). Whether they agree with one another or not, members of this class have the same intellectual furniture, know what the problems are, what the issues are, what the arguments are. Discussion, even debate, is possible. With non-intellectuals—not meant as a pejorative term—there is no point in discussion, there is not enough common ground. The intellectuals have been exposed to the same newspapers, journals, periodicals, books, etc. "Have you read . . . ?" is standard cocktail-party—or even serious—talk.

A considerable amount of the discussion by Mannheim and Schumpeter deals with Intellectuals vis-à-vis capitalism, the labor movement, and the like, and is applicable to the female world only by analogy. But Mannheim's conclusion that in seeking fulfillment of their mission—"as the predestined advocate of the intellectual interests of the whole" (64)—they infuse certain intellectual demands into practical politics does seem to apply. Political discourse is called upon to rise above clichés, glittering generalities, appeals to prejudice and myths, and to confront the results of research. The intellectuals transform "the conflict of interests into a conflict of ideas" (Mannheim, 65). "If they had no other achievement to their credit, this alone would have been a significant accomplishment" (Mannheim, 66).

Much of this applies, with suitable modification, in the female world. In this world the "Intellectual" is the one who does the theoretical thinking. Few women in any of the other social classes challenge or defend the status quo on theoretical grounds. These are the women who write the books, do the research, define the issues, give the speeches, write the briefs, make the reports, circulate the memoranda, write the decisions that change people's minds. It is from among them that most of the theoretical leadership in the female world today is drawn. They are the ones with the training, talent, and intellectual skills to provide the theoretical base for thinking about the problems of women both in their own world and vis-à-vis the male world. Sometimes they achieve Celebrity status, as, for example, in the case of Gloria Steinem or Betty Friedan. If the conceptualization we apply is that of a moving caravan rather than a vertical pyramid, many are avant garde, at the head of the procession. But not all. Some of them bring up the rear. But even in the rear they have to meet the issues as formulated by the avant garde. For although they are by no means homogeneous nor sharing in a consensus, both the avant garde and the rearguard are on the same wavelength.

It is sometimes alleged that women in this class—almost everyone's "whipping-girls"—are interested only in improving their own position vis-à-vis the male world. Actually, concern for women of all classes—working-class, welfare—has a long history and today it is a subject of considerable research interest (Smith-Rosenberg, 1975, 197; Roby, in process). Indeed, it might be said that women in this class have a more comprehensive model of the overall class structure of the female world than do women of other classes. Still, to many women they are intimidating.[10]

Rossi finds three peaks of intellectual feminist activity among women in the history of our country: the mid-nineteenth century; the first two decades of the twentieth; and the period beginning in the late 1960s (1973, 616). The feminists who began to surface in the late 1960s do not hark back in every detail to the earlier feminists but they, like their predecessors, have been performing the archetypical critical function of the intellectual. Their ideas, like a chicken through a boa's body, are being digested slowly all along the way.

There are some women intellectuals who have not identified with the female world. They have had no "class consciousness" as females. They have viewed themselves as writers, scientists, lawyers, judges, administrators, artists, or whatever particular role their discipline assigns to them, but their models and mentors have been male. Some have even served as apologists for the status quo. If they identified themselves with the female world it was to justify and rationalize the lot of women.

Where to place women intellectuals in the social class structure of the female world is even more perplexing than where to place male intellectuals in their world. Lipset found in 1959 that whereas academic men felt themselves to be viewed as having low social status, in public opinion surveys they were actually placed high. "Professors came out fourth among 24 categories, and 38 pecent . . . placed them definitely in the 'upper class' " (1959, 510). Their family backgrounds also placed them in a relatively high status. We know that, because of more rigorous selective processes, academic women come from higher social-class backgrounds than do men (Bernard, 1964). And it is true that on talk shows or in public debate, the apellations "professor" or "doctor" before a woman's name tend to endow her with a modicum of status. But the women we are discussing are not necessarily professors or doctors or even academics. They are simply those women, whatever their positions, who originate the new ideas, spread them, discuss them, promulgate them, and, in general, perform the function of Intellectuals. Although education and/or influence is high in this class, they are placed lower than Celebrities because the range of their influence is more restricted. Their influence is also quite different from that of the Celebrity. Although almost every Celebrity would like to write a book—and many do—or join this class, it is usually a secondary social-mobility goal, an ornament to add to their status as Celebrities.

The Housewife

The nonemployed housewife who does her own work, whatever her husband's income or occupation, is in an equivocal position in the female world. Her status is an example of the disjunction between formal or theoretical status and actual social status. The theoretical status accorded to homemakers themselves is high. They have been assured, since at least Beecher's time and the days of women's sphere, that homemaking is the most important work in the world. Its importance was one of Beecher's most telling arguments in reconciling women to their sphere. Clearly, in a society where families live in separate, individual households, managing them and taking care of their inhabitants are of the utmost importance. Actually, however, the social status accorded to the work of the household, including the care of children, is low and hence it is experienced as low by those who do it. Wilma Scott Hiedi, applying the values assigned to several kinds of functions in the *Dictionary of Occupations*, found that those dealing with housework and child care ranked at the bottom of the list. The social status of the homemaker had declined so drastically that by the 1970s it was a brave woman who—often defiantly—answered that she was a housewife when asked what she "did." As more than half of all adult women are now in the labor force, the nonemployed housewife has become a "minority," a "deviant." An increasing number come to feel denigrated, put down, defensive. "Let's face it," said one housewife to a researcher, "to most women in the movement being a housewife is the lowest of the low—and the homemakers know it" (Howe, 1978, 202).

Statuswise, the nonemployed housewife would thus be placed below the Intellectual or professional or businesswoman because it is only with respect to them that she is likely to label herself "only a housewife." But she should probably be placed above blue-collar or even low-level white collar workers because for many women it is still a sign of status *not* to "have to work." On television game shows she is even complacent. And even at low income levels she probably feels above welfare recipients.

Homemaking is an occupation, as Lopata reminds us (1971), that has no admission requirements, no officially established standards of performance. Anyone can become a housewife. And for a hundred years the destructive effect the occupation of housewife has on her mind and health has been discussed. It is extremely hard for one's self-esteem or self-evaluation to withstand such negative evaluation from the outside world. It is acceptable when one is a member of the majority. It becomes difficult as a member of a minority.

White-Collar, Pink-Collar, and Blue-Collar Workers

Although all three conventional variables for measuring social status—education, income, and occupational prestige—combine to accord fairly low status to white-, pink- and blue-collar workers, they share middle-class status in the present schema. In appearance they may be indistinguishable from business and professional women. They may not "look up" to the business or professional woman but they may be intimidated by them. Service workers are aware of their low position, as, indeed, are other pink-collar workers. Howe did not find social status a primary problem among the pink-collar women she talked to (working conditions and pay were) but the subject did come up spontaneously. Thus, from a beauty shop worker: "People won't tell you this, they think we don't know what they're feeling, but a lot of them think . . . we're lower class." From a waitress: "Oh, yeah. Most people on the outside look down on you. . . . This is the thing I object to about this job more than anything else."

It is puzzling to know what to do with prostitution as an occupation—where, that is, to assign the prostitute in the class structure. Because the site and working hours of prostitutes were so different from those of more conventional women there was—and is—little opportunity for interaction between prostitutes and "respectable" women. Prostitutes therefore develop their own culture, suitable for their own life style. They are also so highly differentiated, from expensive, "high-class" call girls to streetwise but ignorant streetwalkers, that it is difficult to locate them in the class structure of the female world. They probably fall into a standard occupational slot if they are employed or are tallied as nonemployed "spouses" if they told the census-taker that was what they were.

Welfare Recipients

In terms of publicity, welfare recipients deserve "Celebrity" status as much as do the Beautiful People. Some exceptionally clever "cheater" or other is in or near the headlines a good deal of the time. But the position of these "chiselers" in the class structure is low, both in terms of self-evaluation and in terms of the stigma and shame attached to their status since Elizabethan times, when the Poor Laws were administered in such a way as to make the "dole" the last resort. Almost any status was better than that of being dependent on public charity. True, women of the upper middle class—especially as professional social workers—have been trying to mitigate this shame but, although it has been mollified with the ideology of welfare as a right, few women would prefer to remain in this status if there were feasible alternatives. Not the least of the penalties of this low status is the demeaning treatment of the recipients—even those who happen to be, as some of them are, college women—from all the institutions they have contact with, including the very bureaucracies designed to serve them (Belle et al., 1979).

Outcasts

The conception of a society as either a system of interrelated stations or a system of open classes or statuses implies that it can accommodate everyone. There is a place for all, high or low. But it has been clear for millennia that there were always some for whom there was no place. We have already noted old maids, widows, and orphans. Also fallen women, unmarried mothers told never to darken the family's door again. And always the sick, the lame, the blind, the old. When or if they could be neatly tucked into families they became more or less invisible. But in the nineteenth century the new societal structure had a harder and harder time accommodating these misfits, these deviants, these out-of-sync individuals. There really was no place for them. They became the "dependent, defective, and delinquent classes," now numerous enough to call for inclusion in academic courses in the colleges and universities (Bernard and Bernard, 1942).

The low status of these women seems to require no explanation.[11] No one wants to be in their position if she can help it. Some of these women may reject rescue, but that is part of the denigration of their status. We usually try to avoid even looking at the "shopping-bag ladies" on city streets, or at the beggars who accost us. We "store" some outcasts in hospitals for the insane. Powerless, rejected, alienated, lacking in bonds to the structured—even female—world, they are human ciphers. Only recently are they coming to be "repossessed." Shelters are being built to salvage them before they become unsalvageable. There is a respectable research literature on women in jails, nursing homes, hospitals, shelters. Apparently because they are a more recent phenomenon, less is known about the rugged individuals who find the establishment intolerable, the price exacted by it for nonconformity too high, and the rewards for a free-wheeling life sufficient to make it worthwhile. Among them are the bag ladies who find life on the streets congenial—at least preferable to living with resistant sons or daughters. One such woman reported in the Washington press makes the rounds of supermarkets where she rummages through the piles of discarded food. She salvages what she can and trundles it around the city in a cart, dispensing it to less entrepreneurial outcast women on the streets or at the church where they sometimes resort for sleep. Her search for and dispensing of food prevent her from feeling useless. She quotes Shakespeare and does *not* feel low-class. It is other people who classify her thus. The idea that there are women who are successful in the status of outcast is disturbing.

Computation of Size of Classes

It is impossible, with the data available, to determine the precise dimensions of the classes sketched above, especially in view of the criteria we have been using, which, in effect, count oranges with apples. How, for example, can we determine how many women there are in Society? or how many Celebrities there are at any given time? There is a considerable amount of moving up and down in the female world. The difference between the old station concept of social structure and the open-class concept is not that one had status differences and the other hadn't, but that in the station concept, membership was fixed at birth and in the other it is not. The number and relative size of strata are determined by a wide variety of economic and political forces. It would be diversionary to attempt to explore all these forces. But it may be relevant to comment on the nature of the boundaries that delineate the strata.

In an open society like ours, the boundaries are permeable. They may even overlap, as, by analogy, in the civil service system, in which a person may advance within any one grade level step by step but still remain in the same grade even though her salary is higher than that of a woman a grade above her on the organizational chart.

One more comment. It has been pointed out for quite some time that mass production has made it possible for most women to dress well. Except for particularly chic and clothes-conscious women, one can hardly distinguish a young woman of one class from a young woman of another by appearances alone. Even the welfare recipient is frequently indistinguishable from the typist. And women's magazines today—as they have done for decades—beam a never-ending barrage of lessons on decor, etiquette, manners, entertaining, and other cues to class to an enormous and accepting audience. Styles of living become homogenized and boundaries blurred. The size of a class becomes problematical. Despite all these problems, the attempt is made. The results are shown in Table 10-1.

First, Society. In 1892, it consisted of the families of the four hundred people who could be accommodated in Mrs. Astor's Fifth Avenue ballroom. Some forty years ago one writer believed he could encompass Society in sixty families (Lundberg, 1937). Amory in 1961 could vouch for the Coats of Arms of 525 families. The *Social Register*—Society's "Who's Who"—which began in 1887, reached a peak of twenty-one cities in 1925. But how to arrive at an adequate estimate of the number of people included in Society today? On the assumption that, as of 1970, a woman could hardly be an active participant in Society with an annual income of less than $50,000 at her disposal, the number is more or less arbitrarily placed at 203,370, which is the number of nonearning wives in husband-wife households with incomes of $50,000 or more. It might well, of course, be twice that number. In any event, however, it is minuscule.

TABLE 10-1 First Approximation to Class Structure of Female World, 1970*

Class	Number
Society, Celebrities, "Intellectuals"	735,494
Upper Middle	8,321,939
Middle	21,728,314
Lower Middle	12,391,059
Welfare Recipients	2,714,000
Outcasts	1,082,455
Nonemployed Divorced, Widowed, Separated	15,350,000
Unaccounted for	11,596,739
Total Female Population 16 Years of Age and Over	73,920,000

*Source: 1970 Census, Occupational Characteristics, Table 1.

It is especially difficult to determine how many female Celebrities there are, especially since, as noted above, they come and go with such frequency. In 1970 (according to the Census on occupations), there were about 54,000 female actors, athletes, dancers and designers, one population from among whom Celebrities are likely to arise. In addition, there were about 33,000 musicians and composers, almost 40,000 painters and sculptors, and almost 17,000 writers, artists, and entertainers not included above. All told, then, there were, let us say, roughly 144,000 women in the likeliest Celebrity-generating population. If we add a certain number of women who achieve celebrity status in other areas, the eligible population for this class may be, roughly, about 200,000. It is important to note, however, that a large part of the eligible population is unemployed and that those who are employed often have restricted range in which to achieve celebrity status.

In the class of the intellectual élite we include those in the learned professions (clergy, medicine, law), academic women (university and college teachers), social scientists, authors, editors. Not all of them are influential, but they are the population from among whom the influential women arise. In addition there must also be included women in decision-making administrative positions. As of 1970 there were roughly about 332,124 such women. Small, but still larger than either the Society or Celebrity classes. And, in any event, larger than a stricter criterion would warrant. The fifth edition of *Who's Who of American Women* (1968-1969), which would include both this élite and Celebrities, listed only about 22,000 women.

Below this three-pronged élite is a class consisting of the 7,520,317 women in occupations with prestige ratings of forty-five or more and the 801,632 nonearning wives of husbands earning between $25,000 and $49,999, totaling 8,321,939. Next comes a class of women in occupations with scores between thirty and forty on the occupational prestige scale—15,022,820—and the 6,705,494 nonearning wives of husbands with incomes between $10,000 and $24,000, amounting to 21,728,314 women. Following them is a class consisting of the 1,185,965 women in occupations with prestige scores under thirty and the 12,391,059 nonearning wives of husbands earning less than $10,000. In 1970 there were 2,714,000 women eligible for aid to families with dependent children (Ross and Sawhill, 1975, 102). There were other women receiving welfare payments also, but most who do, fall into the AFDC program. It is difficult to arrive at an accurate estimate of the number of women who are outside the class structure, the outcast women, the homeless women, the abandoned women. A rough approximation may be arrived at by looking at women not in households. In 1970 there were 120,913 in rooming houses; 2,270 in flophouses; 259,177 in mental hospitals or homes for the mentally retarded; 630,685 in homes for the aged; and 69,410 inmates of other kinds of institutions, a total of 1,082,455.

These classes account for only 46,973,261 out of the total of 73,920,000 females sixteen years of age and over. Among those who are not included are the 15,350,000 nonemployed separated, widowed, and divorced women who leave on the records none of the clues we have depended on, and 11,596,739 other women for whom sufficient data are lacking. Some of these woman may show up among welfare recipients, some among outcasts. In any event, they would undoubtedly swell the low-income brackets. In 1970 the median income of separated women was $2,814, of divorced women, $4,048, of widowed women, $2,177.

The "Shape" of the Female World

Bernard Barber tells us that a social structure may be pyramidal or diamond-shaped, the first tending to characterize traditional societies and the second modern ones. Traditional societies, being less differentiated, have a relatively small number of status levels and the high positions are few. Modern societies are highly differentiated and there is more room, if not at the top, at least above the bottom. "In a pyramidal structure the majority of roles (and therefore the individuals who occupy them) rank very low" (Barber, 1968, 295). In the modern world, on the other hand, "a number of fundamental social and cultural changes are resulting in what seems to be a general trend in all societies toward an increasingly diamond-shaped distribution of roles along many of the dimensions of their social stratification system." The diamond-shaped structure is associated with "strong pressures toward social equality as well as a need for increasing numbers of middle-ranking functionaries" (295).

One might well raise questions with respect to the relationship between shape and equality. Much depends on the range between top and bottom. Thus, for example, in the hypothetical shapes shown in Figure 10-1, the relatively flat pyramid is related to equality and the elongated diamond is certainly not. In general, however, perhaps Barber's conclusion may be taken as valid in real-life societies and, as a policy, it is probably more desirable to flatten or equalize a shape by raising the bottom levels than by lowering the top levels; but the levels to be raised in a pyramid are probably "heavier" than those in a diamond. In any event, we need not take the relationship between structural shape and either traditionalism or modernism too seriously in order to profit from the insights of the conceptualization. For representational purposes the shape concept serves the useful purpose of enabling us to see the female world from a holistic perspective. Figures 10-2, 10-3, 10-4, and 10-5, based respectively on Tables 9-1, 9-3, 9-6, and 10-1,

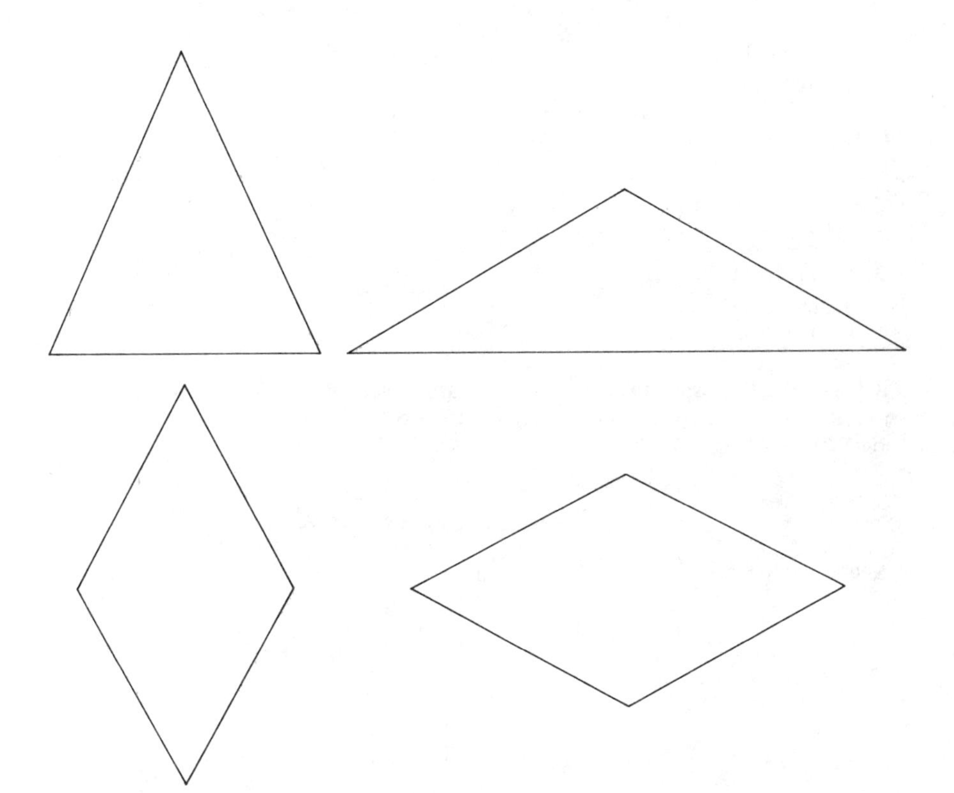

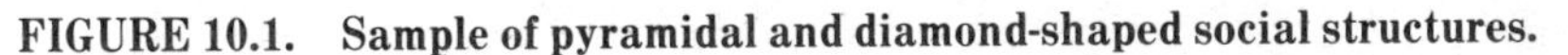

FIGURE 10.1. Sample of pyramidal and diamond-shaped social structures.

show graphically the shape of the female world as reflected in years of schooling, income, occupational prestige, and social class as here measured. Since we have viewed the female world as essentially Gemeinschaft, and therefore traditional, in nature, its social structure should conform to the pyramidal pattern. Only one of the four figures—the one based on income—actually does conform to it.

The educational structure (Figure 10-2) is clearly diamond-shaped. We know that number of years of schooling is increasing for everyone, so that in time those with less than grade-school education will all but disappear, leaving a pyramidal pattern. Such a pattern would not, of course, reflect a traditional society. If the elimination of the lowest levels is going to be matched by an equal increase in college and postgraduate study or continuing education—which seems likely (Astin, 1976)—the probable result would seem to be a moderately flat pyramid, suggesting, however, a tilt toward egalitarianism rather than toward traditionalism.

Income is not a useful index of differentiation in the female world in the sense Barber implies. The shape of the income distribution (Figure 10-3) is—like that of most income distributions—clearly pyramidal, re-

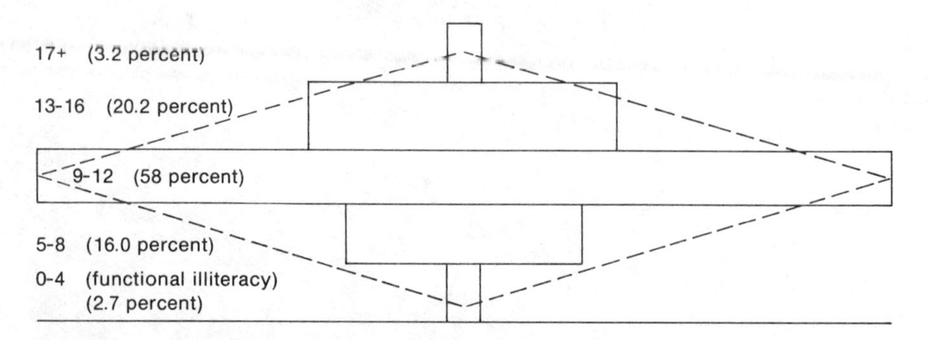

FIGURE 10.2. Shape of female world, years of schooling. Source: Bureau of the Census, Educational Attainment in the United States: March, 1977 and 1976. Population Characteristics, Series P-20, no. 314, Dec., 1977, Table 1, p. 7.

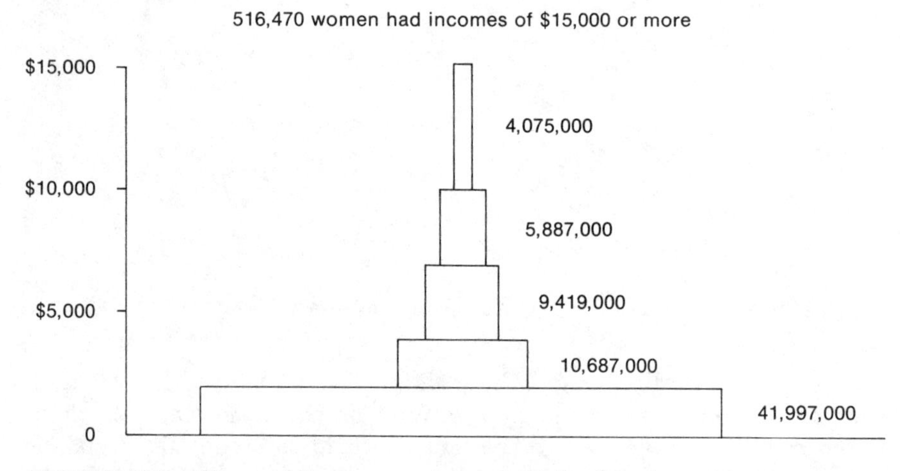

FIGURE 10.3. Shape of the income structure of the female world. Source: Statistical Abstract of the United States, 1977, p. 471.

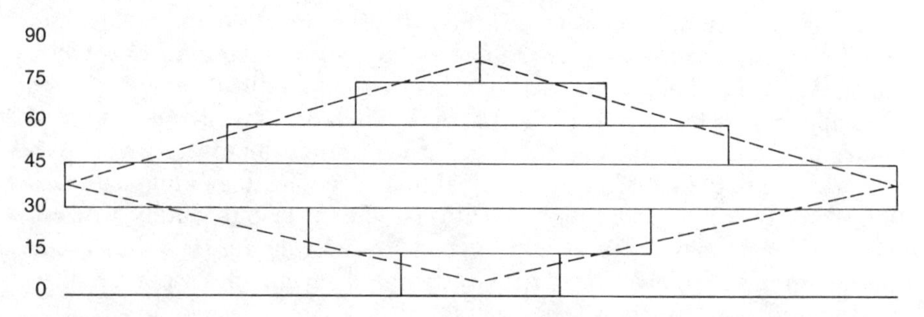

FIGURE 10.4. Structure of the female world: occupational prestige. Source: Occupational Data, 1970 Census; Prestige scores from Report of the United States Civil Rights Commission, Social Indicators of Equality for Minorities and Women (Government Printing Office, August, 1978).

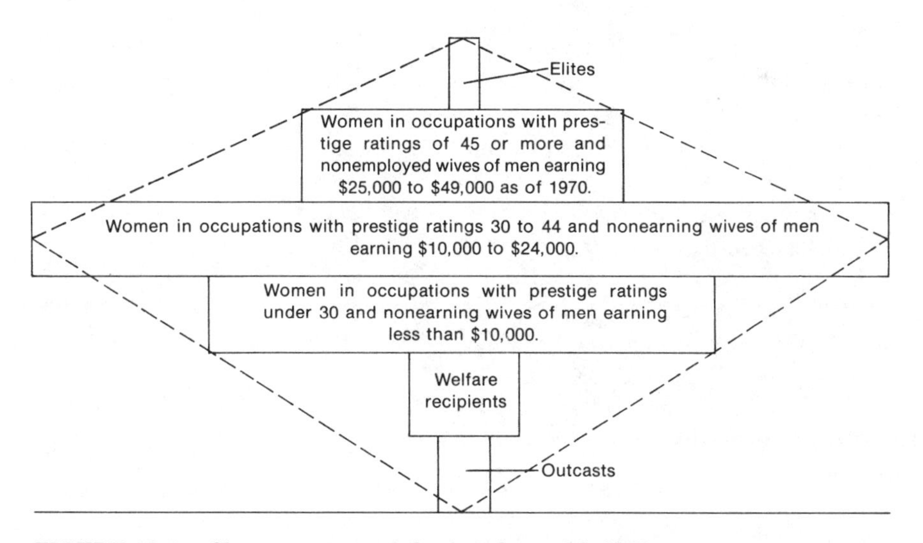

FIGURE 10.5. Class structure of the female world, 1970. Source: Table 9/1. See Addendum for Legend.

flecting, indeed, a fairly undifferentiated structure. Very few women have high incomes. Although many share the high status that goes with high income, that is not the same as having the income in their own right (Chapter 9). Since income in kind—"room and board"—is not included, nonearning wives are low in the income structure.

The shape of the occupational prestige structure (Figure 10-4) reflects a fairly flat diamond. Most women cluster in the occupations at or just below the midpoint—forty-four—of the Temme scale. The fact that there is a ceiling—eighty-eight—for this measure of occupational prestige may have the effect of compressing the several levels. But there is no doubt at all about the pyramidal shape.

In a way, Figure 10-5 compensates somewhat for the defects in Figure 10-3, for here nonearning wives are not relegated to the lower levels but are class-assigned on the basis of their husbands' income. The shape is, as in the case of education and occupational prestige, clearly a diamond. The extremely small number of women in the three-pronged top class cannot begin to provide symmetry vis-à-vis the lowest classes, but, with all the deficiencies—mensural, technical, and conceptual—inherent in the mode of arriving at this figure, the diamond shape still seems incontrovertible. Even if we grant the biases introduced all along the line, it is hard to see how they could have been great enough to force a diamond shape on data not intrinsically amenable to it. The conclusion seems inescapable to me that the social-class structure of the female world is a relatively egalitarian one in the sense that three classes encompass two-thirds of the women who could be accounted for in one way or another and 90.4 percent of those for whom census clues were available. The female world seems to be primarily a middle-class, if not a wholly egalitarian, world.

A social-class system is far too complex to be represented by any one schema. Within any one class level there are numerous groups and cliques, each with its own relative position. Membership in some middle-class groups, for example, is more sought after than membership in other groups. One upper-middle-class sorority ranks higher than another. One lower-middle-class lodge auxiliary ranks higher than another. We shall have more to say of such groups in Chapter 12, but before we leave the subject of social class we turn in Chapter 11 to look at two salient examples of social class: in employer-employee relationships among women in the household, and in the world of volunteerism.

Notes

1. The nineteenth century reserved the concept of class for the middle and working classes, tying class to the production process. Marx finally settled for two—owners of the means of production and workers—but though conflict between these two classes was the central theme of his work, he was not preoccupied with the concept per se (van Beyme, 1972, 1-19).
2. For a discussion of the relationship between class and status, see Lipset, 1968, 202-203.
3. In some countries, such, as England, class has some of the characteristics of an ethnic group. Since each class knows its place, each can interact with the others without looking down or up at the others. Classes have also been viewed as subcultures (Gans, 1962).
4. Amory has traced three centuries of Old Guards complaining of the invading Upstarts. To the survivors, Society was always a thing of the past. It was never what it used to be. Lesser breeds without the law were always in process of displacing the true elect. Society has always been dying. In 1651, the Massachusetts Bay Court was already complaining about women of "meane condition, education, and calling" who were wearing silk or tiffany hoods (31). George Bancroft noted at a party in Jackson's White House that "the number of ladies who attended was small; nor were they brilliant" (28). Tocqueville in the same year observed that "the aspect of Society [had been] totally altered" over the previous sixty years. "The families of the great landed proprietors are almost all commingled with the general mass. . . . The last trace of hereditary ranks and distinctions is destroyed; the law of partition has reduced all to one level" (28-29). In the West, waves followed waves in the 1830s and people were being admitted to Society who would never have been ten years earlier (28). In 1847, an obituary noted that the generation of the deceased—Mr. James Roosevelt—had been "proud and aristocratical . . . the only nobility we had—

now we have none" (27). A Southerner in 1856 sickens at Society in New England, which he finds hardly "fitted for well-bred gentlemen. The prevailing class one meets with is that of mechanics struggling to be genteel, and small farmers who do their own drudgery, and yet are hardly fit for association with a southern gentleman's body servant" (27).

5. Thus in 1868: "It is undeniable that changes, and changes not for the better, have been taking place during the last few years in American social life. . . . The war enabled men to amass fortunes in an incredibly short time. . . . These leaders of gayety flutter in the admiring gaze of the stupid and ignorant masses. . . . Where there is a display of unbounded wealth, such old-fashioned articles as morality and good taste are often despised" (Amory, 26).
6. The changing status relationships between Society and Celebrity status are illustrated by a story that went the rounds some years ago. A Grande Dame Society woman invited Fritz Kreisler, the famous violinist, to perform at a tea party she was giving. His fee was $5,000. No problem. In the course of the negotiations she remarked that of course he would not speak to any of the guests. "In that case," he was alleged to have replied, "my fee will be only half." Mrs. Vernon Castle, a famous ballroom dancer, told a similar story of being engaged to dance at a party before World War I. She found later—after she herself had become a member of Society—that the changing status of Celebrities was the most important change in her time. "Celebrities of today," she noted, "have no idea how socially unimportant you were in the old days" (Amory, 112). The loss of credibility of the whole concept of Society's superiority can be traced in the treatment accorded them by the *Social Register*. Katharine Hepburn and Princess Grace of Monaco were not included; Jane Wyatt was dropped when she went on the stage, but restored when she went on television. Shirley Temple's husband was dropped when he married her (Amory, 130). With the change in composition of the celebrity class, there is a kind of miniregression. Thus, for example, in many exclusive New York City cooperative apartment buildings, Celebrities are not permitted to buy at any price.
7. Lowenthal has traced the changes in the criteria for male popularity in the first four decades of this century as revealed in biographical stories in the *Saturday Evening Post* and *Collier's* magazines. In 1901-1914, almost half (46 percent) were political leaders; by 1941, only a fourth were. Business and professional heroes declined only from 28 to 20 percent (1961, 111). Further, the contents of the stories at the present time do not deal with the serious work of the subjects but rather with the trivia of their private lives (1961, 118-123). An analysis of female celebrities over the same period might show similar trends.
8. Traditional women do not necessarily welcome the intellectual leadership of this intellectual class any more than labor craved the leadership of Intellectuals in the nineteenth century. But Intellectuals did, nevertheless, invade labor politics. They had an important contribution to make. "They verbalized the movement, supplied theories and slogans for it—class war is an excellent example—made it conscious of itself and in doing so changed its meaning" (Schumpeter,77). An analogous relationship exists

between feminists and a large number of women who are "not women's libbers, but . . ." (see Chapter 14).

9. There have, of course, always been talented women who supplied leadership without academic credentials. A recent example is Louise Kapp Howe, who found the academic style stifling rather than stimulating (1977, 227).
10. Early in the 1920s when the League of Women Voters was organizing local chapters in cities around the country, many middle-class women who should have constituted the grassroots stayed away. The leaders, schooled in the suffrage movement, were too high-powered for them.
11. For a historical perspective on the institutionalizing of female outcasts, see Peter N. Stearns, "Old Women: Some Historical Observations," *Journal of Family History* 5 (Spring, 1980): 44-57.

11

Social Class in the Female World: Cases In Point

THE OPERATION AND MAINTENANCE OF THE HOUSEHOLD constitute the largest "industry" in the country in terms of the numbers engaged in it, both as "producers" and as "consumers." In this industry both employers and employees—if there are any—are likely to be women. The work site is a small "firm" or "plant." In this industry there has long been a labor "problem" with consequential impact on the female world, multifaceted and ramifying.

From the point of view of the housewife, the availability of domestic help may make all the difference between entering the labor force and remaining at home. The life style of countless couples today hinges on "the politics of housework" (Mainardi, 1970). The question of who shall do the housework does not equal in urgency the question of who shall rear the children, but it is nevertheless basic. The very existence of the independent household depends on someone's willingness—whether on the basis of love-and/or-duty or of monetary wages—to do the countless chores called for in maintaining it.

The passing of the old live-in servant in the second decade of this century made an enormous difference in family life. Technology was, of course, also involved (Chapter 17), but let no one sweep away the importance of household help in the female world. As long as women are held responsible for household maintenance, the matter of domestic service will loom large in the female world, no matter how it is supplied. On the side of the domestic workers themselves, the matter is by no means insignificant. Though domestic service is declining as an occupation, it remains sizable in the composition of the labor force.

Nor should the macrosociological perspective be neglected. The scarcity of servants has had repercussions on the whole social structure, not only on the women seeking household help and the women seeking household service. Harriet Martineau noted over a hundred years ago, for example, that boarding-house life had become almost compulsory for Americans as a result of the difficulty of getting domestic workers (1837, ii, 245; Salmon, 1897, 55-56). And, at the other end of the social scale, Cleveland Amory believes that today's "servant problem," long "Society's favorite topic, is . . . an argument for the fact that Society has been levelled" (1960, 523). He continues: "The servant, it would seem has, consciously or not, challenged the whole social structure of which he [*sic*] was, for so long, the permanent prop" (524).

Some Demographic Trends

We have noted earlier that although "occupation housewife" is the largest single category of workers in the United States, it does not show up in the extensive literature on the labor force.[1] Indeed, the housewife is not even viewed as part of the labor force at all (Jaffe and Stewart, 1951). But although the housewife does not show up in the labor-force statistics, the paid household worker does. And the worker in this category is almost certainly female. Her precipitous decline in numbers has been among the most remarkable trends in the labor force, with repercussions among the most influential, though not spectacular, of all changes in recent decades.

In 1900 private household workers constituted half of all service workers, a category that itself first appeared in the census of 1870. The number of private household workers reached a peak of about 14 million in 1910 and declined thereafter, fairly precipitously after 1940 (Bogue, 1959, 477). Within these long-time trends, "employment as private household workers . . . tends to fluctuate with economic conditions." Such employment tends, understandably enough, "to bulk especially large during periods of economic depression, and to decrease when there are acute labor shortages " (476). Domestic work, in brief, seems to have been, and continues to be, a last resort for women, taken only when other alternatives are not available, as during a depression.

The demographic character of those engaged in household work continues to change. In the nineteenth century, it consisted overwhelmingly of black and immigrant women. Between 1960 and 1970, the ethnic composition came to include more persons of Spanish origin and other nonwhite, nonblack persons (4.9 percent and 0.9 percent respectively) than in earlier years. There was a correspondingly slight decrease in the proportion of whites and blacks.[2] Domestic workers were becoming older; the median age in 1970 was 49.4 years compared with 44.4 years in 1960. They were slightly better schooled in 1970 than in 1960—9.0 years in 1970, 8.6 in 1960.

A Historical Survey

We noted in Chapter 8 that power was not a suitable dimension for conceptualizing class in the female world. But the relationship between the household worker and her employer, the housewife, constitutes an interesting analogue to the male power paradigm. Thus the history of labor in the male world has had its counterpart in the female world, for the household as a work site had its work-force problems no less than the business or industrial firm. Indeed, this particular "labor problem" long antedated labor problems in the industrial world. The rights of servants and mistresses in the home seemed no less urgent than those of employees and employers in the industrial world. Indeed, the pattern of rights of men in industry, or lack of them, was originally forged on the basis of the earlier common-law definition of master and servant. In neither case was the issue seen in a political context until well into the twentieth century. But the issues were extremely old.

In 1636, for example, Mary Winthrop Dudley was writing to her mother in England asking her to send a different servant ("redemptioneer") to replace the one she had, who had become impossible: "At first coming [to] me she carried her selfe dutifully as became a servant; but since through mine and my husband's forebearance towards her for small faults, she hath got such a head and is grown soe insolent that her carriage towards us, especially myself is unsufferable. If I bid her doe a thing shee will bid me to doe it my self. . . . If I should write to you of all the reviling speeches and filthie language shee hath used towards me I should but grieve you." (Salmon, 1897, 35). In the face of such lack of respect and deference, sanctions had sometimes to be invoked. In 1645, for example, by order of the General Court in Connecticut, one Susan C. was sent to the house of correction, sentenced to hard labor and a coarse diet, "for her rebellious carriage toward her mistress" (Salmon, 36). More than two and a half centuries later, Harland and Van de Water were saying that "mistress and maid . . . were not foreordained from all eternity to be sworn enemies" (1905, 420). They only seemed to be.

By 1880, "literary women" had shed pints of ink over reams of foolscap on the subject of domestic service (Harland, 1880, 132). But it was not until 1897 that the first academic, statistical study of domestic service was published. In it, Lucy Maynard Salmon, a Vassar professor, divided the history of domestic service in America into three periods: the colonial; the first seventy-five years of the Republic, that is from the Revolution to mid-century; and the second half of the nineteenth century. The twentieth-century story has since been told by David M. Katzman (1978).

In colonial times some of the indentured servants or "redemptioneers" were convicts, but some were "free willers." Some were Englishwomen, but some were black, some Indian, and some were Irish (who seemed the most troublesome to their mistresses). "As early as 1718 there was a complaint of the Irish immigrants in Massachusetts" (Salmon, 20). Some of the white women who came were from the "lower classes; some who were not lower class came to prevent disastrous marriages" (21). Some of the "redemptioneers" rose socially at the end of their period of indenture and became prominent members of the community (48). But most were considered "off-scourings" of England and formed a distinct social order, lower than their mistresses. Their descendants, Salmon tells us, became "poor whites" (49). Long after the system was abolished the hard-pressed mistresses looked back with nostalgia to colonial times, when servants knew their place. Not so, says Salmon; they never did know their place. Things were no better in colonial times than they were later. "The social position of all servants was lower than that of their employers, and the gulf between the two was more difficult to span. Service was difficult to obtain and unsatisfactory when secured. Servants complained of hard work and ill treatment, and masters of ungrateful servants and inefficient service, and both masters and servants were justified in their complaints" (53).

The legal relations between master and servant were explicitly defined with respect to length of service, wages, and the mutual obligations of both parties to the contract during the period of service. "But this very definiteness of the contract was due to the fact that the relationship between the two parties was an arbitary one and could not have been preserved without this legal assistance. In default of a better one, the system of white servitude may have served its age fairly well; but its restoration," Salmon warned, if indeed restoration were possible, "would do nothing to relieve in any way the strain and pressure of present conditions" (53).

In the second period, during the first years of the Republic, there were halcyon days, at least in the North. Now the theory and practice of democracy were in harmony. Domestic workers were no longer called servants; they were "help." "The social chasm that had existed in the North between employer and employee, under the system of bonded servants, disappeared. The free laborers, whether employed in domestic service or otherwise, were socially the equal of their employers, especially in New England and in the smaller towns. They belonged by birth to the same section of the country, probably to the same community; they had the same religious belief, attended the same church, sat at the same fireside, ate at the same table, had the same associates; they were often married from the homes and buried in the family lots of their employers. They were in every sense of the word 'help,'" not servants (Salmon, 54-55). Tocqueville himself commented during this period that "the condition of domestic service does not degrade the character of those who enter upon it, because it is freely chosen, and adopted for a time only; because it is not stigmatized by public opinion and creates no permanent inequality between the servant and the master" (Salmon, 57). This idyllic egalitarianism survived in farming communities to the West, but in the South, as blacks replaced whites, the social chasm became impassable. And even in the North the increasing number of foreign domestics began to trouble the pleasant scene.[3]

The third period was ushered in by the "Great" Irish famine of 1845-1849, one of several that brought Irishwomen to this country in large numbers[4]; by the German revolution of 1848, which increased immigration, especially in 1854; by the treaty with China in 1844, which led to an influx of Chinese in the 1860s; and, in general, by the increased mobility of the population, These changes

> introduced a new social, as well as a new economic, element in the North. [They] . . . led to a change in the relation of employer and employee; the class line which was only faintly drawn in the early part of the century between employer and "help" . . . changed into a caste line which many employers believe it to their interest to preserve. The native born American fears to lose social position by entering into competition with foreign labor [Salmon, 64-64].

Just as the Lowell girls did in the mills.

The old free-and-easy "help" egalitarianism was not possible in the new relationship; the European women did not understand it. Thus Salmon quotes Madame d'Arussont, a visiting Frenchwoman, who wrote that "foreign servants are here, without doubt, the worst; they neither understand the work which the climate renders necessary, nor are willing to do the work which they did elsewhere"(60). Like other travellers in the United States, she "found that however subservient domestic servants might be when they left Europe, the first contact with the democratic atmosphere of America wrought a sudden change; subservience disappeared, and the servant boasted of his equality with all." She explained that those educated in America perceive the differences placed between the gentleman and the laborer by education and condition, but the foreigner, taking a superficial view of the matter, sees no difference" (60-61). Salmon also commented on the "subtle change that the democratic atmosphere everywhere wrought in the servants who came from Europe" (61). Without livery or other marks of service, without expected servility, there was no subserviencey of manner. They did not even have to bother to learn new kinds of work. The scarcity of "help" tipped the balance in their favor. A woman was doing a mistress a favor by "going out to work."

Why were native-born women shying away from domestic service, accepting lower-paying jobs instead? A Boston cook earned more than a schoolteacher (Salmon, 102), but teachers were not as scarce as domestic workers. Salmon analyzed the twofold nature of the disadvantages, industrial and social to which domestic workers were subjected. Under the first she specified: no chance for promotion; mechanical, repetitive work; lack of organization; irregularity of hours; limitation on free time; competition with foreign-born and blacks; "interference by those less skilled" (130). But the social disadvantage—low social position—was "far more subtle, intangible, and far-reaching" (165).

The Not-So-Hidden "Injuries of Class"

In *The Hidden Injuries of Class,* Sennett and Cobb write: "Surely . . . the peculiar inheritance of our country—a set of public beliefs about the common dignity of man [*sic*]—ought to serve as a rebuke to all the injustices and denials of class. Surely a nation's public philosophy, founded on the indea that all men [and women] have equal claims on each other's respect, should provide a shield of belief for people; surely this public philosophy ought to work against inferring a man's [or a woman's] dignity from his [or her] social standing" (1972, 251). The "injuries of class" domestic workers experienced were not well hidden. One of the most painful was being called "servant."

A survey in the late 1890s documented this specific complaint: "I fairly hate the word 'servant.' " "I don't like to be called a 'menial.' " "American girls don't like the name 'servants.' " "I know many nice girls who would do housework, but they prefer doing almost anything else rather than be called 'servants' " (Salmon, 155). Salmon traces the history of the word "servant" to get a clue as to why domestic workers hated it so. She did not find the term at all in her 1671 dictionary; by 1720 the dictionary defined it as a "man or woman who serves another"; in 1788, "one who serves"; in 1804, as "one who serves for wages" (Salmon, 69). At first there had been no odium attached to the word.

Salmon sees five factors leading to the abandonment of the term in the first decades of the Republic: the practice of indenturing servants, creating the redemptioneers; the use of the term for slaves; the levelling tendencies of a new country; a literal interpretation of the Declaration of Independence; and the influence of French philosophical ideas on social and political theories (70). "From the time of the Revolution . . . until about 1850 the word 'servant' does not seem to have been generally applied in either section to white persons of American birth" (70-71). Only with the influx of foreign domestics did the term return. By then the taking over of European life styles made possible by growing affluence emphasized class divisions. American women were unwilling to enter such a stigmatized occupation (71-72).

Another not-so-hidden injury of class was the use of Christian names. "It may seem a trifling matter, yet the fact remains that domestic employees are the only class of workers, except day laborers, who are thus addressed. . . . It has become a badge of social inferiority" (156). It still was in 1979 (D. R. Katz, 1979). The symbolism involved in the cap and apron constituted another sore spot: "The wider the separation in any community between employers and employee, the greater is the tendency to insist on the cap and apron" (Salmon, 152). Still another "injury of class" was the fact that domestic workers were made not only to feel their social inferiority but also to acknowledge it. "Not only deference but even servility of manner is demanded as of no other class, and this in an age when social and family relationships are everywhere becoming more democratic, when reverence and respect for authority are sometimes considered old-fashioned virtues, when even undue freedom of speech is permitted to other classes" (Salmon, 158).

Domestic workers felt socially isolated. "A young woman doing housework is shut out from all society, nor can she make any plans for pleasure or study, for her time is not her own" (154). Again, "domestics are not admitted into any society, and are often, for want of a little pleasure, driven to seek it in company that is often coarse and vulgar" (154). And, again: "No one seems to think a girl who works out good enough to associate with, except those who are in domestic service themselves."

Domestic workers were subjected to devastating humiliation as well as to snobbery. "A domestic employee recently went to a public library for a book. The attendant was about to give it to her . . . but when the question was asked and the answer given, 'not a teacher, but a house-maid,' the book was withheld, as servants were required to bring recommendations" (Salmon, 154). Though better paid than many other kinds of worker, domestics, as compared with other service workers in boarding houses, restaurants, and hotels, were underpaid since there were many extra services demanded of them (158). All this adds up to quite a bill of particulars.

The status-related injuries of class were hidden only to those who inflicted them. The recipients saw them with painful clarity. Salmon summed up the situation: "It is this social position with its accompanying marks of social inferiority that, more than any other thing, turns the scale against domestic service as an occupation in the thoughts of many intelligent and ambitious women whose tastes naturally incline them to domestic employment" (163). No wonder young women preferred the freedom and higher status of other work to better wages in service.[5] They did not understand why work that society called the most honorable a woman could do when it was done in her own home without pay became demeaning when done in another woman's home for pay; but they recognized the fact. They saw that discredit came not so much from the work itself as from the conditions under which it was performed, and they did not willingly place themselves in those conditions. They saw "that a class line is always drawn as in no other occupation" (Salmon, 165).

So much, then, for this "labor problem" from the worker's point of view. Most of the voluminous writing on the subject was, however, from the employer's point of view. And much of it did reveal recognition of the ideological paradox of class in a democratic society.

A Disturbed Conscience

The nostalgic situation pictured in the British television series *Upstairs Downstairs* did not widely obtain in the United States. In Britain, with its feudal history, servants knew their place; not only knew it, but appreciated it, valued it, felt no humilitation at the wide status differential between them and the families they served. And, even more important, however benevolent the upper classes might be in their personal contact with servants, there was no ideology of equality to prick the conscience. In the United States, however, where there was no feudal background, the clash of democratic ideology with the status differential was a never-ending source of domestic strain. From Catherine Beecher to the current feminists, women have been uneasy about the status relationships between them and their servants. One of the fundamental issues that the feminists have been concerned with is the use of other women by housewives to relieve them of their own household and child-care responsibilities. How could a woman who believed in a classless society subject another woman to the status of a subordinate being? Was this not reproducing in her own life the whole exploitative pattern she so much opposed? Catharine Beecher was struggling with the same conflict between ideology and practicality in the nineteenth century. The golden days when domestics were "help" rather than servants, when they were the daughters or sisters of neighbors, or at least sister townswomen, were passing. When foreign-born women took their place, the ensuing clash of cultures added to the serious strain on the egalitarian ideology of the halcyon years.

As noted above, the immigrant girls who supplied the market beginning early in the nineteenth century soon lost their European status conceptions and took over the egalitarian ideology they found in this country. They became "uppity." Catharine Beecher—who became, in effect, their apologist—reported a common complaint among their mistresses: these women exhibited "pride, insubordination, and a spirit not conformed to their condition." They not only objected to being called servants, in some cases they even wanted to eat at the same table with the family! "They imitate a style of dress unbecoming their condition; and their manners and address are rude and disrespectful" (1841, 200). Nor did conditions improve with time. Lucy Maynard Salmon, more than half a century later, was reporting the same status confrontations.

Catharine Beecher took it upon herself to explain the situation to housewives in an attempt to mollify the class conflict, to try to reconcile status inequality with ideological egalitarianism. In her book on domestic economy (1841) she devoted a whole chapter to "the Care of Domestics." She told American women that unruly servants were a low price to pay for the benefits of a free society; "if we cannot secure the cringing, submissive, well-trained servants of aristocratic lands, let us be consoled that we thus escape from the untold miseries and oppression which always attend that state of society" (197). And, furthermore, there was a higher sanction involved; "if domestics are found to be incompetent, unstable, and unconformed to their station, it is Perfect Wisdom which appoints these trials, to teach us patience, fortitude, and self-control; and if the discipline is met in a proper spirit, it will prove a blessing, rather than an evil" (197). So, however, difficult, the dilemma of how to reconcile democratic theory with the status of inequality intrinsic in the mistress-servant relationship had to be dealt with. For, as Salmon put it, "democracy among men and aristocracy among women cannot exist side by side; friction is as inevitable as it was between free labor and slave labor in the antebellum days" (1897, 186).

Beecher tried to explain why domestics became so uppity. When the ruder classes make forward and offensive claims, it may be a self-defensive reaction against the low status of their work and must be respected, for

> It should be remembered, that in this Country, children, from their earliest years, are trained to abhor servitude, in reference to themselves, as the greatest of all possible shame and degradation. They are perpetually hear-

> ing orations, songs, and compositions of all sorts, which set forth the honor and dignity of free-men, and heap scorn and contempt on all who would be so mean as to be slaves. Now the term servant, and the duties it involves, are, in the minds of many persons, nearly the same as those of the slave. And there are few minds, entirely free from associations which make servitude a degradation. It is not always pride, then, which makes this term so offensive. It is a consequence of that noble and generous spirit of freedom, which every American draws from his mother's breast, and which ought to be respected, rather than despised. [200]

Still, the low status of domestic work had to be dealt with. Beecher did not rely on appeals to "Perfect Wisdom" alone. She applied the same theoretical rationale to the reconciliation of the mistress-servant status differential as to the subordinate position of women as a whole. "It must be shown" not only that "in this Country labor has ceased to be degrading in any class," but also, and perhaps more important, that

> in all classes, different grades of subordination must exist; and that it is no more degrading for a domestic to regard the heads of a family as superiors in station, and treat them with becoming respect, than it is for children to do the same, or for men to treat their ruler with respect and deference. They should be taught, that domestics use a different entrance to the house, and sit at a distinct table, not because they are inferior beings, but because this is the best method of securing neatness and order and convenience. [201].

And besides, Beecher reassured her readers, servants themselves prefer it that way, They don't really want equality. She herself, for example, had "known cases where the lady of the family, for the sake of convincing her domestic of the truth of these views [about the necessity of different grades of subordination] allowed her to follow her own notions, for a short time, and join the family at meals. It was merely required, as a condition, that she should always dress her hair as the other ladies did, and appear in a clean dress, and abide by all the rules of propriety at table, which the rest were required to practice, and which were duly detailed. The experiment was tried, two or three times; and, although the domestic was treated with studious politeness and kindness, she soon felt that she should be much more comfortable in the kitchen, where she could talk, eat, and dress, as she pleased" (201). The "studied politeness and kindness" were probably harder to bear than relegation to the kitchen.

The lady must not only fulfill her duty to train her servants but she must also do it in a loving and humane way. She should attach them to the family by feelings of gratitude and affection, show a benevolent interest in their comfort as well as their improvement; assume the role of parent. If they are not clean and neat, she must be tactful in imparting new views on propriety. Words of kindness, hope, and encouragement will do more than reproof. Good wages, privileges, and presents will not make up for inconsiderate behavior. The words of a domestic are illustrative: "If we ever did anything wrong, she always talked to us just as if she thought we had no feelings, and I never was so unhappy in my life as while living with her" (206). Compassion was the employer's Christian duty. "Every woman, who has the care of domestics, should cultivate a habit of regarding them with that sympathy and forbearance, which she would wish for herself or her daughters, if deprived of parents, fortune, and home. The fewer advantages they have enjoyed, and the greater difficulties of temper or of habit they have to contend with, the more claims they have on compassionate forbearance. They ought ever to be looked upon, not as the mere ministers to our comfort and convenience, but as the humbler and more neglected children of our Heavenly Father, whom he has sent to claim our sympathy and aid" (206). Love-and/or-duty par excellence.

Like employers in industries with large numbers of immigrant workers, housewives also complained about the "exorbitant wages" servants were demanding (198). Beecher explained the market mechanisms that caused the high wages. "Is it not the universal law, of labor and of trade, that an article is to be valued according to its scarcity and the demand? . . . and why is it not right for domestics to act according to a rule allowed to be correct in reference to all other trades and professions?" (198). Housewives might just as well become reconciled to the situation, for "good domestic service must continue to increase in value, just in proportion as this Country waxes rich and prosperous; thus making the proportion of those, who wish to hire labor, relatively greater, and the number of those willing to go to service, less. . . . It is right for domestics to charge the market value, and this value is always decided by the scarcity of the article and the amount of demand" (198). If the lady understood the law of supply and demand she would have less hard feelings toward her domestics.

It was clear by the end of the century that Beecher's solutions to the "servant problem" were not working. A spate of other solutions bubbled up in the press.

Solutions to the Servant Problem

Some of the proposed solutions, like Beecher's, applied the rules of the integry, "a little practical Christianity," to the relationship (Harland and Van de Water, 1905, 428). But the same authors also suggested the direct opposite, applying the rules of the Gesellschaft to the relationship, that is, putting everything "on a purely business basis" (428). Other solutions included application of the Golden Rule: applying more intelligence, more paternalism (Salmon, 190). Or bringing up more blacks from the South or importing Chinese. Or requiring licensing. Or calling a convention of housekeepers to discuss the subject and what to do about it. Or abolishing public schools beyond the primary grades because, some alleged, "girls are educated above their station." Or adding housework to school curricula. Or establishing training schools for domestics. One solution was "cooperative housekeeping," which sounded radical until it became clear that all it meant was training the daughters of the house to help (Harland, 1880, Chapter 7). More radical was Charlotte Perkins Gilman's "kitchenless house" (Hayden, 1978). "Another plan" specified by Salmon, "perhaps less widely but even more earnestly advocated by its supporters, is that of co-operative housekeeping," not in the sense advocated by Harland in 1880, but rather "the association in a stock company of not fewer than twelve or fifteen families" (190). Salmon devoted four pages to describing this plan which, apparently, appealed to her greatly. But alas, the all but insuperable objection to such cooperative housekeeping as a remedy for the troubles with servants was the fact that most people did not want it (190).

Salmon's study of domestic service ended with the last years of the nineteenth century. She had correctly seen that the problem of domestic work was not a matter of uncongenial personalities that could be solved by changing the attitudes of the individuals involved. It was not a matter of ill will on either side, but a far more fundamental problem of societal structure—political, economic, industrial, social, and educational (168). As currently organized, domestic service was anachronistic. "The difficulties that meet the employer of domestic labor . . . are the difficulties that arise from the attempt to harmonize an ancient, patriarchal industrial system with the conditions of modern life. Everywhere the employer closes his [*sic*] eyes to the incongruities of the attempt and lays the blame of failure, not to a defective system, but to the natural weaknesses in the character of the unfortunate persons obliged to carry it out. The difficulties in the path of both employer and employee will not only never be resolved but will increase until the subject of domestic service is regarded as a part of the great labor question of the day and given the same serious consideration" (129).

Eight decades later David M. Katzman was agreeing with Salmon's diagnosis of the problem, namely that it was not a matter of clashing personalities but rather of great economic and sociological forces. "Until World War I," he notes, "most American servants lived in their employers' homes; the work environment and tasks were thus central to their personal lives. Their employment, living conditions, work tasks, roles, hours, and wages had decided effects on their roles outside the work environment. This complex interrelation of work, environment, and personal life was an anachronism in an industrializing and modernizing society in which workplace and home had become separate and the daily hours of work were rapidly diminishing" (1978, 95). There was, in brief, a kind of historical "asynchrony" between the female world and the economy.

In the framework of the present book, the same point may be made in terms of the lack of fit between the burgeoning Gesellschaft male world and the still surviving Gemeinschaft female world. Whether the housewife was advised to treat the domestic as a member of the family in the Gemeinschaft style or in a businesslike manner in the Gesellschaft style, the result was unsatisfactory. Both were tried; neither was a universal panacea. The problem remains, albeit in somewhat different forms, even today, as we shall have occasion to note in Chapter 14 below.

A Macrosociological Perspective

The story of mistress-maid relationships has recently been viewed from a somewhat different class angle. From this perspective it is seen as, in effect a story of the class upgrading of rural young women, as part of "modernization." Thus MacBride sees "servanthood" not only as a contributing factor in the transition to urbanized living but also as having contributed to what is now looked upon as "human capital." "Modern servanthood, as exemplified in France and England [and, indeed, in our country as well], proved to be a roughly century-long transition which caused the middle class and a large number of servants to come to grips with change," especially urbanization (T. M. McBride, 1976, 16). It was not a forerunner of modern life, but it was a way-station, and even half a century after its demise,[6] traces still persist. "The rise and decline of domestic service consituted a distinct phase in the modernization of western society. . . . The rise of servanthood as an important urban activity accompanied the accelerated urbanization of the late eighteenth to the nineteenth century" (111). It was, McBride believes, "a cross-cultural experience of immense [sociological] significance" (119). Servanthood "was the chief means by which large numbers of people effected the transition to modern urban society" (17).

In addition to helping in the transition to urbanism, the mistress acculturated the immigrant domestic. Leaders of American industry had discouraged the "Americanization" of their immigrant workers, especially the learning of the language, because they did not want to make it easy for workers to communicate freely with one another lest they organize. They tried to forestall the impact of the egalitarian ideology on immigrant workers. But the housewife was eager to have her household worker become "Americanized" as rapidly as possible, in language and skills if not in egalitarian ideology, Every effort was made to acculturate the sometimes literally "coarse and dirty foreigners" (Beecher, 1841, 199).

In addition, the housewife was called upon to educate domestics in their craft, to give them vocational training. "In regard to the great deficiencies of domestics, in qualifications for their duties, much patience and benevolence are required. Multitudes have never been taught to do their work properly. . . . Most persons of this class depend for their knowledge, in domestic affairs, not on their parents, who usually are not qualified to instruct them, but on their employers; and if they live in a family where nothing is done neatly and properly, they have no chance to learn how to perform their duties well. When a lady finds that she must employ a domestic who is ignorant, awkward, and careless, her first effort should be to make all proper allowance for past want of instruction, and the next, to remedy the evil, by kind and patient teaching" (Beecher, 203). The patient lady will be rewarded not only by a more competent servant but—even if the domestic leaves to accept a better-paying position—also by the knowledge that she has created "human capital," which redounds to the benefit of the whole society. "The lady will still have her reward, in the consciousness that she has contributed to the welfare of society, by making one more good domestic" (203). And when or if the servant married she would transmit her improved skills to her children (204). Without denying that domestic service did in fact help to ease the transition to urban life for countless rural women, that it did "acculturate" countless immigrant women, and that it did create a considerable amount of human capital, still the question may well be asked: Was domestic service the best way to achieve these ends? Or was it already anachronistic?

Update

Between 1900 and 1950 much of the work formerly done in the household by the housewife was, as Ogburn and Nimkoff noted years ago, moving out of the home. The practice of dining out was increasing as would the sale of "fast foods" later. Thus, in the first half of the twentieth century, operatives engaged in canning meat products, fruits, vegetables, and seafood increased more than 2,000 percent and laborers in these industries by 416.7 percent (Bogue, 1959, 485). As also did the numbers engaged in miscellaneous tasks of food preparation. The number of waiters, waitresses, and fountain workers increased 680.0 percent; those in personal services, 1857.4 percent (Bogue, 485). Baking too was moving out of the household. The advertising slogan "nothing says lovin' like something from the oven" was coming increasingly to mean something from the frozen pastry compartment at the local supermarket. Drip-dry and crease-resistant fabrics were eliminating much of the need for ironing.

Yet, just as even in a mass-consumer market there are still those who prefer the handcrafted product, so there are still women—especially professional or career women—who need individual home services. And there are still women who need the training to be able to sell such services. Thus as late as the 1960s there were pilot programs in seven cities designed to train domestic workers (MacDonald, 1969). And, there were also efforts to organize them in their own behalf (Chapter 13 below). Equally important, the feminist point of view that work in the home was as deserving of recognition as any other kind of work was having an impact. Professional women, themselves employees, could well appreciate the importance of the services that made their own careers possible. It is only now beginning to dawn on us as a society that if we wish to retain the homemaking "industry," we may have to find a way to subsidize it.

"Paths to Success" in the Female World of Community Service

Altogether different is the glimpse of status in the female world afforded by the work of Arlene Daniels on a "select group of seventy philanthropically inclined women important in a Pacific Coast city" (draft, 1975). Now it is not a matter of wide class—culture, race, ethnic—discrepancy as in the mistress-maid relationship but rather of status in the sense of recognition, in the sense of rising in a career ladder. Daniels describes how a regular career path for upward social mobility in the area of voluntary and community-organization work has evolved among the affluent. This work provides much of the dynamic for haute culture by sponsoring orchestras, art exhibits, museums, and the like. Such a career is overwhelmingly a phenomenon of the female world. Daniels' focus was on "the pathways to success and the formation of special careers" in this volunteer world, and she speculated on "the place of women in highly placed volunteer jobs as a 'female power élite' " (draft, 1975).

One of the background variables she noted was that "any serious volunteer career . . . requires a degree of affluence," whether by way of inheritance, earnings, or husband's generosity. Half of her informants were in the *Social Register,* but there was no consensus among them about their relative social standing. Most had servants. Few admitted to social climbing themselves although one of them occasionally attributed such motives to others. What was clear was that "the Community Leaders needed something to enlarge their existence beyond the home, yet within the traditional scope of expectations for the wife and mother." Crises—illness of self or child, drinking problems, marital unhappiness, or boredom with housework—were often precipitating factors for launching a career of voluntary service. And suggestions from others in their social network often tripped the wire. "I was deeply unhappy in my first marriage. Jane and I had lunch together one day and she said: 'What are you doing?' and I said 'Not much of anything!' And she said, 'So you should consider the Pacific City Government Watchdog Committee!' And I did. I just ate it up. I just liked everything about it. I even enjoyed sitting all day and listening to the City Councilmen." But there was also the love-and/or-duty dynamic of the female world: "To make a decent life for yourself—you must become interested in something. I was brought up to be terribly guilty. [And so] most of my work is causes—that certain people are treated unfairly and that others are not" (Daniels).

Daniels found two general paths to success in voluntary careers: (1) by way of family and organizational affiliations, and (2) by way of opportunities to use special talents which then may lead to "a sense of mission or 'beruf' [calling] created by the realization that they do have a talent."

It is important to know which organizations to choose as a vehicle for upward mobility, for just as some business or industrial corporations are more prestigious than others, so also are some community organizations. In some communities these organizations are fiefs of the socially élite and membership is strictly by invitation, even though members are expected to work hard. In New York City, for example, prestigious organizations include the Metropolitan Opera Board, certain private welfare or health agencies, the School Volunteers, and the like. "Persons choosing among organizations in which to serve" in Pacific City, "know instinctively—or learn after a very short time—what can be a personally acceptable or unacceptable experience. One looks for persons of common interests. Sometimes this goal is met automatically—as in groups formed around common issues, . . . or around common concerns, . . . or some crisis." And it is important to learn that "everything has a status," for movement upward is generally from organizations of lesser importance (smaller, more sectarian, less prestige attached to membership) to greater. Or upward ascent may mean progression through interests related to children's needs to interests of one's own. Daniels describes such an upward ascent that illustrates both kinds of paths to success. It took twenty years and involved a great deal of work as well as the ability to do it well.

Case in Point

MRS. #103: Well, let's start out with the church. From the church I followed my daughter's schooling. She went to private school, so I did parties for the school functions. [I did] the mother's tea, and I was in charge of advertising or doing an Easter Fair, and I helped organize horse shows. Because when you are dealing with the Catholic element—the nuns are so cloistered—so everything had to be done by the parents who would volunteer. I was always a leader and it seems as though I was the one who started things. You start getting experience—one promotion leads to another.

INTERVIEWER: But which way is up?

MRS. #103: Oh, the prestigious boards and the better communities to work in. In school, private school is better than P,T.A.—there are better donations. Well, it is not that it is better, but it is a different class of people . . . a more sophisticated group. I research everything when I start. I want to be the best, I never copy. When you feel you have done it all, you look outside. What's my next move? You don't want to go from one school to another school or from one church to another church because they are still in the same category.

Then I got into the International Center. It maintains ties to other countries. When you are in a private school, you get to know a certain kind of people. You hear about the different organizations that they belong to. And I did decorations for them.

Then I thought it was time to join a club. You are sponsored, you have to have friends. Now it is known as the Gourmet Club. And I joined the Pacific City Reading Society.

All this wasn't easy because [of my ethnic background]. I could not make it through CYWPC [a prestigious civic group]. You have to have a college education for that group. They are very clannish; you have to have gone to [their élite college] or you have to be known by some of them.

I was outspoken, yet very much in demand because of this talent: business acumen and the artistic element.

So I went to the Museum Council and used my business ability giving rummage sales or supervising students who would do the decorating for parties. Then I did the Jonquil Ball. That made my reputation because it is a city-wide affair and the most influential people in the city are connected with it. So when you do work there, you have gotten known.

It was funny when I was approached to do a hotel. The Flower Ball moves from hotel to hotel and the people are transported by bus. I was asked rather gingerly to do a hotel—they thought they were doing me a favor. You have to understand I never had to go looking for jobs. They always came to me.

Everything has a status, even the hotels for the Flower Ball. The Jonquil was the finest. Then the Lilac, the Lily, Daisy, and the Violet. You know what the status is because the Jonquil Hotel has the best orchestra in town. The Lily has the next best, and so on down the line. And the Jonquil had the most expensive sponsor tickets for a table. Glenwood Society sat there. So when they came to me gingerly to ask if I "wouldn't do" a hotel, I said I'd love to and I'd love to do the Jonquil. That really threw them. They heard of my ability but they didn't know

> if they wanted to go along with me that much. So they said they would compromise by giving me the Lilac instead. I said "I don't like it; but I will take it." And it was a big success. Throughout all the buses everyone said, "Go see the Lilac, they have the most interesting decorations." From then on there was no asking and I did the Jonquil for a number of years.
>
> Then the [prestigious art and music] boards approached me and asked me to join. And I have been on [one of the most prestigious boards in the city] for twelve years now. Now I am getting more interested in politics.

By way of contrast to the slow ascents—involving as much effort as many a male career in the economy or polity—Daniels presents another case in which marriage to a wealthy man instantly supplied a woman "with her entrée to the social world that she wanted. . . . With one blow [she] got the position [both socially and in volunteer work] without working her lifetime for it." Other women, even with more money, social position, and/or sponsorship by the proper organizations, might take from five to ten years to reach the highest boards.

The same processes are at work in the case of black women. Elizabeth Burmiller describes them in Washington, D.C.: "The husband makes a big salary, while the wife has time to volunteer her way methodically upward in the correct clubs. She eventually gets noticed, someone already in the Green Book [*Social Register*] recommends her" (*Washington Post,* April 20, 1980.) Burmiller illustrates with the case of one black woman who got her start at a 1971 benefit for Freedman's Hospitals which she co-chaired. It "was a sellout that attracted a large enough number of whites to be considered Washington's first integrated, large-scale fund-raiser, . . . the traditional way, without a sizable fortune or some amount of Washington blue blood, for a family of any color to get tagged for the Green Book." Another black woman began her career doing volunteer work for the National Collection of Fine Arts, then the Washington Performing Arts Society, an "organization where many black women got their starts on the charity ball circuit." When she chaired the Society's Diamond Dinner Dance, covered by *Women's Wear Daily,* her success put her on the map.[7]

Important and pervasive as class is for women in the female world, it is interesting primarily as background for the actual day-by-day lives they lead. It is not in a "class" that women move and have their being but rather in small groups and networks within a general class structure. Sometimes, as members of associations, they may find themselves crossing class lines. And if the issues become broad enough, social movements embracing several classes may occur, resulting in coalitions, if not necessarily solidarity. But sometimes class may itself cleave the female world. Before we turn to these class "faultlines," however, we look in Part IV at the group aspects of the structure of the female world.

Notes

1. Until recently one looked in vain for sociological discussions of domestic and household labor. Helen Lopata (1971) and Ann Oakley (1974) analyzed the work of women in the home in terms of role analysis and Nona Glazer (1977) in terms of its contribution to the social system. David M. Katzman (1978) has given a historical account.
2. Most of the discussion in this chapter deals with white women. For an almost exhaustive study of black as well as white domestic workers, see Katzman, 1978.
3. The importation of women from other countries for domestic service has remained fairly common ever since. The *au pair* girl, usually from Europe, and women from Latin America have been recent examples.
4. It is interesting to note that, almost a century later, Irish women were to prove remarkably successful as labor organizers. Of the fourteen women labor organizers listed in *Notable American Women*, eight were either born in Ireland or of Irish descent (1971).
5. Katzman's examination of the data led him to change his mind about the relative importance of the economic and status dimensions of the problem of domestic service. The economics, he found, were not necessarily primary.
6. Katzman dates the end of the period of the live-in servant at about the time of World War I.
7. The processes may be the same for black women but there are differences in the way they are experienced. There is defensiveness among some of the successful women vis-à-vis others in the black community, who accuse them of élitism, snobbery, and rejection of blacks. (No black person in the Green Book has ever recommended another black for admission.) Still, there are others who hear only "Good for you!" "I'm glad you made it!"

PART IV

The Group Structure of the Female World

In Part IV we look at the female world in terms of its group structure. Unfortunately there is little more consensus on the concept of "group" than there is with respect to so many other concepts we have to use. Homans restricts the concept to small groups: "A 'group' is defined as a number of persons, or members, each of whom, while the group is meeting, interacts with every other, or is able to do so, or can at least take personal cognizance of every other. This requirement, which cannot be met for larger social units, such as armies, justifies calling groups 'small' " (1968, 259). Deutsch, after reviewing the many ways in which the term has been used, finds that they all involve two or more persons who: "(1) have one or more characteristics in common, (2) perceive themselves as forming a distinguishable entity, (3) are aware of the interdependence of some of their goals or interests, and (4) interact with one another in pursuit of their interdependent goals" (1968, 265). In order to accommodate the more sociological usage, which includes more permanent and structured entities, Deutsch adds three more characteristics of groups: (5) they "endure over a period of time, and as a result, (6) develop a set of social norms that regulate and guide member interaction and (7) a set of roles, each of which has specific activities, obligations, and rights associated with it" (265). All conceptualizations agree that the term does not include aggregates, class, type, or any other category imposed from the outside by the observer, such as the entities reviewed in Part III.

However they are conceptualized, groups may be classified in a variety of ways according to a variety of criteria. A generation ago Logan Wilson deplored the lack of a valid classificatory schema. He concluded a survey of group theories with the statement that "the lack of an adequate classificatory scheme precludes the full view of group interactions. . . . Most of the makeshift empirical schemes of classification and analysis have logical inconsistencies, but the logically consistent schemes tend to have the shortcoming of limited applicability" (1945). In the present context, applicability rather than logical consistency is important. Criteria for classification may be: (1) substantive—according to the organizing interest, for example, such as reform, recreation, profession, and the like; (2) structural—according to the principles of organization involved, informal (Deutsch's first four characteristics) or formal (his last three characteristics), and the like; (3) extent—local, national, international; (4) duration—temporary, long-lasting; or (5) origin—self-originated or established by outside agencies—and so on.

On the basis of historical data, Keith Melder distinguished six types of women's groups in the first half of the nineteenth century, which incorporate most of the criteria specified above: family, primarily mother-daughter groups; close friendships; ties growing out of school relations with classmates or "alumnae groups"; religious organizations of women "converted" to good works; voluntary associations, primarily benevolent and reform in character; and, finally, occupational or work-related associations (1977). On the basis of contemporary Norwegian data, Harriet Holter (1978) arrives at a typology based on two criteria: "the degree of consciousness about the problematizing of women's position" and "the degree of formalization and militancy" (1978). She derives five types of group relationships among women: (1) family, kin, and friendship relations; (2) local, community, and traditional voluntary women's associations (that is, groups "organized for others"); (3) women's collectivities in work places, including informal defensive "organizations for protection of own interests"; (4) trade unions, political parties, and other interest groups organized "partially for women's interests"; and (5) women's movements, organized "for changes in women's situation." Holter is well aware that the boundaries between these categories may be diffuse and that one type may sometimes fuse with another. Whatever its defects, however, she still finds this typology useful in her own research in Norway.

In our discussion we use the simple informal-formal categorization, Chapter 12 dealing with the informal, corresponding to groups in Holter's first and Deutsch's first four characterization categories, and Chapter 13, with the more formal, characterized by Deutsch's last three qualities and Holter's last three types. Thus, Chapter 12 begins with the most primary of all groups, family and kinship groups and locale-based networks, which have constituted a large part of the female world until the present, reflecting its lingering Gemeinschaft character. The ideology of women's sphere, with its emphasis on domesticity, did not preclude participation by women in voluntary associations, and such associations came in time to constitute an important part of the structure of the female world, as they do today. Chapter 13 deals with this extension of the group activities of the female world to benevolent associations and, later in the nineteenth century, to the so-called women's club, to the current rapid multiplication of both groups and associations.

When groups expand their scope and activities, they may begin to "move"—that is, they give rise to political and social movement. Sometimes such activities in the female world have moved in to the male world of the economy—as in the case of the Women's Christian Temperance Union, which attacked the liquor industry—or of the polity—as in the case of the suffrage movement. A nod in the direction of such collective behavior is also included in Chapter 13. In Chapters 14 and 15, we comment on several of the major faultlines—structural and issue-related—and some of the homogenizing forces at work in the female world as well as some of the efforts being made to achieve solidarity.

When we were discussing the conceptualization of the class structure of the female world (Chapter 10) we stressed that it had to be holistic, in order to make room for everyone, low or high, outcast as well as dowager. So also in the group structure. There are no groups, radical or conservative, traditional or modern, that can be written out. Traditional women might wish that modern women would just disappear. And, of course, the reverse may be true. Opponents as well as proponents on every issue dear to us, those who disagree with us on issues closest to our hearts no less than those who agree with us, are nevertheless part of the female world. All that variegated, seemingly miscellaneous congeries of groups and associations—do-good, subversive, stodgy, noble—is part and parcel of the female world. We do not have to embrace any of them, but we cannot write them out of the script.

12

Kinship, Network, and Friendship Groups

WE HAVE CHARACTERIZED the female world to date as basically a Gemeinschaft world, in which "blood and soil," or kinship ties and locale are fundamental bonds. Such a view may be in the process of becoming anachronistic, but for the present it is probably still legitimate. We know that kinship ties are fostered primarily by women (Adams, 1971) and that until now women have been largely bounded in their activities and interests by locale. Now that such a large proportion are entering the labor force, the locale bond may be in a process of attrition, although there is at least some evidence to the contrary (Schoenberg, 1978, draft).

Although a great deal has changed in the structure of the female world, the kinship network, especially the mother-daughter relationship, has not wholly disappeared. Both the kinship and the locale aspects of the Gemeinschaft are illustrated in the story of one woman who recounts how they have operated in four generations of her own family.

"Blut" and "Bod" in Four Generations: A Case in Point

Soon after the Civil War, this woman's great-great-aunt, a Southerner married to an Evansville, Indiana man, crossed the Ohio River in the last days of her pregnancy so that her child would be born below the Mason-Dixon line. She was not satisfied with the ritualistic symbol for "Bod" worked out by other Southern women; they would put a bucket of Southern soil under the bed where the child was delivered. When the author's own grandmother, in turn, gave birth she did not return to ancestral soil, but *her* mother—the author's great-grandmother—came to her, again emphasizing the kinship ties. The author's mother delivered her daughter—that is, the author herself—in New Jersey despite her mother's request that she come back to Tennessee for the birth. Instead, the author's grandmother came to New Jersey for the event. "But what came with my grandmother was more than any standard maternity support. As my mother put it, 'she brought all of my background with her. I still knew who I was when Mother was there'" (Cohen, 1978).

True also to the "Bod" aspect of Gemeinschaft, her family did ultimately go back to Tennessee. "I spent a childhood much like my mother's, my friends the children of her friends, almost all born within minutes of the neighborhood in which we played." The author does not think her case unusual: "Certainly the women of my family are not unique; there must be others for whom pregnancy forces a coming to terms with their locus in the family history. . . . We fashion 'support systems,' whether we acknowledge them as such or not, to satisfy our emotional requirements. They demand self-preparation, like carrying the soil of one state to another or . . . crossing a river to comfortable politics."

Kinship Networks

A number of studies in England have shown that this woman's case was, indeed, not unique. "Mum" and her daughters in working-class neighborhoods did constitute a strong Gemeinschaft world until at least a quarter of a century ago. "Kinship networks . . . gave to their individual members considerable reassurance and security. If the wife's mother played a part in helping with her daughter's family she herself could count on the help of her daughter's family when she needed it" (Elias and Scotson, 1965, 47). Townsend observed in another old established working-class district "how many women played a major part in rearing young children for as many as 40 or 50 years of their lives" (Townsend, 1957, 34). One could observe the same pattern in other areas. Among those interviewed in yet another British neighborhood, for example, there were "eighteen elderly women who after their own children had grown up helped to look after their children's children or in other cases after the children of a sister or a sister's daughter"

(Elias and Scotson, 1965, 47). We are told that the same "babushka" or grandmother phenomenon lingers on in the Soviet Union, where the mothers of many of the women in the labor force take care of their daughters' children.[1] In the Chinese courtyard today, many grandmothers also stay home to look after small children when the younger mothers go off to work.

There seems, however, to be a change in process. Friends come increasingly to take the place of relatives in the network structure of the female world, as is highlighted by Johanna Dobkin Gladieux in an interesting study contrasting the composition of social-support networks of traditional and modern women during pregnancy. The general direction of the changes may be inferred from the author's profile of the modern women. They tended to be "more highly educated and to have higher-status jobs than women with more traditionally oriented sex-role attitudes. . . . Modern women were less sensitive to social conventions, and more open to innovation and social change than traditional women. Furthermore, modern women were less apt to practice a religion, and while they wanted to have a baby, they were more prone to have poor or conflicting attitudes about the experience of pregnancy and about marriage. They also tended to want fewer children than their more traditional counterparts. Women with modern sex-role conceptions were also more likely to have infrequent contacts and poor-quality relationships with their own mothers" (1978, 287-288). The contrast, it may be noted in passing, suggests differences between women with professional and working-class or ethnic backgrounds. The differences extended beyond the women themselves to their networks also.

Kinship and Friendship in the Social Networks of the Female World: Case in Point

The social networks of these two categories of women—traditional and modern—"were likely to differ in composition and degree of supportiveness" and thus to affect the quality of the pregnancy experience itself" (Gladieux, 1978, 291). The networks of the traditional women included a large number of relatives; the women themselves were affectively expressive, including others in the pregnancy experience, sharing it, that is, with them. "Ensconced in a close-knit network of relatives or friends who are [themselves] parents, their pregnancy experience tends to be . . . enriching and satisfying. . . . For a traditional woman, pregnancy is not simply an isolated event among many in her life. Instead, childbearing is valued, and takes on an extended meaning. Conveyed to the parturient woman by her relatives, in particular, is the wisdom that comes with seasoned experience. She senses connection to her heritage and recognizes contribution to future generations. . . . Supportive, close-knit systems (especially of relatives and one's own parents) serve a norm-setting function which instills confidence and contentment" (293).

Suggesting the diminution in Gemeinschaft referred to above were the contrasting networks of the modern women in this study. They were more variable than those of traditional women. Among them the network included relatively fewer relatives and more friends, especially work associates who were themselves pregnant, and ties were often based on work-site rather than kinship bonds. For these women "ultimate satisfaction with the experience [of pregnancy] was largely dependent on the interplay between marital relationships and social network factors. . . . The results show that ultimate satisfaction . . . was closely linked to high standing on the dimension of control and autonomy, where, in addition, they had inclusive and affectively expressive relationships with spouses and others" (294). Thus husbands, who supplied affection, and friends, who permitted autonomy, rather than blood ties, constituted the social networks of these modern women in pregnancy.

Although the similarities and differences between the traditional and the modern women varied somewhat according to the trimester of the pregnancy, the author emphasizes the differences in her summary of her overall findings: "women with traditional sex-role conceptions were more certain to have a satisfying, low-anxiety pregnancy experience than women of modern orientation. . . . Because of the norm-setting functions of their [kin] networks, and support within their marriages, they were apt to feel valued and confident during pregnancy, and they looked forward to motherhood. Traditional women felt special and well connected to their pregnancy experience" (294). By contrast, "the modern women ran a greater risk of being dissatisfied with their pregnancy experience" (293).

The author concludes that although "without doubt, there are great benefits and gains associated with women's changing roles in society, . . . there are costs as well," including the attrition of the kinship network. Thus, "for modern women, pregnancy often occurs in an inhospitable context. Detached from their families, and often married to men who share their reservations and hesitancies about childbearing, these women are sometimes cast adrift without the moorings of [kinship] connections that might make their experience more valuable, special, and gratifying" (293). The implication is that social networks in the female world today, organized on the basis of work-site friendships rather than kinship ties, are less suitable for at least the most female of all experiences, pregnancy and childbirth. There is some evidence that women themselves now recognize the alienating effect of our society's mechanization of pregnancy care and childbirth and there is a growing movement to retrieve them for the female world (Chapter 13).

If we had good indices over time of the composition of the social networks of traditional and modern women as defined in the Gladieux study, we would have some idea of the attenuation of Gemeinschaft now going on in the female world. It is not that the female world is becoming transformed into a Gesellschaft world; the relationships in the social networks of both the traditional and the modern women are still, presumably, loving, or at least affectionate. But the kinship component seems to be waning. Still to be determined is the effect of the attempt by women themselves to restore the warmth of family ties to non-kin-based female social networks.

The Kinship Network Issue

Interestingly, the attenuation of kinship ties in modern life was one of the salient issues in family research in the 1950s and 1960s. In 1957, Elizabeth Bott, a British researcher, published a book on *Family and Social Network*, which stimulated widespread interest in networks. She was especially interested in the effect of social networks on conjugal relations. She concluded that when husbands and wives had separate networks, their own relationship tended to be more segregated; when they shared the same networks, their relationship tended to be more complementary or joint.[2] She had found the network concept essential in her research as an anthropologist "because the familiar concepts of group and corporate group of traditional anthropology were not entirely adequate to the field data I was dealing with. The research families did not live in groups. They 'lived' in networks, if one can use the term 'lived in' to describe the situation of being in contact with a set of people and organizations some of whom were in contact with each other and some not" (313).

The concept of social networks caught on and stimulated an extensive research corpus which Bott summarized as of 1971[3] (252-290). Much of this work dealt with sex-role segregation both within the family and in the community. Bott concludes that studies of the geographically nonmobile working class show "marked sexual segregation both inside *and* outside the elementary family" (257), whereas studies of middle-class families in both Britain and the United States show that "married children keep up relationships with their parents and siblings even when physically separated from them" (260). Bott felt that "in spite of the many studies, our knowledge of middle-class families is far from complete" (263).

A considerable amount of network research went far beyond the husband-wife relationships that interested Bott. The concept came to be tied up with a controversy with respect to the nuclear versus the extended family. Much of the research was oriented to demonstrating that the nuclear family, despite spatial separation, was not an isolated unit, as commonly posited, but rather, was firmly embedded in a kin network (Sussman and Burchinal, 1962, 231-240; Litwak, 1965). But the emphasis of much of this work was on male network behavior, dealing, that is, with financial help, or help in upward mobility. Even when the research dealt with the contributions of women in kin networks, their specifically female nature was either not mentioned or treated rather casually.[4] And, interestingly, the male networks did not imply locale-based ties, or "Bod," as the female networks did.

Networks are different from groups per se, though not unrelated. Networks have the effect of expanding the group members' resources. They also have the potential effect of making class barriers more flexible if not wholly permeable. They operate quite simply. Mary is one of a group of, say, four or five friends who help support one another. On this occasion she is asking to borrow a violin so that her daughter can take lessons for a few months, until the family gets caught up on their bills and can buy her one of her own. No one in the group has a violin. But Jane knows someone who might. She calls to ask, and, sure enough, her friend does have one. Countless baby garments and pieces of equipment go from one home to another by way of such networks: Helen's child has outgrown her shirts; Jean knows Dotty, a woman who has just given birth, and within an hour the shirts are on their way to the new mother. It might be a hospital bed for use by an invalid or some expensive appliance for a sick room, or whatever. The network processes messages and often brings replies. It works, of course, like the "old boys" networks. "We're looking for a bright young man for an opening in our St. Louis office. Do you know anyone who . . . ?" He doesn't, but he knows someone who does. The network is a kind of integrating system, bringing into juxtaposition individuals who might never make connections without such a mediating device. It's conceivable that a network might relate women of quite different classes. Thus the daughter of Lucy's maid may be wearing a sweater from the last year's wardrobe of Kim, the banker's daughter, routed by way of a network.

Networks and Communities: "Bod"

The essentially Gemeinschaft nature of the female world is illustrated in the following quotation: "Communities are essentially organizations of homemakers, residential units such as urban neighborhoods, villages, hamlets, compounds or groups of tents. It is difficult to imagine communities without women and children, though one can imagine communities almost without men" (Elias and Scotson, 1965, 146-147). (Like, for example, some of those described in Chapter 3.) The community approach to the female world touches on the "Bod" component of Gemeinschaft. And it is interesting to note that not only the "Blut" or kinship component of the female world but also its "Bod" component seems to be in process of attrition, as is suggested in a growing body of research on networks in urban and suburban communities.[5]

It is not only the sheer propinquity factor in locale that is important but also its tie-up with kinship. Before the automobile rendered us all so peripatetic, the kinship network and locale coincided. Relatives lived within walking distance of one another. Neighbor and kin might be one and the same. Thus, moving to a distant area—to the suburbs, for example—disturbed not only the local ties but also the personal kinship ties, by making them harder to maintain. Moving to the suburbs did not necessarily eliminate neighbors—"nigh-dwellers"— but the ties of mere propinquity did not always or necessarily serve the same functions as kinship ties (Hochschild, 1973).

A considerable body of research deals with the relationships of women in suburbs. The effect on women of mobility, especially from old neighborhoods to suburbs, was in fact, one of the earliest areas of network research. Studies by Tallman (1969), Rainwater and Handel (1964), and by Rainwater (1960) in the 1960s showed the stresses resulting from the break-up of close-knit networks by mobility. More recently it is the effect of stress on women resulting not so much from mobility as from suburban life in and of itself that is being studied. A considerable body of research shows convincingly that living in the suburbs has greater effects on women than on men and that women are more displeased with it (Fischer, 1976; Fischer and Jackson, 1977; Berger, 1960; Gans, 1967; Tallman, 1969). Less mobile, more committed to the home than men, suburban women suffer the stress of distance from relatives and old friends. Gans concludes: "If there is malaise in Levittown, it is female but not suburban" (1967, 226). These women are more isolated than are women in urban neighborhoods.

Sylvia Fava has searched the literature on suburbia as related to women and finds six categories of women especially disadvantaged by suburban living; the aged, teenagers, minority women, corporate wives, the single, and the divorced (draft, 1978). For all of them the stresses of distance from contacts, work, and services are great. "This factor, above all others, appears to be at the root of the suburban problem for women. A recent extensive review of the suburban literature indicates that distance and 'its depressive effects on population potential' are greater for women than for men" (Fischer and Jackson, 1976, 287; Fischer et al., 1977, chap. 7). Fava's review shows for example that while both suburban men and women are more locally oriented than their city counterparts, the increased localism is more marked among the women. "One aspect of this is the 'substitution by women of neighbors in place of friends and relatives,' since only the neighbors are readily available in the suburbs" (Fischer and Jackson, 1976, 286). Fischer and Jackson's analysis notes that "the effects of distance are indirect, in that distance must be translated into access 'from an individual's home to the homes and gathering places of people who are his [her] real and potential associates' " (281). The social networks of suburbanites, especially suburban women, tend to be located closer to their homes because the "cost"—in time and in money—of access to the nonlocal areas is greater than for city dwellers. Fischer and Jackson indicate that "women are less mobile, more committed to the home and include sub-groups with specialized needs not likely to be served among the relatively small number of people in their immediate vicinity" (draft, 1978).

Other research documents these findings. A study by William Michelson "pin-pointed the source of the suburban wives' dissatisfaction; they were increasingly satisfied with the social characteristics of their neighborhood, but increasingly dissatisfied with the locational disadvantages of that neighborhood. Wives, in other words, felt increasingly burdened by the relative isolation of the suburbs while their husbands, who left the neighborhood every day to go to work, remained highly satisfied with both the social characteristics and the locational aspects of the suburban neighborhood" (Fava, draft, 1978).

Working-class women—perhaps the "traditional" women of the Gladieux study—seemed to have more difficulty than white-collar women when they moved to the suburbs, thus distancing themselves from the kinship network of the city. A study of Minneapolis found they had a stronger sense of personal isolation than their city counterparts (Tallman, 1969; Tallman and Morgner, 1970; Warren, 1975). "The problems of the suburban wives stem from loss of the close family and friendship ties characteristic of urban working-class neighborhoods. This network of contacts, on which working-class women depend for personal support and confidence to a greater degree than white-collar women, could not be maintained or reformulated readily in suburbs" (Fava, draft, 1978).

At the other end of the class structure, corporate wives have similar adjustment problems. Now the problem is not so much the severing of kinship ties as it is the severing of roots established in one community when they move to new communities, even when it is just from one suburb to another. Seidenberg has reported on the impact as follows:

"The entire corporate life style encourages her to live solely through and by her husband. . . . The mad rush to the suburbs has added to her miseries by cutting her off from the civic and cultural center. The suburbs are like isolation wards, separated from all but the most superficial contact with fellow human beings and from the vitality of the city. . . . We have created suburban social starvation" (Seidenberg, 1973, 132). A study of depressed women in New Haven found one subgroup consisting of women who had been functioning well before moving from a city to the suburbs: "These women could not adapt even though the move was considered desirable by the family. In these cases, it seems that the depressive illness was intensified or exacerbated by the suburban life style. For example, the low population density and the loss of natural daily social gatherings on the porch, the street or the corner drugstore made sharing experiences and ventilating problems more difficult" (Weissman and Paykal, 1972, 27).

It might be noted in passing that in extreme cases dependence on home ties may become pathological. Agoraphobia, a "morbid fear of public places," is sometimes known as "housewife's syndrome," because it is primarily a women's difficulty. A study of 528 patients found 91 percent to be women, all but 51 of them married (Weekes, 1976). The outside world is seen by such women as a dangerous place. Little girls are taught not to enter it unless they are accompanied. Out there they will not be as protected as they are at home.

Friendship as a Structural Unit

We left the story of female friendship in Chapter 5 with its immanent demise at the end of the nineteenth century. We pick up that thread again here.

We begin by noting that not everyone accepts the idea that female friendships actually did suffer attrition at the turn of the century. Ann Seiden and Pauline Bart believe, rather, that, as noted in Chapter 5, it was only downgrading that they suffered. "There has been," they tell us, "a popular cultural stereotype that women do not like each other very much. It has been said that women do not really trust women friends, do not have grounds for trusting them, do not work well for women supervisors, and are inherently in competition for the available men. This competition is said to override the possibility of genuine friendships" (1975, 192). They trace in some detail the process by which female friendships have come to be thus devalued (193-194). They conclude that female friendship is too basic and important a part of the structure of the female world to be completely undermined. They trace some of the recent efforts to overcome suspicion, mistrust, and competition among women by the ideology of sisterhood. Sisterhood in this sense of "philogyny" (Merton and Lazarsfeld, 1954) is not conceptualized as an alternative to or a support for other relationships but as something new, "a new articulation of one of the primary social bonds whose importance has always been there though denied for good historical and sociological reasons" (196). Women, they note, are rediscovering "the possibility of significant friendship with other women within and without the family . . . something which was disvalued for a short time in history" (194). What is needed now, they argue, is, in effect, its relegitimization.

The devaluation of female friendship, they continue, has extended to neglect of scientific study of the subject. Even sociologists trained to locate "invisible" communities and subcultures have tended to overlook friendship among women. These relationships have tended to be ignored or blurred into family relationships: "female friendships have generally existed as a part of the social structure, sometimes subordinate to family structures, sometimes alongside and independent of family structures, and sometimes as a replacement for family structures. . . . [But] 'familiomorphizing' of such relationships leads to missing some very important points. . . . [Thus] earlier models of social structure did not recognize either that they had an important place in the social structure or that they were worthy of study" (195, 201).

The mystique of the "male bond" denies the existence of a correlative "female bond" (Tiger, 1970), and there is some evidence in the research literature that women have fewer friends than men have (Davidson and Duberman, 1978, draft). But this evidence is not persuasive; structural differences might well account for whatever differences are found. In a study of friendship patterns in Australia and the United States, for example, Robert Bell found that in both countries about the same proportion of men—almost two-fifths—had men friends with whom they spent evenings; but far more American than Australian women (62 percent vs. 28 percent) had female friends. And Veronica Heiskanen found that females in Finland did, indeed, interact with more females and males with fewer males than might be expected on a chance basis (1969, 261). Indeed, it is argued that women have greater "affiliative need" than men (Miller, 1977, Chapter 8).

Differences in the number of women and men who have friendships or in the number of friends they have are less important then differences in the quality of these relationships, which have long been recognized. Here, for example, is how they looked to a woman at the end of the seventeenth century:

> As we [women] are less concern'd in the affairs of the World, so we have less temptation from Interest to be false to our Friends. Neither are we so likely to be false thro' Fear; because our Sex are seldom engag'd in matters

> of any Danger. For these Reasons it is, our Sex are generally more hearty and sincere in the ordinary Friendships they make than Men, among whom they are usually clogg'd with so many Considerations of Interest, and Punctilio's of Honour; to which last perhaps are owing the greatest part of those honourable Actions, which are mistakenly Imputed to Friendship. For something done to salve Honour, commonly puts a Period to all Friendship with unfortunate Persons; whom Men think they may afterward grow cold too without Reproach [Mary Astell, 1697, 132-133].

Men, the author continues, talk about matters of state, politics, religion; and passions can run high (136). They could well learn from women real courtesy, art, wit, and inventiveness (136 ff.).

This was one of the earliest comparisons between the friendships of women and of men. Since that time there have been several others. Women more often show intimate styles of interaction. Their sex-role socialization prepares them for relating to others more intimately as contrasted with male sex-role socialization, which prepares men for one-upmanship. Alan Booth finds that female friendships across the board tend also to be richer in spontaneity and confidences exchanged than men's. "Although spontaneity and affect seemed to characterize the close ties of middle-aged, married, and white-collar respondents, the sex differences in spontaneity and confiding behavior persisted in each category" (1972, 186-187). Some cultures encourage greater intimacy in female than in male friendships.

Cross-sex friendships are discouraged in the female world, certainly among adult, especially married, women. Whether so-called platonic friendships are even possible has long been an interesting topic of debate. But when or if there are such relationships, men seem to confide more readily in women than women in men. Men, in general, are not socialized for close, intimate friendship ties, least of all with women.

We know that in the nineteenth century female friendships supplied the emotional support women did not receive from men, who, as Tocqueville noted, were not then—any more than now—well trained in emotional expression. It has been shown, for example, that women perform the "mental-hygiene" function of marriage for men more than men perform it for women (Blood and Wolfe, 1960). Especially in working-class marriages, as Dair Gillespie has found, for women "social and psychological support emanates . . . not from marriage partners, but from same-sex friends and kin from long-standing and tight-knit social networks" (1971, 457). Mirra Komarovsky's study of blue-collar marriage found the same situation (1962). In her studies of old age, Zena Blau also found that "the wife is the man's only confidante, whereas the woman's closest confidante is most likely to be a woman friend." She concludes that "men satisfy their needs for intimacy largely within the marriage, but women must seek gratification for such needs with their own sex" (Blau, 1973, 73). And a study at the University of Michigan in 1974 found that women supplied emotional support to their husbands twice as often as they received it in return (Warren, 1975, 120).

Since men are not trained to perform the supportive function for women, a void is left in their lives.[6] Esther Harding, a former student of Jung, is quoted as saying that for the most part men are still "quite unable to give women the emotional satisfaction and security they can find with their women friends" (West, 1975, 120). The "strong, silent" type which has been the accepted model for men is not very serviceable as a loving support. As a result, women are now "being forced to re-evaluate . . . their relations with other women," for they are finding that they "need each other as never before " (38). When in stress, not "diamonds" but other women—whether as coworkers, neighbors, or friends, if not relatives—are a girl's best resource. In the 1960s, therefore, a deliberate effort began to create and develop sisterhood.

We noted above in comparing the social networks of traditional and modern women that friends were more important than relatives in modern women's social networks, as contrasted with the pattern among traditional women. In many ways friends in the female world have been more important even than husbands as well as kin. For example, Gladieux found that in the archetypical female experience of both traditional and modern women—pregnancy—"social network variables have a stronger association with pregnancy satisfaction than do marital relationship variables" (292). Most startling of all, however, is the result reported by Bell. American women were asked to specify the three persons they would most like to be with. "The husband was mentioned by 64 percent of the cases, the mother or daughter in 67 percent of the cases, other kin by 38 percent and a girlfriend (or woman friend) by 98 percent" (1975, draft). These findings are probably less surprising when we recall that it has been estimated that American married couples spend an average of only about twenty minutes a week in direct conversation with each other (Holmes, 1972, 357). Even among young college-aged women—stereotypically incapable of strong friendships with one another because of competition for men—the importance of female supports was recognized. Ann Hodge interviewed twenty-two women college students and found that they felt female relationships to be just as important to them as male relationships. "There was a great deal of discussion of the role friendship played in terms of support groups. The women felt that this was an extremely significant aspect of their lives even to the point of actually needing or preferring this support type of relationship over that of the male social relationships." Although they defined marriage as a most desired relationship, "they also tended to agree that this was not enough; they needed their female social relationships" (draft, 1978).

The impact of increasing labor-force participation on friendship does not seem to have been always or necessarily negative. Noteworthy in this connection is the finding that friendships based on the work site may often be the ones that serve the supportive functions of friendship (Warren, 1975). And in the networks of modern, if not of traditional, women studied by Gladieux, friends based on work-site relationships were present in many cases.

In any event, despite the relat_ve neglect of female friendshps in the research literature, it does seem essential in any discussion of the structure of the female world to pay attention to their place in it. Men have been important to women as sources of financial support and also of status in a social world organized on a couple basis. But to see the female world in these restricted terms is to shut out an enormous component in its structure. There are many more female-female relationships in our society than there are female-male relationships. And the part they play not only in the lives of women but also in the structure of the female world is incalculable.

Lest it appear that friendship in the female world is only or even primarily a kind of therapy, the happy kind of relationship it can be not only among working-class women but also among their successful career sisters, the following case in point is offered.

> About twenty years ago I found myself a member of a loosely knit organization dedicated to the care and preservation of homeless cats. All of us on the feline rescue squad ... worked hard at our jobs, but when a cat needed a friend, work stopped and phones rang all over New York until the hapless puss had a home. I thought about my days as a cat benefactor for the first time in years the other night as I was cleaning up after a dinner party. ... All of my guests had been women and the spirit of the evening had carried with it resonances of the long defunct "pussycat underground." . . We used to nurture cats, men, and children; now we seem also to be nurturing ourselves and one another. Successful women had once been our last priority (except for closest friends, of whom we were jealous); now they're among the first. . . . So we sat around that table, picking at the chicken bones and drinking the wine, and there was no paranoia, jealousy, or anxiety in the air. Only mutual support. . . . We talked about how wonderful and creative and successful women are. . . . We were treating each other with the care those pussycats used to receive so many years ago, when all that tenderness and nurturing was looking for a proper outlet and not yet finding it. Not that I still don't love cats. But delight in, and participation in the success of one's women friends is even warmer than a kitten's fur [Fleischer, 1979].

Since many of the supportive services once performed by family and friends have now been taken over by outside agencies—by hospitals, health professionals, nursing homes, schools, insurance, social security, public assistance—what is there left for women to offer one another? The warmth and intimacy that bureaucratized professional services do not supply. In brief, female friendships in and of themselves "can be one of the major 'good things in life' " (Seiden and Bart, 208). They must be relegitimized "so that women and men may take them seriously and recognize that women may well make sacrifices to maintain them" (208).

Surrogate Support Groups

> [T]he city created a new kind of human being—the cosmopolitan—who was able, as his tribal ancestors were not, to relate to others in the new ways that city living made not only possible but necessary. The cosmopolitan did not lose the capacity for knowing others personally. But he gained the capacity for knowing others only categoricially. The cosmopolitan did not lose the capacity for the deep, long-lasting, multifaceted relationship. But he gained the capacity for the surface, fleeting, restricted relationship. It is true, of course, that the transformation from the world of personally known others to the world of strangers has been, and continues to be, an emotionally painful one.
>
> L. Lofland, 1973, 177-178

The female world, like the male world described in this passage, is also having to come to terms with the new kinds of relationships characteristic of modern life. It is attempting to find a modus vivendi between the "deep, long-lasting, multifaceted relationship" and the "surface, fleeting, restricted relationship."

In the absence of the stable old kinship network and with the attenuation of friendship relationships, artificial or synthetic or derivative agencies or networks have to be created to perform the old support functions in new ways. In this transitional period, as women struggle to restructure their world, three kinds of surrogates for the old support groups are relevant here: (1) feminist groups and collectives, (2) self-help groups, and (3) relationships which Peggy Wireman labels "secondary intimate relationships."

The feminist groups comprised of single women—both lesbian and heterosexual—are the most sophisticated, the most aware of what is happening to the structure of the female world, and perhaps the most conflicted about how to deal with it. They try to live according to at least the love-in-the-agape-sense component of the female world without slipping back into the duty-sacrifice component. These women are "isolated from the residential nuclear family adaptation which engages most other women in the world" (Roos, 1978). Indeed, they "warn against the dangers of nuclear family involvement for women." Lacking this age-old basis for security, they actively attempt "to work out alternative protective arrangements." They are handicapped in this effort by the absence of commonly agreed upon rules of procedure, few guarantees of common aims and interests, and custom-based and legal inertia and stabilizers. They find the competition of romantic relationships hard to overcome, for there is a tendency to transform friends into lovers: "a major finding of this research was that women in Berkeley, regardless of their sexual choices, have upgraded their friends closer to the status of lover in order to make a better emotional living," even though "friendship is less polluted by sexist expectations." Friendship, as Seiden and Bart have noted, has few public sanctions. Thus, Roos continues, "while friendship is the relationship of ideological choice in the women's community, few social mechanisms exist for securing sincerity and reliability among friends. The relationship is not well protected, and participants feel less secure than members of family groups, who can imagine some stability in their lives because of the inertia custom and legality provide." But socially sanctioned legal ties do not help women trying to escape oppression. "Berkeley single feminists are forced to make a trade-off between security and freedom in constructing interpersonal relationships." Roos notes that under such adverse circumstances these women also face dilemmas in their work lives. They are disturbed by the conflicts between achievement and equality in the network; achieving women may be accused of exploiting or using the movement; their success humiliates others and leads to invidious comparisons which interfere with ideologically normative warmth. There is no way, as in the family system, for each to share the rewards of any member. Thus "not only is romantic success disruptive to community and network processes, but career success competes as well."

Since the Gemeinschaft ideals are in conflict with the Gesellschaft or capitalistic reality, the members who go into business have a high rate of failure. And "feminist wariness about slipping into old female role behaviors calling for sacrifice of self for the welfare of others further restrains women from helping even tried and true network associates." The lack of workable roles is disconcerting.

Because these women are so verbal, so perceptive and so aware of all the undertones, overtones, insinuations, implications, ramifications of the structure of the female world and so sensitive to the sexism of the male world, they supply us with one of the best maps of the turmoil agitating the female world at the present time. They call our attention to nuances in human relationships that few women and perhaps no men catch without their help. These women are not necessarily happy but "they choose to continue to live with the contradictions feminism engenders." Though they could enter the bourgeois life of conventional women, they do not because they identify with the women's movement and, "to a woman, know themselves as heroic pioneers, as poets and philosophers, as true and complete humans."

Another kind of surrogate for the old kinship group—a category that includes some feminist groups—are the so-called self-help groups which Marcia Guttentag, Susan Salasin and their associates discovered while studying mental-health services for women. They found "many new services springing up that cultivate the ideals and systems of mutual aid. It is no surprise that the majority of these services are geared towards women. The mutual aid concept extends to the process of women helping women—women united on the common ground of their womanhood" (Guttentag, Salasin, et al., 1976).[7] Self-help and the self-help modality are defined as the attempt to solve a shared problem through mutual aid and support. In some cases paraprofessionals or even professionals may also be involved in an administrative, supervisory, or peer relationship (San Diego Center for Women's Studies and Services, n.d.). A support system is defined as "a community or network of people who actively provide emotional support for, and identity with, others experiencing stressful situations" (Guttentag, Salasin, et al., 1968). These groups range widely in scope, from LaLeche League to divorcée groups, from Breast Surgery Rap Groups to Widow-to-Widow programs, from nonfeminist "Philosophy of Christian Womanhood" groups to radical feminist collectives. What they have in common is that they are all based on the assumption that people who share a problem can solve it through mutual aid and support. The model for such self-help is Alcoholics Anonymous.[8]

Gladieux commented, in connection with social networks in pregnancy, that "because of the supposed uniformity of values and the norm-setting and supportive functions of a closely knit social network, . . . a woman's competence, and confidence, in performing the maternal role is increased" (282), as well, we might add, as her competence or confidence in performing other roles as well.

In some ways even more derivative, but in this case not deliberately established for the purpose, is the "intimate secondary relationship," which Peggy Wireman defines as "one which combines certain traits of primary relationships and certain traits of secondary ones. . . . [Such relationships] provide individuals and communities means of adjusting to an urban environment and to rapid social change. They may take the form of neighborhood civic groups, community projects, and the like. They (1) ameliorate the effects of rapid geographic mobility, (2) temper or facilitate changing family patterns, (3) facilitate harmonious relations among a heterogeneous population, and (4) create community integration" (1978, draft). These relationships take place in a public context—that is, in public meeting places—but they often foster close, even intimate friendships. They perform a variety of services for individuals and the community but our concern here is primarily with their function in relation to women.

Wireman illustrates the concept by the situation in Holland. There, "women enter such relationships precisely because they [both provide and] limit intimacy. They offer an alternative to a primary group, yet are not as threatening as entering the secondary relations of a job situation. The lives and identities of Dutch women tend to be tightly oriented to their families. When they want to develop new skills and personal relationships, they frequently become active in voluntary groups. Their excuse for participation is the civic objective and for this reason their husbands permit [*sic*] them to join. Such groups enable them to escape from a boring or conflict-ridden personal relationship. They often are not interested in joining another primary group, such as a 'coffee klatch,' not because of potential threat to their marriages, but because they have found primary relationships to be too confining. Frequently, joining a voluntary group and forming intimate secondary relationships is a preliminary step to obtaining a job, with its [wholly] secondary relationships. In such a case, one of the functions of intimate secondary relationships is to facilitate the emancipation of women. Thus, intimate secondary relationships may fulfill several functions in a society with changing marital roles."

Secondary intimate relationships may either improve a marriage by providing relationships that are stimulating but nonthreatening to a marriage or, on the other hand, they may ease a woman out of a marital relationship. Women may enter into such secondary intimate relationships "to obtain the support needed to face dissolving the marriage."

There may be other transitional or experimental kinds of relationships which attempt, wholly or in part, to supply the affectional ties that kinship and locale groups were traditionally supposed to supply. How and to what extent they succeed we have still to learn. It has long since become a truism that living in this fast-paced world is not easy.

So much, then, for the primary-group, or quasi-primary-group, structure of the female world, the Gemeinschaft world of family, locale, and friends. The evidence seems clear-cut that although kinship ties remain strong in the female world, at least in some segments of it, they seem to be waning for many women. In the transitional period, until we learn to reweave social networks, new "synthetic" or "derivative" forms of relationship seem to be evolving, namely feminist groups, purposively organized support groups, and "intimate secondary relationships." There may be many more as yet unreported.

Some Questions

Is the female world ceasing to be a wholly Gemeinschaft world? Is it ceasing to perform the integrating function of our industrial society, holding the whole social system together? Will it ultimately lose its kin- and locale-orientation altogether? Will fewer and fewer women devote time and energy to maintaining contacts with relatives? What would be the character of local life if there were no women at all at home during the day? If all the eyes in the windows that Jane Jacobs called to our attention were gone? If there were no women interested in garden clubs? If the kinship and locale characteristics of the female world disappeared, would the whole system break down? Or would new, paid professionals evolve whose functions it would be to serve as "family coordinators"—that is, to keep relatives in touch with one another, announcing births, deaths, confirmations, graduations, marriages, reminding them of birthdays, anniversaries, celebrations, health, whereabouts—like the Christmas letters now circulated among friends and relatives, but including problems as well as triumphs—and, in brief, to supply such important services, do all the unimportant, trivial, banal, unprofitable chores which constitute such an important part of the human condition? Are we willing to dispense with these services? If not, what structural surrogates are available to supply them? I find these questions thought-provoking.

Notes

1. In 1959 it was a status symbol in Russia if a child was cared for by a grandmother rather than in a creche (personal observation).
2. "What seems to happen is this. When many of the people a person knows interact with one another, that is, when the person's network is close-knit, the members of his [her] network tend to reach consensus on norms and they exert consistent informal pressure on one another to conform to the norms, to keep in touch with one another, and, if need be, to help one another. If both husband and wife come to marriage with such close-knit networks, and if conditions are such that the previous pattern of relationships is continued, the marriage will be superimposed on these pre-existing relationships, and both spouses will continue to be drawn into activities with people outside their own elementary family (family of procreation). Each will get some emotional satisfaction from these external relationships and will be likely to demand correspondingly less of the spouse. Rigid segregation of conjugal

roles will be possible because each spouse can get help from people outside" (Bott, 1957, 60).

3. Bott classifies the generally relevant studies as: (1) studies of networks and /or conjugal roles in the geographically nonmobile working class; (2) studies containing information about networks and conjugal roles in middle-class families; (3) changes of class, networks, and conjugal roles; (4) studies of family and work; (5) comparative, rural, and tribal studies; and (6) network therapy. She also summarizes studies that specifically discuss or test the conjugal roles/network hypothesis. In this edition, she also notes that despite an enormous corpus of work on networks, many more questions had to be asked and answered before modern network phenomena could be understood. In 1975 a national study in the United States was planned to find "the extent and nature of relationships that keep alive the kin network among persons under 40 years of age and their parents and siblings" (Glick, 1975, 14) but it did not materialize.
4. Services performed by women regularly throughout the year or on occasions are additional functions of the family network. According to empirical studies, these services cover a wide gamut: "(1) shopping, escorting, care of children, advice giving and counselling, cooperating with social agencies on counselling and welfare problems of family members, are types of day-to-day activities performed by members of the kin network. (2) Services to old persons such as physical care, providing shelter, escorting, shopping, performing household tasks, sharing of leisure time, etc. are expected and practiced roles of children [daughters?] and other kin members. These acts of filial and kin responsibility are performed voluntarily without law or compulsion" (Sussman and Burchinal, 1962, 237).
5. The network concept has spread to include professional, economic, and political networks as well as family networks. Indeed, the concept of network has become one of increasing research preoccupation.
6. The void left by the demise of homosociality may correspond to the male anomie which has so preoccupied male students of industrial society. Evidence for the vulnerability of women left stranded shows up in the incidence of stress symptoms, especially among working-class women (Warren, 120-121; Bernard, 1976). Depression, which has reached almost epidemic proportions among women, may be viewed as the female counterpart to male alienation, both related to feelings of powerlessness (Radloff, 1978).
7. At the same time professionals in the area of mental health were also discovering the preventive and therapeutic potential of support systems, comprised not only of professionals and paraprofessionals but also of others in the environment. Such support included "the stimulation of a person's intellectual and emotional development through personal interaction with significant others in the family and with peers and older persons in school, church, and work. In the face-to-face interchanges the person satisfies her needs for love and affection, for limitation and control, and for participation in joint activity which provides opportunities for identification and identity formation. Inadequate provision of . . . such care occurs if there is no opportunity for a person to build relationships with others who can satisfy [her] needs, for instance, if [she] does not have a stable family; if the significant

other people do not satisfy [her] needs, but manipulate [her] in order to satisfy theirs" (Caplan, 1974, 194). A conscious effort was being made to supply such support systems to pregnant women, nursing mothers, divorcées and widows, child abusers, single mothers, abused women, and any woman who needed the kind of support no longer available as it once was in women's sphere.

8. Ten concerns dealt with by forty-six such groups were: widowhood, alcoholism, unwanted pregnancies, rape, mothering, health, career, depression, relationships, and self-realization. The last two, with eleven and seventeen groups, respectively, were the most frequent. About three-fourths (74 percent) of services were for married women, two-thirds (67 percent) for single women, half were for divorced-separated women, and about a third (35 percent) for homosexual women.

13

Groups, Associations, Collective Behavior in the Female World

THE TRANSFORMATION OF SOCIETIES brought about by industrialization increased not only the number of subjects about which nonfamilial and nonlocal groups could be formed but also the facilities which made such organizations possible, and hence the geographic area over which membership could be dispersed. The postal service, for example, was speeded up by the invention of the railroad; later the telegraph and then the telephone vastly improved the means for forming and maintaining non-face-to-face groups. Thus, groups and associations proliferated; Tocqueville in 1840 was already commenting on the propensity of Americans for forming voluntary associations for almost anything and everything:

> Americans of all ages, all conditions, and all dispositions, constantly form associations. They have ... associations of a thousand ... kinds—religious, moral, serious, futile, extensive or restricted, enormous or diminutive. The Americans make associations to give entertainments, to found establishments for education, to build inns, to construct churches, to diffuse books, to send missionaries to the Antipodes; and in this manner they found hospitals, prisons, and schools. If it be proposed to advance some truth, or to foster some feeling by the encouragement of a great example, they form a society. Wherever, at the head of some new undertaking, you see the govern-

> ment in France, or a man of rank in England, in the United States you will be sure to find an association. . . . Americans form associations for the smallest undertakings [1840, 114-115].

It was said in the 1840s that no Boston dinner party was complete until it had formed some reform organization or other. And hardly anything—as Tocqueville implies—was considered beyond the scope of such organizations. Some, such as the antislavery societies, did in fact become major social reform movements.

Women as well as men organized and participated in these associations, and although they rarely occupied decision-making positions in those organized by or with men, they nevertheless profited greatly by the experience. Such movements became schools in collective behavior for women. Through them they "came into direct confrontation with significant male traditions and behavior patterns. . . . Their activities carried them into state and national politics. . . . During these few years [the 1830s]—women abolitionists took a vigorous part in America's social and political dialogue" (Melder, 1977, 61). They not only participated in male organizations but established their own associations as well, and ran them with competence and dispatch. With respect to the penchant for forming voluntary associations the world of women resembled that of men.[1] And for the most part, these were do-good organizations. In Chapter 12 we emphasized the Gemeinschaft nature of the female world; at this point we begin the discussion with comments on its love-and/or-duty aspect.

Philanthropy: Love and/or Duty

We begin with the "organizing for others" which Harriet Holter included in her second category of groups in the female world. The "organizing for others" pattern grew directly out of the "local community . . . embracing the local service of all in the common good . . . and kindness to the weak" (Cooley, 1909, 51). Hannah More, the very preceptress of nineteenth-century ladies, had conceded that philanthropy was a legitimate activity for women; she seemed to have envisioned it in the Lady Bountiful or benefactress tradition of *noblesse oblige*, of the gentry, that is, fulfilling the social obligations of their station. She did not define her teachings as opening a door that would ultimately greatly expand the female world. Voluntary associations in More's day were not a widely known phenomenon in Europe. In many parts of the world such organizations were—and still are—discouraged if not actually banned as threatening to the established order. In the United States, however, they were protected by the Constitution, which guarantees the right of assembly. So they flourished luxuriantly.

It was perceptive of Tocqueville to note the significance of voluntary organizations in American society. Men, he saw, were taking services and functions into their own hands that they did not want taken over by government. Although women, too, as noted above, formed voluntary organizations, and although they, too, became joiners, there was a difference. Their voluntary organizations were not oriented toward their own self-interest, except as participation afforded them channels for "secondary intimate relationships," for self-actualization, for careers, for self-esteem, for escape from boredom. The women in these voluntary organizations were doing the millenial work of the integry, of the female world—taking care of others. Doing good. Or, later in the century, they were doing cultural chores that were beneath the dignity of the male world. They were tolerated as long as they tended to their female business. Some members of the clergy might object to their activities, but by and large no one really bothered enough to cause them concern. They were laughed at by some, joked about by some, but apparently tolerated by most.

Although some of the clergy tried to impede these philanthropical associations when they competed with church activities, they nonetheless flourished, for they were fueled by more than religious fervor. "The dynamics of urbanization, contributing strongly to the creation of the woman-belle ideal, also became the unwitting midwife of female benevolent societies. Women's charities responded to many of the same problems and pressures that called male associations into being. Both were touched by an acute sense of individual impotence to effect social change [as Tocqueville had pointed out] and by pervasive feelings of isolation. But female societies had a heritage uniquely their own and developed along lines quite distinct from their masculine counterparts" (Berg, 1978, 154).

Since the time of the great enclosures in England, which had turned loose on the countryside a host of "sturdy beggars," there had been community—as well as church—efforts to take care of the "deserving" poor. The resulting Poor Laws of the early seventeenth century had been administered by local governments. The dole which they established was already well institutionalized by the time of Malthus, at the end of the eighteenth century. These public relief systems, including the dole, were administered for the most part by men. The idea was to make relief so humiliating that one would do almost anything to avoid it. The settlers in America brought this system with them; there were overseers of the poor in most communities of any size.

In contradistinction to this system, private help, called "charity," was supposed to be motivated by love or, as espoused by Hannah More, by the duty of those who had high position toward those in inferior stations. And early in the nineteenth century women in towns and cities in America did begin to develop a system of voluntary associations that worked outside the harsh public relief system. They began to organize their own independent efforts to help women. Female-headed families, the Biblical "widows and orphans," were among their earliest concerns, as were also aged, indigent females. Prostitutes or fallen women were not neglected. Poorly paid factory girls became a concern. Among the many organizations formed were the Society for the Relief of Poor Widows, the Association for the Relief of Respectable, Aged, Indigent Females, the Moral Reform Society, the Female Benevolent Society, and the Female Charitable Society. They established orphan asylums and, in Boston, a Female Refuge.

Ethnic as well as native-born women formed charitable associations. JoEllen Vinyard, for example, has reported on the situation in Detroit in the nineteenth century:

> Women . . . grouped together, sometimes on religious lines, other times on an ethnic base. . . . The Catholic Female Benevolent Society opened the city's first orphanage in 1834 after cholera left many children without parents. Within two years the Ladies' Protestant Orphan Asylum had opened to house, feed, educate, and instill Protestant tenets in homeless non-Catholic children. Catholic women worked to help the Sisters of Charity maintain St. Mary's Hospital. . . . In the years that followed, the pattern of dual charities was continually repeated. Meanwhile, women of every class and background became joiners. As early as 1850, the altar society of Most Holy Trinity, a working-class Irish parish had 530 members. Throughout the city, women met to sew clothes for their orphans, bake for their food sales and prepare for the annual fairs which supported their own special causes. By the 1880s, there were the Presbyterians' Harper Hospital, the Lutheran Orphan Asylum, the Episcopalian St. Luke's Hospital, church home and orphanage, and the Zoar Asylum of the Zion German Reformed Church. Under Catholic direction there were two orphan asylums, a foundling home, an insane asylum, St. Joseph's Home for the Aged Poor, and St. Mary's Hospital, which had just moved into a new and larger building [Vinyard, 1974].

Nor did Jewish women fall far behind.

> Just as women's natures were expected to be predisposed to piety, they were also expected to be endowed with an extra measure of charity and mercy. Philanthropic concern, particularly on a personal level, was considered an extension of the home and family obligations that women bore, and it became another example of her religiosity and purity. While there had always existed special "women's societies" within the traditional Jewish community, especially for providing the necessary care for the female sick and dead, charity had always been a communal activity, controlled and executed by men. Now many synagogues and most cities and towns boasted a Ladies' Hebrew Benevolent Society. . . . During the Civil War, American Jewish women, like their non-Jewish counterparts, extended their charita-

> ble work. . . . Though small in scale the philanthropic societies established by women throughout the nineteenth century became the forerunners of the great American Jewish women's organizations of the twentieth century [Baum, Hyman, Michel, 1976, 30-31].

In all of these activities the women were, of course, performing the classic function of the female world as integry. But more than charity alone was involved. Although the manifest function performed by all these voluntary associations was to do good, they were more than vehicles for the love-and/or-duty ethos. They constituted, in effect, surrogate and respectable careers for women bored with the isolation of the female world. And in the form of "causes" they remained careers for women until well into the twentieth century (Bernard, 1978, chap. 3). For many a woman there were "virtually no alternatives. Chained to a futile existence fraught with profound conflicts, her discontent manifested itself in illness and in diaries and works of fiction. Finally, as boredom, loneliness, and the craving for identity coalesced into a driving force, women founded networks of societies throughout urban America" (Berg, 154-155). These associations, in brief, served as an antidote for the tedium of their existence. Involvement was a "quest for identity" as well as a response to urban problems. (Berg, 1978, 156).

The problems were certainly there; they were real enough. The aged, the indigent, the underpaid, the sickly, the alcoholic, and the prostitute did need help. The activities of voluntary associations were not "made work." They performed basic community functions. They constituted a legitimate avenue of civic participation outside the home. They were within the sphere of respectable women's duties, yet allowed partial escape from the confining walls of domesticity. The secondary gains in recognition for their own achievements rather than for those of their fathers or husbands were fortuitous. Nor should the benefits to the women's families be overlooked. Volunteer work served as a means to affirm their families' status and importance in the community as well as their own (Goldman, 1972, 34). Thus, whatever the motivation or dynamic or manifest function served by these charitable associations may have been, they performed a number of latent functions also.

One such function was the training which participation gave members in the nuts and bolts of organization. Associations gave women practice in drawing up constitutions and bylaws, in electing officers, in arranging meetings, in assigning duties, in managing funds. The last was especially important, for fund-raising "breached the mythical barrier" between the private and public lives of these women. They also entered public life by exercising the right of petition (Berg, 167).

Nancy Cott raises another interesting question with respect to the functions peformed by work in voluntary associations: Did it contribute to the development of feminism? Did all those experiences in women's clubs and associations contribute to group consciousness? To sisterhood? To female solidarity? To at least a protofeminism? Barbara Berg believes that they did generate a nascent solidarity among participants in the early nineteenth century. "Before 1830, benevolent societies had [only] vaguely perceived a feminine existence separate from the possible relations of her life as wife, mother, sister, and daughter" (193). In associations women extended their sense of solidarity beyond their friends and kin; they "postulated a community of women. They continually emphasized the similarities between themselves and black, Indian, and immigrant women. All women, regardless of background or position, were basically the same; objectified by a society that denied their autonomy. Theirs, then, was a vertical rather than a horizontal, dichotomy, largely shaped by the monolithic precepts of the woman-belle ideal" (267). We have already noted Beecher's efforts to substitute sex for class as a paradigm for organizing society. That ethos, Berg points out, had been used "to compensate for the instability and insecurity of the ante-bellum class structure. The perception of a people separated and stratified by sex, rather than class, intensified the members' belief in the unity of all women. It reinforced the many efforts to help their 'struggling sisters' to a fuller existence and stimulated the growth of a feminist consciousness" (267).

These associations provided other secondary gains as well in the form of support groups. "Membership in an association provided the upper- and middle-class woman, traditionally isolated at home, an opportunity to relate to other women of similar background in an unprecedented manner. Acquaintances and friendships assumed a dimension not found within the stylized tedium of 'social calls.' Energized by a sense of mission, the women of the respective societies drew together. They shielded one another from ridicule and scorn, exchanged ideas on methods, worked hard and long hours to meet deadlines and avert crises, and supported each other in many difficulties arising from work in organized benevolence" (Berg, 161-162).

In ethnic groups, these associations were a meeting ground for old, new, and second generation immigrants which also served as a bridge between classes. As in the associations Berg describes, those in ethnic communities also "offered a dependable recourse and a sense of identity, an arrangement which allowed [female] Detroiters to have confidence in themselves and thus a greater measure of tolerance for their neighbors" (Vinyard, 197). Although philanthropic work fostered competition rather than consensus between ethnic groups, still, by providing ethnic women a chance to gain self-assurance and leadership skills, the church groups helped them move toward integrated community activities.

The wide variety of associations—Bible, missionary, educational, material, industrial, Sabbath-school, infant schools—gave women an opportunity to express individual choice and helped them recognize individual differences among themselves, thus stimulating a sense of community with other women so that "awareness of individuality grew out of unity" (Berg, 166).

Voluntary associations based on philanthropy or charity continued to be a major area for female activities well into the twentieth century. A book on etiquette in 1905 noted that charity was part of a woman's role: "The woman of the family is very often, directly or indirectly, the dispenser of the money devoted to charity. She is the one who decides into what channels it shall go. She has the time for investigating the needs of societies and of individuals. The work too that accompanies gifts of charity more often falls to her lot than to a man. This is a department of service properly belonging to her. She has natural rights in this section of the world's work of which she should be as proud as a patriotic man is of his right to vote" (Harland and Van de Water, 1905, 398). The authors then proceed to instruct women on how to perform in this important area. "Wherever possible the aim of such [charitable] organizations is to help people to help themselves" (400). It is, thus, more than merely a sentimental impulse. But, like other students of the subject, they recognize the secondary gains to be derived: "The opportunity to do good offered by these societies is not only an opportunity to help the poor, but [also] to help one's self, and even in other ways than the one generally acknowledged of broadening one's sympathies and cultivating one's heart. The gain a woman derives in discipline from working in concert with other women is of inestimable value" (400-401).

By now there was also another way to express one's philanthropic impulses, namely in settlement houses. It was "much in vogue . . . for young women just out of college to do a year of social settlement work" (404). Harland and Van de Water had ideas on this subject too: "One should not leave the subject of one's duty to organized philanthropy without a word concerning the work of the social settlement, the greatest philanthropic movement of the day. . . . Unfortunately, fashion and the novelty of the life involved in the experiment [have] made social settlement work attractive to many people for somewhat selfish reasons. . . . They do not know how to get on with poor people and often their ill-disguised curiosity amounts to insolence and hurts those whom it is intended the work should benefit. [Further], these people who, through excitement and love of novelty, leave their homes for settlement work are often needed at home" (403-404).

Actually all these philanthropic and charitable activities were in the process of becoming professional careers. For the first decades of the twentieth century they remained primarily in the female world. They were shaped, conceptualized, trained for by women (Bernard, 1964). Not until the great depression of the 1930s, when the old public —"dole" or "relief," or "welfare," or "assistance"—strand and the newer philanthropy or charity or social work strand converged, did it cease to be an almost exclusive part of the female world. And a challenge had begun to take shape long before that. One of the outcomes of all that participation in associations was that women had begun to become sensitized to the inequity of their own position and the subjugation of many of them to men (Berg, 1978).

A new note began gradually to be sounded. Berg believes that the advent of an activist, non-philanthropy-oriented phase in women's organizations—which she dates as far back as to 1830—marked a sharp break in the sisterhood of the female world, a point that will be commented on further in Chapter 14.

Self-Interest Female Organizations

So long as women limited their organizational efforts to charity or philanthropic activities they were tolerated or ignored if not actively encouraged. So long, that is, as their organizations stuck to their own last, they were acceptable. The clergy might protest when its turf was invaded, but not too strenuously. Only when women began to organize in their own interests were they challenged—only, that is, when they sought change. And especially when they demanded things for themselves rather than for others—the vote, for example—did they begin to be taken seriously. Only then, especially when they attacked the male world, demanding costly reforms, or when they attacked one of the hallowed institutions in the male world—the saloon, for example, or property in the form of slavery.

Much of this activism, based as it was on "philogyny"—the female counterpart of "philanthropy"—was a luxury only fairly affluent women could afford to indulge in. But there was also another kind of organization emerging in the nineteenth century which was more specifically oriented toward self-interest, namely, trade unions. The women involved here were not likely to be socially conscious upper-middle-class—often college-educated—women but women at the machine, the counter, the lathe.

Early in the nineteenth century, the Lowell girls had taken part in "turnouts," or strikes, and demonstrations. But they had not succeeded in forming unions. They had lacked good leadership. As the century wore on women participated in the labor movement to the extent they were allowed. Although they were generally persona non grata in the male unions, some women were permitted to be organizers in the American Federation of Labor. They organized women's locals affiliated with the Knights of Columbus, which included housewives. But hard as they worked for the male unions there was little reciprocation; the interests of female workers received short shrift from the male union leaders. Only recently, in fact, have male-dominated unions begun to show interest in female issues. There was always a problem for the working women of how best to promote their interests: within a hostile male organization or in basically female organizations.[2]

They did try separate organizations. There was, for example, a separate typographical union from 1869 until 1878, but it garnered only forty members and the going was rough all the way. Women organized working women's leagues, national federations, working women's societies, a working women's federal union, as well as working girls' social clubs. They organized an International Congress of Working Women, later known as the International Federation of Working Women. They organized the Women's International League for Peace and Freedom.

Although such sex-segregated organizations did not become the established pattern in the female world, still the basic preference for them as more comfortable for women is understandable. Here is the rationale as expressed in 1915: "Where the conditions of the trade permit it, by far the best plan is to have the women organized in separate locals. The meetings . . . [for] women and girls only draw better attendances, give far more opportunity for all the members to take part in the business, and beyond all question form the finest training ground for the women leaders who in considerable numbers are needed as badly in the women's side of the trade union movement today" (Henry, 1976, 170). In their own locals, women "have the interest of running the meetings themselves. They choose their own hall and fix their own time of meeting. Their officers are of their own selecting and taken from among themselves. The rank and file, too, get the splendid training that is conferred when persons actually—and not merely nominally—work together for a common end. Their introduction to the great problems of labor is through their practical understanding and handling of those problems as they encounter them in the everyday difficulties of the shop and the factory and as dealt with when they come up before the union meeting or have to be settled in bargaining with an employer" (171). In mixed-sex meetings the women felt uncomfortable, they were less likely to participate, they were not likely to be paid attention to.

The female style was not congenial to the men. "Women are less apt to be aggressive in their manner of making demands than are men," said one in 1913 (Matthews, 1976, 172). And "the men have criticized their more patient methods of working gradually toward a desired result. The women hold that their way of handling difficulties results in less friction and gains them a readier hearing in the long run. For the same reason women favor the industrial form of organization [more than twenty years before the CIO]. Jurisdictional disputes do not sap their time and strength. Thus the laundry workers employed in garment factories belong to the union of garment workers and all women who work in binderies are included in one union instead of being divided according to occupation as is common elsewhere" (172).

Literary, Educational, and Civic Clubs

However equivocal the success women had in organizing in their own economic behalf in unions, they were eminently successful in organizing for their own mutual self-improvement, an activity which did not impinge on the male world. The organization of women's clubs became almost a social movement in itself at the turn of the century.

When a visiting Englishwoman was asked what she most admired in the United States she replied without hesitation, the Women's Club (Harland and Van de Water, 1905, 384). Lucy Maynard Salmon, a Vassar professor, commented that "social life everywhere tends towards clubs, societies, and organizations" (1897, 207). She even proposed that domestics "be encouraged to form clubs and societies through which parlors can be provided for social intercourse" (207). Most of the clubs were, of course, primarily for middle-class women, who organized for "literary study, for economic discussion, for the consideration of municipal and social improvements" (Harland and Van de Water, 282). Such clubs were ubiquitous, "to be found all over the country, but particularly do they flourish in the Middle West, where every town and hamlet in the region boasts a woman's club of some sort" (282).

These organizations evoked a considerable amount of ridicule. Even Harland and Van de Water, who approved of them, granted that they were sometimes crude, absurd, and tiresome. Lucy Maynard Salmon was more severe. She called these "literary clubs and classes [which had sprung up and multiplied], offering occupation to their members, but producing nothing and giving at first only the semblance of education and culture, [just] another channel for . . . idle labor . . . in what has been called 'intellectual fancy-work' " (13).

Harland and Van de Water, closer to the middle classes for whom they wrote, were more charitable. In fact, they included in their book on etiquette instruction on the proper way to organize and run recreational, cultural, or charitable clubs. Absurd as some of them might be, "others are fine in themselves, exert a broadening influence over those intimately concerned and are helpful indirectly to the whole community represented by them. . . . It would be hard to estimate how much they have done in creating an atmosphere for the truly artistic and literary element in various communities throughout the United States" (282-283). In fact, "in small communities . . . they may be a means of lifting a whole community to a livelier and more interesting social and intellectual level" (386). Their programs may not have constituted haute culture, but they were "often stepping-stones to improvement in the social life of a community" (384).[3]

True to the female love-and/or-duty ethos, Harland and Van de Water had to invoke the civic-welfare contribution made by such clubs also. "Many women's clubs became important factors in municipal legislation along the lines most amenable to feminine influence. Through such clubs women have helped to solve educational questions, have influenced public sentiment in the direction of cleaning and beautifying the streets, and, in many other ways, have helped to promote law and order" (385-386).

But there were also personal gains to be derived from such club activities. "They lift women out of the consideration of the commonplace, domestic side of existence; they encourage toleration and a give-and-take attitude toward life, in which attitude women are by nature lacking; they open a way for the development of latent talent of various kinds" (384). Their contribution was more, that is, than the "intellectual fancy-work" that Salmon so contemptuously labelled it.

Recent Trends in Group and Association Membership

Our discussion in this Part has been primarily in terms of forms of organization—informal, formal—rather than mainly in terms of the specific substantive interests around which groups are formed. But at least a bow in the direction of the subjects around which women organize is in order here. In his review of trends in groups and association memberships among women Abbott Ferriss (1971) found that women appear to be abandoning some kinds, holding steady in some, and fluctuating in their loyalties to still others. A decline in rural-life organizations is understandable in view of the decline in the rural population (173). The significance of the decline in "hereditary organizations" and in fraternal and ethnic organizations is uncertain; it may be related to the waning Gemeinschaft, to the fading of ethnicity, or to the declining prestige of status-conferring organizations. Ferriss suggests that these "status-symbolic clubs (fraternal, ethnic, hereditary)[4] and 'cultural-social' clubs' " are being supplanted by recreational and work-oriented organizations (173). This may be another aspect of the process we noted in Chapter 12 of the supplanting of kin by friends in the social networks of modern women.

Different organizations have had different histories. Thus, for example, home economics clubs peaked in 1954 and declined thereafter. Membership in the American Legion Auxiliary increased after World War II, reached a plateau, declined, then again increased. Business and professional clubs waxed until 1949, waned in 1962, then recovered. The League of Women Voters grew rapidly through 1952, more slowly since then. The American Association of University Women has shown a steady rate of growth. Fairly stable in membership are general federated women's clubs. But among the expanding groups Ferriss found recreational or sports groups, business and professional groups, and religion-affiliated organizations. In fact, "numerically, religious-affiliated organizations predominate among the memberships women hold. In the aggregate these groups are growing at an annual average rate of 3.1 percent—considerably higher than the rate of female population growth (1.6 percent annually). In 1968, membership in religious groups encompassed almost one-half of all memberships" in the female world (173).

A profile of women affiliated with voluntary associations in 1968 shows that more married than unmarried women were members. And among married women with children under eighteen, 56 percent were members, and half of them—27.4 percent—we know were in the labor force that year (President's Report, 1977, 194). Further characteristics of "joiners" were, according to Ferriss: home ownership rather than renting, urban rather than farm dwelling, high socioeconomic status rather than lower status, more education than only elementary schooling. Members were more likely than nonmembers to be interested in public affairs, to vote, and to support local charities. "Members are more likely than nonmembers to read magazines, and they spend more time reading books, and engage in voluntary public service work more than nonmembers" (172).

Although some of Ferriss' data go back as far as 1940, none goes beyond 1968. And when one considers all the changes that have taken place in the world of women since that time the question arises with respect to the applicability today of the reported situation as of 1968. We know, for example, that there has been almost an explosion of women's groups of all kinds, especially antidiscrimination groups, civil rights groups, radical feminist groups, lobbying groups. Thus in 1976 there were "three national directories which listed thousands of groups that are involved in efforts to gain social justice for women. They include women's centers, national women's organizations and a huge variety of local groups. They include research projects, education projects and labor organizing groups. They include people who are providing services on a day to day basis so that women can have the tools to gain power and independence in this country" (Peters and Samuels, 1976, 59-60).

The reported upsurge in ethnicity may well have reversed the decline in ethnic group membership reported by Ferriss. The ill repute of the Daughters of the American Revolution resulting from its refusal in 1939 to allow black contralto Marian Anderson to sing in its hall, which deterred some young women from joining, seems to be moderating. In brief, we need a new survey of group and association participation by women before we can see this aspect of the current group structure of the female world in accurate perspective. Especially interesting would be an accurate view of the religious groups. Are they continuing to grow as rapidly as in the 1960s? Do they still predominate so markedly? By and large, religious women tend to be traditional. When mobilized they are in a position to exert considerable influence in the female world.

Recent organizations in the female world have had problems working out a style of organization suited to their ideology. Among some the opposition to hierarchy—strongly emphasized in the male world—has been so deeply felt that they have resisted the emergence of leaders or "stars." Among some it led almost to an apotheosis of structurelessness (Freeman, 1975, 119-129, 142-146). Despite strong criticism of such lack of formal structure, some groups persist in the antihierarchical pattern, insisting that what may look like lack of structure is just a different kind of structure. We will have occasion to note Schaef's analysis of the contrast between male and female organizational styles (Chapter 15).

The Latent Integrating Function of Associations in the Female World

Although membership and participation in associations are class-related and may encourage ethnic and racial segregation and thus have divisive impact in the female world, a woman is not always restricted in membership to associations of her own ethnic group, race, or class. Warner and his staff worked out in detail the number of interclass associations there were in Yankee City. He found, for example, that upper-upper individuals participated in six kinds of associations. Lower-upper individuals had memberships in five associations that overlapped with those of upper-upper individuals plus four more that the upper-upper class did not have, but they were excluded from one upper-upper-class association. Each social class was excluded from the highest association of the class just above but added some at the lower end. Only one kind of association had membership from all six social classes. The generalized picture is shown in Figure 13-1.

Thus, in addition to the latent function participation in associations performed for individual women, it also performed, although to a limited extent, the function of making it possible for women from different social classes to have contacts with one another.[5] The nature of those contacts is another matter, as we shall have occasion to note in Chapter 14.

Collective Behavior in the Female World

Of the several categories of collective behavior distinguished in traditional sociology, perhaps fashion—in clothes, décor, entertaining—is the most characteristic of the female world. There have nevertheless been female protests and demonstrations since at least classical times. The women who went on a sexual strike against their husbands under the leadership of Lysistrata may have been only mythical characters. But we know that Roman women did demonstrate against what they considered unfair legislation. They protested, for example, against taxation without representation. An edict of the Second Triumvirate had appropriated wealth from fourteen hundred of the richest women in Rome to pay for war with Brutus and Cassius. At the forum, Hortensia, the daughter of a great lawyer, asked, "Why should we pay taxes when we have no part in the honors, the commands, the statecraft for which you contend?" (Appian, 1910, 62). Women also used direct action to get the so-called Oppian law repealed. This was a sumptuary measure passed during the Punic Wars limiting women's expenditures on clothing and other items: "No woman should possess more than half an ounce of gold, or wear a garment of various colors, or ride in a carriage drawn by horses, in a city, or any town, or any place nearer thereto than one mile, except on occasion of some public religious solemnity"

FIGURE 13-1. Class overlapping in associational memberships. Source: W. Lloyd Warner and Paul S. Lunt, The Status System of a Modern Community (New Haven: Yale University Press, 1942), p. 8.

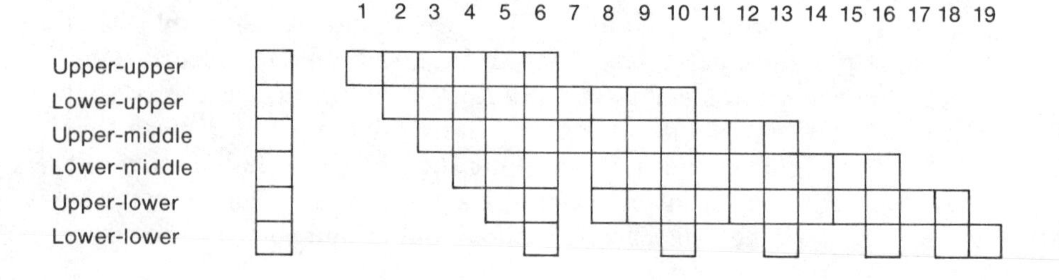

(Livy, 1951, 440). The women protested, much to Cato's horror: "What sort of practice is this, of running out into public besetting the streets, and addressing other women's husbands?" (443).

Since that time women have participated in all kinds of collective behavior not specifically related to the female world itself, including revolutionary movements, abolitionism, the civil rights movement, antiwar movements, and the like, even the gluten-bread movement. Fewer have participated in collective behavior generated within the female world itself.

There are records of crazes, mass hysterias, and other kinds of spontaneous collective behavior but by and large the structure of the female world has not lent itself to them. For our purposes here, it is the more organized forms of collective behavior that are most relevant, especially social movements. Some of the voluntary associations in the female world began to move in the middle of the nineteenth century. "Instead of simply ameliorating social ills and immorality through charity and the promotion of piety, reformers began to speak and write about overturning institutions, inducing drastic changes. . . ." (Melder, 1977, 50).

Social Movements

Lougee notes that there seem to be certain times and places when there is a profound rethinking of the part played by women in the total societal structure. The conceptualization of women's sphere early in the nineteenth century seems to have been one such time. So also was the second half of that century. So, too, of course, have been the 1960s and 1970s and so, no doubt, will be the 1980s. In the first of these periods "movements for moral reform and temperance and against slavery appealed to women because women were the principal victims of the evils which they attacked" (Melder, 1977, 50). These moral-reform movements sought to elevate women to their proper standing but still felt that women should remain in their proper sphere. Women's moral superiority, it was believed, "justified an unprecedented assertion of power by women" (Melder, 53). But it was the old-fashioned fragmented kind of power. These women rejected the women's rights movement. It was not in their script. That was to come later.

The most thoroughly researched social movements in the female world in the nineteenth century were probably the temperance movement and the suffrage movement. Others have attracted relatively minor attention, for example the Bloomer movement, the club-organization movement, the home economics movement, the social-settlement movement, and, in the twentieth century, the women's peace movement led by Jane Addams, the several reform movements led by Florence Kelley and her associates in New York, the social-work movement led by women at the University of Chicago's social service school, and Margaret Sanger's birth-control movement (L. Gordon, 1976).

Of all these social movements in the female world the suffrage or women's rights movement of the nineteenth century and the current women's liberation movement have been among those that have stimulated the most controversy. Feminist scholarship has not yet arrived at a consensus with respect to the significance of the nineteenth-century women's rights movements. A considerable amount of the work dealing with it views it as of fundamental importance in its impact on the female world. Carroll Smith-Rosenberg, on the other hand, dismisses it as relatively unimportant so far as its influence on the female world is concerned (1975, 186). Few women in the nineteenth century knew of Elizabeth Cady Stanton or Susan B. Anthony. They loom large in our image of the female world of the nineteenth century because we are interested in the movement they led. They are important to us. We can see them in context. But most of their contemporaries may never even have heard of them. Or, if they had, probably dismissed their ideas as irrelevant. They were accustomed to the status quo, probably too busy to think of changing it, surely not by way of the ballot with which they had had no experience. Only a relatively few women had received practice in collective behavior by way of participation in the antislavery movement and were thus ready for the women's rights movement, which between 1847 and 1850 had become a "distinct crusade" (Melder, 1977, 143). It was to take more than a hundred years before the issue of women's rights became relevant to enough women to have basic impact on the female world (Bernard, 1976).

Barbara Berg sees the nineteenth-century suffrage movement not as a positive force in the female world but, in fact, as a dysfunctional one, as a great disrupter of the female world, a blow to the female solidarity which had been in process of development by way of the female associations since the early years of the century. She finds a rather notable break in ethos with the rise of the suffrage movement, especially after 1860. "The drive for the vote ruptured the idea of a community of women dedicated to helping one another" (Berg, 1978, 269). It also obscured and vitiated the very "philosophy that had produced the suffrage agitation" (269). The ideology that had been emerging had dealt with "woman's freedom from sex-determined roles, her privilege to control her own life, her right to fulfill her autonomous identity" (269). That social movement, between 1800 and 1860, had also "stood on the threshold of recognizing that the liberation of one class of women depended upon the freedom of all others" (270). But, Berg believes, "in their efforts to secure the ballot, women dismissed or discounted these theories" (269). Foner has shown, further, that the suffrage movement also split the movement to organize women workers (1979).

In a way, this difference of opinion reflects a difference of opinion with respect to the major issues in the female world, now as well as then. Do they center on sex roles, on autonomy, on female identity, or on political equality? As issues they are still controversial. Different diagnoses or analyses lead to different strategies or proposed solutions.

Among the social movements arousing most enthusiasm today are the women's health movement, the movement to retrieve childbirth for the female world, the multifaceted women's liberation movement, and the minimovements at the community level.

The Battle to Protect Female "Turf"

We tend to think of collective behavior in fairly grand terms, of national movements, for example. But in the Gemeinshaft female world they may also be local in scope. And one of the most interesting processes at work in the female world today is the sucking of women, even in the most traditional ethnic enclaves, into the "public" space.

Gans tells us what the situation was like as recently as the late 1950s. In the Italian "village" he studied—the West End of Boston—girls were better educated than their brothers. They not only remained in school longer but they also seemed to absorb more; more of the unmarried girls than of the boys were, therefore, upwardly mobile (1962, 136). School, church, and consumer goods appealed to young women more than to young men (208). If the women entered the labor force it was likely to be as clerical workers (136). So "by virtue of the women's greater receptivity to education, and their premarital employment in the white-collar world, they are likely to take the lead in the process of change" (216). But for most women the weight of their cultural heritage still put a brake on their activities. "Because the wife remains subordinate to the husband in most families, because she is thoroughly indoctrinated in her homemaker role, and because she is hesitant about leaving the house to go to work, she may be unable to implement many of the changes of which she dreams. Her traditional role could act as a brake on her aspirations and perhaps as an accelerator on her frustrations" (216).

Less than two decades later a remarkable change was in process in many such communities. Now the greater education, experience in the labor force, and examples of other pioneering women were beginning to release the old brakes. Even formerly reclusive women were coming out of the kitchen. Many of them made it clear that they were not "women's libbers, but. . . ." They might still define their roles in family terms. But in many cases they came to see that in order to perform even their family roles, especially those of mothers and homemakers, they had to participate in the community. They had to save their neighborhoods. They had to save their schools. They had to learn a lot about the Gesellschaft—about redlining, for example, and credit and taxes. And they had to develop consumership skills, they had to learn to organize, to lobby, to exert pressure. Thus a lot of women who formerly felt that they could ignore the outside world, that they would be taken care of, were learning that they had to get out and fight for what they wanted. They could no longer, even as housewives and mothers, live the sheltered pre-industrial kind of life. More and more issues that arose in the polity were so-called women's issues, like abortion, contraception availability, sterilization. It was difficult for women to maintain their isolation when they felt strongly that these were their issues and that they should therefore have a great deal of say in policies dealing with them.

Nancy Seifer was one of the first to call our attention to the remarkable transformation in working-class and ethnic women (1973). "New threats to neighborhood safety and stability in the 1960s . . . served to drive many working-class women out of their homes and into community activism. Perhaps as women and mothers, they sensed a greater urgency than their husbands; perhaps they had more time (if they were housewives); or perhaps, not having the false pride of manhood at stake, they were more willing to fight and risk defeat at the hands of government officials or politicians. For whatever reason, it was the women who became the troops of the new white ethnic [working-class] organizations that began to take shape at the end of the 1960s in . . . many cities" (18).

Case in Point

Kathleen McCourt has given us a detailed case history of the changes as they occurred in one community, Southwest Side Chicago (1977). Here ethnic women of working-class background found they had to leave their homes in order to protect their neighborhoods against pollution, racism, bad housing, and also in order to deal with old agencies that were no longer serving them adequately. They were part of a national movement back to local control; their adversaries might be citizens' groups, corporate executives, government bureaucracies, or any other part of the male world (15). These women were not politically homogeneous. Some were liberal in the old sense, some conservative. They were not fixated on any specific approach. They used the tactics of the civil rights movement (16) or they imitated black welfare mothers (17). They did not seem to be at all the women we had learned about from Rainwater, Komarovsky, or Gans. They were performing in extra familial roles for the first time in their lives (17). "The working-class woman—especially if she does not hold a paying job—has not felt herself to be a part of any world wider than that of her family. . . . Beyond her immediate family, her friends and contacts in the wider world have been limited. She has not belonged to clubs or participated in groups, either formal or informal. She has tended neither to 'coffee klatch' with her neighbors . . . nor to entertain friends at home in the evening" (18). That old picture is no longer true.

The uprooting of old social networks had led many such women to try out new roles (223). Active and assertive community organization took the place of the old community consensus, "typically masked by a certain quietness and persistence, . . . a structure taken for granted" until disturbed (212). Among the consequences of such participation were not only greater consciousness of and feeling for shared concerns in the local community but also higher self-esteem, a sense of communion among themselves "formed by an actual experience of common feeling" (212).

These women engaging in grass-roots populism, aggressively protecting their "turf"—that is, their neighborhoods—were really attempting to hang on to the Gemeinschaft nature of their female world. They did not see themselves as feminists. They did not want to change their world. Still, they did, in a way, hold to a redemptive role for women. "If this country is to be saved at all, it'll be the women who do it" (114). They could not depend on the male world to reform itself. Indeed, they could not depend on men at all. Thus, for example, the August 28, 1970, newsletter of a block club association carried this sarcastic *sic semper tyrannis* message, expressing the activist women's resentment against the lack of support received from the male world:

FOR WOMEN ONLY

This article is addressed to "women only" due to an incredible fact. THERE ARE NO MEN LEFT.

It might be more correct to state that there are FEW men left. What do I mean? Attend any neighborhood meeting and tell me what gender is prevalent. Women, of course.

"But," you ask, "where are the MEN? Good question—just where are the men? Some are working, surely. Some are sick in bed or in a hospital. Right. WHERE ARE ALL THE REST? . . . Babysitting? Cutting grass?

Ladies, the list of excuses is endless. The truth of the matter is, your "man" is not a man at all. True, he is still of the male species, but any trace of MANHOOD has vanished. . . .

MEN OF THE AREA—UNITE! Show us that you're really out there.

Never fear, Ladies. . . . THERE ARE NO MEN LEFT TO HEAR THE CALL [McCourt, 1977, 42-43].

Notes

1. Female friendship—in fact, female bonding of any kind—has not only been hidden but actually denied. As a corollary, all the values that flow from male bonding itself, which grew originally out of the cooperation required for successful hunting, have also been denied. Tiger demonstrates how and why females could not become hunters and how those who did were selected out of the gene pool because they did not bear many daughters, with their dysgenic genes (Tiger, 1970, 127). So females stayed home and gathered food and therefore did not have to bond and acquire all the organizational skills resulting from hunting. Women anthropologists, not limited by the blinders that make female bonding invisible, have shown a number of examples of female bonding. And a television presentation of pygmy society offers evidence easily demonstrating female skills in bonding and organization. Among the Mbuti pygmies of the central African rain forests, it is true, the men do the hunting. But the women do the fishing. The women gather up the children and gaily go down to the river. They build one dam somewhat upstream and another dam downstream; they then bail out the water between the two dams. The stranded fish are clobbered and carried home in baskets. This activity is as well organized as the hunting projects of the men (*Nova*, Aug. 11, 1977, PBS).
2. The achievement of power, as noted in Chapter 7, has been fraught with many difficulties in the female world. Little by little women are beginning to generate their own resources. Thus consumer groups, largely female in concern, organize housewives' boycotts at the local level. Local neighborhood women learn to shake their fist at city hall on issues close to their hearts. The National Organization for Women, once its numerical base passed the critical mass level, turned to look for coalitions, even with the male world, in its drive for ERA.
3. See Chapter 18 for comments on female patronage of male culture.
4. Placing ethnic, hereditary, and fraternal groups together has validity in the sense that all are Gemeinschaft in character—that is, they are implicitly "kin" based—but they are on quite different levels so far as social status is concerned. Daughters of the American Revolution, for example, are not on the same social-status level as members of an ethnic sodality, though both may be classified as "ethnic." Even when associations turn into social, political, and reform movements, they retain their separate ethnic identities. The suffrage movement was supported predominantly by the Protestant middle class, both as rank and file and as leaders. Temperance movements had advocates in all classes, in all national and religious groups, but their styles of organization differed. Thus the Catholic women organized in their separate parishes while Protestants formed a national Women's Christian Temperance Union (Vinyard, 1974).

5. Moore (1961) found that almost three-fourths (73 percent) of the women who were members of an upper-class hospital board in Chicago were also members of the board of another health and welfare organization; 40 percent were members of a cultural association; and a third (35 percent) of a social association. Domhoff (1971) reports that in 1966 four-fifths of the alumnae of a women's college were engaging in volunteer activities, a fourth (24 percent) by way of churches and another fourth (23 percent) by way of the Junior League (42, 43). In some of these organizations they were mingling only with women of their own class background; but in some, with women of other class backgrounds.
6. The disillusionment with the male world expressed here is analogous on a community level with the disillusionment on a personal level, referred to in Chapter 7, which is often experienced by divorced women when they first confront the misogynist male world.

14

Structural Faultlines

THERE ARE FEW SOCIAL STRUCTURES, if any, that form a seamless whole. The most elementary forms of division of labor and specialization of function, whether by age, sex, talent, or law, introduce cracks that can widen into serious gaps from time to time. The female world is no more immune to such potential cleavages than is any other social entity. In this chapter we look at class, ethnicity, race, and age all of which can produce cracks, even serious fissures or cleavages, in the female, as in the male, world. In the next chapter our attention is directed to the faultlines produced by seemingly intransigent role-related and moral issues. There are, to be sure, connections between the structural and the issue-related faultlines. Positions on certain issues are related to class, race, ethnicity, and age. But the relationship is not close enough to be considered determinative. One finds varying positions on most issues in all classes, races, ethnic, and age groupings.

The Class Faultline

To those who conceptualize the female world as a class—proletariat, for example, vis-à-vis the male world—the whole women's movement may be viewed as a class struggle against oppression. And we do know, from the "turnouts" of the Lowell girls to the union organization work of women, that women have participated in the Marxist type of class conflict. But since most women, as homemakers or subsistence workers, were not even included in the concept of the production process, most of the thinking about class conflict left them out. Our concern here, then, is not with class conflict in the Marxist sense but with faultlines within the female world itself created by class differences.

Class did not greatly trouble the preindustrial world where one was born into one's position and did not try to change it. Because so many class differences expressed themselves in subtle nuances in interpersonal relationships—stance, modes of address, intonation, unwritten codes of all kinds—women, as maids, nurses, domestics, had a good opportunity to learn the subtleties of class behavior.

Most adults spend most of their free time with people and groups of their own class background. There is thus little occasion for the "hidden injuries of class" (Sennett and Cobb, 1972, 251) to do their wounding work. Children in public schools often suffer them, and so, too, as noted in Chapter 6, do young people in adolescent society. But adult women are for the most part protected from contact with classes "above" or "beneath" them. Not many women work for female bosses, and if they do, the class difference is usually not great. Occasionally a beautician will express hostility to her customers who think she is lower class (Howe, 1977, 49). But, except in the mistress-domestic relationship, class differences in the classic sense are not all that salient in the female world.

Far from the barricades was one conflict between working-class women and members of the upper-middle-class élite of the female world who wanted to help them. Although they had a common foe—"management," "employers," "capitalists," "industry"—they confronted it with different perspectives. In *Notable American Women* (1971), for example, there are fourteen women listed under "Labor Leaders" and seventeen under "Labor Reformers." Practically all the labor leaders were of working-class background; almost all the labor reformers were middle-class. The first tended to be organizers, the second, lobbyists and political activists. The issues between them were fundamental—strategy, for the most part—but they were exacerbated in one famous case—the Women's Trade Union League—by interpersonal contacts in which emphasis on the amenities by the upper-middle-class women had an inhibiting effect on the working-class women. The strategic issues took the form of priorities: unionization or protective legislation; separatist organizations or working through male organizations; political or economic pressure; the suffrage movement or the unionizing movement. All these issues were reflected in the Women's Trade Union League, which became, in effect, a paradigm for conflict between the love-and/or-duty ethos of the female world and the self-interest ethos of the male world.

Case in Point: Working-Class Women and Their "Allies"

In 1903, a "small band of enthusiasts who believed that the nonindustrial person could be of service to her industrial sister in helping her find her way through the chaos of industry" organized the Women's Trade Union League (Dye, 1975, 24; Foner, 1979, chapter 16). It was patterned after a British prototype that had been established in 1875 though not fully activated until 1890 (Jacoby, 1974, 73). Although there were some men members in the early years, especially in the British organization, both the British and the American Leagues "quickly became identified as women's organizations with predominantly female membership and leadership" (73). Both engaged in efforts to organize women workers, in legislative activity, and in educational programs. They participated in strikes (Cohen, 1975, 78) and other union activities. But the emphasis here is not on their conflict activities in the industrial scene but rather on the class faultline within the American organization itself.

The Women's Trade Union League constituted "a unique coalition of women workers and wealthy women disenchanted with conventional philanthropic and social reform activities who dedicated themselves to improving female laborers' working conditions and their status in the labor movement" (Dye, 1975, 24). Achieving unionization for women on one side and protective labor legislation and suffrage for them on the other were their—incompatible, as it later proved—goals. Many of the working women were Jewish workers in the garment industry; the upper-class women—called "Allies"—were often from charity organizations, social reform societies, or social settlements, including the New York City Consumers' League, working-girls' clubs, and the Working-women's Society.

This unique organization, which lasted for several decades, "stressed the importance of cross-class cooperation between upper-class and working-class women, and it was the only early twentieth-century women's organization that attempted to build such an egalitarian, cross-class alliance into its organizational structure" (Dye, 25). The only qualification for membership was allegiance to the American Federation of Labor and willingness to work to unionize women workers. The members did not anticipate any difficulties in relating to one another. "Women could, they believed, surmount social and ethnic differences and unite on the basis of their common femininity" (25). They found it easier said than done.

It was not so much class in the economic sense, or even ideology, that was fundamental in explaining the conflicts within the WTUL. It was, rather, class in the interpersonal sense as expressed in language, speech, taste, and the amenities. Although "upper-class cultural domination . . . was always with the WTUL" (Dye, 28), it was certainly not based on a deliberate policy. In fact, "most upper-class members were seemingly unconscious of the genteel atmosphere that permeated the League, despite its unpretentious headquarters in dingy Lower East Side flats." To the working women, however, the class chasm was perfectly clear, as it was to feminists decades later. The WTUL had an aristocratic air about it. The Allies did not see anything incongruous about "juxtaposing 'interpretive dance recitals' with shop meetings or inviting women to stop by for an afternoon of 'drinking tea and discussing unionism.' " No wonder that "on a personal level, the League's gentility undermined workers' self-confidence and made them feel awkward; on an ideological level, the organization's aristocratic character was foreign and often suspect." The working women may not have had a sociological or a social-psychological theory to support them, but, as one of them pointed out, they could sense that "contact with the Lady does harm in the long run. It gives the wrong standard" (28).

But the misconceptions were not on one side only. As one Ally said: "Before I was unconscious about this class and that class and this stupid difference and that stupid difference. Girls were just girls to me, and now you people are putting all sorts of ideas in my head and making me timid and self-conscious" (31). When she was harangued about her condescending activities to bring "culture" to the working girls she defended herself vehemently:

> You cannot push me out and you cannot make me afraid of any working girl sisters or render me *self-conscious* before them, I refuse to be afraid to take them to the Metropolitan Museum and *teach* them and *help* them. . . . I feel no fear in putting my side of the proposition up to any working girl. I'm not *afraid* to tell her that I have something to bring her and I'm never afraid that she will misunderstand or resent what I say. She needs my present help just as the whole race needs her uprising. [29]

The Allies had better education, financial independence, and the advantage of an average ten-year age differential. In spite of their ideals, they found it hard not to show a patronizing attitude. The interactions tended to be one-way rather than mutual: "Instead of working-class members teaching Allies to relate to women workers and to be effective organizers, the opposite was sometimes the case" (29). The working-class members, instead of teaching the Allies how to be effective organizers, lost their own momentum and verve as organizers. The direction of influence was contrary to the one the working women had in mind. Such tendencies did not go ignored or uncriticized. Thus, for example, "Leonora O'Reilly, a working woman with long experience as a garment trades organizer and labor speaker and one of the original members of the League, was particularly vocal in expressing her dislike of college women who came to the labor movement with lofty ideals of feminism and solidarity but who knew nothing about the realities of labor organizing or of working for a living. She was determined that working-class members should not be intimidated by upper-class women's academic and financial advantages" (29).

The working-class critics were right. The Allies did have an inhibiting effect on the working-class organizers, and in some cases made them literally déclassée. Rose Schneiderman and Pauline Newman, for example, though they identified with the East Side immigrant working-class community from which they had come, became alienated from it. Thus Newman wrote of her ILGWU colleagues: "Even as individuals they are not interesting, most of them are unintelligent and 'green,' they have no manners and have no sence [sic]." She no longer felt at home with them. "But the worst of it is that you cannot meet a person with whom you could sit down, and discuss something which is not or does not belong to Russia and because of this I often feel miserable" (Dye, 35).

Part of the difficulty underlying clashes between Allies and workers lay in the fact that the two groups had different conceptions of *class*. The importance of class differences was usually far more obvious to working women than to Allies. Upper-class members were not as acutely aware of class antagonism within the League and often downplayed the importance of social background. Many were even confused by the emphasis workers placed on class differences. They did not see all that much difference between classes.[1] In this emphasis on egalitarianism, or, rather, commonality across class lines, Dye thinks they were "typical of the early twentieth-century women's movement" (25-26).

Regardless of class, commonality was a major ideological theme. "Unlike mid-nineteenth-century feminists who had inveighed against the notion of a separate sphere for women and who had argued that both sexes shared a common humanity, early twentieth-century feminists, suffragists, and social reformers stressed the importance of sex differences." (Dye, 26). Reta Childe Dorr, a WTUL member, expressed this philosophy in these words: "Women now form a new social group, separate, and to a degree homogenous. Already they have evolved a group opinion and a group ideal. . . . Society will soon be compelled to make a serious survey of the opinions and the ideals of women. As far as these have found collective expressions, it is evident that they differ very radically from the accepted opinions and ideals of men. . . . It is inevitable that this should be so" (Dye, 26).

Nevertheless, League members, like other feminists in the early twentieth century, were often vague when they tried to define this female sisterhood. They usually used the term to convey the idea that social class was less important than gender for understanding a woman's status. To them, as to Beecher, the primary social dichotomy was rooted in differences between women and men, not between classes. Women, some League members argued, shared distinct emotional qualities: they were more gentle and moral than men, more sensitive and responsive to human needs. League members also argued that women, regardless of class, could empathize with one another because they belonged to an oppressed social group. This belief in sisterhood "provided the ideological impetus for the League's formation and helps explain why many women joined the organization" (26).

The women soon learned that such classless sisterhood was easier dreamed of than implemented. "Beyond a basic commitment to unionizing women workers and to the AFL, there was little upon which women in the League could agree. Far from behaving in sisterly fashion in their day-to-day affairs, members were often at odds with one another over League objectives and policies. . . . Personal animosity and rancor accompanied debates over WTUL priorities" (26). Angry letters, threats to resign, attack and defense were frequent. The women were, in brief, "a contentious lot" (27).

Some historians have interpreted the discord as the result of class conflict. William Chafe, for example, argues that "Reformers viewed the WTUL's primary function as educational, and believed that the interests of the workers could best be served by investigating industrial conditions, securing legislative action, and building public support for the principle of trade unionism. Female unionists, on the other hand, insisted that organizing women and strengthening existing unions represented the League's principal purpose. One group perceived the WTUL as primarily an instrument of social uplift, the other as an agency for labor organization" (1972, 71).

Although Dye grants the importance of the class interpretation of the conflicts within the WTUL, she does not see it as wholly adequate. It is too simplistic to explain the complex situation. The working-class members and the Allies did not always line up on issues according to class:

> A member's social background did not dictate her stand on League policies. On every important issue, alignments were unclear. Suffrage, traditionally regarded as a middle-class issue, was an important priority for

> many working-class members. Rose Schneiderman and Pauline Newman were the first members to devote themselves full-time to the suffrage campaign. Ally Helen Marot, on the other hand, resisted the League's growing emphasis on the importance of the vote. Protective labor legislation, an issue that was enormously important in the League's history during the 1910s and 1920s, was a more controversial issue than woman suffrage, but on that issue as well, there were no clear class alignments. Allies and workers could be found on both sides of the question. In short, one cannot argue that only upper-class League members supported such reform issues as protective legislation while only workers supported labor policies such as direct organizing. There is no evidence for the view that working women saw the League as a labor union and Allies viewed it as a social reform organization (32-33).

Because of this lack of synchronization between class and position on issues, Dye sees ideological and policy conflicts as basic components in the conflicts that rent the League. It could never reconcile "dedication to women as an oppressed minority within the work force and . . . commitment to the labor movement as a whole. Belief in sisterhood, League members discovered, was not always compatible with a belief in the importance of class solidarity. . . . Were women workers oppressed because they were workers or because they were female? In effect, many controversies . . . were in large part a reflection of the League's struggle to synthesize feminism and unionism" (27). The members had a dual commitment, to organized labor on one side and to the women's movement on the other (33). How to reconcile sisterhood with working-class solidarity was a prime difficulty. If a woman worked for protective legislation or the suffrage or separate unions for women, she was charged with dividing the working class. But if she did not support women's issues, she was accused of ignoring the special problems of women in the work force. Neither the League nor its individual members ever resolved the dilemma.[2] (33). During the period 1903 to 1914, policy centered on integrating women into the labor movement as workers; the next decade was concentrated on suffrage and protective legislation. Policy was couched in either/or terms: the working woman was either exploited as a worker or she suffered as a woman. "Caught between two alternatives, League members frequently were unable to define their purpose or their role" (36).[3]

The League endured until 1950, when it was disbanded owing to lack of financial support after suffering a serious decline in the 1930s and 1940s (Jacoby, 1975). In the end, Dye notes, it "had only limited success in achieving its goal of an egalitarian cross-class alliance. Although the League went farther than any other women's organization in establishing sustained relations with working women and in grappling with the problems a feminist alliance posed, its internal affairs were rarely harmonious" (36).

Almost a quarter century after the demise of the Women's Trade Union League, feminists were again attempting to come to terms with social class. This time the scene was different. So was the issue. It was not whether to work for the suffrage or to strengthen the union but how to reconcile the class differences among women that were impeding the feminist movement itself. Many of the women with working-class backgrounds had now gone to college. They had a sophisticated eye for locating the stress points. They were articulate. They were not easily put down.

Case in Point: Working-Class Women and Their Feminist "Oppressors"

Although there had been a considerable corpus of theoretical writing on class by radical feminists—some of it from a macrosociological perspective, some of it in the form of an exegesis on the work of Marx, some of it dealing with socialist aspirations to a classless society, some of it an analysis of the position of women in the male world based on the Marxist paradigm of a female underclass vis-à-vis the male bourgeoisie—still, the whole class issue remained intractable in their own lives. However they disposed of it on a macrosociological level, there it still was, alive and flourishing in their interpersonal lives as revealed in their relationships with one another. It became a serious preoccupation. Trying hard to achieve feminist solidarity, they had found both class and race inequalities standing in the way, race proving easier to deal with than class. It troubled them.

Why, the middle-class women puzzled, were they and working-class women having such a hard time working together, despite their sincerest efforts? Why was there so much hostility toward the "upper-middle-class white woman"—almost everyone's whipping-girl, as we have pointed out (Chapter 10)—among working-class women and particularly among black women, especially when these upper-middle-class white women believed that they had the interests of all women at heart? Certainly black women's, working-class women's, and housewives'. What was it about class, they wanted to know, that made it so difficult for even the best-willed among them to overcome it? Why did it foil their best-intentioned efforts to work together? When they realized that the theoretical approach was not enough, that some of the answers lay nearer to home, they looked—as feminist canons prescribed—to their own experience and zeroed in on the subtleties of class behavior among themselves.

In 1972 a group of—white—feminists met to work out answers to these questions in interpersonal discussion (Bunch and Myron, 1974). Feminists had begun their movement quite naive regarding the class issue: "At first, it 'did not exist.' Like most Americans, feminists [like the Allies in the WTUL] believed that we lived in a classless society, with equal opportunity for all hard-working people (or at least for all worthy whites)." But the myth collapsed when "working- and lower-class women grew more conscious of being oppressed in the movement [itself] and raised the class issue" (8). That is, just as women had become aware of their own oppression in the civil rights and antiwar movements, so working-class and lower-class women were becoming aware of oppression in the predominantly female feminist movement.

The white upper-middle-class feminists recognized the validity of this charge; there was, indeed, a class issue among women. True, they did not understand it or know what to do about it. But they did know that "the class system . . . not only puts some women in a position of power over others but also weakens all women" and that it was therefore "crucial to the future of feminism" to understand and resolve it. Lack of understanding of the class issue had the effect of alienating lower- and working-class women, who then formed "groups and alliances among themselves" (Bunch and Myron, 1974, 8-9), whereupon, they were accused of being divisive.

Yes, class was divisive, replied the lower- and working-class women, but not because they were beginning to make their objections heard. It was divisive "because the more privileged white, middle- and upper-class women have not recognized how they and the movement are oppressive and have not taken effective action to eliminate or at least work against class, race, and heterosexual oppression" (10). Working-class women could not be blamed for reacting to the class structure that caused their oppression. But blame was not the issue. Class involved "much more than Marx's definition of relationship to the means of production" (Bunch and Myron, 1974, 15).

"Class involves your behavior, your basic assumptions about life, your experiences (determined, in turn, by your class) . . . how you are taught to behave, what you expect from yourself and from others, your concept of a future, how you understand problems and solve them, how you think, feel, act. It is these behavioral patterns cemented in childhood that cause class conflicts in the various movements. It is these behavioral patterns that middle-class women resist recognizing although they may be perfectly willing to accept class in Marxist terms, a neat trick that helps them avoid really dealing with class behavior and changing that behavior in themselves. It is these behavioral patterns which must be recognized, understood and changed" (Brown, 1974, 15). The onus lay with middle-class women because they "have not taken effective action to eliminate or at least work against class." The issue: "How will we eliminate the cause of these divisions—classist behavior, class power, and class privilege—not how to shut up those who are bringing the problems out of the closet" (10).

Among the first responses to these charges by the guilt-stricken upper-middle and middle-class feminists was "downward mobility," which took the form of romanticizing the lower-class woman, of patronizing her, and rejecting their own class privileges. The assumption by these feminists of a kind of pseudo-poverty was a form of according high status by imitation. It was the direct opposite of the pattern followed by the middle-class women in the WTUL, who had hoped to raise the cultural level of the working-class members, not "drop down" to it.

The feminist working-class women would have none of this. They resented and derided the whole concept of downward mobility. Whatever the solution to the class issue might be, it was *not* to be found in voluntary downard mobility in consumer behavior, which, in their eyes, was "a mockery of working-class life." It was poverty made fashionable. Actual behavior remained the same. "Those who don't comply with this 'hip' lifestyle are looked down upon. It is in the establishment of hierarchies that the middle class betrays itself—they always have to look down on somebody, a habitual attitude of power."[4] The upwardly mobile young woman wanted no part of this phony pose. "I don't want to live with mattresses on the floor, ragged clothes, dirt, and spaghetti for supper every night. How anyone can imitate poverty and give it the flavor of 'inness' is so alien to me that it is disgusting. I don't want to be above anybody but I do want decent housing, nice clothes and good food" (Brown, 1974, 19). Downward mobility took many insulting forms. "Middle class women parody our speech to prove how they are no longer middle class. This is as unforgiveable as a white person putting on a broad black 'accent' " (21).

The original motive for downward mobility among middle-class women may have been an attempt to change their ways, but it had a fatal flaw: "They could *afford* to become downwardly mobile. Their class privilege enabled them to reject materialism." But for those who had grown up without material advantages, deliberate, self-conscious downward mobility was infuriating. Here were upper-middle-class women flaunting their rejection of what the working-class women had never had and still couldn't get. Downward mobility, furthermore, had the dangerous effect of preventing high-achieving working-class women from enjoying the material privileges available to the middle-class women. Before downward mobility, working-class women had been invisible to the middle-class women or, if visible, considered trash; after downward mobility they were regarded as "counterrevolutionaries" if they did not follow suit and still wanted to improve their life style. It was inverse snobbism either way. Deliberate downward mobility was "the other side of the capitalist coin, or, to put it more bluntly, the East Village is second-generation Scarsdale" (Brown, 1974, 21). The advice of this (successful) working-class woman to her middle-class sisters was: "If you have money, sister, don't deny it, *share* it. If you have advanced skills don't make pottery in your loft, teach us those skills. If you have good clothes don't walk around in rags, give us some of your clothes. Downward mobility is a way to deny your material privileges, to prove how 'right on' you are. We know that any time you get tired of poverty you can go right back [to those privileges]" (21).

Equally offensive to the working-class women was the theoretical rejection of the intellect in favor of emotion. Downward mobility in consumer behavior, "the greatest insult yet devised by middle class people against the working class," was bad enough; it was unendurable when tied to intellectual downward mobility, "married to the mistrust of the mind and a worship of the emotional."

> A woman who thinks and analyzes is accused of being a power-hungry "heavy" in the movement while a woman who cries at every meeting is embraced as a true sister. Many middle class women, fearing that intellect will be mistaken for middle class behavior and remembering *their* college experience, bury their brains in a morass of "vibes," "gut feelings," and outright hysteria. This is dogmatically declared "true woman" behavior since men don't express their feelings. Serious organizing to end our oppression is suspect, ideological struggle is heresy; feelings are the way, the light, and the truth—even when they result in political stagnation. Such an idea spells death to real political change if people cling to it. [Brown, 19-20]

Truly an ironic twist. Women emphasizing rather than minimizing sex differences. Women apotheosizing the old emotional feminine stereotype, not in the name of sex but of class. The working-class woman's grievance lay not in the use of intellect but in its misuse. "It isn't intellect that working class women mistrust in middle class women, it is how middle class women use their intellect to rationalize holding onto class behavior that hurts us. Or simply, we mistrust bullshit, not brains" (20).

These working-class women—or, rather, women with working-class backgrounds—were different from those the Allies had worked with in the WTUL. They had gone to college and could both use its advantages and understand its limitations. College challenged the working-class woman's whole life experience; its snobbism and its jargon ran counter to her working-class style. She endured hundreds of slaps in the face—not only the sexism that even the middle-class woman suffered—but also the classism of the college (Brown, 18). Some working-class women who went to college rejected their class background, took over middle-class values and became upwardly mobile. Others wanted only to escape the trauma of their parents' lives, not to become like middle-class women. "Perhaps the most outrageous aspect of the middle class women's views on education and the working class women is their unspoken assumption that we went to college because we were upwardly mobile—in other words, we wanted to be like them. Only a woman far removed from bread and butter reality could harbor such an assumption" (18).

The middle-class feminists in their "sheer arrogant blindness" did not recognize that a college education did not erase the stigmata of class. The fact that many women fight their way "out of inadequate schools into the universities and become 'educated' in no way removes the entire experience of our childhood and youth—and working class life. A degree does not erase all that went before it" (Brown, 16). True, with a degree they could get better jobs, but their pasts remained the same and their ways remained intact (17). A white middle-class woman would not tell a black woman with a college degree that she was no longer black, but she tells educated working-class women that they are no longer working class. Why?[5]

The answer to this question was not simple. Middle-class women resented the violation of the stereotype of working-class women—that they were inarticulate, shy, passive, uninterested in ideas—when, unintimidated, they spoke up in rap sessions. Or they rejected the working-class woman's own analysis of her oppression because it was not couched in sociological language. Keeping working-class women bottled up in the stereotype was a way to retain their own class power. "Disbelief of a working class woman's analysis of her class oppression is one more way to undermine us—we don't 'know enough' to analyze our own goddamn oppression, we need a middle class woman to do it for us in fancy sociological language" (Brown, 17).

Shades of Newman and Schneiderman! None of the—sometimes bumbling—criticism levelled against the upper-middle-class feminists by outside attackers came as near to hitting them where they were most vulnerable as this passionate in-house onslaught. Even this egalitarian movement in the female world was not immune to the class faultline.

Update on Household Workers

Although the nineteenth-century system of organizing domestic service disappeared from the American scene after World War I, it remained in the form of the day worker. We noted in Chapter 11 how, from colonial times on, throughout the nineteenth century, "ladies" or "mistresses" and "servants" fought out a class war in the privacy of the household. Then, and ever since, women as employers have complained of the behavior of employees, and employees of employers'. Whatever the ethnic or racial composition of the domestic labor force and whatever its age or its educational achievement, the difficulties persisted. In the twentieth century the private battle spread to the political scene. We pick up here the story we left in Chapter 11.

In 1935, when the Social Security system was inaugurated, there was a great outcry, especially in the South, that now there would be no black women left to cook in white women's kitchens. Whatever legislation was proposed that mollified the lot of the black female labor force—a large proportion of which was in the household-service category—the same complaint was heard. And when female unemployment was being discussed—especially black female unemployment—there was always someone to say that there were plenty of jobs in the suburbs if only the black women really wanted to work, insinuating that if they didn't prefer to be subsidized by welfare they would be out there in the white women's kitchens.

Case in Point

Dorothy Bolden had been a maid, North and South, for forty-two years. She had been active in the civil rights movement in the early 1960s, but it was her skill in dealing with the busing issue in 1965 that led to her recruitment in the movement to improve the lot of the domestic. When the Urban League learned of what she was trying to do for domestics, it saw the potential for its own program and called a meeting to which all kinds of people, black and white, came. Bolden listened to them and felt they were all wrong, so she decided to stand up and "tell it straight." She told the middle-class activists "that they actually didn't know what they were talking about" (1976, 161); not one of them had ever worked as a maid, never knew what that "labor field really was." Nor did the domestics themselves know much about the overall situation. They didn't even know the price they wanted for their services and how much money they should try to get. Her advice: "Go out and bring us back something you think we can deal with" (160).

After this 1965 meeting, Bolden herself spent a lot of time talking to and about domestics. From this experience she arrived at an asking figure of $15 plus carfare a day.

Establishing the asking price for a day's work was one thing; getting it accepted was another. "After we set the price, you had to teach those women how to ask for it. If you were making ten dollars a day, you had to learn how to communicate with the lady and tell her about the cost of living. If she didn't want to pay it, you'd just have to find a new job that's willing to" (161). Bolden did not support protest as a weapon. "We women didn't believe in it. . . . Because if thirty thousand women get [to be] without a job, and that's how many maids there are in Atlanta, where else have we got to go to? So we couldn't go out demonstrating, and we weren't ramrodding anything down anybody's throat. Just if we weren't getting paid, we just walk off the job. So this is the way the fifteen dollars came around" (161).

The employing women were by no means amenable to the wage demands. "I had telephone calls coming in from employers calling me a bitch. Or they'd say, 'The bitch wasn't worth that type of salary' " (163). Bolden listened patiently, responding with "kind words that would erase their ugly words, so we would hit it off pretty good after that" (163).

Bolden was wary of the media. "They could have said, 'This is a radical woman here, bringing on disturbance between the employers and employees' " (162). She wanted the women themselves, not the media, to define their movement and barred the press from their meetings.

There were meetings and, against her own wishes, Bolden was made founding president of the National Domestic Workers, Inc. (161). The group was not national despite its name, but Bolden nevertheless did engage in fairly widespread organizing activities, especially in the South (162). The word "union" was deliberately rejected as part of the organization's name. The women had learned "how much 'union' frightens people" (162-163), especially in southern textile towns. Even to the women themselves it meant "coming in to stampede and bargain and harass and talk about striking and this kind of thing" (163). They didn't want to be bothered by a union that collected money from its members but provided no perceptible benefits. They didn't want anyone talking to their employers but themselves.

Bolden soon broadened her activities. She became a kind of employment agency, attempted to upgrade the field of domestic service, worked in Georgia in 1971 for a homemakers' skills training program, aimed to establish a career ladder, wrote a manual for maids. She was "trying to give them a guide on what it's really all about, and how the relationship with employers should be established in it—how they should work together, being two women, and that kind of thing" (166).

As of 1976, National Domestic Workers, Inc. had not become "national," but it had survived and was providing "a voice for domestic workers, serving as a buffer between them and their employers and helping employers and employees to find each other" (Seifer, 1976), 175).[6] Bolden's dream of training programs had not attracted federal funding. But National Domestics, Inc. had called a conference on the implementation of Title XX of the Social Security Act which had as one of the outcomes the formation of a new group, Common Cause for Justice for Low Income Women.

By the end of the decade, the idea of unionizing domestics, at least in the North, was no longer so frightening. And just as the term "servant" had been anathema to women in the nineteenth century, so were the terms "maid" and "girl" becoming anathema in the late twentieth century. Some women who did household work were now calling themselves, and asking to be called, "household technicians" (Katz, 1979). Under the leadership of another black woman, Carolyn Reed, Household Technicians of America was being organized in major cities, with a thousand women already meeting weekly in five chapters in New York City (45). Salary ($30 to $35 a day in New York City) was a primary demand, and the hope was that household workers would soon be included in state collective-bargaining legislation. There were also demands for more contracts, including specific job specifications.[7] Working conditions, fringe benefits, including vacations, pensions, and health plans, good equipment to work with, wage incentives—the whole shopping list of standard union issues—were among the items called for. This group was being wooed by the Service Employees International Union, but Reed resisted turning leadership over to a male-led union that could never understand the women's point of view.

Race as well as class issues motivated Reed. "One of these days I'm going to do some research on what some of these big-shot feminists pay their people who work for them." "Carolyn," Shirley Chisholm once said, "represents the black women who take care of feminists' babies while they're out fighting the white male." Playing on the guilt feminists feel about hiring black women, Reed says to them, "pay me real well and treat me with respect, and you'll get over your guilt" (Katz, 1979, 49). Reed's goal was to raise the status of household service, as sanitation men and other uniformed forces had done, so that it would become a real career choice for young women rather than, as now, a last resort.

Meanwhile, on a small scale, the Marxist solution was beginning to emerge, the "industrialization" of at least the cleaning component of household service. Entrepreneurs, both men and women, were hiring skilled and well-equipped teams to "mass produce" household cleanliness. Within a short period of time such a team, with their own efficient equipment, could clean a household with competence and speed. Expensive, to be sure, but there was no reason why this kind of service should be cheap, no matter who was doing it.

To what extent the style of class conflict waged by Bolden and Reed is determined by the nature of the "industry" they are in and to what extent by the sex of those involved or the race faultline is an interesting question. In any event, the contrasts and similarities of the current scene to the nineteenth-century situation (Chapter 11) invite thoughtful attention. Unionizing domestics was not among the solutions offered at the turn of the century. If the effort succeeds it will have achieved a good deal more than the mere improvement of the lot of household technicians who work for pay. It will stimulate recognition of the value of such work even when not done for pay.

The Ethnic Faultline

Whatever the nature of class as an issue in the female world and whatever the nature of the cleavages it engenders, it has had wide ramifications, becoming inextricably tied in with both ethnicity and race.

The female world, like the male, has been fragmented into numerous ethnic enclaves. As early as the 1840s, Catharine Beecher, as we have noted, spoke of ethnic servants as "dirty" foreigners, in a literal sense. Leaders of the suffrage movement in the latter part of the nineteenth century were opposed to immigration, revealing a kind of ethnicism, even racism (Rossi, 1973, 473).[8] And the distances between and among ethnic women themselves remained as long as language, residence, and endogamy exerted their boundary-maintaining effect.

Ethnic faultlines showed up among working women early in the twentieth century.[9] We have already commented on the ethnic component of the mistress-maid faultline in the household. A similar faultline showed up among women in the industrial labor force, hampering the organization of women workers. Thus, for example, "at the turn of the century the American working class was a mixture of scores of different nationalities. Each national group brought to the workplace cultural attitudes and stereotypes vis-à-vis other nationalities which made organizing difficult. Employers exploited these differences, even deliberately hiring from a mixture of nationalities to make unity less likely" (Henry, 1976, 173). A case in point is a study of flower-making. In this industry "Italian women predominated but Jewish workers played a leading role in the struggle for unionization. The Italian women often came from peasant cultures where patriarchal power was strong. Many of the young Jewish immigrants, by contrast, had been industrial workers of some sort in the ghettoes of eastern Europe, many of them participants in radical labor movements in their homelands. They tended to be more urban than their Italian counterparts, and correspondingly they often fell into arrogance toward their fellow and sister workers" (173). Item: A Jewish worker, commenting on the unwillingness of Italian women to organize, said, "If they were more civilized, they wouldn't take such low pay. But they go without hats and gloves and umbrellas" (175).[10] Nor did such attitudes endear them to their sisters in the WTUL. Thus, reporting the results of an election for president of the League in 1914, Pauline Newman explained to Rose Schneiderman why she had lost. Nothing, she said, had been left undone by the opposition, including pointing out that Rose was a socialist, interested in the suffrage, and a "Jewes" (Dye, 1975, 30).

A study of the men's garment industry in Chicago in the first decade of the century offers glimpses of ethnicity as it shaped up at that time. Jewish women in that industry were especially active in the labor movement. Thus, during a strike, though they constituted only about 10 percent of the female work force, they constituted two-thirds of the female participants (Cohen, 1974, 78). A partial—though only partial—explanation of this high rate of activism may lie in the fact that only 15 percent of the Jewish women workers were married as compared to 60 percent of the Italian women and 30 percent of the Polish women. According to Cohen, further, the "Jewish women were notably poor workers" and were not especially interested in improving their trade skills. Rather, they were interested in improving their education to move up and out of the industry (80). They were already, by a kind of "anticipatory socialization," in the middle class. We have already noted the aspersions cast by one Jewish worker on the Italian women. Even in the WTUL, the loyalties of the Jewish women were sometimes more feminist—that is, middle-class—than ethnic. Thus, Newman commented to Schneiderman: "No matter how much you are with the Jewish people, you are still more with the people of the League, and that is a relief" (Dye, 35).

The long tentacles of ethnicity reach far beyond the labor force and ramify widely throughout the female world, revealing themselves especially in the faultline between ethnic women and feminists. The theory on which the ethnic women have based their lives—often theological and hence Biblical—is lightyears away from the theory on which the feminist movement has based itself—economic, sociological, psychological, anthropological, political—that is, scientific. In some cases the issues and the symbols used to dramatize them by feminist women seeking change have seemed remote to ethnic women, even trivial. They had no stake "in protesting the exclusion of women from the executive suite, political office, and professorships. They had little interest in symbolic demonstrations to allow women to frequent men's bars or in protests against companies which refused women credit cards in their own name" (Seifer, in Samuels, 1975, 9). Sometimes the ethnic faultline was related to the housewife-professional faultline, the housewife feeling herself denigrated by the achieving women, put down, made to feel that her self-worth demanded labor-force participation (Chapter 15).

By the 1970s, however, the inevitable homogenizing forces—education, labor-force participation, the mass media—began to narrow the faultline. Feminists were calling attention to the balkanized state of the female world. The women's movement had not created the ethnic cleavages but had made women more aware of them. Both feminists and the ethnic women embraced activism, each in their own way. Thus, while condemning the "women's libbers," the ethnic women could themselves practice "women's lib" under a different theory. They, too, could confront city hall if or when they felt that their own values were being threatened (Chapter 13).

The Race Faultline

The class aspect of the race faultline has already been touched on. It is difficult to disentangle one from the other. There are some students of the subject, in fact, who tend to identify the two, emphasizing class almost to the exclusion of race. Still, quite beyond class there has been on both sides the haunting, hovering, omnipresent, and intractable fact of race prejudice, even, in many cases, hatred. Its persistence has been a long-time preoccupation of feminists, who have invested a considerable amount of effort to overcome it.[11]

In the past the grueling racism blacks had to endure generated violent—literally nauseating—hatred among many black women against all whites, but especially against white women. During the early desegregation era, instances of grueling cruelty were reported in the media. When one girl sat down at school, no one sat beside her. Or they moved away when she sat down. One white girl surrounded her seat with purse, scarf, and books to prevent a black girl from sitting near her. Such instances had the effect of making her feel very black and very stupid, wholly inferior. If the others laughed, one girl was sure everyone was laughing at her. She wanted to cry, to scream. She wanted to strike them because they made her feel so rejected. But she knew she could not. That would show how mad she was. So she hated them for making her feel that way and herself for letting them make her feel that way. Understandably, such anger and hostility persist into adulthood. Thus Lillian Smith tells of one charming, sensitive, intelligent black woman who became physically ill in the presence of white people "and has immense difficulty coming to terms with the resentment of her childhood" (1949, 130). Still, other black women manage to overcome the hatred. At least one woman, years after she had been subjected to the most horrendous trauma when schools in Little Rock, Arkansas, were being desegregated a generation ago, shows none of the stigmata such torments might well have left.[12]

Although some black women, caught between sexism and racism, express rejection of the feminist point of view in many respects, they accept it in others. Thus, in response to a poll, more black women (57 percent) than white women (26 percent) said they "really want a career" (Greider, 1978).[13]

One of the objections to the feminist movement among black women reflects the class faultline. For example, we find Dorothy Bolden telling the National Women's Political Caucus: "We're not on your agenda. We're not in your by-laws. We're just scrubwomen and you're not even considering motivating us" (Seifer, 1976, 170). There wasn't any love in the women's movement, as there had been in the civil rights movement (171). Black women were invisible. "You don't see me. You never have seen me because I'm off at seven o'clock in the morning. I'm catching a bus and I'm not off until black dark, and you're gone home and I'm probably serving you your dinner. What kind of help are you offering me?" (171).

It was a fair enough question. The invisibility of black women was not merely a matter of work timing. It had a political history. The suffrage movement—though early associated with abolitionism—had become overtly racist by the end of the century. In 1903, Belle Kearney, a Southern suffragist, argued at a National American Woman Suffrage Association convention that "the enfranchisement of women would insure immediate and durable white supremacy.... The South is slow to grasp the great fact that the enfranchisement of women would settle the race question in politics" (Jacoby, 1975, 129). With this point of view, "in order not to antagonize Southern congressmen and suffrage supporters, black women were consistently discouraged from participating in the suffrage movement" (129). Nor, unfortunately, had the situation entirely disappeared three-quarters of a century later. Although the modern feminist movement has shown great concern for the welfare of minority women, it has been constrained in its efforts by the same political forces as those operating early in the century. At the turn of the century suffragists realized that "whether they liked it or not, these groups of men [Southern congressmen] did have the vote, and it made more sense to have them as allies than as enemies of the women's cause" (129). In the 1970s and 1980s it is state legislators who hold the votes with respect to the Equal Rights Amendment. Many black women were waiting for more vocal support from feminists before they offered support.

Among the issues between black women and feminists has been one concerning sex roles, black women arguing that their grievance was not the oppression of black females by black males but the oppression of black males by the society at large, which had had the effect of emasculating black men and defeminizing black women. They were struggling with the image of the powerful black matriarch, a white-created myth that had had damaging repercussions on them and their relationships with men. While white women were engaged in a great effort to prove that they were strong, powerful, capable, black women felt they had to deny their strengths (Wallace, 1979, 46). Their goal was better jobs for black men so that their women could be supported instead of having to do tedious, menial work themselves. The white feminist movement was not their solution. Black women do not seem involved in actually fighting the feminist movement so much as reminding it of its limitations so far as they are concerned.

Real as the faultline between black and white women as employee and employer has been and is, and real as the differences are with respect to political action, the most painful cleavages between them have been, and continue to be, those having to do with relationships with men. A generation ago, anthropologist Melville Herskovitz estimated that at least 80 percent of those classified as black in our country had some "white blood" in their veins. The figure would probably be higher today. From all we know about the mores of race relations in the past, practically all of this "white blood" was undoubtedly contributed by men. No one knows how many white women saw light-colored babies born in the slave cabins, knowing that their husbands were the fathers. In recent years, however, the shoe has been on the other foot. Now it is more likely to be black women deploring the number of white women who are dating and marrying black men, thus adding to the already considerable demographic deficit of men in the black population (Jackson, 1972).

Sexual relations of black men with white women had long been interpreted by white men as an attack on them. Now they were seen by black women as a weapon against them. "Black men often could not separate their interest in white women from their hostility toward black women" (Wallace, 1979, 48). White women were, in effect, weapons in a conflict between black men and black women. Interracial sexual relations had a dual impact: "Since 1966, the black man had two pressing tasks before him: a white woman in every bed and a black woman under every heel" (West, 1979). The bitterness of black women toward these white women was strong and deep: "Black women made no attempt to disguise their anger and disgust, to the point of verbal, if not physical, assault in the streets—on the white woman or the black man or both" (Wallace, 1979, 48).

It would be inappropriate for a white feminist to attempt to contribute to the difficult task of black women theorists grappling with the paradoxes of their situation as blacks, as women, and—at least for some—as feminists. It may not be out of line, however, to note that at the crest of the civil rights movement some white women flaunted their relationships with black men as badges of their lack of race prejudice If they were using these relationships as a weapon it was more likely to be aimed at their parents or the white status quo in general than against black women.

In any event, the idea of black and white women using men—white or black—as weapons in their own private battles—whether against peers or parents—is not an inspiring one.

The Age Faultline

When few people lived to the age of sixty, most spent a relatively small part of their lives in three-generation families or households. And since for most of human history technological changes were slow as measured by the individual life span, age and experience could be a plus in terms of wisdom and knowledge. Now that an increasing number of women live to eighty and beyond—there were 3,289,000 of them as of July, 1978 (Bureau of the Census, April, 1979)—we hear more and more about four-generation families if not households and about the anxieties of the middle generations. And as technology changes faster and faster, there is a wider gap between old and young. Culture forms of the young seem incomprehensible to the old and vice versa.

At midcentury our attention was being called to some of the changes taking place in our generational orientation. Until fairly recently we lived, so to speak, in vertical or generational time—oriented toward parents, grandparents, forebears. But increasingly we were becoming more peer-oriented, living primarily in horizontal relationships (Riesman and others, 1950). Especially cogent were the educational differences that accentuated age differences, for far more of the younger generation had been exposed to college, which made a big difference in attitudes and values (Chapter 9). Thus a 1969 study by Yankelovich found that on some issues—abortion, homosexuality—college and noncollege young people differed from one another more than either group differed from their parents. On other issues—premarital and extramarital sexual relations—they differed from their parents more than from one another (17). Unfortunately these data were not broken down by sex so we cannot specify the situation in the female world. The generations confronted one another not only as parents and children but also as age "strata."

All kinds of sociological entities—parties, publics, interest groups—have come to be seen in terms of their age composition. The tendency toward age segregation is deplored by many. When painful decisions about the allocation of scarce resources for health care have to be made, the elderly—most of whom are women—do not have a great deal going for them.

Homogenizing Trends

There was a commonly expressed fear in the early years of democracy that the result would be a great levelling with consequent loss of great achievements. "In few [of the civilized nations of our time] have great artists, fine poets, or celebrated writers been more rare [than in the United States]. Many Europeans . . . have looked at [this fact] as a natural and inevitable result of equality; and they have supposed that if a democratic state of society . . . were ever to prevail over the whole earth, the human mind would gradually find its beacon-lights grow dim, and men would relapse into a period of darkness" (Tocqueville, 1840, 35). From a somewhat different perspective, Herbert Spencer arrived at a different conclusion. He promulgated a "law" to the effect that industrialized societies were moving from a condition of undifferentiated homogeneity to one of increasing heterogenity, with the implication that this trend was a sign of progress. Where there is great homogeneity, schismogenic differences, though they may be great, will tend to be few, and faultlines, though they may be wide, will also tend to be few. Consensus is likely to prevail among the undifferentiated components.

Neither the Tocqueville nor the Spencer approach seems applicable to the female world. Still, a brief glance at differentiating and homogenizing trends may be in order here. Is the female world, for example, becoming more or less homogeneous, with respect, first of all, to the indexes of socioeconomic status?

With respect to years of schooling, the answer may be a fairly unequivocal yes, the female world *is* becoming educationally more homogeneous. We noted in Chapter 9 that in the not-too-distant future there will be few American women with less than high-school education and almost none with less than elementary education. Since the faultline between literacy and illiteracy is psychologically far greater than that between high school and college, great as that is, it would seem that we may legitimately conclude that so far as this index of socioeconomic status is concerned, the female world is becoming more homogenized. The Allies of today would have far less advantage over the young working-class women than they had in the days of the WTUL. In fact, in feminist circles the young working-class woman may herself be a college graduate.

With respect to income, the trend data are blurred by the impact of inflation which makes comparisons hard to interpret. It is not permissible to compare one period with another since the value of the income has changed over time. But it is legitimate to compare the proportion at any given income levels at any one time with the proportion at any given income levels at another. And the trend seems to be in the direction of reducing the spread in the proportions in low and high income brackets. In 1966, for example, there were seven times as many women with incomes under $5,000 (87.5 percent) as with incomes $5,000 and over (12.5 percent). In 1973, the proportions of women with incomes under $5,000 (70.6 percent) was only 2.4 times that of women with incomes $5,000 and over (29.2 percent). The median income had risen 61 percent; the proportion with incomes under $5,000 had declined by a fifth (19.3 percent); and the proportion with incomes $5,000 and over had increased one and a third times (134 percent) (Women's Bureau, 1969, 132; 1975, 128). It is true that inflation had pushed some women into the $5,000 and over bracket, thus overemphasizing the change. But still it cannot be wholly discounted.

When most women were housewives the occupational structure of the female world was fairly homogeneous. The entrance of so many of them into the labor force means that it is becoming more occupationally differentiated. New faultlines appear as a result; these will be commented on briefly in Chapter 15. Among women in the labor force, the occupational distribution remains remarkably constant over time; still, there has been a slight (extremely slight) trend in the direction of reducing the proportion in the low-prestige occupations and increasing the proportion in the high-prestige ones. Between 1959 and 1974, for example, professionals increased slightly (from 12.1 to 15.6 percent) while operatives and service workers declined slightly (from 15.4 to 13.1 percent and from 23.5 to 21.6 percent, respectively) (Women's Bureau, 1975, 84).

In a massive sort of way, then, it does seem that slow-moving but nevertheless discernible trends are homogenizing the female world so far as indexes of socioeconomic status are concerned. My own interpretation would attribute a considerable amount of the reduction in heterogeneity to education, especially of such working-class women as Rita Mae Brown, who have attended college and are in a position to assess the operation of class factors, to make us aware of them and hence less likely to accept them. The kinds of class conflicts that plagued the WTUL persist, but the upper-middle-class women are now more eager to get rid of them than they had been in the past.

We mentioned the effect of mass production in the clothing industry, which has made apparel—for example, the hats and gloves that meant so much to the Jewish girl quoted above—less and less a symbol of class. Here there surely has been homogenization; the T-shirt and jeans have almost become a universal uniform. And even though they are in the process of becoming fashion items by the "designer" touch, they do, overall, still have a levelling effect. Bolden was especially pleased with the diminishing class differences in appearance among black women. "There's been a great deal of change. . . . You can't tell a maid from a secretary anymore. In the past, if a black woman was a maid you could tell by the way she dressed. Now they don't carry the shopping bags as much, they go neater, and they look more lively and intelligent" (1976, 167).

One more class-related converging trend, namely in divorce rates. Among female professionals the divorce rate—unlike the rate among professional men—has tended to be high (Glick, 1975, 7). But it was rising more slowly among this group than among other women, so that "the percent divorced among upper-group women was tending to converge with that for other women by increasing more slowly than the average" (7).

Within the female world there have been some converging trends with respect to race. The rates of school enrollment among white and nonwhite females are becoming more similar, especially in the high-school years, when the rate of increase among nonwhite females between 1940 and 1950 was almost twice as great (170 percent) as among whites (Bogue, 1959, 332). This educational convergence between races is especially significant because of the relationship between years of schooling and income. Here, too, there appears to be a converging trend. In 1939, the median wage or salary of nonwhite women was less than two-fifths (37.0 percent) that of white women; by 1972, it was almost nine-tenths (86.8 percent) (Bernard, 1975, 211.) In 1970, black women with eight or fewer years of schooling had median earnings only three-fourths (73.4 percent) as high as those of white women with the same number of years of schooling (Bernard, 1975, 207), but among women with college degrees, black women had incomes almost as high as those of white women (96.7 percent) (207).

These trends in schooling and income are related to convergence in occupation. In 1973, for example, "more than half (55 percent) of the minority-race women workers who were under 35 were employed in white-collar jobs, while less than 32 percent of those 35 and over held such jobs. Among white women, these proportions were 65 and 63 percent" (Women's Bureau, 1975, 104-105). Almost twice as large a proportion of white as of minority women thirty-five and over were in white-collar jobs. Among younger women, only about a fifth more were. A further indication is that the proportion in clerical jobs among nonwhite women (36 percent) was approaching that of white women (39 percent).

The convergences in some (but not all) demographic aspects of race are important because they can have indirect impact on social relations. We know, for example, that the gap between white and nonwhite women has considerably narrowed in such a basic demographic variable as the mortality rate. In 1900, nonwhite females had a crude death rate 51 percent greater than that of white females (Bogue, 1959, 177); by 1977, it was 45.2 percent greater (National Center for Health Statistics, 1979, Table 10). In 1900 the life expectancy of nonwhite females at birth was about two-thirds that of white females (69 percent) (Bogue, 183); in 1975, it was 93.7 percent (Statistical Abstract, 1977, 65).

The live birth rates of white and nonwhite women have not, however, been converging. If anything, the difference has been widening. In 1940 the live-birth rate among nonwhite women 15 to 44 years of age was 132.8 percent higher than among white women; in 1975, it was 141.7 percent higher (Statistical Abstract, 1977, 56). Only in the higher parities (fourth pregnancy or more) was there convergence between 1950 and 1975. Nor was there convergence in proportion married. In 1960 among white women the marriage rate was 108.9 times higher than among nonwhite women; in 1976, it was 120.3 higher (Statistical Abstract, 1977, 74). There was, however, convergence in the percent in the status of divorce; 56.2 percent as many among white as among nonwhite women in 1960, 74.3 percent in 1976.

Neither the probable outcome of the homogenizing racial trends nor their significance for the female world can, of course, be delineated with much certainty. It seems likely that nonwhite and white women will become increasingly similar in education, income, and occupation, but what such similarities will mean for the female world as a whole is not obvious. Are the worlds of nonwhite and white women really converging on the work site? In marriage patterns? In the family? The answers are not yet forthcoming.

It is even harder to document convergence among ethnic groups. The old "melting-pot" model has long since been discounted. Still, the research on ethnic working-class communities suggests that ethnicity does tend to bleach out. It tends to become an almost recreational—even quaint—reminder of *temps perdu* rather than, as in the older generation, a passionate reality. As Arthur Shostak has noted, the young ethnic women resonated to Gloria rather than to Edith Bunker. It may be noted, though, that even in Gloria's world, the ties were still predominantly within the family rather than with friends.

It is not likely that the class, race, ethnic, age faultlines in the female world will soon disappear altogether, Or, more to the point, that new ones will not appear. But that there are some homogenizing trends which may tend to narrow their width, if not always their depth, seems probable. In any event, there will always be others to take their place—ideological issues, for example—that can create equally wide faultlines and generate even more passion. Chapter 15 glances at some of them.

Notes

1. It will be recalled that Harland and Van de Water also commented on the lack of understanding the young social-settlement workers showed vis-à-vis the poor (Chapter 13).
2. My own mother, who worked in the garment industry as a girl in the late 1880s, was permitted by her mother to march in suffrage parades but never, repeat never, permitted to participate in union activities.
3. The debate between the separatist and integrationist perspectives persisted throughout the century, taking different form with different issues. Should women join forces with other reform movements or concentrate on their own cause? Women's rights or abortion? Should they concentrate on protective legislation for women or work with men on working-class unionization?
4. She was well on her way to becoming a best-selling author (Rubyfruit Jungle).
5. On the macrosociological level, radical feminists had an answer to this question in an interpretation of class as a way of perpetuating the inferior position of women. "Women in peasant, agricultural, and lower-class cultures are often called 'dominant' because they retain some of that matriarchal strength. Male supremacist societies must try to eliminate this female strength. The primary means of doing this both in the United States and in other countries is through the domination and promotion of middle-class values, including an image of the female as a passive, weak, frivolous sex object and eager consumer. The class system thus not only puts some women in a position of power over others but also weakens all women. Analyzing these and other ways that patriarchy, white supremacy, and capitalism reinforce one another is crucial to the future of feminism" (Bunch and Myron, 1974, 8).
6. Interestingly enough, a new issue was surfacing, "a rising demand from employers for the women to 'live in,' while most domestic workers want to be able to live with their own families" (Siefer, 1976, 175). This somewhat surprising regression to the nineteenth-century live-in pattern, which, as Katzman has noted, was already long-since anachronistic, was doubtless related to the distance which suburbanization was interposing between the work site in the suburban housewife's household and the home of the domestic in the central city. The great distance took a lot of time for transportation. The live-in aspect of domestic service did not show any marked renascence.
7. It will be recalled that "specificity" and "contract" were among the characteristics that differentiated the two polarities described in Chapter 2. Among the specifications Reed and her union called for were no dog walking and window-washing only with proper pay and in compliance with building regulations. "If you want somebody to do your laundry . . . or to take care of your kids, that's fine. But you can't have it for nothin' " (Katz, 1979, 49). Child-care: "If you are in the child-care position, that's fine, but we shouldn't be mothers" (49). Home economists had long been doing job

analysis; the "household technicians" were now bringing their own job description to the task.

8. Rossi accounts for this parochialism in terms of the small-town backgrounds of many of the leaders and their malaise at the growing political power of immigrants, which, they thought, could be countered by women like them: "The women's movement . . . drew deeply on its roots in small-town America and reacted far more strongly to what had been lost as the United States embarked on its romance with industrialization than to what the future might hold or to the price attached to industrialism for the millions of women less fortunate than themselves. Though they wrote and spoke as if they were equally concerned with women at all levels of society, the nineteenth-century women's rights spokeswomen rarely knew or deeply cared for the lot of women outside their own social class. . . . Consequently their feminism was linked to status politics rather than to class politics. When the chips were down during the last stage of the suffrage movement, they did not draw back from the anti-immigrant ethos then abroad in the country but bent it to their own political ends, arguing that the best women of the country—middle class, educated, moral, Protestant—would, if given the vote, help counteract the political power of the growing numbers of new citizens among the immigrants" (1973, 473).
9. It is interesting to note that race and ethnicity fragmented not only the industrial labor force but also the world of the prostitute. Thus, for example, in Virginia City until at least the mid-1870s, women who lived in the "small whitewashed cabins set below the town's main thoroughfare . . . maintained strict social [class] boundaries among themselves. European- and American-born women looked down on Chicanas and Latinas, charging higher prices and occupying better locations. Within this upper-status group, women were ranked according to their youth (few of the early prostitutes were less than 25 years old) and attractiveness. As a group, the western Europeans were novelties and tended to attract wealthier customers than Americans" (Goldman, 1972, 34-35).
10. Conceptually, ethnicity and class have close relations. "In the early years of the century the lower classes in cities were often immigrants. . . . The emphasis in thinking was therefore on their ethnicity more than on their class. . . . With time, however, the old immigrant component in the community became greatly attenuated. The children might still live in ethnic areas but they looked and acted like everyone else. They became, in research and in theory, blue-collar workers, the working class or the lower-middle class rather than immigrants or ethnics. The fading—though not the disappearing—of ethnicity as such thus left the class rather than the ethnic characteristics of this generation highlighted" (Bernard, 1973, 55).
11. Race prejudice on the part of white women vis-à-vis black women seems to be somewhat different from that of white men. On January 18, 1976, *Bill Moyers' Journal* dealt with "Rosedale, New York, The Way It Is." It was about a community's response to the purchase of a house by a black family. The camera panned the faces of a wide variety of ethnics as they sang "God Bless America," envisioned, obviously, as all white, and it showed the unabashed hatred as paraders chanted "Kill Simpson." The women, in-

terviewed on their doorsteps, expressed the warmth they felt for one another; there was genuine affection among them. They just did not want their cosy, intimate relationship disturbed. There was no hatred for Mrs. Simpson as a woman. Certainly no call for her blood.

12. And, alongside of the resentment, hostility, and anger some black and white women have felt toward one another, there has been, at least in some cases, genuine affection, however wide the status differential between them. Anne Firor Scott, after recounting the antagonism between mistress and slave, reminds us that there was also affection. "It is possible to jettison nine-tenths of the sentiment about Negro mammies and still have substantial evidence of what was not, after all, a surprising phenomenon. Women who lived and worked together often formed bonds of friendship and mutual dependency across the color bar. 'An affectionate friendship that was to last for more than sixty years,' one man wrote of his mother and a slave. 'She was a member of the family,' wrote a Mississippi woman, and another, 'she loved me devotedly and I was much attached to her.' A visiting Englishman commented upon the close relationship between the Calhoun ladies and their slaves" (Scott, 1970, 47-48).
13. This career orientation seemed paradoxical not only because it seemed to contradict the antifeminist point of view but also because it did not correspond to the seemingly greater kin and locale orientation among black than among white women, as reported in a market research survey. Although fewer black than white women (36% vs. 58%) said they could always count on their neighbors, they too expressed "a strong desire for a sense of community and nostalgia for the simpler life of the past" (Greider, 1978). They were more likely than white women to "keep in touch." Thus, according to this study, "black women . . . are more nostalgic than white women about the past. They care more about scattered relatives in distant parts of the country. They buy more of the so- called 'keep-in-touch' products—greeting cards, stationery, snapshot cameras, film."

15

Issue-related Faultlines

CUTTING ACROSS ALL structural cleavages are the faultlines based on issues. The usual way of dealing with such faultlines would be in terms of ideology. The topic would be stated as "ideological faultlines," and, in a certain sense, issue-based faultlines are frequently ideological and often, in the female world, religious. But the purpose here is to be specific rather than abstract, to emphasize the concrete issues themselves rather than the theoretical ideologies on which they rest.

Any hard-and-fast distinction between structural and issue-related or ideological faultlines is impossible to make for issues may divide women of any class, race, ethnic, or age group. There are few if any issues that line up women completely by any of these structural categories, with all those on one side in the same class, all those on the other in another. Antiracism is as near as any. It would probably line up all black women on one side, but many white women would also line up on the same side.

In a certain sense, faultlines based on class, race, ethnicity, and age and those based on issues are two ways of looking at the same phenomena. In one case the focus is on the structural variables (classes, races, ethnic groups, age brackets) and we ask: How do they line up on certain issues? Do more women in higher than in lower socioeconomic classes tend to favor *X*? Do more white than nonwhite women oppose *Y*? And so on. In the other case the emphasis is on the issues and we ask: What is the class, race, ethnic, and age composition of those who line up on different sides of given issues? Are those who favor *Z* predominantly in upper or lower socioeconomic classes? Are those who oppose *W* mainly nonwhite or white? In the first case, we say, "Republicans favor low federal budgets." In the second, "People who favor low federal budgets will vote Republican."[1] We have not attempted to hew too rigorously to this approach.

Moral standards and values of many kinds give rise to specific issues that can take a variety of forms, all of which may create fissures. Abortion, for example, sex roles, and lesbianism have been among such cross-class, cross-race, cross-ethnicity, cross-age "schismogenic" moral issues in recent times. What is characteristic of these "schismogenic" issues is that they are intractable and easily become the rallying ground for "single-issue" lobbying groups. They generate a great deal of emotion and are often not at all amenable to the usual processes of dealing with divisive matters. In addition to issues dealing with morality and sex roles that have produced faultlines in the female world there seem to be differing temperamental or personality characteristics among women that predispose some—"modern"—women to favor certain life styles and other—"traditional"—women, to favor other life styles. We look briefly at this phenomenon also.

Female Sex Roles as Issues

The standard definition of the family for research purposes is often in terms of a household consisting of a husband who is an income earner, a wife who is nonemployed, and children under the age of eighteen. This corresponds fairly well with the popular image of the contemporary nuclear family. A great deal of thinking is in terms of this picture. It is, in fact, perhaps the usual way of thinking about the family.[2] Actually, as we saw in Chapter 5, this family constitutes only a relatively small percentage of all husband-wife households. Husband-wife families with children under eighteen in which the man is the sole earner constitute only about a fifth of all husband-wife families (19.4 percent). Granting only for the sake of argument—a concession not all women are willing to make—that mothers of small children should remain in the home to take care of them, what should be the role of the women in the other 81 percent of husband-wife families may become a real issue, for the lives of women have drastically changed since the so-called demographic revolution. The number of years during which the household fully occupies any woman's time has declined almost precipitously.

The issue between mistress and maid, housewife as employer and domestic worker as employee, described in Chapter 11, is only one that housewives have had to face. In the late 1960s and in the 1970s a new issue emerged between the housewife—increasingly "homemaker"[3] rather than housewife (Bernard, 1979)—and, this time, the employed mother. As more and more mothers entered the labor force, fewer women were left at home in the neighborhood to perform the age-old integry functions. Ordinarily the working mothers were conscientious about making provision for the after-school care of their children. But breakdowns in routine—if school closed early on account of some special event, or if there is no school at all owing to a teachers' conference, or if traffic delays a mother's return from work, or whatever—were common, leaving the home-based mothers of other children there to meet the crisis. As a result, according to Howe, "mothers at home often feel a little critical of mothers who are away when the kids come out of school. I used to be that way myself when I was home in the suburbs with my kids and it seemed like all the children whose mothers were on jobs would land up at my house. Those of us at home would often have to take over the supervision of these kids in a lot of ways. Breaking up fights or bandaging knees or deciding who was going to use what at the playground or just talking to them. Then some of us mothers at home volunteered at an after-school center, and I thought then, listening to how the women talked about the other mothers at work, that it was unlikely that sisterhood could exist between these two groups" (1977, 196-197).[4]

Related to this issue of the homemaker versus the working mother was one related to the feminist position with respect to homemaking as she interpreted it. To the homemaker the feminist seemed to stand for a position that was denigrating nonemployed women; she seemed to be looking down at them, making them feel defensive, even apologetic. There seemed to be an implication that homemaking was not a genuine choice but a last resort because the homemaker could not do better. Women who had always taken it for granted that all women were housewives—like the Indian tribe whose name for themselves meant human being—were taken aback when being a housewife came to be, as they thought, viewed as deviant. Or even, to use Parsons' term, "residual," a pattern "to be followed most closely by those who are unsuccessful in competition for prestige in other directions" (1942, 611). The homemaker felt she was being pressured. At social events, for example, she resented being asked what she "did." "Let's face it, to most women in the movement, being a housewife is the lowest of the low—and homemakers know it" (Howe, 1977, 202). An anonymous letter to a newspaper editor expressed the feelings of countless homemakers: "I deeply resent the implication that I am lazy, shallow, or just plain crazy for staying home. . . . The assumption that personal fulfillment for women can be found only in the active pursuit of a career degrades homemaking and motherhood to the status of a desirable but expensive hobby. . . . For all that has been written about the decline of the American family, society is increasingly intolerant of those women who wish to devote their lives to its support" (*Washington Post*, June 7, 1978).

Howe believes a class issue is involved here. "To what extent, if any," she asks, "was the feminist position about 'the drudgery of housework' also an expression of class attitudes—of (1) an elitist disdain for manual labor that one also often finds among upper-class men and (2) a commitment to 'careers' as the one route to 'success' that is more typical of the upper classes?" (205). As a matter of fact, whenever it is feasible, even homemakers try to shift a good deal of the menial work involved in housekeeping to others, including domestics. And few, as we noted in Chapter 11, undertake it as a life work if there are suitable alternatives. Still, it cannot be denied that there are many women—71 percent according to a study cited by Howe—who derive a high level of satisfaction from the work of the homemaker overall (206).

Actually the feminist movement was not putting down the homemaker. In contrast to those who called housework "shit work" were those who were sensitively tuned to the vulnerability of the homemaker. Their sensitivity grew as their knowledge of the true dimensions of her position grew. The homemaker's plight, in fact, became a major issue in the feminist platform. At its first meeting in 1966, NOW was demanding "the right of women in poverty to secure job training, housing, and family allowances on equal terms with men, but without prejudice to a parent's right to remain at home to care for his or her children; revision of welfare legislation and poverty programs which deny women dignity, privacy, and self-respect." Plank 13 of the National Women's Conference in 1977 stated as a principle that "marriage is a partnership in which the contribution of each spouse is of equal importance and value." The homemaker should have her own rights under Social Security. And in the unfortunate case of "displacement" by widowhood, divorce, or desertion, programs should be made available to help her achieve self-sufficiency. Women had always taken it for granted that their husbands were legally obliged to support them; the feminists showed them that a husband could give his wife only bread and water to eat and drink and rags to wear, but the courts would not interfere. The feminists told housewives how few resources were available to them in the case of death, divorce, or desertion by a spouse. The feminists told them of their Social Security disabilities. Not all homemakers were ready for such a frightening message. Some punished the messenger in the age-old style.[5]

Sexual Morality as an Issue in the Female World: Case in Point

Among the associations formed early in the nineteenth century were some, as we have noted, that directed their efforts in behalf of fallen women (Melder, 1977; Berg, 1978). But as the century wore on and sexuality became taboo as a public issue, ladies were less and less inclined to identify with prostitutes. Even, or perhaps especially, in the pioneer West. Marion Goldman (1972) paints a picture of the structural cleavage in the female world between "upright," respectable women and "painted ladies" in the West in the nineteenth century. Although a great deal has been written about the economic conflict between the cattlemen and the farmers on the frontier, little has been written about an analogous social conflict within the female world.

Both the upright women and the prostitutes had their own separate worlds, and "an elaborate code of manners emphasized the enormous social distance between them. . . . A respectable woman seen in or near the restricted district even in broad daylight courted disgrace, while any prostitutes walking in the residential areas would be totally snubbed. When matrons encountered shady ladies in the shopping district, they were expected to treat the bad women as if they didn't exist" (Goldman, 38). These informal pressures were later supplemented in the mid-1870s by legal codes which "served to keep painted women in their appropriate places" (38). Still, both of these separate worlds had functions to perform in the total community. Sometimes they conflicted. Interestingly enough, over the classically female love-and/or-duty ethos as expressed in the dispensing of charity.

In the nineteenth-century frontier towns the higher-status painted ladies had come, in the absence of large numbers of upright women, to perform some of the traditionally female nurturing functions in the community. "Since they were almost the only women in town they . . . assumed integral roles in community life such as nursing the sick, doing charity work, and organizing much-desired general recreations such as picnics, parades, and dances. . . . The legendary harlot heroines of the Old West derived much of their fame from good deeds of this type. While working for charity and group leisure, prostitutes performed broadly 'maternal' functions for the whole community rather than for their own nuclear families" (Goldman, 35). As the number of upright women increased, however, this function became an issue.

The respectable women were especially miffed by the charitable work that had become part of the prerogatives of the upper echelons in the prostitute's world. It vexed the upright women, for "if prostitutes had been permitted to continue charitable work, such activities would not have remained a route to recognition for respectable women. The high-mindedness and personal goodness associated with charity work could easily have been questioned if socially ostracized women routinely performed such deeds.[6] Moreover, if prostitutes and good women went about these duties side by side the good women would be socially tainted by association with the bad women. Thus, the town's matrons had to choose between forcing prostitutes out of volunteer work or abandoning one of the few routes of recognition open to them." (37).

By gaining control of charity and philanthropy the upright women both maintained their social distance from shady ladies and sustained their social dominance. "As they cared for the sick during frequent mine disasters, took charge of orphans, and organized general recreation, they appropriated a good deal of power, making decisions affecting the lives of almost everyone in the community. Upper- and middle-class women's appropriation of these activities affirmed the ascendency of their social class and values" (Goldman, 37). The success of both informal and formal controls over the prostitutes' world rested on the "general belief in the popular dichotomy between worthy and debased women" (38). Without such a moral base, the relatively small upright women's world could not have succeeded even to the extent it did.

According to Goldman's study,

> The single most striking characteristic of the process of legislation of female morality in Virginia City was that both prostitutes and reputable women assumed their respective roles in the conflict because of the same economic and ideological forces. Reputable women gained their socioeconomic status and security from their husbands' positions. Prostitutes, too, were entirely dependent upon men for their livelihoods and professional standing. Both groups had been forced into these positions of dependency because the occupational structure and its supporting ideology offered no possibility for women to earn a comfortable living and community esteem at the same time. While respectable women succeeded in crowding prostitutes out of civic life and separating them from the community, the painted women's confinement in the restricted district was nothing more than a distorted image of the respectable woman's insulation in her family parlor. Both groups of women suffered from being classified as either good or bad; both groups were dependent upon men not only in a financial sense, but [also] for their respective identities. This sexual ideology not only contributed to both the spread of prostitution and the growth of forces opposing it, but [it also] served to isolate all women from full and meaningful participation in the social world. [Goldman, 39]

An almost 180-degree turnabout has taken place in some segments in the female world vis-à-vis prostitution as an issue since that time. Certainly among feminists today the position has become one of protecting the prostitute against exploitation rather than distancing themselves from her. The attitude is not, like that of the voluntary associations early in the nineteenth century, one of saving "fallen women" but one of not blaming the victim. In the meanwhile, another issue has surfaced in the female world with a strong moral—also political—component, namely lesbianism.

Lesbianism as an Issue

Lesbianism as an issue in the female world has an interesting history. We have noted that strong bonds of affection were not only tolerated but even encouraged in women's sphere in the nineteenth century. Loving relationships remained acceptable for decades. Female homosociality was as matter-of-fact as male homosociality. But, as noted in Chapter 5, it suffered an eclipse in the twentieth century. Friendships between women came to be derided or denied as impossible because of their competition for men. And lesbianism, along with intimate friendships between women, became taboo. When it came out of the closet in the late 1960s the cleavage lesbianism caused in the female world reached almost crisis proportions. As an issue it had two aspects, one moral and one political.

For nonfeminist women the issue was moral, defined in traditional terms, often based on biblical morality: lesbianism was morally wrong, sinful, even a crime. There were others who, though they also thought it morally wrong, could nevertheless see it as an issue of civil rights.[7]

Among many feminists, on the other hand, the issue was wholly political. But political in an unfamiliar way. Girls, they reminded us, learn quite early the importance adolescent society attaches to female attractiveness to males in achieving status (Chapter 6). And Glen Elder had demonstrated the advantages women could achieve by way of men in marriage (Chapter 7). Jean Lipman-Blumen had explained the preference women exhibit for men in terms of the greater access to all kinds of resources derivable through men (1976). Catering to men, in brief, was one of the best ways to share in the privileges of the male world. The whole fabric of laws, institutions, conventions, and other norms woven by these relationships was what political lesbians called the "institutions of heterosexuality." Even granting that reproduction demanded conception, and that conception demanded the fertilization of the ovum by the sperm—almost invariably by way of sexual intercourse—still, the whole superstructure built on this admittedly biological base was not itself biological but cultural. The whole apparatus which reduced women to "winning," "seducing," "attracting" men was a humiliating part of that superstructure. The lesbians and their feminist supporters wanted none of it. "Most of our privileges as women are granted to us by our relationships to men (fathers, husbands, boy friends) whom we [lesbians] now reject" (Bunch and Myron, 1975, 33). And now that reproduction was coming increasingly under control, so that male participation in the fertilizing process could be reduced to a brief incident or two in a lifetime—or even eliminated by laboratory impregnation—the whole superstructure of heterosexual institutions was becoming more and more anachronistic.[8] Unobstructed by relationships of love, fear, or dependence on men, the perspective of these women was unflinching. And, to many other women, frightening.

There was also a psychological aspect to the lesbianism issue. To many women it was antimale, "man-hating." The perspective from which feminists wrote made men "the enemy." It exposed certain phenomena that most women had never seen before. And, either out of love or fear, they did not want to see them now. They had always seen the emperor's clothes, even his crown and scepter. They were accustomed to his regalia. They did not want it stripped away as these feminists seemed to be doing. Many averted their eyes or dropped their heads. Even if they could no longer see the clothes clearly, they were not about to become regicides, to weaken the male structure that supported them. There were others, however, who could no longer feel safe and secure once they had seen the emperor without his imperial trappings. But, with no alternative sources of security or safety, they kept their knowledge to themselves. They were unwilling to take on the emperor. They felt they could, however, take on the lesbians.

There were a few who were impressed by the lesbian analysis, though not converted to it. They hoped to be able to discuss the matter with the emperor. More self-confident, less dependent on men, they were willing to parley with "the enemy." Would he settle for, let us say, a pair of jeans and a T-shirt? Something, for example, like the clothes they themselves were wearing?

The lesbian interpretation of heterosexuality, not as a biological given but as an institutional prescription for the relations between the sexes, a cultural artifact, was one of the major shocks in the female world, creating a faultline not only between lesbians and traditional women but also between lesbians and other feminists. It all but split the feminist movement. It was not until 1977 that the feminist movement was able to come to terms with the lesbian issue. At the First National Women's Conference in Houston that year, support of lesbianism was one of the resolutions accepted. Plank 23 was couched in civil-rights terms. Its official report read: "Congress, State, and local legislatures should enact legislation to eliminate discrimination on the basis of sexual and affectional preference in areas including but not limited to, employment, housing, public accommodations, credit, public facilities, government funding, and the military. State legislatures should reform their penal codes or repeal State laws that restrict private sexual behavior between consenting adults." (1978, 89). But the real—psychological—wallop was in the small print: "A woman who does not choose to play a traditional or male-centered secondary role may find herself labeled too strong, too aggressive, too masculine, and finally, a lesbian. The fear of the effects of that label may limit the non-lesbian woman in the expression of her individuality. Only when the word 'lesbian' has lost its power to intimidate and oppress will women feel free to be strong and independent human beings" (National Women's Conference, 89). Knowing full well how heavy an incubus it would be in working for the ERA, the delegates nevertheless refused to reject the women who espoused it.[9]

Issues and Structural Faultlines

Issues vary widely among themselves in many ways, in the subject matter they deal with, in the amount of emotion they engender, in the seriousness of the differences involved. Some are amenable to continuing debate; they are in a process of "maturing." New data, new experiences are still coming in so debate is still profitable. Positions are still susceptible to modification by new information. When no new additions are forthcoming to knowlege or experience so that "debate" comes to consist only of the repetition of arguments both sides know and/or feel they can rebut, an issue may be called "postmature." It has no place to go. If neither side is ready to concede validity to any part of the other side, further debate is fruitless.

In such an impasse the two sides can harden and take on the features of a structural division as ineffable as a biological one like race. Abortion seems to be an example of such an issue. Leaders on both sides know all the arguments of the other side. New medical techniques are discounted in advance by opponents. They already, for example, resist amniocentesis or conception in a laboratory glass for fear that defective fetuses in one case or the unused fertilized ovum in the other will be discarded, procedures that, in their view, come under the heading of abortion, which they call murder.

Political, Not Religious, Faultline

We noted in Chapter 12 that Catholic as well as Protestant women established their own social and do-good organizations and institutions in the nineteenth century, as, of course, did Jewish women. But I have found no research reports of a religious faultline within the female world. Women have shared such collective religious prejudices as those of the Know Nothings and, no doubt, anti-Semitism. Still, perhaps because the Catholic Church felt itself to be under seige for so long and Jewish women lived in ghettoes for so long, women of different religious faiths were fairly isolated from one another and had little if any contact with one another. Whatever faultlines separated them were truly ideological as well as cultural. Ideological differences persisted but they did not deeply touch the lives of women as women. And, of course, there have been both traditional and modern women within all the major faiths.

True, there have been political issues—contraception, abortion—on which the Catholic Church takes a strong position. Many women protest the political clout exercised by the Church, especially on legislation dealing with abortion. But the rift is not between non-Catholic and Catholic women. For there are many Catholic women who share with non-Catholic women opposition to the Church's political support of antiabortion legislation.[10]

Traditional and Modern Women

On the basis of a number of themes found in many parts of the world, Inkeles and Smith characterize modernity as including: openness to new experience, readiness for social change, flexibility, information seeking, high educational and occupational aspirations, among other qualities (1974, 19-24). These researchers sought to delineate "the process whereby people move from being traditional to becoming modern personalities" (5). A modern society "needs participating citizens, men and women who take an active interest in public affairs and who exercise their rights and perform their duties as members of a community larger than that of the kinship network and the immediate geographical locality" (4). The modernization process can produce profound cleavages in a traditional society between those who cling to the old and those who embrace the new.

An analogous cleavage may be said to develop in the female world in our own society as its Gemeinschaft character becomes eroded. The study by Gladieux, which focused on the most "female" moment in a woman's life—the birth of her first child—showed a preponderance of kinship members in the traditional woman's social network (Chapter 12). The modern women's network, it will be recalled, was constituted preponderantly of friends, often from the work site, rather than of relatives. The several issues discussed above also seem to divide women along traditional-modern lines.

If we conceptualize the difference between modern and traditional women in terms of relative attachment to the Gemeinschaft, as the work by Gladieux suggests, we find that it is increasingly difficult for traditional women, even the most conservative, to resist "modernization." They have to become open to new experience, be ready for social change, develop flexibility, seek information, plan. Much as they may deplore participation in public—especially political—action, they have to meet the challenge. Even the opponents of the National Women's Conference in Houston in 1977 "learned political skills . . . and got out of the kitchen by organizing rallies, writing leaflets and holding press conferences" (Rosenfeld, 1977). The antiabortion women imitate the old civil rights tactics of civil disobedience and go even further, invading abortion clinics, burning them, in most nontraditional ways. There is no way they can remain passive and homebound.

"Traditional" and "Modern" as Structural Components of the Female World

There seems to be a tendency for issues to cluster, all of one cluster appealing to one set of women and all of another to a different set of women. Thus traditional women tend to share a common position on many issues and modern women tend to share a different position. In a figurative way, issues may thus be said to create structural divisions, as in the above example of abortion. This figure of speech cannot be carried too far. It is possible to be traditional on some issues but modern on others. Traditional, for example, with respect to sex roles but modern with respect to equal pay.

The issues that divide traditional and modern women seem, nevertheless, to line women up on the basis of certain personality traits. The contrast between traditional and modern women runs through the whole female world. It is not limited by class, race, ethnicity, or even age. At one end of the class structure a detailed and perceptive study of the Work Incentive Program (WIN) of the 1960s found both traditional and modern women among the predominantly black, lower socioeconomic-level women, those eligible for participation in the program. "A traditionalist mother feels obligated, principally, to home and family. . . . She expects to be supported by virtue of her position as a woman and as a mother" (Klausner, 1978, 15). She will accept employment if necessary, even in low-level occupations. Klausner distinguished three categories of traditionalist women: (1) the adjusted, to whom motherhood was the core identity, and who conformed to the supportive traditional mileu around them; (2) the incompetent traditionalist, who could not operate successfully in the labor force and who was, therefore, not exposed to modernizing influences; and (3) temporary traditionalists in process of modernizing (15). In contrast to the traditionalist mother, "a mother committed to a modernizing life style sees herself as responsible for the economic provision and protection of her children. The modernizing tendency is reinforced through the discipline of job requirements and by the variety of social influences to which work exposes her" (15).[11] The kinds of work these modernizing women do—blue- or white-collar—promote modernizing life styles by way of the social relations they provide. When traditionalist women work, it is often an extension of household chores—domestic service, waitresses, nurse's aides (16)—which protects them from more change-inducing stimulation. Modern women seek training in other occupations.

Both traditionals and moderns are also found at higher as well as lower socioeconomic levels, as a fairly extensive corpus of research on high-school, college, and professional women shows (Bernard, 1971, 9-13). Thus, in a study of high-school girls the moderns "tended to be more receptive than other girls to the new, to growth, and to change; they were less conventional and conforming" (Bernard, 10). Another study, this time of college women, also found modern women more unconventional and independent. Still another found them more achievement-oriented (10). Rossi found them more egalitarian but less nurturant and also less dependent; they valued the world of ideas more; they were occupationally competitive (11). Ginsburg found moderns characterized by striving for autonomy (11). A study at Cornell found them more nonconformist and unconventional (11). At Vassar, intellectual, unconventional, independent, "perhaps rebellious" (11). And so on.[12]

Definitive data on the relative number of women in the categories "traditional" and "modern" are not available. The research up to the early 1970s showed about 7 or 8 percent of girls and young women to be moderns and about a fifth to a fourth traditionals. The others ranged between. But the proportions change from time to time.

To see a faultline between traditionals and moderns does not imply consensus among those on either side. Among the moderns, for example, some are willing to roll with the punches; some insist on ideological purity at any cost. Some proclaim sisterhood loud and clear but nevertheless feel justified in "trashing" any who violate a single tenet of the code.

In Chapter 14 we spoke of homogenizing trends among women in income, race, education, and the like. Can women with ideological differences achieve solidarity?

Solidarity

The fate of solidarity, let alone of female solidarity, in the fragmented modern world is the subject of an enormous literature. The concept itself may be viewed as the sociological counterpart of the more social-psychological concept of homosociality. The contrast between the pre-urban, preindustrial world of small, solidary kin and locale-based groups on one side and the urban, industrial, impersonal world on the other was, as noted in Chapter 2, a major preoccupation of social thinkers in the nineteenth century. It is a curious fact, therefore, that nowhere in this literature is *female* solidarity examined. Since it has been assumed that women are incapable of "bonding" (Tiger, 1970), the literature on solidarity has been almost exclusively about men.

Mayhew traces the history of the concept from Durkheim to Parsons, illustrating it with examples from a variety of areas—race, kinship, labor, class—but not sex. We learn that in the French tradition, solidarity became synonymous with fraternity, that its loss leads to the widespread alienation of men. No references to sisterhood or alienation of women. Solidarity, in brief, has been studied as an exclusively male phenomenon. And, indeed, in the form of bonding described by Tiger, a kind of male solidarity has been able to survive, even thrive, in the modern world despite the alienation so voluminously discussed.

Actually the story of female solidarity has been somewhat different from that of male solidarity. The impact of the Gesellschaft or contract or cash-nexus world has, as we have had frequent occasion to note, been somewhat delayed and the development of surrogate forms of solidarity retarded.

The solidary groups women have lived in conform to the forms that Mayhew says are necessary for an integrated solidary system: (1) attraction, which refers to a network of individuals who have primary ties of affection for one another; (2) loyalty, which refers to groups whose aims one shares and feels must be protected; (3) a sense of membership or inclusion, which refers to a feeling of identification with the group; and (4) association, which refers to the sharing by individuals and groups of a common cause, though not necessarily of group membership (1971, 74-75). The first three of these criteria cover the groups discussed in Chapters 12 and 13. It is the wider "solidary system" of individuals and groups sharing a common cause though not necessarily group membership that is problematical.

Female solidarity even under the most auspicious circumstances is peculiarly vulnerable to the social impact of crosscutting. Crosscutting refers to the potential conflict among members of the numerous interest groups in a society which claim their loyalties, thus tending to prevent the polarization that might result if all the interests of one group coincided and diverged from the interests of all others. The possible strengthening impact of crosscutting on the solidarity of a social system overall is counterbalanced by the weakening effect it has on the component elements. Crosscutting in the present context prevents the "battle of the sexes" from polarizing a society, but it can also prevent strong bonding among women. Too much crosscutting can fragment any system.

The history of the women's movement in the nineteenth century is a case in point. Abolitionism, or whatever other reform movement might need the support of women, crosscut their own movement. In the New Left of the 1960s the same crosscutting occurred: the women were expected to choose loyalty to the New Left's male-defined goals over loyalty to their own goals as women. At the International Women's Conference in Mexico City in 1975 and Copenhagen in 1980, women were again subjected to crosscutting: loyalty to male-specified, government-formulated goals—anticolonialism, North-South issues—crosscut loyalty to women's goals for themselves such as improved education and health. The classic example of crosscutting is the plight of black women, many of whom feel that loyalty to blacks crosscuts loyalty to women, or vice versa. We noted a similar situation in the case of the WTUL, in which loyalty to the women's suffrage movement crosscut loyalty to the movement to organize working women.

Crosscutting renders the individual woman vulnerable to cooptation. Many women find female solidarity hard to reconcile with almost any of the other competing pulls on them: ethnic, racial, religious—and male. Perhaps especially male. Men seem better able to "gang up" against women than vice versa. Loyalty to the corporation more easily takes precedence over loyalty to the family in the case of men than of women; some top men in industry are quite candid in admitting it. Loyalty to a woman's family crosscuts almost every other loyalty and usually wins.[13] Much as a woman favors "equal pay for work of equal value," she is still resentful when an unmarried woman earns as much as her husband, who is a father of four.

Ethnic or working-class women and "upper middle-class élite" women deal with different kinds of men. Working-class women are dealing with men who are especially vulnerable. It would be diversionary to go too deeply into the hazards of the male role, but being a "good provider" has always been a basic specification in our society. Implicit in the "good provider" role is the complementary role of the person or persons being provided for, customarily a wife and children. But being a "good provider" depends on a host of forces far outside the immediate control of the man involved (Bernard, 1981). He is vulnerable to layoffs, temporary or longterm loss of work, unemployment, elimination of his job, hostile employers. The nineteenth-century need for female support is still a reality in the lives of many working-class men. The wife is not likely to feel like adding to his burdens. His vulnerability is obvious to her. She is inclined to support him, even when, as sometimes happens, he abuses her. It is often recognition of his weakness, not of his strength, that puts her on his side. Some black women express the same feeling.

Crosscutting creates what might be called the "I'm-not-a-women's-libber-but" syndrome, exemplified, for exampled, by Dorothy Bolden:

> I'm pround that women began to get up and let them know that we can shape this world into a form together, but some of them are trying to be men. If God wanted you to have everything that a man has, he would have given it to you. A woman is a helpmaker. She's not to get up and dominate man. I can't see things like pushing a man out of a job. . . . I've been a free woman all my life. I've been making my own decisions, but I respect yours and I'll go halfway with yours. But a man is your protection. . . . He takes on the full responsibility [for supporting the family]. So why do you think that he's taking your rights? . . . I like to see a woman making a decent salary. If she's doing a man's job in an office or any other place, I feel she needs to be equally paid. Everybody ought to be equally paid on this earth for what they're sweating for. But not just to prove a point that a man is pouring cement so I want to pour cement too. This is why men are not respecting us anymore. The womanhood has lost something. . . . I think the majority of men have got hang-ups about women coming in and taking over men's jobs and it builds resentment until she catches hell [1976, 171-172].

Sometimes the "I'm-not-a-women's-libber-but" syndrome takes the form of professing acceptance of the goals of the women's movement but not of its methods, especially its confrontational methods.

Still, crosscutting does not necessarily fragment the female world. Women who line up against one another on some issues may line up together on others. Thus, for example, nine women in the Virginia House of Delegates, though they disagreed on the ERA, could agree on legislation to establish the concept of "marital property" in case of divorce (Barker, 1979). Although the leader of one antiabortion group rejected Ellie Smeal's invitation to meet with pro-choice groups to explore common goals, at least some women of the "right to life" persuasion were willing.

Granted then that female solidarity is difficult to achieve, is it even possible? Can the female world "get it all together"? Hostile critics sometimes view as their trump card the fact that there are such marked differences among women that overall solidarity is impossible. Small solidary groups may be the very essence of the Gemeinschaft female world, but is more possible? A more encompassing unity? A genuinely integrated female world?

Despite the faultlines sketched above, women do seem to be learning how to bond, after their own fashions. Not only in the traditional form of intimate small groups but also in the more organized form of sharing a common cause, though not necessarily group membership. Thus, for example, in June 1975, a coalition of almost a hundred women's organizations with a membership of about thirty million was formed "to pool their talents and resources for common goals, abolish the barriers dividing women, and gain strength for [their] cause through numbers" (Brozan, 1975). It issued a National Women's Agenda, through which "the national women's community has come together in an unprecedented demonstration of unity and focus. Each organization feels strengthened by the fact that its own goals are reflected in the National Women's Agenda, supported by so many women" (Women's Action Alliance, 1976).

The common goals specified by the Agenda were not blatantly feminist but general goals that any liberal could subscribe to, namely: (1) fair representation and participation in the political process; (2) equal education and training; (3) meaningful work and adequate compensation; (4) equal access to economic power; (5) quality child care for all children; (6) quality health care and services; (7) adequate housing; (8) just and humane treatment in the criminal justice system; (9) fair treatment by and equal access to media and the arts; (10) physical safety; and (11) respect for the individual. The preamble recognized differences in programs and goals among the participating organizations, but saw an overriding unity: "Diverse as we are, we are united by the deep and common experience of womanhood." These women not only recognized their diversity but even insisted upon it. The membership list included such seemingly strange bedsisters as: La Leche International, the Leadership Conference of Women Religious, the League of Women Voters, Lesbian Feminist Liberation, Lesbian Mothers' National Defense Fund, Lutheran Church Women, and the National Black Feminist Organization. An organization that ran a gamut from Hadassah and YWCA through Junior League and United Auto Workers, from Camp Fire Girls to Appalachian women, was in a position to involve a great many women who individually would not be in a position to participate actively in the women's movement. Whatever it took to get almost a hundred organizations to sign the same document could not help but strike a blow for female solidarity, however long the road ahead might prove.

Important as the Agenda was, it was soon overshadowed by another attempt at solidarity, the First National Women's Conference in Houston in 1977. Epochal as the Conference was, however, it should not in any way belittle the Agenda. The Agenda did not have the political backing or the media access of the Houston Women's Conference. The Agenda had to woo and persuade and win widely disparate groups to sign a common program. It was an heroic effort and, in many ways, a greater, though subtler, achievement than the 1977 Houston Conference.

But the Houston Conference was a landmark. For the first time women of all ages, ethnic backgrounds, races, classes, religions came together under one roof to debate female issues. And it passed twenty-five resolutions ranging in controversiality from how to collect statistics that would be useful for women to the elimination of discrimination against homosexuals. The emotional high experienced by the women delegates was extraordinary. Here was sisterhood in its most exciting form. But not yet 100 percent solidarity. On some issues, yes. Who could oppose enforcement of laws against discrimination in education? On some issues, not yet. There were still some women who feared the ERA. And on some issues like Medicaid for abortion—no, never![14]

At the moment there is no way to predict the outcome of such female groping for solidarity. Women are learning as they go. It took workers a long time to learn the best way to organize. Women may, as the male advertisers reassure them, have come a long way, but the shape of the female world they are in the process of building is not yet wholly clear. It is growing by an organic process, according to its own logic. With no way to prove it, I would say that the world women are in the process of building will not be exclusionary, it will not be "misandrous" or antimale, and it will not be aggressively competitive. What it will be is harder to say. But whatever the ultimate form it takes, a great deal rides on it. Including—to update the motto of the French Revolution—liberty, equality, and humanity.

Coda

"Intrapsychic" interpretations are ordinarily not congenial to sociologists, but one seems relevant here. A distinguished sociologist, W. I. Thomas, noted some years ago that we are all subject to certain ambivalences; we want new experiences, adventure, excitement, but we also want security.[15] When new experiences—like plague and famine—are less likely to be pleasurable than calamitous, the search for security may prevail over the search for new experiences for most people. But when new experiences are more likely to be pleasurable than disagreeable, security may take the form of sheer boredom, and new experiences then seem more desirable.

Today, despite the greater prevalence of options, there are traditional women who still want the protection and security available to them (if not always attainable) in marriage. They do not want "to deny themselves full enjoyment of many of the real gratifications [for example] of being petted, pampered, admired, and taken care of" (Keniston, 1971, draft). And they are willing to forego the new experiences involved in self-fulfillment. Conversely, among the modern women who opt for new experiences there are times when they, too, long for protection and security, when they, too, would like to have someone they could trust to "take care" of them. But they have "to define these gratifications and the needs that lie behind them as dangerously infantile, childish, and regressive." Thus both types of women may long for options they have already foreclosed for themselves. The traditional woman does not want to surrender her security; still, she covets the interesting contacts the modern woman, especially the successful professional, has. The modern successful professional woman does not want to give up her work; still, there are times when she longs for the protection and security of the "taken-care-of" traditional woman. The traditional woman resents the modern woman, envies the satisfactions she enjoys; the modern woman who is finding self-fulfillment in her work may nevertheless envy the protected, sheltered, even pampered traditional woman. Both would like the best of both worlds; but neither is willing to pay the price for the other world. As Gladieux noted, "there are great benefits and gains associated with women's changing roles in society, but there are costs as well" (1978, 293).

Notes

1. The distinction may be made in methodological terms. In one case the structural variables are the "independent variables" and positions on issues the "dependent variables." In the other case, attitudes on issues are the "independent variables" and the structural categories are the "dependent variables." The first asks, to what extent do positions on issues "depend" on class, race, ethnicity, age? The second asks, what is the class, race, ethnic, age composition of those who, for example, believe "women's place is in the home"?
2. The American Home Economics Association has a more realistic definition of the family: "AHEA defines the family unit as two or more parents who share resources, share responsibility for decisions, share values and goals, and have commitments to one another over time. The family is that climate that one 'comes home to,' and it is this network of sharing that most accurately describes the family unit, regardless of blood, legal ties, adoption, or marriage" (*A Force for Families*, n.d.). This was the definition of the family which so enraged the conservatives referred to in Chapter 5.
3. "About the need to clean up my language. 'Homemaker isn't so hot either,' Faye, one of [Howe's] informants, said, " 'but it's probably the best we have. A hell of a lot better than that godawful housewife' " (Howe, 1977, 201).
4. The faultline between domesticity and career is older than industrialization. Lougee has described how it showed up in the time of the salonières. The followers of Fenelon wanted women reared to become hardworking, frugal mothers. They would deprive women of independence and posited a strict hierarchy and "harsh isolation within marriage" (Lougee, 1976, 187). All this was antithetical to the *bel esprit* represented by the salonières.

Nor does this faultline take the same form among black women as among white women. Among blacks it was not housewife versus career woman. Many wanted to be only housewives.

5. We mentioned in Chapter 7 the shock some women experience after years of being sheltered from contact with the male world by a loving husband. Not until they lose such protection does the "click" occur that suddenly reveals to them what the feminists were talking about. They learn about it in their contacts with welfare agencies, for example, or job-hunting, trying to get a loan, whatever. In the mid-1970s a documentary film, *Janie's Jane*, pictured the radicalization of a working-class woman who had always been someone else's protected "Jane"—her father's, her husband's. After her husband left her and her small children, she moved from the anti-"women's libber" position to that of an organizer as she learned from her own experience how vulnerable women, particularly working-class women, really were vis-à-vis the male world.
6. The relationship of Melanie Wilkes and Belle Watling in *Gone with the Wind* is illustrative of this status situation. Melanie scandalizes the good ladies of Atlanta by "receiving" Belle, as a gesture of appreciation for the madam's protection of Melanie's husband.
7. Charlotte Bunch stated the argument for supporting the lesbian position that went beyond the civil-rights argument: "Feminine support of gay rights is also crucial to the philosophy and success of feminism because of the role that homophobia has played in keeping women in their place. All women, no matter what their sexual preference, are restrained in many areas of life by the threat of being called 'lesbian' and of facing the economic and social consequences that go with that label. When women can give unflinching support to gay rights, that form of control over women's behavior will dissipate. Lesbian-baiting will never end just because feminists deny a connection between the issues; it will only end when women deny it the power to threaten them" (1978).
8. Even so far as the function of producing sexual pleasure was concerned, heterosexuality as institutionalized in our society was not satisfactory for most women. It had come to be defined primarily in terms of penetration, suitable for male pleasure but not necessarily for women in achieving orgasm (Hite, 1976). Some argued that women, knowing the female body, were far better able than men to perform this function for other women.
9. There were class cleavages in the lesbian community as well as elsewhere. Rita Mae Brown reports on the class differences which kept lesbians apart and "at each others' throats": "Behavior born of privilege granted from white, upper-class male heterosexuals is destructive to women and must be ended. . . . In the past those of us from working-class backgrounds tried to make this clear to straight sisters. We are now making it crystal clear to our middle-class lesbian sisters. . . . Don't waste our time by trying to prove you are an exception because your father was working class and your mother was middle class. . . . Stop trying to wriggle out of those middle-class ways. . . . Change them. You are your own responsibility" (1974, 22-23).

10. On the day Pope John Paul II was celebrating the Mass in Washington, there appeared "An Open Letter Concerning Human Rights to His Holiness, Pope John Paul II" sponsored by Catholics for a Free Choice, "a nationwide organization of women and men both practicing and inactive Catholics, laity and clergy. . . . of all ages, ethnic backgrounds and occupations" (*Washington Post*, Oct. 7, 1979). They asked the Pope to instruct the Church officials "to refrain from their attempt through political action to impose Church teaching on all citizens." They argued that an amendment to the Constitution banning abortion would impose the religious views of a minority on all Americans.
11. In a forthcoming study (Free Press, 1981), Zena Blau reports that the IQ and achievement-test performance of black children was related to whether their mothers were in the labor force, for how long, and whether they had any social contacts with whites. These mainstream contacts apparently affected everything from worldview to child-bearing practices. As well as, of course, expectations. There is no reason to doubt that similar results would be found for other groups.
12. The explanations for the differences tended to be in terms of "needs" or of socialization, according to the researcher's discipline—psychology or sociology—background.
13. In the contest for loyalty, the male world enforces the choice by women of family and the company by men. In one study, for example, executives were asked whether they would promote candidates with excellent records, but including among other qualifications that their primary loyalty was to their families. Almost half of the respondents (45 percent) said they would not promote such a man. When the same *vita* was said to be that of a woman, 58 percent said they would not promote her. Nor would they hire a woman for a job that called for long absences from the home, since that was where her primary obligations lay (Rosen, Jerdee, and Prestwick, 1975, 562-572). Sheila Kamerman has also found that if women do not express primary loyalty to home responsibilities they are considered deviant and therefore not hired at all, but if they are hired, no allowance is made for their domestic responsibilities (1979).
14. The leaders who conceived the idea for the Conference and brought it off knew that more was needed. President Carter set up a National Advisory Committee to advise him on implementing the resolutions. The members of this Advisory Committee took their mandate seriously, established local, state, and regional networks to spread information, and worked on legislative programs. They won on some issues, lost on others. At the end of the first year after Houston, the "score" stood as follows: success on pregnancy disability, civil service reform, teenage pregnancy, and flexitime; failure on welfare reform, veterans' preference, family violence, jobs for women, and, of course, Medicaid funds for abortion. The Committe had helped in securing an extension for ERA, had projected welfare and health needs for the future, and had worked on the needs of women that would have to be dealt with in any national health insurance bill. It was also thinking ahead to the Conference of Women's Issues in 1980. In 1979, the

implementation of the Houston planks suffered a setback when the Advisory Committee set up by the president lost its chairwoman, Bella Abzug.

The dismissal of Abzug had important consequences in raising public consciousness with respect to political issues. The apparent assumption under which President Carter had been operating was that women did, indeed, have their own special issues, and he was willing to let them deal with those questions. But he did not think they should butt into the major —male—issues, like, for example, the budget. The Commission did not agree. They saw all issues as female issues or, at least, as having a female angle. They were not about to limit their concerns to issues specified by the President. More than half resigned. The work of the Commission in implementing the Houston recommendations was impeded, but an important point had been made. A few months later, the executive secretary of the President's Interdepartmental Task Force on Women, Nancy Gordon, was noting that the Federal budget is an every-person issue but there are some parts of it that impact more on women than on men (Gordon, 1979). Inflation, for example, hit women harder than men because there were more women than men among the poor, the unemployed, and those on fixed incomes.

15. Psychologists have an analogous but not identical concept of ambivalence between the need for achievement and the need for affiliation which, in a society like ours, may similarly be ambiguous, one, in effect, costing the other. There is evidence of tension whichever choice one makes. There is, for example, the housewife who works longer on weekends, presumably to show how important her work is (Vanek, 1974), and the activist community worker who is more conservative with respect to the female family role than less activist women (McCourt, 1977).

PART V

The Culture of the Female World

Like other such fundamental sociological concepts as social structure, class, and group, the concept of culture lacks consensual definition. In 1934 Ruth Benedict, following a proverb of a Digger Indian, called it "the cup of life" (1934). Almost a half-century later the term "culture" was being widely used in this technical or anthropological sense as well as in the more popular sense of the arts, high or popular.

For some students of the subject, the theory of culture patterns and that of social structure are parallel. "Both are holistic theories in the sense that they try to cover all aspects of society and culture—law, politics, economy, technology, kinship and social organization, art, literature, language, religion, philosophy, science, and so on" (Singer, 1968, 532). And both hark back to the "father of anthropology," Edward Tylor, who in 1871 defined culture as: "that complex whole which includes knowledge, belief, art, morals, law, custom, and any other capabilities and habits acquired by man [sic] as a member of society" (1958, 1). Singer includes "social structure as a theory of culture" (1968, 530), and

Parsons sees culture as determining social structure (Blau, 1975, 17). It becomes a toss-up, therefore, whether culture should be viewed as an aspect of structure or structure as an aspect of culture. To complicate the matter further, in actual research, as distinguished from theory building, the term has been elaborated and extended to include subcultures; we hear of a youth culture, of ethnic culture, of class culture, of capitalistic culture, of black culture, of the culture of aging, the culture of a school, of poverty, and what have you.

Culture is dealt with here as coeval with social structure, not independent of it but different enough from it to warrant separate discussion. And out of the welter of topics included in the concept of culture from Tylor to Singer, only four are selected for attention here: language, technology, the arts, and ethos or values. Even in this restricted sense there is, admittedly, a fallacy implied in talking about "female culture" as though it were the same for all classes, ethnic groups, and races, for it can vary greatly even within a given class, ethnic group, or race. And, like other cultures, it has varied over time. The discussion here is limited to female culture primarily in our own society, with only occasional nods to other times and places.

The first chapter in Part V (16) deals with the rock-bottom, fundamental basis of the culture of female world—as of any other human world—language. Anthropologists have long been teaching us how language shapes our very mentality, how we perceive, think, feel in terms of our language. It is impossible to think of any human society without dealing with the language that serves to make abstract communication possible. The differences between the languages of the female and male worlds have been noted for more than a generation. Psychologists, sociologists, and students of literature have also added recently to the work of linguists in forwarding our understanding of the way language shapes behavior in the female world. We now know, for example, that the female world in our own society cannot be understood at all without some knowledge of how it is affected by the hostile American English language.

When one speaks of technology one is referring to an enormously complex entity, a kind of *ding-an-sich* (thing in itself), a unified whole made up of a staggering set of interrelated processes and products. So to speak of technology and the female world is almost like speaking of air and the female world. Technology is all-pervasive, a multifaceted, widely ramifying conglomerate of things, ideas, and processes. It is almost impossible, therefore, to assess its precise impact on anything, for nothing escapes its effects. No matter how far away one runs to escape it —to the mountains, to a distant island, to the farthest archipelagoes, as some attempt to do—sooner or later modern technology catches up. Monster to some, savior to others, it is simply there, inescapable, omnipresent. So, in this dense jungle of artifacts—tools, weapons, machines, engines, missiles, atomic power plants, neutron bombs, and especially computers—banking, credit, corporations, not to mention immunization, antibiotics, amniocentesis, and scores of other biological techniques for saving human life, we carve out only one little swath here: technologies in the household and their effect on the female world.

Although art—fine, popular, folk, performing, pictorial, auditory, dramatic, whatever—relies on technology, it differs from it in that technology is a means to an end (which, to be sure, can be art itself) while art is an end in and of itself. It gives life significance, delight, catharsis, insight, escape, release, meaning. Not all art to all people. Different social classes, different art. Different ages, different art. A statue that evokes the profoundest emotion, perhaps ecstasy, in one part of the world may be repulsive or funny in another. What is moving to some people is boring to others.

Different sexes, different art? That is the question in Chapter 18. Although some radical feminists have rejected the conceptualization of the female world *as* a culture (Chapter 2), they have not rejected the idea that the female world *has* a characteristic culture of its own—in the sense of art, music, drama, literature—separate and different from that of the male world. Some women, both traditional and modern, have accepted the idea but shamefacedly, with embarrassment and apologies, even contemptuously, judging female culture to be of low quality, denigrating it more than they probably would if it were the culture of some exotic, faraway place. Whatever evaluation is made of this female culture, it does reflect the inner values, the longings, the dreams of women and cannot be dismissed as unimportant. Chapters 18 and 19 are concerned with this component of female culture.

In Chapters 20, 21, and 22 we turn to another basic component of female culture, its ethos. Although we have referred to the love-and/or-duty ethos throughout our discussion, at this point we focus on it in more detail. "Ethos," the *Oxford English Dictionary* says, is "the prevalent tone or sentiment of a people or community," its "character, ideal excellence." In terms of values, as measured on instruments, women rate high on religious, social, and aesthetic values (Tyler, 1968, 210). But the approach in these chapters is somewhat different from this measurement one.

In Chapter 3, the discussion of the love-and/or-duty dynamic of the female world mentioned the three Greek categories of love, based respectively on *eros*, *philos*, and *agape*, the first sexual, the second friendly, the third humanitarian. Some attention has already (Chapter 13) been directed toward the second of these—philanthropy or charity—in the female world. In Chapter 20 we look at the *eros* component and in Chapter 21, at the *agape* form, as illustrated in the political behavior and humanitarian values of the female world. The kinds of behavior called for by the love-and/or-duty ethos may be subsumed under the term "stroking." This is a term sometimes applied to what Bales, in his study of task-oriented groups, called "expressive" behavior (Bales, 1951). It is essentially giving, supportive, compliant behavior. The consequences for women are far reaching. In Chapter 22, attention is paid to some of the challenges currently being directed by women toward the love-and/or-duty ethos itself.

16

Language: Words and Deeds

THE IMPORTANCE OF verbal communication in human relations has been recognized since at least Biblical times, with the story of the famous Tower of Babel. The social solidarity that a common language gave human beings made them arrogant; they felt they could do anything, even reach heaven. The Lord was infuriated by this challenge. With only one tongue, "nothing will be restrained from them which they have imagined to do" (Genesis, 11:1-9). So He confounded their language. The more we study and learn about language and speech the better we understand the Lord's reaction.

Verbal language sets human beings off from other primates, even the most intelligent. Language determines what we see and how we see it. Before we have a word for something we can hardly see it at all. Once it is named we see it everywhere. Abstract as well as concrete things. Until, for example, the terms "male chauvinism" or "sexism" were applied to certain taken-for-granted forms of behavior, no one—or hardly anyone—saw them. Once there was a word for such behavior, more and more people did see it, in some cases by a sudden process, akin to Paul's conversion, the "click" (O'Reilly, 1972, 54-56). Understandably, language and its use constitute a basic component of any culture. Indeed, a major branch of cultural anthropology deals specifically with lingustics.

Only relatively recently, however, has the importance of language in the female world come in for careful scientific scrutiny. Although gender was a common variable in anthropological studies of language in the nineteenth century, it was not until the turn of the century that speech differences by sex were added to studies of gender (Bodine, 1975, 130).[1] Almost a quarter of a century later the subject was revived and extended by Oscar Jesperson (1922). But it is only in the last decade or so that a cadre of serious students of the subject have uncovered for us one of the most illuminating aspects of our own language—its sexism—and its pervasive effect on women, on how they think and feel, and the way language structures and limits their world. These researchers taught us, for example, how hostile the American-English language is to women, how demeaning it is, and how inadequate for expressing women's own experience, especially their sexual experience. Women have also learned how handicapped they are in the use of spoken language, and how all these factors are reflected in styles of interaction between them and men. It is, in brief, by way of language and its use that we come to get an insider's perspective on the female world.

A Hostile Language

Language is one way in which the misogyny of the male world, referred to in Chapter 2, finds expression. We know, for example, that no matter how the female world in our society is conceptualized, it uses a language that is hostile to it,[2] for the American-English language, as Jesperson noted a long time ago (1922), is a male language. "Whatever Adam called every living creature, that was the name thereof" (Genesis, 2:19). This "power to name" is, as Stimpson has noted (1979), of inestimable importance. Thus women have to use a misogynist language, one not friendly to women, a language, for example, that has more vernacular animal words—like "bitch," for example—for them than it has for men (Eble, 1972). Greer calls it a "language of women-hatred" (1971), noting that words like "witch," originally applied to both sexes become pejorative when applied only to women. Conversely, words which originally applied pejoratively to women only lose their pejorative significance when they come to apply to men also, as illustrated by the word "shrewd-shrewish" (Strainchamps, 1971). There seems to be in American English, in fact, a tendency toward what Schulz calls "pejoration," a tendency, that is, for words that designate women to become debased (1975). The love-and/or-duty ethos of the female world becomes "masochism" and its locale-orientation, "claustrophobia."

A Sexually Denigrating Language

The hostility is shown also in the denigrating language of sex. Feminists have reviewed the use of language as a way of depreciating women (Todasco, 1973). There are more derogatory terms for women for which euphemisms must be substituted to avoid implicit downgrading, according to Robin Lakoff, as illustrated by the euphemistic "lady" for "woman" (1975). Lawrence notes that obscenities, until recently almost the sole prerogative of the male world, nearly always derogate women with "undeniably painful, if not sadistic, implications" (1974, 33). A study of over two thousand "dirty jokes" here and abroad found that most were originated by men; there was no place for women in such folklore except as the butt of humor.[3] "It is not just that so preponderant an amount of the material is grossly anti-woman in tendency and intent, but also that the situations presented almost completely lack any protagonist position in which a woman can identify herself—as a woman—with any human gratification or pride" (Lawrence, 1968). There are at least 220 terms in English for sexually promiscuous women contrasted with about 22 for promiscuous men (Stanley, 1972). Offensive expressions referring to women, like tramp, piece of ass, pig, pussy, reflect male disgust and contempt. A study of insults used by men in 200 languages reported far more directed against women than against men (Gregerson, 1977). Since World War II, one researcher claims, sex insults have increased (Faust, 1970). More recently, the male-controlled media have coined words that trivialize the women's movement, such as "libber," "lib-lady," "libbies" and the like (Eble, 1973).

A Subordinating Language

The American-English language not only is sexually denigrating of women but is also a vehicle for asserting male superiority. It reflects women's inferior position in the male world (Lakoff, 1975). Elbe notes that since "during the course of the development of the English language the male has been the dominant sex, it is not surprising . . . to find . . . this dominance coded into the language" (1972). Thus words referring to male behavior have connotations of power; those referring to female behavior connote weakness. Men bellow but women purr; men yell, women scream; men get angry, women fret (Key, 1972), men growl, women squeal (Farb, 1973). Franzwa analyzed the meaning of different words that had reference to masculinity and femininity and found that those referring to femininity—such as "sweet" or "pretty"

— were weak and "good," almost pejoratively, whereas those referring to masculinity were strong and either "good" — e.g., "capable" — or, almost admirably, "bad" — e.g., "dominating" (1974, draft).

A Sexually Inadequate Language

The American-English language is inadequate for expressing a wide gamut of female experience, which puts women at a great disadvantage in understanding themselves, let alone in communicating with others. The language is not designed for the way they feel, an inadequacy particularly notable in the area of sex itself.

About three-quarters of a century ago, Elsie Clews Parsons called to our attention the fact that among English-speaking peoples "women have no words, secret or otherwise, to describe [even] some of the simplest sex characteristics and expressions" (1913, 156; Eble, 1972, draft), whereas the language supplied men with some 1,200 synonyms for the word "intercourse" alone (Stanley, 1973, 6).[4] Such language deficiency has hampered women greatly in dealing with their own sexuality, not to mention that of males. There are, for example, no colloquial words for vagina, for clitoris, for orgasm, to serve the female world as there are for such gender-specific but non-sex-tainted phenomena as menstruation, pregnancy, childbirth.

If, for example, a girl consulted the *Oxford Dictionary*, all she would learn about orgasm is that it is: (1) violent excitement of feeling, rage, fury; a paroxysm of excitement or rage (1663). Or that it is (2) excitement in an organ, or part, accompanied by turgescence; specifically, the height of venereal excitement in coition (1684). If, her curiosity unabated, she looked up "turgescense," she would learn that it is: (1) the action or condition of swelling up: the fact or state or condition of swelling up; the fact or state of being swollen; (2) figuratively (a) progressive swelling to inflation, pomposity, bombast (1806). If, still puzzled, she looked up "coition" (1541), she would learn that it is: (1) going or coming together; conjunction (1761); (2) sexual conjunction, copulation (1615). And if, though somewhat discouraged by now, she looked up "copulation" she would find that it is: (1) the action of coupling or condition of being coupled; connection; union (1752); (2) the union of the sexes in the act of copulating (1483). Copulating, she would note, means uniting in sexual congress (1632). The simple, straightforward — albeit hostile — "fuck" she would not even find in the dictionary at all until 1969. And though she would presumably know the word and what it meant, she would never — again, until recently — say it. It was — and still is for most women — a dirty word and, like curse words, swearing, profanity, and obscenity, forbidden in their world.

Only when it became demystified in the 1960s and 1970s, when almost every other hostile adjective used by either sex seemed to be "fucking," did the hostile, aggressive, denigrating meaning of the word "fuck" become clear.[5] "Fuck you!" was the ultimate insult. "You fucking____" expressed the ultimate in anger or contempt. Only when women began to use the word and thus emasculated it did it lose its power. Only then did it become clear what the feminists meant by insisting that rape was not so much a sexual act as an act of aggression, as the very archetype of male hostility and misogyny.

Not until the early 1970s did women begin to take their own sexual education and protection into their own hands. Women who had never even heard the word "orgasm," let alone experience it, learned what it was all about, challenging the male definition, showing how it differed from their own. They learned a vocabulary for their own anatomy, their own physiology, their own sexuality. It vastly extended their knowledge of themselves (Boston Health Collective, 1976). And hence of their own world.

A Female "Genderlect"

Is there a female language? Early linguists, dealing with exotic languages, sometimes implied that there were separate and different languages for the two sexes among some peoples, though Jespersen, an early student of the subject, rejected this idea (Bodine, 1975, 131). Still, on the basis of evidence for the existence of "systems of co-occurring, sex-linked linguistic signals in the United States," Kramer suggests research on "genderlects" or "sexlects" (1975). Not only is there a standard American-English language used by men about women, there is also a traditional language used by women themselves. Certain words, as we noted above, are forbidden. But others—nice, pretty, darling, charming, sweet, lovely, cute, precious—are suitable only for women[6] (Kramer, 1975, 52-53).

On the basis of written language, V. Tiger and Luria distinguish two kinds of language within the female world, one for the "inlaws," the traditional or folk subworld of women, and the other for the "outlaws," or more modern women. The sound of the first:

> is what we term womantalk, that chastising, advising, chattering talk by means of which women join together to sew and mend and patch and stitch the seams of daily life. Womentalk is this hodgepodge, the colored afghan embracing the community which is women's own. What we think of as woman's gossip, girl talk, bitchery, old wives' tales or chattering is, seen from the generic perspective, woman's wisdom: the subterranean lore of communal life. Womantalk unearths the encrusted nuggets of woman's

> lore. It describes what has been termed the community of women. But . . . not all voices sing in unison. So within this community there are inlaws and outlaws, and we can identify them by their voices, by the sounds they create. Who is the inlaw within the community of women? She is the woman living in harmony with the laws of her land, its customs, its conventions, its taboos. Unlike the outlaw, the inlaw within the community of women participates—without self-awareness—in continual communal analysis, through the languages of the female life in her time [1978, 2-3).

It is interesting that the women authors of this passage take over the pejorative male vocabulary—bitchery, gossip, chattering—to characterize this womantalk. But the voice of the inlaws is also "soothing, moving, instructive, repetitive," as contrasted with the voice of the outlaws, which is "shrill, strident, carping" and "rends the air with calumny, complaint, and grievance" (4). These characterizations illustrate how recourse to the male pejorative vocabulary slants the perspective even of women viewing themselves.

Speech

It is, however, as much in the use of spoken language as in either vocabulary or writing that the worlds of women and of men differ from each other. And both are also different when women and men speak to one another. Some of the differences are fairly trivial. Thus the speech of women seems more refined, more correct, more proper, more precise. But some of the differences are not trivial; the speech of women is less forceful. Lakoff, for instance, believes that women use more tag questions at the end of sentences—like "isn't it?" "don't you think?" "wouldn't it?"—which have the effect of softening their impact. They are "midway between an outright statement and a yes-no question . . . less assertive than the former, but more confident than the latter" (1975), though Kramer asks for more empirical studies on the subject before accepting Lakoff's thesis (Thorne and Henley, 1975, 48).

A common observation is that women's speech is "concerned with internal states" while men's is more action-oriented (Barron, 1971), that the vocabulary and speech patterns of the female world permit more expression of feeling, and such expression is more acceptable than it is in the male world. Thorne and Henly review the research:

> Men who are discontented with traditional notions of masculinity often refer enviously to the greater ability of women to express emotions and to engage in personal self-disclosure. Mark Fasteau writes of "the personal communication," the easy expression of feelings, that women have developed among themselves, but which is relatively absent among men.[7] Some language studies can be fitted into this theme. Brend found that women

> have a wider range of intonation, using a high level of pitch that men usually avoid. This . . . level of pitch may be associated with emotional expressiveness, as may tag questions. Gleser *et al.* [1959] analyzed samples of speech and found that females used significantly more words implying feeling, emotion, or motivation. The findings and speculations of Wood, Barron, and Bernard are also relevant to the claim that women's speech is more emotionally expressive than that of men [1975, 26].

Balswick and Peek also find that the female world permits positive expressivity whereas the male world frowns on it (1971, 363-368). Pleck has summarized much of the thinking on the subject (1976, 229-244). The sociology of emotion is not yet developed fully enough to tell us all we would like to know about this aspect of female culture (Hochschild, 1975, 280-307).

A caveat is therefore in order here. The implication from laboratory studies of small groups is that expressivity is warm, supportive, loving, that it shows solidarity, raises others' status, gives help, is rewarding, tension releasing, agreeing, accepting, understanding, complying (Bales, 1950). But there is also a negative aspect of expressivity, shown in the same laboratory studies in the form of disagreeing, rejecting, withholding help; showing tension, withdrawing; showing antagonism, deflating others' status, defending or asserting self (Bales, 1951, 9). There is no evidence that men do not exhibit such negative expressive behavior. Actually men are permitted a great deal of expressivity or feeling of this negative form. In fact, the original laboratory research on instrumental and expressive role behavior in small groups was done with male subjects.[8] Men are permitted to express a great deal of emotion and feeling, especially hostility, competitiveness, combativeness, whereas women are not permitted such negative expressivity. For just as positive emotional-expressive behavior in men is underemphasized in the literature so also is its negative aspect underemphasized in women. Presumably all of the behaviors delineated in the laboratory studies of small groups can occur in either the male or the female world. All we may be able to say is that one is more permissible in the male world, the other in the female.

Whether or not women's speech shows more emotion than men's, it does tend to be more integrative (Barron, 1971). In general, the conclusion seems valid, though not yet unequivocal, that women tend to use speech to build upon rather than challenge the other's statements. Bardwick, for example, finds communion characteristic of the female world in contrast to separation, which is more characteristic of the male world (1974, 60). The female world is characterized by intimacy, which psychologists contrast with the more superficial "sociability"[9] (1966, 175). In the female world, that is, speech seems to be used more collaboratively, supportively. Hirschman, for example, though she did not find certain expected sex differences in speech, did find that women more than men indicated support, attention, understanding, or agreement by the use of "*mm hmm*" (1975b). This characteristic was more marked in female-female speech than in speech in mixed-sex groups (1975b).

Contrasting with the collaborative, supportive character of women's speech is the male style, which tends to be one of argumentation, parry and thrust, one-upmanship, challenge, attack and defense, debate, competition.[10] Points may not be conceded; once made, they have to be insisted on even if they are not correct; face must be saved; deference must be exacted; opposition must be shown up or put down (Bernard, 1968, chap. 6). Corroborative of this characterization was a study of male and female speech which found more hostile terms used by men, more supportive ones by women (Eble, 1972, draft).

Collins offers a market analogy as a paradigm for male conversation (1975, 135). He has made an analysis of what he calls "conversational resources and conversational costs"—an approach which in itself is characteristic of the male world—in which he traces the interactions involved in the male "conversational market." He tells us that "the basic premise is that everyone moves toward the best available exchanges for creating his subjective status. But by no means is everyone able to get others to help him create a conversational world in which he can continuously show off, receive deference, and enjoy himself. Some persons must settle for lesser realities in which they are merely audiences and supporters of conversational heroes, or participants in tawdry worlds of minimal conversational interest. Where one stands depends on the resources that he brings to the market" (1975, 135).

Collins' use here of the generic male pronoun is quite accurate. Current research suggests that women are far less likely than men to show off or receive deference. Quite the reverse, in fact. Freedman tells us that "males everywhere tend to demean women, belittle their accomplishments, and, in the vernacular [clearly laden with symbolism] 'put them down.' I have not heard of a culture in which the males do not engage in this chauvinistic sport" (1979, 61). The market style of conversation is not congenial to most women. It makes them feel uncomfortable. Conversation under these circumstances is not enjoyable.

Quite in contrast to the Collins model are accounts of women's rap sessions. One study found several significant strategies.

> The first of these involves politeness rules and breaches thereof. The women seemed to value decorum highly, they asked permission to speak . . . and tried to make sure that others were completely finished before another woman began. There may be some difference at this point between the male and female codes, men tending, in women's view, to be less polite. A

> woman once told me that she never got to speak in a seminar because she kept waiting to make sure the male students were finished talking; they never were. The women in the rap group took pains to see that everyone spoke, often asking for the response or comments of someone who had not spoken much, and they disliked any one person dominating the meeting [Kalcik, 1975, 4-5].

So far from demanding deference, these women began and ended with apologies for talking at all or for talking too long. Support was expressed not only linguistically—by way of comments during and after another woman's story, questions asked to show interest as much as to get answers—but also paralinguistically, in the form of sympathetic noises, facial expression, and gestures (Kalcik, 1975, 5). The female world is less inclined to see conversation as a market situation. It is less marked by disputation. It is less likely to view an adversary relationship as a good way to get at the facts of a case.[11]

The way the female world uses language in speech reflects a characteristic style of bonding, collaborative rather than combative or competitive. Laboratory studies have shown that in games of strategy men play a more aggressive game and women a more collaborative one[12] (Vinacke and associates, 1959, 343-360; 1961, 61-75; 1963, 75-88). Such differences in styles of interaction may help to explain men's rejection of women in work groups. Horner reports, for example, the inability of young men to function in a situation structured along female interaction patterns. An experiment had been set up which "put men and women in cooperative kinds of conditions to work with each other ... in order to examine whether some of the psychological barriers that women have in competitive situations would be alleviated or be controlled and if women could actualize in the situation." The situation worked well for the women, but the men couldn't take it. "For months before they had been talking about how empty the competitive kinds of activities were and they were putting down competition and all of that. Finding themselves, however, in a very simple cooperative situation with a woman, for whatever reasons, made them, the men, experience tremendous feelings of powerlessness" (Horner, 1974, 4).

Consequences for Women of Language and Speech Patterns

The consequences for women of having to use a language hostile and denigrating to them and styles of speech expressing this hostility and denigration have not been trivial. In an experiment conducted at the Pennsylvania State University, for example, two graduate students in the speech department were selected, one woman and one man, who were judged by the faculty to have equally good communication skills.

Each was given two identical lectures to deliver to two classes in introductory sociology, one on a topic presumably of greater interest to women, one to men. Each person spoke to one group on the first topic and a week later to the other group on the second topic. The students were told in advance that they would be examined on the contents of the lectures. So far as sheer acquisition of facts was concerned, the students did equally well on lectures delivered by the man and by the woman. But they qualified the facts learned from the woman. Comments like: "she said thus and so," "she made the point that . . . ," "she stated that. . . ." appeared more often with respect to the woman than with respect to the man. The facts that came from the male lecturer were accepted as more authoritative (Bernard, 1964, 255-257).

On a wider stage the disability becomes more serious. Murphy refers to the fact that women do not have access to the forum in the male world (1962, 1077). This crippling handicap has been explained in terms of women's trained incapacity. For women in their world are not only taught a woman's language but also a female style of using it, a style that avoids strong, forceful statements. They are encouraged instead to use expressions suggesting uncertainty and triviality of subject matter. They do not make strong assertions. They have to have "assertiveness training" even to protect themselves, let alone to exercise leadership. Thus these trained-in defects become strong inhibitors of leadership skills. Unable, therefore, to speak precisely or forcefully, they are at a disadvantage in serious discussion (Lakoff, 1975).

A survey of etiquette books written for women beginning in the fourteenth century finds the same inhibiting rules of behavior prescribed for them—not to talk too much, to repress anger, to listen patiently, to show deference to men, to be humble and respectful (Bornstein, 1978, 132-137). Eble has documented in detail how girls and women in our own country from colonial times on have been instructed by etiquette books how not to speak with authority on any topic (1975, draft). As late as 1970, the *New Seventeen Book of Etiquette* was still advocating the feminine ideal of meekness and politeness. Understandably, therefore, women find it difficult to relinquish "followship behavior" (Tiger, 1970, 75). Even in their own world, let alone in the male's (D. Smith, 1975, draft).

Talk as Change

After all the effort of the women's movement, the question is sometimes raised: Has behavior itself really changed? Or is it just talk that has changed? Whether behavior has or has not changed—and there is evidence that it has—we know that there has been a "talking" revolution. Shock waves have been sent through the female world not only by the use of previously forbidden words but also by the reintroduction of whole areas of once forbidden topics. Subjects that were once unmentionable by ladies—sexuality, orgasm, abortion, rape, wife abuse—have come to be spoken of openly, without self-consciousness or embarrassment. This is not a trivial change, for talking itself is important behavior. And, perhaps more to the point, not talking about a thing is also communicative. Silence and censorship—by self as well as other—can convey as much as words.

Until recently a vast, dark "underworld" underlay the female world, a world too awful to speak of, a world that was literally "unspeakable." Silence protected an unknown amount of wife abuse, rape, sexual harassment on the job, alcoholism. Family closets have been notoriously full of such skeletons—even live bodies—that no one ever mentioned. That would have been bad form. They were family secrets that the mores forbade revealing.

The "talking" revolution has now made it possible for the victims of such behavior to talk about it. It is no longer too awful to speak of. Women learn that what they had considered both individual and shameful was in fact widely shared. Being able to talk not only makes it possible to put their heads together to resolve the difficulties but also to relieve the guilt of those who thought only they were beaten, only they were anorgasmic. Abuses could no longer be swept under the carpet and thus protected.

There are still many people who prefer not to know about the darker side of the female world. Talking about certain aspects of it seems to them to condone the behavior or, by recognizing it, to strip it of negative sanction or condemnation. "Let lesbians be, but they shouldn't flaunt their homosexuality." So long as they remain in the closet, they're tolerable. They should stay there. "I know that there have always been abortions, but now they're *talking* about it" was the way one woman expressed herself. So long as abortion was hidden, not discussed, not in the public prints, it too could be tolerated. Just talking about it encouraged it in her view. It meant it was permissible to have an opinion on it.[13]

Body Language

It is not only verbal language that has attracted research attention in connection with the female world but also nonverbal or so-called body language, which can be quite as communicative as speech.[14] The body language of seduction and flirtation in both sexes is an ancient and well-known lore. Skill with props—the fluttering fan, the glove, the veil, the handkerchief—and in the use of the eyes, mouth, and nostrils was part of the training of many girls in the eighteenth and nineteenth centuries. Sometimes these nonverbal body-language messages were given far greater credence than verbal language, even when they contradicted each other.

At the present time serious consequences can ensue from misreading of body language. In the days when flirtatiousness was sanctioned and no nice girl was supposed to admit she was "willing," there was some logic in asserting, as the song had it, "Your lips tell me no, but there's yes, yes in your eyes." But today the standard male justification for rape is based not on "she led me on" but rather on "she didn't fight hard enough" or "her protests were not convincing." Insufficient physical resistance is not the same as the body-language come-on represented by the conventional seductive behavior of an earlier day. The disparity in size and strength often makes refusal in any language, physical or verbal, ineffective.

But only relatively recently have the political or power, as contrasted with the playful, aspects of body language come in for research scrutiny. The first systematic book on the subject did not appear until the late 1970s (Henley, 1977), and its title was *Body Politics*, to emphasize the power aspects of body language. Since there is so little power in the female world, body politics is not a prevalent hazard there. It is when men and women confront or interact with one another—usually on male turf—that the full expression of body politics comes through. The resources men bring with them, not only physical—larger size and louder voice—but also social—the support of their world—give them great initial advantage. They can make women feel uncomfortable or unsupported with even minimal gestures. Not sexual seduction but sexual domination is the focus of concern in body politics.

Here, too, of course, the history is long, longer even than history. For among subhuman animals the language of power and domination has attracted considerable study. Indeed, a large component of male social organization among subhuman animals consists of gestures of dominance and submission. And much of the apparent conflict among them is mainly gestural or symbolic communication. Even among human beings, the raised arm threatening a blow and the response of cringing submission are as old and as well known as their loving opposites, the outstretched arms, the warm embrace. Not recognition of the existence of nonverbal language but the subtleties of its forms in our society today constitute the current focus of attention. Especially as they impinge on women.

Body politics deals with the way we sit, use space, stare, cock our heads, or touch one another (Henley, 1977, vii). These are not trivial or minor aspects of interaction. They are part of the pattern of domination and submission. Indeed, the whole apparatus of protocol—which determined how members of different "stations" in life in status-organized societies must behave—included precise rules to guide the body language of superior and inferior. Who bowed to whom, who took precedence in a line, who took the initiative in shaking hands—these and scores of other kinds of behavior constituted the "grammar" of body language. Inferiors should not "presume." Superiors should not exploit. In the United States, which did not have a feudal tradition accustoming everyone to a status conception of society and its structure, there was a general freedom which foreign observers perceived as very bad manners. People did not seem to know their place, who was higher, who was lower. The numerous etiquette books published in the nineteenth century attempted to impose some order on this apparent disorder.

These books did not have the myriad categories or the analytic sophistication of current researchers. Instead of the fine points of body politics they spoke generally of manners, demeanor, style, courtesy, politeness. They were addressed to women and they were on the side of those who wanted social life to be smooth. They were written for women in the home who had to find a modus vivendi between the democratic ideology of equality and the inequalities among members of the household—between servants and mistresses, for example, as noted in Chapter 11; between adults and children, older and younger, weaker and stronger, sick and well, as well as between women and men.

Catharine Beecher was one of the first to deal with body politics in the home. She noted in 1841 that "certain grades of superiority and subordination are needful for individual and for public benefit" (1977, 122). This principle had not been adequately appreciated. Thus "all the proprieties and courtesies which depend on the recognition of the relative duties of superior and subordinate have been warred upon, and thus we see, to an increasing extent, disrespectful treatment of parents from children, of teachers from pupils, of employers from domestics, and the aged from the young" (123). There were clear-cut rules of precedence that ought to be followed, "a style of deportment" appropriate to different relationships (125):

> It is suitable for a superior to secure compliance with his wishes from those subordinate to him, by commands; but a subordinate must secure compliance with his wishes, from a superior, by request. It is suitable for a parent, teacher, or employer, to admonish for neglect of duty; it is not suitable for an inferior to take such a course to a superior. It is suitable for a superior to take precedence of a subordinate, without any remark; but in such cases, an inferior should ask leave, or offer an apology. It is proper for a superior to use the language and manners of freedom and familiarity which would be improper from a subordinate to a superior [125].

Lack of compliance with these rules of precedence and status constituted the major defect in American manners. Children sometimes behaved toward their parents in a style appropriate only between equals;

servants behaved toward their employers in a style not appropriate to their inferior position. Being inattentive when spoken to, staring, yawning and gaping in company, not looking a speaker in the face, and insubordination were among the evidences of bad manners or, in the modern idiom, body politics. Although the democratic rule was that superiors—in age, station, or office—took precedence over subordinates, still, "the feebler sex has precedence of more vigorous man"(125). Only, of course, in the realm of manners. In the social system, as noted in Chapter 4, women were subordinate.

"The 'trivia' of everyday life—touching others, moving closer or farther away, dropping the eyes, smiling, interrupting—are commonly interpreted as facilitating social intercourse," and that was Beecher's goal. But she also recognized their function as, in the modern idiom, "micropolitical gestures, defenders of the status quo—of the state, of the wealthy, of authority, of all those whose power may be challenged" (Henley, 1977, 3). Essential even in a democracy like ours.

The kinds of behavior we now see as part of the language of the body, the language Henley has in mind when she speaks of body politics, is becoming more perceptually clear to us. Differences in nonverbal behavior are seen as learned differences deriving from differences in power (Henley, 2). Much of the nonverbal language of women vis-à-vis men derives from their inferior position, as that of men vis-à-vis women derives from their superior position.

Women, it has been found, are better able than men to understand nonverbal signals, whether they come from a female or from a male. Perhaps because "nonverbal behavior seems to play an especially important part in women's lives, many studies have found women to be more sensitive to nonverbal cues than men are" (Henley, 13). And it has been suggested that subordinates in general tend to be more sensitive to nonverbal signals than superordinates. They have to be; it may be a matter of survival. Such differences are sometimes interpreted as sexual rather than as status or power-related. But the fact that the boss touches the secretary more than she touches him is as likely to be a status as a sex gesture (17). Some of the salient aspects of gender and nonverbal behavior emphasized by Henley are: "female sensitivity and the importance of nonverbal cues in women's lives: . . . [the way] women's nonverbal behavior may be used against them to justify attack; [the fact] that females and males seem to bodyspeak different nonverbal languages and [the fact] that [although] these differences are learned, they may be maladaptive" (18). She notes that such differences resemble the differences that have been found between the actions of the powerful and powerless" (18).

Henley summarizes her survey of the research literature in a table on the gestures of power and privilege, showing how nonverbal behavior differs between equals, nonequals, men and women (Table 16-1).

TABLE 16–1 Examples of Gestures of Power and Privilege*

Nonverbal Behaviors	Behaviors Between Status Equals		Behaviors Between Status Nonequals		Behaviors Between Men and Women	
	Intimate	*Nonintimate*	*Used by Superior*	*Used by Subordinate*	*By Men*	*By Women*
Address	Familiar	Polite	Familiar	Polite	Familiar?†	Polite?†
Demeanor	Informal	Circumspect	Informal	Circumspect	Informal	Circumspect
Posture	Relaxed	Tense (less relaxed)	Relaxed	Tense	Relaxed	Tense
Personal space	Closeness	Distance	Closeness (option)	Distance	Closeness	Distance
Time‡	Long	Short	Long (option)	Short	Long?†	Short?†
Touching	Touch	Don't touch	Touch (option)	Don't touch	Touch	Don't touch
Eye contact	Establish	Avoid	Stare, Ignore	Avert eyes, Watch	Stare, Ignore	Avert eyes, Watch
Facial expression	Smile?†	Don't smile?†	Don't smile	Smile	Don't smile	Smile
Emotional expression	Show	Hide	Hide	Show	Hide	Show
Self-disclosure	Disclose	Don't disclose	Don't disclose	Disclose	Don't disclose	Disclose

*Source: Nancy M. Henley, *Body Politics*, Power, Sex and Nonverbal Communication, © 1977, p. 181. Reprinted by permission of Prentice-Hall, Inc., Englewood Cliffs, New Jersey.
†Behavior not known.
‡Who waits for whom; who determines the length of the encounter; who ends the conversation, etc.

The overall picture illustrates Roger Brown's generalization to the effect that toward inferiors one uses the form suitable between intimates; toward superiors, the form suitable toward strangers (Henley, 180). On all ten items of behavior, the forms used between men and women correspond to those used between superior and subordinate. Among most of the items of nonverbal behavior (address, demeanor, posture, personal space, time, and touching), the intimate form corresponds to the form used by men and superiors, the nonintimate form, by women and subordinates. For three—facial expression, emotional expression, and self-disclosure—the intimate form corresponds to those used by the man or superior, the nonintimate, to those used by the woman or inferior. Eye-contact is equivocal.

Body language is sometimes used by a subordinate to "make a statement" without direct confrontation, with its built-in disadvantage. Clothes, stance, posture, coiffeur, cosmetics, grooming, sitting position—foot on desk, knees far apart—proclaim a rejection of stereotyped femininity. In some cases women have identified themselves as political lesbians, an extreme form of body language, to convey their utter rejection of the male world.

Both verbal and body language, then, constitute a basic and all-pervading component of female culture, profoundly influencing if not determining, all other aspects. In quite a different way, another component of culture, technology, is also pervasive, with wide ramifications throughout the female world, as we shall see in Chapter 17.

Notes

1. An annotated bibliography (1975) by Thorne and Henley of 131 items in the by-now extensive research literature on sex differences in language, speech, and nonverbal communication includes: vocabulary and syntax, phonology structure, conversational patterns by sex, dialects and varieties in language, sex as a variable in multilingual situations, language development, and nonverbal aspects of communication. The discussion in this chapter relies heavily on this rich resource.
2. Apparently the German language is also hostile to women. Thus Ferdinand Tönnies finds that "yelling and screaming, jubilation and bemoaning, like laughing and weeping in words, are the expression of the feminine soul" (1957, 163).
3. So thoroughly ingrained in the male world is the insulting, degrading point to dirty jokes that they cannot understand why these jokes are not funny to women. They expect women to laugh at them and they feel offended if women show displeasure. Why don't they have a sense of humor?
4. One woman in her forties recalled an experience in a graduate seminar in which she had used the word "screw" with no conception of its meaning; she had learned only in the last year what the word "cunt" meant.

5. To the definition "to have sexual intercourse with" the *Heritage Dictionary* in 1969 added in its entry for "fuck," among other definitions: "to deal with in an aggressive, unjust, or spiteful manner" and, followed by "up," "to mishandle, bungle" and "to meddle, interfere."
6. The use of formerly forbidden words—long a part of the male world's language (Polsky, 1967; Collins, 1975, 247)—became almost required in the early years of the liberation movement. This "vocabulary of shock" (Eble, 1975) was used to overcome the stereotyped prissiness of feminine language but also to assert a right to the use of strong language to add emphasis, to call attention to what was being said, and to stress one's commitment to it (Conklin, 1974).
7. The envy Fasteau shows of self-revelation among women may be overdrawn. It is commonly assumed that women reveal themselves more readily than men. Actually there has been, at least until recently, great reticence among women about many aspects of their emotional lives. We are only now learning how much wife abuse has been endured by women, how much alcoholism in husbands. A long history of etiquette books taught women not only to accept verbal and physical abuse from a husband but also "to conceal his defects from others" (Bornstein, 1978, 135). The misery of the wallflower has to be carefully disguised.
8. Instrumental, as contrasted with expressive, behavior included such items as giving suggestions, direction; implying autonomy of others; giving opinions, evaluations, analysis (Bales, 1951, 9).
9. A study of elementary school children found relationships in the female world to be affectionate and even when competitive, not invidious. The girls did not, like the boys, feel they had to be first, to win or lose face. On one occasion when a girl won a race her friend told her she had deliberately held back so she could win. Instead of anger and resentment at such a seeming put-down, the winning girl said, without sarcasm, "that was nice of you" (Best, forthcoming).
10. Competition, like the verbal duel, is a characteristic form of bonding in the male world: "Competition . . . performs an integrating function. . . . The fact that entities are competing for the same thing means that they belong to the same public or group. They are 'in.' Those who refuse to enter the competition are expressing a rejection of the values being competed for; they are 'out.' . . . In brief, submitting to competition is one way of indicating affiliation, acceptance of common values. To remain out of the competitive race, conversely, is to express contempt or lack of homage for the values of others. Competition thus creates conformity" (Bernard, 1962, p. 75).
11. Clinical as well as laboratory evidence documents these kinds of differences. Anne Schaef, on the basis of fifteen years of therapy with women, sees interaction in the female world and in the male world as representing different systems of myths, collective representations, collective beliefs. The male world believes that it is possible to know and understand everything; that it is possible to be logical, rational, and objective; and that it is not legitimate to use subjectivity. The center of the male world is seen as the self and its work, with temporary lapses to include a female who is then incorporated in the male self. Relationships—people—constitute the

core of the female system. Time is conceived of differently in the two systems. It is intimately related to instruments in the male world; time is what the clock measures. In the female world, Schaef notes, it is a process of cycles, of passages. One does what needs to be done whenever it needs to be done. The male system favors hierarchical relationships; the female, peer relationships until proved inefficacious. The male system tends to define intimacy physically, the female system, verbally, in terms of talking together, sharing. Decision making in the male system is linear, facilitating quick, simple decisions which are, however, more vulnerable to sabotage. In the female system it is more scattered, multivariate, more likely to get off the track, to bring in seemingly extraneous considerations. The female system, Schaef thinks, though it takes more time, arrives at a more creative solution, better supported, more innovative. There is, she believes, as much need for training in such consensual decision making as in Robert's *Rules of Order*, itself also a verbal form of interaction. Whereas women are familiar with the male system, men are not likely to recognize the female system. They may see it operate, but they interpret what they see as mere fragments of random or deviant non-male-validated behavior.

12. In another study, however, it should be pointed out, Lirtzman and Wahba found that when "talking, signaling, or communication by any means were absolutely prohibited" in coalition formation, leaving only assigned weights as the criterion, women could be just as competitive, aggressive, and exploitive in laboratory games as men. They speculate that, once coalitions are formed, "in the ensuing bargaining and allocation of rewards, we might expect that the accommodative [female] style would be exhibited" (Lirtzman and Wahba, 1972, 406-11).
13. Sociologically speaking, she was correct. As soon as people are permitted an opinion on a norm, it has ceased to be in the mores.
14. For a visual presentation of communication by body language, see Goffman, 1979.
15. Men tend to interpet the meaning of female behavior as though it is identical with male, especially in the area of sex. Thus a male myth arose that in effect justified rape. Women might say they did not want sexual relations but, according to male interpretation, their bodies were saying yes.

17

Household Technologies

THE NEW PRODUCTIVE TECHNOLOGIES outside the home, which at the end of the eighteenth century and the beginning of the nineteenth inaugurated what came to be known as the Industrial Revolution, had a direct impact only on the minority of women who entered the labor force as industrial workers. Far more immediate for most women were the effects of the new household technologies, many of which, it might be noted, were invented by women.[1] Yet the industrial revolution in the household seemed less important than the change from hand-powered tools in the cottage to power-driven machines in the factory because it involved such homely things as, say, yard-pump water versus indoor plumbing, and because we are not used to thinking of housewives as part of a labor force. Cowan corrects our perspective: "The change from the laundry tub to the washing machine is no less profound than the change from the hand loom to the power loom; the change from pumping water to turning on a water faucet is no less destructive of traditional habits than the change from manual to electric calculating. It seems odd to speak of an 'industrial revolution' connected with housework . . . but despite this oddity, I think the term is altogether appropriate" (1976, 9). She reminds us that the uniquely female technologies have been so "neglected . . . that we know more about the bicycle than about the baby carriage" (1977, 24).[2] As a result of inadequate research on the effects of household technologies, "in certain crucial respects we do not fully understand the impact of technology on women" (Cowan, 1974, 250).

The story of household technology is full of paradoxes, differing approaches leading to different conclusions. Among the questions raised are these: Did the new household technologies save time? If so, what was done with the time saved? If they did not, why not? Did the new technologies destroy "traditional habits," as Cowan has suggested? Did the new technologies modernize the household? The women? The answers are by no means unequivocal.

Technology and Time

Inkeles and Smith, in their research on modernization, emphasize attitude toward time as a basic criterion of modernity. In this sense, Catharine Beecher was among the earliest modernizers. The importance of time was, in fact, one of the central tenets of the Protestant ethic. Time and tide waited for no man. Time was money. Procrastination was the thief of time.

Beecher suggested ways to save time. Combining functions, for example, saved time, as when charitable sewing or visiting the poor were made recreational (*sic*) activities. Using odd moments helped too. It was astonishing, she said, "how much can be accomplished by a little planning and forethought in thus finding employment for odd intervals of time" (1841, 175). She saw the importance of scheduling the household so as to synchronize its activities with the rapidly growing interdependence of the economy. Early rising, for example, was important not only for the welfare of the family itself but for the whole community. "All that great portion of the community who are employed in business and labor find it needful to rise early; and all their hours of meals, and their appointments for business or pleasure, must be accommodated to these arrangements. Now, if a small portion of the community establish very different hours, it makes a kind of jostling in all the concerns and interests of society. The various appointments for the public, such as meetings, schools, and business hours, must be accommodated to the mass, and not to individuals. . . . Thus it is manifest that late rising not only injures the person and family which practice it, but interferes with the rights and convenience of the community in which they reside" (111-112).[3]

As it turned out, the amount of time saved by scheduling was eclipsed by the time saved (or potentially saved) through use of the new household equipment provided by technology. The Rumford stove, for example, which could be used for both cooking and heating, made a clean, efficient kitchen possible in the central core of the home; it didn't need to be relegated to the dark, damp cellar or basement or back house. Even minor items such as a paring and coring device (1838) and an egg-beater (1857) could save time. Folding beds, home elevators, chopping machines, and churns were at least labor-saving if not necessarily always time-saving aids. (They were, incidentally, also status symbols [Andrews and Andrews, 1974, 317].) The later innovations—the dishwasher, the clothes washer, and later the automatic washing machine, the laundromat, the supermarket, frozen foods, the home dryer, for example—"pale into insignificance when compared to the quantum change from oil lamps to electric lamps, coal stoves to gas stoves, kitchen heating to central heating, outdoor plumbing to indoor plumbing, not having a bathroom at all to having one, canning tomatoes to buying canned tomatoes, making dresses to buying them, baking bread to buying it, living with servants and living without them" (Cowan, 1976, 164).

What did women do with these potentially time-saving devices? A variety of things. First and foremost they raised the family's standard of living. It began to be noted some time ago that although labor-saving technologies did, indeed, save human muscle-power, they did not necessarily save time. More than a generation ago, for example, Folsom pointed out that although "we have been enabled to have more conveniences in our homes, yet it takes more time to take care of the modern home" (1943, 581). He challenged the idea then current that technology had vastly reduced the housewife's work. "A great deal of scorn has been heaped upon the idle, bridge-playing woman, but this 'freeing of women's time by machinery' has been grossly exaggerated" (581-582). Actually a version of Parkinson's Law prevailed.[4] Whatever the level of household technology, the work expanded to fill all the time available for it. Or the standard of living rose. Changes of clothes, formerly scheduled weekly, came to be scheduled daily when laundering was so easy and ironing not required. Thus a woman who had just bought an ironing mangle warned her neighbors not to follow her example. Before she had the mangle her family had been satisfied to sleep on unpressed sheets; now they wanted the sheets to be ironed. Folsom noted that as a result of the "greater elaboration of living" (580), city women were spending more time on homemaking and family care than rural women who had fewer household amenities. Later studies have corroborated this point.[5] Joann Vanek, for instance, has found that the amount of time devoted to homemaking expands and contracts according to the amount of time husbands spend at home or at work, expanding especially on weekends, when husbands are not at work.

The potential for using up the saved time was exploited by advertisers. "A glance at any woman's magazine testifies to the enormous importance of making today's home a place of beauty, culture and spotless cleanliness. . . . Interior decorating, gardening, preparation of varied and attractive menus, personal beauty care, and chauffeuring, entertaining, and otherwise catering to children—all take far more time than they used to" (Smuts, 1959, 28). "Saved time" in the household, Smuts notes, is also used to help husband and children in their pursuit of happiness. "The focus of women's tasks at home has shifted. Less occupied with meeting the physical needs of her husband and children, the wife is now expected to help them pursue the elusive goal of happiness. . . . There is no doubt that [these functions] consume time and energy, and that society imposes at least some of them upon . . . women" (28).

All these activities can become vastly elaborated. "Preparation of varied and attractive menus" now expands to classes in exotic cooking; "personal beauty care" now expands to include not only the hairdressing salon but also the health club. exercise classes, weight watchers, jogging. "Interior decorating" may involve needlepoint and other time-consuming versions of the traditional feminine crafts. Whether it is "society" or the advertisers who impose these tasks on women is a point we will comment on presently.

Child care was another use to which the "saved time" was put. When it was safe to give a child the run of the town or yard, the child did not require its mother's constant watchful eye. And when it was taken for granted that children could walk to just about any place they had to go, the mother did not have to accompany them. In time, chauffeuring children came to be one of the most time-consuming activities of the housewife. Cowan has also shown how advertisers taught women to invest the "saved time" in child care.[6] If a mother brought the advertiser's product she would have more time to pay attention to her children (1974, 251).

We have already noted some of the other uses made of the time saved by technology in the household, namely, the performance of "vicarious leisure" and "conspicuous consumption" for affluent husbands (Chapter 9). Even less affluent husbands found it important to have wives who did not "have to work" and who could instead spend their time window shopping or going to movies or, later, watching television.[7] Or reading, including not only novels but also manuals and periodicals addressed to the housewife, bringing her both scientific knowledge and advertisements to control her purchases.

Elaboration of their families' standard of living was not the only outcome of the new household technologies for women. We have already referred (Chapter 13) to the large number of benevolent associations and civic and cultural clubs that flowered in the nineteenth century. These outside activities became increasingly available to less affluent women also. By the twentieth century, even working-class women could engage in "committee work for parent-teacher associations; fund raising; supervising Boy Scout, Girl Scout, and other organized children's activities; political organizing at the local level; participating in school and community improvement groups; helping to run cooperative nursery schools, and all of the other things that today take so much of the time of many married women" (Smuts, 29). We noted earlier that such clubs and activities were the butt of a good deal of humor, but Smuts reminds us that they contributed importantly to the social fabric as well as introducing the "kitchen-bound housewife to the problems of the world about her" (31).

Even so, toward the end of the nineteenth century the activities made possible by the time saved by the new technologies began to seem dull and unchallenging. Many women were bored with their lives. "Even before 1890, there were signs that some women were finding time heavy on their hands" (Smuts, 30). Some of the more affluent young women went to college. But the emptiness of their lives when they graduated made some of them—Jane Addams is the archetype—literally ill (Chapter 22). It was in this group that social service became a lifetime career. Whether or not the new household technologies led to labor-force participation, labor-force participation did change the way time was used. If the non-employed housewife elaborated her household's standard of living, the employed woman simplified it: no ironing, shorter hair to reduce time spent on care, simpler clothing, a less formal style of entertaining. Fewer small dinner parties that might take three days of preparation; a single annual party instead, one that might even be catered.

Household Technologies and Labor-Force Participation

Conventional wisdom has it that one of the uses to which the time saved by household technologies was put was participation in the labor force. Cowan challenges this assumption. The data neither confirm nor disprove it. She cites the only two studies (Long, 1958, 120-123, and Oppenheimer, 1970, 29-39) that attempt to support it and finds neither convincing. Oppenheimer did find a relation between the rise in married women's labor-force participation and the rise in number of household appliances, but there was a twenty-year gap between these phenomena. Cowan concludes that "two generations of American women used their electrical appliances to create more 'satisfying' homes, and it was only in the third generation that women began to suspect that the satisfaction was a ruse" (1974, 249). She comes down on the side of a less than impressive relationship between household technologies and labor-force participation. "The initial effect [of the new technologies] was to raise standards of houshold care and to transfer several functions that had previously been performed outside the home, or by paid employees, to the purview of the housewife. Concurrently, time-priorities changed for housewives; whatever time they saved—let us say in cooking—they were expected to translate to other tasks, primarily child care. Consequently, therefore, there appears to be no immediate relationship between the growth of household technologies and the indicator of social change with which it is ordinarily thought to be associated—that is, with the entrance of married women into the labor force" (1974, 251).

Household Techologies and Domestic Service

A great many of the household innovations introduced in the post-World War II years, although well beyond the point of diminishing returns, did save time and thus provided an alternative to the domestic service that had always been in short supply, as well as to the sharing of tasks by maiden aunts and adolescent daughters, as in the past (Cowan, 1976, 158). Even before the Great Depression, the housewife was described as "cheerfully and resolutely" doing her housework herself (Cowan, 149). The servant remained in fiction and even in house plans, which still provided "maid's rooms." "But the days when a housewife of moderate means fully expected that she would have at least a maid of all work, and probably a laundress and nursemaid, were clearly over" (149).

The departure of servants made a difference in even the architecture of the home. When there had been servants, the kitchen, for example, had been "a dreary room, often in the basement of the house." Now that the kitchen had become "the housewife's [not the servant's] domain, it had to be prettied up" (Cowan, 1976, 150). Today it has become as much a decorator's domain as the living room.

A Great Paradox: Science and Heart

It was not only the mechanical household gadgets themselves, important as they were, that had an impact on the female world. The scientific mind-set that accompanied the burgeoning industrial technologies was also influential, though in a subtler way.

The theoretical bases for the practical or industrial arts may vary widely in different societies. They may rest on magic, on inherited lore, on chance, or, like Charles Lamb's apochryphal roast pig, on accident. Anthropologists find it is as interesting if the medicine man utters incantations over burnt entrails as if he applies antibiotics supplied by the Red Cross.

In the present context, the relevant—household—technology rested on scientific grounds. The mind-set that accompanied it in the eighteenth and nineteenth centuries was one that used science rather than tradition as the approved measure of legitimacy. This meant that the specific technologies were, presumably, subject to rational tests; they were impersonal; they worked or they did not work according to scientific tenets. It was possible to check the results against results based on, say, tradition or magic. The new technologies implied a kind of mentality not irreversibly tied to tradition or to inherited lore. They implied an openness to change. Branca has characterized these new attitudes as even more important in the modernization process than changes in the nature of work itself (1975, 145). In the context of the home, the nineteenth century's new adulation of science led to a great paradox.

The factory was a Janus-headed puzzle to the housewife, both enemy or threat and model to follow. On the one hand it was a symbol of scientific technology, admirable as a model for the household; on the other, it was a symbol of the new economic order and, as such, a force undermining tradition. A variety of defenses, as Andrews and Andrews (1974) point out, had to be erected against it: nativism in politics, for example, revivals in religion, romanticism in literature, and, more relevant here, the cult of domesticity, discussed in Chapter 4. The home became, in effect, a counter-symbol to the factory. This development involved the "sentimentalization of domestic life, the elevation of the woman to a sanctified position as ruler of the home, the romanticizing of childhood, and the subsuming of values like piety, thrift, and moderation under the rubric of 'domestic virtues,' ... all components of a developing mythology or ideology of 'domesticity.' ... This tendency—called by William Taylor the 'domestic transformation of American society'—was rooted in a desire sometimes stated explicitly, sometimes obviously subconscious, to defend a national lifestyle against the kinds of disorienting change the factory most directly symbolized" (1974, 311). It was technology, then, that "stimulated the new perception of the home as a moral center and the woman as its divinely appointed ruler" (313).

But the factory, though it represented the harshness of the Gesellschaft against which the home had to defend the family, also represented the prestige of science, and this was seized upon as a means of upgrading the instrumental contribution of the housewife. Thus, the home became not only the realm of the heart, as prescribed by the cult of domesticity, but also, increasingly, a symbol of science, taking the factory as a model. "To the nineteenth-century American the most tangible symbol of the technological order which developed out of eighteenth-century science was the factory. . . . Factories became fit symbols of the social and intellectual developments which produced them; they came to represent . . . the forces of change which were restructuring American Society; new ways of organizing labor, . . . new attitudes toward time, . . . and a new economic model with profound implications for social organization and basic patterns of thought" (Andrews and Andrews, 1974, 310).

It was in this respect that the factory came to serve as a model for the housewife in her efforts to improve the status of household management by professionalizing it. Technology offered a source of aid in elevating the woman's role as a professional housekeeper because "domestic science . . . drew on exactly the same assumptions and values as did such disciplines as chemical and mechanical engineering—and hence seemed to promise the same status to the housewife as the engineer received" (Andrews and Andrews, 1974, 317). Lydia Maria Child was already speaking of the kitchen as a laboratory. "Technology represented to nineteenth-century women anxious to elevate the woman's status a potentially powerful ally. Technology was seen . . . as a friendly source of assistance in the movement to secure for women an elevated role in society" (quoted in Andrews and Andrews, 1974, 313).[8]

The Women's Building at the Philadelphia Centennial Exhibition in 1876, Andrews and Andrews note, displayed not only such expectable exhibits as painting, statuary, mechanical inventions, and the arts and crafts of women but also an engine run by a woman which operated all the machinery in the building. They find it "extraordinarily interesting that at the first international exhibition at which women had the use of an entire separate pavilion in which to celebrate themselves they chose to emphasize machinery" as well as domestic artifacts (325).

Meanwhile, in another part of the forest, the problems of coming to terms with science as related to homemaking were being tackled in a somewhat different way. Women were no longer waiting for science to come to them. They were aggressively going out to "domesticate" it themselves. The movement to bring science into the household became formalized, even institutionalized, in the home economics movement. Catharine Beecher had a long line of successors—the home economists—who did in fact contribute a scientific component to the female world. With no loss to its female character.

The Domestication of Science

In the 1880s a group of women assembled at Lake Placid in the first of a series of meetings that eventuated in the formation of the American Home Economics Association. Bent on applying science and technology to the home, they were among the prime movers in the "domestication" of science. The colleges of home economics in the land-grant universities were, in fact, parallel to the colleges of agriculture and engineering. Like students in those colleges, the students in home economics colleges measured, experimented, surveyed. They applied time-and-motion techniques to home management, which was taken as seriously as farm management was. They studied the use of time in the household. They tested food for nutritional and caloric value. They pursued the instrumental aspect of the housewife's role with great dispatch. And when they later turned to the expressive or "heart" aspect, their approach was equally scientific. Family relations and child development were also studied through the use of strictly scientific canons.[9]

As it turned out, the colleges established to bring the fruits of science to the homemaker as they were being brought to the farmer had a hard time hewing to that line. The tendency was always in the direction of professionalizing the curriculum, cutting down on the transmission of the practical household skills of cooking and sewing and upgrading research and business and industrial applications. Women trained in these colleges as home economists were needed as professionals on the staffs of women's magazines, in group-feeding programs, businesses, the Peace Corps, and nutritional programs around the world (East, 1978). Where their professional interests were concerned, they had power and knew it: "Just ask any congressman involved in writing vocational legislation" (East, 1978). Here were women archetypically "modern" in their acceptance of the rationality of science and its practical application in the household, yet dedicated to applying it to the archetypically humane—"heart"—goals of the traditional female world.[10]

But they also remained archetypically traditional. One of their leaders, Marjorie East, found the same defects in the home economists as feminist critics were finding among other women: they were trained to think of themselves as unimportant, incapable of the highest achievement, believing that household management was women's work and therefore not very important. "Home economics has been of women, by women, and for women, which makes it, by the same definition, not that important." She summarized the results of sixty-four studies on home economists; they were found to be "expressive, friendly, and sociable; open and adaptable to other people's opinions; family oriented in . . . [their] private lives; not ambitious or highly motivated toward power or influence; conservative and traditional; practical, prudent, useful, orderly, reliable; not abstract, intellectual, or theoretically oriented" (East, 1978). The wrong people to achieve her definition of the goal of home economics, to apply "rational thought to home life for improving that matrix for human development."

These women were not feminists.[11] They were in no way identified with the women's rights movement of the nineteenth and early twentieth centuries, and they were latecomers to the twentieth-century feminist movement. Some, in fact, were positively hostile to it. Why? The question has not yet been researched, but the answer may not be hard to find. These women had an honored and respected female world of their own. It was *theirs*. They were neither ashamed of it nor embarrassed by it. They did not have to fight for recognition; the male world willingly granted them legitimacy. Since the male world did not want to take over the functions of the colleges of home economics until much later, when they had become more prestigious and changed their name, there was little competition with the male world. The home economists did not feel a need for the feminist movement. Its application of science and technology to the human needs of home and family was in no sense as paradoxical as it might seem. In a way, this female world simply coopted the male emphasis on science and technology and applied it to its own ends.

Andrews and Andrews believe that "linked as she was to technology, a powerful symbolic as well as actual force, the housewife was by the end of the nineteenth century a new social type whose influence on American life has been only imperfectly appreciated" (1974, 325). True, but also perhaps in a somewhat unexpected way—that is, as herself a co-optee, the object of manipulation by the advertisers, who, as Cowan notes, became the new ideologues (1974, 21).

The New Ideologues

In time it came to be the advertiser who defined the female domestic role. When laundresses and nursemaids disappeared from the scene, they left a wide berth for the sales pitch for soaps, cleaning equipment, processed foods, appliances. In the nineteenth century housework had been seen as a science; now it became a craft, a creative endeavor, the housewife an artist, not a drudge, a sophisticated consumer rather than a producer (Cowan, 1976, 152). As early as World War I, under the aegis of the advertiser, housework began to be seen as an expression of the housewife's personality rather than as a chore. And not the least of the advertiser's contribution was teaching the homemaker how to use the home to implement the love-and/or-duty ethos. It was a time "in which the affections of a mother-in-law were won by toilet tissue, and the dying amorousness of a disinterested husband was fanned to flame by walnut cake" (Cohn, 1943, 127). Nothing, a television commercial tells the housewife, says lovin' like something from the oven, and the food processors were willing to supply what went into the oven, as servants had once done. The advertisers played up the love component of the love-and/or-duty ethos of the female world. Whereas before that time housework in a servantless home was viewed as a series of chores or trials that the housewife had to do until she could find a servant, now housework became "an emotional 'trip' " (16). It became, that is, a way to express one's love. Thus "laundering was not just laundering, but an expression of love; the housewife who truly loved her family could protect them from the embarrassment of tattle-tale gray. Feeding the family was not just feeding the family, but a way to express the housewife's artistic inclinations and a way to encourage . . . affection. Diapering the baby was . . . a time to build the baby's sense of security and love for the mother" (16).

From her study of advertisements in women's magazines, Cowan found that in the late 1920s they began to appeal to the housewife's fears rather than to her strengths; they became less informative; they played increasingly on guilt, which is, of course, the flip side of duty. "One anxious emotion ever creased her [the housewife's] brow—guilt. She felt guilty a good deal of the time, and when she wasn't feeling guilty she was feeling embarrassed; guilty if her infant didn't gain enough weight . . . guilty if her children went to school in soiled clothes . . . embarrassed if her nieces and nephews accused her of having body odor, guilty if her son was a laggard in school, guilty if her daughter was not popular with the crowd (her mother having failed to keep her dresses properly ironed)" (Cowan, 1974, 155). And the threshold for guilt continued to drop. "In earlier times a woman could [be] made to feel guilty if she had abandoned her children. . . . In the years between the wars American women apparently began to feel guilty if their children were seen in public in scuffed shoes" (155). Or, even later, if their husbands' shirts had "ring around the collar." If children were deprived of television, parents were told when television was new, their intellectual development would be handicapped; today they are told that if the children are deprived of their own personal $600 computer they will similarly fall behind those who have such advantages. Cowan recognizes, of course, that though "advertisers may have stimulated these guilt feelings, . . . they could not have created them singlehandedly; the guilts must have been there or advertisers would not have found that they could be successfully played upon" (155).

Have the New Household Technologies Modernized the Household?

We know that "science" did not improve the status of homemaking to a professional level, as, according to Andrews and Andrews, the women had hoped. Nor did the new technologies "modernize" the household. "Middle-class, much less working-class, households neither are nor [ever] were rational organizations" (Davidoff, 1976, 138). Hareven concurs; despite all the technological innovations, "housework remained nonmodern" (1976, 201). Cowan elaborates:

> Despite all the changes that have been wrought in housework, and they have been many, the household has resisted industrialization with greater success than any other productive locale in our culture. The work of men has become centralized, but the work of women remains decentralized. Several million American women cook supper each night in several million separate homes over several million separate stoves—a specter that should be sufficient to drive any rational technocrat into the loony bin, but that does not do so. . . . Out there in the land of household work there are small industrial plants that sit idle for the better part of every working day; there are expensive pieces of higly mechanized equipment that are used only once or twice a month; there are consumption units that trundle out to their markets weekly to buy eight ounces of this nonperishable product and twelve ounces of that one. There are also workers with no job description, time clocks, or even paychecks. Cottage industry is alive and well and living in suburbia [1977, 30].

Whatever may have happened to women in the paid labor force, at least to the middle-class homemaker, industrialization came finally to emphasize not the Gesellschaft structure but an intensification of the Gemeinschaft. In Chapter 2 we suggested that the female world could be conceptualized in terms of one side of the several Parsonian pattern variables—diffuseness, for example, as contrasted with specificity; affectivity as contrasted with affect-neutrality; ascription as contrasted with achievement. In the household, according to Cowan, we find increasing diffuseness instead of increasing specificity; increasing affectivity instead of affect-neutrality. These points are documented in her analysis of the middle-class household in the 1920s. "The work force [in the household] became less rather than more differentiated as domestic servants, unmarried daughters, maiden aunts, and grandmothers left the household and as chores which had once been performed by commercial agencies (laundries, delivery services, milkmen) were delegated to the housewife. The individual workers [housewives] also became less specialized; the new housewife was now responsible for every aspect of life in her household, from scrubbing the bathroom floor to keeping abreast of the latest literature in child psychology.

The housewife is just about the only unspecialized worker left in America" (1976, 23). Nor was her work becoming "modern" in the sense of affect-neutrality. "Instead of desensitizing the emotions that were connected with household work, the industrial revolution in the home seems to have heightened the emotional context of the work, until a woman's sense of self-worth became a function of her success at arranging bits of fruit to form a clown's face in a gelatin salad" (1976, 23; Bernard, 1972, chap. 10). Similarly with respect to the achievement component of industrialization: "We socialize our men to aspire to feats of mastery over nature, we also socialize our women to aspire to feats of submission to nature. . . . Men build; women inhabit. Men are active; women are passive. . . . We have trained our women to opt out of the technological order as much as we have trained our men to opt into it" (Cowan, 1977, 31-32).

Cowan's critique of homemaking as a "cottage industry," Davidoff's characterization of it as nonrational, and Hareven's view of it as nonmodern are by no means new judgments. During the nineteenth century, for example, there was considerable criticism of the wastefulness involved in having separate, individual households, each with its own separate, individual fire, its own separate, individual kitchen, its own separate, individual garbage pail. And there were numerous suggestions for cooperative living arrangements, including, of course, new communities based on then-current ideologies (Bernard, 1942, chap. 21). Charlotte Perkins Gilman wrote advocating the kitchenless home and Lucy Maynard Salmon, cooperative housekeeping. But such suggestions for organization and use of technology did not take hold. Apparently not enough families were willing to forego their own separate, individual—wasteful—households. Cowan elaborates: "In the early days the new technology could have been used to communalize housework. The first vacuum cleaners [1859] were large mobile units; they were brought into a home by a team of skilled operators to take over the housewife's cleaning chores. The new washing machines [1873] could have been placed in communal laundries where paid employees would take over the housewife's washing chores, and the editors of *The Ladies Home Journal* [even] advocated that this be done. Those same editors also advocated retention of the wartime communal kitchens, so that the wasteful process of cooking each family's meals separately would be eliminated. . . . The new domestic technology, communalized or not, could have freed American women to do productive work outside their homes" (Cowan, 1976, 164-165). But it did not.[12] Cowan attributes this rejection of communalized technology to the power of the feminine mystique (165).

The new technologies seem to have taken a step in the direction of more "fast foods," more prepared frozen foods, more dining out,[13] "meals on wheels," and the like. But few households seem willing to give up their individual refrigerators, stoves, garbage disposals. Attempts to industrialize household cleaning operations are beginning but are not yet generally available. Traditional habits still hang on. The ethos of the Gesellschaft is still resisted by the Gemeinschaft in the home.

Some Trauma of Becoming Modern

It was not always easy for women to become "modern." Branca, on the basis of British experience, calls the nineteenth-century middle-class Victorian woman the first "modern" woman, in the sense, for example, that "she expressed a growing reliance on science" (1975, 151), that she was more secular and therefore less bound by old religious tenets than women in other classes (147). But at the same time she was being deprived of support from kin networks and church-related groups as a result of the mobility and urbanization that accompanied industrialization. She could enjoy the advantages of the new sewing machine in the home and take a keen interest in problems of community sanitation. But as an innovator she was also subject to a great deal of unfavorable comment—then as now. The journals she now had time to read included criticisms of her along with recipes. She could accept chloroform for childbirth, artificial feeding, contraception, and seek "to define herself . . . as an individual and to gain new control over her body" (151). But she did not have public sanctions to back her (152). These early "modern women," as a result, "suffered considerable anxiety as they tried to develop a new life style" (153).

Nor were all of them successful in coping with the changes being introduced into their world. They felt insecure in their family roles, especially in the maternal role (Branca, 148). Despite the many manuals telling them how to rear their children, despite the authoritative and presumably scientific advice so liberally dispensed in the women's journals—perhaps because of it—many of these women became severely depressed. Branca cites a letter in 1870, for example, from "a sufferer of low spirits," seeking advice from other women regarding her problems with depression and alcohol. "Health manuals often warned women about the ill effects of alcohol" (148). An article in a medical journal noted that "one of the principal causes of alcoholism among women was domestic problems" (148). Other articles deplored the use of "drowsy syrups," without which many women were unable to function (149). Some women seemed to be dependent on sedatives or stimulants such as opium, morphia, and valerium (149). Branca concedes that the evidence is only impressionistic but feels it cannot be wholly ignored. In the United States we know that elixirs consisting primarily of alcohol—like Lydia Pinkham's—were common in the nineteenth century; drug addictions supported by patent medicines were prevalent until well into the twentieth century. The successful "modern" woman probably used activism rather than dependency to deal with the anxieties caused by rapid change.

So much, then, for the engineering technologies. The biological technologies—especially those having to do with reproduction—have impinged on the female world in a somewhat different way. Here women were among the leaders in modernization. Thus, although "the preindustrial character of women's work in the home persisted long after the larger society had become industrialized" (Hareven, 1976, 201), the story in the bedroom was somewhat different. Hareven raises the question "as to whether under certain historical conditions, women, rather than being the last to modernize, may actually have been in the vanguard. In the area of family limitation, for example, women may have taken greater initiative than men" (1976, 205). In political and industrial change, men were in the vanguard, but in family, child-rearing, personal values, socialization, women led the way (205).

The Biological Technologies

Historically, the female world has been more involved with the biological technologies—plant and animal foods and fabrics, domestic animals, healing techniques, childbirth—than with the more mechanical ones—weapon-making, for example—and, on the current scene, more with the spate of technologies having to do with contraception, abortion, and aging than with nuclear power. Even such a simple artifact as the speculum, which makes it possible for women to examine the insides of their own bodies, seems to have enormous interest for women and influence on their feelings about their bodies. Nor should the comfort and convenience of such humble and mundane technologies as those involved in the manufacture of sanitary pads and tampons be overlooked. Nor of the well-designed brassiere.

Important as all the biological technologies were for the female world, they pale in significance when compared to improved contraceptive technologies. "The advent of birth control is perhaps the most obvious sign of the development of new attitudes, and by releasing some energies from traditional functions it sets the stage for other developments" (Branca, 1975, 151). Probably nothing has had greater impact on the mores of the female world and, furthermore, on its overall structure than control of fertility, now becoming increasingly feasible. For as long as most of a woman's life was spent in gestation, lactation, and infant and child care, the sexual division of labor accommodated itself to that fact. The worlds of men and of women developed along these functional lines and created mentalities, characters, and personalities suitable for them. But the advent of widespread—ultimately, mass—feasibility, if not universal acceptance of contraception in the nineteenth and twentieth centuries, together with the restructuring of work in urbanized, industrialized societies, marks a turning point in human history as momentous as the invention of the plow. As the plow—among other inventions—did, contraception reorients the relations between the sexes, with profound impact on the worlds of both. Biological differences between the sexes remain and will continue to remain incontrovertible facts of life. But they less and less determine the nonreproductive functions of women and the consequent division of labor. What such changes will ultimately do to the female world remains to be seen.[14] In the meanwhile it is hard to remember that not too long ago the use of artificial means of contraception was an issue in the female world.[15] It is taken for granted now.

Nor should we be too cavalier about amniocentesis, which makes it possible to discover genetic defects (as well as the sex) of the fetus in utero, giving women the choice of abortion if they wish it, sparing themselves the long years of sacrifice involved in the care of defective—even if loved—children. Or the surgical techniques—however backward until women themselves insisted on their modernization—that have saved the lives of women suffering from breast cancer.

Shulamith Firestone speculated a few years ago about the artificial womb that would take over the whole gestation process; and there has been talk of the "renting" of the womb of one woman to gestate the ovum of another woman. Since the fertilization of an ovum in the laboratory in 1978, these extensions of biological technologies no longer seem far-fetched. A whole new discipline of bioethics has sprung up to assess their possible moral impact on both the male and the female worlds.[16]

The advances in biological technologies have had great impact on the very bodies of women. Some years ago I pointed to the emergence of what I considered a "new sex," a sex consisting of women still in the prime of life but now released from the demands of child bearing and child rearing. They were vital, vigorous, beautiful, alive. Women in their forties who were still achieving, still creative; women in their fifties; even women in their sixties and seventies (Bernard, 1968, 25-27). The female population includes a growing number of this "new sex." Indeed, they contribute a growing part of the leadership in the female world. The tired old stereotypes clearly no longer hold. Few of the old clichés coined when most women were in the child-bearing years for most of their short lives remain valid. A world with such a population is bound to be different from a world with a physically worn out population.

The Feminist Perspective on Technology

As in so many areas of concern, feminists are way out front in the area of technology. In the late 1970s they were calling for more input from women in the direction of its course. "What," they were asking, "is a feminist definition of appropriate technology? Appropriate for whom? Appropriate for what? At what cost? Says who? Who pays the bill? What does it mean in the development of tools/technologies that help people take control of their lives? Women are rarely the developers or the designers of the technologies we use. How can women as producers, designers, as consumers influence new technologies? Where do women want to go technologically? What are our fantasies for the future? How do we demythologize the notion that 'technology' is inaccessible so that women will increasingly envision themselves also controlling alternative technologies? What are the points of access for women for use, development and control of alternate technologies?" (flyer for Conference on Women and Technology: Designing Our Future, Washington, D.C., 1979). Their concerns far transcended the household; the whole human environment as it impinged on women was their beat.

Notes

1. Mary Hannah Hawkins, on the basis of an analysis of the numerous patents taken out by American women, found that most of them dealt with household activities, "including everything from home heating devices, kitchen supplies and bathroom fixtures to appliances for washing, drying and ironing clothes" (n.d., 88). Among them are: the ice-cream freezer (Nancy Johnson, 1843); the sad-iron (Mary Ann Cook, 1848); the butter worker (Lettie Smith, 1853); the washing machine (Ellen Boyce, 1862); the floor warmer (Clarissa Britain, 1863); the dish drainer (Clarissa Britain, 1864); the vegetable grater (Sarah McGill, 1866); the mop wringer (Mary Carpenter, 1866); the reservoir cook stove (Sarah Clark, 1868); the ironing table bureau (Margaret White, 1870); a compound for cleaning silk (Karolina Fries, 1870); a dishwashing machine (Catherine Woodruff, 1872); a wall or window washer (Elizabeth Bradley, 1873); a carpet cleaner (Sarah Stearns, 1876); an invalid bedstead (Annie Evans, 1882); the window guard (Bertha Schmitt, 1883); a washing compound (Annie Rhoads, 1884); the dust pan (Fanny Marsh and Mary Margerum, 1886); a wire dust whip (Eliza Ann Terry, 1887); the bedclothes holder (Susan Henning, 1887); and the toaster, (Julia Downey, 1887).

It might be argued that such household inventions have little impact on the greater world. Actually, they may reverberate widely. Cleanliness, a large component of the care of households, is an example. Until the middle of the eighteenth century, "most people in all classes had lice and diseases associated with dirt. The concern with personal and domestic cleanliness, with the stricter ordering of things and people in the house . . . emerged as an important way of marking the middle classes off from those below them, well before the germ theory of disease was discovered" (Davidoff, 1976, 127).

2. In 1957 I summarized some of the simpler technologies as they affected mother-child relationships as "the three c's:" "the net effect of the three c's —carriages, carpets and cans . . . was to separate the child from contact with his mother's body. Carriages took the baby out of the shawl for transportation purposes. Carpets symbolize abundance in the form of more expensive household furnishings which demand protection against the child's depredations. . . . And, finally, canned baby food . . . tended to put the child in front of the mother rather than next to her in feeding" (Bernard, 1957, 376).
3. If she were writing today she might well be asking the outside world to accommodate itself to the household by way of more flexible work schedules rather than the other way round.
4. Parkinson's law: "Work expands to fill the time allotted to it" (Webster's *New Dictionary of the American Language*, 2nd College Edition, 1970).
5. "It is . . . possible that as the functions performed by families have shrunk, social expectations about a woman's role have actually increased—that women are now expected to keep their families better clothed, better housed, better fed and better adjusted—and that these increased expectations have placed new demands on a woman's time by increasing the number of functions that she is expected to perform—from nutritionist, to comparison shopper, to electrical repairwoman, to semi-professional psychiatrist" (Cowan, 1974, 248).
6. "[F]rom the point of view of a woman's time, the functions have not disappeared at all: the suburban mother does not have to teach her children to read and to write, to spin and to sew, but she does have to drive them back and forth to all the schools, extra-curricular classes, lessons and social engagements that modern socialization requires, which may be just as time-consuming and less personally rewarding" (Cowan, 1974, 248).
7. A good deal of the time saved at present is invested in waiting for services of one kind or another. Even among women who are in the labor force, schedules have to be accommodated for the countless kinds of services that have to be called in. In 1976 Ellen Goodman was commenting on the situation: "The Working Mother . . . knew . . . that she had willfully violated a cardinal rule of American life: No Working Person Must Ever Need Anything Serviced. Or Repaired, Delivered, Picked Up or Otherwise Touched at Home. . . . There was absolutely no coincidence between the times they delivered and the times she was at home. . . . The entire service industry was geared to the myth that every house had its housewife and that this housewife's patriotic duty was to be thrilled at the idea of hang-

ing around scraping her yellow, waxy, buildup off the linoleum while she waited for deliverers, installers and fixers" (Dec. 20, 1976). In December 1961, I wrote in a letter to one of my children: "Yesterday I had to spend waiting around for service people of one kind and another—Salvation Army to haul off the accumulated newspapers, Edna to clean the house, a man to measure the radiators for covers, and a plumber to investigate a leak in the third-floor bathroom." The generally accepted belief has been that the time of the housewife was at everyone's disposal. Elise Boulding sees "waiting-for" within the family as a gift (1977).

8. The irony of the situation seems to have escaped contemporary observers, but a British researcher, Leonore Davidoff, reminds us of it: "Capitalists, as public men, were supporting the cult of domesticity, while at the same time, as rational entrepreneurs, they were recruiting women workers into their mills and mines through the back door" (1976, 133-134).
9. See Bernard, *Academic Women* (1964) for a brief sketch of home economists as contrasted with their peers in the women's liberal arts colleges (Chapter 2).
10. Ellen Richards, an MIT-trained scientist and an early pioneer in home economics, established a food program in the poor districts of Boston and was greatly disappointed when they rejected her well-planned nutritious food.
11. Ellen Richards, for example, was proud of her use of feminine wiles to manipulate the men at MIT. "Perhaps the fact that I am not a Radical or a believer in the all powerful ballot for women to right her wrongs and that I do not scorn womanly duties, but claim it as a privilege to clean up and sort of supervise the room and sew things, etc., is winning me stronger allies than anything else. Even Professor A. accords me his sanction when I sew his papers or tie up a sore finger or dust the table, etc. Last night Professor B. found me useful to mend his suspenders" (Carolyn Louise Hunt, 1958, 1-2). Lucy Maynard Salmon was too bashful to accept an honorary degree from the University of Michigan (MacCracken, 1927, 30-31). In 1979, a psychologist, Florence Denmark, discovered that academic men actually found outspoken and assertive women more attractive than conciliatory women. Nevertheless, the conciliatory person was preferred for actual appointment.
12. Although Marx himself foresaw the industrialization of domestic service and thus the release of women for labor-force participation, the impact of the technologies of the household on the female world has not been a major theme of Marxism.
13. A quarter of a century ago a team of my students at The Pennsylvania State University made a study of the relationship between the number of meals students ate with their families at home and their scores on a personality test. There did seem to be a relationship. The more meals eaten at home with the family, the better the students' scores.
14. We do not include here the even wider ramifications of fertility control. Marvin Harris, a neo-Malthusian, believes that "modern contraceptive and abortion techniques . . . may have come too late" (1977, xi). He is concerned about the pressures of population on environmental resources and believes that "we have only begun to pay the penalties for the environmental

depletions associated with this new round of [industrial] intensification, and no one can predict what new constraints will be needed to transcend the limits of growth of the industrial order" (xi).

15. There are differences of opinion still with respect to contraceptive techniques. For many centuries they were primarily in the control of men and only secondarily in the control of women. More recently hormonal and mechanical methods have given the control largely to women. Some men resent relinquishing this privilege, so long a male prerogative. And many women resent the assignment of this responsibility exclusively to them, especially in view of the potential hazards involved. Research on new ways to assign the responsibility is in process. And in the meanwhile a relatively old technique, vasectomy, is growing in popularity.
16. As yet far from being taken for granted is abortion. The technology of abortion has improved greatly until now it is said that a properly managed abortion is less dangerous than term delivery. But the emotional and political issues surrounding this particular area of technology are so searing that further progress may be braked. At least temporarily.

18

"Culture" in the Female World: The Literary and Fine Arts

Some Distinctions

In addition to the anthropological conceptualization of culture—as comprised, that is, of language, technology, values, symbols, the arts and crafts—there is another that sees it mainly in terms of aesthetic creations. There is a hazard in the use of the same term in both of these senses. The aesthetic approach calls for evaluation, for the application of critical standards, for judgment of the quality of the work. Culture in the aesthetic sense is conceptualized as high, or "haute," on one side, and folk, on the other. According to "Veblen's Law," culture is high in terms of the expense required for either its production or its appreciative consumption. In general, a taste or skill that calls for years of "cultivation" is considered higher than one that can be picked up with little or no training. As a corollary, practical skills and arts that produce utilitarian products, however beautiful, are not as high as those that produce only to delight, even though the practical skills may take considerable time to acquire. Somewhere between high and folk culture is popular (mass) culture, which crosses class lines. Even when it is literate, it makes few if any pretensions to permanent appeal or value.

This evaluative approach is not used here. The concern is not with aesthetic quality. To understand the culture of the female world the work of less accomplished artists as well as of great ones is important. Sometimes, in fact, the work of the former tells us more—the novels of, say, Jacqueline Susann more than those of Katherine Anne Porter. Inclusion here does not imply an accolade. Important as the status aspects of culture are, they belong in a different context. Both "good" and "bad" art are intrinsic aspects of female culture and equally valuable as clues for understanding the female world. The "culture" discussed here has to do with the creative work that offers escape, excitement, delight, catharsis, enlightenment, self-understanding, consolation, reconciliation, inspiration, alleviation of pain, insight, uplift, fantasies, to name only a few of the many functions served by any art form, "high" or "low."

A distinction should be made at the outset between my use of the terms "female culture" and "culture of the female world." A large component of the "culture of the female world" includes products created by men. The ramifications of this fact are extensive. It means, for example, that a considerable part of the cultural diet consumed by women in what they see, hear, and read portrays them mostly as they look to men, in a male context, in situations of interest to men. "Female culture," on the other hand, refers to that part of the culture of the female world which is created by and for women themselves.[1] The male world has, in general, shown less interest in and concern with female culture than the female world has exhibited toward male culture.

Women as Patrons and Consumers of Male-Created Culture

The female world contributes a considerable amount to the support of male-created and oriented culture. In the more communal aspects of high culture women have, in effect, served as "patrons" of the arts since at least the days of the salonières. The female world was structured to accommodate male culture. Gaye Tuchman has summarized the part women have played in the creation and support of male culture. "The importance of women to the French literary world in the seventeenth and eighteenth centuries has long been stressed. As hosts, sponsors, and authors in the earlier periods and as hosts and sponsors in the latter, women have been credited with providing an institutional framework through which literary and philosophic figures could meet to exchange ideas. . . . The salon provided a regular, stable context for intensive associations and explorations, guiding the analysis of ideas. This context was particularly important as the class basis of literature changed, as the 'man of letters' [became] a bourgeois bohemian or professional" (1975, 180). And so, too, in painting and sculpture (180).

In the United States the female world has also been a strong supporter and patron of male culture, in its own, if not in the salonière, way. The new leisure class of women referred to in Chapter 8 may not have run salons, but they did take over the support of orchestras, opera, theater, galleries, libraries, museums, and other cultural amenities, along with their charitable and philanthropic activities, heading drives to raise money for these institutions as well as subsidizing them themselves. They have been strong patrons of drama and dance. Running benefits and balls to support cultural events became intrinsic to the life style of wealthy women. Such support of culture was an early and continuing activity for the "vicarious leisure" Veblen described as acceptable for wealthy women. Indeed, foreign observers sometimes commented on the fact that affluent women constituted the only leisure class in the United States; without their support there would be no culture at all. More than a half-century after Tocqueville, Bryce concurred with his conclusion: "In a country where men are incessantly occupied at their business or profession, the function of keeping up the level of culture devolves upon women." (1891, 612). And another half-century later, a book on manners and morals in America had as one of its subheadings, "My culture is in my wife's name" (Cohn, 1943, 72).

Women have been not only the supporters of male culture but also its major consumers as well. A considerable number of the books women read, the movies and plays they see, the television and radio programs they watch, the records they listen to, the dances they perform are created by men. And, with few exceptions, the contents reflect a male perspective on the world even when they deal with women. This is a culture expressive of the male world, reflecting its view, its conceptions.

Recently women have begun to protest the image of women reflected in male-created culture. They find much of it harmful for the self-image of women. Indeed, one of the most salient aspects of female culture at the present time is a kind of revolt against the portrayal of women in male culture—some of it, especially in contemporary rock culture, blatantly misogynist—and an attempt to salvage female culture of the past and encourage it in the future.

Salvage Operation

One of the most common taunts used to put women down is the question: Why are there no female Beethovens, Reubens, Michelangelos, Newtons, Shakespeares, Kants, Tolstoys? Women are given music lessons, painting lessons, taught to read and write. Why, then, no great creative geniuses? Ignoring the most obvious answer, that few women have had the time or leisure, we note that creativity calls for a special matrix in which it can take hold and flourish, as the sociology of scientific and artistic creativity has helped us to see. Women have been not only excluded from such matrices (Chapter 1), but, more significant, positively discouraged from even thinking of gaining access to them. Thus, for example, Robert Southey, poet laureate of England, told Charlotte Brontë: "The daydreams in which you habitually indulge are likely to induce a distempered state of mind; and in proportion as all the ordinary uses of the world seem to you flat and unprofitable, you will be unfitted for anything else. Literature cannot be the business of a woman's life, and it ought not to be. The more she is engaged in her proper duties, the less leisure will she have for it even as an accomplishment and recreation" (Goulianos, 1973, xv). An almost identical lecture was delivered to a modern writer in 1890.[2]

Even in the rare cases in which women overcame such discouragement their work was not understood. Some of them wrote about their own world, which was totally foreign to men, "a world in which women's revelations, if they were anything but conventional, might not be welcomed, might not [even] be recognized" (Goulianos, xiv). Most men can know women only as they think, feel, and behave in the presence of men. They cannot know women as they think, feel, and behave in the female world, apart from men. Therefore men could not resonate to women's writings, for they dealt with "childbirth, . . . housework, . . . relationships with men, . . . friendships with other women. They wrote about themselves as girls and as mature women, as wives, mothers, widows, courtesans, workers, thinkers, and rebels" (Goulianos, xi). All these subjects, approached from the female perspective, looked unfamiliar, different from the way they looked to most men.

Thus the standards used to judge female work were inappropriate. The perspective could not be right. Or, if it was, the result was trivial, the work insignificant. It was therefore either ignored or contemptuously dismissed.[3] In all the arts, the gatekeepers at every step of the route to achievement were men. They were entirely engrossed in their own male world. They could not be distracted from it. Certainly not by anything so strange as female work.[4] So the obstacles to creativity for women were all but insuperable.

Goulianos has shown us how these pressures have operated in the case of writing before the eighteenth century. In her search for women's writings over time—many of them hidden in rare book rooms in antiquated editions—she met with disinterest and even ridicule from learned male academics (1973, xiii). The persistence of such treatment of female work—even in some cases down to the present—gave her great insight into the kind of treatment creative women had to contend with in the past. The cavalier disdain reflected in Carlyle's put-down: "Who ever reads an American book?" had been the fate of women's work for centuries.

In the 1970s women were self-consciously attempting to restore female culture of the past and to nurture the current creativity of women. Researchers were scouring libraries and archives to uncover literary works, and feminist presses were presenting them to an appreciative public. In the fine arts women were searching the history of painting and sculpture, rescuing and exhibiting work long relegated to oblivion by male art historians. They were establishing collective galleries to display the work of women artists. One such gallery, Artemesia, was opened in 1973 in Chicago with the express purpose of "encouraging the development of art created by women . . . changing the attitudes about art by women and educating the public about the role of women in the history of art" (Rojak, 1977, 15).

The discussion in this chapter deals primarily with female culture in the sense of culture created by women, especially with the literary arts, mainly fiction. During the eighteenth century an enormously important event occurred that was to have incalculable impact on female culture: the emergence of the novel. Numerous currents and eddies have ruffled the literary culture of the female world since then. Great historical events have come and gone, fictional genres—sentimental, gothic, local-color, realist, naturalistic—have waxed and waned, style has succeeded style. Through all these changes authors and audience have engaged in a complex pattern of interaction. The novel has entertained its readers, held up models for them, defended them, excoriated them, subverted them, offered them escape, reconciled them to their fate, fomented rebellion, interpreted their world for them, told them who they were and who they ought to be. Has been, in brief, a fundamental cornerstone in female culture.

The Preeminence of the Novel in Female Culture

Although the novel as we know it was invented in England by Samuel Richardson in the middle of the eighteenth century, most novels thereafter were written by women (Tuchman, 185). Fiedler tells us that "the moment at which the novel took hold coincides with the moment of the sexual division of labor which left business to the male, the arts to the female" (1960, 6). And, interestingly enough, women as authors were remarkably successful. "When women became the chief authors as well as the chief characters of the novel, a real change took place," a change amounting to a genuine revolution. "Never before had there been an art form in whose production women played so predominant a part." Indeed, men saw them as strong competitors in this "branch of business." They even imitated the women authors "in order to bid for their audiences" (Fiedler, 54). Hawthorne himself "was not averse to taking a leaf from their book" (64). He felt the competition so strongly that he called the women authors "d____d female scribblers." "The manufacture of novels is the first business in the modern world into which women were permitted to enter in large numbers, and in which, competing on an equal footing with males, they achieved financial success" (55). No wonder Fiedler concludes that "the birth of the novel is . . . a critical moment in the emancipation of women" (54-55).

True, the novel, however popular and enjoyed, was not viewed as a serious art form until the time of Flaubert. In America it was viewed as the work of amateurs and improvisors, designed for entertainment and the teaching of morality (5), often a "great engine in the hands of the field of darkness" (10). And "on its most obvious level, the novel was a kind of conduct book for the daughters of the bourgeoisie, aimed at teaching obedience to parents and wariness before potential seducers" (10). In any event the novel was the first case of "mass" art, different from folk art (8).

The male authors had pretensions to art; the female authors wanted to teach women. So, "from the first, the United States possessed two literatures, two types of novels . . . : the novel of sentimental protest and that of sentimental gentility, the masculine novel and the feminine, the anti-bourgeois and the philistine" (96). The first failed, the second succeeded: "The former [male] kind . . . fails, for its basic assumptions demand that it triumph as art or be lost; the latter [female kind] succeeds, for its basic assumptions demand only that it triumph as a commodity—and it need only become a best-seller to be fully itself" (96). And the most spectacular bestseller ever was one of the first published in this country, *Charlotte Temple* (1791) by Susanna Haswell Rowson, which went through no less than two hundred editions (Birdsall, 1971, 203).

The two literary traditions—gentility and protest—differed not only in basic assumptions but also in orientation. The gentility novel was bourgeois, the protest novel antibourgeois. "Where the . . . bourgeois sentimental novel is woman-centered and feminist, the . . . anti-bourgeois sentimental novel is male-centered and anti-feminist" (89). One is conservative and antiintellectual, the other radical and antiphilistine."The whole drift of the anti-bourgeois tradition is in the direction of substituting a male mind for the female one at the center of the novel" (85). The female tradition asked the reader to identify with the female character; the male tradition, with the male character.

Readers and Writers

An old variation of the chicken-and-egg question which sometimes surfaces among students of culture is: Does art imitate life or does life imitate art?[5] It is an interesting point of departure for discussion, however insoluble. If art imitates life, then we should look at art—in the present context, fiction—as a reflection of the female world it "imitates," and the focus of concern should be on the world of the reader. If life imitates art, then we should look at the artist—in the present context, novelist—who presents the models that are imitated in life by the reader.[6] There is, of course, no clear-cut and unequivocal answer to this question. We learn different things about the female world if we focus on the readers or on the writers. Both may tell us important things about it. In any event, whichever imitates the other, the result is not a carbon copy.

In England at the beginning of the eighteenth century few young women could read; by the end of the century female literacy had become so general that even servant girls were reading novels and well-born girls read scores of polemics and homilies for their improvement as well (Watt, 1963). We noted in Chapter 17 that reading, especially novel reading, was among the uses to which women put the time saved when technology and affluence relieved them of some of the household tasks in the nineteenth century. The novel thus became a major component in female culture. Indeed, we are told that "during the middle decades of the nineteenth century, the world of novels and poetry became as much a part of the sphere of women as the tasks of child rearing and school teaching" (Kett, 1977, 138). Late in the century, Bryce said of women writers that "fiction, essays, and poetry are naturally their favorite provinces" (1891, 612).

When lending libraries brought books within the economic scope of middle-class women the female reading public was even further extended. In England literary discussion of books came to be substituted for card games (Tuchman, 1975, 185). Women in America came to form "not only the larger part of the reading public, but an independent-minded part, not disposed to adopt the canons laid down by men" (Bryce, 613). Bryce was somewhat patronizing, noting that women were "eager and assiduous readers of all such books and periodicals as do not presuppose special knowledge in some branch of science or learning" (612). Many of the women's clubs referred to in Chapter 12 were, and still are, book review or literary clubs.

Readers are not, of course, a homogeneous population. The world constituted by the readers of books is as complex as the demographic structure of the female world itself. Looking at readers does not, therefore, give us a simple portrayal of a homogeneous world. The upper-middle-class woman is probably more likely to buy books than is the middle- or lower-middle-class woman. The books she borrows from the public library are probably different also, reflecting a different world. The older woman probably buys and borrows different books from those selected by younger women. Professional women no doubt buy and borrow different books from those bought and borrowed by beauticians. And so on. So which readers do we look to in attempting to get a fix on the culture of the female world? And what segment of the female world is the artist imitating?

Nor are writers a homogeneous group; like readers, they are a highly selected one.[7] They have, at least, to be literate. And persistent. And, to be successful, "tuned in" to the lives—hopes, fears, longings, nightmares—of their readers. C. H. Cooley, a sociologist, noted a long time ago that "the reader should feel that the author's mind and purpose are congenial with . . . [her] own, though in the present direction they go farther, that the thought communicated is not at all alien, but so truly . . . [hers] that it offers an opportunity to expand to a wider circle, and become a completer edition of . . . [herself]" (1909, 337). The protagonists in the successful novel offer readers "glorified images of themselves" (Fiedler, 54). Popular writers have better antennae than most of us, catch trends more acutely. Whether empathically or cynically, they zero in on the readers' dearest fantasies.

In either case—life imitating art or art imitating life—what about all the work that never reaches the reader? What about the mute, inglorious Miltons, writers born to bloom unseen—or unread? What, again, about the part played by the gatekeepers—until recently, mostly male—who decide what will and will not be published? And what about the manuscripts destroyed by their authors?[8] There may be large segments of female culture never revealed in fiction. We do not encourage or nurture many writers who could write the books, They do not have the time or money or ambience to engage in that activity. Tillie Olsen has told us about the silences of these women (1965).

Still, whatever the odds, a great many women have been successful as novelists. By the end of the nineteenth century, Bryce was reporting that "the number of women who write is infinitely larger in America than in Europe" (612).[9] And he attributed the "fondness for sentiment, especially moral and domestic sentiment, which is often observed as characterizing American taste in literature," to the influence of women (612).[10] The women who wrote successful sentimental novels in the nineteenth century not only entered the literary scene but came to dominate it.[11] They wrote the great bestsellers. Many were urban, ambitious; some made a lot of money—often more than their husbands—and were, in fact if not in theory, heads of their households. They were examples of "the new woman" in many ways, assertive, activist, even entrepreneurial. Three representative authors of the nineteenth-century sentimental novel are selected here for illustrative comment: namely Susanna Haswell Rowson (1762-1824), Mrs. Emma Dorothy Eliza Nevitte Southworth (1819-1899), and Mary Jane Hawes Holmes (1825-1907).[12]

Rowson's best-selling novel, *Charlotte Temple*, has been called "a subtle protest against the dependent status of women in her day" (Birdsall, 1971, 203). But she also wrote fictionalized moral tracts for the *Boston Weekly Magazine.* In addition to fiction, Rowson wrote textbooks in spelling, geography, and history for the Young Ladies Academy, which she established in Boston, the first in this country to offer girls more than an elementary education. Much of her writing was done as a result of dire necessity. Her spouse was "not an ideal husband" (202), and when he failed in business they went on the stage together. She wrote the plays, including one, *Slaves in Algeria, or a Struggle for Freedom* (1794), in which a "group of American women, captured by North African pirates and held for ransom, eventually make their escape" (203). Like many other authors of sentimental novels, she was a do-gooder, "expressing her humanitarian convictions by serving for some years as president of the Boston Fatherless and Widows Society" (203).

Mrs. Southworth was extraordinarily prolific and financially successful.[13] Like so many other contemporary women, she taught school before her marriage, but she was not, like her friend Harriet Beecher Stowe, a reformer. Nor was she a feminist, though one of her most memorable female characters, Capitola in *The Hidden Hand* (1850), manages—like Rowson's captured women—to save herself from the most oppressive circumstances, circumstances from which the standard heroine would have had to be rescued by a man. She was a match for any many in bravery and boldness (Hofstadter, 1971, 328). Mrs. Southworth has been judged to be one of the best writers among the sentimental novelists of the nineteenth century. "She used the creaky machinery of the Gothic romance—ghosts, abductions, trapdoors, thieves' dens, deserted houses—with freshness, and though her stories do not depart from the melodramatic conventions of her day, they are full of lively incident" (Hofstadter, 1971, 328). Mrs. Southworth's marriage ended in separation. She returned to Washington and was on her own thereafter.

Mary J. Holmes, like both Rowson and Southworth, was a teacher. Though not really a reformer, she was a do-gooder, founding temperance and literary clubs and a reading room in the village of Brockport. During the depression of 1893, she organized a soup kitchen for the unemployed. In her novels she tried "to avoid the sensational" and never dealt "in murders, or robberies, or ruined girls but rather in domestic life as I know it to exist." She always meant to "write a good, pure, natural story, such as mothers are willing their daughters should read, and such as will do good instead of harm" (Griswold, 1891, 63-64, cited in Urness, 1971, 208). What is especially noteworthy in the present context, though, is that "unlike many other women writers of her time, whose plots centered on conflict between man and woman," Mrs. Holmes wrote about the relationships between and among women, whether as rivals or as sisters, as equal opponents worthy of one another's steel. Like both Rowson and Southworth, Holmes was enormously successful.[14]

These were the women who were so in tune with the women of their time that whatever they wrote seemed to resonate in the minds of their readers, whether about women captured by pirates, abducted heroines, or good, pure women, We "know" what the "real" female world was like in the nineteenth and early twentieth centuries from the law, legislation, newspaper reports, documents, and other records of all kinds that fill the historical archives. We get a "feel" for it not only from the women who wrote about it and the response to their writings by readers as shown in the sales, but also from the contents of the novels themselves, from the themes that pervaded them.

The Seduction Theme in Women's Novels

Since the time of the first great novel, Samuel Richardson's *Pamela*, the seduction theme has been one of the major motifs of the sentimental novel, persisting even to the present day. It postulates a cult of virginity in which the sexual purity of a woman is her major asset. The preservation of virginity in the face of almost insuperable odds becomes the counterpoint theme to seduction. Female purity was apotheosized by both male and female authors as the only kind of female morality that counted. A woman might be mean, despicable, harsh, cold, whatever; but if she was virginal or chaste she was counted a "good" woman. If she was generous, kind, tender but not virginal or chaste she was counted a "bad" woman.[15] Even today, despite the recent upsurge in acceptance of the erotic in the media, the cult of virginity still retains a wide constituency. It is estimated, for example, that 14 percent of all women in the United States read the novels of an Englishwoman, Barbara Cartland, all of whose more than two hundred books have virginal heroines and who has stated her belief that "the world is waiting for the new standards of purity, beauty, and love" exemplified in her books (Fleischer, 1977).

The intentions of men in novels of seduction had to be carefully scrutinized and assessed early in any relationship. Only if they included marriage could they be considered honorable. Working girls were especially vulnerable. Or daughters in families in precarious financial circumstances. Or loving, gentle, but passionate girls who "stooped to folly." If a woman succumbed to the man's seductive wiles she might be told never to darken the door of her father's home. The temptations could take any number of forms—love, comfort, jewels, career promotion—and so also could the methods—deceit, misrepresentation, whatever. It was to be taken for granted that men wanted only one thing from women; not all were willing to pay for it with marriage. In time, the seduction theme became the butt of humor among the sophisticated. But Fiedler reminds us that it was still in evidence in a 1955 bestseller, *Marjorie Morningstar*, and that *Charlotte Temple* was still in print until a few years ago.

The seduction theme has been interpreted as representing the sexual encounter as a battle of the sexes, "an almost irreconcilable struggle between the male, who desires sexual satisfaction without marriage, and the female, who desires marriage, if not without sex, at least with as little of it as possible" (Fiedler, 39). In this great struggle, the powerful—men—were on one side, the powerless—women—on the other (40). If the Horatio Alger myth of upward mobility epitomized the essence of male culture, so did the virtuous girl's victory over the villain's seductive ploys characterize female culture as portrayed in the sentimental novel.

A counterfoil to the seduction theme is the theme of the girl looking for a suitable marriage, encapsulated in the first chapter of Jane Austen's *Pride and Prejudice:* the business of a mother—Mrs. Bennet in this case—was to get her daughters married. When, as noted in Chapter 6, marriage was the only dignified status, when a girl could do so much better by way of marriage than by her own efforts, finding a good husband was a major preoccupation in the female world. "In light of the novel's predominantly feminine audience, it is scarcely surprising that its ideal theme should be love and marriage, and that its ideal protagonist should be a woman—no grand lady, but some girl, passionate and pure" (Fiedler, 7). The search for suitable men to marry could also take numerous forms. At first a girl had only to prove she would be a loving, useful, helpful mate; later she had to devise more devious ways "to marry a millionaire."

The "Taking Care" Theme in Women's Novels

A second and, in my opinion, more important—though less blatant—theme in novels written by women is the love-and/or-duty motif, which sees the relationship between the sexes not as a Dionysian encounter, as in the seduction theme, but from a more Apollonian perspective, showing men not as paragons of macho power but just the reverse, a perspective that shows women suffering not from male potency and assault but from male weakness and failure (Fiedler, 218).

The selflessness and service called for by the love-and/or-duty ethos is faithfully portrayed in the sentimental novel. The heroines conform to its precepts, ostensibly at least. But under the cover of conventionality there is another message. While going through the motions of the standard female roles the women manage, somehow or other, to rescue men by their superior coping ability. The picture that comes through is one in which the heroines, though properly pious, retiring, domestic, docile, and archetypically feminine, are actually quite capable, not passive, women. The selflessness-and-service pattern demanded by the love-and/or-duty ethos is shown to function in quite unexpected ways. It has been analyzed by Patricia Meyer Spacks (1976) under the rubric of "taking care." We follow her analyses here.

In Jane Austen's *Persuasion*, for example, Mrs. Croft exemplifies how women "take care" unobtrusively, without fanfare or boasting. Thus, while driving in a carriage, the Crofts are about to run into a post, but by Mrs. Croft's "cooly giving the reins a better direction herself," by her taking control, that is, "they happily passed the danger; and by once afterwards [again] judiciously putting out her hand they neither fell into a rut, or ran foul of a dung-cart; and Anne, with some amusement at their style of driving, which she imagined no bad representation of the general guidance of their affairs, found herself safely deposited" (Spacks, 106). Spacks comments that though such careless driving might be a matter of amusement to Anne, it reveals the nature of male-female relationships. "Mrs. Croft's technique is notably self-effacing; she does not claim the right to control, but unobtrusively exercises it when necessary" (106).[16] Like Mrs. Croft, the heroines in American sentimental novels conformed to the stereotyped model of the modest, nonassertive woman; but in a crunch, they were capable of saving the day when the men fell short (Wood, 1972). Thus Huldy, in Harriet Beecher Stowe's "The Minister's Housekeeper," keeps house for Parson Carryl, who, like so many of the author's men, is "a helpless creature." The point and humor of the tale lie in his total dependency on Huldy's "lightning-quick feminine intuition to extricate him from the pitiful plight to which his ponderous brain has led him and in which his pathetic masculine pride threatens permanently to trap him" (Wood, 10-11). When he tries to get a turkey to hatch a hen's eggs, Huldy is convulsed with laughter. "Men," Wood notes, "were apparently good for a laugh, if not for much more" (11). There was no hand of steel at the helm, but there was one concealed in a velvet glove. If women had to rescue men, they did it in a way that hid the fact. In these novels, "such combined assertion [of control] and concealment is the feminine ideal" (Spacks, 106). One "takes care" of men in a double sense: by protecting them and by sparing them the humiliation of having to recognize that they are being protected.[17]

In the case of Anne in *Persuasion,* "the reward of her virtue is quite appropriately a marriage in which she too [like Mrs. Croft] may hope to guide the carriage away from posts, to avoid ruts and dung carts by judicious extensions of the hand, to help, and be valued for helping, her husband, without ever claiming leadership. By 'taking care' of her own conduct and of the appearance she creates, she wins the privilege of taking care of a husband" (Spacks, 109). As Huldy does also, with no aggressiveness on her part at all (Wood, 11). The novels of Elizabeth Gaskell are also used by Spacks to illustrate "the necessity and the charm of a woman's 'taking care,' the arduousness with which she trains herself, and is trained for proper self-forgetfulness in the role of wife and mother" (110).

Spacks notes that "the glorification of altruism as feminine activity" reaches extraordinary heights in Louisa May Alcott's *Little Women.* "The good woman *serves,* she subordinates herself always to the will of others—to husband, to employer, but also to the poor family down the street—she demonstrates her worthiness by sacrificing her self, in the most literal sense: one comes to feel that no *self* remains for the book's ideal woman" (124). Even Jo, who resents the model of femininity imposed on her, has to justify her writing on altruistic—feminine—grounds. By earning money she can help "take care of" her family.

"Taking care" was not always seen as a virtue by later writers. Spacks notes that in its less admirable forms it encourages passive and negative behaviors like endurance and denial rather than the more activist, positive ones, such as attempting to alter circumstances. Such a limited pattern represents "the highest emotional possibilities of the commitment to 'taking care' of others" (134). Taking care can also exacerbate guilt. In Ellen Glasgow's *Vein of Iron,* Spacks points out, "since women have the enormous responsibility of taking care of the entire masculine world, they are manifestly responsible if anything goes wrong. Men are not to be blamed for anything" (132). But such taking care can also be used exploitatively, as a ploy for achieving control. In Glasgow's early novels, for example, "women discover the potential for exercising control at both extremes of submissiveness: by allowing themselves to be dependent, taken care of, and taking care of others. Both versions of the traditional female role suggest the devious ways an oppressed group may find to make an impression on the world" (Spacks, 130).

Not all the women in the sentimental novels conformed to the love-and/or-duty ethos. In Mrs. Gaskell's *Wives and Daughters,* Hyacinth is selfish, but this is understandable considering the penury of her early life. To her stepdaughter "she exemplifies feminine selfishness, and all the moral evils selfishness in a woman brings in its wake. Her empathic capacities if ever she had any, have atrophied; she can now feel only for herself" (Spacks, 114). But the author does not punish her. "She gets most of what she wants—ease, power, freedom" (115) and, equally to the point, she is no unhappier than any of the other characters in the book. By the turn of the century, Kate Chopin, in *The Awakening* (1899), was not only noncondemnatory but actually supportive of the heroine's insistence on cherishing herself.[18]

By 1927, in Virginia Woolf's *To the Lighthouse*, the love-and/or-duty ethos became an intrinsic aspect of the character of some, but not all, women. Mrs. Ramsay, quite content with her life dedicated to others, and career-oriented Lily Brisco are presented by Spacks as representative of a metaphysics of female altruism in which moralizing about what women should or should not do or be is irrelevant. Mrs. Ramsay has spent her life giving, Lily finds such giving not something to aspire to but rather something despicable. Yet even she could see the "glow, the rhapsody, . . . the most supreme bliss" it conferred on "the giving woman" (Spacks, 138). Spacks finds that Woolf's point is not, like Glasgow's, "that women are naturally good or noble or even enduring; rather, that their responsiveness to others, their capacity to offer help and sympathy, may be an essentially impersonal flowering of their natures, a manifestation of their own needs, not merely a reaction to others" (139). The selfless service prescribed by the love-and/or-duty ethos of the female world is seen as not a societal imperative but as merely the expression of the natural—instinctive?—character of some but not all women.

Spacks makes an especially subtle and perceptive analysis of the ambiguities in the whole "taking care" syndrome. Her students were disturbed by it. They found it hard to accept "the effective power of apparent humility" and the suggestion that "the represssions implicit in self-sacrifice" may be as rewarding as a career (141). But the most interesting aspect of "taking care" in the present context seems to me the fact that men had to be protected from knowing that they were being taken care of. Spacks, explicating Mrs. Ramsay in Woolf's *To The Lighthouse*, has this to say: "Men always, from the feminine point of view, lack something. Fundamentally, they lack understanding, are simple creatures even in their intellectual accomplishments; and they must have something, someone to protect. So the wise, benevolent, controlling woman, the eternal mother, who comprehends even if she cannot communicate the meaning of experience, in her mind reduces all masculine accomplishment to the level of children's games. She is never openly contemptuous, only patronizing; she does what is expected of her" (137).

Women readers of the sentimental novel were thus confirmed in their conviction that men, despite their bluster, were just little boys grown tall who had to be taken care of, who had to be protected from their own inadequacies. This message was the very stuff of the literary culture of the female world. This was what women understood among themselves and knew, in a quiet, unarticulated, almost conspiratorial way, must be kept secret, certainly from men.[19] The female world this culture fed and nourished and represented was the world described by Cott and Smith-Rosenberg (Chapter 4), the world men entered as aliens. It represented the freemasonry among women, the "tacit fellowship and sympathy" (*Heritage Dictionary*, 1969) they felt without having to verbalize it. This was a shared but private world women knew and experienced, cut off from men. This was the great female secret. It was not an example of the cliché—"behind every achieving man there is a woman who helped make it possible"—which everyone was willing to concede, nor of the facts that, Barrie told us, every woman knew. It was not the fame and achievement of men that women shared but their hidden mistakes and failures, which they protected the men from having to face.

Local Color Novels

A third theme that comes through in the writings of female novelists, especially in the so-called local-color genre, had to do with the encroachments of Gesellschaft on their world. Male novelists, Fiedler notes, wrote about men who had fled the cares and responsibilities of home. "The typical male protagonist of our fiction has been a man on the run, harried into the forest and out to sea, down the river or into combat—anywhere to avoid 'civilization,' which is to say, the confrontation of a man and woman which leads to the fall, to sex, marriage, and responsibility. One of the factors that determine theme and form in our great books is this strategy of evasion, this retreat to nature and childhood" (xx-xxi). Women local-color novelists wrote about the women left behind. They wrote about the transformation of their kin- and locale-based world by the new urban, industrial order. For the men had left not, as Fiedler says, to retreat to nature and childhood, but for the West or for the cities. The authors of many of these novels lived in backward or remote parts of the country rather than in cities. Life in a dying rural area from which so many of the men had fled was often hard. These women were realists, and in this sense their work had sad overtones. The local-color novelists were social historians as well as novelists, as Dickens was, and their books, like his, contained criticisms of the old values and systems as well as of the new ones.[20]

The absence of men in the worlds these women wrote about is especially relevant. The heroines were women "whom society has deserted and abandoned, stranded in the nearly manless backwater of northern New England and the rural South" (Wood, 1972, 17-18).

Since the impact of Gesellschaft continues to reverberate in areas not yet urbanized, the local-color genre has survived in modified form. Zona Gale (1874-1938), who spent her childhood in Portage, Wisconsin, had a successful career in New York but returned to Portage in 1911. Her stories of Friendship Village "sentimentally emphasize the virtues of small-town life" (Rideout, 1971, 8). Her work "helped in the reinterpretation of middle-class small-town life" (9). Willa Cather (1873-1947) reported on the psychological and emotional accompaniments of the passing of the frontier. A recurrent theme in her work is "the story of those who attempt to escape from its parochialism and then experience an overpowering nostalgia to return. In due course this was reexpressed as . . . a bitter elegy over the substitution by a new generation of shoddy marketplace [Gesellschaft] values for the earlier heroism and courage" (Edel, 1971, 301). She also wrote of a lady who "has outlived a pioneer experience and finally succumbs to the counterfeit of the new times" (Edel, 307). The novel which won a Pulitzer Prize for Cather in 1922, *One of Ours*, also dealt with the decline of the pioneer tradition.

Ellen Glasgow's novels told the chronological story of Southern history from Reconstruction on. Although she lived a cosmopolitan life, with contacts on two continents, her home base was the family residence in Richmond, Virginia. In the years following World War I, "her voice joined with those who found no lasting values in modern urban life and who, with a bitter nostalgia for the past, turned back to a faith in a solitary communion with the land" (Kaufman, 1971, 47). Glasgow became more feminist as she grew older; in her last novel, *In This Our Life* (also a Pulitzer Prize winner), the leading female characters had names like "Stanley" and "Roy" and the men were little more than temporarily ornamental. Edith Wharton is also considered to have some affinity with the local-color tradition, but the changes she wrote about were not those resulting from the impact of Gesellschaft on old rural communities, but rather the changes in the New York she knew when good taste was eclipsed by vulgarity (Auchincloss, 1971, 572).

The Gothic Tale

The failure of the French Revolution, fruit of the great Enlightenment, was a crushing blow to idealistic writers early in the nineteenth century. One response was a return to the past in the so-called Romantic

Movement in literature. The interest in the medieval past had started earlier in the eighteenth century but merely then as a new fashion, beginning with a great interest in chivalry, plate armour, lancet windows, and later, in old ballads and antique poetry. It evolved, finally, into the novels of Sir Walter Scott, probably the most widely read, especially in the prewar American South. The Romantic Movement led also to the gothic novel, which, like the sentimental novel, was invented by a man, Horace Walpole, but was soon taken over and standardized by women writers. It was, in fact, a " 'female scribbler,' Ann Radcliffe . . . who, in the late eighteenth century, first managed to make a success of gothic fiction" (Fiedler, 107). One of the most successful of all gothic tales—*Frankenstein*—was in fact written by a woman.

In the sentimental novels, the "moral and domestic sentiment" which Bryce referred to in the American novel did, in fact, prevail. These novels portrayed life situations that most women faced at one time or another: unwelcome love, unrequited love, rejected love, abandonment, painful choices, disillusionment, disappointment, resignation. These were common themes that women could resonate to. Not so the themes in the gothic novel. It was filled with spinetingling mystery, haunted castles, bandits, ruins, terror, and maidens in flight. Heroines were subjected to the passionate advances of a highly romantic but unsuitable lover—a neurotic or a foreigner or someone very much out of their class. Seduction might take the form of abduction, which conveniently took the moral issue out of their hand. The gothic novel was written for pure entertainment, as far from polemics or didactics or out-and-out moralizing as possible. It was sheer fun. But it was also much more.

Fiedler notes that just as the sentimental novel was contested by two conflicting parties, philistine and antibourgeois, so also was the gothic novel. Both confronted similar, though opposite, tasks. The essentially genteel sentimental novel could be exploited for antiphilistine ends only with difficulty: the antibourgeois gothic novel could "only with difficulty be adapted to the needs of the sentimental middle class" (107). He proposes an interesting solution to this dilemma of the antiphilistine or antibourgeois protagonist. The authors sent coded messages. "Though they may have whispered their secret to friends, or confessed it in private letters, in their actual works they assumed what camouflage prudence dictated. They *wanted* to be misunderstood" (xxv). Fiedler is referring here to Mark Twain, but his point—the uses of literary subversion—is relevant to other writers as well.

Since the gothic was on the side of the underdog, it could be used in almost any context. Fiedler sees it as reflecting not a battle between the sexes but the struggle of antibourgeois standards against bourgeois philistinism.[21] The gothic novel was like the classic Western, in which either the Indian or the cowboy could be cast as the villain. In the gothic the bad side could be made so appealing that although it had to lose—that was the "camouflage prudence dictated"—it won. In this sense the gothic tale was subversive.

Katherine Ellis (1976) shows how the gothic atmosphere made morally subversive behavior acceptable, how it provided a "kind of cover" for impulses that would never have been permitted in more realistic settings. In the course of an abduction, for instance, a great deal of titillating erotic behavior could occur, obviously meant to be disapproved of by the reader but deliciously exciting in the process.[22] Some modern versions of the gothic novel are, in fact, essentially "soft porn," in which the seduction takes the form of rape. The titles—*Love's Tender Fury, Moonstruck Madness, This Loving Torment, Dark Fires*—hint at dark sexual messages. One successful author of this current version of the gothic, Rosemary Rogers, has been characterized as the "queen of rape and romance" (Hendrickson, 1979). And so, in their way, were the authors of early gothics.[23]

No wonder parents disapproved of novels.[24] The seducer is made so attractive and the seduced heroine is portrayed as so appealing that, as Hannah More pointed out, the reader is carried in her imagination to a point not so far from sharing the act itself, living with the heroine through a kind of vicarious seduction. The morally subversive nature of such novels could not help but seem to parents as having a morally deteriorating influence on their readers.

Heroines in at least some modern gothics have been "subverted" in a feminist direction. Barbara Michaels, author of present-day gothics, tells us that her "Heroines are all intelligent, independent women, who are as apt to rescue the hero as be rescued by him" (quoted in Hendrickson, 1979). Another author of present-day gothics, Phyllis Whitney, tells us about her heroines also: they "have always gone after what they wanted.... They are becoming stronger in their own identities by the end of each book" (quoted in Hendrickson, 1979). (She then explains that "perhaps their author is becoming more 'enlightened.' ")

The gothic could be subversive not only with respect to erotic love but also with respect to filial duty. Ellis sees the gothics as portraying the child, not the parent, as the one who is right. The maiden-in-flight,[25] a common convention in gothics, was "a symbol through which the authors could portray, in a covert fashion, the imprisonment that is the underside of economic dependence.... In the triumph of children over parents the reader is shown the triumph of pure feeling . . . over the confining prejudices and institutions that fallen man has created,"in brief, over the establishment (55). Reading gothics was, in effect, a vicarious protest against filial duty, against the bourgeois family which sequestered woman in the home (52). "Protective camouflage" might make the parents appear to win; but the reader was on the daughter's side.

Along with the standard themes in the sentimental, local-color, and gothic novels there have also been some novels that have gone counter to the mainstream, novels, for example, about the "New Woman," the woman to whom love was not the major value in her life. An English novelist, Dinah Mulock Craik, represents this "subversive feminism."[26] Although she wrote the standard story of women's suffering and endurance, she was especially concerned about unmarried women, about teaching them self-reliance and self-development (Showalter, 1975). "Her advice was brisk and bolstering; avoid false pride, get yourself educated and trained, don't worry about what men will say" (14). She taught sisterhood across the class board. "When she thought of the single woman, she thought not only of the orphaned young lady, or the governess, or the authoress, but also of the cook, the housemaid, the seamstress—and the prostitute. In a chapter on 'Female Servants' she insisted that the moral bonds of sisterhood should govern the relationship between employers and domestics" (14). She recognized female depression, anxiety, hypochondria, fear of aging (15). Although her novels concentrated on married bliss and "the need for women to submit to their husbands," still she also insisted that "each woman was responsible for her own happiness" (20). Even single women could be happy in and by themselves (19). Later on, in America, Edna Ferber was also to write about strong, self-reliant women who could make it on their own.

Short Stories

Many nineteenth-century novels first appeared as serials in magazines. Women, like other readers, thus became accustomed to reading fiction in magazines, short stories as well as novels. The short story has been characterized as "especially adapted to the American temperament and the American *Kultur*" (Pattee, 1918, 367). Though it had a fairly long history back to folk tales, it did not come into its own until the late nineteenth century. "The period between the Civil War . . . and the outbreak of the Great War in Europe in 1914 may be termed . . . the Era of the Short Story" (367).

The evolution of the short story in America began with Hannah More's "colourless, formless, undramatic" tales, which were "subservient only to the interest of virtue" and "peculiarly adapted to flourish in the Puritanic atmosphere of the new nation" (368). Washington Irving, Nathaniel Hawthorne, and Edgar Allen Poe gave the new genre literary luster, but is was Rose Terry Cooke (1827-1892) who, in the 1850s and 1860s, gave it a more realistic slant. And women have embraced this form of fiction both as producers and consumers ever since. Vernon Parrington tells us, in fact, that "the American short story . . . is largely provided by women for women" (Cohn, 1943, 182).

Rose Terry Cooke, a New England woman, started out as a poet, but although her poetry was published it did not prove to be her major talent. Her reputation came to rest primarily on her short stories, precursors of the local-color genre. "Her characters are an odd collection of solitary spinsters and vanished types" and "men grown 'cussed' from their fight with nature" (Lintner, 1971, 378). The women in her stories were "cruelly warped and broken by their hard lot" (378). Her stories, though grim, are not altogether without humour. Cooke was a raconteur rather than a master of the short story. Hard pressed for money, she ground out much of her work without inspiration, as didactic potboilers. Still, when free of pressure, she could turn out work good enough for the literary periodicals, such as *Harper's* and *Atlantic.*

The authors of the sentimental novels wrote numerous short stories. The local colorists, in fact, were known more for their short stories than for their novels. Some of the classic short stories in American literature were from the pens of women writers, such as Sarah Orne Jewett's "A White Heron" (1866) and Freeman's "A New England Nun" (1891). The current state of the short story is considered in Chapter 19.

Genres in any art form have lives of their own. Thus William Peterfield Trent and his associates claim that romance prevailed in this country in the 1830s, sentimentalism in the 1850s, realism in the 1880s, and naturalism at the turn of the century (1936, 95). Still, such a neat chronology does not seem to fit the writings of women. All the genres Trent lists survive. The literary style of the past is no longer acceptable, but the gothic tale still flourishes. The themes of the sentimental novel also recur over and over again in present-day novels. The love-and/or-duty ethos still pervades the popular stories. How much sacrifice of my family for my career may I claim? How much "taking care" must I engage in? How can I best find self-fulfillment? How much must I give? The impact of Gesellschaft on the female world finds expression in the dilemmas of the working wife, the working mother. Both authors and readers are still wrestling with the old core problems of the female world: How to transform the love-and/or-duty ethos to suit the constantly changing demands conditions are making. And how to come to terms with Gesellschaft.

The "Distaff Faulknerians"

Women were receiving messages from novels—those written by women but also some written by men. The books of the male and female authors presented images of women that were quite different. The male authors shied away from portraying "any full-fledged, mature women" (Fiedler, xix). Fiedler summarizes the types of women that were characteristic of American novels: Fair Maiden, Dark Lady, Good Good Girl, Good Bad Girl, White Witch, Golden Girl, goddess, bitch, castrating woman, vampire, lady with the whip, New Woman (273 ff.). These were "symbols of the [male] rejection or fear of sexuality" (xix). Fiedler feels that sentimentalism, which he views as a universal calamity, a blight (45), made it impossible to draw convincing portraits of women (273). The "image of the golden girl-child dies the hardest death of all in the American psyche" (324). But even she could not survive the reaction against the old school of sentimental novel. Even she finally "yields before the general onslaught on the concept of pure womanhood" (324).

The demeaning image of women in so many novels written by men was not without impact on women themselves. Fiedler reminds us that if Faulkner had written of blacks with as much hostility as he expressed when writing of women, "his books would have been banned in every enlightened school in the country" (309).

Any novel—or film, for that matter, or television program—can serve as a projective test. Different people see different things in it. And this is especially so in the case of literary works. *The Merchant of Venice*, for example, is a quite different drama from the one most of us know when Shylock is played as a comic figure (as some scholars claim was Shakespeare's intention). In this connection it is interesting to note how the work of certain women novelists in the twentieth century have been interpreted.

Fiedler sees Katherine Anne Porter, Eudora Welty, and Carson McCullers as a first generation of "distaff Faulknerians" and Elizabeth Spencer and Flannery O'Connor as second-generation writers of that gothic tradition (450). This interpretation is intended as an accolade. Wood, on the other hand, sees these women as representatives of the local-color tradition. But Audrey T. Rodgers sees their work as an attempt to portray the defects in the fictional female image so starkly as to shock women into change. These writers, she claims, tried to shake women loose, to free them from their bondage by telling them that they were to blame for their fate. They "indicted women for not seizing the reins in their own behalf and for succumbing to the belief that they are, indeed, living embodiments of the stereotypes spun from the male imagination" (Rodgers, 1979, 248-249). The women who show up in the work of Flannery O'Connor ("Greenleaf," "Good Country People"), Dorothy Parker ("Big Blonde"), Eudora Welty ("Why I Live at the P.O."), and Katherine Anne Porter ("Flowering Judas") "act out the preconceived roles of temptress, nun, or mindless romantic," thus perpetuating such clichés as "the fiction that women hate women" and thus betraying "themselves as they betray others" (249).

These writers, she argues, "call women to account" by assaulting such caricatures "with scathing wit and contempt" (249). Along with playwrights like Lillian Hellman (*The Little Foxes*) and Clare Boothe Luce (*The Women*), fiction writers were choosing "to expose these bitches, temptresses, and destroyers" in order to show "the insidiousness of such self-betrayal" (250). They held up images of how women perceived themselves to show how women perpetuated the grotesque image of themselves reflected back in so much current writing. Katherine Anne Porter put it in these terms: "My aim is to find the truth of my own life and the facts of it" (250). And Clare Boothe Luce explained in a television interview why she wrote so cruelly about women—let women look at their own lives, at one another. Let them see through their own eyes, not through the eyes of male stereotypes. And judge themselves.

Angry Women

Whichever view is held, it is true that there did follow, later in the century, a quite different genre in female culture. If the "distaff Faulknerians" excoriated women, the "angry exposé" novelists unmasked the stereotypes they hid behind. The subversion in Rita Mae Brown's books, for example—*In Her Day, A Plain Brown Rapper*, or *The Hand that Cradles the Rock*—is no longer covert as in the gothic tale, no longer latent or in code; it no longer pays tribute to the conventions; it no longer sentimentalizes the sorrows, griefs, and pains of its heroines. It proclaims them, shouts them from the housetops, often angrily. Nor does it blame women for them. The later novelists—Sylvia Plath, Doris Lessing, Marilyn French—write about women not dispassionately as "they" or "them" but, though gramatically in the third person, almost passionately, as we or us or I. They are not objective observers but intimate participants in the scene. They identify with their characters.

The male world was dumbfounded when it became possible for women to express their emotions and feelings so vehemently. Despite the commonly held theory that women are more open and revealing than men in the expression of their emotions, women have actually not been allowed to express their feelings, certainly not their hostile, angry feelings. Men have been permitted, even expected, to bluster, roar, and swear violently. Women have had to control such emotions. They were allowed to cry, to be sure. The popular poetry written by women in the nineteenth century tended to be filled with tears. And certainly the readers of sentimental novels were supposed to cry. But even here, pride or fear often caused them to suppress their feelings.

The wallflower has had to smile cheerfully despite the anguish of her rejection. The battered wife has had to hide her pain. As had also the wife of the alcoholic. Or the neglected wife. Or the abandoned wife. Or . . .

Now the anger that had so long been suppressed gushed forth. Women were no longer "laughing" at the insults directed toward them, to avoid the charge that they "had no sense of humor." They were no longer having to pretend that they were amused by male jokes at their expense. Literary critics were amazed to find how often the major characters in novels by women went mad, committed suicide, suffered profound depressions, or turned to other women. To the outside world's amazement, female culture—which had always seemed so placid, so satisfied with the status quo, so complacent, even so cheerful—was revealed as a cloak for pain. These writers were not the women the male world had known, the women who put up such a brave front in their presence. "I have been criticized for my recent books," Beauvoir was saying. "Some women complained that I did not present positive heroines, because I showed mostly broken, unhappy women. I did so because that is how I see and feel today's feminine condition. I have no desire to present heroic, militant women who I feel are nonexistent and utopian" (1978, 32). No subterfuges; no covert messages, no codes, Since we aim for subversion, let it be open, aboveboard, inescapable. No gloss.

Poetry

Until recently relatively little critical attention—except in the case of such stars as Elizabeth Barrett Browning and Emily Dickinson—has been paid to poetry in female culture as compared even with prose. A considerable part of it, to be sure, was mere versifying. But there were serious poets also.

One study of nineteenth-century British poets finds depicted in their work not only conventional, conservative roles, such as daughter, wife, mother, but also certain deviate roles, such as the fallen woman, *femme fatale*, spinster, working woman, and even "New Woman" (Hickok, 1977), the first group overshadowing the second by far.

> The bulk of women's poems tended to reinforce conservative ideals; poems which expressed protest or even doubt about the tenability of those ideals were relatively few. Nevertheless, a small but vigorous countertendency gained momentum throughout the century. Thus, a curious state of tension exists in nineteenth-century women's poetry between the ideal of passive, domestic, male-oriented womanhood and the reaction against that ideal. Although poetry depicting women in their most socially acceptable roles—dutiful, submissive wife; devoted, angelic mother—seldom contra-

> dicted convention, there *was* a real tradition of protest, however subtle. Also, while reluctant to offer outright endorsement of alternative roles, the popular women poets nonetheless shifted their attitude towards "unprotected" women from hostility to sympathy. It becomes no longer necessary to depict the fallen woman as irrevocably damned, the spinster as ridiculously unattractive, or the *femme fatale* as unmitigatedly evil. The working woman's cause is not only recognized, but sometimes loudly propounded [Hickok, 1977].

Despite such growing acceptance of "deviant" female roles, however, "the 'New Woman' failed to enlist the popular women poets' sympathies"(3). A woman might "fall," remain unmarried, be a siren, even enter the labor force, but agitate for women's rights? Perish the thought. Hickok concludes that "the conservatism of many . . . women poets' representations of women stemmed from their personal acceptance of contemporary ideals of womanhood, their feminine sense of a 'mission' to lead society towards an ideal goal, and a lack of life experiences, caused by their sheltered existences. Additionally, the demands and expectations of their middle-class audience and of the prevailing literary double standard were inhibiting factors" (Hickok, 1977). Despite their limitations, however, Hickok believes that the literary subculture created by these poets devised a "cluster of female traditions which remain appropriate forms of female self-expression today."

Current students of women's poetry find its themes and images different from those of men's poetry. Despite the great volume of "verses" and "versifying" in the nineteenth and early twentieth centuries, there was also a considerable amount of serious experimentation and innovation. The work was communicative rather than obscure, as some more recent work has been characterized. The conflicts were different from those expressed by men poets. They were not necessarily parochial or even, strictly speaking, American but tended to be universal. They were not always resolved, nor did the poets promise that they were even resolvable. Many of them might well be unresolvable, a part of the human condition.

Some women poets now, as then, write of their relationships with husbands, lovers, mothers, fathers, sisters, brothers, children, other women. Some, of their minds, their ideas; some, of their bodies, their senses; some, of their homes. Some are humorous, others serious. Spacks sees writing as an escape for women. "Women dominate their own experience by imagining it, giving it form, writing about it" (1976, 413). Writing poetry represents a special way of expressing what they are experiencing, learning.

The poetry these women wrote was popular; it found an audience. It sold better than poetry by men (177). "The law of supply and demand has greatly benefited the woman poet in America" (Watts, 5). To be sure, this popular poetry—read primarily by women—was looked down on. Bryce was extremely surprised by it. "In poetry . . . many whose names are quite unknown in Europe have attained widespread fame" (Bryce, 1891, 613).

The women poets who wrote in the first half of the present century—such as Amy Lowell, Edna St. Vincent Millay, Hilda Doolittle, Sara Teasdale, Elinor Wylie, Dorothy Parker—are characterized by Audrey T. Rodgers as sensitive artists who nevertheless had to struggle against the bonds imposed on them by their profession (1979, 253). In another study, this time of eight American poets writing since 1912, women poets are described as in a double bind, caught in an inherent conflict between their roles as women and as poets. Amy Lowell, herself a distinguished poet, thought "women who write poetry" a "queer lot" because they were both outsiders and still part of a special minority (Gabelnick, 1978, draft). Juhasz reminds us that even Dickinson "had to deny herself as a woman to be a poet" (1977, 715). Rodgers finds that—perhaps because of this role dilemma—the poetry of many women early in the century is "glib, overly sentimental, brittle, or vaguely distressed, . . . deficient in depth and credibility, never approximating the portrait of women in the fiction or the later poetry" (252). There is no palpable image of woman in these poems. Roles like "flirt, ecstatic, or neurotic are donned and shed at will, like so many changes of dress." Rodgers sees Millay as celebrating herself in the flapper role "with a slickness that belies real feeling." Lowell she sees as "weighed down by the heavy baggage of sentiment . . . or upheld in antiseptic frigidity." The women in Wylie's poems, she believes, "bear no resemblance to women in real life." Parker, she thinks, hides behind "acerbity and wit."

Why, one asks, had the women poets of the nineteenth century not suffered such a double bind? Gabelnick hints at a possible explanation: the old women's sphere with its built-in supports had now begun to suffer attrition. Bowles asks, "Did the masculinist tradition encourage them to stay away from other women?" (1978, 714). The heart of the matter, Gabelnick concludes, was a longing for creative community, for the support system so essential for creativity. These poets, not in the major mainstream, did not share in the great renaissance of American poetry exemplified by the work of T. S. Eliot, Ezra Pound, William Carlos Williams. "They appear totally oblivious to the 'new poetry' and the 'new criticism' " (Rodgers, 253).

As in the case of the novel, so also in the case of poetry, the second half of the century saw an explosive rebirth. Women poets began to find one another. "Using their own sense of disaffiliation with the larger artistic community, women built new connections among themselves. Exposing their anger, their isolation, their ignorance, they connected with one another yet remained individuals" (Gabelnick). With this new "sisterhood," poetry provided an even richer soil than prose for the search for female identity (Rodgers, 258). Poetry became more genuine in the expression of emotion, more honestly self-critical, even more painfully confessional than in the past. It came to "reveal the stress of ambivalence," it became more openly autobiographical, franker, more strident, less reticent, less witty (Rodgers, 253). It brought "a surge of anger, bitterness, self-loathing, violence, melancholia, and desperation" but also "a heady self-awareness manifested in endless celebrations of the body and the emotions" (253). In the work of some, poetry transcends the self; Sylvia Plath, Anne Sexton, Denise Levertov, Adrienne Rich, for example, "like all artists . . . speak for themselves, for other women, and ultimately for that within us which is shared by all human beings" (253). Two poets who ended their own lives explicitly rejected the core female identities. Plath's mouthpiece is an angered and hating woman who "lashes out at men, marriage, motherhood" (Rodgers, 255). Sexton, in a poem "Consorting with Angels," writes of a woman who was "tired of being a woman,/tired of the spoons and the pots,/tired of my mouth and my breasts,/ tired of the cosmetics and the silks" (Rodgers, 262). Adrienne Rich, on the other hand, celebrates the women who carry on the struggle: "Attention has got to be paid by women to what it means to be a woman. . . . What *we* think it ought to mean, what *we* think it has meant, *our* interpretations" (Rodgers, 256).

Critics ask of the new poetry women are writing: Is it poetry? Juhasz replies that such a question is the essence of sexism, resulting from a "culture that has made rules for everything, including art, that upholds values" (714). She rejects such sexual parochialism. "The traditional criteria for poetry have described the poetry that men have made; it has been 'universal' because it has described the experience of MANkind" (714). Meanwhile there seems to be a great upsurge in creativity among women poets, the depth and impact of which, Gabelnick believes, "will take many decades of the twenty-first century to understand."

The Fine Arts

Some of the earliest human artistic work was done by women in the form of decoration of pottery or designs braided into basket containers or woven into rugs or textiles of one kind or another. Recently the folk arts of stitchery have been rediscovered. Norma Papish has combed museums over the world and called to our attention the skill and talent expressed not only in great tapestries but also in old embroideries and laces. The art of quilting has been accorded museum recognition. But in the fine arts, the study of female culture has until now been neglected. In discussing the visual arts as a component of female culture the approach must be somewhat different from our approach to the verbal arts.

Unlike the novel, painting and sculpture have never been a major component of female culture. Although drawing was part of a cultivated girl's training, the culture of the female world has relied almost wholly on the products of male artists. The pictures or statues women have bought have been created by men. It is only recently that the artwork done by women in the past has begun to be resurrected. Thus interpretations of female culture vis-à-vis painting are only now beginning to become available. Our discussion here is therefore mainly historical and ideological, with minimal attention to the substantive content of female painting.

Since all the standards for judging sculpture or painting, for example, have been established by men—or by women artists trained by men—there has been little space in female culture for a distinctively female art. The work of few women painters and sculptors has been recognized; the products of only a handful have found places in the galleries.

A tradition of discouragement analogous to that of other aspects of female culture has prevailed in the area of the fine arts. Just as Brontë and Glasgow were advised to stop invading male turf and to return to their true métier, just as being poets had isolated women from the domestic world of women, so also in the case of painters. An art critic in the 1920s relegated women as a whole to the fringes of the creative community; "Women painters, like women poets, women novelists, women musicians, women politicians, women prisoners have been only lesser men" (cited in Mitchell, 1978, 681). They may have been good imitators, but they did not have "the initiative or the ability to blaze new paths for themselves." When a choice had to be made between art and one's duties and obligations to family, art usually lost out. And those who persisted, such as Jane Wyeth and even Georgia O'Keeffe, had to wait until they were well along in years before adequate recognition was forthcoming. Until recently women painters were relegated to a special category, not quite in the male sphere but tangential to the real thing. ("She's a good painter—poet, writer, scientist, what-have-you—for a woman.") Now that O'Keeffe's position is unchallengeable, "criticism by men rarely refers to her as a 'woman painter,' a phrase which should denote a painter of the female figure. Whether this is due to an increasing consciousness of female potential, embarrassment about sexual bias, or the fact that O'Keeffe, in her 90s, has entered the rather neuter sphere of the aged, it is nonetheless a welcome departure from previous habits of expressions" (686).

All of this is the result of a long history, a story which Harris and Nochlin (1976) and, more recently, Germaine Greer (1979) have put together in their histories of women artists. Century by century, these authors recount the circumstances that fostered or denied women's artistic talents.

Especially interesting in the history of women artists is the curious form Spacks' "taking care" paradigm took. Greer documents case after case in which the work of a woman artist—daughter, wife—was turned over to her father or husband to be signed and sold by him. She did this to please—to "take care of"—him. That was what a dutiful woman was expected to do. Greer implies, as Woolf does in the case of Mrs. Ramsay, that this represented willing self-sacrifice, as legitimate a source for personal fulfillment as recognition of the artistic work itself. Whatever the reason, the practice of attributing the work of women to men resulted in the "loss" of female names from the register of great artists.

After the thirteenth century, Harris and Nochlin tell us, when small shops run by master craftsmen were replaced by larger shops apart from their dwellings, women were no longer exposed to craftsmanship and the chance to learn the skills of the several crafts. Their status was reduced as their work was transformed into male trades. In the fourteenth century women were cutlers, leatherworkers, butchers, ironmongers, glovers, bookbinders, even goldsmiths. The widows of draftsmen were allowed to continue their shops, but "the wives of painters, sculptors, and goldsmiths rarely participated in a workshop or ran it after their husbands' death, for these were highly skilled crafts requiring a long apprenticeship" (14). Women were not admitted to the guilds, and since no work was allowed at home, the women could not learn (15). Circumstances differed in different countries from the sixteenth to the eighteenth centuries. In Italy, copying and decorating of texts was done by cloistered nuns away from stimulation, so their work was not innovative. Conditions were somewhat better in Flanders, for "the medieval pattern of wives, and occasionally daughters, following their husbands' and fathers' professions seems to have persisted . . . at least until the sixteenth century" (25). Also in the north, the misogyny of a celibate priesthood was abating and with the Reformation literacy began to spread. Thus in the seventeenth and eighteenth centuries women first emerged as serious professional artists, trained in workshops of established artists (26). By the early eighteenth century they also had a chance to attend private drawing sessions which reduced the cost of hiring models (26-27). But "custom, prejudice, and practical problems . . . continued to make it virtually impossible for a gifted woman to train herself properly, to believe in her gifts as ardently as a man, or to devote herself to her career as completely as a man" (28). Among the "prejudices" which hampered women artists was "the belief that women did not even have the potential for artistic genius," which Harris and Nochlin think is enough to explain "their absence from the earlier history of Renaissance painting" (28).

Nevertheless, a few women did overcome these constraints in the sixteenth, seventeenth, and eighteenth centuries. Some were even financially successful. Some, lacking any model for successful spinsterhood, left their profession at marriage (29). Fathers and husbands who profited from the success of women did not oppose them, but others, like male novelists, did not welcome their competition. The male artists, who controlled the most prestigious and profitable commissions, tolerated the women so long as they remained on the fringe and were therefore not much of a threat. Or they were condescending and patronizing. Women's work was "all right for a woman" (30). But by the eighteenth century there were enough successful women painters to pose an economic threat to the men. Even when women were admitted to the academies, in the eighteenth century, they were not allowed to attend drawing classes, hold office, compete for prizes, or teach. Some academies did not even allow women to attend meetings. The only privilege they were granted was the prestige of membership and permission to exhibit in the salons (37). Even in the nineteenth century in France, women were excluded from the École des Beaux Arts and the Class of Fine Arts of the Institute (46) and were restricted by "feminine propriety" from exhibiting in the salons (49). Their training was second rate and criticism of their work was patronizing. In England women were denied membership in the Royal Academy; they had a hard time getting serious instruction (51).

Harris and Nochlin contrast the impact of Condorcet and Rousseau on the position of women. Condorcet in 1790 was asking, "Why should people prone to pregnancy and passing indispositions be barred from the exercise of rights no one would dream of denying those who have gout or catch cold easily?" (45)—a question which reminds us of the same question modern women have been asking about benefits for pregnancy leave and leave for prostate surgery. Rousseau had a different view. His "notion of woman as the 'natural' guardian of the home militated strongly against her achievement of status as an independent being, in the arts as elsewhere" (45).

Summarizing their extensive research, Harris and Nochlin note that until the nineteenth century women artists were deprived of access to training, a serious handicap. Where academic training mattered less, women did well (43). The successful artists were those who had access to the court and aristocratic circles. The salons helped. Women were especially good at pastels, portraits, and flowers, and they flourished when these genres were in demand.

Nor is the story over. As recently as 1974 Lise Vogel was asking why the recognition of even so great an artist as O'Keeffe had taken so long and why women artists themselves have taken so long to learn to seek their own approach, independent of that of the male tradition. "Why," she was asking, "has art, perhaps more than any other field, lagged so far behind the general movement for change initiated by modern feminism?"(3) Where, specifically, were "the books, articles, or collections of essays presenting a feminist critique of art?" And why, she continued, were "there no monographs and virtually no articles on women artists written from a feminist perspective?"(3). And the reproductions and slides of the work of women artists, where were they? And the syllabi and bibliographies dealing with the issues of women, art, and feminism, why were they so hard to find? What did it mean that there were almost no feminist art history courses in the schools? Where were the feminist art historians and critics? Why were there so few of them? What were women artists doing today? Especially those who considered themselves to be feminists. "What *should* a feminist artist, critic, or art historian do?"(3). How create a woman's art in the face of so many obstacles?

Despite the discouraging situation reflected in these searching questions, Vogel admitted that feminism was finally beginning to reach the art world. The most obvious evidence was the increasing, though still small, "number of exhibitions devoted to women artists, both past and present" (7). Attempts were being made to mount exhibits of "the image of woman" in art, "although these shows have tended so far to range from incoherence to outright sexism" (7). The more established art magazines were beginning to publish articles on women artists and on the feminist art movement, and new periodicals had also been started, such as *Women and Art, A Feminist Art Journal*, and *Womanspace Journal*. Cooperative galleries were being set up, like ARC (Artists, Residents of Chicago) Gallery, a collectively run gallery founded to exhibit women's art (Broughton, 1977, 15). A few "women and art" courses were beginning to be offered in connection with the women's studio movement. Conferences were being held and several sessions on the topic of "women and art" were being dutifully alloted at the annual meetings of the College Art Association. The commitment in art scholarship to see art in its social context was converging with the rise of feminism.

There was also a flurry of formal organization among artists. One artist, Charlotte Robinson, was stimulated by the National Women's

Conference in Houston in November, 1977, to organize a coalition of artists to tackle the nitty gritty of the artistic career. She had by now begun "to see what the women's movement could accomplish for women in the arts. First of all, it teaches them to take themselves seriously. It gives them people to talk to. How do you get a gallery? How do you get the government to change the tax laws to give artists a fair break? An old-girl network helps" (Richard, 1979). She did the basic work of organizing. She made phone calls, wrote letters, attended meetings. She learned and "had a lot of fun." She was so successful in her efforts that in little more than a year after Houston the Coalition of Women's Art Organizations represented more than 60,000 members; the Women's Caucus for Art was making awards for Outstanding Achievement in the Visual Arts in the Oval Office of the White House, and the president himself was calling it a historic moment. Women artists, he said, "had for too long been ignored." All this was at least an auspicious start.

But only a start. What was all this flurry of activity *for*? Was it primarily to get access to the channels of training, gallery exhibiting, teaching posts? For some, perhaps, that was it. But some artists, critics, and art historians were asking more pointed questions. What, for example, might a feminist point of view mean "for the creation of art and for cultural criticism and history" (Vogel, 7)? Who was the audience for art, for criticism, for history, for teaching? Women only? Men also? Equally central, if not more so, was the ideological issue: What do you mean, female art?

Ideological Issues

Some years ago, psychologists confronted with questions of a similar nature replied that psychology was what psychologists studied. Mainardi expresses the same approach in answer to the question about female art. She argues that women "who have been gerrymandered out of the very definition of art must be free to *define* art, not to pick up the crumbs from The Man's table.... We must begin to define women's art as *what women* artists *do*, not try to slip and squeeze ourselves through the loophole of the male art world" (1977, 23). The difficulty is that what women artists do depends on the training they have had, the models they have been exposed to, the criteria they have been taught to apply. Defying the canon is not all that easy. With no ideological perspective women artists will simply imitate the subjects and the techniques that have suited and pleased men.

Another answer rested on a theory of a characteristically female aesthetic or sensibility, "involving an imagery and formal style specific to women. Proponents insist that an authentic artistic language is being created, corresponding to the distinct social experience of women, independent of 'male defined' art" (Vogel, 1974, 32). Such a point of view is described by Broughton: "Women's art reflects the unique shape and space of woman. The creative expression of experience, as made whole by women, is full and round; the shape of breasts and vaginas. It is autobiographical; a reflection of the infinitely intimate and searingly personal" (1977, 15). She quotes Lucy R. Lippard's concept of "female imagery" which is biologically derived from body identification and forms: "Women's art is round, organic, autobiographical, with orifices and vaginal openings" (15). Frances Schoenwetter, a sculptor, is quoted as being "interested in birth, death, things from which we stem" (15), and as believing women's art to be different from men's.[27]

Opponents of this female-sensibility perspective reject it on the grounds that it is opportunistic, restrictive, and limiting, rehabilitating an artistic ghetto. It is based on two premises. The first is the assumption "that an individual's experience is primarily and perhaps completely determined by gender. Women and men are held to inhabit utterly separate worlds, and variations of class or ethnic experience are considered clearly subordinate to gender distinctions. The second assumption is that whatever exists today must be essentially unchangeable; the babble of the sexes is felt to be eternal and ahistorical. It follows, then, that the only way women artists can operate is to accept these terms and develop their own strength, autonomously and in apparent opposition to men" (Vogel, 23).

Harris and Nochlin come out against a specific female sensibility; but they cannot rule out the fact that since artists must express the experiences they have been subjected to, the female experience of women will be different from the male experience of men. "There are no particularly stylistic features associated with the work of women artists . . . although it is also clear that in specific historical situations women artists have been encouraged to turn to certain areas of activity more than others," such, as flower painting (64). Women artists, further, are not all of a piece; they are as different from one another as they are from men. Thus one woman painter paints a peasant woman as the embodiment of fatalistic conservatism; another, as a symbol of revolt (65). "In the face of the enormous range and variety of paintings by twentieth-century women, it would indeed be futile, if not impossible, to talk of a "woman's style' or a "feminine sensibility' " (59). The whole tenor of their book "argues consistently against such 'innate' or 'essential' proclivities on the part of women artists, or indeed against the existence of any specifically feminine tendencies whatever, apart from specific historical contexts. That motherhood should have played such an important role in women artists' iconography is hardly remarkable, historically it has been the central life experience for most women, cutting across barriers of class, period, and nationality. Yet even in the case of this most universally popular of subjects, the variations on the theme are more striking than the similarities"(66).[28]

Having thus made the case against any specific style or sensibility, they nevertheless find that being a woman is an important factor in the work of women artists. "To discard obviously mystificatory, essentialist theories about women's 'natural' directions in art is by no means to affirm that the fact of being a woman is completely irrelevant to artistic creation. That would be tantamount to declaring that art exists in a vacuum instead of in the complex social, historical, psychological, and political matrix within which it is actually produced. The fact that a given artist happens to be a woman rather than a man counts for something; it is a more or less significant variable in the creation of a work of art, like being an American, being poor, or being born in 1900. Like any other variable, little can be predicted on its basis in isolation from the specific context in which it exists" (59-60).

Since I am not myself an artist and therefore not entitled to take a stand on this issue, I may be intrusive when I say that it does not seem to me that women artists developing their own strength implies opposition to men or a battle of the sexes as Vogel states the position (23). I must admit, however, that I might have reacted differently if my work had been denied showing in "male-run and male-dominated art galleries." I think women artists will discover what female art is as they learn to value their own experiences and learn to indulge in what delights them, whatever the canon prescribes.

Notes

1. A great many aspects of even female culture are omitted from this far from exhaustive overview. An enormous body of nonfiction writing by and for women is not dealt with, nor are books on self-help, self-improvement, health, beauty, food, diet, child care, child rearing, marital adjustment, gardening, housekeeping, sports of all kinds, travel, on and on. Almost all middle- and upper-middle-class girls take ballet lessons or lessons in other forms of dancing and there have been great female choreographers—Isadora Duncan, Ruth St. Denis, Katherine Dunham, Agnes deMille, Martha Graham—but they are not discussed here either. Nor is serious music. Each of these subjects warrants a whole chapter.
2. Spacks quotes from Ellen Glasgow's autobiography her devastating experience with Price Collier, of Macmillan's, in 1890: "He told me frankly that there was no hope for me with Macmillan. No, it would not do the slightest good if he read my manuscript; he could tell, without reading it, that there was not a chance of Macmillan's accepting the book. 'The best

advice I can give you,' he said, with charming candor, 'is to stop writing, and go back to the South and have some babies.' And I think, though I may have heard this ripe wisdom from other men, probably from many, that he added; 'The greatest woman is not the woman who has written the finest book, but the woman who has had the finest babies' " (129).

3. Fiedler (1960) tells us, for example, that when the novel was taken over by women, it became degraded, sank into an artistic underworld (56), that female authors were the enemies of psychology and technique and candor (57)—also of tragedy (58).
4. An analogous situation with respect to the work of women in the social sciences today often prevails. On lists of publications on academic vitas, research dealing with feminist issues is often discounted as unworthy as a basis for promotion or tenure (Bernard, 1979, 271-272).
5. An analogous question is sometimes raised with respect to fashion. Do fashion designers "dictate" fashion? Or do they simply offer a range of designs among which the buyers select what suits them, thus establishing the fashionable? Some years ago a team of my students tackled this question with respect to hemlines. They found that although the designers did present differing hemlines, women did not raise their hemlines as high or lower them as low as was "dictated." They did select among the lengths offered, but only those that pleased them.
6. Two illustrations of the relationship between art and life, offered by Fiedler, may be relevant. "In life as in books . . . ladies learned to be pale and forbearing and forgiving; in life as in books, men learned to play at lechery . . . , to smoke, drink, tell smutty stories, and plot escapes from the females" (64). "In America, . . . the use of women as symbols of piety and purity led to an unfortunate series of misunderstandings. With no counter-tradition, cynical or idealizing, to challenge it, the sentimental view came to be accepted as quite *literally* true, was imposed upon actual woman as a required role and responded to by men as if it were a fact of life rather than of fancy" (51). In the first, there was an echoing back and forth between "life" and "art." In the second, "life" was imitating "art." Of course, "art" imitates "art" also. Thus, Fiedler tells us, the encounter between Lovelace and Clarissa in the first great novel of seduction "was reported over and over—or at least imposed itself upon life in the perceiving mind—until that encounter, and its actors, had become stereotypes from which no American author could entirely escape" (73).
7. A spot check of half a dozen local libraries in an urban community found differences or similarities by sex according to the area of the city served. In one, the patronage was primarily by women, mainly because it was in an area of older residents, most of whom were women. But the librarian found little if any sex differences in the kinds of books borrowed. Both men and women borrowed adventure stories, war novels, historical romances, and mysteries. Some women were also borrowing books on money and management. In another branch, located in an apartment house area with many single (unmarried, widowed, separated, and divorced) women, the female borrowers favored fiction over nonfiction, especially gothic and historical novels; the male borrowers preferred war novels. Both borrowed myster-

ies and adventure stories. But also the great classics, like, for example, *War and Peace*. Other branches showed variations of these two patterns according to the demographic composition of the area served.

8. Ellen Glasgow, for one, destroyed manuscripts when discouraged by unfriendly criticism (Kaufman, 1971, 46). Among all the female diary keepers and letter writers of the nineteenth century there must have been quite a company who also tried their hands at writing novels. When we look at novels for insights we are looking at a more or less selected, undoubtedly biased, sample.
9. The biographical dictionary *Notable American Women* (Harvard; Bellamy Press, 1971) lists 220 names under "authors," not all novelists. In the 213 years between 1607-1820, there are 12; in the 39 years 1821-1860, 61; in the 39 years 1861-1900, 79; and in the 50 years 1900-1950, 68 (all deceased). The first and last periods cannot be compared with the middle two because the time span differs and also because many writers in the first half of the present century are still alive and therefore ineligible for inclusion. But it may be noted that in the 39-year period 1861-1900, the number of authors increased at a rate about a third (30 percent) over the rate of increase in the 39-year period 1821-1860. Ann Douglas Wood offers this partial explanation for the influx of women into the profession of writing between 1800 and 1860: "They were attracted to literature because it was very much a profession, but one that could be made to look *un*professional. It enabled its practitioners to do a man's job, for a man's pay, in a woman's clothes. Authorship until the late eighteenth century had not been a profession in the modern sense of the word. It had been a matter of finding a paying patron rather than of pleasing a reading public, a state of affairs which early apologists for America used to explain the barrenness of literature in this new country where men were too busy creating a nation to patronize the arts" (1972, 6). A competitive literary market obviated the need for a patron. In a sense, a different kind of gatekeeper took over. Now profit rather than personal prejudice determined who was in a position to be published. This contrast corresponds to Ralph Turner's distinction between "sponsored" and "contest" competition (1960, 856-857) and my own contrast between "judgmental" and "autonomous" competition (Bernard, 1962, 64-65).
10. These successful writers were not a peculiarly American phenomenon. After the first wave of Victorian women novelists in England (the Brontës, Mrs. Gaskell, George Eliot) there came a number of women, born between 1820 and 1840 (Margaret Oliphant, Charlotte Yonge, Mrs. Henry Wood, Dinah Craik, among others), who were "novelists with a purpose—self-disciplined and steadily productive over many years, active in journalism as well as in literature" (Showalter, 1975, 5). These women, "despite their [own] achievements in the literary marketplace, . . . generally opposed organized movements for women's rights and stressed an individualistic need for personal strength" (5). Their own lives were, except for their professional success, strictly according to the Victorian code, and their novels "celebrated the domestic, the bourgeois, and the conventional" (5).
11. For a discussion of ten successful writers in the nineteenth century, see

Wood (1972, 3-46). There is an issue among students of literature with respect to how much attention need be paid to the biographical and historical context of an artistic product. Some argue that only purely aesthetic criteria should be applied, that biographical and historical data are irrelevant for appreciating the aesthetic value of a novel or poem, that Shakespeare's sonnets are as beautiful whether we know anything about Shakespeare and his age or not. Others argue that it is only when we put it into historical perspective and invoke biographical data that we can fully appreciate it. I tend to favor the second point of view, although I do recognize that sometimes too much reliance on minute scholarship can overwhelm the great work itself, that sometimes the volumes of exegesis, tracing of meanings, of "influences," and so on can kill any aesthetic pleasure the work itself might generate. Still, in the present context, it is not the aesthetic quality of the novels we are concerned with but their contribution to the culture of the female world.

12. I selected Mrs. Southworth and Mary J. Holmes because their books were still avidly read in the early decades of this century. My sister, five years my senior, and I devoured them.
13. Mrs. Southworth was the most popular author for *The Ledger*, itself the most popular story journal of its day. Her income rose to $10,000 a year, a large sum in the 1850s.
14. Mary J. Holmes received $4,000 to $6,000 for each story she wrote for *The New York Weekly*, a rival to *The Ledger*, for which Mrs. Southworth wrote. "The sales of her books were immense, totaling over two million copies" (Urness, 1971, 208). They went through edition after edition, and libraries had to keep twenty to thirty copies of each title on the shelf.
15. In the male literary tradition, if not in real life, there was the complementary erotic theme of the prostitute with the heart of gold which reached the female world in Margaret Mitchell's Belle Watling in *Gone with the Wind.*
16. Wood sees the sentimental novel as dealing in a disguised way with a power struggle between the sexes in which the outcome is predictable (1972, 10).
17. Compare with the etiquette books for working women referred to in Chapter 9.
18. See Chapter 22 for the growing challenge of the "taking care" ethos.
19. See Chapter 19 for lore on this topic in female culture.
20. Wood lists ten of the best-known local colorists as representative: Alice Brown (1857-1948); Rose Terry Cooke (1827-1892); Mary Wilkin Freeman (1852-1930); Sarah Orne Jewett (1849-1909); Celia Thaxter (1835-1894); Kate Chopin (1851-1904); Grace King (1851-1932); Mary Murfree (1850-1922); Ruth M. Stuart (1849-1917); and Constance Femimore Woolson (1840-1894) (1972, 13-14).
21. *Frankenstein*, according to Fiedler, was designed to shock the bourgeoisie into seeing its smug world as a chamber of horrors (117).
22. Gladstone's nightly search of the streets of London for prostitutes to redeem has also been seen as supplying latent sexual excitement along with manifest do-goodism.

23. Other writers of gothic tales, on the other hand, reject this form. Phyllis Whitney comes "to the defense of the innocent 'Gothic,' " telling us that "not one heroine in any of my books has ever been raped. This is true of most writers in our field" (1979, 25). Another, Barbara Michaels, writes: "I've been writing Gothic novels for more than 15 years, and I've never written a rape scene" (1979, 25.).
24. Schoolgirls in the nineteenth century used to hide the novels of George Sand under their mattresses because they were forbidden. Other gothic and sentimental novels no doubt suffered the same fate.
25. The maiden-in-flight might be viewed as the female counterpart of the Rip Van Winkle myth of the male-in-flight, called to our attention by Fiedler. The maiden could not escape from domesticity on her own, as a man might, but she could do so by way of abduction.
26. Although Craik wrote fifty-two books, she is best known for a melancholy fable, *The Little Lame Prince*. Her *John Halifax* (1856) is still in print in England.
27. An interesting example of one difference between the male and the female perspective in art is offered by the case of Judy Chicago's magnum opus, "The Dinner Party." In male paintings, breasts and buttocks are apotheosized; the vulva as a subject has been left to the pornographers. In Chicago's work the vulva appears as a beautiful, delicate flower, viewed aesthetically rather than pornographically. Whether intended or not, the result in effect destroys the pornographic value of the pictures in Larry Flynn's *Hustler* magazine.
28. Some years ago in an unpublished study I reported on all the mother-child pictures that I could find, from the earliest madonna-and-child paintings down to contemporary advertisements. In the earliest ones it was almost impossible to distinguish where one figure left off and the other began; mother and child were a single entity. In some of the pictures the child gazed up at his mother; in others he gazed calmly out at the world. In the advertisements of the 1950s, the mothers were holding the child out in front, emphasizing his separate identity. One nineteenth-century Picasso was especially interesting. The upper part of the child's body is in the traditional close body-contact position; the lower part is turned away from the mother, reflecting a kind of schizoid relationship of both closeness and distance.

19

Popular and Folk Culture

Women's Magazines

We noted in Chapter 18 that many of the authors of novels in the nineteenth century were also writing short stories for magazines. Mrs. Southworth and Mary J. Holmes were, in fact, pitted against one another by the *Ledger* and the *New York Weekly* in the competition for readers. For the social history of female culture a great deal can thus be quarried out of the run of the mill contents of women's magazines. We noted in Chapter 17 what Cowan learned from studying the advertisements in women's magazines.[1] The fiction in these magazines is equally illuminating.

The short stories in these magazines were written according to a formula. Whether by men or by women, they were tailored to specifications laid down by mainly male editors. Thus, in 1890 the criteria for the short story laid down by *The Ladies' Home Journal* were that: "(a) it must interest you; (b) it must show the bright rather than the dark side of life; (c) it must glorify virtue in women and honor in men; (d) the good must be rewarded and the wicked punished; (e) it must make you feel that you are meeting real people who elevate your thoughts; (f) it must be the kind of book that you can give your daughter, one that will point the way to a noble life" (Cohn, 1943, 199-200). Cohn concluded that a half century later this was still the formula for fiction in women's magazines. Of the two great themes of short stories, romantic love and adventure, the first has been especially characteristic of those written by and for women.

Cohn, reviewing a century of magazine fiction, found the year 1888 to be a kind of turning point, as indicated by the stories in *Godey's Lady's Book.* He arrived at this conclusion by examining three representative tales, two published in 1878 and one in 1888. In one 1878 story, "the heroine, grave, cold, and unmarried at twenty-eight, gives up her fiancé without a struggle and practically forces her younger sister upon him as she tells him that she is middle-aged and unattractive" (185). In the second 1878 story, Becky, a hired girl, nurses a male victim of a train wreck who is unconscious most of the time. When he recovers he thanks her tenderly and promises to return. He never does, of course, but the hired girl dwells content for the rest of her life in memory of the one month when "she had tasted the happiness of heaven," the one month in which "she had had her 'story' " (187). "The mere act of waiting on a man [even an unconscious one!] was supposed to lift her into a higher sphere, and the privilege of loving him—[even] if unloved in return—was enough to give her a satisfied peace for life" (187). The third story, published in 1888, "is so different in tone, manner, and morals from its predecessors that a hundred years seem to have passed" (188). "How Lutie Managed It" is about a woman's revolt against the drudgery of rural housekeeping. Lutie marries Will and comes to his farm only to find housekeeping involves more than collecting ferns and sketching. Baking, cooking, cleaning, preserving are just too much. And when she sees Annie, her sister-in-law, toiling from four in the morning until ten at night she is shocked. "Lutie! Lutie!" Annie cries, "If it wasn't for the children I'd pray to be at rest in the churchyard" (188). Lutie lays down the gauntlet to her husband: servants and leisure or no more marriage. She wins. Not only for herself but also for Annie. No suggestion is made that husbands share the labor. No mention of more labor-saving appliances; just a shifting of the drudgery from one woman to another. But the general idea was radical enough to seem revolutionary.

Cohn contrasts these stories with stories published in the 1940s. "In the 1870s women lived and breathed for men, surrendered their happiness to a man's caprice, and were supposed to regard youth and beauty as fleeting gifts. Men could do no wrong; they were the bestowers of light whom women should be glad to serve as superior beings. 'Women age more rapidly than men,' says Margaret,' " in one of the stories. "Now it is the other way around" (186). But when Cohn actually analyzes the 1940s stories the heroines do not seem, after all, to have come such a long way. He summarizes the doctrines espoused by women's magazines: "(a) a woman's place is in the home; preferably a home where she can have lots and lots of nice babies; (b) . . . even if a woman is singularly gifted—as for surgery—she would be more content removing eyes from potatoes in her own little kitchen than appendixes from patients in a hospital; (c) . . . beautiful women are ill-advised to enter the professions, while plain ones take refuge in them as in a cloister; and (d) . . . even beautiful and gifted women long for what you—the reader—already have. Namely, a husband and a home, and therefore any housewife is better off than this talented but thwarted woman" (198-199).

Cohn ends with a kind of requiem for the female reader's mental and emotional life: "You are saddened when you think how many women living on a diet of women's magazines—fed but not nourished—fall victims to mental pellagra. You are depressed when you realize that those who swallow their fiction pills undoubtedly feel a momentary glow, only to be let down in the end because they have derived little from their reading which enriches their lives or squares with experience" (205).

Two decades later, in 1963, a bombshell was to explode in the form of another examination of women's magazines, this time by an ardent feminist, Betty Friedan. She unmasked the feminine mystique as implictly and explicitly taught in their contents. In 1939, she found, the heroines of stories in the four major women's magazines (*Ladies' Home Journal, McCall's, Good Housekeeping, Woman's Home Companion*) "were career women—happily, proudly, adventurously, attractively career women—who loved and were loved by men" (1963, 38). As nurses, teachers, artists, actresses, copywriters, saleswomen, they showed spirit, courage, independence, determination, strength of character. Although there was usually a love story involved, the major theme was one of women "marching toward some goal or vision of their own, struggling with some problem of work or the world" (38). These women—Friedan labels them "New Women"—were rarely housewives. The New Woman did not necessarily lose her man by her commitment to her work. Friedan reminds us that these stories were not written for career women but for housewives. "The New Woman heroines were the ideal of yesterday's housewifes; they reflected the dreams, mirrored the yearning for identity and the sense of possibility that existed for women then" (40). If the reader could not achieve the goals of the career-woman heroines, at least she dreamed of them for her daughters. The last example of the New Woman Friedan found in the women's magazines was in 1949. Thereafter she disappeared from the scene. "By the end of 1949, only one out of three heroines in the women's magazines was a career woman—and she was shown in the act of renouncing her career and discovering that what she really wanted to be was a housewife" (44). A decade later, Friedan found not a single heroine with a commitment to any kind of work, art, profession, or mission; only one in a hundred heroines had a job (44).[2]

On the basis of the stories of the 1950s, Friedan reports that "the image of American women seems to have suffered a schizophrenic split" (46). The heroine as a separate self disappears, even as the subject of her own story. "The end of the road is togetherness, where the woman has no independent self to hide even in guilt; she exists only for and through her husband and children" (47).

Friedan's passion was one of the first signs of the renascence of the feminist movement. She did not condone even the momentary glow from the fiction pills. They were no longer to serve as unchallenged placebos. Still, the addiction remained. Among the preliminary findings of a current unpublished study of women's magazines was that although their editorial contents have kept pace with modern trends of thought about women, their fiction has retained a more traditional flavor (Cantor, forthcoming).

The Trues

The era of the "Trues" began soon after World War I.[3] Although the contents of the stories in the slick women's magazines may change with the times, there is a genre—originated in 1919 with *True Story*—which retains an almost total preoccupation with the central core of the lives of its many readers: religion, babies, marital problems, sexual problems. Since the stories in the Trues are presumed autobiographical, the names of the authors are not published. The readers of the Trues, as described by the editor of a number of them, are remarkably conservative. They are young, under thirty-two, with incomes of $8,000 to $10,000, most with high-school education, and a "fair share" with some college exposure; some are in rural, especially Bible-belt, communities. This editor believes the stories she publishes paint a fairly accurate picture of the kind of lives these women lead, their values, their preoccupations. Her readers substantiate her belief. "This could be my story," they often write to tell her. If this is in fact the case, here is the kind of women they are: "not in the least ashamed when they engage in what used to be known as illicit sex; most anxious to marry and have children; thoroughly, overwhelmingly, and frighteningly dependent on men for their emotional well-being; beginning to make a few small stabs at independence, and certain that a divine, benign deity watches over their every move, so that everything will turn out for the best" (Bachrach, 1978). If these readers really do represent young women today, they have not come a long way at all. They do not, in fact, come through as much different from Cohn's heroines of the 1870s or Friedan's of 1950. Still, there are those "few small stabs at independence."

The Pervading Sadness of Female Literary Culture

Ruth Benedict characterized Dobuan culture as hostile, suspicious, paranoid; Kwakiutl culture as competitive; Zuñi culture as blandly ceremonial (1934, 23). If it is possible or legitimate to characterize such "patterns" of culture, then female culture as reflected in female writings may be described as basically sad. Although happy endings have characterized women's fiction—sometimes as in Becky's case in 1878, not really happy, just made to seem so—they are not arrived at without a painful struggle. There is relatively little humor, irony, sarcasm, sardonicism, or cynicism in women's fiction. There is a great deal of pain and grief, however glossed. The pervasive mood is sadness. Female culture reflects the "worlds of pain" (Rubin, 1976) in which its women readers live.

Few women have written in the comedic vein; few comedians are women. Music-hall entertainers in the nineteenth century could make a male audience laugh and in the late 1970s female stand-up comedians were beginning to appear in night clubs and on television. Their style was fresh and their materials often genuinely funny. Their targets included, among other female-oriented experiences, advertisements addressed to women, marital complications, pregnancy, virginity, drugs, the insensitivity of men, the seduction techniques of men. There were rapier thrusts, as when the response to an advertisement in which a woman is humiliated by the ring around her husband's collar asks in turn why he didn't wash his neck (originally published in *Ms.* magazine). Erma Bombeck was developing her own comedic genre which gently poked fun at the thousands of frustrating details of daily domestic life. But there are as yet few popular female humor magazines.

Much of the comedic material in the culture of the female world is written by men. A great deal of the humor of America's most popular female television comedian, Carol Burnett, is based on bitter, cruel sketches in which an elderly crone makes fun of her husband's impotence, or in which mother-and-daughter set-tos result in mutual psychological mauling. Or, in the case of another famous comedian, Lucille Ball, it was about a daffy woman forever becoming involved in idiotic situations. This was not female humor but the humor of male writers vis-à-vis women. As is the humor about mothers-in-law, golddiggers, and all the other stock female characters of male culture.

The Soaps: Radio and Television

The soap opera—watched by an estimated 22 million people daily—is the oral and, in the case of television, also the visual counterpart of the Trues. More than a generation ago it was already being called "the most popular form of entertainment ever devised . . . a form prepared for and wallowed in almost entirely by women" (Cohn, 1943, 129). Like novel reading, listening to soap operas on radio or watching them on television was another use to which the time saved by household technology was put. Cohn explains the popularity of the soaps as due to the relief they offer to the tedium of the housewife's day and to the fact that by watching the suffering of other women she can feel relatively well off by comparison (137).

Lopate contrasts the soaps with another popular entertainment, the game show, which is an intrusion from the male world. The game show often degrades the participants. "For the game shows, the focus of both the eroticism and the infantilization is the M.C., with his power to bestow goods. In a world which can grant more [commodities] than one could ever want, the response of child-like excitement is the signal that the contestants willingly give up their autonomy, isolation, and potential power for the privilege of being taken care of" (Lopate, 1976, 80). The viewer is in the position of being invited to enjoy the degradation of her sisters. The same cannot be said of soaps.

The soap opera, even when written by men, may be viewed as a bona fide component of female culture. It may violate all the canons of ordinary everyday life, but it does faithfully reflect the traditional love-and/or-duty ethos of the female world, as well as its kin- and-locale orientation.

Cohn, analyzing the contents of radio soap operas a generation ago, found the formula to include this basic love-and/or-duty component. The heroine, for example, shows a "gluttonous desire for self-sacrifice"; she "neglects her own headache and goes around curing the headaches of others" (134-135). There must, of course, also be a romantic interest, but the heroine must "suffer and suffer," for "every problem is a woman's problem" (134).

Kin are also fundamental components of the soaps. Family members "interact, connect up and form new families, and break up and go back to their families of origin. Inside the soaps, there is no way to be outside a family" (Lopate, 76). Thus, "the family of origin holds solid when the children's marriages break. When trouble arises between parents, the children gather together. A breakup in a marriage is never definitive or permanent. Sisters and brothers, in-laws and exmates, are continually involved in each other's lives. Ties of kinship and affinity are the determining structures" (76). It is, in brief, the kind of world most women long for, "a world where husbands and wives still talk to each other after years of marriage, where brothers care for sisters, and where children concern themselves with the lives of their parents. The main concern of people's lives—whether they are women or men—is their relationships with those who are dear to them" (79).[4]

The soaps also reflect the locale aspect of Gemeinschaft. Propinquity is of the essence. Most take place in small towns or suburban areas, and characters who live in cities are "within close proximity to one another. Dropping in on a friend, relative, or lover is always possible" (79). Personal communication is always available. People are not separated by great distances; the logistics of interrelationships are simple. Thus "everyone—not just women—has time to deal with the personal and emotional problems of those who are dear to them. . . . There is always time to talk, to get things straight" (78) and straightened out.

Such emphasis on kinship and locale in television soap opera, it must be pointed out, does not result from the insights of their authors or producers. The Gemeinschaft world of the soaps may, to be sure, be dictated to some degree by the nature of the female world of its viewers, but it reflects even more powerfully the nature of the medium itself. Some of the emphasis placed on the strength of kinship ties "emanates from the necessities of designing continuity into a soap opera. There can be only a limited number of characters if the soap is to hold together dramatically over time. Characters who go off to work or marry someone outside the primary network would either be lost to the story or would create an ever increasing addition of new characters. When a new character does enter the soap, it is often as a primary character's new romance, ward, or mate. Thus, the soap opera as a genre is based on the lives of two or three families" (76). The same structural limitations dictate the emphasis on locale. The characters cannot be too dispersed. They have to be available. "Dropping in" is an essential ploy. As a result, "the characters do not have to suffer the isolation and aloneness that is part of the adult state as we know it" (81). But neither do they achieve the rewards of adult power and autonomy.

As illustrative of the lives lived in the soap operas, the events in two of them during one week are offered here. The date happened to be 1978 but it could just as well have been 1977 or, for that matter, 1984.

> Steven in "The Doctors" does not share Carolee's enthusiasm for her career. Doreen is ill but refuses to see a doctor. Steve promises to keep her illness a secret. Nola is working on her problem with alcohol. Dorothea persuades Greta to have natural childbirth.
>
> Faith of "Ryan's Hope" dreads the thought that her pregnancy will trap her with Tom forever. Dee swears out a complaint against a man who robbed her and attempted rape. On the pleasanter side, she enjoys a reun-

> ion with an old friend, Siobhon. But Siobhon has given Johnny an Irish wolfhound as a gift, which displeases Maeve and Mary. Nancy's father encourages her interest in Pat.

A third vignette is an account not of a week in a television soap but in a real-life situation. These events happened in a real family:

> Arlene learns that Alison has surrendered all the property rights the court granted her in her divorce. She makes plans for Alison and the three children to come to live with her in her new home. The three little girls are delighted to be away from the mobile home park. Two days later Alison leaves the new home giving no address where she can be reached. The children are grief-stricken, crying a good deal of the time. Arlene takes custody of the children when she learns that Alison has returned to Michael, a man with a prison record and into drugs. When Alison learns of the loss of custody, she returns home, badly beaten up. Arlene makes arrangements for her to get into a therapy group at a local women's center. When Alison leaves again, Arlene has her committed to a hospital where she can secure treatment for severe depression and suicidal tendencies.

Millions of women follow the trauma in the lives of the characters in soaps. Like the real-life story recounted above, they reflect the nitty-gritty, the dense matted fiber of relationships they all know. These are experiences that they have had, or that someone they know —a friend, sister, daughter—has had, experiences that constitute a large part of the life of many women in the female world.

Cohn wondered why women did not protest the soaps' insult to their intelligence. Still, he did note that even in the 1940s such protests were beginning. "A large number of women . . . have publicly denounced soap-opera sponsors for 'underestimating the nation's taste and intelligence,' for 'stupidity,' and for not 'knowing women' " (139). And *Time* Magazine in May, 1942, was expressing the belief that a change was coming: "Little by little, with gingerly audacity, CBS has been edging toward a radio revolution, based on the radical assumption that listeners—even housewives—have brains" (quoted in Cohn, 128).

From Cantor's analysis of the industry, the failure of that "gingerly audacity" could have been predicted.[5] The structure of the industry itself renders change almost impossible. In the 1940s as now, "the sponsors said nothing in reply but merely looked at the charts of their rising sales and so were content. . . . Using air-waves that are not God's gift to them or to soap manufacturers but that, theoretically, are the possession of the people," they justify this debauchery of public taste by pointing out that these profitable programs subsidize the high-culture programs offered in the evening (Cohn, 137-138). The protests against the radio soap operas, beginning to build a generation ago, have now taken a more structured form, including as targets not only the image of women the soaps project but also the organizational structure of the industry that makes it so resistant to change.[6]

Cinema

Although daytime theater and moving picture audiences tend to include many women, neither theater nor cinema for the most part reflects female culture accurately, let alone sympathetically. There have been relatively few women dramatists or producers—Rowson was one of those few—and the work of women—such as Lillian Hellman, Clare Boothe Luce, Elaine May, Ida Lupino, and Lina Wertmuller—has not portrayed the world women live in from their own point of view. It has taken over the male perspective on the human scene, often even expressing male-type contempt for the female characters, as, for example, in *The Little Foxes, The Women*, and *Swept Away*.

In recent years there has been considerable feminist interest in the nature of the female characters portrayed in moving pictures. Joan Mellen notes, for example, that "one searches in vain in the contemporary cinema for a new perception of women which assumes their capacities and value. An international and rapidly developing women's movement has induced the cinema to be only slightly more self-conscious about its patronizing and hostile portrayal of women as flawed creatures" (1973, 15). It is, however, only the packaging, not the message itself that has changed. "Simpering dependence, subordination" are replaced by more toughness and less demureness, but emotional emptiness is still the message. Although in the 1940s, Hollywood was producing stories about strong, autonomous career women "in open struggle to assert the right to such aspirations and showing boundless energy in achieving them" (17), Mellen attributes the success of these films to the times when women were needed in the labor force and their abilities were therefore encouraged and appreciated. But in the 1950s cinema female characters were again "simpering, dependent hysterics" or "undulating sexual manikins" (24). In so-called "new" films, "women are no longer coy, but they lack all personal integrity" (25). No replacement for the relinquished "place" in the home has been found. Women have not achieved inner peace. They have become shrill and unseemly instead of coy. Pornography and sadism burgeon, "for the counterpart to taming women by making them domestic servants has been the illicit fantasy of women as lascivious gratifiers" (25). The women's movement is coopted, its ideology used against women.

All this male-oriented work is part of the culture of the female world since women as well as men patronize it, though it is not female culture itself, not created by women or representative of their perspective. The female world is, in effect, in a state of cultural seige, helplessly trying to hold back the destructive impact of the image of women. Efforts on the part of organizations of women have not been notably successful.

Songs

Songs offer a somewhat different perspective. A collection by Jean Page (1979) of songs—country, western, gospel—written for and by women singers reveals with vivid rawness the special world of pain these women inhabit. Unfaithful men, deserting men, drunken men, unloving men parade through them. Unappreciated, let alone unrequited, love is a pervasive motif. Kitty Wells sings of the woman who falls to pieces whenever she sees the man who wants them to be just friends as though they had never kissed, or of the woman in a barroom who forgets that she is still a wife and loses her wings, all because of her husband's neglect. Loretta Lynn sings of the woman warning her man not to come home a-drinking with loving on his mind; too many nights she has lain awake crying; if he wants the kind of love he gets out on the town, he doesn't need any of hers. Shel Silverstein sings about the woman who is always pregnant and Lorene Allen of the liberation now possible by way of the pill. Dory Previn sings about the humiliation of women who are dependent on men for their sense of self. But still, despite all these painful trauma, the basic love-and/or-duty ethos persists: take care of men, they're only children after all. Thus Tammy Wynette and Billy Sherill urge women to stand by their man, to give all their love to him. It may be hard to be a woman and men do a lot of things women can't understand. But if a woman loves a man, she should be proud of him because, after all, he's just a man. Dolly Parton sings of the long-suffering wife whose sacrifice and devotion had always been taken for granted and who suddenly, without warning, leaves home for good. A new twist on the old desertion theme. Now it is the wife's turn. Joni Mitchell deals with women with both heart and mind; and her typical protagonist is looking for respect, for affection, even passion, whereas her lover seeks only stimulation. Still, she is always there, in accord with the ethos of female culture, like the woman in the Wynette-Sherill song, to support him when he needs her. Melissa Manchester sings of equality. She sings of a woman and her lover who make it through the night and so, with characteristic optimism, she believes that there are better times ahead (Graustark, 1978, 60). Joan Baez's songs reflect certain philosophical themes in female culture: compassion for the poor and for minorities.

Quite different is the perspective available from a study by Mary Hornby of forty lesbian love songs. "What is reflected in the published lesbian love songs are the words and impressions of women who live in a female world sung to other women living in their own forms of the female world. This continuity of the female experience creates the space for peculiarly female notions of love and relationships" (Hornby, 1978, draft). One lesbian group, The Deadly Nightshade, sings satirical songs. The lesbian poets have found the answer to the old dilemma. They do not have to choose between love and art. They can embrace both. They have found their creative community. In Gabelnick's words, they have connected with one another, yet remain individuals.

Hornby finds four primary relationships pervading lesbian poetry —mother, sister, lover, and friend—each including aspects of each of the others. Lovers are nurturing and comforting, like a mother. They comfort, hold, rock. As among the female utopias (Chapter 21) and in the work of the poets commented on above, home is an important element, as is familiarity also. The themes of trust and continuity are central. Respect and loyalty are important. Lifetime relationships are sought; "forever," "eternity," "infinity" are common time spans. Tenderness and passivity do not exclude strength and independence. Even the admired, self-sufficient lover is expected to need emotional comfort. Seduction rather than conquest is the valued style, mutuality and sharing rather than exploitation are the preferred relationships. All images used are female: soft, voluptuous, never forceful and conquering. Sometimes nonsense syllables or vocal nonwords are used to convey sensation rather than meaning; bird calls and hollers are used to establish a sense of unity beyond words. Sometimes legendary rituals are invoked such as witchcraft, goddess worship, black magic, African spirituals.

Oral Folk Culture

Before universal literacy, oral story telling, singing, tall tales, as well as jokes, yarns, word games, legends, fairy tales, and myths, constituted a rich storehouse of oral folk culture. As well as rich bodies of lore about how to live, and aphorisms, mottoes, and the kinds of reminders of virtue that showed up on samplers. Not to mention superstitions, charms, and protective incantations. A considerable part of this culture must have been by and for women and girls, especially the lore that related to the central core of the female world, namely, childbirth. There had to be ways of dealing with the evil eye if it threatened a child. There had to be "secrets" that produced good bread. Or special ways of taking care of plants and gardens. Unfortunately, female folk culture has been ignored by anthropologists; only now are women beginning to retrieve it. For here, as in high culture, the application of male standards and criteria has tended to seive the distinctly female products out of the research effort. When female folklore has been noted at all, it has been downplayed. "Usually in Western societies it is the male genres that have been used to define the recognized universe of artistic expression within a group. . . . Female experience forms either fit the male mold or they are relegated to a non-legitimate, less-than-experience category" (Farrer, 1975, xv-xvi). Even women, if they have been trained by men, see the female world contemptuously, as when "womantalk" is characterized as "bitchery" (Chapter 16). What, for example, might be viewed as a "tall tale" among men would be dismissed as mere exaggeration among women; stories and yarns that among men were likely to be viewed respectfully among women were likely to be viewed as mere gossip or "clotheslines" and hence unworthy of scientific attention (xvi).

Kalcik calls our attention to the fact that in the study of folklore—where ignoring women would seem to be least likely—female stories have been dismissed as not "real" stories but "just gossip" or "women's talk" (1975, 7, 11). When a woman folklorist studied them she found them quite valid, "a uniquely women's genre" whose structure paralleled "the rhythm of many women's lives, filled . . . with small tasks and constant interruptions from children, husbands, telephone repairmen." She could see their structure as "a group product" with "roots in women's sense of powerlessness and their realization that they need to work together" (11). Such an insight was seived out of the male folklorist's net.

Other selective processes were also at work. Hertha Grudde, for example, offers another reason why tales told by women have not appeared in folk research. The culprit was not always the tunnel vision of the male researcher. Sometimes it was the shyness of the women themselves, especially in responding to male questioners. In her own work on Low German tales, she had to work out special ways "to discover the women story-tellers, . . . to overcome their shyness and their fear that they were being held up to ridicule" (Thompson, 1946, 411-412).

Still, despite initial blind spots, some male scholars have given us appreciative portraits of female tellers of folk tales. Stith Thompson writes that in some societies (Ireland) men tell the folk tales; in others (East Prussia) women do (Thompson, 1946, 408). And "some collectors have found interesting stylistic differences in the stories told by men and by women" (453). Thompson presents a case in point, comparing the styles of a male and a female folk-tale teller. He found the male's story "full of many subjects, and rich in added episodes and details"

(453), the female's "meager in details, unified, and self-sufficient" (453). The male, interestingly, had only four tales, but he elaborated them in such detail that they took up ten times as much space as the female's did in the researcher's notes. Some of these differences may result from a kind of specialization by sex, so that certain kinds of tales may be told only by men, others only by women (453).

Thompson analyzes one female tale-teller who occupied a very special position.

> She is not much concerned with the tricks of Marchen style, its formulas and repetitions. She often summarizes events rather than narrating them at length and she is not always careful to preserve the traditional story intact. With these negative [according to male criteria?] qualities it would hardly seem possible that she should be a great narrator. Her power lies in two directions. She visualizes her characters so that they take on life. The supernatural is so minimized that even in that realm ordinary human life is imagined. Her realization of the dramatic situation comes from her interest in the background and the psychology of the action. She fills the tale with homely details of life as she has known it as servant girl and as housewife. Her knowledge of the experiences of the exiles in prison and in their later life crops out in many a scene. She thinks of every important episode dramatically and describes all the psychological reactions. In short, for her the folktale is a form of living art and she puts into the telling of it all her knowledge of life and understanding of human nature. Perhaps this is as far as such a traditional form can be modified by the individual tale-teller without changing its entire nature and becoming creative literature. [Thompson, 453]

This female tale-teller, in brief, has taken the folk form up to the very boundary of individual—as contrasted with folk—creativity. She improvises, bored with the traditional stylized tricks, formulas, and repetitions; she dramatizes, playing up the psychological aspect of the action. She even demystifies the supernatural, reducing it to ordinary human life. Servant girl, housewife, and exile in prison, she knows them all. All this unencumbered with details, coherent, complete in itself. There must have been a great many such talented tellers of folk tales in the long millennia before literacy transformed the creative scene.

Although mothers must have been important sources and bearers of fairy tales, the great compilations have been made by men so that in their literary, as distinct from their folk, form, they reflect a male image of the female world. It is a world filled with wicked witches, cruel stepmothers, mean sisters, cheating mothers on one side and helpless victims who have to be rescued by valiant heroes on the other. Farrer quotes Ferris to the effect that "if past folklore studies . . . had been done by women rather than men, an extensive 'feminine' tradition . . . might have been recorded" (xi). Only now are feminist scholars attempting to correct the balance by offering traditional folk tales culled from a variety of cultures about women who are clever, witty, resourceful, strong, courageous, achieving, and successful, with "role models a-plenty."[7]

There is undoubtedly a vast folk world still waiting to be explored, not only coming down from preliteracy times but also expressing itself all around us today. Beverly J. Stoeltje, for example, has delineated a female genre which she labels the "kernel story" and has illustrated it in connection with the frontier experience. She found three female types in these stories—the refined lady, the helpmate, and the bad woman—and also three male types—the cowboy, the settler, and the bad man. Out of these six components came an image of the frontier that finds expression to this day in cinema, television, and novels. She found practically no conversation between the sexes (1975, 25-41). Farrer quotes Kalcik, who has studied *kaffee klatsches* (female supermarket and park-bench talk) and finds them characterized by a peculiarly female style which she calls a "collaborative genre," in which "the performer role is passed from one group member to another, often in what appears to be in the middle of an utterance" (xvi-xvii).[8] (This style seems to relate to the style of interaction noted in Chapter 16 in which the listener builds on, rather than challenges, the speaker.)

Female Lore

Lore has a distinguished etymology. The term once referred to learning, erudition. It has now been reduced to "a body of traditional facts or beliefs and superstitions about whatever subject." And because it is traditional, it withstands scientific assault. One knocks on wood whether or not one accepts the lore that explains the practice. Lore includes knowledge based on personal experience—one's own or someone else's, taken on faith—and the wisdom distilled from that experience. It may deal with almost anything—love, marriage, weddings, motherhood, the body, menstruation, relations with men—that concerns the major foci of female life.

Signs and tests of love are important. So are dreams. They help a girl learn who loves her. The moon is important in the lore about love, as are other odds and ends such as snails, four leaf clovers, amulets, cats, what have you. There is a voluminous folklore dealing with weddings. For the bride, "Something old, Something new, Something borrowed, Something blue, And a new dime in the shoe." Salt in the glove is also advised. All fun and games today, but once taken quite seriously.

Anything related to menstruation has, until recently, been exclusively a topic for the female world and hardly even allowed there. The monthly flux is mysterious enough to mothers themselves. The chances are that the girl will learn about it from peers or sisters, along with a considerable amount of lore.[9] With the relentless barrage of advertisements for everything from sanitary pads to "feminine hygiene" products and with books streaming from the presses on everything from contraception to orgasm, it would seem that there is nothing left for female lore to transmit orally from one female to another. Still, well-hidden, there remains the unwritten knowledge or wisdom or superstitions that women have accumulated from one another and passed on. Kalcik found a number of such items in her study of rap sessions. "When I had my first period, my mother told me I would have to stop jumping rope, so for a long time I thought if I wasn't careful my stomach would fall out somehow" (Farrer, 1976, 4). Other examples of the lore transmitted among females: "I thought that if you had sex on Sunday you could never get pregnant." "If you dance around after intercourse, it's almost impossible to get pregnant."

Equally interesting has been the lore about men and marriage handed down from mothers to daughters. It teaches that men are undependable, irresponsible, unreliable. Lurking in the dark underground of female lore there still remains the old seduction theme of the sentimental novel: "Never trust men as far as you can throw them. . . . Men want only one thing;[10] watch out. All they want is to take advantage of you" (Pildes, 1977). But also present is the "taking care" motif Spacks found in the novel. Women, Pildes says, "are taught to consider men . . . insensitive, emotionally inadequate and highly needful of nurturing and pampering, requiring special handling like babies or convalescents." Other examples of alleged female lore include such items as: "Men may play around with fast girls, but they marry the conventional ones"; "don't be too free and easy with men or they'll take advantage of you"; "be coy"; "play hard to get"; "it's just as easy to fall in love with a rich man as with a poor one"; "make him pay for your favors"; "don't have sexual relations with a man until he has committed himself."[11] Pildes found that women were shown "how to trick men, how to demonstrate false affection and/or sexual passion, how to trap them into giving money and social security." It is the long shadow of the old nineteenth-century sentimental novel neatly preserved in modern dress. Not, on second thought, very modern after all.

One of the interesting trends today is the slashing attack some women are making on the female lore which, in their opinion, has had hurtful rather than helpful effects on them. The vast mother-lore, for example, which seized on the love-and/or-duty core of the female ethos and apotheosized motherhood, has come in for serious criticism (by men, it may be noted, as well as by women). Mother-love, taken for granted along with the love due to mothers by their children, has been vehemently challenged. "I have always lied to my mother. And she to me. How young was I when I learned her language, to call things by other names?" is the way one book begins (Friday, 1977, 1). The lack of transmitted lore is now played up. The silences, that is, rather than articulateness, about femaleness. Modern women are attempting to replace the lore based on the angelic mother of the nineteenth century, on the cult of true womanhood, with a more modern conception of lore, one more consonant with its original meaning of learning, erudition.

Women in all aspects of culture at the present time are engaged in a great effort at self-understanding. They have known themselves only through male eyes for so long that it is difficult for them to learn to see themselves through their own, to understand their own experiences, to define themselves, to come to terms with themselves. They are so used to old ways that they are sometimes frightened at what they learn about themselves and the implications of this new knowledge. Like blacks, homosexuals, Jews, and other minorities, women have tended to be self-hating for so long that they find it hard to be themselves. They tremble at the thought of facing up to male misogyny. They are fearful of the price they may have to pay for the self-knowledge which is said to set one free. It will take some time before all the forces work themselves through. Female culture both reflects and charts the course these forces are taking. In any event, female culture will never be the same again.

Notes

1. The power of the advertisers extends beyond their impact on sales. Gloria Steinem tells us that "publications for women are expected to offer 'supportive editorial copy' to complement ads for such products as clothes, food, or cosmetics. . . . This dependence on ad content also explains why the editors of other women's magazines, even those newer ones for 'career women,' have been largely unable to do without cooking, fashion, and beauty articles" (1979, 6). Fiction is quite secondary as a clue to female culture. It is merely a ploy to attract readers of advertisements. The new magazines Steinem refers to include: *Self, McCall's Working Mother, Working Woman, Women Who Work,* and *New Woman.* The audiences they reach are minuscule compared with those of the "seven sisters: *Family Circle, Good Housekeeping, Redbook, McCall's, Ladies' Home Journal, Better Homes and Gardens,* and *Woman's Day*" (Unsigned, 1979, 64).

   The new magazines are beamed to special rather than, like the old ones, to general audiences. *Self,* dedicated to fitness, is aimed at "the woman who wants to be good at everything, and has to keep physically and emotionally fit to do her best" (65). Its chief competitor is *Cosmopolitan. New Woman* aims to help "women find out who they want to become and then helping them become what they want" (132). *McCall's Working*

Mother is "tailored to their [working mothers'] main need—time—and their main desire—family" (123). The reader is younger than the reader of the older magazines, more career-oriented, better educated, and with a higher income. *Working Woman*, the fastest growing magazine in the country, is aimed at the same readers as *Cosmopolitan* and intended to help "working women with information on how to advance and giving them reassurance and inspiration" (137). *Savvy* is directed to the executive woman but is designed to be more than an office manual (138). From the point of view of the advertiser, magazines are judged almost exclusively in terms of how many potential consumers they can deliver. "Lifestyle has become more important than traditional demographics" (140). When queried about the appropriateness of cigarette ads in a fitness magazine, the editor commented, "We're greedy" (132). The same picture of advertising impact could be painted in the case of television.

2. It is interesting to note that the stories Friedan was analyzing were far from imitating life. Just as the heroines were retreating into the home, women in real life were beginning to stream into the labor force.
3. There are several groups of Trues. One—the McFadden trues—is edited by Florence J. Moriarty and consists of: *True Love, True Romance, True Confessions, Modern Romances, Secrets, True Story,* and *True Experience.* Another, from Sterling Library, is edited by Susan Silverman and includes *Real Confessions* and *Modern Love.* Others are *True Romantic Confessions* and *Secret True Confessions* (Bachrach, 1978).
4. Relations between members of the same sex are rarely discussed in the soaps; if they are, it may be in connection with a third person they are both fighting for. But commiseration is shown in times of stress. Especially fulfilling for women viewers are stories in which men commiserate with one another about the loss of a dearly loved wife (Lopate, 1976, 80).
5. Muriel Cantor summarizes numerous studies of the contents of television programs. Except for the soaps, all show a preponderance of male characters (draft, 1978). The women are in limited and less prestigious roles. They are presented "as lacking independence." They are rarely shown in nontraditional occupations.

   The portrayal of women in television commercials has been made an issue by women's groups who have used their research in challenging the licensing of certain channels. Four such studies, as summarized by Cantor, "provide evidence that women are not portrayed as autonomous, independent human beings, but are primarily sex-typed. . . . Advertisers are lagging far behind [real-life] role changes in their portrayal of women." Later studies bringing the data up to 1978 report little change. Despite recent agitation by women's groups, the prospects for change are not encouraging. If anything, things are getting worse. For "although there is a new kind of woman out in the real world, her image is not being portrayed. Moreover, the gap between reality and what the media portray is widening" (George Gerbner, quoted by Cantor, 1978).
6. Cantor asks: If more women were creating and producing television programs, would it make a difference? She concludes that it would not. Women creators and producers would be as subject to the norms of this male-

oriented industry as men are. "It is unlikely that programming will change unless there are important structural changes in the way television is produced." She then adds: "Two things are working against change: one is the deep-seated cultural tradition for the subservience of women, and the other is the way the broadcast industry is structured. Entrenched bureaucracies are difficult to penetrate. With the industry contracting production and with the networks able to control the prime-time schedule, the prospects for change are limited." The same kinds of structural barriers may, with modification, be applied to other areas of culture.

7. One such book, edited by Ethel Johnston Phelps, is called *Tatterhood and Other Tales* (Feminist Press, 1978). The publishers tell us that "the stories . . . were chosen for a special characteristic that singles them out from other fairy and folk tales. The protagonists are heroines in the true and original meaning of the word—heroic women distinguished by extraordinary courage and achievements" (intro.).
8. Kalcik found the darker side of oral female culture in the content of rap sessions: low salaries, slow promotion, humiliations, disparaging treatment by male professors and by other students in school, difficult situations with dating, marriage, living together. There was also self-discovery involving the exchange of information on physiology, about which many of the women seemed poorly informed.
9. See, for example, Delaney, Lupton, and Toth, *The Curse, A Cultural History of Menstruation* (New York: Mentor, 1976). The subject seems to have preoccupied men more than women.
10. So widespread is this bit of lore that when the editors of *True* wanted a catchy title for one of their stories, they chose "He's Marrying You for Only One Thing." But it turned out to be that the "one thing" in this case was simply immigration papers.
11. Richard Dawkins, a sociobiologist, has also worked out a logical evolutionary rationale for this body of lore. He classified the behavior prescribed in this lore into two categories: the "domestic-bliss strategy" and the "he-man strategy," finding an evolutionary basis for both. In the animal world, the first category attempts before copulating to test the male for his patience, fidelity, and willingness to share in the rearing of offspring. "Any male who is not patient enough to wait until the female eventually consents to copulate is not likely to be a good bet as a faithful husband. By insisting on a long engagement period, a female weeds out casual suitors, and only finally copulates with a male who has proved his qualities of fidelity and perseverance in advance. Feminine coyness is, in fact, very common among animals, and so are prolonged courtship or engagement periods" (Dawkins, 1978, 161). Some female birds, in fact, refuse to copulate until the male has built them a nest or provided them with a considerable amount of food.

    In the second, or "he-man," strategy, Dawkins continues, having given up the idea of securing help from the father, a female settles for good genes from her mate for her children. "If a female can somehow detect good genes in males, using externally visible clues, she can benefit her own genes by allying them with good paternal genes" (169). What are the criteria she will look for? Survival ability as measured by age, strong muscles, physical attractiveness, ability to win fights, good territory, high status. On the basis of animal behavior, Dawkins thus explains a considerable part of the lore of the female world to his own satisfaction. Still, after having a lot of fun working out his genetic theories he concludes that "man's way of life is largely determined by culture rather than by genes" (177).

20

The Ethos of the Female World: Eros

"EROTIC," THE *OXFORD ENGLISH DICTIONARY* says, means "of or pertaining to the sexual passion," and its entrance into the English language is dated 1651. Eroticism has posed a paradox for women over many decades, for sex and sexuality have tended to be negative values in the female culture of our society. In Hite's survey of almost three thousand women, over 95 percent "indicated that they had been brought up with the idea that sex was 'bad,' or at the very least a subject that was never mentioned—implying that it was bad" (Hite, 1976, xxix). As subjects of sober discussion, sex and sexuality, especially female sex and sexuality, are still taboo in large segments of the female world. Courses in sex education are either banned from many school systems or restricted to anatomy and physiology. Sex-related words are censored on television. Nor, as we have noted, is there even an adequate vocabulary in female culture for discussing female sexual experience.

With so little communication, each woman has tended to feel that she was unique, alone, different in her sexuality. Whole generations did not even know there was such a thing as female orgasm, let alone ever experiencing it. So sexuality came to be defined entirely in terms of male sexuality. "Sex" has meant penetration, the most efficient route to male orgasm but not always the most satisfying for women, rather than the stroking, cuddling, hugging, and caressing that do give women erotic pleasure. Only recently have we learned that relatively few women achieve climax by way of penetration. "Somehow it is all right for a woman to demand equal pay, but to demand equality in sex is not considered valid" (Hite, 1976, 293). To say all this does not deny the overwhelming importance assigned to sex appeal, to beauty, to glamour in female culture, a set of values inextricably tied in with love and romance.

In contrast to the discussion in Chapter 18 of romantic love in the literary culture of the female world, eros is viewed here in a sociological context, especially as related to another basic component of female culture, the quest for beauty.

A Male Preserve

Although some of the greatest love poetry has been written by women—Sappho, for example, and Elizabeth Barrett Browning—most of the writing on the subject of love has been by men and it has been about erotic love in the male world. So also with sex. "Most of the novelistic attitudes toward sex were really set in the second half of the eighteenth century by Richardson's quivering 'feminine' sensibility, Fielding's bluff 'masculine' sensibility, and Sterne's leering lubriciousness" (Freedman, 1978). Byron told women that "man's love is of man's life a thing apart, t'is woman's whole existence." True, it was a woman, Eleanor of Aquitaine, who established the chivalric Courts of Love, but the male troubadors codified, spread, and glorified the lessons they had learned.

To arrive at a female view of the nature of love we might apply a projective test, asking subjects to complete this sentence: "Love is____." The titles of books written by women classified under "love" in the Library of Congress catalogue may, figuratively speaking, be taken as such a projective test of the concept of love in female culture. Love is: a challenge, a fever, a flame, a four-letter word, a funny present, a gamble, a hopscotch thing, a laugh, a light burden, a little child, a pie, a place, a poem, a special way of feeling, a riddle, a wild assault; love is: always new, dangerous, forever, free; an antic, lovely, terrible thing; all, enough; for the living; a certain season; like an acorn; . . . Lovely, that is, but also funny; a thistle, but also a flame; a four-letter word, but also a special way of feeling; antic, but also terrible; a gamble, but also a poem; and so on. In brief, a dream and a nightmare. A fairly accurate reflection of the human condition.

A Paradox

We spoke above of erotic love as presenting a paradox in the female world. The specifically erotic dimension of love has tended to be played down in female culture. There has been, in fact, almost a cult of female virginity before marriage and chastity afterward. A woman might have been mean, despicable, harsh, cold, whatever; but if she was virginal or chaste she was counted a "good" woman. If she was generous, kind, tender but not virginal or chaste she was counted a "bad" woman.[1] We noted in Chapter 4 that women in the nineteenth century were viewed as morally superior to men, especially in the realm of sex. They were therefore the more guilty when they violated the mores. The double standard was justified on these grounds. "It received support . . . from a genuine conviction that women were, naturally and habitually, morally superior to men; and so, much more culpable when they fell. The Victorians no more thought it unfair to blame a woman more than a man for unchastity than a commander-in-chief would think it unfair to punish an officer more severely than a private for running away from the enemy" (Freedman, 1978).

Even today, despite the growing acceptance of eroticism in all the media, the cult of virginity still has wide support in the female world. Ira Reiss has found that women are less permissive in their attitudes toward sexual behavior than are men. There did not seem to be any radical increase in the proportion of nonvirginal women entering marriage in the half-century between the 1920s and the 1970s (1971, 407), but in the 70s the proportion of women engaging in premarital sex relations did increase (Reiss, 1971; Bernard, 1975, 238-240).[2] More interesting as an index of cultural—rather than behavioral—change was the fact that the marital status of young women at sexual initiation was becoming "increasingly irrelevant." There was a great deal of talk about the pros and cons of premarital sex relations, indicating that the cult of virginity had definitely subsided. Still, for a large proportion of women it was still a major value. A substantial proportion of young women interviewed on television were still saying that "they would wait for marriage." The virginal heroines in Barbara Cartland's novels referred to in Chapter 18 remain popular today. But so, of course, do the heroines in the soft porn gothics of Rosemary Rogers. We have, in fact, in Cartland and Rodgers almost archetypical examples of two approaches to erotic love, one supportive of the established status quo and the other subtly subversive of it, "loving" and "being in love."[3]

Erotic love remains in equivocal status in the female world. There is more insistence among women than among men that sexual behavior be accompanied by love or affection. There is fear of male sexuality unaccompanied by feelings of tenderness and warmth. There is repugnance of becoming merely depersonalized "sex objects."

Subversive Love

It is not always easy to figure out what love has really meant in the female world. The Athenians viewed "being in love" as a kind of aberration. This sense is retained in such folk phrases as "mad about you," "crazy about you," "madly in love," "wildly in love," "lovesick," "not in her right senses," "moonstruck," and the like. In another place I once characterized the condition of "being in love" as showing many of the earmarks of trance or dissociation phenomena (Bernard, 1942, 390 ff). The lover often displays illusions, delusions, fixed ideas, compulsions, obsessions, euphoria, elation, and melancholia for shorter or longer periods of time. Sumner pointed out that the Greeks envisioned such a state of madness as inflicted "through the caprice or malevolence of some god or goddess" (1906, 362). Individuals in this condition are called "charmed," or "fascinated," or "bewitched," terms originally implying the intervention of a supernatural power. One "loses" one's head in this condition. The outsider cannot understand what she "sees" in him, or he in her. Shakespeare's Titania falls in love with the donkey-headed Bottom, illustrating in fantasy form some of the symptoms of this aberration. "We often say that a girl is in love with love rather than with the particular man she thinks she loves, or we say that love is blind—Titania does not love the donkey-headed Bottom, she is in love with a self-created illusion" (Bernard, 391).

To a girl in love her man is wonderful, handsome, the epitome of male attractiveness. To the outsider he is just an ordinary man, like millions of others or often a donkey, much worse than most. Attacks of "falling in love" come and go with a rhythm of their own, seemingly independent of outside conditions. The particular man who brings on this state may be more or less accidental; he just happened to be there when the madness struck (Bernard, 392).

No amount of scientific research dispels the folk belief in a kind of "chemistry" between certain individual men and women that attracts them to one another. No amount of sociological or anthropological analysis can theorize this "being in love" out of existence. "Malinowski cites cases . . . among the Trobriand Islanders; some resulted in suicide. Even among the Dobu, where we should scarecely expect a high degree of love, Fortune points out that boys and girls do occasionally defy public opinion and form forbidden alliances" (Bernard, 389).[4] It cannot be legislated out of existence no matter how subversive it may be, not only to a status quo, as in the case of the Montagues and the Capulets, but also to the whole mate selection process and the stability of marriages and families, as in the case of Anna Karenina and Vronsky.

Erotic Love Versus Filial Duty

In traditional families, a young woman might be torn between the love of a man and parental duty. A standard character in old-fashioned stories was the young woman who had to sacrifice marriage to take care of her parents. Even today there are many young women—Jewish, Catholic, ethnic—who explain to young men, "I do love you! But I can't marry you! I just couldn't do that to my parents!" Such a clash between family loyalty and erotic love is an especially poignant form of a classic conflict between role obligations and "human nature," in this case exemplified by love.

In the didactic literature of female culture, choosing duty above love was rewarded, but sometimes in the romantic literature the kudos went to the choice of love over duty. George Sand's novels, for example—indeed, the whole Romantic movement of the early nineteenth century—favored sentiment or love over duty. Thus George Sand taught that the love-motivated hour a woman spent with her paramour was morally superior to the many hours each night she dutifully spent with her husband. A. O. J. Cockshut summarizes the situation in his comments on Jane Austen: "Passionate people are supposed to ignore duty, and dutiful ones are supposed to lack passion. This is a very agreeable doctrine. It suggests to the respectable that they have little passion, and it suggests to the wayward that their moral deviations are due to an excess of passion, that is, to an intenser life. Jane Austen shows that often, and perhaps typically, the reverse is true. Strong characters in her books generally have strong feelings. Weak characters have weak feelings" (quoted by Richard Freedman, 1978).

As a matter of fact, whatever the romantic novels may have taught, when there had been a real-life conflict in the female world, duty, even sacrifice, had tended to weigh more heavily in the balance than erotic love. It was the daughter who gave up marriage to take care of elderly parents. And even in the twentieth century it was, after all, the British princess, not the king, who surrendered love for royal duties. The conflict between love—especially erotic love—and duty still remains.

What our society has done is coopt erotic love. Mate selection was once a family affair, and learning to love the spouse came after rather than before marriage. It still is a family affair in many parts of the world today. Young women students in Beirut, for example, once confided in my then-colleague Margaret Matson, who was teaching there, that they felt sorry for American girls who had to find their own husbands. They themselves were relieved of this onerous task by their families. But in our society "being in love" has been almost the only acceptable reason for marrying. To marry for any other reason is viewed as calculating, cold, wrong. Some feminists object to the notion of love; they see it as a way of persuading women to settle for the illusion of romance rather than autonomy, for a fantasy rather than reality. They see the glorification of romantic love in female culture as a way of conning women into a position in which they are exploited, a way of preventing them from perceiving their status in its true perspective. Still, there seems to be no way to write the values of erotic love and romance and "being in love" out of female culture. Women, for good or ill, are going to "fall in love" with men, whatever the consequences.[5]

Among immigrant groups in the past being a good provider and moderately sober were major qualifications sought in husbands. Marriage was too important to leave to the mercy of romantic love. Too much was at stake. Although "being in love" came to be the conventional reason given for marrying among later generations, in real life young women still knew that when it came to seeking a marriage partner, romantic love was not enough; it was not the only value to seek in a relationship with a man. But desire for release from such restrictions on marital choice is now becoming fairly widespread. It is one of the reasons many young women today seek to achieve economic independence. If a trade-off is needed between economic support and love, they want to be able to choose love.

The degree of eroticism in any male-female relationships may vary. Whether love is possible between men and women without any erotic component has been argued for many years. Can men and women be loving friends with no physical attraction between them? From time to time we hear of brother-sister kinds of relationships between nonrelated men and women, or of male-female friendships that are loving but not erotic. Women sometimes find such relationships with homosexual men. Among the elderly marriage sometimes has a companionable but nonerotic quality. Such nonerotic but loving relationships may be more sought after in the female than in the male world.

Pauline Love

It is interesting to note that in Paul's famous hymn to love, the first part deals with activities that do not constitute love—prophesying, moving mountains, giving away goods, feeding the poor—while the second part deals with passive states that *do* constitute love. The first, male; the second, female. Thus Pauline love is essentially a female kind of love: "Love suffereth long, and is kind; love envieth not; love vaunteth not itself, is not puffed up, doth not behave unseemly, seeketh not its own, is not provoked, taketh not account of evil; rejoiceth not in unrighteousness, but rejoiceth with the truth; beareth all things, believeth all things, hopeth all things, endureth all things. Love never faileth." Whether or not Paul was addressing women here, the ideal he was describing was the embodiment of the love-and/or-duty ethos of the female world.

Personal Beauty as a Value in Female Culture

A motion picture popular some years ago dealt with Bluebeard's eighth wife. At their marriage she demanded that he bestow a fortune upon her. He acceded, thus guaranteeing her economic independence of him. The result was that he never tired of her, as he had of his first seven wives. Truly a cautionary tale. And one that an increasing number of women since the time of Charlotte Perkins Gilman—at the turn of the century—have tried to hammer home to women: Your economic dependence on men is your undoing.[6] It also helps to explain the importance of personal beauty in female culture.

Despite the vast body of proverbs, mottoes, sermons, didactics, and polemics that has arisen to reconcile women to lack of beauty—"beauty is only skin deep," "character is more important than beauty," "vanity is a weakness of character,"—beauty remains a strong value in female culture, well nigh irrepressible. Even when frivolity is seriously frowned upon in the hard work of building a new social order, as in the Communist world, the moment there is a let-up in repressive measures against beauty, a whole industry pops up to cater to it.[7] Even in China, the moment it became possible to do so, the young women began to spend a large proportion of their earnings at the beauty parlors (*Los Angeles Times*, 1977). A phenomenon so pervasive and so enduring has understandably attracted the attention of a wide variety of social observers.

In his *Descent of Man*, Darwin spent some time arguing the case for "the influence of beauty in determining the marriages of mankind" (1952, 571). Unlike the courtship pattern among lower animals, in which the males vie for the favor of the female so that she is the agent of selection, among human beings the male has gained the power of selection. "Women are everywhere conscious of the value of their own beauty; and when they have the means, they take more delight in decorating themselves with all sorts of ornaments than do men. They borrow the plumes of male birds, with which nature has decked this sex in order to charm the females. As women have long been selected for beauty, it is not surprising that some of their successive variations should have been transmitted exclusively to the same sex; consequently that they should have transmitted beauty in a somewhat higher degree to their female than to their male offspring, and thus have become more beautiful, according to general opinion, than men" (584).[8] Richard Dawkins, a modern neo-Darwinian, is also puzzled by the fact that whereas in lower species it is the male who is colorful and the female drab, among human beings the reverse is true (1978, 177). "What," he asks, "has happened to modern western man? Has the male really become the sought-after sex, the one that is in demand, the sex that can afford to be choosy? If not, why not?" (178). Any attempt to offer a detailed answer to Dawkins' questions would be diversionary, but at least a comment may be in order in the context of the importance attached to beauty in the female world, quite aside from its role in natural selection.

Men do not have to compete very hard when the economic dependency of women makes their survival depend on marriage. It is certainly true that beauty in women became supremely important when there was little place for a woman outside her own home, and few opportunities for economic survival, much less comfort, unless provided by a husband. And it is true, as noted in Chapter 8, that until recently a woman could do better for herself by way of marriage than through her own efforts. Beauty matters. It may be that the competition among women for husbands is a temporary—historically speaking—aberration, a deviation from the Darwinian model, that as "being taken care of" by men in marriage becomes less and less essential for women, beauty will become a less urgent value in their world. They will increasingly be in a position to be the selecting rather than the selected ones.

In any event, however valid the sexual-selection theory might be for animals, it does not seem to have validity for human beings. Beautiful women may, indeed, be sought as marital partners, but they are not assigned a reproductive role; their fertility rate is not high. Gini, for example, found a generation ago that at least in Italy the fertility of the most beautiful women was less than that of other women (1938, 575-576), possibly because they avoided having children as a threat to their beauty.

Still, even when mate selection was a family rather than an individual affair and property or dowry as well as beauty was involved, a beautiful young woman was probably more valuable than a plain one and could doubtless command a better "price."

Still, the emphasis on beauty persists even after marriage. Freud saw it as a form of narcissism, which is a way of naming but not explaining it. In reply to an old question—do women dress for men or for women?—the Freudian answer might be, for women, namely for themselves.

Parsons presents an intriguing alternative suggestion. He sees the glamour, or beauty, pattern as, in effect, a compensation in female culture for exclusion from the male occupational world, as a chance, that is, to strive and achieve success in an area that does not compete with men. "The glamour pattern has certain obvious attractions since to the woman who is excluded from the struggle for power and prestige in the occupational sphere it is the most direct path to a sense of superiority and importance" (1942, 610). But there are ineradicable difficulties associated with it: it is self-limiting to youth. If the glamour pattern is "strongly entered upon, serious strains result from the problem of adaptation to increasing age."

Because cultivating and preserving beauty can be a costly endeavor, a considerable amount of the value assigned to it has to do with the conspicuous consumption Veblen described so long ago. Beauty, whether in clothes or body, is expensive and hence was an index of a father's or husband's success. Even Parsons commented on the common stereotype at mid-century "of the association of physically beautiful, expensively and elaborately dressed women with physically unattractive but rich and powerful men" (610). The trade-off of female youth and beauty for male wealth and power has been a common theme in popular culture for many years.

Cohn, writing at about the same time as Parsons, sees advertising as stimulating the emphasis on beauty, if not actually creating it. "In the woman's world of America, beauty is more than an abstraction. It is a concrete fact expressed in terms of hundreds of millions of dollars annually spent for things that 'beautify.' It is thousands of persons employed by one of the country's largest industries; little girls, scarcely adolescent, getting their hair done in beauty parlors; masseurs going from apartment to apartment of the urban well-to-do. . . . This national phenomenon, this almost fanatical zeal for the appearance of the body, and these expenditures for bodily care unapproached elsewhere merit our attention for whatever light they may throw upon our manners" (1943, 174-175) as well as our mores and values.

Clothes are an important part of beauty and constitute as great a preoccupation in the female world as the body that wears them. Interestingly enough, women themselves have had relatively little input in clothes design. Mrs. Amelia Bloomer's "pantalettes," inspired by the actress Fanny Kemble, did not attract a wide following when introduced at mid-century; nor did Dr. Mary Walker's trousers, jacket, shirt, stiff wing collar, bow tie, and top hat meet more than ridicule. There have been few women among the great designers. Yet one of the best-loved garments has been one designed by a woman, Coco Chanel, whose classic jacket has been bought and cherished by millions of women year after year. When Mary Quant rose to popularity in the early 1970s, she all but abolished the skirt, reducing it to little more than a ruffle at the bottom of a chemise. Even the enormous prestige of Marlene Dietrich was not enough to overcome conservative rejection of the female pants suit for several decades. It has sometimes been alleged that male designers show their misogyny in the clothes they foist on women. In the world of *haute couture* a woman's body becomes little more than the stage on which the designer exhibits his work. Whatever the complexity of the world of costume, beautiful clothes remain an important value in female culture. Success in the area of sensing fashion trends, finding good clothes, wearing the right thing is the kind of success women can appreciate in one another; it is in this sense that it is sometimes argued that women dress for one another, not men. It is a form of competition and, as do other forms, it offers its own kind of exhileration.

In many ways the value placed on beauty in female culture is, like the value placed on erotic love, actually subversive rather than in line with other values of the female world. It is not pursued out of either love or duty. It is more self-oriented than the characteristic other-oriented philosophy of agape. Still, in view of the structural restraints on women, it is quite understandable, even pardonable, as Mary Astell noted at the end of the seventeenth century: "In Women, the object of . . . [Vanity] is their Beauty, and is excusable in those that have it. Those that have it not may be pardon'd, if they endeavour at it; because it is the only undisputed advantage our Sex has over the other, and what makes 'em respected beyond all other Perfections, and is alone ador'd" (1697, 61).

Whatever theory is invoked to explain it, to the young women in prime time, beauty is a value of transcendent importance. Coleman, as noted in Chapter 6, was indignant at the emphasis on it in adolescent society, which he found dysfunctional in many ways. It detracted from the real business of schools, namely, education and training for adult roles; it made for low self-esteem among many girls. With fine sarcasm, he commented:

> Perhaps, at least for girls, this is where the emphasis *should* be: making themselves into desirable objects for boys. Perhaps physical beauty, nice clothes, and an enticing manner are the attributes that should be most important among adolescent girls. No one can say whether girls should be trained to be wives, citizens, mothers, or career women. Yet in none of these areas of adult life are physical beauty, an enticing manner, and nice clothes as important for performing successfully as they are in high school. . . . If the adult society wants high schools to inculcate the attributes that

> make girls objects to attract men's attention, then these values of good looks and nice clothes . . . are just right. If not, then the values are quite inappropriate [1959, 51-52].

Whether the beauty value in female culture is permitted or discouraged, it is far too complex to be interpreted in simplistic or particularistic terms. It has different significance at different ages, in different roles, at different times. Whatever the biological component may be in beauty itself, there is certainly a socialization component in the value placed upon it. Early in life the pink world starts to process the little girl to value it. She learns early the punishment meted out to the unattractive child. And also the fact that there are few areas of life in which injustice is more blatant and failure more painful than in the area of physical beauty. There are few agonies more excruciating than the wallflower's. Or the fading beauty's.

A great deal has happened since the time when Parsons and Coleman wrote. Whether or not the questions Coleman asked would evoke the same replies today we do not know, nor whether the glamour pattern functions the same way today as it did when Parsons described it in the early 1940s. In the late 1960s and in the 1970s there was a strong rejection among avant garde women of the whole glamour pattern. They were as austere in their rejection of artificial beauty aids as any other revolutionary group. Cosmetics were eschewed. Legs and underarms went unshaven. Hair was left uncurled and often uncombed. Jeans or overalls were worn instead of skirts. Conventional beauty was rejected as too artificial. The natural look was emphasized. These were strong political statements. And certainly the use of personal appearance to create "sex appeal" was rejected. Such political statements persist among some young women today. One rarely sees among feminists the elaborate lacquered hairdos of the past, the vividly made-up faces, the four-inch spike heels. Such embellishments show up more frequently among older women. Or celebrities. Or among the young who do not yet recognize and understand the political statement that was being made.

Notes

1. In the male literary tradition, if not in real life, there was the complementary erotic theme of the prostitute with a heart of gold which reached the female world in Margaret Mitchell's Belle Watling. Leslie Fiedler has traced two contrasting motifs in the American novel—one dealing with the pure blonde, blue-eyed White Maiden and the other with the passionate Dark Lady (1960).
2. Ira Reiss projected a proportion of 65 to 70 percent for the immediate future (1971, 407).

3. There is an almost inexhaustable number of ways to classify love. Chivalric love is not the same as romantic love, Dionysian love is not the same as Apollonian (Bernard, 1942, chap. 15), and so on (Hunt, 1959).
4. This emphasis on the universality of the "being-in-love" phenomenon does not imply that it is not also a cultural phenomenon. Both loving and being in love have had codes which prescribe how individuals must behave, even to pining away for unrequited love.
5. Erotic love between women may have been acceptable in the nineteenth century. At least the inference has been made by some students of female friendships at that time that they were actually lesbian relationships. Smith-Rosenberg has considered this possibility in her discussion of the passionate contents of the letters they wrote to one another (1975, 1-27). The conventions of the time permitted not only passionate language but also a considerable amount of physical contact among women.
6. Scheherazade used a different technique to keep her husband's attention, if not his love. She charmed with her tales. In addition, she kept him in suspense, that is, unsure of her.
7. I happened to be in Moscow when Paris couture was invited in to help establish a fashion industry. The fashion shows were avidly attended; the women devoured each offering with unconcealed delight. A Soviet poet was urging "a cult of women's charms" (Selvinsky, 1967). But, conversely, conservative Muslim women in Iran in 1978-1979 returned to traditional body-covering garb as a strong political statement.
8. For a discussion of sex appeal, see Bernard, 1942, chap. 15. Darwin's explanation for the greater beauty of women than of men is, of course, absurd, depending as it does on the inheritance of acquired characteristics. As a matter of fact, when infant mortality was high, woman were probably in greater demand for their reproductive capacity than for sheer beauty.

21

The Ethos of the Female World: Agape

EVEN HANNAH MORE, the doyenne of proper female behavior in the nineteenth century, had given her imprimatur to "benevolence" and, as noted in Chapter 13, women had tackled some of the personal casualties of nineteenth-century capitalism, or Gesellschaft by way of their associations. Toward the end of the century this *philos*-oriented form of the love-and/or-duty ethos moved in the direction of *agape*—in the direction, that is, of a broad-gauged humanitarianism. It became increasingly activist, both politically and nonpolitically, even reformistic. And it became more sophisticated as more and more college women became exposed to radical new ideas.

Of special significance was the movement toward the professionalization of social activism. Academically trained women began to transform this kind of activism into careers. It began to be paid for, thus, in effect, bringing it into the cash nexus or exchange economy. Although a considerable amount of agape remained in the form of voluntary services, it is still significant that much of it became professionalized.

Some of the leaders were looking to down-to-earth research as a basis for their activism, but many of those working to extend agape to the rights of women found that the time-hallowed other-oriented ploy was more effective. Among the earliest agitators for women's rights the arguments rested on a right that they insisted was as legitimate for women as for men. The suffrage was not something men had a right to bestow or withdraw. It was not something women had to earn or deserve or justify. Some input into the running of the polity in support of their interests was the right of all citizens, female as well as male. Opponents argued, however, that in their role as wives, women did not have to participate in the polity themselves; their interests were adequately protected by their husbands.

Only when the grounds of justice got them nowhere did these women turn to a line of argument that better fit the agape ethos of female culture. Political equality, for example, would make women better wives (Freeman, 1975, 19). Or help them reform the world. "It was only when women argued that they needed it [the suffrage] as a social good, to help 'clean up' society, that the idea of suffrage became widely acceptable" (Freeman, 19n).

Agape as Societal Redemption

"The very intensity of our feeling for home, husband, and children," Julia Ward Howe declared in 1888, "gives us a power of loving and working outside of our homes, to redeem the world as love and work only can" (1888, 9). And a considerable number of the early feminists, who believed that women were morally superior to men—purer, more altruistic—accepted this concept of the redemptive function of women in the polity: "The reformist women sought the vote not to free themselves but to reform society. They thought that with it working people could clean up their sweatshops, the traffic in liquor could be stopped, child labor eliminated, and society generally bettered. They were so concerned with fighting other people's battles that they could not conceive of themselves fighting solely their own" (Freeman, 1975, 18).

Opponents answered this female social-redemption argument by stating that even if women did vote, they would only vote as their husbands told them to anyway (Duverger, 1955, 129). There would therefore be no improvement or even change in the polity as a result. Or, if they voted independently, since they were not as intelligent as men, they would be unduly swayed and their vote would therefore have a disastrous effect on policy (Tiger, 1970, 259), voting for the wrong things for the wrong reasons. And anyway, women already had all the power they needed in their role as mothers; the hand that rocked the cradle ruled the world, as the saying goes (Hess and Torney, 1967). Further participation in the polity would coarsen and degrade women and render them unfit for the gentler roles of wife and mother. In attenuated form, arguments similar to these, so reminiscent of the ideology of women's sphere, still reverberate at the present time.

But some of the politicians themselves also believed the redemption argument. They fought against granting the suffrage to women in fear that by bare chance women just might succeed in cleaning up the political system.[1] There was, therefore, a sigh of relief when they noted that for many years not only were women not voting in large numbers, but that even when they did, nothing much changed. The amount of violence at polling places did decline and minor changes did occur in other aspects of the system, but no change was as spectacular as the politicians had feared.

It is true that for some time after women were granted the vote the rate of participation in the polity was low.[2] Summarizing eleven studies, all done before 1969, Costantini and Craik tell us that "the political behavior literature is replete with evidence that at all levels of political action from discussing politics to voting, to political letter-writing, to holding party or public office, women participate less than men. They appear to be less informed politically, and to display a lower sense of political involvement and political efficacy" (1972, 218). Still, on the basis of this research, the authors add that "women have tended to defer to the political judgment of men, in this country and elsewhere; sex roles have been so defined that politics is primarily the business of men." Since these studies were made, the proportion of women who vote has increased markedly and in the case of at least some of them, especially the young, has overtaken the proportion of men who do (Lansing, 1973, 59-76; Bernard, 1975, Table 8.6; Janowitz, 1978, 104).[3]

Even though there was no articulated theory or actual attempt to "redeem" society, neither was there a strong female lobby of women to press for their own interests. When, after the passage of the Nineteenth Amendment, the leaders of the suffrage movement formed a League of Women Voters, it was not designed to exert pressure in behalf of women's issues. It was, on the contrary, strictly, even blatantly, nonpartisan, an educational organization for voters in general in behalf of issues of general concerns, not necessarily women's specific concerns.[4] There still was not a "woman's vote," that is, a self-interested vote in behalf of women's own interests.

Only in the 1970s with the resuscitation of interest in the Equal Rights Amendment did women begin seriously on a large scale to learn the skills of political participation, of lobbying, of letter-writing, of assembling to petition redress of wrongs, of exerting pressure in their own behalf rather than exclusively in behalf of others.[5] They did not see that it was women's peculiar obligation to clean up the ills of government or of society (Carden, 1974, 169). They did not think they had to prove themselves morally superior or even equal to men in order to warrant more say in policy formulation. Their case rested, in brief, not on greater moral qualificatons or promises to be or do good but, as in the early years, on justice. They began to exercise the right to formulate their own issues rather than accepting the formulation of issues by men[6] and also to exercise the right to formulate the "women's" angle on all issues, to make clear, that is, the impact of any program on women and the female world.

Equality as a Value in the Ethos of the Female World

Although equal rights was a battle cry of the women's suffrage movement from at least the middle of the nineteenth century, equality as a general principle has not been a salient value in female culture. We noted Catharine Beecher's invocation of Tocqueville to justify both mistress-maid inegalitarianism and sex inegalitarianism in general. We referred in Chapter 10 to the dilemma housewives faced in reconciling the mistress-maid inequality with the American democratic ideal.

Even how to conceptualize equality between the sexes is perennially frustrating. Even equal legal or political rights, the easiest kinds of equality to conceptualize, are difficult to achieve, especially when the implementation costs money and the poor are less likely than the affluent to be able to afford them.[7]

The ideology of women's sphere had solved the problem of inequality by making it very clear that female subordination—essential for societal stability—did not imply female inferiority (Chapter 4). And the female world seemed to accept that stance. But the ideology that powered the suffrage movement did not accept that solution. Nothing less than complete political, legal, and economic equality was the goal of its leaders. The implications of such equality are still being worked out in the 1980s as we hammer through the meaning of the Equal Rights Amendment.

Recently there appeared a critique of the whole concept of equality. The authors note that feminists have succumbed to the Western male world view with respect to equality, justice, and progress; they suggest Islamic thought as an alternative and propose, inter alia, a "strategy of mutualism and complementarity," of acknowledging "inequalities in a non-invidious way . . . to undergird programs presently based on an unrealizable goal or ultimate good of equality" (Nelson and Oleson, 1977, 6). One corollary to this position is the acceptance of all-female occupations as desirable (5).

Quite aside from the whole issue of legal, political, and economic equality is another kind of equality that is slowly working its way through the public mind. It has to do with what used to be called "manners and morals," a point of view that should not be viewed as trivial. It is a kind of equality that expresses itself in personal interaction, the kind we examined in Chapter 16 in our discussion of body politics. It will be achieved when men pay attention to women talking to them, even when what the women are saying seems irrelevant to them; it will be achieved when they come to see its relevance, when even if they find female thinking boring and dull, they recognize that, *sub specie aeternitatis*, it is as valid as their own. When they recognize that they hold up only half the sky and that the part help up by women is as real and as important as their own. When it is no longer expected as a matter of course that women will laugh at male dirty stories which put women down on pain of being accused of having no sense of humor. When resistance to "chair," chairperson," "she/he," and other language changes dies out. When it is no longer taken for granted that the male perspective is the only one, the female perspective "different" or "deviant" and therefore ignorable. When men become sensitized not to interrupt, not to monopolize, not to patronize. When, in brief, men grant women the everyday "human" rights expected by equals.

Agape as Social Activism: The Academic Approach

Not all extensions of agape were political in character. Indeed, many of the most activist women were not strong proponents of women's suffrage. But in the colleges at the turn of the century new ideas were brewing which had the effect of greatly expanding the social realm of agape.

A new educational ideal for women was worked out in the women's colleges in the fifteen years between 1890 and 1904 (Antler, draft, 1978) which came to be defined as "fitness for an active and useful life." Culture was no longer the passive absorption of knowledge or learning, as it had been earlier. It now implied activism. Now, that is, it involved "a sympathetic and mature understanding of social problems outside the college campus and the motivation to become a part of their solution." College should inspire students "to the service of others," develop the "sympathetic and altruistic virtues" and get rid of petty and selfish ones (Palmer, quoted in Antler, 1978). For this generation of college women, "achieving identity—or finding their 'true selves'—was to come . . . through the experience of relating to the social world *outside* them." Although only a relatively few women went to college, "their influence on public opinion and public life was far out of proportion to their numbers. . . . As later events were to prove, it was university women who . . . assumed leadership of broad social movements concerned with improvements in the status of women" as well as other oppressed people.

There had, of course, been a fairly long history of "social activism" in the form of philanthropic and reform associations earlier in the nineteenth century (Chapter 13). But now the activism was based increasingly on new conceptualizations of social structure. These young women were invading male precincts. "At Vassar," for example, "women began flocking into the rapidly expanding departments that dealt with economics, once considered a man's field, and social problems" including socialism and labor problems as well as charities and corrections. The idea that women's work could "be as great as men's" was expressed (Antler). Service, community responsibility, key concepts in the female world's ethos, characterized the lives of this generation of college women as they did those of noncollege women. "The ideal of service as the goal of education continued to gain ground. The 'cry for the social sense,' as the Vassar *Miscellany* defined it in 1907, reflecting a 'vague sort of responsibility felt by the individual for the community in which he [*sic*] lives,' now had several institutionalized outlets" in the form of practical service as well as in socialist and suffrage clubs and, especially social settlements.

In the second decade of the century something new was being added. The emphasis on the social services was beginning to become professionalized. The services were no longer to be mere expressions of the female world's philos or agape but true vocations, even occupations. Already in the first decade there was "a new campus movement aimed at crystallizing vague demands for service into definite opportunities for remunerative employment" (36). "Friendly visiting" became paid social casework; working with immigrants became social-settlement work. But pay did not change the philanthropic and humanitarian bias of these new professions in the female world.

Jane Addams, Sophonisba Breckinridge, Julia and Edith Abbott, to name only a few of the best known of many women, were to create a new kind of agape expressed as humanitarianism. They were not afraid to hurl research facts at wrong-doers in or out of government. They did not necessarily follow the suffrage route, but they acted. In addition to bringing the female ethos of solicitous attention to bear on a wide variety of helpless or needy people, they wanted to improve the lot of these people. Agape took on an advocacy form. It became politically activist, even reformistic. These women were not afraid to shake their fists at city hall. Or to participate in strikes of mill workers, as

Vida Scudder of Wellesley did. The women's colleges became, in President Coolidge's words, "hotbeds of radicalism."

Agape-Oriented in Spite of Themselves

It is interesting to note—and illustrative of the power of the agape ethos of female culture—that whether they promised it or not, the contribution of women to general policy then tended to be and has continued to be altruistic, on the humanitarian or agape side, and their contribution to political life thus quite in keeping with the agape dynamic. There is a sizable body of research to document this trend.

A Harris poll in 1972, for example, reported that women were "significantly more compassionate" than men about social issues such as hunger, poverty, problems of the aged, and racial discrimination. "Women . . . are much more inclined . . . to vote and to become active not only for their own self-interest, but for the interests of society, the world, and most of all, out of compassion for humanity" (Harris Poll, 1972, p. 75). And, despite findings that women tend to be more conservative than men, a 1975 survey of the seventeen Congresswomen found them tending toward the liberal side of many issues. They supported wage-price controls, gun control, more speed in integration, better health care, support for education, mass transit, aid to the poor, more housing. They opposed highway construction and arms expenditures (Unsigned, July 1, 1975). In 1976 Costantini and Craik, in an analysis of the voting record of the nineteen women members of Congress, also showed them to be more liberal than their party leaders[8] (Fritchey, 1976). And, finally, a brief overview of the records of the ninety-five women who have served in the U. S. Congress shows that many "stood out for their strong indentification with humanist issues: peace, child care, health and welfare" (Tolchin, 1976).

At the state level the agape of female culture was also evident. Thus a study of fifty women state legislators found that although they did not have a "distinct female style,"[9] they did seem to have an agape approach. That is, "they paid particular attention to health and education" (Unsigned, *Carnegie Quarterly,* 22 Summer, 1974, 4). They concentrated on community needs rather than on special interests' needs. They were not agape in their orientation on ideological grounds for they "uniformly tended to see problems as technical rather than ideological, and they emphasized pragmatic cooperation and a public-service approach to politics" (4). They brought to politics "a problem-solving orientation rather than an ideological one" (3). They were agape in their approach, that is, not on a basis of principle; they simply applied the agape dynamic of female culture. It came to them "naturally," it came to them culturally. They had been socialized in a prefeminist ambience; they were not "women's libbers," did not even emphasize women's issues (although they did all support ERA).

The participation of women in party politics as well as in government itself has also been shown to be more public-service-oriented than self-oriented. Thus, for example, Costantini and Craik report that "politics for the male leader is evidently more likely to be a vehicle for personal enhancement and career advancement. But for the woman leader it is more likely to be a 'labor of love,' one where a concern for the party, its candidates, and its programs assumes relatively greater importance. If the male leader appears to be motivated by self-serving considerations, the female leader appears to be motivated by public-service considerations" (234-235). These women, in brief, were not "in politics" to capture positions for themselves but for others, mainly for men. They conform to a pattern which Lipman-Blumen and Leavitt label "vicarious" or relational rather than direct achievement (Leavitt, Lipman-Blumen et al., 1977). As Fritchey notes, "women are seldom afflicted with machismo, the most dangerous vice of male presidents" and, perhaps, of most male political leaders as well.

The future may be different when women participating in the political process do not come up by way of the volunteer route. "There may be a significant change in that more women are running, they are younger, and those seeking higher offices are almost all lawyers" (Kirkpatrick, 1974, 3). Although they will be better prepared, however, they will, Kirkpatrick concludes, still remain handicapped (3). Will they still retain the agape orientation?

The Two Cultures

The agape political behavior of women is so different from that of men that at least one researcher speaks of two political cultures: "political sociologists assume that since women are members of the same polity as men, they are members of the same political culture as well. . . . Within any one nation, the differences between men and women are differences of degree. And . . . the differences of degree are accounted for in terms of the social attributes of women rather than the political system itself. The alternative thesis is that women live in a different political culture from men, a culture based on differences in political socialization, differences in political opportunity structures, and the way in which the media of communication define each of them. . . . These add up to a female design for political living that is dissimilar from that of the male. . . . Like other subcultures with similar experience, the political culture of women has its own way of understanding the political world. Kept out of power, they bring other criteria to bear on public issues and persons in public life" (McCormack, 1975, 24-25). The author, Thelma McCormack, then proceeds, on the basis of her analysis of female voting behavior, to describe the—agape—nature of female political culture: its responses are more moral than pragmatic, status- rather than class-oriented, more concerned with continuity than with change, with the legitimation and normative uses of power rather than with its acquisition.[10] She concludes that these differences between the female and the male political cultures are differences in kind, not merely of degree.

McCormack does not judge either of the two political cultures superior to the other. Both, she believes, are flawed. The chief pathology of female political culture is its ignorance of public life; that of male political culture, its obsession with expediency. "The overall effect of the dualism," she believes, "is to diminish the quality of political life, for since there is no real political community, only a bundle of constituencies, political institutions drift and are never fully accountable" (26). She concludes that "a two-culture theory of political behavior may serve to correct the biases of political sociology" (27), but ultimately she looks for "a third political culture in which authority and power are two sides of the same coin" and are fully integrated. Such a political culture awaits the achievement of social equality between the sexes (28). She warns women against the temptation to adopt a male identity, against overcompensation, against seeking an identity neither male nor female as "experts."

Elise Boulding makes a similar point when she reminds us that just "giving women equal opportunity with men to do all the things that men now do" would not make "the world more peaceful and just" (1977). Individuals of whichever sex who were in positions to dominate or exploit others would still be able to do so. What needs change is not merely the sex of its occupants but the structure itself.

Many men now also agree that women should be fully represented in "every area of decision making, problem solving, or institution building—if for nothing else, just to make sure that their interests . . . are not being neglected or overridden" (Platt, 1976). And in some areas they should be more than equally represented "to correct the distortions that men throughout history have imposed on our attitudes and our institutions" (Platt, 1976).[11]

The upsurge in recent years of the new orientation among women which justifies struggling for recognition of their own issues and of the female input in all issues (Chapter 14) does not mean, in brief, that the old "redemptive" or at least other-oriented stance has disappeared. Although many women simply want more of what they have been deprived of under the status quo, the fundamental argument for more input into policy by women is for many still in terms of a better world for everyone—in a man's words, "to correct the distortions that men . . . have imposed in our attitudes and our institutions" (Platt, 1976). The experience of women, Platt continues, in their current roles or in their rejection of these roles, no matter how they change, gives "them a better understanding of the problems than most men have. This may be true in such areas as the rights of minorities, distributive justice, the rights of patients and the dying, child-care centers, consumerism and product safety, ecology and pollution control, new family and neighborhood structures, the rights of the old, part-time and flexible working hours, the use of leisure, religious reform, education throughout life, world famine, and food and its distribution, population, health care and development in the poorer countries, and peace keeping" (1976). This agape on a worldwide scale is a heavy charge on female culture.[12]

In addition to the real-life female communities described in Chapter 3, there have also been imagined or literary communities of women, no less interesting than the real-life ones for understanding the female world. Or more disturbing to the status quo.

Female Utopias

> A community of women is a rebuke to the conventional ideal of a solitary woman living for and through men, attaining citizenship in the community of adulthood through masculine approval alone. The communities of women which have haunted our literary imagination from the beginning are emblems of self-sufficiency which create their own corporate reality, evoking both wishes and fears [Auerbach, 1978, 5].

Some women have engaged in creating such literary communities, expressing the longings and dreams of female culture—and its critique of the status quo—in the form of utopias.

Utopias do not have to be constrained by reality. They are not intended as blueprints. "Utopia is not simply a planned society in the sense of contemplated changes in the existing social structure. Utopia is society planned without restraint or handicap of existing institutions and individuals. The utopist may populate . . . [her] fictional state with a race of men [and women] wiser, healthier, and more generous than any society has ever been. The utopist may take advantage of . . . [her] fictional license, and often does, to construct a configuration of institutions the like of which the world has never known. The fiction of utopia therefore allows the utopist to reach as far toward the ideal as . . . [she] can stretch the limitations of . . . [her] language and . . . [her] environment. Utopia is not merely a society reconstructed according to specifically planned changes, nor is it predictive of what changes may or must come about in an existing social structure" (Patrick and Negley, 1952, 4-5).

In Chapter 2, Mancur Olson was quoted to the effect that what looked like utopia to the sociologist looked like a nightmare to the economist and vice versa. The several utopias presented here, describing feminist ideals of society, might well look like nightmares to a characteristically macho-oriented male of our society today. But examining them might also help him understand what a nightmare present-day society is to many women.

The utopian literature is the flip side of much of the women's writing on exploitation and oppression; it deals with their visions rather than with their nightmares. Utopias written by women give a different kind of glimpse into the political culture of women from that given by McCormack. They show how their authors would arrange a society if they had the power.

The discussion here is based on an analysis by Carol Pearson of seven utopias, all but one published since 1974.[13] Despite seeming divergence among them, there is still a surprisingly large area of consensus. Overall they tend to be egalitarian, communitarian, and nonviolent, the kind of world in which the authors and their female readers would feel comfortable. They fit women, are congenial, obviate the necessity of being constantly on guard. Pearson notes that the imagery tends toward circles rather than toward angles; "better" tends to mean "central" rather than "higher." In these fantasies, "coming home" of the alienated means being won over by women.

The feminist utopias explicitly or implicitly replace the price dynamic of the cash nexus economy with the love-and/or-duty dynamic of the integry. "In none of these feminist utopias was there any difference in income according to the kind of work done" (Pearson, 1977). Pearson notes that just as women are "able to design societies without dominance, because they lack the experience of dominating, so, too, it may be that women find it easier than men to imagine societies in which people work without being paid and without an atmosphere of competition for scarce, privileged jobs." In this way the female utopias reconcile the incompatibility between the integry and the economy in favor of the integry. In Pearson's words, "feminist utopias do away with the division between inhumane market place and the humane hearth and pattern the entire society on the principles which ideally have governed the home."

The polity no less than the economy is transformed. It tends to be anarchistic, and decentralized.[14] Its scale is small. It is, in effect, a mirror image of the big, bureaucratic, centralized, dehumanized, hostile, conflict-ridden, dangerous male world women contend with in real life.

There are no formal government or laws. "Characteristically, feminist utopian societies are either so small that everyone knows one another, or people live in a number of small groups which function like extended families . . . Kinship networks between these 'families' are the basic pattern of macrocosmic social organization rather than states, so formal government is not needed. Since there are no cities there is no need for centralized bureaucracies, no controlling centers. Suggestions, not orders, are used to achieve consensus. Pearson quotes the author of one utopia, *The Dispossessed*, to the effect that women do not have to learn to be anarchists; men do. In another utopia, "the anarchists are so individualistic they are incapable of [even] forming a mob!" Order is maintained "maternistically." Not, that is, by force or threat but by convincing citizens that the leader's advice is in their best interest. And it is, for the "women have been socialized to govern not for their own benefit but for the families they govern and serve. The socialization to serve and to sacrifice one's own needs for those of others makes it possible for women to envision a society in which people cooperate instead of competing, and nurture each other instead of dominating one another. Every citizen is loved and nurtured as children (ideally) are."

Religion, too, is female-centered. "God . . . is an earthmother goddess. . . [who] rather than [being] a force in opposition to evil . . . represents life in all its fluidity and contradictions." Religious experience is "going home to mother." Pearson reminds us of the implications for women of worshipping a same-sex divinity. "There is no overstating the difference between worshipping a God who is seen as like oneself [rather than] as fundamentally different." People in the feminist utopias receive the same unquestioning and nurturing love from their female deity as the love children receive from their mothers.

The family as paradigmatic for societal organization is clearly central in feminist utopias. Not, however, the nuclear family or patriarchy. The socialization of children is crucial. "Children are never illegitimate, because they all have mothers." There is "an almost total lack of restraints" in child rearing. Children "are encouraged by example and discussion to grow and experiment, cautioned to avoid [only] action which could destroy them." The biological mother is not the sole caretaker of her child; everyone shares in child rearing. Freed from the constraints of duality—yin-yang, good-bad, right-wrong, vice-virtue,—"morality is based upon one question: 'How do we manifest potential?' " In addition to communal responsibility for children there is a low birth rate. One utopia integrates men into the child-bearing and child-rearing system by allowing them to be mothers; in another, only the mother is recognized as a parent; in most, the mother-daughter bond is the crucial one, but the actual biological tie in most is severed or deemphasized.

A pervasive theme in these utopias is freedom from fear of rape or assault. Either men themselves or at least male sex-role patterns are eliminated, for "male violence, connected with the desire to 'master' others, . . . is antithetical to a feminist utopian vision." Nor do sex-linked tasks or even male characteristics appear in these utopias. In Bryant's *Kin of Ata*, although "there are words for male and female . . . they are almost never used. Everyone is called simply 'kin.' " Class and race privileges, it goes without saying, are eliminated along with sex privileges.

Sex differences are not assumed in these feminist utopias. Men are either eliminated or converted. "The most common plot structure of the feminist utopia novel is the conversion story in which a male narrator comes to see a feminist society as superior to a masculinist one. . . . In giving up the need to 'master' and control the woman within and women without, the male hero becomes fully human. Like [that of] the female hero, his liberation may be experienced as 'coming home to mother.' . . . Feminist utopias suggest that the death of patriarchy and the birth of a new, more fully human consciousness is and will occur, in men as well as in women." This, then, is a reflection of the kin-and-locale nature of the female world and its love-and/or-duty ethos as illustrated in utopias written by women.

The values of female culture may also be inferred from the images women have expressed of a future which does not make such drastic demands on our credulity as do utopias.

Female Hopes and Dreams

Elise Boulding does not shrink from the idea of women's dreaming for the future. Although she does not attribute intrinsic superiority to women, she does recognize that the past millennia during which women have lived on the underside of history has equipped them well for the task of restructuring the future. The underside becomes a special resource. "The future is society's free fantasy space, its visioning space, its bonding space. It is space in which minds can learn to grapple with complexities that are destroying the overside" (1976, 789). Life on the underside may have inhibited women from innovation in the past (790) but it has not damaged their human potential (782). She therefore looks to women for innovation and creativity for the future where having lived so long on the underside becomes a special resource. Women, she argues, must be trained to use this free-fantasy, this visioning, not for redeeming the errors of the past but for creating better futures on the overside. Thus, even though women do not claim ethical superiority, their long experience in the "underside" predisposes them to see the conditions necessary for a more just world. Women seem to be bound by their agape culture even in spite of themselves.

What would the world be like in the future if women had more say in it? When pressed to think in terms of their own hopes and dreams the picture is one of quite modest proportions. Here is the way Gloria Steinem saw it in 1970. The economic system would be changed to one more nearly based on merit. There would be "free access to good jobs —and decent pay for the bad ones women have been performing all along, including housework." A four-hour workday would result from greater skill and, in the absence of cheap labor, mechanization of repetitive, low-level jobs would result. The polity would be tempered by the participation of women in the direction of moderating aggression. Consumers and children would get more legislative attention. In return for surrendering some ruling-class privileges, men would be relieved of the strain of power and responsibility. Equal participation in the church would be taken for granted and "full participation of women in ecclesiastical life might involve certain changes in theology, such as, for instance, a radical redefinition of sin" and, one should also add, of divinity itself. Because there is no longer any urgency with respect to population growth, a number of alternative family patterns become feasible: "couples, age groups, working groups, mixed communes, blood-related clans, class groups, creative groups. Single women will have the right to stay single without ridicule, without the attitudes now betrayed by 'spinster' and 'bachelor.' Lesbians or homosexuals will no longer be denied legally binding marriages." The traditional family would not be abolished nor would the option to be a housewife. They would remain available choices for those who preferred that life style, for men as well as women. Child rearing would be based on talent, not sex. Parental responsibility would be equalized. With greater political representation by women, "the country's machismo problems would be greatly reduced." Not that violence would be wholly eliminated, but it would be minimized.

A "utopia" written not in terms of the story of an ideal society but in terms of a possible future for our own society was presented by Shulamith Firestone in the same year, 1970. Since her emphasis was primarily on a critique of current sexuality, the political implications were suggested rather than explored in depth. Four goals mark her approach: (1) technology, including an artificial womb, will free women from the tyranny of child bearing and will give to everyone, including men and children, a share in the child rearing role: (2) economic independence and self-determination for everyone; (3) "the total integration of women and children into the larger society" (271); and (4) sexual freedom and freedom of love, under which, "with full license human relationships eventually would be redefined for the better" (271). Although in the transition to the new society "adult genital sex and the exclusiveness of couples" might have to be maintained, new structures would restructure our psychosexuality and in the new society there would be no need for an incest taboo. In time we would return to "a more natural 'polymorphously perverse' sexuality.'" This would permit more genital sex for children, but since genital sex would not be so central, sex would not be a problem (272). Whereas the fictional utopias imply, in effect, a form of matriarchy, or at least a social structure operating along female lines, Firestone's seems to contemplate a complete integration of sexes and ages.

The hopes and dreams about the future from the perspective of women in the arts—painting, sculpture, art history, architecture and design, theater, dance, music—are revealed in the replies of women to questions about the year 2000 (Tripp, 1975). For themselves they want release from the isolation which the male art world has relegated them to; they want more recognition from museums, dealers' shows, loan exhibitions, and teaching faculties; they want art history to be rewritten to include the work of "lost" artists; they want more participation by women in the business and production aspects of art. They do not expect any of these goals as gifts; they must be achieved by women themselves.

But in all of this dreaming in their own behalf, they do not violate the agape ethos. They want no élitism; they want art humanized; they want art integrated into our daily lives; they want technology used to make this possible; they want more leisure for everyone to enjoy the arts; they want better representation of minorities and, in the dance, of "straight" men. They look forward to the time when "a feminist today . . . will be a humanist" (135).

A foretaste of what it would feel like to live if not in an actual utopia, at least in a less threatening world was experienced by women who attended the National Women's Conference in Houston in November of 1977. One woman reporter commented on how it felt: "An all-female world meant there were no lewd remarks to contend with, no self-conscious jokes about women's libbers, and for the first time there were more women's bathrooms than men's. I found myself less preoccupied with my appearance than I usually am and totally without the fear that I usually have in a strange city of being vulnerable to physical attack. . . . The all-female environment at the conference gave us a misleading but intriguing glimpse into what a world with power shared equally might hold. The generally civilized behavior of the delegates, the concern about important human issues and the serious attitude that most delegates took toward their work—all this was impressive" (Rosenfeld, 1977). She also reported on the impact of this world on a male fellow reporter, who found himself "talking to women about their jobs, their thoughts, their lives, without regard to how attractive or single they may be."

Religion and the Church in Female Culture

Since so many of the vital events in human life—birth, physical maturation, marriage, death—involve women's bodies and are almost universally marked by religious rites, the female world is almost intrinsically related to religion. Even when women were not literate, they had to have some religious instruction since they were responsible for the training of children. The family as paradigm and as implementer of faith has thus implicated women deeply in religion.

Eros was downplayed in early Christianity, but agape, like charity, was important. Although religions have generated as much hatred and violence as universal brotherhood, sisterhood, or love, Christianity has been at least theoretically committed to love. Both faith and the church, or the organization that embodies that faith, have tended to be central in female culture. Nine out of ten women surveyed in 1978 professed faith in God, and two-thirds prayed every day (Hyer, 1978). Almost 70 percent of the women surveyed in 1978 said they turned "to God first for comfort and guidance in time of trouble" (Hyer). Whether or not these findings corroborate the Marxist tenet that religion is the opiate of the people, faith has as a matter of fact served to reconcile women to their fate.

The local or parish church looms large in female culture, for the kin-and-locale characteristics of the Gemeinschaft world encompassed the parish as well as the home. Thus even in times and places when the locale of the female world has been most restricted, the institutional church has been an important concern, including responsibility for a good share of the menial housekeeping jobs required to keep church buildings in order. Though the church has been less reassuring than the deity—only 5 percent of the women surveyed tended to turn to the clergy for comfort in time of trouble—it has served nevertheless as an important extension of an otherwise restricted life space. Thus in times and climes when women's place was in the home they used the church as an arena for wider participation.

The female world also, by way of the church, assumed responsibility for many of the good works—visiting the poor, charity, the care of the sick—that were done in the community (Chapter 13). The church thus served as the matrix for a considerable amount of organization in the form of auxiliaries, associations, clubs, and the like. A survey in 1968, for example, showed how large such religious groups loomed in the female world. From it, as we saw in Chapter 13, Abbott Ferriss concluded that "in the aggregate these religious groups are growing at an annual average rate of 3.1 percent—considerably higher than the rate of female population growth (1.6 percent annually). In 1968, membership in religious groups encompassed almost one-half of all membership" in the female world (1971, 173).

Still, along with this faith in God and proliferation of church-related groups, "growing doubt about the institutions of religion" were also being reported in 1978. More and more women were finding it hard "to base their moral decisions on traditional religious precepts" (Hyer). Religious rules on divorce, contraception, and abortion, for example, were producing more and more resistance, especially among more conservative denominations. Many women were torn between the desire to retain their church affiliation and the desire to bring it into line with current trends.[15]

Some women went beyond moral precepts and attacked theology itself. They challenged the very conceptualization of deity. They did not accept its maleness nor the whole misogynist ideology of most Western religions. The issue of ordaining women was so sensitive that actual schism took place in some denominations—among the Episcopalians, for example—and was threatened in others. As yet, however, these avant garde issues have not had great impact on the culture of the female world. It was morality, not theology or ecclesiastical rules, that was raising the fragmenting issues (Chapter 15).

Notes

1. Credit was, in fact, given to the women's vote for the passage of the so-called Prohibition Amendment.
2. A Chicago study in 1923 showed why. In the mayorality election in that city, three-fourths of those who had not even registered were women. Illness, either of themselves or others they had to care for, was the commonest reason given. Disbelief in women's voting was given by about 9 percent, including 1 percent who gave husband's objection as the reason (Merriam and Gosnell, 1924).
3. There is, predictably, disparity among women in proportion who participate in the political process, white-collar workers showing the highest rate (47.0 percent) and blue-collar workers the lowest (20.0 percent) as of 1972.
4. In some cities the women in the League of Women Voters were so high-powered that they intimidated less well-educated women. The Women's Party exerted but minor influence.

5. Jean Baker Miller, a revisionary psychoanalyst, has given thoughtful attention to the theory of self-interest as applied to women. She argues that the cripplingly poor self-image women suffer from is not justified, that what have been defined by male standards as weaknesses in them—their greater need for bonding, their emotional expressiveness, their empathy, for example—can actually be their basic strengths. She reassures women that it is legitimate to recognize their own needs and to work to see that they are met (1976).
6. They wanted: protection for women against rape; better health services, including contraception and abortion; an end to discrimination in education, vocational training, job opportunities; protection against "displacement" as housewives in middle life and recompense for their work in the home; credit on the same terms as men. They wanted into the Social Security system in their own names. They wanted a better public image in the media; an end to put-downs; changes in language and in forms of address. These women were finding issues that stunned the world, so long had many of them been swept under the carpet.
7. This issue gained some salience in the mid-1970s when government funds for Medicaid programs providing abortion to indigent women were withdrawn by the federal government and in many states. What good, feminists asked, was a right if one could not afford to exercise it?
8. It must be recognized that constituencies that sent women to Congress were themselves undoubtedly more liberal than party leaders. Another distinction invites attention, namely, the distinction between liberalism and humanitarianism, women tending to be more humanitarian but not necessarily more liberal.
9. Although their political style may not have been "female," it did include "the art of getting people to work together, to compromise, and to strive for common goals" (Unsigned, *Carnegie Quarterly*, 2-3). And they did have "a strong feminine identity" (3).
10. A distinction between strength and power might be useful. Women have had to be strong whether or not they had power.
11. The distortions that have to be corrected—as contrasted with evils that have to be redeemed—were of this nature: "There is a general feeling now that the contribution of Western men has tended to be objective, technological, manipulative, concerned with things not people, with death rather than life, with thought rather than feeling, with punishment rather than positive reinforcement, with decision rather than ongoing assessment, with intervention rather than nurturance, ecological rhythms of birth and death and open-ended growth. Men should correct such distortion in themselves, of course, but it would seem to be an area of world outlook where women at least may be less blinded by the past, and where they could be of enormous help" (Platt, 1975). Cf. Jean Baker Miller's argument, note 4 above.
12. A society operating according to the values of female culture would not, it seems to me, be so preoccupied with bigness. The scale would be smaller. I do not think women feel comfortable when things become too big. Bigger is not necessarily better from their perspective. It is interesting to note that

a great many men also are coming to reject the male world's preoccupation with bigness. One of the major prophets of diminished size is, in fact a man —E. F. Schumacher—whose book *Small Is Beautiful* (1973) became a best seller and attracted attention especially under the rubric Intermediate Technology.

13. Mary Bradley Lane's *Mizara: A Prophecy* (Boston: Greg Press, 1976, 1890); Charlotte Perkins Gilman's *Herland*, serialized originally in *The Forerunner* 5, no. 6, (1915); Marge Piercy's *Woman on the Edge of Time* (New York: Knopf, 1976); Joanna Russ's *The Female Man* (New York: Bantam, 1975); Dorothy Bryant, *The Kin of Ata Are Waiting for You* (New York: Moon Books/Random House, 1976, 1971); Ursala LeGuin's *The Dispossessed* (New York: Avon, 1974); Mary Staton's *From the Legend of Biel* (New York: Ace, 1975); James Tiptree, Jr.'s "Houston, Houston, Do You Read?" in *Aurora: Beyond Equality*, Vonde N. McIntyre and Susan Janice Anderson, eds. (Greenwich, CT: Fawcett, 1976); Ursala LeGuin, "Is Gender Necessary?" in *Aurora*, 1976, 134-135.
14. The strongly decentralized form of so many female utopias is especially interesting in view of the conclusions of Negley and Patrick with respect to the crucial nature of centralization based on their examination of—male—utopias. In general they find that centralization is viewed as indicating progress, decentralization, retrogression. "The fundamental distinction which is involved between the progressive and retrogressive utopias—and it is a rather important distinction—seems to rest on a basic disagreement as to the essential value of centralization or decentralization in the social framework of institutions. . . . It is of primary importance to note whether the values which he [the utopist] proposes as ideal are supposed to result from an increased centralization of the political structure or whether he is advocating a process of decentralization. Progressive utopias generally emphasize centralization, and retrogressive forms usually decry centralizing tendencies as destructive of values. . . . The problem of centralization vs. decentralization is not only the important basic issue, but it is perhaps the most significant principle of analysis and classification of utopian speculation in respect to its political or philosophical implications" (1962, 6-7).
15. In 1980 the story of Sonia Johnson, a devout, fifth-generation Mormon woman, highlighted the emotional bind in which many deeply religious women found themselves. She was excommunicated from her Church because of her challenge to the methods used by its hierarchy against the ERA, to which she was deeply committed.

22

The Ethos of the Female World: Challenge and Change

CHALLENGES BY WOMEN of the male world—of the polity, for example, in the form of the suffrage movement and of the economy in the form of the abolition and the temperance movements—had begun in the nineteenth century. But challenges within the female world itself were different, more difficult. The achievement of reform in family law and the acquisition of the suffrage were hard enough. But changing the love-and/or-duty ethos of the female world was to prove just as hard as changing the legal and political constraints of the male world, if not harder. Still, by the turn of the century, the costs of this ethos were beginning to be assessed by avant garde women. And judged high.

Some Implications of the Love-and/or-Duty Ethos

In an economy that operates on a cash nexus basis, one can live by the love-and/or-duty ethos only if one has financial support. Thus, for example, women can be humanitarian, charitable, or philanthropic only when they are financially independent or are being "taken care of" by others they can count on. Moers has pointed out, for example, that

Mrs. Shelby in *Uncle Tom's Cabin* was able to be opposed to slavery because her husband was prospering from it (1973, 59). Thus, young women who look forward to a philanthropic—or agape-oriented—life of service to their familes and to their communities must feel that there will be someone to support them in such a life. In an abstract context, there is justification for a society's having some roles such as these, whose occupants are above the battle. Hereditary monarchs do not have to worry about being elected and so can support the general good rather than special interests. Justices with a lifetime appointment are similarly freed from the pressures of lobbyists. In an analogous way, the wife who is supported by her husband can be on the side of the angels in her social and community activism, whichever side he is on.

Some Costs of the Agape Ethos

The joker lies, of course, in the fact that though individuals in such above-the-battle roles are free to follow general welfare or agape policies, they too are ultimately dependent on those who support them. A king can be overthrown; a justice can be recalled; a wife can be forced to cease and desist if her activism displeases her source of support. She is not really a free agent. The need to be taken care of can become a heavy albatross, leading a young woman to downplay her career plans. It almost forecloses the possibility of autonomy, as the plight of so many abused if not abandoned women abundantly demonstrates. It encourages dependency, which is itself related to depression (Bernard, 1976; Radloff, 1979). It delays or diverts a woman from experience in the outside world.

It has other hazards as well, for lifetime dependence on others for support is risky at best and is becoming more so. As of the late 1970s and early 1980s, the odds that a marriage would survive until death dissolved it were just about even in some parts of the country. Further, the level of support a wife can count on is indeterminate; at present in many states it is only as high as the husband chooses to make it. If he decides that a crust of bread, a glass of water, and a shabby outfit are enough, the court is generally loathe to intervene unless his wife is willing to leave him. Husbands might consent to subsidize old-fashioned charity and community service but not to subsidize reforms they viewed as threatening. Like ERA, for example. Movements in behalf of women have never been generously financed by the male world. And adding to the complexities on the current scene is the male liberation movement, which is challenging the "breadwinner" or "good provider" male role.

The love-and/or-duty ethos is inherently nonegalitarian in effect. It calls for a serving role. Anyone who lives by it must always be compliant, doing for others, "stroking." "Stroking" is the term sometimes applied to what Bales in his study of task-oriented groups (1951) called "expressive" behavior: showing solidarity, raising the status of others, giving help, rewarding, agreeing, concurring, complying, understanding, passively accepting. These are the kinds of behavior women are socialized to engage in; they are likely to characterize a love-and/or-duty ethos. They are the kinds of behavior that keep a group at peace in contrast to instrumental behavior, which keeps it at work. But the peace may be bought at a high price; it may result in exploitation.

The love-and/or-duty ethos is handicapping in the polity as well as in the economy, for it precludes the acquisition or exercise of power as we know it in the male world. Individual women may achieve power—history supplies examples such as Deborah the General or Queen Elizabeth the First among others—but in a world in which the love-and/or-duty ethos prevails, such behavior violates its fundamental tenets and puts one at a disadvantage. One can, of course, use power in a variety of ways, not only ruthlessly as a tyrant might, but also lovingly as a father might, or for good ends as a benevolent monarch might. Thus, although power does not necessarily contravene the love-and/or-duty ethos, the love-and/or-duty ethos may contravene the use of power, for if one is constrained to deal with others on a love-and/or-duty basis, it is difficult to attempt to control or to coerce them against their will.

Some Psychological Costs of the Duty Ethos

The duty as well as the love component of the ethos of female culture has its costs in the form of guilt or anger and resentment. Duty—stern *daughter* of the voice of God—can keep a woman in a marriage long after it has become destructive to her. If a wife is mistreated she is easily convinced that she is to blame; she has somehow or other been negligent in performing her duties. Many battered women have attested that they hesitated to leave home for a long time because they were convinced that they were somehow or other at fault, that they had brought the mistreatment on themselves. And until recently there was a widespread tendency for the public to agree with them. They "blamed the victim."

In this manner the duty component of the female world's ethos may have an emotionally crippling impact on those who espouse it by generating guilt. Selflessness, taking care of others, has been the prescribed rule. "To absorb, to retain, to be nourished, to grow—all this is to receive," women were taught not too long ago. "This is happiness. To give of what you have and are — of yourself — that others may be better and happier — this is blessedness. By a beautiful provision of nature, self-denial and work offered in this spirit and for this purpose ennoble instead of dwarfing heart and intellect" (Deland, 1911, 58). The power of this teaching is still being recorded in the notes on female patients in therapy sessions. Thus, for example, a psychiatrist finds that "in psychotherapy women often spend a great deal more time talking about giving than men do. Women constantly confront themselves with questions about giving. Am I giving enough? Can I give enough? Why don't I give enough? They frequently have deep fears about what this must mean about them. They are upset if they feel they are not givers. They wonder what would happen if they were to stop giving, to even consider not giving. The idea is frightening and the consequences too dire to consider. Outside of a clinical setting, most women do not even dare to suggest openly such a possibility" (Miller, 1976, 49). So far from never having to say they are sorry, women who adhere to the duty component always have to say they are sorry. And feel sorry. Since the ethos frequently calls for selflessness, even sacrifice, and giving, giving, giving, if they are tempted to look after their own interests rather than those of others, they feel guilty. Wives can be made to feel guilty if they want to "do their thing" even if no one would be hurt by it. Daughters can be made to feel guilty if they seek to follow their own interests even if this would in no way injure other members of the family. So also in the case of mothers vis-à-vis their children.[1]

The violation of role prescriptions is common enough in all roles. It can be especially guilt-generating in the kin-oriented female world. The adult daughter is guilt-ridden because she is not doing more for her ailing mother, or sister, or brother. The professional woman is guilt-ridden because she spends time with her work that could (should?) be spent with her family, or vice versa. Women have so many — sometimes cross-cutting — obligations, responsibilities, and loyalties (Chapter 15) that no matter what they do there is plenty of room for guilt. They should have done more. Guilt, to repeat, is the inexorable flip side of the love-and/or-duty ethos.

Not to be omitted from the balance sheet of psychological costs is the vulnerability of women to charges — often valid — of interference, of bossiness. Under the guise of duty — sincerely believed in — a woman might perform acts that violate the dignity of others. "It hurts me more than it hurts you" has become a cliché expressing this manifestation of the love-and/or-duty ethos. Or "spare the rod and spoil the child," another classic form of this hazard. Like convinced cultists, the duty-bound often attempt to impose their ethos on others. As socializers of children and moralizers, women feel duty-bound to impose their own norms on their families, often including husbands. Duty is often also a guise for aggression, as it is a rationale for dependency, There is, finally—as also in the case of love—the danger of exploiting others' sense of duty. "You owe it to me; it's your duty . . ." as son, daughter, husband.

Nor, in this complex tangle, is all this prescribed love-and/or-duty necessarily good for its recipients. Even Deland, who was bemoaning the change in the nature of duty early in the century, recognized that it was not always benign. "Our mothers," she noted, "had a monopoly of unselfishness; they gave, instead of received; they grew in grace, but it was at the expense of their families" (58). So much self-sacrifice demoralized the recipients. It turned well-meaning husbands into brutes and children into tyrants. Nor—and this was a stinger—were such self-sacrificing women conscientious about the rights of children *not* to be born. This was an assault on the very cornerstone of the female world, its maternal role.

Some duty-bound women may be embittered, knowing that they are paying a heavy price to perform what they see as their responsibility as daughters, wives, mothers. They may become angry, hostile, resentful. The obedient daughter does her duty as she has been taught to see it but seethes inwardly. She minds being the one—not her brother—who is expected to care for their disabled older parents. The duty-driven individual may be as merciless as the most achievement-driven. Either may perform harsh acts. To say, therefore, that the female world operates on a love-and/or-duty dynamic does not imply that all the women in it are angels or saints or loving, serving goddesses or embodiments of the "true womanhood" celebrated in women's sphere in the nineteenth century. Still, it cannot be denied that a large proportion of women do, whatever the cost, conform to the requirements of that ethos, or try to.

Agape versus Filial Duty

Not included in any of the three Greek categories of love—eros, philos, or agape—was familial love. Perhaps it was simply taken for granted. Or perhaps it was implicit in Gemeinschaft itself. Or perhaps duty was enough. But in the Christian tradition familial love was the very model of love: the fatherhood of God, the motherhood of Mary, the brotherhood of man. Not many demands could legitimately conflict with those of the family.

When the female world was almost wholly a kin- and locale-oriented one, the behavior motivated by love-and/or-duty was, so to speak, *en famille.* One served one's family of course because one loved them. But also out of duty. In both cases it was beside the point. One did what one had to do for one's kin whether one loved them or not. So there was rarely any occasion for conflict between love and duty. They converged. Nor need there be conflict between duty toward one's family and philos. When even Hannah More recognized the validity of including the poor or lower classes in the orbit of the ministrations of the female world, there was little occasion for conflict between such philanthropic love and duty to one's family. Perhaps some husbands or some clergy may have objected to the time women devoted to their benevolent associations early in the nineteenth century, but by and large this activity seems to have generated little conflict.

As individuation became more feasible, however, especially with the spread of higher education, it became clear that agape, in the humanitarian or social activism sense, and filial duty did not always coincide, that sometimes there might be a conflict between what love prompted one to do and what filial duty ordered one to do.

The Struggle for Redefinition of the Ethos of Female Culture

A revolt against the costs of the female ethos—personal, economic, political, psychological—was already beginning at the turn of the century. Young college women, pioneer members of an intellectual élite, were the first to respond to the conditions that were eroding the love-and/or-duty ethos. "Higher education played a critical role in enabling women to begin to construct a new identity [and ethos] for themselves both within the context of male endeavor and outside it" (Antler, 1978). It was to take a century for the issues involved to become relevant to enough women to impact on public policy. Still, even after a century the solution is by no means clearly defined.

We have met these avant garde women before. They were among the "modern" women whose social networks were less kin-related than more traditional women's (Chapter 12). They were among the "Allies" in the WTUL, bringing class values to working girls (Chapter 14). They were the "outlaws" referred to in Chapter 16. They were among the women who were "domesticating science" in the land-grant universities (Chapter 17). They were among the college-educated women transforming agape into social activism (Chapter 21). Their present-day counterparts are members of the educated intellectual élite, the "upper-middle-class, college-educated" women who are, as already noted (Chapter 10), everyone's whipping girls today. At this point we see them early in the century wrestling with another aspect of the female world, "modernizing" the love-and/or-duty ethos, especially as it related to freeing women from the domination of the kinship aspect of the female world, specifically the "family bond," attempting to make more autonomy possible. These were women who did not *have* to go out to work. they were the women who *wanted* to, who wanted careers. Even, if need be, at the expense of marriage. The women for whom there was no excuse, as there was for women from less affluent homes, to enter the work world. Women who wanted "self-fulfillment," as it was called before it became "self-actualization." The women who gave "career women" a bad name (Helsen, 1972).

The first generation of college women had had to fight strong opposition to the very idea of higher education for women at all: it would have an adverse effect on their femininity; they would cease to be true women; their health would suffer. There were the same arguments used with respect to women's participation in the labor force or in politics. These women had to be highly motivated. They had to have conviction. They had to want learning no matter what the cost, for the cost was high. In the 1870s and 1880s, they found college life lonely, isolating. They were viewed as deviant, "psychological invalids," as their counterparts in the 1960s were viewed as "crazies." Although they themselves insisted on their femininity, they also insisted on defining it in their own way, not as innocence, purity, or sensibility but as knowledge-based. "The attainment of knowledge would allow them not only to become the intellectual companions of men," a distinctly feminine, that is other-oriented, goal, but it would also—mark this—"provide a means by which they could order, transform, and direct their own lives" (Antler, 1978), a distinctly self-oriented goal. Far out.

"To Direct Their Own Lives"

Ibsen's Nora was one of the most dramatic forerunners of the rebels against sacrificial duty. She was affirming a duty to herself that shocked the public. In a much-quoted passage she proclaimed that above all she had a duty to herself. She was no longer satisfied with prescribed role behavior. She had to think things out for herself.[2] True, this was a man's statement of the case, but apparently it struck a chord with many women. And the freedom they were seeking was not only from control by husbands but also from what came to be called "the family bond." The story of Jane Addams and several of her contemporaries is taken as illustrative of the conflict—between their obligations or duties to their families and their wish for autonomy and independence—to which college-educated women were subjected in the late nineteenth and early twentieth centuries.

Adams (1860-1935) graduated from Rockford College in 1881. Although her health had previously been good, now, with nothing to engage her time, she became ill. "I seem to have reached the nadir of my nervous depression and sense of maladjustment. I am filled with shame that with all my apparent leisure I do nothing at all" (Antler). When her brother died, the responsibility for his family fell on her shoulders, but even this did not seem to mitigate her feelings of futility. Not until 1887, after her second trip to Europe, where she learned about settlement houses, did she discover what she wanted to do. "Refusing to return to her family to resume the role of dutiful daughter, sister, and aunt, she took rooms instead with Ellen Starr in a Chicago boarding house to prepare for the launching of their settlement."

M. Carey Thomas[3] (1857-1935), later president of Bryn Mawr, was another example of the conflict between family demands and desire for autonomy. Her postcollege depression was so serious that she thought of shooting herself. Her mother accused her of being "utterly and entirely selfish," an accusation in no sense designed to alleviate her anguish. Rheta Dorr (1886-1948)—an early prototype of the "investigative reporter"—is another example of a woman who had to be a self-helper, an independent individual, free of parental obligations.[4]

Not all college-educated women, however, experienced such conflict. Either their families made no restraining demands on them or, as traditional women, they felt no wish for autonomy or independence. For them marriage was a satisfactory solution. They were content with the dependency that accompanied the love-and/or-duty ethos of the female world.

For others, however, the desire for autonomy was disablingly intense. Especially for the more modern ones for whom the "need to break away from parental control before establishing autonomy became a necessity" (Antler). It was a genuine enough issue to give rise to a new conceptualization of duty, one that included duty to one's self.

A New Concept of Duty

It had taken an enormous corpus of sermons, lectures, homilies, and the like in the nineteenth century to keep women on the harsh path of selfless duty. These "positive reinforcements" were now losing their persuasive power for the avant garde of college-educated women, many of whom had read or heard enacted Nora's impassioned speech—"I believe that first and foremost I am an individual"—and resonated to it. In developing a new definition of the female ethos, advocacy of self-interest was, of course, unthinkable. So the new point of view had to be couched in terms of duty. Duty, however, to one's self.

Margaret Deland[5] explained what was happening early in the century. Two forces—one self-oriented, one other-oriented—both considered good, were at work to change the feminine ideal; a sense of individualism and a sense of social responsibility (1911, 59). Admirable as both might be, they were having damaging effects. "These two forces—a woman's sense of her right to her own life . . . and her sense of her ability to help others . . . —both so noble and so full of promise—sometimes threaten the very springs of life" (59). And this conflict was reflected in the prevailing discontent among women (59).

> The young woman of today is supplementing a certain old-fashioned word, *duty*, by two other words, "to myself." Sometimes just being happy, just enjoying herself, seems to be a duty—but for the most part, our girls are not so trivial as that. They feel that education and the grasping of opportunity are duties; the cultivation of the mind, or, for that matter, cultivation of the soul; the finding a vocation, the joining a sisterhood, the going off to take care of lepers. Noble impulses, all of them; but contrast them with the old ideal, and you will notice one thing—in all such expressions of individualism, the family is secondary [58].

Social activism was taking precedence over filial duties.

"The new ideal attacks the old. . . . Our girls know how to say, 'I want,' and 'I will,' or sometimes, 'must,' but they are not learning to say 'I ought' " (62). They are quite different from preceding generations. "The mothers of forty or fifty years ago had no theories about improving the world (except the heathen) outside their own respectable doors; but they had strength, and patience, and tenderness, and courage, and *selflessness*. (That, I think would be the name of their ideal—selflessness.) Can we remember that selflessness, and see no difference between it and the present feminine individualism?" (58).

The cause of this new concept of duty, Deland alleged, was higher education. " 'You—*you*—YOU—' the higher education cries; 'never mind other people; make the most of your own life. Never mind marriage; it is an incident; men have proved it so for themselves; it is just the same for women. Never mind social laws; do what your temperament dictates—have affairs, enjoyment even. But do your duty to yourself!' " (62). The author then asks, in effect, what price self-development. "What," she asks, "Is the relative value to society of individual development which comes at the cost of family life? . . . Is there any culture, of mind or soul, to equal that which comes from the simple doing of one's duty?" (62). Then the crucial question: what is duty? The answer was framed in terms of an altruistic criterion. To such questions as "Is this culture for myself or for others?" the dutiful answer was, for others (63).[6]

Duty to self versus duty to family ceased in time to be a source of conflict for unmarried women. By the middle of the century this kind of conflict between family and career no longer plagued them. But it still raged in the breasts of many women in the form of family versus job or career if they were married and especially if they were mothers. Duty to her family took precedence over every other in a woman's life.

It was one thing for gifted and affluent young women to challenge the filial-duty imperative of the female world's ethos. It was momentous that they were able to break the umbilical cord to the family. But it is also important to note that even when they implemented the new concept, "duty to self," it still took the form—not as Deland had feared it might, of frivolity or immorality—but, actually, of the traditional agape guise of social service of one kind or another, as settlement workers or social-work professionals, as social reformers, as pioneers in welfare plans.[7] Until well into the century, self-fulfillment was still taking that serving form.

We reviewed in Chapter 21 the humanitarian slant of women's political behavior today. And whatever may have been the agitation for promulgating a new self-oriented definition of duty to include the duty to one's self, the ethos of female culture has remained essentially altruistic, still philos- and agape-oriented. Higher education did not water down, let alone obliterate, its altruistic ethos. It still remains other-oriented. Thus Carol Gilligan, for example, in a study of women in and around a university community—whose orientation, according to Deland's charge against higher education, should be highly self-oriented—found that they were still other-oriented. Asked, for instance, to tell what morality meant to her, one woman replied: "When I think of the word morality, I think of obligations" (Gilligan, 1977, 485). And another, morality "has to do with responsibilities and obligations and values" (488). Still duty-bound. Still, three-quarters of a century after Deland's charge, obligations, responsibilities. The fearful naysayers who had lamented the consequences of higher education for women could be reassured. The "me-generation" did not seem to have overwhelmed the female world.

But an awareness of the costs of the ethos of the female culture was growing. Challenges were multiplying. In the 1970s the demands of academic women were beginning to express themselves in so-called women's studies. A generation of college women were beginning to be exposed to the fruits of a wholly new genre of scholarship in history, anthropology, political science, economics, sociology, which was helping them define themselves and their own world from their own perspective, in terms of their own experience. And evaluate the costs of the ethos of their world. Women were increasingly coming to resent the iron chains of duty, the unmitigated selflessness demanded of them. They wanted out. Not to have to feel responsible if something went wrong. Not to have to feel that if they had not done what they did or if they had done what they should not have done, all this would not have happened. If it rained on the day of the picnic, not to have to feel it was their fault. In brief, not always having to say or even feel that they were sorry.

What Kind of Female World?

We have already noted (Chapter 5) that there is by no means a consensus among feminist scholars with respect to women's sphere in the nineteenth century with its cult of domesticity and true womanhood. No more is there consensus today with respect to the female world. There are some women who see the rewards of the love-and/or-duty ethos and the penalties of its loss. They covet for women today the love and support supplied by the bonds of womanhood in the nineteenth-century world of love and ritual; the relegitimization of female friendships and the cultivation of sisterhood seem to them of utmost importance (Chapter 12). But there are others who see the costs involved in the ethos of the female world, not only within the female world itself, vis-à-vis the family, but also—increasingly—vis-à-vis the economy and the polity, who see it as an incubus, not as a haven. They want none of it. Why, they ask, should women not be paid in the coin of the (male) realm for their contribution to the family as well as on the work site? Why should they be expected to supply the emotional support people ask for without pay any more than professionals are? Some of these issues will be touched on in Chapters 23 and 24.

This, then, has been the love-and/or-duty ethos of female culture. It is clear that, powerful as its grip still is on many, perhaps most, women, it no longer goes unchallenged. By the 1960s, the 1970s, and the 1980s, it was facing not only the challenge of Nora's passionate insistence on a right to be an autonomous, responsible adult human being but also a challenge based on the costs—personal, economic, political, psychological—it imposed on those who conformed to it. The Gemeinschaft world which had nurtured and protected it was increasingly being encroached upon by the Gesellschaft as more and more women entered the labor force and were exposed to it.

In contrast to the selflessness demanded by the ethos of female culture was the self-interest that pervaded the Gesellschaft. In that world, self-interest was not only permitted, it was, as we shall note in Chapter 23, almost mandated. Its inhabitants have a dispensation against the sin of self-interest (Dumont, 1977). It is the very keystone of the structure of both the economy and the polity. Self-interest—preferably enlightened, but in any event self-oriented—is the bottom line in economic and political interchanges. Taking care of one's own interests is a basic rule of that game (Chapter 23).

Confronting the ethos of the male world on a massive scale called for a profound reevaluation of the female world. It called for a great deal of soul searching. How much change did women want in their own world? What kind of change? What were the alternatives? To take over the ethos of Gesellschaft? To modify it to make it more comfortable for women? For example, since almost half of the labor force were women, the economy was as much theirs as men's and therefore such policies as flexible hours, paid maternity leave, pregnancy benefits, and any other policy that lightened their load—whether profitable or not, whatever the cost-benefit—were perfectly legitimate. Agape was as legitimate as profit. So which option to choose? Modify the female world's ethos? Or the male world's?

Questions of this kind proved to be hard to deal with. They constitute major issues in the female world in the 1980s.

Notes

1. One daughter of such a guilt-ridden mother, disaffected by her mother's ongoing apologies, her constant appeals for assuaging her conscience, rebuked her: it was arrogant of her to feel so guilty. Who did she think she was, anyway? God? She wasn't all that powerful. She couldn't have made that much difference if she had done A instead of B. So drop the guilt trip!
2. The famous passage in Ibsen's *A Doll's House*, translated into English in 1883, was Nora's reply to her husband's *obiter dictum*, "First and foremost you are a wife and mother." Her answer: "That I don't believe any more. I believe that first and foremost I am an individual. . . . I'm not content any more with what most people say, or with what it says in books. I have to think things out for myself and get things clear."
3. Martha Carey Thomas (1857-1935)—she dropped the gender-identifying "Martha" and came to be known by the more gender-neutral "Carey"—was born into an affluent Baltimore family of Quaker persuasion. After taking a degree at Cornell she went to Germany and was the first woman doctor from the University of Zurich. She was chosen president of the newly established college for women, Bryn Mawr, and became known for her insistence that its standards equal or excel those of the best male colleges. "Her two main causes had been woman suffrage and women's education. In the first, though a latecomer, she had for a time been a leader. In the second, she had initially been an inspiration, though Bryn Mawr was to seem increasingly less significant as an experiment owing to the widening acceptance of coeducation, with which she had had nothing active to do. Her most important impact was as a pioneering example to many restless, able, career-oriented girls of her own time: the militantly individualistic, triumphantly sexless women who became conspicuous in America early in the twentieth century" (Veysey, 1971, 449). This quotation is from a sketch by a male author. It is unlikely that a woman would have called the women of the early years of the century "triumphantly sexless."

4. The mother-daughter struggles which Antler has traced seem to reflect an effort by women to escape the "family bond" and might well be viewed as an early rebellion against the patriarchal family.
5. Margaret Deland (1857-1945) was a writer who, as the wife of a Boston businessman, "rose to the second or third rank of Boston's business and intellectual life," a somewhat patronizing comment regarding someone who was, by the same author, viewed as a "female Howells." As a girl in Maple Grove, Pennsylvania, she "was given 'new ideas' like that of female independence." By the age of twenty she was already self-supporting as a teacher of drawing in the Girls' Normal College of New York (later Hunter College). She met "advanced young women from Boston" but did not take on their qualities. She avoided extremes in her view of woman's rights: resolute in her own freedom, she never supported woman suffrage." Nor, for that matter, universal male suffrage. Helping unmarried mothers was one of her major causes. "She was daring in the pursuit of conventional ideas" (Levenson, 1971, 454-455). The quotations from Deland in the text suggest the conflicted perspective from which she was viewing women early in the century. "Her thought was determined more by personal need than by logic or tradition" (455).
6. It is interesting to note how tenaciously the Deland thesis has hung on. It was being repeated in a somewhat different context in 1979 (Berger, 1979, 64-67).
7. It may be legitimate to view social work as an expression of philos and to see social reform as an expression of agape. A considerable amount of the social activism of the women Antler discusses was a salvage operation, picking up the pieces after a rampant and unbridled capitalism had destroyed a good many social and societal props. For a sketch of the academic aspects of this social activism, see Bernard, 1964, Appendix A, 242-250. Mary Jo Deegan has brought this sketch up to date (1977, draft). Antler's focus is mainly on the women's colleges in the East; Deegan's is primarily on the coeducational universities of the middle west, especially the University of Chicago. Deegan shows that the deflection of the outstanding women academics from the more theoretical to the more social-work or agape orientation was as much the result of exclusion from the theoretical disciplines as of personal preference.

PART VI

The Economy, the Polity, and the Female World

From the point of view of the original design of this book—as factual a description as possible of the female world—the goal, however inadequately, has been achieved. The age and marital-status structure of the female world has been sketched (Chapters 6 and 7). The status structure, including its educational, occupational, and income components, has been delineated and its class structure roughly portrayed (Chapters 8-11). The group composition, including faultlines—both structural and ideological—has been outlined (Chapters 13-15). And four major aspects of its culture—language, household technology, arts, and ethos—have been examined, at least superficially (Chapters 16-22).

Because the purpose has been to deal with the female world as an autonomous entity in and of itself rather than as a counterfoil to the male world there has been only a minimum amount of reference to the male world. There has been, in fact a conscious attempt to avoid invidious comparisons between the worlds of women and of men. The male world has been invoked only when it was needed to explain some aspect of the female world—the influence on it, for example, of male misogyny and exclusivity—or to serve as a control. Nor is there here proposed any expansive discussion of it at this late date. Still, any discussion of the female world at this particular moment does call for some attention to it because in order to rethink their own world, women must increasingly understand the changes taking place in the male world as well as in their own.

The male world seems to be at odds with itself and this fact has repercussions in the female world. We began in Chapter 2 with a brief sketch of an ancient ideological polarization in the male world, the poles of which I labelled "male" on one side and "female" on the other. It continues into the present, with increasing recognition that however adaptive the macho ethos may once have been, it has become less and less so. Increasingly there are those in the male world itself who seek to free themselves from the bind that imprisons them. The male world even looks in the direction of the female ethos to extricate itself. Because of the importance of these trends in the male world, Part VI extends some attention to them. Chapter 23 looks at the economy or Gesellschaft, 24 at the polity, and Chapter 25, at ways of relating them with the female world.

23

The Female World and the Economy

THE ECONOMY HAS BEEN an almost exclusively male preserve since at least the eighteenth century and perhaps even earlier. And it has operated according to a totally different ethos from that of the female world, an ethos of self-interest. Adam Smith's treatise *The Wealth of Nations* (1776) showed that if every man followed his own best interest, if he tended strictly to his business without outside interference, the national product would be maximized. A century and a half later the president of a major corporation echoed Adam Smith's theme: "What's good for General Motors is good for the country." The picture that came through was of an orderly, self-regulating system in which exchange maximized individual well-being and thus benefited all parties as well as optimizing productivity. Everyone came off better than before in such transactions, having always exchanged something he valued less for something he valued more. The system was inherently benign in nature in this cheerful portrayal.

Under Malthus, however, the sunny descipline of economics became a "dismal science." He showed that workers were doomed to perpetual poverty because, since they needed many children to help support the family, they tended to breed up to the level of subsistence. The elaboration of these paradigms in the nineteenth century combined with the work of biologist Charles Darwin to produce the doctrine of Social Darwinism, which, in effect, apotheosized a dog-eat-dog, devil-take-the-hindmost ethos. Still, the new system seemed to work. It was dynamic, creative, and productive. I do not think that the female world could have created nineteenth-century capitalism. I do not even think most women have been comfortable in it. It was, I believe, a male creation all the way.

In this chapter we take a long running jump to show how technology shaped the capitalist economy; we look at the self-interest ethos of this system and at the "economic man" it created. The question is then asked: as more and more women participate in the labor force for more and more years of their lives, what effect will the male ethos have on the female world and on women themselves?

Women and Technology

Until fairly recently there were few productive technologies in which women could not engage, few productive skills that they could not learn. It is not the purpose here to trace in detail the contribution of women to human technology, but a momentary glance is in order. Since prehominid days, technologies dealing with food have been typically a concern of the female world. It has been women as much as if not more than men who have fed the human species.[1] Women must have been among those who scavenged the carcasses left by surfeited large animals. They were almost certainly the ones who learned how to find and dig up edible roots, to gather berries, nuts, and seeds.[2] They might very well have been the ones who discovered that seeds produced edible food.[3] It is generally conceded that women invented the digging stick and thus hoe agriculture. They may have created stocks of food when they invented containers—baskets, pottery—to transport and store them in. And, thus, parenthetically, they may have invented the idea of property, the origin, according to some theorists, of all our woe. They may also have trapped small animals. They may, further, have chipped flint, made arrowheads, spearheads, even bows. Why not? Reconstructions of prehistoric times usually cast men in these roles, but there seems to be no proof that some of these crafts may not have been practiced also by women. If women had not been preoccupied almost exclusively with bearing and rearing children and feeding everyone, we do not know how human culture would have developed.[4] There is no reason to believe that females have been incapable of inventiveness and creativity (Mason, 1898).[5]

The human species was doing fairly well with its slow-growing technologies for countless millennia when one great technological advance—the harnessing of artificial power—in one small part of the globe in one particular moment in its history—the middle and late eighteenth century—accelerated the development of technology so enormously that it is rightly called a revolution, perhaps the most widely ramifying and influential in human history until that time. It even changed the way humans saw the world. It encouraged the concentration of population in towns and cities. It transformed the nature and locale of much of the work of the world. It changed relationships within families. In brief, it introduced the modern world, a world like no other ever known before. A world, as a matter of fact, that is only now beginning to reach most of the human species. It changed the stage on which the human drama—birth, socialization, marriage, reproduction, death—was played out. It created and nurtured the kind of society that Tönnies labelled the Gesellschaft, or capitalistic society (1957, 258). And, most relevant in the present context, a particular ethos to regulate it.

One of the themes of the present volume is that the female world has resisted the impact of Gesellschaft and its ethos longer than the male world has. Here we deal with women's experience with this ethos and ask to what extent they take over the characteristics of Gesellschaft when they enter the labor force, to what extent the ethos of the Gesellschaft impacts on the ethos of the female world, and what challenges it poses.

The Ethos of Gesellschaft

The productive technologies that prevailed until the latter part of the eighteenth century had been of a sort that individuals in families could manage by themselves. True, the division of labor and teamwork had been part of the productive process for millennia, but for the most part an individual could still produce with his own tools at his own bench in his own bailiwick. And so could his partner, his wife, with her tools, in her bailiwick. With the emergence of power-driven machinery and the engineering technology to deal with it, at the end of the eighteenth century, the organization of production began to take on a different character. The workers who had done their spinning and weaving at home on their own spindles and looms, on raw materials brought to them and taken from them by agents, were now assembled in a common location to spin and weave on someone else's machines.

That was important enough in and of itself. But of equal significance in the present context was the process that made the factory (often just a shed to protect the machinery) and the machines available in the first place. The factories and the machinery were expensive; not many could afford them. A whole technology for assembling capital was needed to build them before there could even be factories. At first families might be able to supply the capital, and no doubt some of the earliest factories and mills were family establishments.[6] But as factories and mills improved and as engineering technology snowballed and called for larger and larger investments, new kinds of technologies—banking and credit, for example—had to be developed to provide them. Workers, furthermore, had to be found and trained to operate the machines.[7] That is, another kind of technology—for organizing land, labor and capital—had to be invented to enable the engineering technology to do its work.[8]

This financing and organizing might have been done in a number of ways. It might have been done by governments themselves. It might have been done by cooperatives. It might have been done by rich families. As it turned out, the way that won out—a way not available to women[9]—was that of a number of "rugged individualists" or entrepreneurs, one by one or organized in combination, with a minimum of oversight by government (and even that long delayed). Adam Smith's classic treatise on the wealth of nations (1776)—written just before the great spurt in industrialization—persuaded policymakers that this was the best way to do it. A whole genre of writing, from Mandeville's *Fable of the Bees* to the utilitarian philosophy of Jeremy Bentham, concomitantly exalted a kind of self-interest that found social justification in Smith's great work. The common weal would best be served if everyone acted in his own self-interest. Combined with what Weber called the Protestant Ethic, this philosophy produced what Tawney called the acquisitive society and what Tönnies labelled Gesellschaft. This new system transformed men who were born to a certain place in society and knew better than to try to change it into men who, once the new industrial order began to open channels, were eager to take advantage of them to rise in the economic ladder.

It has been noted (Ross, 1920) that different periods of time call forth and honor different kinds of achievement. At one time religious leaders are the most highly honored; at another, warriors; at still another, great artists, musicians, or poets.[10] Beginning at the end of the eighteenth century, the great entrepreneurs, bankers, industrial leaders—masters of the financial organizational, marketing technologies—became the prevailing type of hero in our country.[11] The Gesellschaft was their creation; it suited them; they dominated it and fought off all attempts to interfere with its operation. A new kind of ethos came to dominate commercial and industrial relationships, the ethos of capitalism, of the market, based on monetary exchange, on a "cash nexus," subject to careful accounting. It created "economic man," rational, efficient, calculating, for whom profit rather than kinship bonds determined decisions. Allow the market, not sentiment, to control what and how much is produced. The market will regulate itself better than government.

Capitalism—as it came to be called—was a beautifully self-regulating system. Later, in the hands of the so-called Social Darwinists, the new ethos almost apotheosized the industrial and financial leaders who had amassed the capital, built the factories, trained the workers, encouraged the inventions, and thus vastly increased their own and the national wealth. For a long time the rugged individualist pursuing his own interests was king in the United States. Social theorists for more than a century have been tracing out all the ramifications of the new ethos on the human species. The Darwinian rubric, "struggle for existence," rationalized a great deal of inhumane behavior. The classes owed nothing to each other (Sumner, 1952). Every man for himself and the devil take the hindmost seemed a rational rule. The work world was harsh, competitive, uncaring. In time, to be sure, when the results of this ethos began to show up in shocking health problems, when reformers—many of them women—began to show legislators what the human costs were, when Marx explained what had happened, modifications began. But the competitive self-interest ethos remained. Considerably faded from its most virulent nineteenth-century form, the ethos still characterizes the male world. In almost caricature form, it is still apotheosized by modern writers. Thus, for example, Ringer recommends getting rid of outmoded notions like duty and charity (1977). Korda promulgates a Hobbesian view of the world as a dangerous place; a man must achieve power to live comfortably in it. "No matter who you are, the basic truth is that . . . your gain is inevitably someone else's loss, your failure someone else's victory" (Korda, 1975). Power is essential to protect oneself against the cruelty and ruthlessness of others; kindness betokens weakness, justice invites defeat, power pays off. A man must learn and practice the rituals, symbols, and games of power. He must not have compassion, sympathy, pity, remorse, for these are signs of weakness. A sense of justice may lead to defeat. The nice guy is a weakling.

The engineering technology was, then, only part of the great revolution at the end of the eighteenth century. So also were the organizational and financial technologies which put the engineering technologies to work. And the scientific world view. All were important. But the most profoundly influential part of the new industrial order was the ethos that underlay it.

These and other effects of that great complex of revolutions in the male world have been almost endlessly studied and researched, especially their impact on class structure, on the relationship between the worker and his tools, on the distribution of rewards, on alienation, on anomie, on culture—on every aspect, in fact, of the male world. The contrast between the preindustrial, often nostalgically idealized, Gemeinschaft or kin-based local economy and the modern Gesellschaft or capitalist economy has been a major preoccupation of urban and community sociologists for well over a century. But until recently the specific impact of the Gesellschaft on the female world per se has received only secondary, indirect, derivative attention, if any, perhaps because the impact was so delayed. Among the questions that now arise are these: How have all the changes brought about by the new technologies affected the kin- and locale-based female world? How, specifically, have they influenced the love-and/or-duty ethos? With respect to developing countries today, Inkeles and Smith emphasize that modernizing requires liberating people from restrictive kinship and local ties (1974, 4). Does this apply also to "modernizing" the female world?

Why the Delay in the Impact of Gesellschaft?

The new technologies that so revolutionized the male world have, until recently, had primarily indirect rather than direct impact on the female world. Although they did open up some channels, the new industrial order that resulted from them cut women off from some other channels previously available to them in the female world. The local markets, for example, where a woman could participate in the economy as a more or less independent agent by selling goods she had made or grown—textiles, produce, eggs, butter, cheese. Or by way of the agent who had bought the product of her spindle or loom. The new technologies changed the work site for many women. They came in time to change relationships within the family. But the major impact came slowly.

At least two hypotheses suggest themselves as explanations for the delay in the impact of the Gesellschaft on the female world, one having to do with what may be called the critical mass hypothesis and the other with the nature of the work women did in the labor force. The first hypothesis resorts to a diffusion model (Bernard, 1976). In any population, several categories of individuals may be distinguished on the basis of readiness for change, namely: the avant garde or innovators; the early accepters; the early majority; the late majority; and the laggards. The change cannot begin its upward thrust until a critical mass of individuals has been achieved. That is, there have to be enough individuals influenced by the forces making for change—in the present context, number of women in the labor force, for example—before enough momentum can be achieved to propel the change more rapidly. It then shoots upward as a growth curve does until even the laggards are caught up in it. The characterization of groups of people in terms of amenability to change in the "critical mass" hypothesis is a bit too psychological in the present context. It implies more deliberate choice than was actually exercised in most cases, but it is useful.

As applied to the present question, we note from Table 23-1 that the proportion of all American women who were in the labor force[12]—where they could be directly exposed to the Gesellschaft—was small throughout the nineteenth century. As late as 1870, in fact, there were fewer than two million (Jaffe and Stewart, 1951, 160) constituting only 13.3 percent of all females *ten* years of age and over and 14.7 percent of the work force. And even two decades later, in 1890, only 15.5 percent were in the labor force. Nor did the percentage increase very rapidly in the early twentieth century. Not until the late 1970s did it become roughly equal to the proportion not in the labor force. More than half the adult members of the female world, in brief, until yesterday, were not directly involved in the labor force at any one given point in time. Even in the decade of the 1940s, during the great upsurge of women employed in war time industries, the proportion rose only 17.4 percent, from 28.2 percent in 1940 to 33.1 percent in 1950. Between 1950 and 1960 it rose 21.1 percent. By the end of the 1970s, as noted, about half of all women were in the labor force. The "critical mass" seemed to have been reached in the 1960s, when the proportion was between a third and two-fifths.

TABLE 23-1 Female Labor-Force Participation Rate and Proportion of Labor Force Female, 1870–1977*

Year	*Labor-Force Participation Rate*	*Proportion of Labor Force Female*
1870	15.5	14.8
1880	16.3	15.2
1890	19.2	17.2
1900	20.4	18.1
1910	—	—
1920	24.1	20.4
1930	25.1	22.0
1940	28.2	25.3
1950	33.1	28.9
1960	37.8	35.0
1970	43.4	38.1
1978	49.1	40.1
(1990)	(54.8)	(44.0)

*Source: 1890-1950, Donald J. Bogue, *The Population of the United States* (New York: Free Press, 1959), p. 423; 1960-1970, Women's Bureau, *1975 Handbook* (Washington: Government Printing Office, 1975), p. 11. Figures for participation rates for 1978 and 1990 from Ralph E. Smith, *The Subtle Revolution* (Washington, D.C.: The Urban Institute, 1979), p. 14. Figures for proportion of labor force female for 1978 and 1990 from Employment and Training Report of the President (1978), pp. 159, 253. The earlier years refer to females fourteen years of age and over, the more recent years to females sixteen years of age and over.

The relatively small proportion of women in the labor force at any one time conceals the fact that a much larger number of women participated in the labor force at some time or other in their lifetime. But not under circumstances calculated to have much impact on the female world. For in the nineteenth and early twentieth centuries, females in the labor force consisted largely of a stream of young—"prime-time" and younger—women passing through the occupational structure between school and marriage. They did not see themselves as more than temporary sojourners in the outside Gesellschaft world. In 1900-1902, women's labor-force life averaged only 7.6 years. By 1939-1941, it was 12.2 years (Jaffe and Stewart, 1951, 317). By 1960 it ranged from 17 years for a woman who had four or more children to 45 years for a woman who had never married (Garfinkle, 1969). This lengthened period of time in the labor force was in turn related to the growing number of women who continued to be in the labor force after marriage. The proportion of women in the labor force who were married rose from 4.6 percent in 1900 (Jaffe and Stewart, 249) to 62.3 percent in 1974 (Women's Bureau, 1975, 17). And for mothers, the length of time in the labor force grew even more. In fact, a far greater portion of a woman's work life may occur after, rather than before, she has raised her family and reentered the labor force (Garfinkle).

Another hypothesis explaining the delayed impact of the Gesellschaft on the female world has to do with the nature of the work women performed in the labor force. Except early in the industrializing process, relatively few of the women in the labor force were in occupations that subjected them directly to the Gesellschaft. Although early in the nineteenth century a large proportion of employed women were in the mills and factories, this proportion declined to only a fourth by the end of the century (Baker, 1964, 79). Most of the work women did was in a personal setting—teaching, nursing, typing, retail selling, personal service (Baker, part 2). And as long as women remained in segregated sectors of the labor force, the rules prescribed for them in the female world followed them into the work site, and they still conformed to its norms (Chapter 9). The stenographer performed some personal tasks, as a wife might; she was, in fact, sometimes called an "office wife." The salesgirl obeyed the floor manager as she might her father or some other authoritative male. Although the young women were paid wages and to this extent were following the cash-nexus set of norms, their duties and obligations were often diffuse, many of them more than the job description called for, including the usual supportive services expected of women.

We noted in Chapter 9 how, for example, the female world thus continued to envelop women even when they entered the labor force, how its norms surrounded them and continued to shape their behavior. The etiquette books quoted there reflected the world a woman continued to inhabit, a world in which she was still expected to be the "angel," not only of the home, as in the era of women's sphere, but also of the work site, supporting, replenishing, building up. She was, in brief, still bound by the norms of the female world.

Nor did labor-force participation change the familial or kin-based orientation of these young women. They lived at home, and often the money they earned was contributed to the family or used for family ends, for household expenditures, to help pay off the mortgage, for a dowry. Their earnings were, in effect, surrogates for the actual services they would otherwise be offering in the home. As late as the 1920s, working girls were still turning over most of their earnings to their families (Bernard, 1942, 90). The working wife generally continued to perform as household manager. The female world was, no doubt, affected to some extent by the "tour of duty" of young women in the labor force, but its ethos was not fundamentally changed. Whatever changes there were, they were not great enough to affect the values, ideals, motivations, beliefs, attitudes, expectations, norms, and rules of the female world. Despite the impact of the college-educated career women, the female world remained still primarily a kin- and locale-based world.

It was not until the middle of the twentieth century, when a critical mass had been achieved, that the ethos of the female world began to show the impact of the Gesellschaft. Now that virtually all women were in the labor force at some time or other in their lives, and about half of them or more at any given time, the impact on the female world was becoming strong enough to elicit serious concern about its consequences for women. Ideological factors also no doubt played a part in alerting women, whatever their work and however long their stay in the labor force, to the disadvantages to which their conformity to the norms of the female world subjected them in a harshly competitive, profit-based system motivated by self-interest. Women were having to work out their relationship to the Gesellschaft. It was not a new concern in the male world; it had bothered men for a long time.

"Foreign and Terrible to Her Original Inborn Nature"

Not too long after Alexander Hamilton expressed his satisfaction with the work of women and children in factories, where they were "rendered more useful . . . than they would otherwise be" (1791), they were beginning to be discouraged from entering the work force. The American economy was a male creation, tailored along male lines of organization and assuming male styles of relating. The entrance of women into this male preserve was seen as the intrusion of a foreign element that had to be closely controlled, segregated in limited enclaves. In 1828 the *Boston Courier* announced that "powerful necessity is rapidly breaking down ancient barriers, and woman is fast encroaching, if the assumption of a right may be deemed an encroachment, upon the exclusive domination of man." Assuming that the times were "out of joint," this paper sarcastically suggested that soon "our sons must be educated and prepared to obtain a livelihood in those dignified and more masculine professions of seamstresses, milliners, cooks, wet nurses, and chambermaids" (Baker, 84).

The horrendous effect of female labor-force participation, as male trade unionists saw it, was emphasized by the statement of the National Trades Union: " 'The system of female labor' was 'the most disgraceful escutcheon on the character of American freemen, and one that, if not checked by some superior cause, will entail ignorance, misery and degradation on our children to the end of time' " (Baker, 84). In Philadelphia, a speaker at an NTU meeting hoped "that the time might soon come 'when our wives, no longer doomed to servile labor, will be the companions of our fireside and the instructors of our children; and our daughters, reared to virtue and usefulness, become the solace of our declining years' " (84). As late as 1875, C. D. Wright, chief of the Massachusetts Bureau of Labor Statistics, thought that "married women ought not to be tolerated in the mills at all . . . for it is an evil that is sapping the life of our operative population, and must sooner or later be regulated, or, more probably, stopped" (Baker, 84).

Throughout the nineteenth century the argument was made that entering the labor force would have a bad effect on women. They would become coarsened. They would lose their femininity, even their virtue. They would no longer be able to perform the "heart" function, to be companions at a man's fireside. The rough, tough work world would make them unfit to perform their true womanly roles. They would take over the ethos of the Gesellschaft. They would become "economic women."

In 1887 Tönnies himself was already asking about the effect of the Gesellschaft on female character. "As woman enters into the struggle of earning a living, it is evident that trading and the freedom and independence of the female factory worker as contracting party and possessor of money will develop her rational will, enable her to think in a calculating way, even though, in the case of factory work, the tasks themselves may not lead in this direction. The woman becomes enlightened, coldhearted, conscious" (1957, 166). This is unnatural, for "nothing is more foreign and terrible to her original inborn nature. . . . Possibly nothing is more characteristic and important in the process of formation of the Gesellschaft and destruction of Gemeinschaft. Through this development the 'individualism' which is the prerequisite of Gesellschaft comes to its own" (166).

Did all these changes have the anticipated coarsening effect on women? Have women indeed lost their womanliness? There is no convincing reason to believe that they have. In fact, the research on women well into the twentieth century has shown that they are still performing the "heart" function, still emotionally supportive, still stroking. Not until almost the last third of the twentieth century were women being taught to subscribe to the ethos of the Gesellschaft, how to take over the Gesellschaft personality characteristics (Chapter 22).

A study looking for evidence on the "masculinization" theory of female personality today showed that although the activities of recent cohorts of college women were "clearly becoming increasingly like males' previous patterns," in personality variables women were still high on the characteristically female affiliation dimension. Although there was some decline between the classes of 1964 and 1978, "the affiliation motive was higher in females in both classes. . . . The 'masculinization of female personality' hypothesis is not supported" here (Stewart and Salt, draft, 1978). Interestingly, on the power-motive dimension, "women scored higher than men . . . in 1964, but lower in 1978," suggesting, if anything, recent nonmasculinization rather than the opposite.

That women will, indeed, change can be taken for granted. But it is evidence of our blinders that we think the only way to change is to become like men, that there are no other alternatives. Women will change, but in their own way. There are other ways to be a woman than a male way. Women are learning those ways.

Options

We referred in Chapter 22 to the questions confronting women today: What kind of world do they want? Do they want to repudiate the female world altogether and embrace the ethos of the male world? Or do they want to salvage their own world but in modified form, to cut its costs? As long ago as the beginning of the century the same problem was puzzling women. Even then, "the 'sphere' of woman was anomalous and confused. With some exceptions women themselves were confused no less than society at large about what they could and should be doing" (Baker, 85). The issues became relevant for more and more women as the century progressed. They are no easier to deal with today than they were then. But proposed ways of dealing with them have become more differentiated.

A substantial body of research shows in glaring detail how disadvantaged women socialized into the ethos of the female world are in the economy.[13] They are easily exploited and discriminated against. They are trained to be nonassertive, compliant, agreeable, to serve others. Living in the female world not only fails to prepare women for living in the Gesellschaft, it makes them unfit for it. Children who have been taught to be kind, gentle, supportive in the home have to learn to be tough, competitive, aggressive in the "outside" Gesellschaft world. Some women therefore repudiate the female world. Conforming to its norms is counterproductive in the Gesellschaft. Instead they advocate a policy of taking over the Gesellschaft self-interest ethos. Rather than teach women to be devious, manipulative, exploitative, as the old office etiquette books did, the new books were teaching them how to do well in the Gesellschaft by following its rules of efficiency, rationality, profit. They should become, as Tönnies had feared they might, rational and calculating.

Some women did not repudiate the female world and what it stood for but they did want more say in the management of the economy. It began to dawn on them that now, with such a large proportion of women in the labor force, there was no reason intrinsic in the nature of things that running the economy should necessarily be an exclusively male prerogative. The economy belonged to women as well as to men. They had as great a stake in it as men had. If their lives required certain work conditions—such as good day care for young children, flexitime, job sharing, pregnancy and maternity benefits—then these conditions should have been provided as a matter of course, whether or not they were profitable.

If the ethos of the female world disappeared, if it ceased to perform its integrating function, would the whole societal system break down? Or would the male world modify its structure to take on the supportive function? Would it listen as sympathetically as women have done? Would the male world incorporate the altruistic ethos into the economy—see to it, for example, that bureaucracies set up to perform helping functions did not harm rather than help their intended beneficiaries, or at least inject more humane procedures into them? Or will women entering the economy by their mere presence be the transmitters of change? If so, how? Is there some critical mass of women in the labor force which determines when the female style affects the structure of the male world?

Some women reject the whole Gesellschaft ethos. They feel uncomfortable with it and want no part of it. The new relationships they experiment with among themselves do not resemble the Gesellschaft.[14] Like many disaffected men, they experiment with small enterprises, boutiques, handicraft, consultancies, professional services. Tönnies did not think Gemeinschaft was a lost cause. "The possibility of overcoming this female individualism and arriving at a reconstruction of Gemeinschaft exists. Women's growing consciousness . . . can develop and rise to a moral-humane consciousness" (166). Unfortunately he did not specify how this was to be done. A considerable number of women are now working on this seemingly intractable problem.

Will Success Spoil the Female World?

Meanwhile a subtle and perhaps, in the long run, more significant process has been going on. Instead of softening the Gesellschaft, the reverse process has been taking place, namely, one of "economizing" the female world, importing into it certain principles of the Gesellschaft, substitution of the monetary exchange "cash-nexus" for the love-and/or-duty ethos. Just as activist women early in the century were transforming agape into a salaried profession, so today women are coming to be paid for the kinds of care they used to give freely.

Thus, more and more activities and services that were once offered by women as favors or performed as duties are now becoming marketable; women are asking that they be paid for them. We even think now in terms of finding ways to pay housewives for their services.[15] The Gesellschaft standards of worth are being taken over by the female world. In brief, the caring services until now performed on the basis of love- and/or-duty in the integry increasingly move into the economy where they become saleable commodities. The old personal network fades into the cash nexus. In a recent novel (*Summer before the Dark*) Doris Lessing describes how the heroine discovered the monetary value of the caring she had always supplied on a love-and/or-duty basis. She was astonished to learn that the caring that her family had always taken so much for granted was worth a considerable amount of money to the international civil service.That world paid her to care; she had a marketable skill. She was not doing anything different from what she had always done for her family at home. But now she was being appreciated; value was assigned to the caring; she was being paid for it. Similarly, the care of children, of the disabled, of all lowly or helpless people is little by little being transferred from the female world to the cash-nexus economy. Not always, it may be added, with favorable results.[16] The question may well be raised: can it be regarded as "caring" if it is paid for?

Conflict of this kind is not, of course, unique to the female world. The male world is also set up to generate it. Vulnerability to such conflict is, indeed, endemic in the human condition.

Modernization

As related to developing countries, the phenomena of change in the female world we have been discussing here in terms of the Gemeinschaft-Gesellschaft paradigm are often dealt with in terms of a newer and more fashionable paradigm, "modernization." About a half-century ago the material culture of the simpler peoples was a major topic of research; invention and the diffusion of culture traits were widely studied; the origin and spread of a number of such traits were traced and generalizations about the process arrived at. More recently, however, the focus of interest has drastically changed as the so-called simpler peoples were, in effect, being folded into the orbit of the industrialized Western world. The normal channels of diffusion were not operating. Although missionaries had been spreading the Christian religion and modern medical science, although colonial administrators had been imposing Western administration, sanitation, and schooling on the "developing" peoples of the Third World, now that colonial empires had passed away the problem was to help these people take over and master the technical accoutrements of the modern world themselves. A major concern of researchers thus came to be "modernization." In 1949, President Truman had laid down his Point Four Program to bring modern science and technology to these newly emerging countries; the Economic and Social Council of the United Nations was also funding modernizing programs. Modernization was in. A host of social scientists from several disciplines went to work to deal with the problems. The 1960s were to be the "decade of development" (Inkeles and Smith, 1974, 3).

Hareven notes that the concept of modernization tends to be a catchall category. Sometimes it is synonymous with industrialization, sometimes it includes a broader spectrum than mere industrial development. "Most definitions fall within two areas: (1) personal modernity, which concerns changes in individual attitudes and behavior, and more 'rational' decision making; (2) societal modernity, which describes such large-scale social shifts as economic development, new communications, higher rates of literacy, and secularization" (1976, 191). As related to women and the female world, we discussed the first of these in Chapter 17. At this point we shall deal with the second or societal aspect. In both kinds, it soon became evident that modernization consisted of more than merely introducing modern technologies. Much more.

The Societal Aspects of Modernization

The analogy between societal modernization and "modernization" of the female world is more than a mere figure of speech. In both cases a preindustrial society must be psychologically and sociologically "retooled" (Lerner, 1963). Psychologically, as Inkeles and Smith pointed out, the individual must free himself (or herself) from kin- and locale-based ties; for "a modern nation needs participating citizens, men and women who take an active interest in public affairs and who exercise their rights and perform their duties as members of a community larger than that of the kinship network and the immediate geographic locality" (Inkeles and Smith, 1974, 4). And sociologically the societal structure must become achievement-oriented, emphasizing specialization and universalistic criteria (Hoselitz, 1964). Actually, it might be noted in passing, the impact of modernization programs as designed by the West has often been calamitous for women. In bringing Western sexist biases to a developing country, these programs have, for example, given technological training to men, who were not the farmers, and deprived the women, who were, of the new and necessary skills (Boserup, 1970). As in the case of the developing countries, "modernization" of the female world calls upon old kin- and locale-based systems to come to terms with new ways of relating. In both cases, traditional and modern individuals confront one another; in both cases, there is nostalgia for the old along with adoption of the new (Lerner, 1963).

The intent here is not to disparage modernization or, in the present context, to argue against it for the female world. The point, it seems to me, is that if it is to occur, "modernization" in the female world should be guided by the female world itself, timed to its pace, and oriented in the direction it chooses. Modernization need not be imposed on the female world in a way that deprives it of the supports that have sustained it in the past.

Notes

1. There seem to be differences of opinion among researchers on the relative contribution of women to the production of food. One study, on the basis of Murdock's *Ethnographic Atlas*, finds women averaging 44 percent of the subsistence activities (Aronoff and Crano, 1975, 17). Another study of six culture regions finds a range of 24.5 to 43.5 percent, averaging 34.9 percent (Sanday, 1973, 1682-1700); still another study of the same six regions, shows a range of 18 to 42 percent, averaging 31 percent (1974, 207-214). Elise Boulding estimates that when sedentary agrovillage life began, perhaps 12,000 years ago, women contributed as much as 80 percent (1976, 97). Leakey and Lewin estimate that hunting provided only about 30 percent of the food in the hunting-gathering economies (1978). Precise calculations are of course impossible. Rae Blumberg gives the most recent and exhaustive overview of the female contribution to agricultural systems in her detailed historical and current survey (1980).
2. Clifford Jolly (1970) believes that among early prehumans a premium was placed on the ability to "manipulate objects of very small size relative to the hand," such as seeds. Thus, says Wilson, "man became bipedal in order to pick seeds" (1975, 569). Since women have smaller hands than men it must have been women who first picked the seeds.
3. My own (admittedly playful) theory of the discovery of horticulture follows this scenario: Tired of having her cache of food greedily eaten up by the

children as soon as she brought it home, and before she had invented baskets and pots to store the seeds in, one woman hid her seeds and berries in a hole in the ground. Others followed suit. Then, years later, one brilliant woman noticed that whenever she hid her seeds near the entrance to the cave, where the sun reached them, sprouts appeared, but whenever she hid them in the dark rear of the cave they did not. "Don't be silly," her sisters may have said; "it's just coincidental." So she experimented. And year after year it happened as she predicted. She had invented, or discovered, horticulture. The Greeks had a somewhat different story. They named this woman Ceres.

4. Kropotkin interestingly discusses how different the industrial revolution would have been if it had come at the time of the medieval city, in which mutual aid was prevalent. He even suggests that the decay of the mutual-aid system delayed the industrial revolution (1975, 37-39).
5. See E. Boulding in Chapter 3 above on the creativity of women in courtyard life. Female macaques were the first to learn to wash sweet potatoes provided to them by researchers. The young learned from them, and the practice spread among all but the old. ("Wild World of Animals," ABC television program, Feb. 25, 1979).
6. For an illustration of industrialization, including financing, by a Mexican family, see Larissa Adler Lomnitz and Marisol Perez Lizaur, *Family History*, 1978, 352-409. See also Chapter 3 above for the story of the convent which served as a great financial institution in Mexico.
7. Coming to terms with the Gesellschaft was by no means easy for the workers. The new industrial system called for a worker subject to a different kind of discipline from that of the preindustrial era. It took some time to develop that kind of worker. The story of Robert Owen, a British industrialist and philanthropist, is often cited as an example. He was one of the first of the great entrepreneurs who were carrying out the changes we call the industrial revolution. Some factories had used paupers and their children, supplied by overseers of the poor. They were sometimes locked inside the factory so that they could not escape. Owen wanted none of that. He built decent houses for his workers and devised an elaborate scheme of rewards and demerits to train them. It was an ad hoc experiment. In the context of the present concern for modernization, Inkeles and Smith consider the study of the process "whereby people move from being traditional to becoming modern personalities" one of the most important research tasks for social psychology (1975, 5)
8. Veblen was among those who made a big distinction between the mentality of the engineer and that of the businessman (1904, 1914, 1919).
9. If industrialization had been a female enterprise it would probably have been accomplished differently. The standards might have been different. Size and speed might have been less important than other criteria. The resulting economy would probably have been on a smaller scale and the tempo somewhat slower. The ethos might well have been closer to that of Marx than to that of Smith; "from each according to ability and to each according to need," is a rule that most mothers apply to their children. The larger, stronger child is expected to do more; the less able child is not de-

prived. The system would probably have been less productive and the society correspondingly less affluent. Profit would not have been the major criterion in decision making.

10. Leo Lowenthal has traced the succession of types who became heroes in popular culture in this century (1961).
11. In England, where land remained the basis for high status, the men whose wealth came from the new industrial order bought estates and became part of the landed classes. Scions of the old landed gentry and nobility who had once exercised their "need for achievement" in hunting, games, and athletic sports becoming to a gentlemen, and who had looked down on "trade" and other nonagricultural pursuits, came in time to be as money-motivated as the upstarts.
12. The very term "labor force" is relatively new, having entered the research vocabulary only in the 1930s (Jaffe and Stewart, 1951).
13. Women in the male professions were among the most vocal in portraying the disadvantages women suffered from in the male world. But "Heaven help the working girl" reflected the folk recognition of the defenselessness of a young woman socialized to comply, to obey, to conciliate, when confronted with demanding male employers.
14. An inconspicuous example, by no means generalizable, is offered by a group of Southern women mill workers who did not like the Gesellschaft atmosphere of the mill where they worked. They quit and organized their own little work setting, working according to their own pace, at their own hours, in a congenial sisterly and supportive atmosphere. They were unexpectedly successful. They received more orders for their work than they could fill, competing on the basis of the quality of their product (television documentary, 1977).
15. Women clinical psychologists, with training equal to that of men, find more resistance to pay commensurate with their skills. They are performing a service that women have been performing for milennia. So why should they be paid for it? There is a real conflict here, both in the women themselves, who feel the ambiguity of their position, and in the inconsistency between the ethos of the female world—give, nurture, heal—and the ethos of the male world—demand payment for services.
16. "Bleeders-for-hire," for example, include more individuals with poor health records than volunteer donors do; a class factor is usually involved.

24

The Female World and the Polity

Making Decisions

Just as the classical paradigms posited an "economic man" to run the capitalistic system, so did the classical paradigms posit his political counterpart, "political man." But whereas economic man rejected conflict—it interfered with production—his political counterpart almost gloried in it. Spencer was sure that industrialization would rid the world of war because it would integrate nations into a mutually advantageous economic system. The political Social Darwinists, however, thought peace was just a dream, and not a beautiful one at that. They apotheosized a fantasied law of the jungle, red in tooth and claw. A tough-minded ethos guided the thinking of this male world of power. The polity, like the economy, has been a male preserve.

The function of the polity has to do with making societal or group decisions, with enforcing them, modifying them, interpreting them. There are countless ways of structuring these processes, of determining who makes, enforces, and interprets decisions. Some ways produce compliance, others, resistance, resentment, and hostility. Until recently, few women have been in these societal decision-related positions.

There are usually a great many people who wish to make the decisions and consequently there is an ongoing struggle among them for the right or privilege to do so. A considerable amount of aggression, competition, conflict, coalition-formation, strategy, is called for to achieve these positions. All of these are "political" processes and may go on in all kinds of social groupings, from a small local club to a nation or, in fact, on the world stage itself. We limit ourselves here to the current scene in our own society. Not everyone has the qualities called for in the struggle for decision-making power.[1] But apparently more men do than women (Maccoby and Jacklin, 1974). It is the preponderant number of aggressive, competitive, want-to-win-at-any-price individuals among men as compared with the number among women that gives the polity its overwhelming male character and its macho style.

In the United States women began to knock at the door of the polity in the nineteenth century, reminding it that they were not even recognized in the Constitution. It took a long, painful, militant battle for them to gain even a toehold in it. And not until well into the present century did the suffrage become a constitutionally protected right of women. We saw in Chapter 21 how women have responded. The same arguments that had been used against their entrance into the economy had been used against their entrance into the polity.[2] In neither case did all the doomsday predictions materialize. Only recently are women beginning again to claim that the polity, no less than the economy, is as much theirs as men's. They constitute more than half its membership. They are taxpayers. They are consumers. There are no issues that do not impact on their lives at one point or another. All issues are female issues, from the national budget to abortion legislation. The decisions the polity wrestles with impinge on them from birth to death. From the hospitals where they are born and give birth to the schools they attend and those their children attend to the site where they work to the supermarket where they shop for the family's provisions to the Social Security benefits they earn or inherit to the nursing homes in which they die. Little by little women are learning how to participate in the polity. Only recently are rules being evolved to mitigate the disadvantages they have been under in playing the ruthless "political game."[3]

The men who protested that giving the suffrage to women would "unsex" them or coarsen them knew that the polity was a harsh, rough arena, governed by an ethos far removed from the gentler one of the female world.

The Ethos of the Polity

The polity, reflecting as it does a male ethos, embodies enormous preoccupation with the quest for power. History as a male scholarly pursuit has concentrated on the aspects of the discipline which have to do with war, violence, kings, emperors, expanding empires, consolidating kingships, aggression, all primarily male concerns. Kropotkin notes that fascination with these aspects of history has completely overshadowed more peaceful, mutual-aid aspects: "The self-assertion of the individual or of groups of individuals, their struggles for superiority, and the conflicts which resulted therefrom, have . . . been analyzed, described, and glorified from time immemorial. . . . History, such as it has hitherto been written, is almost entirely a description of the ways and means by which theocracy, military power, autocracy, and, later on, the richer classes' rules have been promoted, established, and maintained. The struggles between these forces make, in fact, the substance of history. . . . On the other side, the mutual-aid factor has been hitherto totally lost sight of; it was simply denied, or even scoffed at, by the writers of the present and past generations" (1975, 37-38).

Friedrich Nietzsche articulated the archetypical male political ethos. It was he who promulgated the doctrine of the superman. Power was the *ultima thule* of the superman. There was nothing but contempt for the weak. The great man was silent, inexpressive, cold, distant, inscrutable. "A great man . . . is colder, harder, less cautious and more free from the fear of 'public opinion,' he does not possess the virtues which are compatible with respectability and with being respected, nor any of those things which are counted among the 'virtues of the herd.' If he is unable to lead, he walks alone. . . . He asks for no 'compassionate' heart, but servants, instruments; . . . He knows that he cannot reveal himself to anybody: he thinks it bad taste to become familiar; and as a rule he is not familiar [even] when people think he is. When he is not talking to his soul, he wears a mask. He would rather lie than tell the truth, because lying requires more spirit and will. There is a loneliness within his heart which neither praise nor blame can reach, because he is his own judge from whom [there] is no appeal" (1964, 366-367). From warriors we must learn to die for the interests we are fighting for; "we must learn to sacrifice numbers, and to take our cause sufficiently seriously not to spare men"; and we must "practice inexorable discipline, and allow ourselves violence and cunning in war" (379). The very prototype of the strong, silent man, self-sufficient, contemptuous of the weak.

Nor did this ethos have any respect for women. In fact it charged that *their* ethos was actually the most selfish of all: "Behold this love and pity of women—what could be more egoistic? . . . And when they do sacrifice themselves and their honour or reputation, to whom do they sacrifice themselves? To the man? Is it not rather to an unbridled desire? These desires are quite as selfish, even though they may be beneficial to others and provoke gratitude" (221). Woman "requires a religion of the weak which glorifies weakness, love, and modesty as divine" (300). She conspires against the strong. And she exploits her motherhood. "Women avail themselves of children for the cult of piety, pity, and love:—the mother stands as the symbol of convincing altruism" (300).

It was not Nietzsche, however, so much as the Darwinian theory of evolution that undergirded the overriding male political ethos of the nineteenth century. Darwin himself was not a Social Darwinist. He rejected the school of philosophy which made selfishness the basis of all human behavior (1952, 316). There was too much in both human and prehuman behavior that went counter to it. Still, the insistence on seeing self-preservation or self-interest as the key to all human behavior in the economy and power-seeking in the polity has persisted among male thinkers. The corpus of theory that has supported this point of view has been based not on political economy, as in the case of "economic man," but rather on primatology and anthropology. A fairly sizable number of books has shored up this interest, the most popular being those by Konrad Lorenz, Robert Ardrey, Desmond Morris, Lionel Tiger, and Robin Fox. There is enormous preoccupation in this school of thought with power, with the male struggle for dominance, and often an invidious undertone of admiration for the "princely" alpha male in a troop of primates. A human interpretation is sometimes implied when it is not overtly expressed. There is an inordinate emphasis on control of others in the male world. Its ethos calls for a great deal of aggression, territorial defense, struggle for dominance. Decisions are made by and for the powerful. And woe betide the weak.

Although many ethologists and primatologists do not necessarily accept this interpretation and use of their work,[4] it still exerts enormous appeal in the public mind and is often applied almost literally to the human scene. And because in our society the male world has this ideological bias, because aggressiveness is valued, because achievement is glorified, and because winning is seen as not everything but the only thing, it is difficult for the polity in our society to impose reins either on itself or on the economy.

The Roszaks encapsulate the story of this male ethos in the past century. "In no small measure the last hundred years stand as the historical crisis of masculine dominance. During this period, under the pressure of advancing industrialization, the sexual stereotypes have played into the political life of the modern West with a special force.... The critical moment in this psychic dimension of history ... covers the two or three generations that precede the outbreak of the First World War" (1969). During those years there was a hard-boiled, militaristic style: militarism, imperialism, and racism took on the character of secular religions. Nietzsche's philosophy was appropriated as a cult of "sadistic bullying." There were numerous spokesmen for violence, many celebrations of war and warriors. Humanitarian values were "contemptuously" swept aside. The world stage was dominated by "bully boys and great predators" like Bismarck, Lenin, Kipling, Andrew Carnegie, Teddy Roosevelt, and Cecil Rhodes. For Jack London, the world was "a jungle, a battleground, a gladiatorial arena" (92). Invocations of blood and iron, power and bellicosity raised brute force to a supreme metaphysical principle. "The period leading up to 1914 reads . . . like one long drunken stag party where boys from every walk of life and every ideological persuasion goad one another on to ever more bizarre professions of toughness, daring, and counterphobic mania" (92). Although the harsh toughness the Roszaks excoriate has for some time been in process of mitigation, as recently as the 1940s the Third Reich was still apotheosizing it. The master race embodied the combativeness, aggressivity and belligerency celebrated in the cult; its members were the natural rulers over the inferior races of the world.

On a less blood-and-thunder note, the same macho theme is played out on the national scene today. Books on how to achieve power, how to dominate, how to intimidate become bestsellers. Those who have mastered power play the game twenty-fours hours a day with everyone from parking-lot attendants to wives, waiters, traffic cops, fellow workers, those above and those below them in the corporate structure. Even in the halls of our own Congress, a newspaper reporter tells us, House-Senate conferences "in their rawest form . . . are brawling, ego-driven tests of will; wrenching clashes of philosophy, muscle and politics" (Sinclair, 1977).

Such an ethos tends to create a certain kind of character. Thus Robert Ringer recommends getting rid of outmoded notions like duty and charity (1977) and "winning by intimidation" (1978). Korda also sees life as a zero-sum game; if you win, I lose. This is the reflection of an ethos lacking compassion, sympathy, or pity (1975). (We might say in passing that it is this conception of power that has given it a bad name in the female world.) Winning, climbing, achieving are prime values. Successful managers are characterized by "their drive to excel over fellow employees" (Engel, 1977, 55). They are hungry for power: "The drive to accomplish, the urge to compete, ambition, determination, dynamism —these are only facets of the overriding characteristic that sets super-executives apart. That characteristic can be summed up in one word: hunger" (56). The head of ITT still works up to twenty hours a day "in pursuit of greater wealth and power." Tycoon Norton Simon, already worth more than $100 million, is still a driven man.

Case in Point

A close associate of former President Nixon reports on the aftermath of his downfall. He quotes his great hero as he described how it felt to be so driven by the male ethos:

> We knew very young what the dream [of power] was all about and how to win it. Being hungry helps, but it isn't nearly enough and in some cases, it isn't even necessary. . . . I was not a good athlete and that was the very reason that I tried and tried and tried. To get the discipline for myself and to show the others that here was a guy who could dish it out and take it. Mostly, I took it. But once you learn that you've got to work harder than everybody else it becomes a way of life as you move out of the alley and on your way. In your own mind you have nothing to lose so you take plenty of chances and if you do your homework many of them pay off. . . . You find you can't stop playing the game . . . because it is part of you and you need it as much as an arm or a leg. . . . So you are lean and mean and resourceful and you continue to walk on the edge of the precipice because over the years you have become fascinated by how close to the edge you can walk without losing your balance. . . . You've got to be tough. You can't break . . . even when you know there is nothing left. You can't admit, even to yourself, that it is gone. . . . A man doesn't cry. . . . I don't cry. . . . You don't cry [Clawson, 1979].

Roszak sees the same male power-worshipping ethos in the writings of Hemingway and Mailer, with their cult of bullfighting and prize fighting and brawling, in "the ceaseless need [of the male] to prove how tough, how *really* tough one is" (1969, 93). The popular media also fuel this "ceaseless need." The very concept of maleness is associated with violence. In Tiger's words, "Notions of valid maleness are widely associated with the hard military virtues, with various activities such as hunting, speeding, fighting, and the extraction of substantial sums of money from either natural resources or people" (1969, 46).

Natural and Sexual Selection: A Brief Excursus

Natural selection was the great theoretical rationale for the male power ethos. There was no appeal from it. It justified the power and privilege of the "fittest," defined as the strongest, even the most ruthless. Darwin himself, as we noted above, was not a Social Darwinist. In fact he observed that sometimes qualities that were adaptive up to a point could be elaborated to a level at which they became maladaptive instead. Furthermore, there was another kind of selection at work in the animal world, sexual selection, which operated on quite different principles and selected different kinds of characteristics than strength or "fitness." Natural selection, Darwin pointed out, dealt with qualities that helped their bearers overcome or destroy others of their own sex; sexual selection, with those that helped attract females. "Sexual selection . . . depends, not on struggle for existence in relation to other organic beings or to external conditions [environmental limitations], but on a struggle between the individuals of one sex, generally the male, for the possession of the other sex. The result is not death to the unsuccessful competitor, but few or no offspring. Sexual selection is, therefore, less rigorous than natural selection" (43). The result of natural selection might be death to the unsuccessful party, thus irretrievably cutting his genes out of the gene pool; the result of sexual selection, however, would only reduce not eliminate the contribution of the unsuccessful individual to the gene pool. Natural selection was based on eliminating an opponent; sexual selection, on winning a partner. Killing a competitor in a fight would do no good if the female would not accept the killer. "The power to charm the female has sometimes been more important than the power to conquer other males in battle" (375). Natural selection, in brief, made for tougher males; sexual selection, for more attractive males.

There was, Darwin taught, a limit to what natural selection could do. "In regard to structures acquired through ordinary or natural selection, there is in most cases, as long as the conditions of life remain the same, a limit to the amount of advantageous modification in relation to certain special purposes" (374). In the present context, for example, the purpose of reaching the top of the corporate or political ladder. Sometimes, as noted, the qualities acquired by natural selection may actually become maladaptive—for example, the horns of certain stags (374). Or, in the case of modern man, the win-at-any-price mentality. In any event, "natural selection will determine that such [maladaptive] characters [as, for example, the Korda-Ringer mentality] shall not be acquired by the victorious males, if they would be highly injurious, either by expending too much of their powers, or by exposing them to any great danger" (374.)

The relevance of this brief digression is that the male political ethos, however it is conceived, may now have reached the point where its component elements are in fact injurious, "by expending too much of their [males'] powers" (374). The power-driven male, operating on a never ending one-upmanship basis, who has to be victorious over all others no matter what, may be analogous to the stag with maladaptive horns. Darwin's hedge—"as long as the conditions of life remain the same"—no longer obtains. Conditions *are* changing. Getting to the top, beating all others, winning whatever the cost may call for the investment of so much energy, so many resources, that relatively little is left over for family, even reproduction.

Nor can sexual selection be counted on to come to the rescue. It is assumed that "generally, the most vigorous males, those which are best fitted for their place in nature [read: the corporation], will leave most progeny" (Dawkins, 1978, 43), an assumption not justified in human society. It may be true that, as Henry Kissinger is quoted as saying, power is the greatest aphrodisiac, for powerful men do indeed seem to have their pick of beautiful women. Still, there is no evidence whatever that they contribute more genes to the gene pool. (Consider the case of Henry VIII.) The very richest men in our society may have more children than less wealthy men, but by and large the differential fertility between rich and poor favors the poor. And if we think in terms of female fertility the differentials are marked not only with respect to income but also with respect to education and occupation. If men were really motivated by a desire to contribute to the gene pool—to be "gene-fit"—they would concentrate on "charming the female" rather than on destroying one another.

Past Not Necessarily Prologue

Although the darker side of the male world—its history of gratuitous slaughter, terrorism, torture—does not escape the notice of the female world, it cannot be denied that its achievements to date in science, technology, the arts, philosophy, however biased in the male direction, have been admirable. It has produced a wide variety of intellectual systems, and there is no reason to believe that it has exhausted all its potential. These male achievements, like the stag's horns in early stages of its evolution, have in large part been adaptive. Still, though the male ethos may have stimulated superb achievements in the past, it may not necessarily do so forever. Shakespeare's "what is past is prologue" (*The Tempest*, II, i, 253) is not necessarily true. What is adaptive at one time may not be so at another. "How many trends and processes, which we now increasingly see have gone too far, were at some time an embodiment and manifestation of profoundly positive human aspiration and striving" asks one critic of the direction the male world is taking (editorial, *Intermediate Technology*, 1976).[5]

With respect to one of the major enterprises of the male world, warfare, historians find it less and less functional in this day and age. It may once have served defensible functions, although at prohibitive cost. "It has at times stimulated science, invention, and the art," but it has also "destroyed civilizations and initiated dark ages." At the present time, however, "war is more likely to deteriorate the quality of life than to improve it" (Wright, 1968, 466). Probably about a tenth of all deaths in the first half of this century were war-related. And, as Spencer pointed out a long time ago, in an integrated international economic system, war no longer made economic sense. Marvin Harris also concurs in the judgment that war is anachronistic today. "Merely because all human beings in the world today and in the known past have lived in warmaking sexist societies or societies affected by warmaking sexist societies is not reason enough to cast human nature in the image of the savage characteristics which are necessary for waging successful war. The fact that warfare and sexism have played and continue to play such prominent roles in human affairs does not mean that they must continue to do so for all future time" (1977, 66). It is just possible that in order for human beings to survive under some of the conditions they were subjected to in the past, an ethos that was competitive, territorial, aggressive, driven to win, to dominate, had to be cultivated—and for many individual men it did have to be cultivated with a vengeance—and nurturance played down.

Despite what looks—at least to outsiders, especially women—like the demonstrable futility of war, there are some who still share William James' revulsion at the thought of too much peace. The prospect of a warless world is terrifying to them. They argue that without war there would probably be more murder, terrorism, and general violence. To them the male need for a moral equivalent of war seems urgent. If men aren't killing one another in "decent" wars, he implies, they will do so out of boredom. Although the female world does not wholly preclude fighting—vide Deborah, Joan of Arc, the Abbess Rundegard—I do not remember ever hearing or reading about any woman who bemoaned the possibility of eliminating war; a felt need for war does not characterize the female world.

From the perspective of the female world, the preoccupation of the male world with power and dominance takes on the aspect of an almost neurotic compulsion. As it also does, of course, to many individual men who find the whole male ethos of dominance and aggression uncongenial. Having to deal with it can be frustrating to them as well as to women. They do not seek to conform to its tenets. Impatient to get on with the job, they, like many women, have watched other men in committee meetings spend more energy on the latent agenda—one-upmanship—than on tackling the tasks before them on the table.

Although books like those of Korda and Ringer—which practically burlesque the male ethos—do, to be sure, constitute an embarrassment to many men, still the message does seem to fit the macho image and to appeal to many. The fact that such books are written and avidly read must mean, however, that a great many men do not have the imagination or skill to carry out the message. They have to learn how from books; they buy thousands of copies.

A really crucial moment arrives when these men, rather than seek to conform to it, begin publicly to question the very nature of the male ethos itself, as some have recently begun to do. They find the whole ethos of dominance and aggression, of winning, winning, winning, uncongenial. They resent the pressures exerted on them to accept it. They deplore the brutality of male adolescent hazing. They reject the machismo written into the stereotyped male role (Farrell, 1975; Pleck, 1976; David and Brennan, 1976; Brenton, 1966). This is not, however, the old meekness that was to inherit the earth; this is not about turning the other cheek; this is not about Christian humility. This is about the very definition of maleness and an attempt to redefine it in terms suitable for the modern world.[6] It's about time. For, as Carolyn Heilbrun puts it: "What is important now is that we free ourselves from the prison of gender and, before it is too late, deliver the world from the almost exclusive control of the masculine impulse" (1973, xiv). We have permitted it too long. "By developing in men the ideal 'masculinized' characteristics of competitiveness, aggressiveness, and by placing in power those men who most embody these traits, we have, I believe, gravely endangered our own survival" (xvi). Nor is this merely a literary figure of speech.

For it may be that we have now arrived at a moment when the male ethos has become maladaptive rather than adaptive, anti rather than prosurvival in its impact. Quite a lot of people seem to think so. They think that an ethos that stimulated so much achievement in the past must find new ways to express itself. War and violence will stop "when their productive, reproductive, and ecological functions are fulfilled by less costly alternatives (Harris, 1977, 66). Such alternatives now lie within our grasp for the first time in history. Granted that it was something in the male ethos that impelled the male world to achieve prodigiously, this recognition does not necessarily mean that it must go on endlessly even when its operation may now have become maladaptive.

Among the changes that are rendering the old male ethos maladaptive are those relating to the greatest male successes, levels of productivity that are beginning to threaten the good earth itself. Warfare is only one way the human species could destroy itself. There are others.

The New Nemesis: K-Extinction

A sociobiologist, Edmund Wilson, distinguishes two kinds of extinction to which a population or species may be exposed, r-extinction, at the beginning of its history, and K-extinction, at a much later time, when it has reached the limits of its ecological resources. In the r-extinction situation, mutual defense and cooperative foraging and nest building serve to maximize survival (1975, 107). Populations in this situation tend to be young and to have extensive kin relationships; altruism and mutual help tend to prevail. In the K-extinction situation, however, mutual aid becomes minimized (108). At a time when a population is vulnerable to r-extinction, high fertility rates are necessary; at a time when it is vulnerable to K-extinction, as in densely populated areas, fertility need not—must not—be encouraged.

At least one theorist, Marvin Harris, argues that K-extinction—a term which he does not himself use—is a constantly recurring threat in human history. He sees the new technologies of production developed to meet the needs of a population constantly pressing on the limits of productivity. He aims "to show the relationship between material and spiritual well-being and the cost-benefits of various systems for increasing production and controlling population growth" (1977, xi).[7] This is where women prick up their ears; Harris is now approaching their beat. "In the past," he continues, "irresistible reproductive pressures arising from the lack of safe and effective means of contraception led recurrently to the intensification of production. Such intensification has always led to environmental depletion, which in general has resulted in new systems of production—each with a characteristic form of institutionalized violence, drudgery, exploitation, or cruelty" (xi). Hunters exhausted the game they hunted; slash-and-burn cultivators interfered with the ecological processes that renewed the soil and thus destroyed the arable land; we have squandered our own fossil fuels. Like the sorcerer's apprentice, the male world has carried even originally adaptive practices to maladaptive limits. We are caught, in effect, in an economic nightmare, an intolerable bind. But, Harris asks, must we go on forever repeating the old cycle, forever seeking to find new techniques of production and push them "far beyond their optimum"?

Harris is not optimistic. The new technologies of contraception may have come too late. Although the best way to achieve a good solution to the population-resources equation would be control of population size, this is so hard that intensification of production has been used instead (4-5). "Contemporary societies are committed to the intensification of the industrial mode of production. We have only begun to pay the penalties for the environmental depletions associated with the new round of intensifications, and no one can predict what new constraints will be needed to transcend the limits of growth of the industrial order" (xi).

Time for a Change?

There seem to be periodic crises in human history when old adaptations no longer serve, when, in fact, they actually become dysfunctional. The late twentieth century seems to be such a time. Both the economy and the polity seem unable to deal adequately with a world in which few, if any, of the old paradigms seem to work.

In Chapter 22 we looked at the modern feminists' rejection of the redemptive role of women on the ground that there was no need for women to assume such a role, that they had no more responsibility for solving the ills the male world has brought on us than did men themselves. Certainly women as individual human beings could not—and did not—claim, as nineteenth-century women had done, to be intrinsically more virtuous than men. But they did not believe that their participation in the polity would be harmful, as Lionel Tiger suggests it would be: "Given cross-cultural data about the political role of females, it may constitute a revolutionary and perhaps hazardous social change with numerous latent consequences should women ever enter politics in great number. Even a but partly female-dominated polity may be beyond the parameters of 'healthy' possibility, given the basic conservatism of species" (1970, 259). Tiger does not specify the tipping point at which women would become hazardous for the polity.[8]

But not all men share Tiger's concern about female participation in the polity. Some welcome it. And it is interesting to speculate, as we do in Chapter 25, on the possibilities if a female style of arriving at decisions did come to have serious input in the polity.

Notes

1. Although "women are as attracted to power as are men," according to Matina Horner (1974, 3), they differ from men, according to David Winter, in their use of it. "Women," he says, "do not equate power with physical aggression, excessive drinking, or sexual conquest. Don Juan . . . is an exclusively male pathology of power activation" (1979, vii). In the male ethos, " 'conquest' of women and the conquest of cities are metaphors for each other." When women achieve power, Rosabeth Kanter found, they exercise it in their own way; they are neither more sensitive and humane than men nor more overbearing (1979, 1). The way power is exercised depends on the organizational structure. One must "change the basic organization structure that destroys both men and women. . . . Organizations . . . must contribute to the development of people, not destroy them" (Porter, 1979, 1), an approach which seems to accord with the ethos of the female world.
2. I was in high school in the years before the 19th Amendment was added to the Constitution. Our women teachers were staunch feminists. There was gentle but outspoken Mrs. Gray, my English teacher, who, year after year, repeated the same story. "A woman was entertaining a conservative guest at tea. He was declaiming on the absurdity of woman suffrage. 'Why, just think of it! Imagine your cook voting!' His hostess smiled back sweetly and replied, 'I often think of it. You see, he does.' "
3. Both political parties reform their procedures to accommodate more women participants in important decision-making activities, such as national con-

ventions. The Democratic Party calls for equal representation. Women remain handicapped more by paucity of funds to finance campaigns than by strictly structural features. The serious discrimination is on the part of large contributors to campaigns.

4. Wilson criticizes earlier work as inefficient and misleading. Konrad Lorenz (*On Aggression*), Robert Ardrey (*The Social Contract*), Desmond Morris (*The Naked Ape*), Tiger and Fox (*The Imperial Animal*) "selected one plausible hypothesis or another based on a review of a small sample of animal species, then advocated the explanation to the limit" (551). He characterizes Raymond Dart's work on apes as "very dubious anthropology, ethology, and genetics" (255). He notes also that "overt aggressiveness is not a trait in all or even a majority of human cultures" (254). Leakey and Lewin also reject the myth of man as "killer ape" (1978). The acceptance of a myth does not necessarily rest on its "truth" or factual basis.
5. The same point—that what is desirable at one point may be inadequate at another—is made in the area of science by David Riesman: "Competitiveness is so very American or more broadly Western in its style that I am led to wonder whether it bears some relation to our progress in scientific work, or rather whether, if women had a larger influence on that work, other sorts of discoveries might not be made, other laws emphasized, and altered patterns of scientific and academic organization preferred or discovered. . . . It could be argued that it took a particular set of sex-role attitudes as well as specific religious and cultural values for Western science and technology to develop initially, although to continue the work, one might speculate as to whether a different pattern of attitudes might not be productive" (1964, xix-xx).
6. "Male Liberation" groups patterned along the lines of Women's Liberation groups were springing up across the country. One of them, called Free Men, in Washington, were seeking to "find alternative ways to define male roles" (Thompson, 1977). They rejected the imperatives: "Push your way to the top"; "Be the breadwinner"; "Stick in there and fight"; "Men don't cry." They rejected the drinking component: "To drink someone under the table" is considered a masculine feat. Presented only as food for thought, and certainly not as a hypothesis, is the idea that just as the primordial fetal stuff would remain female if not prodded by the male hormone, so the "real" nature of humanity or "human nature" would probably be more like "female" human nature than like the "nature" that has to be achieved with so much effort as "male" nature is, if it were not prodded from infancy on to be aggressive, competitive, dominant. Even with all the effort invested in making boys achieve this goal, it is doubtful if most men are all that macho.
7. Harris is not presenting a revamped version of the Malthusian paradigm. He is not talking about a race between the pressures of sheer numbers on subsistence. We know that in industrialized countries as subsistence has increased as a result of modern technologies reproduction rates have declined. Indeed, improved standards of living have been advocated as the best way to control population growth in the Third World. On the contemporary scene it is the standard of living that presses on resources. A major issue among theorists today has to do with the optimal rate of growth of in-

dustrial economies. A rapid rate of economic growth is profitable for some people. It results in more goods but it also presents the threat Harris is warning about.

8. We note in passing that Tiger seems unable to see a polity that is neither male-dominated nor female-dominated. This inability is one of the fallacies of polarized thinking, to see all gender-related issues as either/or.

25

Relating the Two Worlds

A Prophet's Roar

A quarter of a century ago sociologist Pitirim Sorokin was already calling alarmed attention to the way the ethos of the male world was functioning; people, he said were

> prone to believe in the power of the struggle for existence, selfish interests, egoistic competition, hate, the fighting instinct, sex drives, the instinct of death and destruction, all-powerful economic factors, rude coercion and other negativistic forces. . . . We are highly skeptical in regard to the power of creative love, disinterested service, unprofitable sacrifice, mutual aid, the call of pure duty and other positive forces. The prevalent theories of evolution and progress, of the dynamic forces of history, of the dominant factors of human behavior, of the 'how' and 'why' of social processes, unanimously stress such negativistic factors as the above. . . . Sensate minds emphatically disbelieve the power of love, sacrifice, friendship, cooperation, the call of duty, unselfish search for truth, goodness, and beauty. These appear to us as something epiphenomenal and illusory. . . . We are biased against all theories that try to prove the power of love and other positive forces in determining human behavior and personality; in influencing the course of biological, social, mental, and moral evolution; in affecting the direction of historical events; in shaping social institutions and culture [1954, 47-48].

This moral blast at the ethos of the male world was being echoed almost a generation later in connection with the endangered environment. Thus Bezdek and Strodtbeck were reminding us of the possibility "that the values consistent with short range competitive enterprise may be inappropriate for solving the problems of a highly developed society" (1970, 491). Maybe old ways, appropriate under one set of circumstances, were no longer adequate. They asked, "Can the motivation which conquered the frontier and developed the industrial base of society be redirected and used to balance the ecosystem? Can new organizational goals be imposed on the pragmatic achiever?" They were not sure. Perhaps something new must be added. A more feminine motivational emphasis? At least they raised the question: "Will the solution to problems like that of environmental control require a new motivational emphasis, one that is more idealistic, and, heretofore, considered more 'feminine'?" (491).

Others were coming to the same conclusion. Did the economy have to be so harsh? Sennett and Cobb were noting that affluent societies did not have to be efficient at the price of human values; they could afford to be less efficient than the male ethos demanded they be (1972, 261). Competition was not all that essential. They ask: "Can people be expected to work without hierarchical rewards, without symbols of achievement?" (262). And "Could it be that, in abolishing a hierarchy of rewards, a society might bring these feelings [of love] back into the productive forms of men's [*sic*] lives?" (262).

"Women's Ways": Cases in Point

What are the more "feminine" ways that Bezdek and Strodtbeck are calling for? And is there any assurance that they can actually serve the purpose Bezdek and Strodtbeck have in mind? What reason is there to believe that they are even useful?

Annie Oakley may have been right when she sang to her male counterpart, "Anything you can do I can do better"—a form of braggadocio that proved her point—but for most women a more nearly accurate version would probably be: "Anything you can do I can do, too, but I'd do it differently." There are many ways to skin a cat. Or manage an economy. Or operate a polity. Sometimes the way women do it might even be better than the other ways.

There are bits and pieces of research, however limited in practical applicability controlled research necessarily has to be, that at least give us hints with respect to the efficacy of the female style. These cases-in-point are not intended as a justification for greater sharing by women in decision making in the polity, as proof that they deserve it, or as a demonstration of their worthiness, as in the old redemptionist argument. I do not believe women have to prove their credentials for full participation. It is their right. But it is reassuring to know there is evidence that their participation can improve the quality of decisions.

It may be a far cry from the research laboratory to the real world, but not too far to be relevant. One study, for example, found that laboratory games structured according to the tenets of the male ethos as delineated by Peter Blau's exchange model produced expectably sexist behavior in both men and women. The goal sought in this rigidly structured game was exchange of social control. The goal of a second, more open and liberally structured, game was more consonant with the style of the female ethos: that is, exchange of trust and information. In this second type of game, scores were consistently higher and interplayer differences in scores significantly smaller than in the rigidly stereotyped male kind of game. The authors conclude that "sexist behavior is a response to the structure of the game [social system] and the rules [norms] of play [interaction]." And, further, that "a change in game structure and rules results in a change in game behavior—regardless of social psychological attitudes" (Osmond and Martin, 1973, draft).

Another laboratory study of game behavior produced similar results. In Chapter 16 we reported the aggressive, power-oriented style of male behavior in laboratory game situations as contrasted with the more accommodative or collaborative style of females. The results obtained are relevant at this point: the payoff from the female style was better than that from the male style:

> In terms of which style produces a better outcome, it is quite clear that the female arrives at a relatively more favorable position than does the male (most striking when she forms the minority). Male strategy may be called self-defeating when it encounters female strategy. By competing against each other in the majority situation, the males place the female at an advantage, for their attempts to exploit her merely mean that she more often obtains points through coalition. One male may defeat the other, but the female thereby gains. In groups with a female majority, the same result does not occur, because, evidently, the aggressive play of the male minority, seeking to exploit his rivals, forces the two females into a comparatively solidary alliance against him, either as a simple means to avoid undue competition (i.e., to solve the problem of outcome in the female manner) or as a defense against his perceived strength. In either case, he loses. [Vinacke and Bond, 1961, 73].

In brief, "all of these phenomena may be understood as a function of male 'exploitative' strategy vs. female 'accommodative' strategy. The former appears to be self-defeating when it encounters the latter" (74).[2]

A third experimental study had to do with success in a pencil-and-paper test dealing with survival problems on a desert. Six teams of five individuals each, with different sex-ratios—five women: no man; four women: one man; three women: two men; two women: three men; one woman: four men; five men—were asked to rank fifteen items according to their importance for survival in a contrived desert situation, first individually, without group discussion, and then together as a team after group discussion.[3] The individual scores for each team were averaged, so that there were two scores for each team, one the average of the five individual, prediscussion scores and the other the postdiscussion, consensual team score. The standard of correctness was the ranking of an experienced expert on survival in desert conditions. The lower the score, the more nearly it coincided with his rankings. The averaged prediscussion individual scores were about the same for men (69.9) and women (69.1). The all-female team score (53.8) was better than the all-male team score (62.8). Although team discussion improved the performance of both sexes, it improved female scores (15.3) more than twice as much as it improved male scores (7.1).[4] The "male bond" did not seem to work as well among the men as the "female bond" did among the women. As I read the results it seems to me that perhaps the women were more open to the arguments made by other members of the group, more amenable to persuasion by discussion, that the men may have been more reluctant to change their minds or concede a point in discussion, that having once made a point it was harder for the men to admit that another point of view might be better.[5] I picture the men therefore as less amenable than women to correction by group discussion.

In another study, this time observational, Raphaela Best found that while a group of third-grade boys were fighting it out to see who was going to be in charge of the line-up for watching the long-awaited hatching of chicks, and thus missing the whole show, the girls, unencumbered by the need to boss the operation, were quietly watching the whole process in an orderly fashion (forthcoming). Again, a branch bank run by women in a Maryland suburb, designed to serve its customers in ways reassuring to them rather than intimidating, grew faster than any other branch. And, finally, the radical women who dissociated themselves from the macho Weathermen in the 1960s had greater ultimate success in terms of survival and duration of impact than the men themselves had.

The style of the female world, in brief, can pass even the male-world test—winning. It may be in fact that the win-at-any-cost competitive pattern of the male ethos detracts from rather than adds to its efficiency and productivity. It is just possible, as Bezdek and Strodtbeck imply, that incorporating the style of the female world into the economy and the polity would have a benign rather than (as Tiger fears) a hazardous effect. On the male as well as on the female world. For it does appear that where important issues are being delineated and great decisions being made, the contribution of the female as well as of the male style could greatly improve the result, whatever the content of the decision itself might be. It is not the substance of the issue alone that is important but the style of arriving at it as well. It may well be desirable as Bezdek and Strodtbeck imply, that there be enough representatives of the female world in legislatures and on benches to have an impact on both the decisions and the styles of arriving at them. Granted then, that incorporating the style of the female world would be desirable, is it feasible?

The Possibility of Cultural Change: Cases in Point

The inertia of culture seems to trap us in the present pattern of relationship between the ethos of the male world and the ethos of the female world. Still, we do know that whole cultures sometimes do change, and fairly rapidly at that.

Some years ago Margaret Mead described the Arapesh of New Guinea, among whom both men and women were nurturing in the way we define as female. But only a few years earlier they had been head hunters, a far cry from a female kind of pursuit. She later revisited and reported equally remarkable changes in other cultures she had studied originally a generation earlier. Since then a reversal of the kind of change reported among the Arapesh—from an essentially female style to a male style—has also been reported this time among the Fore in Papua, New Guinea.

In the early 1960s E. Richard Sorenson lived among the Fore and recorded their life on film. They gathered and gardened for a living. Although he himself does not label Fore society of the early 1960s as maternal, he does say that women constituted a "benevolent sanctuary" to children. There were "no chiefs, patriarchs, priests, or medicine men." The single men's house sheltered ten to twenty men, boys, and friends; several smaller women's houses provided shelter to the women and small children. The older boys and young men explored and roamed, but also gardened. There was a "spontaneous urge to share food, affection, work, trust, toils; and pleasure was the social cement that held the Fore hamlets together" (1977, 107). Friendship ties were more important than kinship bonds. When land was plentiful the Fore left a place rather than fight for it, though when land became scarce they would fight if they had to. But they considered warfare a curse (41). There was a division of labor, the men and boys doing the selecting of the garden sites, the slashing and burning, and the fencing; the women and girls cleared the weeds and grass, prepared the soil, transplanted, cultivated, and harvested. There were no monetary units. "Sharing was informal and voluntary among friends and close associates. There was no attempt to quantify value to facilitate repayment. With outsiders exchange took the form of feasts" (76).

This almost archetypically "female" kind of world disintegrated with the coming of a road which opened the Fore up to the outside world, introducing coffee culture to them and bringing them into the world market economy. The Fore world—from child rearing to forms of social bonding—was completely transformed. Now there were "repeated incidents of anger, withdrawal, aggressiveness and stinginess" (114). Sorenson attributes the changes to differences in child-rearing practices introduced after the coffee revolution. But far more was involved. A "male" style succeeded the old "female"-style world. Exchange superseded sharing. The sexual division of labor changed. It was primarily the men who went forth into the outside world to work on the coffee plantations, who learned how to cultivate the coffee, and who brought it back to their own communities. The transformation did not involve a dissolution or abolition of the sexual division of labor but rather a reformulation of it.

The new "male" society that came with the coffee revolution was wealthier in that it supplied the community with more material goods. But it was also more competitive, less loving, less relaxed. There were, in brief, costs as well as benefits from the change.

Changing Times

Granted that change in a highly complex society like ours is altogether different from that of change among the Fore and that we could hardly expect so much change in style so rapidly. Still, change in our society has been occurring ever since the beginning of the nineteenth century. If the pristine self-interest ethos of the Gesellschaft had been left to operate in full force, the whole system would long since have collapsed. It was too lethal; it left too many casualties. When the catastrophic concomitants of the new capitalistic system had first begun to surface in the nineteenth century, a wide variety of reform movements with a wide variety of programs had arisen to pick up the pieces left in the wake of rampant industrialization. Women had done much of the salvage work, the "friendly visiting," the philanthropy, the social work, the social reform that had kept the new economy viable. The self-interest ethos had not been permitted to operate in pristine form. It had had to be restricted. The current cries of men like Sorokin, Bezdek, Strodtbeck, Sennett, and Cobb remind us that the time may now be ripe for accelerated change.

For some time now the economy has been moving in the direction of the pole here labelled female. The ethos of the Gesellschaft is becoming more congruent with the ethos of the female world. A "people-oriented" style of management has been found essential in administering the economic system. It began to evolve in the 1920s in the form of a so-called human-nature-in-industry movement[6] even before women were in a position to make their views felt. By the first quarter of the century workers were already protesting the social and psychological conditions of the work site. Researchers were asking what was on the workers' mind and they were telling anyone who would listen what it was. In the present context all this can be seen retrospectively as a recognition of the values embodied in the female ethos, a concern for workers as human beings. It was still motivated, however, by self-interest since it was profit—not love and/or duty—that ultimately motivated the human-nature-in-industry good deeds.

We are now being told that the newer kinds of work call for qualities reflected in the female ethos; that such qualities are needed at all occupational levels, and not only vis-à-vis workers but vis-à-vis everyone. Qualities heretofore condemned as feminine are now in demand. Whether brought to bear on either the economy or the polity by men or by women or by both or by some intrinsic logic of the systems themselves, the female style may prove to be just what a lot of doctors—male and female—have been ordering for quite some time. This conclusion is not intended to resuscitate the redemptive role of women but to suggest that the direction present-day economic and political trends are taking may just happen to coincide with the style and ethos of the female world.

If it is, indeed, true that the "logic of events" is leading in the direction of greater recognition of the style of the female world, is there any need for women to push it themselves? If the economy and the polity increasingly are being pulled in the direction of the female ethos, if the necessity for altruism is crowned with scientific recognition, even accorded adaptive status (Wilson, 1975), if some men are even converts to the female approach, should women complain if this movement is not recognized as such? If they are not given a share of the credit?

There is a story that circulates in the female world, so common that it has become a cliché, of a woman who has proposed an idea to a male group only to have it fall on deaf ears. They listen politely but then as politely ignore the suggestion. Several minutes later the same idea is proposed by a male member of the group and now it is enthusiastically embraced. Should the woman be elated that her idea has prevailed? Or should she be angry that she is not credited with it? The first response would conform to the old interpretation of the female culture's ethos. A woman should be satisfied with a "redemptive" role. Right—in the form of her idea—has prevailed. Why care who gets the credit for it? Shouldn't she just rejoice in knowing that the ethos of the female world is infiltrating the male world? Or is that much self-effacement beyond the call of—even feminist—duty? Yes, it is. We want, in Jean Baker Miller's words, "a new form of living . . . [and] the ways of achieving this new form of living will . . . have to include more mutuality, cooperation, and affiliation, on both a personal and a larger social scale" (1976, 113). The new ways should not be manipulative or have to be bootlegged in as though illegitimate.

No Promise of Utopia

Despite the dreams of the utopists and idealists, there is no all-purpose, perfect way for the two worlds to relate to one another; no ultimately true, correct, basic, permanent, final way toward which we are groping and which we will some day achieve. The relationship between the two worlds in gathering societies was just as "true" as that between male and female peasant worlds in the middle ages or male and female Victorian worlds in the nineteenth century, or male and female worlds in the recent past. However different the relationship between them, they are all "true." But a relationship that is suitable for one age is not necessarily so for another.

To say that the relationship between the worlds will change does not mean that they will necessarily converge, that they will come to resemble one another in all ways, that they will become identical, indistinguishable, that all differences will disappear. They will no doubt continue to differ. And they will relate to one another in different ways. Sometimes a whole culture may "tilt" in the direction of the male ethos, sometimes in the direction of the female, sometimes in a direction different from both.

Carpe Diem

I am sometimes criticized by my *consoeurs* for what seems to them my irrational optimism. How can I sustain such a mood in the face of so many setbacks in the female world, so much defeat, so much backlash, such slow headway? The obstacles from the male world—in both economy and polity—sometimes seem all but insuperable. Well, for one thing because I have lived a great many years and know how long it takes to effect change, how bumpy the road is, and how much patience it takes. For another thing, I retain my faith in human intelligence. I think, for example, that the male world can change. If it is capable of putting a man on the moon, it is surely capable of modifying itself.

I allow a male—a sociobiologist to boot—to state my case here on the assumption that it will have more credibility coming from a "hawk"—representing the male world—than it would coming from a "dove"—representing the female world.[8]

> [E]ven if we look on the dark side and assume that individual man [*sic*] is fundamentally selfish, our conscious foresight—our capacity to simulate the future in imagination—could save us from the worst selfish excesses.... We have at least the mental equipment to foster our long-term selfish interests rather than merely our short-term selfish interests. We can see the long-term benefits of participating in a "conspiracy of doves," and we can sit down together to discuss ways of making the "conspiracy" work. We have the power to defy the selfish genes of our birth.... We can even discuss ways of deliberately cultivating and nurturing pure, disinterested altruism—something that has no place in nature, something that has never existed before in the whole history of the world [Dawkins, 115].

Translated into the idiom of the present context, his message is that the male world is capable of participating in the goals of the female world. It can learn that its own best interests lie in sharing the values of the female world. I believe that the "doves"—regardless of their sex—are becoming increasingly persuasive.

Some moments in history seem to be more open to change than others. As Harris sees it, "We are rapidly moving toward such an opening" (195). The present is a time when "a mode of production . . . is reaching its limits of growth and a new mode of production must soon be adopted." It may be a propitious time for "reining in" the male ethos. The odds for success, I recognize, may not be favorable. Still, "in the meantime, people [read: women] with deep personal commitments to a particular vision of the future are perfectly justified in struggling toward their goals, even if the outcome depends on both luck and skill; the rational response to bad odds is to try harder" (Harris, 196). *Carpe diem* might well be the best motto.

Notes

1. Some women resist the idea that there is anything specifically "feminine" about ecology, that "planet-keeping" is in line with "housekeeping." Still, it was a woman, Rachel Carson, who warned us of the silent spring, and although most of the environmental scientists are men—because most sci-

entists are—this earth-keeping movement appeals to more women than moon-walking does. And when a college of home economics wanted to give recognition to its expanded perspective, it called itself a college of human ecology.

2. When communication among players was forbidden in coalition formation, using only assigned weights as criteria, women performed just as competitively, aggressively, and exploitatively as men. The authors speculate, however, that after the coalitions have been formed, "in the ensuing bargaining and allocation of rewards, we might expect that the accommodative [female] style would be exhibited" (Lirtzman and Wahba, 1972.)
3. The data are from the Desert Survival Problem, developed by Human Synergistics. It is designed to teach the nature of effective human action by exploiting the values of group discussion. Guidelines included three don'ts: not to vote, which tends to split groups into winners and losers; not to make easy compromises which might be based on erroneous assumptions needing challenge; and not to compete within the group since either the group wins or no one does. The do's included: listening and paying attention to what others in the group were saying; bringing underlying assumptions into the open for discussion; encouraging others, especially the quieter members, to participate since the contributions of everyone were needed. Consensus was arrived at when each member of the group could say: "Well, even though it may not be exactly what I want, at least I can live with the decision and support it." A prescription for the truly female style.
4. A single "intruder" or "token" of the other sex had the greatest impact on averaged individual scores for both sexes. Thus, introducing the first female lowered the average individual scores of the preponderantly male group by 1.7 score points; introducing the first male to the preponderantly female group lowered the score by 1.2 score points. This reduction may have resulted from the "token" or "solo woman" and "solo man" effect, the equivocal position of these "oddballs" resulting perhaps in poorer performance on their part. Or, conversely, it may have resulted from the discombobulation resulting from an abrupt change in the organization of the group. Adding the second or third male or female did not change the averaged individual scores and what changes there were in the group scores were in the direction of improvement. If there were three males and two females or three females and two males, the averaged individual scores were about the same (67.8 and 67.3 respectively). Beyond the "tipping point" one way or the other, performance seemed to improve. The team that did the best was one consisting of three females and two males—it did almost as

Team Composition	*Averaged Individual Scores*	*Team Scores*	*Difference*
5 females, 0 males	69.1	53.8	+ 15
4 females, 1 male	67.9	58.4	+ 9.5
3 females, 2 males	67.3	54.3	+ 13.0
2 females, 3 males	67.8	64.8	+ 3.0
1 female, 4 males	71.6	62.0	+ 9.6
0 females, 5 males	69.9	62.8	+ 7.1

well as the all-female team—and the mixed team that did the worst consisted of two females and three males.

5. It is puzzling to an admittedly biased outside observer to contrast the male picture of the Dionysian corporate world as a vast jungle of power-hungry climbers with the female picture suggested by the women in this experiment, of an Apollonian system of teams working together, winning perhaps on some issues, losing on others. If the first, who would willingly want to be part of it? If the second, even an archetypical member of the female world could find it congenial.
6. Ellen Goodman has encapsulated the conflicting pressures on an entrepreneur and manager in this time of transition. In his school of business administration he had been taught that management was a matter of profits and losses; in actual practice he finds it a matter of "cost-accounting" personal problems. "Every day this boss has to decide at what point the best interests of his employees conflict with the best business interests of his company" (1978). He has to reconcile a "male ethos" with a "female ethos," concern with efficiency and concern with the family problems of his employees.
7. I originally intended to include an epilogue to this book in which an attempt would be made to relate the sociobiological research on altruism to the love-and/or-duty ethos of the female world. The idea was discarded, however, as too diversionary. I did not wish the major emphasis to be deflected from description to a controversial theory of causation.
8. The reader has no doubt already noted that I have relied almost exclusively on male sources for the contents of the male ethos.

Bibliography

Abbott, Lyman. "The Home-Keeper." In *The Home Builder*. New York: Houghton-Mifflin, 1906. Reprinted in Marion Harland, ed., *Home Making*. Boston: Hall and Locke, 1911.

Abram, A. "Women Traders in Medieval London." *Economic Journal* (London), June 1916, 276-285. Reprinted in Susan Groag Bell, ed., *Women from the Greeks to the French Revolution*. Belmont, Calif.: Wadsworth, 1975.

Acker, Joan. "Women and Social Stratification: A Case of Intellectual Sexism." *Amer. Jour. Sociol.*, 78, 1973, 936-945.

Adams, B. N. *Kinship in an Urban Setting*. Chicago: Markham, 1968.

______. "Isolation, Function, and Beyond: American Kinship in the 1960s." In Carlfred Broderick, ed., *A Decade of Family Research and Action, 1960-1969*. Minneapolis, Minn.: National Council on Family Relations, 1971, 163-186.

Adler, Freda. *Sisters in Crime*. New York: McGraw-Hill, 1975.

Adler, Polly. *A House Is Not a Home*. New York: Rinehart, 1953.

Alan Guttmacher Institute. "Special Report: The House Committee on Population," *Perspective*, June 9, 1978, 1-2.

American Home Economics Association. *A Force For Families*. Washington, D.C., n. d.

Amory, Cleveland. *Who Killed Society?* New York: Harper, 1960.

Andrews, William D., and Deborah C. Andrews. "Technology and the Housewife in Nineteenth Century America." *Women's Studies*, 3, 1974, 309-328.

Andrewski, Iris. *Old Wives' Tales: Life Stories of African Women*. New York: Schocken, 1971.

Angrist, Shirley S., and Elizabeth M. Almquist. *Careers and Contingencies.* New York: Dunellen, 1975.

Antler, Joyce. "Culture, Service, and Work: The Changing Ideals of Higher Education for Women during the Progressive Period." 1978. Draft.

______. " 'After College, What?': New Graduates and the Family Claim." 1979. Draft.

Antler, Stephen, and Joyce Antler. "Social Policy and the Family: An Analysis of Programs Designed to Aid and Protect Family Life, 1890 to the Present." 1979. Draft.

Appian (Horace White, trans.). In Emily James Putnam, *The Lady.* New York: Sturgis and Walton, 1910.

Ardener, Shirley, ed. *Defining Females.* Somerset, N.J.: Halsted Press, 1978.

Ardrey, R. T. *The Territorial Imperative.* New York: Atheneum, 1966.

Arenal, Electa. "The Convent as Catalyst for Autonomy: Two Hispanic Nuns of the 17th Century." 1979. Draft.

Arkin, William. "Prolegomenon to the Study of 'Brother' as a Male Family Role." *The Family Coordinator*, 28, Oct., 1979, 630-637.

Aronoff, Joel, and William D. Crano. "A Re-Examination of the Cross-Cultural Principles of Task Segregation and Sex Role Differentiation in the Family." *Amer. Sociol. Rev.*, 40, 1975, 12-20.

Aronson, Naomi. "Fuel for the Human Machine: The Industrialization of Eating in America." Brandeis University doctoral dissertation, 1978.

As, Berit. "On Female Culture: An Attempt to Formulate a Theory of Women's Solidarity and Action." *Acta Sociologica*, 28, n.d., 142-161.

______. "Toward a Theory of Female Culture: An Exposition of Master Suppression Technologies." Paper given at Conference on Work and Employment: Toward What Kind of Society? Lisbon, 1979. Draft.

Astell, Mary. *An Essay in Defense of the Female Sex.* 3rd ed., with additions. London: A. Roper and R. Clavel, 1697.

Astin, Helen, ed. *Some Action of Her Own, The Adult Woman and Higher Education.* Lexington, Mass.: Lexington Books, 1976.

Auchincloss, Louis. "Edith Newbold Wharton." In Edward T. James, ed., *Notable American Women.* Cambridge, Mass.: Belknap Press, 1971, 570-573.

Auerbach, Nina. *Communities of Women, An Idea in Fiction.* Cambridge, Mass.: Harvard University Press, 1978.

Babcock, Barbara Allen, and Ann E. Freedman, Eleanor Holmes Norton, and Susan C. Ross. *Sex Discrimination and the Law: Causes and Remedies.* Boston: Little, Brown, 1975.

Bachrach, Judy. "From 'Super-Macho' to 'Pure Femininity.' " *The Washington Post*, Dec. 19, 1977.

______. "True Confession." *The Washington Post*, July 17, 1978.

Badek, Evelyn Gordon, "Salonières and Blue-Stockings." *Feminist Studies*, 3, Summer 1976, 185-199.

Badran, Margot. "Huda Shacrawi: Memoirs of an Egyptian Nationalist and Feminist." Paper presented at Berkshire Conference, Mt. Holyoke College, 1978.

Bahr, Harold. "Changes in Family Life in Middletown, 1924-1977." Paper presented at American Sociological Association meetings, 1978.

BAKER, ELIZABETH FAULKNER. *Technology and Woman's Work*. New York: Columbia University Press, 1964.

BALES, ROBERT. *Interaction Process Analysis: A Method for the Study of Small Groups*. Reading, Mass.: Addison-Wesley, 1950.

BALKAN, SHEILA, and RONALD J. BERGER. "The Changing Nature of Female Delinquency." In Claire B. Kapp and Martha Kirkpatrick, eds., *Becoming Female: Perspectives on Development*. New York: Plenum, 1979, 207-227.

BALSWICK, JACK O., and CHARLES W. PEEK. "The Inexpressive Male: A Tragedy of American Society." *Family Coordinator*, 20, 1971, 363-368.

BANE, MARY JO. *Here to Stay: American Families in the Twentieth Century*. New York: Basic Books, 1976.

BARASH, DAVID P. *Sociobiology and Behavior*. New York: Elsevier, 1977.

BARBER, BERNARD. "Social Stratification: Introduction." *International Encyclopedia of the Social Sciences*, vol. 15. New York: Macmillan, 1968, 288-295.

BARDWICK, JUDITH J. "Androgyny and Humanistic Goals." In M.L. McBee and K.H. Blake, eds., *The American Woman: Who Will She Be?* Beverly Hills: Glencoe Press, 1974.

BARKER, KARLYN. "Delegates Give Big Vote to Marital Property Bill." *The Washington Post*, Jan. 26, 1979.

BARNHART, ELIZABETH. "Friends and Lovers in a Lesbian Counterculture Community." In Nona Glazer, ed., *Old Family/New Family*. New York: D. Van Nostrand, 1975, 90-115.

BARRON, NANCY. "Sex-Typed Language: The Production of Grammatical Cases." *Acta Sociologica*, 14, 1971, 24-72.

BASCH, FRANÇOISE. *Relative Creatures. Victorian Women in Society and the Novel*. New York: Schocken, 1974.

BATTLE-SISTER, ANN. "Conjectures on the Female Culture Question," *Jour. Mar. and Fam.*, 33, 1971, 411-420.

BAUM, CHARLOTTE, PAULA HUMAN, and SONYA MICHEL. *The Jewish Woman in America*. New York: Dial Press, 1975.

BAZIN, NANCY TOPPING, and ALMA FREEMAN. "The Androgynous Vision." *Women's Studies*, 2, 1974, 185-215.

BEAUVOIR, SIMONE DE. Interview reported in *Atlas World Press Review*, April, 1978, excerpted from *Le Monde*.

_____. *The Second Sex*. New York: Bantam, 1953.

BEECHER, CATHARINE. *Treatise on Domestic Economy*. New York: Schocken Books, 1977.

BELL, ARTHUR. "Asexuality, Everybody's Not Doing It." *The Village Voice*, Jan. 23, 1978.

BELL, ROBERT. "Female and Male Friendship Patterns." Paper presented at Sociological Association of Australia and New Zealand University of Waikato, Hamilton, 1975. Draft.

BELL, SUSAN GROAG, ed. *Women from the Greeks to the French Revolution*. Belmont, Calif.: Wadsworth, 1975.

BELLE, DEBORAH, et al. *Lives in Stress: Context for Depression*. Cambridge, Mass.: 1979. Draft.

BELOTTI, ELENA GIANINI. *What Are Little Girls Made Of? The Roots of Feminine Stereotypes*. New York: Schocken, 1976.

BENEDICT, RUTH. *Patterns of Culture*. New York: Penguin, 1934.

BENET, MARY KATHLEEN. *The Politics of Adoption.* New York: Free Press, 1976.

BERG, BARBARA J. *The Remembered Gate, Origins of American Feminism: The Woman and the City, 1800-1860.* New York: Oxford, 1978.

BERGER, BENNETT. *Working Class Suburb.* Berkeley: University of California Press, 1970.

BERGER, BRIGITTE. "What Women Want." *Commentary,* March 1979, 64-67.

BERGER, PETER, and THOMAS LUCKMAN. *The Social Construction of Reality: A Treatise in the Sociology of Knowledge.* New York: Doubleday, 1966.

BERMAN, CLAIRE. "Why Can't a Woman Be More Like a Man?" TWA *Ambassador,* 10, 1977, 20, 22.

BERNARD, JESSIE. *American Family Behavior.* New York: Harper, 1941.

______. *American Family Behavior.* New York: Harper, 1942.

______. *American Community Behavior.* New York: Dryden, 1949; Holt, Rinehart, and Winston, 2nd ed., 1962.

______. *Social Problems at Midcentury.* New York: Dryden Press, 1956.

______. *Academic Women.* University Park, Penn.: Pennsylvania State University Press, 1964; Meridian, 1970.

______. *Women and the Public Interest.* Chicago: Aldine, 1971.

______. *The Sex Game. Communication between the Sexes.* Englewood Cliffs, N. J.: Prentice-Hall, 1968; Atheneum, 1972.

______. *The Future of Marriage.* New York: World, 1972; Bantam Books, 1973.

______. "Adolescence and Socialization for Motherhood." In Sigmund E. Dragastin and Glen H. Elder, Jr., *Adolescence in the Life Cycle, Psychological Change and Social Context.* Washington, D.C.: Hemisphere Publishing Corp., 1975.

______. "Change and Stability in Sex-Role Norms and Behavior." *Journal of Social Issues,* vol. 32, no. 3, 1976a, pp. 207-224.

______. "Homosociality and Female Depression." *Journal of Social Issues,* vol. 32, no. 4, 1976b, pp. 213-238.

______. "Where Are We Now? Some Thoughts on the Current Scene." *Psychology of Women Quarterly,* vol. 1, no. 1, 1976c, 21-37.

______. "Models for the Relationship between the World of Women and the World of Men." In Louis Kriesberg, ed., *Research in Social Movements, Conflicts and Change.* Greenwich, Conn.: JAI Inc., 1978, 291-340.

______. "Crisis, Revolution, and the Politics of the Family." *Transaction-Society,* forthcoming, 1980a.

______. "Policy and Women's Time." In Jean Lipman-Blumen and Jessie Bernard, eds., *Sex Roles and Social Policy.* Beverly Hills, Calif.: Sage Publications, 1979, 303-333.

______. "The Good-Provider Role, Its Rise and Fall." *The American Psychologist,* vol. 36, no. 1, Jan., 1981, 1-12.

______, and L. L. BERNARD. *Origins of American Sociology.* New York: Crowell, 1942.

BERNSTEIN, MARCELLE. *The Nuns.* Philadelphia: Lippincott, 1976.

BEST, RAPHAELA. *One World, Shared Worlds.* Forthcoming.

BEZDEK, WILLIAM, and FRED STRODTBECK. "Sex-Role Identity and Pragmatic Action." *American Sociological Review,* 35, 1970, 491-502.

BIGNER, JERRY J., "Fathering." *The Family Coordinator,* 19, 1970, 470-483.

BIRD, CAROLINE. *The Spirit of Houston. The First National Women's Confer-*

ence. An Official Report to the President, the Congress and the People of the United States. Washington, D.C., 1978.

BIRDSALL, RICHARD D. "Susanna Haswell Rowson." In Edward T. James, ed., *Notable American Women*. Cambridge, Mass.: Belknap Press, 1971, 202-204.

BLAKE, JUDITH. "The Changing Status of Women in Developed Countries." *Scientific American*, 231, Sept. 1974, 136-147.

BLAU, PETER. *Exchange and Power in Social Life*. New York: Wiley, 1964.

______, ed. *Approaches to the Study of Social Structure*. New York: Free Press, 1975.

BLAU, ZENA SMITH. *Old Age in a Changing Society*. New York: Franklin Watts, 1973.

______. *Black Children-White Children: Competence, Socialization and Social Structure*. New York: Free Press, 1981.

BLAXALL, MARTHA, and BARBARA REAGAN. *Women and the Workplace: The Implications of Occupational Segregation*. Chicago: University of Chicago Press, 1976.

BLOCK, JEANNE. "Issues, Problems and Pitfalls in Assessing Sex Differences: A Critical Review of The Psychology of Sex Differences." *Merrill-Palmer Quarterly*, 22, 1976, 283-309.

______. "Another Look at Sex Differentiation in the Socialization Behaviors of Mothers and Fathers." In Julia A. Sherman and Florence Denmark, eds., *The Psychology of Women: Future Directions in Research*. New York: Psychological Dimensions, 1979, 29-88.

______, and VALORY MITCHELL. "The Impact of a Decade on Social Change on Two Generations." 1978. Draft.

BLOOD, ROBERT O., and DONALD M. WOLFE. *Husbands and Wives, The Dynamics of Married Living*. New York: Free Press, 1960.

BLUMBERG, RAE LESSER. "Women and World Development: Veil of Invisibility, World of Work." *International Journal of Intercultural Relations*. In Press. Also in Irene Tinker and Michele Bo-Bramsen, eds., *Women and World Development*. Washington, D.C.: Overseas Development Council, 1976.

______. *Females, Farming, and Food: Rural Development and Women's Participation in Agricultural Production Systems*. Washington, D.C.: Office of Women in Development, FAO, 1980.

BODINE, ANN. "Sex Differentiation in Language." In Barrie Thorne and Nancy Henley, eds., *Language and Sex*. Rowley, Mass.: Newbury House, 1975, 130-151.

BOGUE, DONALD. *The Population of the United States*. New York: Free Press, 1959.

BOLDEN, DOROTHY. "Forty-two Years a Maid." In Nancy Seifer, ed., *Nobody Speaks for Me, Self-Portraits of American Working Class Women*. New York: Simon and Schuster, 1976, 136-177.

BOOTH, ALAN. "Sex and Social Participation." *Amer. Sociol. Rev.*, 37, 1972, 123-192.

BORNSTEIN, DIANE. "As Much as a Maid." In Douglas Buttorff and Edmund L. Epstein, eds., *Women's Language and Style*. Akron: Akron University Press, 1978, 132-138.

BOSERUP, ESTER. *Woman's Role in Economic Development*. New York: St. Martin's Press, 1970.

BOSTON WOMEN'S HEALTH BOOK COLLECTIVE. *Our Bodies Ourselves*, rev. 2nd ed. New York: Simon and Schuster, 1976.

BOSTON WOMEN'S HEALTH COLLECTIVE. *Ourselves and Our Children*. New York: Random House, 1978.

BOTT, ELIZABETH. *Family and Social Network; Roles, Norms, and External Relationships in Ordinary Urban Families*. New York: Free Press, 1957, 1971.

BOULDING, ELISE. "Familial Constraints on Women's Work Roles." *Signs*, 1, 1976, 95-118.

______. *The Underside of History: A View of Women through Time*. Boulder, Col.: Westview Press, 1976.

______. "Women and Social Violence." In *Violence and Its Causes: Theoretical Aspects of Recent Research on Violence*. Paris: UNESCO, 1977.

BOULDING, KENNETH. "The Grants Economy." *Michigan Academician*, 1, 1969, 3-11.

______. *The Economy of Love and Fear, A Preface to Grants Economics*. Belmont, Calif.: Wadsworth, 1973.

BOURGUIGNON, ERIKA, ed. *A World of Women. Anthropological Studies of Women in the Societies of the World*. New York: Praeger, 1979.

BOWLES, GLORIA. "Criticisms of Women's Poetry: An Addendum." *Signs*, 3, 1978, 713-718.

BRANCA, PATRICIA. *Silent Sisterhood, Middle Class Women in the Victorian Home*. Pittsburgh: Carnegie-Mellon University Press, 1975; London: Croom Helm, 1975.

BREDEMEIER, KENNETH. "Burning Tree Remains a Male Bastion." *The Washington Post*, April 14, 1975.

BRENTON, MYRON. *The American Male*. New York: Coward McCann, 1966.

BRODER, DAVID S. "The Coming Debate: Equity—or Efficiency?" *The Washington Post*, Oct. 26, 1977.

______. "Let 100 Single-Issue Groups Bloom." *The Washington Post*, Jan. 7, 1979.

BRONFENBRENNER, URIE. Testimony before the Senate Sub-Committee on Children and Youth. September 25, 1973. In *American Families: Trends and Pressures*. Washington, D.C.: Government Printing Office, 1947, 147-180.

______. "Man Is, A Woman Is. . . ." *The Washington Post*, Nov. 26, 1976.

BROUGHTON, PATRICIA. "Moving Mountains." *Mountain Moving*, no. 2, Winter 1977, 15.

______. "News item." *Moving Mountains*, no. 2, Winter 1977.

BROWN, BARBARA A., ANN E. FREEDMAN, HARRIET N. KATZ, and ALICE M. PRICE. *Women's Rights and the Law*. New York: Praeger, 1977.

BROWN, RITA MAE. "The Last Straw." In Charlotte Bunch and Nancy Myron, eds., *Class and Feminism*. Baltimore: Diana Press, 1974, 13-23.

BROWNMILLER, SUSAN. *Against Our Will: Men, Women, and Rape*. New York: Simon and Schuster, 1975.

BROZAN, NADINE. "An Agenda for Feminists." *New York Times*, June 20, 1975.

BRYCE, JAMES. *The American Commonwealth*, rev. ed., vol. 2. London: Macmillan, 1891.

BUNCH, CHARLOTTE. "ERA Debate: A Tendency to Blame the Victims." *The Washington Post*, Aug. 5, 1978.

BUNCH, CHARLOTTE, and NANCY MYRON, eds. *Class and Feminism*. Baltimore. Diana Press, 1974.

BUREAU OF THE CENSUS, *Statistical Abstract of the United States*. Washington, D.C.: Government Printing Office, 1977.

BURGESS, JANE K. "The Single-Parent Family." *The Family Coordinator*, 19, 1970, 136-144.

BUREAU OF LABOR STATISTICS. "Married Persons' Share of the Labor Force Declining, BLS Study Shows." Press Release, March 8, 1977. *Employment and Earnings*, July, 1979, vol. 26, no. 7, July, 1979.

BURKHART, KATHRYN WATTERSON. *Women in Prison*. New York: Popular Library, 1976.

BUTTORFF, DOUGLAS, and EDMUND L. EPSTEIN, eds. *Women's Language and Style*. Akron, Ohio: University of Akron Press, 1978.

CAHN, ANN FOOTE, ed. *Women in the United States Labor Force*. New York: Praeger, 1978.

CALIFORNIA COMMISSION ON THE STATUS OF WOMEN. *Impact ERA. Limitations and Possibilities*. Millbrae, Calif.: Les Femmes Publishing, 1976.

CAMPBELL, ARTHUR A. "The Role of Family Planning in the Reduction of Poverty." *Jour. Mar. and Fam.*, 30, 1968, 236-245.

CAMPBELL, D'ANN. "Women's Life in Utopia: The Shaker Experiment in Sexual Equality Reappraised—1820 to 1860." *The New England Quarterly*, 51, 1978, 23-38.

CANBY, HENRY SEIDEL. *The Age of Confidence*. New York: Farrar and Rinehart, 1934.

CANTOR, MURIEL. "Television Drama and Commercials." Draft of paper for National Institute of Mental Health, 1978.

______. *Sex and Sexual Violence in Women's Fiction*. In process.

CAPLAN, GERALD. *Support Systems and Community Mental Health: Lectures on Concept Development*. New York: Behavioral Publications, 1974.

CAPLAN, PATRICIA, and JANET M. BUJRA. *Women United, Women Divided. Comparative Studies of Ten Contemporary Cultures*. Bloomington, Ind.: Indiana University Press, 1979.

CARDEN, MAREN LOCKWOOD. *The New Feminist Movement*. New York: Russell Sage, 1974.

______. *Feminism in the Mid-1970s*. A Report to the Ford Foundation. New York, 1976.

CARLSON, C. "Family Background, School and Early Marriage." *Jour. Mar. and Fam.*, 41, 1979.

______. "The Shifting Relation of Work and Marriage Decisions." Paper presented at Population Association of America, 1979.

CARTER, HUGH, and PAUL GLICK. *Marriage and Divorce: A Social and Economic Study*. Cambridge, Mass.: Harvard University Press, 1970.

CASSELL, JOAN. *A Group Called Women: Sisterhood and Symbolism in the Feminist Movement*. New York: McKay, 1977.

CAUFIELD, MINA DAVIS. "Universal Sex Oppression? A Critique from Marxist Anthropology." *Catalyst*, nos. 10-11, Summer, 1977, 60-77.

CHADWICK, BRUCE A. "Converging and Diverging Lifestyles of Working and Business Class Families in Middletown, 1920-1970." Paper presented at American Sociological Association, 1978.

CHAFE, WILLIAM H. *The American Woman, Her Changing Social, Economic, and Political Roles 1920-1970*. New York: Oxford, 1972.

______. *Women and Equality, Changing Patterns in American Culture*. New York: Oxford, 1977.

CHAPPELL, C. BRADFORD. "Status Attainment Process of Women in Middletown in 1978." Paper presented at American Sociological Association, 1978.

CHERLIN, ANDREW. "Work Life and Marital Disruption." In George Levinger and Oliver Moles, eds., *Divorce and Separation*. New York: Basic Books, 1979, 151-166.

CHICAGO, JUDY. *Through the Flower*. New York: Doubleday, 1974.

CHILD, LYDIA MARIA. *The Frugal Housewife*. Boston: Carter and Hendee, 1829. Reprinted in Kirk Jeffrey, *q.v.*

CHILMAN, CATHERINE. *Adolescent Sexuality in a Changing American Society*. Washington, D.C.: Department Health, Education, and Welfare, 1978.

CHODOROW, NANCY. *The Reproduction of Mothering. Psychoanalysis and the Sociology of Gender*. Berkeley: University of California Press, 1978.

CLARK, GRACIA. "The Beguines, A Medieval Women's Community." *Quest, A Feminist Quarterly*, 1, 1975, 75-77.

CLARK, MICHELLE. *Introduction to Mary Wilkin Freeman, The Revolt of Mother and Other Stories*. Old Westbury, Conn.: The Feminist Press, 1974.

CLAWSON, K. W. "A Loyalist's Memoir: Ken Clawson's Account of Richard Nixon." *The Washington Post*, Aug. 9, 1979.

COBBE, FRANCES POWER. *The Duties of Women*. Farmingdale, N.Y.: Dabor Services, Inc., 1979. Original, 1881.

COCKSHUT, A. O. J. *Man and Woman: A Study of Love and the Novel 1740-1940*. New York: Oxford, 1978.

COHEN, JEAN LAWLOR. "A Family's Generations of Motherhood." *The Washington Post*, May 14, 1978.

COHEN, MIRIAM. "Role of Women in the Organization of the Men's Garment Industry, Chicago, 1910." In Dorothy G. McGuigan, ed., *New Research on Women at the University of Michigan*. Ann Arbor: University of Michigan, 1974, 77-84.

COHEN, STANLEY. "The Assault on American Victorianism in the Twentieth Century." Paper presented at Colloquium of the Woodrow Wilson International Center for Scholars, Smithsonian Institution, 1975.

COHN, DAVID LEWIS. *Love in America*. New York: Simon and Schuster, 1943.

COLEMAN, EMILY. "Infanticide in the Early Middle Ages." In Susan Mosher Stuard, ed., *Women in Medieval Society*. Philadelphia: University of Pennsylvania Press, 1976, 47-70.

COLEMAN, JAMES. *The Adolescent Society*. New York: Free Press, 1961.

______. "The Affluent Young—No Children, No Heroes." Interview in *San Francisco Chronicle*, March 31, 1978.

COLLINS, RANDALL. *Conflict Sociology*. New York: Academic Press, 1975.

COLEMAN, R. C., and LEE RAINWATER. *Social Standing in America*. New York: Basic Books, 1978.

CONKLIN, NANCY FAIRES. "Toward a Feminist Analysis of Linguistic Behavior." *The University of Michigan Papers in Women's Studies*, 1, 1974, 51-73.

COOK, BLANCH WIESEN. "The Personal Is the Political: Women, Alternative Lifestyles and Political Activism." Paper presented at Berkshire Conference, Bryn Mawr, 1976.

COOLEY, C. H. *Social Organization, A Study of the Larger Mind.* New York: Scribner, 1909.

COOLIDGE, MARY ROBERTS. *Why Women Are So.* New York: Holt, 1912.

COOMBS, LOLAGENE. "Preferences for Sex of Children among U.S. Couples." *Perspectives*, 9, 1977, 259-265.

COSTANTINI, EDMOND, and KENNETH H. CRAIK. "Women as Politicians: The Social Background, Personality, and Political Careers of Female Party Leaders." In Martha Schuch Mednick and Sandra Schwartz Tangri, eds., "New Perspectives on Women," *Jour. Soc. Issues*, 28, 1972, 217-236.

COTT, NANCY. *The Bonds of Womanhood.* New Haven: Yale University Press, 1977.

COTTRELL, FRED. *The Railroader.* Stanford, Calif.: Stanford University Press, 1940.

COWAN, BONNIE. "The Forgotten Women of Women's Lib, A Feminist's Critique." 1978. Draft.

COWAN, RUTH SCHWARTZ. "A Case Study of Technological and Social Change: The Washing Machine and the Working Wife." In Mary Hartman and Lois W. Banner, eds., *Clio's Consciousness Raised.* New York: Harper Torchbooks, 1974, 245-253.

______. "The 'Industrial Revolution' in the Home: Household Technology and Social Change in the Twentieth Century." *Technology and Culture*, 17, 1976, 1-25.

______. "Two Washes in the Morning and a Bridge Party at Night: The American Housewife between the Wars." *Women's Studies*, 3, 1976, 147-172.

______. "Women and Technology in American Life." In William B. Pickett, ed., *Technology at the Turning Point.* San Francisco: San Francisco Press, 1977, 23-33.

COXE, MARGARET. *Claims of the Country on American Females.* Columbus, Ohio: 1842, 1, 29. Present citation, Melder, 1977, 2.

CRONKITE, RUTH C. "The Determinants of Spouses' Normative Preferences for Family Roles." *Jour. Mar. and Fam.*, 39, 1977, 575-585.

CUBER, JOHN, and PEGGY HARROFF. *Sex and the Significant Americans.* Baltimore: Penguin, 1965.

CURTIN, RICHARD, and PHYLLIS DOLHINOW. "Primate Social Behavior in a Changing World." *American Scientist*, 66, 1978, 468-475.

DANARAJ, SHANTA. "Son Preference in Taiwan: Verbal Preference and Demographic Behavior." In Dorothy G. McGuigan, ed., *New Research on Women.* Ann Arbor: University of Michigan, 1974, 136-137.

DANIELS, ARLENE KAPLAN. "Room at the Top: Contingencies in the Volunteer Career." 1975. Draft.

______. "Feminist Perspectives in Sociological Research." In Marcia Millman and Rosabeth Moss Kanter, eds., *Another Voice.* New York: Anchor Books, 1975, 340-380.

______. "Development of Feminist Networks in the Professions." *Annals of the New York Academy of Sciences*, 1979.

______. *Invisible Worlds of Women: Careers in Volunteerism.* In process.

DARWIN, CHARLES. *Descent of Man*. Chicago: University of Chicago Press, 1952. Original, 1871.

DAVENPORT, BASIL, ed. *The Portable Roman Reader*. New York: Viking, 1951.

DAVID, DEBORAH, and ROBERT BRANNON. *The 49 Percent Majority*. Cambridge, Mass.: Addison-Wesley, 1976.

DAVIDOFF, LEONORE. "The Rationalization of Housework." In Diana Leonard Barker and Sheila Allen, eds., *Dependence and Exploitation in Work and Marriage*. London: Longman, 1976, 121-151.

DAVIDSON, LYNNE R., and LUCILE DUBERMAN. "Same-Sex Friendships: A Gender Comparison of Dyads." 1978. Draft.

DAVIS, KINGSLEY. *Human Society*. New York: Macmillan, 1949.

______. "The Continuing Demographic Revolution in Industrial Societies." In Seymour Martin Lipset, ed., *The Third Century, America as a Post-Industrial Society*. Stanford, Calif.: Hoover Institution Press, 1979, 37-64.

DAWKINS, RICHARD. *The Selfish Gene*. New York: Oxford, 1978.

DAY, JANE ROGERS. "Goodbye America." *Negro Digest*, Oct., 1963.

DEEGAN, MARY JO. "Women in Sociology: 1890-1930." 1977. Draft.

DEGLER, CARL. *At Odds*. New York: Oxford, 1980.

______, ed. "Introduction" to Charlotte Perkins Gilman, *Women and Economics, q.v.*

DE HUSZAR, GEORGE B., ed. *The Intellectuals. A Controversial Portrait*. New York: The Free Press, 1960.

DELAND, MARGARET WADE (CAMPBELL). "Change in the Feminine Ideal." *Atlantic Monthly*, May, 1910, 289-302. Reprinted in Marion Harland, ed., *Home Making*. Boston: Hall and Locke, 1911, 57-63.

DELANEY, JANICE, MARY JANE LUPTON, and EMILY TROTH. *The Curse, A Cultural History of Menstruation*. New York: New American Library, 1976.

DEMAUSE, L. "The Formation of the American Personality through Psychospeciation." *Journal of Psychohistory*, 4, 1976, 1-30.

DEMOS, JOHN. "The American Family in Past Time." *The American Scholar*, 43, 1974, 422-446.

DENMARK, FLORENCE. "Growing Up Male." In Eleanor L. Zuckerman, ed., *Women and Men, Roles, Attitudes, and Power Relations*. New York: The Radcliffe Club, 1975, 89-101.

DEUTSCH, MORTON. "Group Behavior." *International Encyclopedia of the Social Sciences*, vol. 6. New York: Macmillan, 1968, 265-276.

DEVORE, IRVEN. "Primate Behavior." *International Encyclopedia of the Social Sciences*, vol. 14. New York: Macmillan, 1968, 351-360.

DOBROFSKY, LYNNE R. "The Wife: From Military Dependent to Feminist?" *International Journal of Women's Studies*, vol. 1, no. 3, Winter-Spring, 1978, 248-258.

______. "Women's Power and Authority in the Context of War." *Sex Roles*, 3, 1977, 141-157.

______, and CONSTANCE T. BATTERSON. "The Military Wife and Feminism." *Signs*, 2, 1977, 675-684.

______. "Prolegomena to the Study of 'Sister' as a Female Family Role." 1979. Draft.

DOMHOFF, WILLIAM. *The Higher Circles*. New York: Vintage, 1971.

______. "The Women's Page as a Window on the Ruling Class." In Gaye Tuchman, Arlene Daniels, and James Benet, eds., *Hearth and Home: Images of Women in the Mass Media.* New York: Oxford, 1978.

DOUVAN, ELIZABETH. "Family Roles in a Twenty Year Perspective." Paper presented at Radcliffe Centennial Conference, 1978.

DOYLE, B. W. *The Etiquette of Race Relations in the South.* Chicago: University of Chicago Press, 1937.

DRINKER, SOPHIE. *Music and Women: The Story of Women in Their Relation to Music.* New York: Coward-McCann, 1948.

DUBIN, ROBERT. "Workers." *International Encyclopedia of the Social Sciences.* New York: Macmillan, 1968, 564-572.

DUBLIN, THOMAS. "Women, Work, and the Family: Female Operatives in the Lowell Mills, 1830-1860." *Feminist Studies*, 3, 1975, 30-39.

______. *Women at Work.* New York: Columbia University Press, 1979.

DUBOIS, ELLEN CAROL. *Feminism and Suffrage. The Emergence of an Independent Women's Movement, 1848-1969.* Ithaca, N. Y.: Cornell University Press, 1978.

DUMONT, LOUIS. *From Mandeville to Marx.* Chicago: University of Chicago Press, 1977.

DUVERGER, M. *Political Role of Women.* Paris: UNESCO, 1955.

DYE, NANCY SCHRAM. "Creating a Feminist Alliance: Sisterhood and Class Conflict in the New York Women's Trade Union League, 1903-1914." *Feminist Studies*, 2, 1975, 24-38.

EAGLETON INSTITUTE OF POLITICS. Conference on American Women and Politics, Rutgers, 1974, report in *Carnegie Quarterly*, 22, Summer, 1974.

EAST, MARJORIE. "Home Economics: A Profession? A Discipline?" Proceedings of the Conference on Current Concerns in Home Economics Education, Urbana, Ill., April, 1978, 3-6.

EBAUGH, HELEN ROSE FUCHS. *Out of the Cloister, A Study of Organizational Dilemmas.* Austin, Texas: University of Texas Press, 1977.

EBLE, CONNIE C. "How the Speech of Some Is More Equal than Others." Paper presented at Southeastern Conference on Linguistics, 1972.

______. "If Ladies Weren't Present I'd Tell You What I Really Think." Paper presented at Southeastern Section, American Dialect Society, 1972.

______. "Some Broadminded Remarks on Language." Paper presented at University of North Carolina, 1972.

______. "How to Name a Revolution." Paper presented in 1973 at Southeastern Conference on Linguistics, abstracted in Thorne and Henley, 1975, 226.

______. "Girl Talk: A Bicentennial Perspective." Paper presented at Southeastern Conference on Linguistics, 1975.

EDEL, LEON. "Willa Sibert Cather." In Edward T. James, ed., *Notable American Women.* Cambridge, Mass.: Belknap, 1971, 305-308.

ELDER, GLEN. "Appearance and Education in Marriage Mobility." *Amer. Sociol. Rev.*, 34, 1969, 519-533.

______. *Children of the Great Depression.* Chicago: University of Chicago Press, 1974.

______, RICHARD ROCKWELL, and DAVID J. ROSS. "Psychological Patterns in Marital Timing and Divorce: Comparisons across Forty Years." Paper presented at meetings of Society for Study of Social Problems, 1978.

ELIAS, NORBERT, and J. I. SCOTSON. *The Established and the Outsiders, A Sociological Inquiry into Community Problems*. London: Frank Cass and Co., 1965.

ELLIS, KATHERINE. "Charlotte Smith's Subversive Gothic." *Feminist Studies*, 3, Spring-Summer, 1976, 51-55.

EMMERICH, DUNCAN, ed. *The Folklore of Love and Courtship*. New York: American Heritage Press, 1970.

ENGEL, PETER H. "Movers and Doers: Anatomy of a Successful Manager." TWA *Ambassador*, 10, 1977, 55, 56.

EPSTEIN, CYNTHIA. *Woman's Place, Options and Limits in Professional Careers*. Berkeley: University of California Press, 1970.

FABE, MARILYN, and NORMA WIKLER. *Up against the Clock, Career Women Speak on the Choice to Have Children*. New York: Random House, 1979.

FAHEY, MAUREEN. "Block by Block: Women in Community Organizing." *Women*, 6, n.d., 24-29.

FARAGHER, JOHN MACK. *Women and Men on the Overland Trail*. New Haven: Yale University Press, 1979.

FARAGHER, JOHNNY, and CHRISTINE STANSELL. "Women and Their Families on the *Overland Trail*." *Feminist Studies*, 2, 1975, 150-166.

FARLEY, LINN. *Sexual Shakedown: Sexual Harassment of Women on the Job*. New York: McGraw-Hill, 1978.

FARRELL, WARREN. *The Liberated Man*. New York: Bantam, 1975.

FARRER, CLAIRE R., ed. *Women and Folklore*. Austin, Texas: University of Texas Press, 1975.

FAVA, SYLVIA. "Women's Place." Paper presented at American Sociological Association, San Francisco, 1978.

FERGUSON, MARJORIE. "Imagery and Ideology: The Cover Photographs of Traditional Women's Magazines." In Tuchman, Daniels, and Benet, eds., *Hearth and Home*. New York: Oxford, 1978, 97-115.

FERNEA, ELIZABETH WARNOCK, and BASIMA QATTAN BEZIRGAN, eds. *Middle Eastern Women Speak*. Austin, Texas: University of Texas Press, 1977.

FERRISS, ABBOTT L. *Indicators of Trends in the Status of American Women*. New York: Russell Sage Foundation, 1971.

FIEDLER, LESLIE. *Love and Death in the American Novel*. New York: Meridian, 1960.

FISHER, ANNE E. *Women's Worlds, NIMH-Supported Research on Women*. Rockville, Md.: National Institute of Mental Health, 1978.

FISCHER, CLAUDE S. *The Effect of Urban Life on Traditional Values*. Working Paper 222, Institute of Urban and Regional Development, Berkeley, 1974.

——, and MAX JACKSON. "Suburbs, Networks, and Attitudes." In Barry Schwartz, ed., *The Changing Face of the Suburbs*. Chicago: University of Chicago Press, 1976.

——, et al. *Networks and Places. Social Relations in the Urban Setting*. New York: Free Press, 1977.

FISCHER, JUDITH L. "Relationship Styles among Singles and Marrieds." Paper presented at Society for Study of Social Problems, 1978.

FLEISCHER, LEONORE. "Cats, Careers, and Caring." *The Washington Post*, Jan. 7, 1979.
______. "What Makes the World Go Round." *The Washington Post*, Oct. 30, 1977.
FLETCHER, JOSEPH. "Love Is the Only Measure." *Commonweal*, 83, 1966, 427-432.
FOLSOM, JOSEPH K. *The Family and Democratic Society*. New York: Wiley, 1943.
FONER, PHILIP S. *Women and the American Labor Movement, from Colonial Times to the Eve of World War I*. New York: Free Press, 1979.
FRANZWA, HELEN H. "Woman's Place in Semantic Space." 1974. Draft.
FREEDMAN, DANIEL G. *Human Sociobiology*. New York: Free Press, 1979.
FREEDMAN, RICHARD. Review of A.O.J. Cockshut, *Man and Woman: A Study of Love and the Novel 1740-1940*. In *Book World, The Washington Post*, July 16, 1978.
FREEMAN, HAROLD E., and GENE G. KASSEBAUM. "The Illiterate in American Society: Some General Hypotheses." *Social Forces*, 34, 1956, 371-375.
FREEMAN, JO. *The Politics of Women's Liberation*. New York: McKay, 1975.
FRIDAY, NANCY. *My Mother/My Self*. New York: Delacorte Press, 1977.
FRIEDAN, BETTY. *The Feminine Mystique*. New York: Norton, 1963.
FRIEDMAN, REENA SIGMAN. "Prostitute's Progress." Review of *The Maimie Papers, Lileth*, no. 5, 1978, 40-41.
FRITCHEY, CLAYTON. "The Women's Caucus." *The Washington Post*, April 24, 1976.
______. "The True Champions of Family Life." *The Washington Post*, Dec. 3, 1977.
FULENWIDER, CLAIRE KNOCHE. *Feminism in American Politics*. New York: Praeger, 1979.
FURSTENBERG, FRANK, JR. *Unplanned Parenthood: The Social Consequences of Teenage Childbearing*. New York: The Free Press, 1976.
GABELNICK, FAITH. "Making Connections: American Women Poets on Love." 1978. Draft.
GAGNON, WILLIAM. "Prostitution." *International Encyclopedia of the Social Sciences*, vol. 12. New York: Macmillan, 1968, 592-598.
GALBRAITH, JOHN KENNETH. "Economics of the American Housewife." *Atlantic Monthly*, 232: 78-83, August, 1973.
GANS, HERBERT J. *The Urban Villagers, Group and Class in the Life of Italian-Americans*. New York: Free Press, 1962.
______. The Levittowners. New York: Pantheon, 1967.
GARFINKLE, D. "Work in the Lives of Women." Proceedings of the International Population Conference, London, 1969, vol. III, 1601-1613.
GETZ, J. GREG, and HANNE K. KLEIN. "The Frosting of the American Woman: Hairdressing and the Phenomenology of Beauty." Draft of paper presented at Society for Study of Social Problems, New York, 1980.
GIALLOMBARDO, ROSE. *The Social World of Imprisoned Girls, A Comparative Study of Institutions for Juvenile Delinquents*. New York: Wiley, 1974.
GIELE, JANET. *Women and the Future*. New York: Free Press, 1979.
GILDEN, WILLIAM. "Instant Love! Fans Meet Soaperstars." *The Washington Post*, July 24, 1978.
GILDER, GEORGE. *Sexual Suicide*. Chicago: Quadrangle, 1974.

______. "Naked Nomads." *Commentary*, 58, Nov. 1974, 31-36.

GILLESPIE, DAIR L. "Who Has the Power? The Marital Struggle." *Jour. Mar. and Fam.*, 33, 1971, 445-459.

GILLIGAN, CAROL. "In a Different Voice: Women's Conception of the Self and of Morality." *Harvard Educational Review*, 47, 1977, 481-517.

GILLIGAN, JOHN J. "Women and Their Importance to the Third World." *The Washington Post*, June 24, 1978.

GILMAN, CHARLOTTE PERKINS. *His Religion and Hers*. New York: Century, 1923.

______. *Women and Economics*. New York: Harper Torchbooks, 1966. Original, 1898.

______. *The Home, Its Work and Influence*. Urbana: University of Illinois Press. 1972. Original, 1903.

GINI, CORRADO. "Beauty, Marriage and Fertility." *Human Biology*, 10, Dec., 1938, 575-576.

GIORDANO, JOSEPH, and MARION LEVINE. "Mental Health and Middle America. A Group Identity Approach." New York: Institute on Pluralism and Group Identity, Nov., 1975.

GITHENS, MARIANNE, and JOSEL L. PRESTAGE. *A Portrait of Marginality, The Political Behavior of the American Woman*. New York: David McKay, 1977.

GLADIEUX, JOHANNA DOBKIN, "Pregnancy—the Transition to Parenthood: Satisfaction with the Pregnancy Experience as a Function of Sex Role Conceptions, Marital Relationship, and Social Network." In Warren B. Miller and Lucile F. Newman, eds., *The First Child and Family Formation*. Chapel Hill: Carolina Population Center, 1978.

GLAZER, NATHAN, and DANIEL PATRICK MOYNIHAN. *Beyond the Melting Pot*. Cambridge: MIT and Harvard University Press, 1963.

GLAZER, NONA. "Housework: A Review Essay." In Nona Glazer and Helen Youngelson Waehrer, eds., *Women in a Man-Made World*. Chicago: Rand McNally, 1977, 360-369.

______. "Affirming Sex Inequality: Portrayals of the Employed Woman's Domestic Labor in a Mass Periodical." 1979. Draft.

______. "Toward a Theory of Women's Social Class: Domestic Work." 1979. Draft.

GLENNON, LYNDA M. *Women and Dualism*. Philadelphia: Longmans, Green, 1979.

GLESER, GELDINE C., LOUIS A. GOTTSCHALK, and JOHN WATKINS. "The Relationship of Sex and Intelligence to Choice of Words: A Normative Study of Verbal Behavior." *Jour. Clinical Psychology*, 15, 1959, 182-191.

GLICK, PAUL C. "Some Recent Changes in American Families." Bureau of the Census, Special Studies Series P-23, no. 52, Summer, 1975.

GOFFMAN, ERVING. "The Arrangement between the Sexes." Theory and Society, 4, 1977, 301-331.

______. *Gender Advertisements*. New York: Harper and Row, 1979.

GOLD, MARTIN, and DAVID REIMER. "Changing Patterns of Delinquent Behavior among Americans 13 through 16 Years Old: 1967-1972." *Crime and Delinquency Literature*, 7, 1975, 483-517.

GOLDMAN, MARION. "Prostitution and Virtue in Nevada." *Society*, 10, Nov.-Dec. 1972, 28-32.

GOODE, W. J. *After Divorce*. New York: Free Press, 1956.

______. Celebration of Heroes: Prestige as a Control System. Berkeley: University of California Press, 1979.

GOODMAN, ELLEN. Column in *Washington Post*, Dec. 20, 1976.

______. "Who's Really Anti-Male?" *The Washington Post*, March 24, 1979.

GORDON, ANN D., and MARI JO BUHLE. "Sex and Class in Colonial and 19th Century America." In Berenice Carroll, ed., *Liberating Women's History*. Urbana: University of Illinois Press, 1976, 278-300.

GORDON, LINDA. "Are the Interests of Men and Women Identical?" *Signs*, 1, 1976, 1011-1018.

______, ROSALYN BAXANDALL, and SUSAN REVERBY. "Boston Working Women Protest, 1869." *Signs*, 1976, 803-808.

GORDON, NANCY. "Institutional Responses: The Social Security System." In Ralph E. Smith, ed., *The Subtle Revolution*. Washington, D.C.: The Urban Institute, 1979, 223-256.

GOTTSCHALK, EARL C., JR. "Exploding the Myths about the American Family." *Family Circle*, Dec. 13, 1977.

GOULIANOS, JOAN, ed. *By a Woman Writ*. Baltimore: Penguin Books, 1974.

GRAUSTARK, BARBARA. "Newsmaker" item. *Newsweek*, July 10, 1978.

GREEN, CHESTER L. and GLORIA P. GREEN, eds. *Employment and Earnings*. Washington, D.C.: Bureau Labor Statistics, July, 1979.

GREEN, M. M. *Ibo Village Affairs*. N.Y.: Praeger, 1964, part III, Women's Organization.

GREER, GERMAINE. *The Female Eunuch*. New York: McGraw-Hill, 1971.

______. *The Obstacle Race*. New York: Farrar, Straus & Giroux, 1979.

GREGERSON, EDGAR. "Social Linguistics." Paper at New York Academy of Science Conference on Language, Sex, and Gender, 1977.

GREGORY, JANE. "The Return of the Debutante: Is Coming Out Coming Back?" *The Washington Post*, Feb. 11, 1979.

GREIDER, WILLIAM. "Old Racial Stereotypes Perish in the Marketplace. Black Women . . . Are More Nostalgic Than White Women about the Past." *The Washington Post*, April 12, 1978.

GUTTENTAG, MARCIA, SUSAN SALASIN, et. al. *Women-to-Women: Alternative Services in Mental Health*. 1968. Draft.

______. *Sex Differences in the Utilization of Publicly Supported Health Facilities: The Puzzle of Depression*. Harvard University, 1976. Draft.

GUTTMAN, DAVID. "Men, Women, and the Parental Imperative." *Commentary*, 56, 1973, 59-63.

GUTTWILLIG, JACQUELINE G. "The Equal Rights Amendment and Alimony and Child Support Laws." Citizens' Advisory Council on the Status of Women, 1975.

HACKER, HELEN. "The Feminine Protest of the Working Wife." *The Indian Journal of Social Work*, 31, Jan. 1971, 401-406.

HAMILTON, ALEXANDER. *Report on the Subject of Manufactures*, vol. I, 1791. New York: Williams and Whiting, 1810, 192.

HAMILTON, RICHARD. *Restraining Myths, Critical Studies of United States Social Structure and Politics*. New York: Wiley, 1975.

HAMMOND, DOROTHY, and ALTA JABLOW. *Women in Cultures of the World*. Menlo Park, Calif.: Cummings Pub. Co., 1976.

HAREVEN, TAMARA K. "Modernization and Family History: Perspectives on Social Change." *Signs*, 2, 1976, 190-206.

HARLAND, MARION. *Our Daughters: What Shall We Do with Them?* New York: G. W. Carleton, 1880.

______, and VIRGINIA VAN DE WATER. *Everyday Etiquette, A Practical Manual of Social Usage*. Indianapolis: Bobbs-Merrill, 1905.

______, ed. *Home Making*. Boston: Hall and Locke, 1911.

HARRIS, ANN SUTHERLAND, and LINDA NOCHLIN. *Women Artists: 1550-1950*. New York: Knopf, 1976.

HARRIS, LOUIS, and ASSOCIATES. *The 1972 Virginia Slims American Women's Opinion Poll*. New York: published by the authors, 1972.

HARRIS, MARVIN. *Cannibals and Kings, the Origins of Culture*. New York: Random House, 1977.

HARWOOD, RICHARD. "Change Is Slow for Saudi Women, but Prosperity and Modernism Are about to Pierce the Veils Dividing the Sexes." *The Washington Post*, Feb. 12, 1978.

HASSELBART, SUSAN. "Some Underemphasized Issues about Men, Women, and Work." Paper presented at American Sociological Association, 1978.

HAVIGHURST, ROBERT, and ARTHUR W. CHICKERING. "The Life Cycle." In Arthur W. Chickering, ed., *The Future American College*. Forthcoming.

HAWKINS, MARY HANNAH. "19th Century Household Patents by Women." In Lisa Leghorn and Betsy Warrior, eds., *Houseworker's Handbook*. Cambridge, Mass.: Woman's Center, n.d.

HAWRYLYSHYN, OLI. *The Economic Value of Household Services*. New York: Praeger, 1979.

HAYDEN, DOLORES. "Charlotte Perkins Gilman and the Kitchenless House." Paper presented at Berkshire Conference, 1978.

HAYNES, S. G., and M. FEINLEIB. "Women, Work, and Coronary Heart Disease, Prospective Findings from the Framingham Heart Study." *American Journal of Public Health*, 70 (Feb. 1980), 133-144.

HEFNER, ROBERT, and ASSOCIATES. "Sex-Role Transcendence." Ann Arbor: 1975. Draft.

HEILBRUN, CAROLYN G. *Toward a Recognition of Androgyny*. New York: Knopf, 1973.

HEISKANEN, VERONICA STOLTE. "Community Structure and Kinship Ties: Extended Family Relations in Three Finnish Communities." *International Journal of Comparative Sociology*, 10, 1969, 251-262.

HELSEN, RAVENNA. "The Changing Image of the Career Woman." *Journal of Social Issues*, 28, 1972, 33-46.

HENDRICKSON, PAUL. "Rosemary Rogers, the Princess of Passion Pulp." *The Washington Post*, March 22, 1979.

HENLEY, NANCY M. *Body Politics: Power, Sex, and Nonverbal Communication*. Englewood Cliffs, N.J.: Prentice-Hall, 1977.

HENNIG, MARGARET, and ANNE JARDIN. *The Managerial Woman*. New York: Anchor/Doubleday, 1977.

HENRY, ALICE. "The Woman Organizer." In Baxandall, Gordon, and Reverby, eds., *America's Working Women*. New York: Vintage, 1976.

HERNTON, CALVIN C. *Sex and Racism in America, An Analysis of the Influence of Sex on the Race Problem*. New York: Doubleday, 1965.

HESS, R. D., and J. V. TORNEY. *The Development of Political Attitudes in Children*. New York: Doubleday, 1967.

HICKOK, CATHLEEN CLAIRE. "Representations of Women in the Work of Nineteenth-Century British Women Poets." Doctoral dissertation, University of Maryland, 1977.

HILL, CHARLES T., ZICK RUBIN, and ANNE PEPLAU. "Breakups before Marriage: The End of 103 Affairs." Paper presented at American Psychological Association, 1977.

HILLER, E. T. *Social Relations and Structures*. New York: Harper, 1947.

HIRSCHMAN, LYNETTE. "Female-Male Differences in Conversational Interaction." Abstract in Barrie Thorne and Nancy Henley, eds., *Language and Sex, Difference and Dominance*. Rowley, Mass.: Newbury House, 1975a, 254.

______. "Analysis of Supportive and Assertive Behavior in Conversation." Abstract in Barrie Thorne and Nancy Henley, eds., *Language and Sex: Difference and Dominance*. Rowley, Mass.: Newbury House, 1975b, 288.

HITE, SHERE. *The Hite Report, A Nationwide Study of Female Sexuality*. New York: Macmillan, 1976.

HOCHSCHILD, ARLIE. *The Unexpected Community*. Englewood Cliffs, N.J.: Prentice-Hall, 1973.

______. "The Sociology of Feeling and Emotion: Selected Possibilities." In Marcia Millman and Rosabeth Moss Kanter, eds., *Another Voice*. New York: Anchor, 1975, 280-307.

HODGE, ANNE. "Loneliness: The Relation of Attribution Theory and Female Loneliness in the Female World." 1978. Draft.

HOFFMAN, LOIS WLADIS. "Changes in Family Roles, Socialization, and Sex Differences." Paper presented at National Council Family Relations, 1976.

HOFSTADTER, BEATRICE K. "Emma Dorothy Eliza Nevitte Southworth." In Edward T. James, ed., *Notable American Women*. Cambridge, Mass.: Belknap Press, 1971, 327-328.

HOLMES, DONALD J. *Psychotherapy*. Boston: Little, Brown, 1972.

HOLTER, HARRIET. *Sex Roles and Social Structure*. Oslo: Universitetforlaget, 1970.

______. "Typology of Women's Relations and Associations with Each Other: Five Categories." Paper presented at International Sociological Association, Uppsala, 1978.

HOMANS, GEORGE CASPAR. "The Study of Groups." *International Encyclopedia of the Social Sciences*, vol. 6. New York: Macmillan, 1968, 259-265.

HOPKINS, MARY ALDEN. *Hannah More and Her Circle*. Philadelphia: Longmans, Green, 1947.

HORNBY, MARY. "Lesbian Songs." Draft, 1978.

HORNER, MATINA. *Comments in Research Trends and Needs in Women's Education and Career Development*, ed., Helen S. Astin and Yvonne Guy. Occasional Paper no.1, Johnson Foundation, Wingspread, Racine, Wis., 1974, p. 4.

HOSELITZ, BERT F. "Social Stratification and Economic Development." *International Social Science Journal*, 16, 1964.

HOUSE COMMITTEE ON POPULATION. Witnesses Discuss Consequences of Aging of Baby Boom, US Population Trends. Washington, D.C.: Alan Guttmacher Institute, June, 1970.

HOUGHTON, WALTER E. *The Victorian Frame of Mind 1830-1870.* New Haven: Yale University Press, 1957.

HOWDEN, MELISSA A. "My Evidence, Women's Art? Art Made by Women? Does It Matter? If So, Why?" 1978. Draft.

HOWE, FLORENCE. "Women and the Power to Change." In Florence Howe, ed., *Women and the Power to Change.* New York: McGraw-Hill, 1975, 127-171.

HOWE, JULIA WARD. Opening Address, 14th Annual Report of the Association for the Advancement of Women, Woman's Congress, Detroit, 1888, p.9.

HOWE, LOUISE KAPP. *Pink Collar Workers: Inside the World of Women's Work.* New York: Avon, 1977.

HRDY, SARA B. "Male-Male Competition and Infanticide among the Langurs." *Folia Primat.* 22, 1974, 19-58.

______. "Infanticide as a Primate Reproductive Strategy." *Amer. Scientist,* 65, 1977, 40-49.

______. *The Langurs of Abu, Female and Male Strategies of Reproduction.* Cambridge, Mass.: Harvard University Press, 1977.

HUBER, JOAN. "Looking Back, Looking Ahead: Generational Views of the Women's Movement." Introduction to Ann Foote Cahn, ed., *Women in the U.S. Labor Force.* New York: Praeger, 1979.

HUNT, CAROLYN LOUISE. *The Life of Ellen H. Richards.* Washington, D.C.: American Home Economics Association, 1958.

HUNT, MORTON. *The World of the Formerly Married.* New York: McGraw-Hill, 1966.

HUNT, BERNICE, and MORTON HUNT. *Prime Time, A Guide to the Pleasures and Opportunities of the New Middle Age.* New York: Stein and Day, 1975.

HUTCHISON, E. P. *Immigrants and Their Children 1850-1950.* New York: Wiley, 1956.

HYER, MARJORIE. "Poll of Women Cites Wide Faith in God." *The Washington Post,* April 21, 1978. This poll appeared in the May 1978 issue of *McCall's.*

______. "Catholic Women's Move for Reform Goes beyond Ordination." *The Washington Post,* Nov. 13, 1978.

______. "Catholic 'Network' Teaches Tactics for Religious Lobbying." *The Washington Post,* July 23, 1979.

HYMAN, PAULA. "The Volunteer Organizations: Vanguard or Rear Guard?" *Lilith,* no.5, 1978.

INKELES, ALEX, and DAVID H. SMITH. *Becoming Modern, Individual Change in Six Developing Countries.* Cambridge, Mass.: Harvard University Press, 1974.

JACKSON, JACQUELINE. "Where Are the Black Men?" *Ebony,* 27, 1972, 99-102.

JACOBS, ALBERT C., and ROBERT ANGELL. *A Research in Family Law.* No publisher given, 1930.

JACOBS, RUTH HARRIET. *Life after Youth. Female, Forty—What Next?* Boston: Beacon, 1979.

JACOBY, ROBIN MILLER. "Feminist and Class Consciousness in the British and American Women's Trade Union League, 1890-1925." In Dorothy G. McGuigan, ed., *New Research on Women at the University of Michigan.* Ann

Arbor: University of Michigan, 1974, 77-84.

______. "The Women's Trade Union League and American Feminism." *Feminist Studies*, vol. 3, Fall 1975, 126-140.

JAFFE, ABRAM L., and CHARLES D. STEWART. *Manpower Resources and Utilization, Principles of Labor Force Analysis*. New York: Wiley, 1951.

JAMES, EDWARD T., ed. *Notable American Women, A Biographical Dictionary*. Cambridge, Mass.: Belknap Press, 1971.

JANOWITZ, MORRIS. *The Last Half-Century, Societal Change and Politics in America*. Chicago: University of Chicago Press, 1978.

JEFFERSON, LARA. *These Are My Sisters, A Journal from the Inside of Insanity*. New York: Anchor, 1975.

JEFFREY, JULI ROY. *Frontier Women: The Trans-Mississippi West, 1840-1880*. New York: Hill and Wang, 1979.

JEFFREY, KIRK. "Marriage, Career, and Feminine Ideology in Nineteenth-Century America: Restructuring the Marital Experience of Lydia Maria Child 1828-1874." *Feminist Studies*, 2, 1975, 113-130.

JESPERSON, OSCAR. *Language: Its Nature, Development and Origin*. London: Allen & Unwin, 1922.

JESSIE, SALLY ANN. "A New Women's World." 1978. Draft.

JOHANSSON, SHEILA RYAN. "Sex and Death in Victorian England." In Martha Vicinis, ed., *A Widening Sphere*. Bloomington, Ind.: Indiana University Press, 1977, 163-181.

JOHNSON, WINNIFRED BURT, and LEWIS M. TERMAN, "Personality Characteristics of Happily Married, Unhappily Married, and Divorced Persons." *Character and Personality*, 3, 1935, 297-310.

JOHNSTON, JILL. *Lesbian Nation, the Feminist Solution*. New York: Simon and Schuster, 1973.

JOHNSTON, TRACY. "Who Is the Sweetheart of 1978?" *Ms.*, 6, 1978, 58ff.

JOLLY, CLIFFORD. "The Seed-Eaters: A New Model of Hominid Differentiation Based on a Baboon Analogy." *Man*, 5, 1970, 5-26.

JOLNA, STACY. "Jacees Group Sues to Keep Women in Unit." *The Washington Post*, Dec. 21, 1978.

JONES, MARY GWLADYS. *Hannah More*. New York: Greenwood Press, 1968.

JOSEPHSON, HANNAH. *The Golden Threads: New England's Mill Girls and Magnates*. New York: Russell and Russell, 1949.

JUHASZ, SUZANNE. "The Critic as Feminist: Reflections on Women's Poetry, Feminism, and the Art of Criticism." *Women's Studies*, 5, 1977, 113-130.

KALCIK, SUSAN. "Personal Narratives in Women's Rap Groups." In Claire R. Farrer, ed., *Women and Folklore*. Austin: University of Texas Press, 1975, 3-11.

KAMERMAN, SHEILA B. *Parenting in an Unresponsive Society*. New York: Free Press, 1979.

KANTER, MARILYNNE. "The Psychological Implications of Never-Married Women Who Live Alone." 1978. Draft.

KANTER, ROSABETH MOSS. *Women and Men of the Corporation*. New York: Basic Books, 1977.

______, and BARRY A. STEIN, eds. *Life in Organizations*. New York: Basic Books, 1979.

KATZ, DONALD. "Carolyn Reed and the Backstair Revolt." *New York*, June 11, 1979, 45-50.

KATZ, JOSEPH. "Home Life of Women in Continuing Education." In Helen Astin, ed., *Some Action of Her Own*. Lexington, Mass.: Lexington Books, 1976, 89-106.

KATZMAN, DAVID M. *Seven Days a Week*. New York: Oxford, 1978.

KAUFMAN, MARJORIE R. "Ellen Anderson Gholson Glasgow." In Edward T. James, ed., *Notable American Women*. Cambridge, Mass.: Belknap Press, 1971, 44-49.

KELLY, RITA MAE, and MARY BOUTILIER. *The Making of Political Women*. Chicago: Nelson-Hall, 1978.

KENISTON, KENNETH. "Themes and Conflicts of 'Liberated' Young Women." Karen Horney Memorial Lecture, New York City, March 24, 1971.

KETT, JOSEPH F. *Rites of Passage, Adolescence in America 1790 to the Present*. New York: Basic Books, 1977.

KEY, MARY RITCHIE. "Linguistic Behavior of Male and Female." *Linguistics*, 88, 1972, 15-31.

______. *Male/Female Language*. Metuchen, N. J.: Scarecrow Press, 1975.

KING, CHERI A. "Candle-Passing Ceremony." 1978. Draft.

KIRKPATRICK, JEANE J. *Political Woman*. New York: Basic Books, 1974.

KLAUSNER, SAMUEL Z. *Six Years in the Lives of the Impoverished: An Examination of the WIN Thesis*. Philadelphia: Center for Research on the Acts of Man. 1978.

______. Testimony before Senate Finance Committee, Nov. 15, 1978. (Deals with Modernizing and Traditional women.)

KLEIMAN, DEVRA G. "Review of E. O. Wilson, *Sociobiology: The New Synthesis*, *Signs*, 3, 1977, 493-495.

KLEIN, J. "The Family in 'Traditional' Working-Class England." Abstract in Thorne and Henley, eds., *Language and Sex, Difference and Dominance*. Rowley, Mass.: Newbury House, 1975, 265-266. Orig. in J. Klein, *Samples from English Culture*, vol. 1. London: Routledge & Kegan Paul, 1965, 103-113.

KOLODNY, ANNETTE. "Literary Criticism: A Review Essay." *Signs*, 2, 1977, 404-421.

KOMAROVSKY, MIRRA. *Woman in the Modern World*. Boston: Little, Brown, 1953.

______. *Blue-Collar Marriage*. New York: Random House, 1962.

KORDA, MICHAEL. *Power! How to Get It, How to Use It*. New York: Ballentine, 1975.

KOZLOFF, JOYCE, and MAY STEVENS, eds. *Women Artists on Women's Artists*, Special Issue of *Women's Studies, An Interdisciplinary Journal*, 6, 1978.

KRADITOR, AILEEN, ed. *Up from the Pedestal*. Chicago: Quadrangle, 1968.

KRAMER, CHERIS. "Women's Speech: Separate but Unequal?" In Thorne and Henley, eds., *Language and Sex, Difference and Dominance*. Rowley, Mass.: Newbury House, 1975, 210.

KRAMER, JOHN H., and CYNTHIA KEMPINEN. "Erosion of Chivalry? Changes in the Handling of Male and Female Defendants from 1970 to 1975." Paper presented at Society for Study of Social Problems, 1978.

KROPOTKIN, PIETR ALEKSEEVICH. *The Essential Kropotkin*, Emile Caporeya and Keitha Templous, eds. New York: Liveright, 1975.

KUMMER, HANS. *Primate Societies, Group Techniques of Ecological Adaptation*. Chicago: Aldine, 1971.

LACEY, W. K. *The Family in Classical Greece*. Ithaca, N.Y.: Cornell University Press, 1968.

LAFFERTY, J. CLAYTON, PATRICK M. EADY, JOHN M. ELMERS, and ALONZO W. POND. *The Desert Survival Problem. A Group Decision Making Experiment for Examining the Increasing Individual and Team Effectiveness*. Plymouth, Mich.: ELM, 1973.

LAGEMANN, ELLEN CONDLIFFE. "Educational Biography: An Approach to the History of Women's Education." Paper presented at Berkshire Conference, 1978.

LAING, R. D. *Self and Others*. 2nd ed. New York: Pantheon, 1971.

LAKOFF, ROBIN. *Language and Woman's Place*. New York: Harper and Row, 1975.

LANCASTER, JANE BACKMAN. "Play Mothering: The Relations between Juvenile Females and Young Infants among Free-ranging Vervet Monkeys." *Folio* Primatologica, 15, 1971, 161-182.

______. "In Praise of the Achieving Female Monkey." In Carol Tavris, ed., *The Female Experience*. New York: Ziff-Davis, 1973, 5-9.

______. *Primate Behavior and the Emergence of Human Culture*. New York: Holt, Rinehart, Winston, 1975.

LANDIS, PAUL. "Sequential Marriage." *Jour. Home Economics*, 42, 1950, 625-628.

LANSING, MARJORIE. "Women: A New Political Class." In Dorothy Gris McGuinan, ed., *A Sampler of Women's Studies*. Ann Arbor: Center for Continuing Education of Women, 1973, 59-76.

LANTZ, HERMAN. *People of Coal Town*. New York: Columbia University Press, 1958.

______. "Pre-Industrial Patterns in the Colonial Family in America: A Content Analysis of Colonial Magazines." *Amer. Sociol. Rev.*, 33, 1968, 413-426.

LASLETT, PETER. *The World We Have Lost*. London: Methuen, 1965.

LASSER, CAROL. "Lifecycle and Class: Domestic Service and the 'Girls' of the Salem Female Charitable Society." Paper presented at Berkshire Conference, 1978.

LAVRIN, ASUNCION. "Women in Convents: Their Economic and Social Role in Colonial Mexico." In Berenice Carroll, ed., *Liberating Women's History, Theoretical and Critical Essays*. Urbana: University of Illinois Press, 1976, 250-277.

LAWICK-GOODALL, JANE. *In the Shadow of Man*. Boston: Houghton-Mifflin, 1971.

LAWRENCE, BARBARA. "Dirty Words *Can* Hurt You." *Redbook*, May, 1974, 33.

LAWS, JUDITH LONG. *The Second X*. New York: Elsevier, 1979.

LEACH, EDMOND R. "Social Structure, The History of the Concept." *International Encyclopedia of the Social Sciences*, vol. 14. New York: Macmillan, 1968, 482-489.

LEACOCK, ELEANOR. "Class, Commodity and the Status of Women." In Ruby

Rohrlich-Leavitt, ed., *Women Cross-Culturally: Change and Challenge*. The Hague: Mouton, 1975.

LEAKEY, RICHARD E., and ROGER LEWIN. *People of the Lake. Mankind and Its Beginnings*. New York: Anchor-Doubleday, 1978.

LEAVITT, HAROLD, JEAN LIPMAN-BLUMEN, SUSAN SCHAEFER, and REUBEN HARRIS. "Vicarious Achievement Orientation." Paper presented at American Psychological Association, 1977.

LECKY, WILLIAM EDWARD HARTPOLE. *History of European Morals*. London: Watts, 1869.

LEE, HELEN JACKSON. *Growing Up Black*. New York: Doubleday, 1978.

LEE, PATRICK, and NANCY GROPPER. "Sex-role Culture and Educational Practice." *Harvard Educational Review*, 44, 1974, 369-410.

LEMASTERS, E. E. *Modern Courtship and Marriage*. New York: Macmillan, 1957.

______. "Revolt of the Blue Collar Wives." *Playgirl*, Sept. 1975, 40-41 ff.

LERNER, DANIEL. *The Passing of Traditional Society: Modernization in the Middle East*. New York: Free Press, 1963.

LEVENSON, J. C. "Margaret Deland." In Edward T. James, ed., *Notable American Women*. Cambridge, Mass.: Belknap Press, 1971, 454-456.

LEVINE, MURRAY, and ADELINE LEVINE. *A Social History of the Helping Services: Clinic, Court, School, and Community*. New York: Appleton-Century, 1970.

LEVINGER, GEORGE, and OLIVER MOLES, eds. *Divorce and Separation in America*. New York: Basic Books, 1979.

LEWIN, KURT. "Some Social-Psychological Differences between the United States and Germany." *Character and Personality*, 4, 1936, 278-308.

LIEBOWITZ, RUTH P. "Voices from Convents: Nuns and Repentant Prostitutes in Late Renaissance Italy." Paper presented at Berkshire Conference, 1978.

LINNER, BIRGITTA. "Teaching Sex and Personal Relationships in Swedish Schools." *Social Change*, no. 7, Sept. 1978. Available at Swedish Embassy, Washington, D.C.

LINTNER, SYLVIA CHACE. "Rose Terry Cooke." In Edward T. James, ed., *Notable American Women*. Cambridge, Mass.: Belknap Press, 1971, 378-379.

LIPPARD, LUCY R. *From the Centre: Feminist Essays on Women's Art*. New York: Dutton, 1976.

LIPSET, MARTIN SEYMOUR. *Political Man*. New York: Doubleday, 1960.

______. "Social Class." *International Encyclopedia of the Social Sciences*, vol. 15. New York: Macmillan, 1968, 296-316.

LIPMAN-BLUMEN, JEAN. "Observations on the Current Status of the Women's Movement in the United States." Paper presented at International Sociological Association, Uppsala, 1978.

______. "Ideology, Social Structure, and Crisis." 1979a. Draft.

______. "Emerging Patterns of Female Leadership: Must the Female Leader Go Formal?" In Matina Horner, ed., *Perspectives on the Patterns of an Era*. Cambridge, Mass.: Harvard University Press, 1979b.

______. "Bernard, Jessie." *International Encyclopedia of the Social Sciences*, vol. 18. New York: The Free Press, 1980, 49-56.

LIRTZMAN, SIDNEY I., and MAHMOND A. WAHBA. "Determinants of Coalition Behavior of Men and Women: Sex Roles or Situational Requirements?" *Journal of Applied Psychology*, 56, 1972, 406-411.

LITWAK, EUGENE. "Extended Kin Relations in an Industrial Democratic Society." In Ethel Shanas and Gordon Streib, eds. *Social Structures and the Family: Generational Relations*. Englewood Cliffs, N.J.: Prentice-Hall, 1965.

LIVY. *Cato on Extravagance* (Cyrus Edwards, trans.). In Basil Davenport, ed., *The Portable Roman Reader*. New York: Viking, 1951.

LOFLAND, LYN H. *A World of Strangers: Order and Action in Urban Public Space*. New York: Basic Books, 1973.

LOMNITZ, LARISSA ADLER, and MARISOL PEREZ LIZAUR. "The History of a Mexican Urban Family." *Family History*, 3, 1978, 392-409.

LONG, CLARENCE D. *The Labor Force under Changing Income and Employment*. Princeton: Princeton University Press, 1958.

LOPATA, HELENA ZNANIECKI. *Occupation Housewife*. New York: Oxford, 1971.

______. *Widowhood in an American City*. Cambridge: Schenkman, 1973.

______. "Couple-Companionate: Relationships in Marriage and Widowhood." In Nona Glazer, ed., *Old Family/New Family*. New York: D. Van Nostrand, 1975, 119-149.

LOPATE, CAROL. "Daytime Television: You'll Never Want to Leave Home." *Feminist Studies*, 3, 1976, 69-82.

Los Angeles Times, May 3, 1977.

LOUGEE, CAROLYN C. *Le Paradis des Femmes: Women, Salons, and Social Stratification in 17th Century France*. Princeton, N. J.: Princeton University Press, 1976.

LOWELL, JAMES RUSSELL. "On A Certain Condescension in Foreigners." In *Lowell's Works*, vol. 1, 1966, 293-328. Original date, 1869.

LOWENTHAL, LEO. *Literature, Popular Culture, and Society*. Englewood Cliffs, N. J.: Prentice-Hall, 1961.

LUBOVE, ROY. *The Professional Altruist: The Emergence of Social Work as a Career*. Cambridge: Harvard University Press, 1965.

LUNDBERG, FERDINAND. *America's 60 Families*. New York: Vanguard Press, 1937.

LYND, ROBERT, and HELEN LYND. *Middletown*. New York: Harcourt, Brace and World, 1929.

______. *Middletown in Transition*. New York: Harcourt, Brace and World, 1937.

MACCOBY, ELEANOR, and CAROL NAGY JACKLIN. *The Psychology of Sex Differences*. Stanford, Calif.: Stanford University Press, 1974.

MACCRACKEN, HENRY NOBLE. *Address at Memorial Service for Lucy Maynard Salmon*. Poughkeepsie: Vassar College, 1927, 30-31.

MACDONALD, DUNCAN. "Arriving: The Household Professional." *House Beautiful*, 111, March, 1969, 88-89.

MAINARDI, PAT. "The Politics of Housework." In Robin Morgan, ed., *Sisterhood Is Powerful*. New York: Vintage Books, 1970, 447-454.

______. Editorial, *Moving Mountains*, 1977, 23.

MANDLE, JOAN. *Women and Social Change*. Princeton: Princeton Book Co., 1979.

MANNHEIM, KARL. "The Sociological Problem of the 'Intelligentsia.' " In George B. deHuszar, ed., *The Intellectuals, A Controversial Portrait*. New York: Free Press, 1960, 62-68.

MARCH, ARTEMIS. "Female Invisibility in Androcentric Sociological Theory." Paper presented at American Sociological Association, 1978.

MARCUS, JAN. "Art and Anger." *Feminist Studies*, 4, no. 1, Feb. 1978, 69-98.

MARTIN, WENDY, ed. *The American Sisterhood: Writings of the Feminist Movement from Colonial Times to the Present.* New York: Harper & Row, 1972.

MARTIN, WENDY. "Seduced and Abandoned in the New World, The Fallen Woman in American Fiction." In Wendy Martin, ed. *The American Sisterhood.* New York: Harper & Row, 1972, 257-272.

MARTINEAU, HARRIET. "From Eastern Life: Present and Past." In Jean Goulianos, ed. *By a Woman Writ: Literature from Six Centuries by and about Women.* Baltimore: Penguin, 1973, 199-212. Original, 1848.

______. *Society in America.* New York: Saunders and Atley, 1837.

MASON, OTIS TUFTON. *Women's Share in Primitive Culture.* New York: D. Appleton, 1898.

MATTHIASSON, CAROLYN J., ed. *Many Sisters: Women in Cross-Cultural Perspective.* New York: Free Press, 1974.

MATTHEWS, LILLIAN. "Women in the Trade Unions in San Francisco." *University of California (Berkeley) Publications in Economics*, vol. 3, no. 1, June 10, 1913. Present citation, Baxandall, Gordon, and Reverby, eds., *America's Working Women.* New York: Vintage, 1976.

MATTHEWS, SUSAN. "A Woman's Refuge: A Personal Experience." 1978. Draft.

MAYHEW, LEON. *Society, Institutions and Activity.* Glenview, Ill.: Scott, Foresman, 1971.

MCBRIDE, THERESA M. The Domestic Revolution, *The Modernisation of Household Service in England and France 1820-1920.* London: Croom Helm, 1976.

MCCARTHY, BARRY. *What You (Still) Don't Know about Male Sexuality.* New York: Crowell, 1978.

MCCLELLAND, DAVID C. *Studies in Motivation.* New York: Appleton-Century-Crofts, 1955.

MCCONNELL-GINET, SALLY, RUTH BORKER, and NELLY FURMAN, eds. *Language in Women's Lives: Literature, Culture, and Society.* Forthcoming.

MCCORMACK, THELMA. "Toward a Nonsexist Perspective on Social and Political Change." In Millman and Kanter, eds., *Another Voice: Feminist Perspectives on Social Life and Social Science.* New York: Anchor, 1975.

MCCOURT, KATHLEEN. *Working-Class Women and Grass-Roots Politics.* Bloomington, Ind.: Indiana University Press, 1977.

MCDONNELL, ERNEST W. *The Beguines and Beghards in Medieval Cultures.* New York: Octagon Books, 1969.

MCGINNIS, LYNDA M., and MCGINNIS, PATRICK R. "Primate Behavior and the First Infant." In Warren B. Miller and Lucile F. Newman, eds., *The First Child and Family Formation.* Chapel Hill, N. C.: Carolina Population Center, 1978, 24-34.

MELDER, KEITH. *Beginnings of Sisterhood: The American Women's Rights Movement, 1800-1960.* New York: Schocken Books, 1977.

MELLEN, JOAN. *Women and Their Sexuality in the New Film.* New York: Horizon Press, 1973.

MERRIAM, CHARLES E., and HAROLD FOOTE GOSNELL. *Non-Voting: Causes and Methods of Control.* Chicago: University of Chicago Press, 1924.

MERTON, ROBERT. *Social Theory and Social Structure*. New York: Free Press, 1957.

______, and PAUL LAZARSFELD. "Friendship as a Social Process: A Substantive and Methodological Analysis." In Morroe Berger, Theodore Abel, and C. H. Page, eds., *Freedom and Control in Modern Society*. New York: Van Nostrand, 1954.

MESSER, MARY BURT. *The Family in the Making*. New York: Putnam, 1928.

MICHELSON, WILLIAM. "Intention and Expectations in Differential Residential Selection." *Jour. Mar. and Fam.*, 35, 1973, 184-196.

MILES, HENRY. *Lowell As It Was and As It Is*. Lowell, Mass.: Powers & Beagley, 1845. Present citation, Thomas Dublin, "Women, Work, and the Family," *Feminist Studies*, 3, 1975, 30-39.

MILLER, ANITA. *Impact ERA: Limitations and Possibilities*. Millbrae, Calif.: Les Femmes Publishing, 1976, for the California Commission on the Status of Women.

MILLER, JEAN BAKER. *Toward A New Psychology of Women*. Boston: Beacon Press, 1976.

MILLER, JOANNE, CAROL SCHOOLER, MELVIN L. KOHN, and KAREN A. MILLER. "Women and Work: The Psychological Effects of Occupational Conditions." 1978. Draft.

MILLER, S. M., and PAMELA ROBY, "Strategies for Social Mobility: A Policy Framework." *The American Sociologist*, June 1971, 18-22.

MILLMAN, MARCIA, "Autobiography and Social Mobility, Life Accounts of Working-Class Daughters." Paper presented at Society for Study of Social Problems, San Francisco, 1973.

MILLS, C. WRIGHT. *The Power Elite*. New York: Oxford, 1959.

MITCHELL, CARROLL. "On Aronoff and Crano's Re-examination." *Amer. Sociol. Rev.*, 41, 1976, 1071-1072.

MITCHELL, MARILYN HALL. "Sexist Art Criticism." *Signs*, 3, 1978, 681-687.

MOERS, ELLEN. "Money, the Job, and Little Women." *Commentary*, Jan. 1973, 57-65.

MOLES, OLIVER. "Marital Dissolution and Public Assistance Payments." In George Levinger and Oliver Moles, eds., *Divorce and Separation*. New York: Basic Books, 1979.

MOORE, JOAN W. "Patterns of Women's Participation in Voluntary Associations." *Amer. Jour. Sociol.*, 46, 1961, 592-598.

MOORE, KRISTIN A., and SANDRA L. HOFFERTH. *The Consequences of Age at First Childbirth: Final Research Summary*. Washington, D.C.: The Urban Institute, 1978.

______, SANDRA L. HOFFERTH, STEVEN B. CALDWELL, and LINDA J. WAITE. *Teenage Motherhood: Social and Economic Consequences*. Washington, D.C.: The Urban Institute, 1979.

MORE, HANNAH. *Strictures on the Modern System of Female Education*, vol. 2. London: T. Cadell, Jr. and W. Davies, 1799.

MORRIS, JAN. *Conundrum*. New York: New American Library, 1974.

MOWRER, ERNEST R. *The Family: Its Organization and Disorganization*. Chicago: University of Chicago Press. 1932.

MOYNIHAN, D. P., and NATHAN GLAZER. *Beyond the Melting Pot*. Cambridge,

Mass.: MIT Press, 1963.

MUNRO, ELEANOR. *Originals: American Women Artists*. New York: Simon and Schuster, 1979.

MURPHY, ROBERT F. Review of Denise Paulme, ed., *Femmes d'Afrique*. In *American Anthropologist*, 64, 1962, 1077.

MURRAY, ROBERT H. *Studies in the English Social & Political Thinkers of the Nineteenth Century*. Cambridge: W. Heffer & Sons, 1929.

MYRDAL, ALVA, and VIOLA KLEIN. *Women's Two Roles*. London: Routledge and Kegan Paul, 1956.

MYERSON, ABRAHAM. *The Nervous Housewife*. Boston: Little, Brown, 1929.

MYRON, NANCY, and CHARLOTTE BUNCH, eds. *Lesbianism and the Women's Movement*. Baltimore: Diana Press, 1975.

MYERS, JUNE. "To Fifty and Beyond—at Your Own Risk." *Heliotrope*, Summer 1979, 1, 3.

NATIONAL CENTER FOR HEALTH STATISTICS. "Final Natality Statistics, 1976." *Monthly Vital Statistics Report*, 26, Supplement, no. 12, March 29, 1978.

______. "Final Marriage Statistics, 1976." *Monthly Vital Statistics Report*, 27, Supplement, no. 6, Sept. 13, 1978.

______. "Annual Summary for the United States, 1977, Provisional." *Monthly Vital Statistics Report*, 26, no. 13, Dec. 7, 1978.

NATIONAL COMMISSION FOR MANPOWER POLICY. *Women's Changing Roles at Home and on the Job*. Washington, D.C.: Special Report no. 26, National Commission for Manpower Policy, September, 1978.

NATIONAL COMMISSION ON THE OBSERVANCE OF INTERNATIONAL WOMEN'S YEAR. *The Spirit of Houston*. Washington, D.C.: The State Department, 1978.

NATIONAL COMMISSION ON WORKING WOMEN CENTER FOR WOMEN AND WORK. *National Survey of Working Women: Perceptions, Problems and Prospects*. Washington, D.C.: National Manpower Institute, June 1979.

NATIONAL COUNCIL OF WOMEN OF THE UNITED STATES. *Transactions, 1881*. Farmingdale, N. Y.: Dabor Services, Inc., 1979.

NATIONAL WOMEN'S ACTION ALLIANCE (flyer). "What Is the U.S. National Women's Agenda?" 1975.

NATIONAL WOMEN'S AGENDA COALITION. Working Paper, Aug. 31, 1976.

NELSON, CYNTHIA, and VIRGINIA OLESEN. "Veil of Illusion: A Critique of the Concept of Equality in Western Thought." *Catalyst*, nos. 10-11, 1977, 8-36.

NEUBECK, GERHARD, ed. *Extra-Marital Relations*. Englewood Cliffs, N.J.: Prentice-Hall, 1969.

NIETZSCHE, FRIEDRICH. *The Will to Power* (Anthony M. Ludovici, trans.). New York: Russell and Russell, 1964.

NORLAND, STEPHEN, and NEAL SHOVER. "Gender Roles and Female Criminality: Some Critical Comments." *Criminology* 15, 1977, 67-87.

NORTON, ARTHUR J., and PAUL C. GLICK. "Marital Instability: Past, Present, and Future." In George Levinger and Oliver Moles, eds., *Divorce and Separation in America*. New York: Basic Books, 1979.

OAKLEY, ANN. *Sex, Gender & Society*. New York: Harper & Row, 1972.

______. *Women's Work: A History of the Housewife*. New York: Pantheon, 1974.

O'CONNOR, PETER A. "Household Head and Type of Household: Stockton, California, 1880." Paper presented at Pacific Sociological Society, 1973.

OGBURN, W. F., and MEYER NIMKOFF. *Technology and the Changing Family*. Boston: Houghton-Mifflin, 1955.

OKUN, ARTHUR M. "The Polarizers Are Hard at Work." *The Washington Post*, Nov. 27, 1978.

OLSEN, TILLIE. *Silences*. New York: Delacorte, 1978.

OLSON, MANCUR. "Economics, Sociology, and the Best of All Possible Worlds." *The Public Interest*, 12, 1968, 96-118.

OOMS, THEODORA, and TERESA MACIOCHA. *Teenage Pregnancy and Family Impact: New Perspectives on Policy. A Preliminary Report, June 1979*. Washington, D.C.: The George Washington University Institute for Educational Leadership, 1979.

OPPENHEIMER, VALERIE K. *The Female Labor Force in the United States*. Berkeley: University of California Press, 1970.

______. "The Sociology of Women's Economic Role in the Family." *Amer. Sociol. Rev.*, 42, 1977, 387-406.

______. "Rising Educational Attainment, Declining Fertility and the Inadequacies of the Female Labor Market." In C. Westoff and R. Parke, eds., *Demographic and Social Aspects of Population Growth*. Washington, D.C.: Government Printing Office, 305-329.

O'REILLY, JANE. "Click!" *Ms.*, Spring, 1972. Reproduced October, 1980, 69-70.

ORTH, PENELOPE. *An Enviable Position: The American Mistress from Slightly Kept to Practically Married*. New York: David McKay, 1972.

ORTNER, SHERRY B. "Is Female to Male as Nature Is to Culture?" In Rosaldo and Lamphere, eds., *Woman, Culture and Society*. Stanford, Calif.: Stanford University Press, 1974, 67-88.

OSMOND, MARIE W., and PATRICIA Y. MARTIN. "From Closed- to Open-Systems: Game Simulation of Sex-Role Behavior." 1973. Draft.

PAGE, JEAN, ed. "Country & Western Songbook: A Feminist Interpretation of Woman in Country/Western Music." 1979. Draft.

PAPANEK, HANNA. "Purdah in Pakistan: Seclusion and Modern Occupations for Women." *Jour. Mar. and Fam.*, 33, 1971, 517-530.

______. "Purdah: Separate Worlds and Symbolic Shelter." *Comparative Studies in Society and History*, 1973, 289-325.

PARK, ROBERT E., and HERBERT A. MILLER. *Old World Traits Transplanted*. New York: Harper, 1921.

PARRINGTON, VERNON. *Main Currents in American Thought*. New York: Harcourt, Brace, 1927-1930.

PARSONS, ELSIE CLEWS. *The Family*. New York: Putnam, 1906.

______ (pseudonym, John Main). *The Old-Fashioned Woman: Primitive Fancies about the Sex*. New York: Putnam's, 1913.

PARSONS, TALCOTT. "Age and Sex in the Social Structure of the United States." *Amer. Sociol. Rev.*, 7, 1942, 604-616.

______. *The Social System*. Glencoe: Free Press, 1951.

______, and ROBERT BALES. *Family, Socialization, and Social Process*. New York: Free Press, 1955.

Patrick, J. Max, and Glenn Negley, eds. *The Quest for Utopia: An Anthology of Imaginary Societies*. New York: Henry Schumann, 1962.

Pattee, Fred Lewis. "The Short Story." In W. P. Trent, John Erskine, S. P. Sherman, and C. Van Doren, eds., *The Cambridge History of American Literature*, vol. 2. New York: Macmillan, 1936, 367-395.

Paulme, Denise, ed. *Women of Tropical Africa*. Berkeley: University of California Press, 1971.

Pearson, Carol. "Women's Fantasies and Feminist Utopias," *Frontiers*, 2, no. 3, 1977.

Perlez, Jane. ". . . and What Ever Happened to the Most Popular Girl in Your Class?" *Ms.*, 6, 1978, 59 ff.

Perlman, Helen Marris. *Relationship: The Heart of Helping People*. Chicago: University of Chicago Press, 1979.

Peters, Barbara, and Victoria Samuels. *Dialogue on Diversity: A New Agenda for American Women*. New York: Institute on Pluralism and Group Identity, 1976.

Peterson, Rebecca, Gerda Wekerle, and David Morley. "Work and Environment: An Overview of an Emerging Field," EDRA 7, Vancouver, May 24, 1976 and Habitat Forum of the UN Conference on Human Settlements, June 5, 1976.

Phillips, Dayton. *Beguines in Medieval Strasburg: A Study of the Social Aspect of Beguine Life*. Ann Arbor: Edwards Bros., Inc., 1941.

Pildes, Judith. "Our Mothers' Daughters." 1977. Draft.

Piotrkowski, Chaya S. *Work and the Family System: A Naturalistic Study of Working-Class and Lower-Middle-Class Families*. New York: Free Press, 1979.

Platt, John. "Women's Roles and the Great World Transformation." In Guy Streatfeild, ed., *Women and the Future*. Binghamton, N. Y.: Center for Integration Studies, 1976.

Pleck, Joseph H. "The Male Sex Role: Definitions, Problems, and Sources of Change." *Journal of Social Issues*, 32, 1976, 155-164.

Pollak, Otto. *The Criminality of Women*. Philadelphia: University of Pennsylvania Press, 1950.

Polsky, Ned. *Hustlers, Beats, and Others*. Chicago: Aldine, 1967.

Pomeroy, Sarah B. *Goddesses, Whores, Wives, and Slaves: Women in Classical Antiquity*. New York: Schocken, 1975.

Popenoe, David. "Urban Sprawl: Some Neglected Sociological Considerations." Paper presented at Eastern Sociological Society, 1977.

Popenoe, Paul. "Can the Family Have Two Heads?" *Sociology and Social Research*, 18, 1933.

Population Reference Bureau. *Interchange*, Feb. 1979.

Porter, Elsa. Roundtable Discussion in Radcliffe Symposium on Women and Power, An Exploratory View, moderated by Irene Tinker. Washington, D.C., 1979, 46.

Power, Eileen. "Women in Nunneries." In M. M. Postan, ed., *Medieval Women*. Cambridge: Cambridge University Press, 1975.

President's Report. Employment and Training Report of the President. Washington, D.C.: Government Printing Office, 1977.

Putnam, Emily James. *The Lady*. New York: Sturgis and Walton, 1910.

QUINN, JANE BRYANT. "Managerial Men and Women Are Found Remarkably Alike." *The Washington Post*, July 17, 1978.

RADICALESBIANS. "The Woman Identified Woman." 1970. Draft.

RADLOFF, LENORE. "Sex Differences in Depression: The Effects of Occupation and Marital Status." *Sex Roles*, 1, 1975, 249-266.

______. "Risk Factors for Depression: What Do We Learn from Them?" In Deborah Belle and Susan Salasin, eds., *Mental Health of Women: Fact and Fiction.* New York: Academic Press, 1979.

RADLOFF, LENORE SAWYER, and DONALD S. RAE. "Susceptibility and Precipitating Factors in Depression: Sex Differences and Similarities." *Journal Abnormal Psychology*, 1979.

______. "Brief Report: Depression and the Empty Nest." *Sex Roles*, vol. 6, no. 6, Dec. 1980, 775-781.

______. "Components of the Sex Difference in Depression." In R. G. Simmons, ed., Research in Community and Mental Health, vol. 3. Greenwich, Conn., in press.

RAINWATER, LEE, RICHARD C. COLEMAN, and GERALD HANDEL. *Workingman's Wife: Her Personality, World and Life Style.* New York: Oceana Publication, 1959.

REUBEN, DAVID. *Everything You Ever Wanted to Know about Sex But Were Afraid to Ask.* New York: McKay, 1969.

REISS, IRA L. *The Family System in America.* New York: Holt, Rinehart, Winston, 1971.

RICH, ADRIENNE. *Of Woman Born.* New York: Norton, 1976.

RICH, SPENCER. "Enrollment Hits New Low for the '70s." *The Washington Post*, May 13,1979.

RICHARD, PAUL. "Women in the Arts, Charlotte Robinson, Worker-in-the-Trenches." *The Washington Post*, Jan. 31, 1979.

RICHIE, JEAN. *Apple Seeds and Soda Straws: Some Love Charms and Legends.* New York: Henry Z. Walsh Inc., 1965.

RIDEOUT, WALTER B. "Zona Gale," In Edward T. James, ed., *Notable American Women.* Cambridge, Mass.: Belknap Press, 1971, 7-9.

RIESMAN, DAVID. *The Lonely Crowd.* New Haven: Yale University Press, 1950.

______. *Introduction to Jessie Bernard, Academic Women.* University Park, Penna.: Pennsylvania State University Press, 1964.

RINGER, ROBERT. *Looking Out for Number 1.* New York: Funk & Wagnall's, 1977.

______. *Winning through Intimidation.* New York: Crown, 1978.

RIZZARDI, CAROL. "The Feminist Holy War: Religion—the First and Final Frontier." *Moving Mountains*, a Feminist Quarterly, 2, Winter, 1977, 16-17, 30-31.

ROBINSON, LILLIAN S. *Sex, Class, and Culture.* Bloomington, Ind.: Indiana University Press, 1978.

ROBY, PAMELA. "Sociology and Women in Working-Class Jobs." In Marcia Millman and Rosabeth Moss Kanter, eds., *Another Voice.* New York: Anchor, 1975, 203-239.

______, and VIRGINIA KERR. "The Politics of Prostitution." *The Nation*, April 10, 1972, 463-466.

ROBY, PAMELA. Unpublished study of working women in the United States.

RODGERS, AUDREY T. " 'Portrait of a Lady': Images of Women in Twentieth-Century American Literature." In Eloise Snyder, ed., *The Study of Women: Enlarging Perspectives of Social Reality.* New York: Harper and Row, 1979, 228-261.

ROOS, JOAN. "Sisters, Sweethearts, and Security: Some Dilemmas Encountered by Berkeley Single Feminists." 1975. Draft.

ROSALDO, MICHELLE ZIMBALIST, and LOUISE LAMPHERE. Introduction to Rosaldo and Lamphere, eds., *Women, Culture and Society.* Stanford: Stanford University Press, 1974.

ROSEN, BENSON, THOMAS H. JERDEE, and THOMAS L. PRESTWICK. "Dual-Career Marital Adjustment: Potential Effects of Discriminatory Managerial Attitudes." *Jour. Mar. and Family,* 37, 1975, 565-572.

ROSEN, RUTH, and SUE DAVIDSON, eds. *The Maimie Papers.* Old Westbury, Conn.: Feminist Press, 1977.

ROSENFELD, MEGAN. "Houston: Reflections on an All-Female World." *The Washington Post,* Dec. 2, 1977.

ROSS, E. A. *Principles of Sociology.* New York: Century, 1920.

ROSS, HEATHER, and ISABEL SAWHILL. *Time of Transition.* Washington: The Urban Institute, 1975.

ROSSI, ALICE. "Transition to Parenthood." *Jour. Mar. and Fam.*, 30, 1968, 26-39.

______. "A Biosocial Perspective on Parenting." *Daedalus,* 106, Spring, 1977, 1-31.

______, ed. *The Feminist Papers.* New York: Bantam, 1973.

______, and ANN CALDERWOOD, eds. *Academic Women on the Move.* New York: Russell Sage, 1973.

ROSSMAN, MARTIN. "It's Invisible: Once—A Magazine for Teens." *San Francisco Chronicle,* Sept. 5, 1978.

ROSZAK, BETTY, and THEODORE ROSZAK, eds. *Masculine/Feminine.* New York: Harper & Row, 1969.

ROTHBLATT, DONALD N., DANIEL J. GARR, and JO SPRAGUE. *Women and the Suburban Environment.* New York: Praeger, 1979.

ROTHMAN, SHEILA M., *Woman's Proper Place: A History of Changing Ideals and Practices, 1870 to the Present.* New York: Basic Books, 1978.

ROULETTE, THOMAS G. "Islam: From Rugs to Steel Mills." *The Washington Post,* Jan. 31, 1979.

RUBIN, LILLIAN. *Worlds of Pain.* New York: Basic Books, 1976.

______. *Women of a Certain Age.* New York: Basic Books, 1979.

RUBLE, DIANE N., and E. TORY HIGGINS. "Effects of Group Sex Composition on Self-Presentation and Sex Typing." *Jour. Soc. Issues,* 32, 1976, 125-132.

RUX, JULIA. "Celibacy: An Alternative to Sex-Typed Dyadic Relationships." 1978. Draft.

RUZEK, SHERYL BURT. *The Women's Health Movement.* Praeger, 1978.

SAEGERT, SUSAN, and GARY WINKEL. "The Home: A Critical Problem for Changing Sex-Roles." Paper presented at American Sociological Association, 1978.

SAFILIOS-ROTHSCHILD, CONSTANTINA. "The Study of Family Power Structure: A Review 1960-1969." *Jour. Mar. and Fam.*, 32, 1970, 70-90.

SAHLI, NANCY. "Smashing: Women's Relationships before the Fall." *Chrysalis,* no. 8, 17-27, 1978.

SALMON, LUCY MAYNARD. *Domestic Service*. New York: Macmillan, 1897.

SAMUELS, VICTORIA. *Nowhere to Be Found: A Literature Review and Annotated Bibliography on White Working Class Women*. New York: Institute on Pluralism and Group Identity, Working Paper no. 13, 1975.

SANDAY, P. R. "Toward a Theory of the Status of Women." *American Anthropologist*, 75, 1973, 1682-1700.

SAN DIEGO CENTER FOR WOMEN'S STUDIES AND SERVICES (flyer). N.d.

SAPIRSTEIN, M. R. *Emotional Security*. New York: Crown, 1948.

SAWHILL, ISABEL V., ed. *Women's Changing Roles at Home and on the Job*. Washington, D.C.: National Commission for Manpower Policy, 1978.

SAXTON, RUTH. "Life for Women in a Men's Paradise . . . 1840-1851." 1978. Draft.

SCANZONI, JOHN. "An Historical Perspective on Husband-Wife Bargaining Power and Marital Dissolution." In George Levinger and Oliver Moles, eds., *Divorce and Separation in America*. New York: Basic Books, 1979, 20-36.

SCHAEF, ANNE. "The Female and Male Systems." Paper presented at Women's Studies Conference, University of Maryland, 1978.

SCHATZMANN, LEONARD and ANSELM STRAUSS. "Social Class and Modes of Communication." *Amer. Jour. Sociol.*, 60, 1954, 329-338.

SCHEPPELE, KIM LANE. "Feminism as a Response to Sociological Ambivalence." Paper presented at Sociologists for Women in Society, 1977.

SCHLAFLY, PHYLLIS. *The Power of the Positive Woman*. New York: Harcourt, Brace, Jovanovich, 1979.

SCHLESINGER, ARTHUR M. *Learning How to Behave: A Historical Study of American Etiquette Books*. New York: Macmillan, 1946.

SCHOENBERG, SANDRA P. "Older Adults as Anchors in City Neighborhoods." 1978. Draft.

______, and IRENE DABROWSKI. "Factors Which Enhance the Participation of Women in Urban Neighborhood Social Life." Paper presented at American Sociological Association, 1978.

______. "The City Woman and Her Neighborhoods." 1979. Draft.

SCHOFIELD, WILLIAM. *Psychotherapy: The Purchase of Friendship*. Englewood Cliffs N.J.: Prentice-Hall, 1964.

SCHULENBURG, JANE TIBBETTS. "Clio's European Daughters: Myopic Modes of Perception." In Julia A. Sherman, and Evelyn Norton Beck, eds. *The Prism of Sex*. Madison, Wis.: University of Wisconsin Press, 1979, 33-54.

SCHULZ, MURIEL R. "The Semantic Derogation of Woman." In Thorne and Henley, eds., *Language and Sex, Difference and Dominance*. Rowley, Mass.: Newbury House, 1975, 222-223.

SCHUMACHER, E. F. *Small Is Beautiful: Economics As If People Mattered*. New York: Harper and Row, 1973.

SCHUMPETER, JOSEPH A. "The Sociology of Intellectuals." In George B. de Huszar, ed., *The Intellectuals, A Controversial Portrait*. New York: Free Press, 1960, 69-79.

SCOTT, ANNE FIROR. *The Southern Lady, from Pedestal to Politics 1830-1930*. Chicago: University of Chicago Press, 1970.

SCOTT, J. P. "Social Behavior, Animal." *International Encyclopedia of the Social Sciences*, vol. 14. New York: Macmillan, 1968, 342-351.

SEIDEN, ANNE M., and PAULINE BART. "Woman to Woman: Is Sisterhood Powerful?" In Nona Glazer, ed., *Old Family/New Family*. New York: D. Van Nostrand, 1975, 189-228.

SEIDENBERG, ROBERT. *Corporate Wives, Corporate Casualties?* Garden City, N.Y.: Anchor, 1973.

SEIFER, NANCY. *Absent from the Majority, Working Class Women in America*. New York: National Project on Ethnic Research, 1973.

______. "The Working Family in Crisis: Who Is Listening?" New York: Institute on Pluralism and Group Identity, 1975.

______. "The Key to Our Future: Coalition Building." In *Women's Agenda*, 1, Feb. 1976, 12-13.

______. "Where Feminism and Ethnicity Intersect: The Impact of Parallel Movements." New York: Institute on Pluralism and Group Identity, Feb. 1976, Working Paper no. 16.

______. "Equal Rights and Working Class Women." New York: Institute of Human Relations, n.d. Draft.

SELIGMAN, M. E. P. "Depression and Learned Helplessness." In R. J. Friedman and M. M. Katz, eds., *The Psychology of Depression: Contemporary Theory and Research*. Washington, D.C.: Winston and Sons, 1974, 83-113.

SELVINSKY, ILYA. Quoted in *The Washington Post*, April 13, 1967.

SENNETT, RICHARD. *Families against the City: Middle-Class Homes of Industrial Chicago, 1872-1890*. Cambridge, Mass.: Harvard University Press, 1970.

______, and JONATHAN COBB. *The Hidden Injuries of Class*. New York: Knopf, 1972.

SHAW, LOIS B. "Economic Consequences of Marital Disruption." 1978. Draft.

SHEEHY, GAIL. *Passages: Predictable Crises of Adult Life*. New York: Dutton, 1976.

SHERMAN, JULIA A., and EVELYN NORTON BECK, eds. *The Prism of Sex*. Madison, Wis.: University of Wisconsin Press, 1979.

SHILS, EDWARD. "Intellectuals." In *International Encyclopedia of the Social Sciences*, vol. 7. New York: Macmillan, 1968, 399-415.

SHORK, ERIKA. "History's Economic Outcasts, The Inexorable Relationship between Economic and Social Roles." *Atlas Report*, April, 1978, 33. Adapted from *Die Zeit*, Hamburg.

SHOSTAK, ARTHUR, and WILLIAM GOMBERG, eds. *Blue Collar World*. Englewood Cliffs, N.J.: Prentice-Hall, 1964.

SHOWALTER, ELAINE. "Dinah Mulock Craik and the Tactics of Sentiment: A Case Study in Victorian Female Authorship." *Fem. Studies*, 2, no. 2-3, 1975, 5-23.

______. "Feminism's Awkward Age: The Deflated Rebels of the 1920s." *Ms.*, 7, 1978, 64ff.

SILVER, CATHERINE BODARD. "Salon, Foyer, Bureau: Women and the Professions in France." *Amer. Jour. Sociol.*, 1973, 836-851.

SILVERMAN, ARLENE. "On Losing a Neighbor." *California Living*, Nov. 5, 1978, 44.

SILVERMAN, PHYLLIS R., ed. *Helping Each Other in Widowhood*. New York: Health Science Publishing Company, 1975.

SIMON, RITA. *The Contemporary Woman and Crime*. National Institute of Mental Health. Washington, D.C.: Government Printing Office, 1975.

______. "American Women and Crime." *Annals American Academy Political and Social Science*, 423, Jan. 1976, 31-46.

SMITH, DOROTHY E. "An Analysis of Ideological Structures and How Women Are Excluded: Considerations for Academic Women." Paper at Women's Studies Conference, University of Alberta, 1975.

______. "A Sociology for Women." In Julia Sherman and Evelyn Norton Beck, eds., *The Prism of Sex*. Madison, Wis.: University of Wisconsin Press, 1979.

SMITH, LILLIAN. *Killers of the Dream*. New York: Norton, 1949.

SMITH M. B. *The Single Woman of Today: Her Problems and Adjustment*. New York: Philosophical Library, 1962.

SMITH, RALPH E. *The Subtle Revolution*. Washington, D.C.: The Urban Institute, 1979.

______. Women in the Labor Force in 1990. Washington, D.C.: The Urban Institute, 1979.

SMITH-ROSENBERG, CARROLL. "Puberty to Menopause: The Cycle of Femininity in Nineteenth Century America." In Mary Hartman and Lois W. Banner, eds. *Clio's Consciousness Raised*. New York: Harper Torchbook, 1974, 23-37.

______. "The Female World of Love and Ritual: Relations between Women in Nineteenth-Century America." *Signs*, 1, 1975a, 1-28.

______. "The New Woman and the New History." *Feminist Studies*, 3, nos. 1-2, 1975, 185-198.

SMUTS, ROBERT W. *Women and Work in America*. New York: Columbia University Press, 1959.

SNYDER, ELOISE, ed. *The Study of Women: Enlarging Perspectives of Social Reality*. New York: Harper and Row, 1979.

SORENSON, E. RICHARD. "Growing Up as a Fore Is to Be 'In Touch' and Free." *Smithsonian*, vol. 8, May 1977. 107-114.

SOROKIN, PITIRIM. *Altruistic Love: A Study of American "Good Neighbors" and Christian Saints*. Boston: Beacon Press, 1950.

______. *The Ways and Power of Love*. Chicago: Henry Regnery, 1954.

______. *Social and Cultural Dynamics*. Englewood Cliffs, N.J.: Bedminster Press, 1962.

SPACKS, PATRICIA MEYER. *The Female Imagination*. New York: Avon, 1976.

SPITZE, GLENNA. "Role Experiences of Young Women: A Longitudinal Test of the Role Hiatus Hypothesis." *Jour. Mar. and Fam.*, 40, 1978, 471-480.

SPRADLEY, JAMES P., and BRENDA J. MANN. *The Cocktail Waitress: Woman's Work in a Man's World*. New York: Wiley, 1975.

STANLEY, JULIA P. "Paradigmatic Woman: The Prostitute." Paper presented at South Atlantic Modern Language Association, 1972.

STANNARD, UNA. *Mrs. Mann*. San Francisco: Germain Books, 1978.

STANSELL, CHRISTINE. "Women on the Great Plains 1865-1890." *Women's Studies*, 4, 1976, 87-98.

STATISTICAL ABSTRACT OF THE UNITED STATES 1977. Washington, D.C.: Government Printing Office, 1977.

STEARNS, PETER N. "Old Women: Some Historical Observations." *Journal Family History*, 5, Spring, 1980, 44-57.

STEINEM, GLORIA. "The Good News Is: These [College Years] Are *Not* the Best Years of Your Life!" *Ms.*, 8, Sept. 1978, 64-68.

______. "What Is a New Ms.?" *Ms.*, Nov., 1979, 4.

STEWART, ABIGAIL J., and PATRICIA SALT. "Changing Sex Roles: College Graduates of the Sixties and Seventies." 1978. Draft.

STIMPSON, CATHERINE. "The Right to Name." In Julia Sherman and Evelyn Norton Beck, eds. *The Prism of Sex.* Madison, Wis.: University of Wisconsin Press, 1979.

STINCHCOMBE, ARTHUR. "Social Structure and Organizations." In James March, ed., *Handbook of Organizations.* Chicago: Rand McNally, 1965, 142-193.

STOELTZE, BEVERLY L. " 'A Helpmate for Man Indeed,' The Image of the Frontier Woman." In Claire R. Farrer, ed., *Women and Folklore.* Austin: University of Texas Press, 1975, 25-41.

STOLLER, ROBERT J. *Sex and Gender: On the Development of Masculinity and Femininity.* New York: Science House, 1968.

STONE, MERLIN. *When God Was a Woman.* London: Quartet Books, 1976. British edition entitled *The Paradise Papers.*

STRAINCHAMPS, ETHEL. "Our Sexist Language." In Vivian Gornick and Barbara K. Moran, eds., *Woman in Sexist Society.* New York: Basic Books, 1971, 240-250.

STRONG, LESLIE D. "Alternative Marital and Family Forms." *Jour. Mar. and Fam.*, 40, 1978, 493-503.

SUMNER, W. G. *Folkways.* Boston: Ginn, 1906.

______. *What Social Classes Owe to Each Other.* Caldwell, Ohio: Caxton, 1883, 1952.

SUSSMAN, MARVIN B., and LEE BURCHINAL. "Kin Family Network: Unheralded Structure in Current Conceptualization of Family Functioning." *Marriage and Family Living*, 24, 1962, 231-240.

SWERDLOW, AMY. "The Greek Citizen Woman in Attica Vase Painting: New Views and New Questions." *Women's Studies*, 5, 1978, 267-284.

SWIFT, PAMELA. "Pregnancy — Status Symbol." *Parade*, June 22, 1977.

SZALAI, ALEXANDER. *The Use of Time: Daily Activities of Urban and Suburban Populations in Twelve Countries.* The Hague: Mouton, 1973.

______. "Women's Time. Women in the Light of Contemporary Time-Budget Research." Paper distributed as an official document at the Mexico City United Nations International Women's Year Conference, 1975.

TALLMAN, IRVING. "Working-Class Wives in Suburbia, Fulfillment or Crisis?" *Jour. Mar. and Fam.*, 31, 1969, 61-72.

______, and RAMONA MORGNER. "Life Style Differences among Urban and Suburban Blue-Collar Families." *Social Forces*, 48, 1970, 334-348.

TALMON, YONINA. "Social Aspects of Aging." *International Encyclopedia of the Social Sciences*, vol. 1. New York: Macmillan, 1968, 186-196.

TEMME, LLOYD V. *Occupation: Meaning and Measures.* Present citation from U.S. Civil Rights Commission, *Social Indicators of Equality for Minorities and Women*, 1978, 94-103.

TERRY, ROBERT M. "Trends in Female Crime: A Comparison of Adler, Simon, and Steffensmeier." Paper presented at Society for Study of Social Problems. San Francisco, 1978.

TETER, D. PARK. "Future Shock in Iran." *The Washington Post*, Dec. 10, 1978.

THOMAS, W. I. *The Unadjusted Girl.* Boston: Little, Brown, 1923.

THOMPSON, STITH. *The Folktale.* New York: Dryden Press, 1946.

THOMPSON, VERNON C. " 'Men's Lib' Seeks Alternatives to 'Macho Image.' " *The Washington Post*, October 31, 1977.

THORNE, BARRIE, and NANCY HENLEY, eds. *Language and Sex: Difference and Dominance*. Rowley, Mass.: Newbury House, 1975.

THWING, CHARLES FRANKLIN, and CARRIE F. BUTLER THWING. *The Family: An Historical and Social Study*. Boston: Lee and Shepard, 1887.

TIGER, LIONEL. *Men in Groups*. New York: Vintage, 1970.

TIGER, VIRGINIA, and GINA LURIA. "Inlaws/Outlaws: the Language of Women." In Douglas Butturf and Edmund L. Epstein, eds., *Women's Language and Style*. Akron: University of Akron Press, 1978, 1-10.

TILLION, GERMAINE. *Ravensbruck: An Eyewitness Account of a Women's Concentration Camp*. New York: Anchor, 1975.

TOCQUEVILLE, ALEXIS DE. *Democracy in America*, vol. 2. New York: J. and H. J. Langley, 1840.

TODASCO, RUTH, and others. *An Intelligent Woman's Guide to Dirty Words*. Chicago: Loop Center Y.W.C.A., 1973.

TOLCHIN, SUSAN J. *Women in Congress 1917-1976*. Washington, D.C.: House of Representatives Report no. 94-1732, June 25, 1976.

TÖNNIES, FERDINAND. *Community and Society* (Charles P. Loomis, trans. and ed.). New York: Harper Torchbooks, 1957. Original, 1887.

TOWNSEND, PETER. *The Family Life of Old People: An Inquiry in East London*. New York: Free Press, 1957.

TRAHEY, JANE. *Women and Power*. New York: Rawson, 1978.

TRESCOTT, JACQUELINE. "Black Feminist on the Front Line." *The Washington Post*, Feb. 7, 1979.

TRIPP, MAGGIE, ed. *Woman in the Year 2000*. New York: Arbor House, 1974.

TUCHMAN, GAYE. "Women and the Creation of Culture." In Marcia Millman and Rosabeth Moss Kanter, eds., *Another Voice*. New York: Anchor, 1975, 171-202.

______, ARLENE DANIELS, and JAMES BENET, eds. *Hearth and Home: Images of Women in the Mass Media*. New York: Oxford, 1978.

TURK, MIDGE. *The Buried Life: A Nun's Journey*. New York: World, 1971.

TURNER, RALPH. "Sponsored and Contest Mobility." *American Sociol. Rev.*, 25, 1960, 855-867.

TYLER, LEONA E. "Sex Differences." *International Encyclopedia of the Social Sciences*, vol. 7. New York: Macmillan, 1968, 210.

TYLOR, EDWARD B. *Primitive Culture*. Glouster, Mass.: Smith, 1958.

UDY, STANLEY H., JR. "Social Structural Analysis." *International Encyclopedia of the Social Sciences*, vol. 14. New York: Macmillan, 1968, 489-495.

UNGER, RHODA K. *Female and Male: Psychological Perspectives*. New York: Harper & Row, 1979.

Unsigned. "Political Woman: Public Role and Personal Challenges." *Carnegie Quarterly*, 22, 1974, 3-5.

Unsigned. "Women Lawmakers Are More Liberal." *The Washington Post*, July 1, 1975.

URNESS, CAROL L. "Mary Jane Hawes Holmes." In *Notable American Women*, Edward T. James, ed. Cambridge, Mass.: Belknap Press, 1971, 208-209.

VAN BEYME, KLAUS. "Class, Class Struggle." *Comparative Encyclopedia of Marxism, Communism, and Western Society*. New York: Herder and Herder, 2, 1972, 1-19.

Vanek, Joann. "Keeping Busy: Time Spent in Housework, United States, 1920-1970." Ph.D. dissertation, University of Michigan, Ann Arbor, 1973.

______. "Time Spent in Housework." *Scientific American*, Nov., 1974, 116-120.

Veblen, Thorstein. *Theory of the Leisure Class*. New York: Macmillan, 1917. Original, 1899.

Veevers, J. E. "Voluntary Childlessness: A Review of Issues and Evidence." Paper presented at meetings of International Sociological Association, Uppsala, 1978.

Veroff, Joseph. Unpublished study, 1950, referred to by David C. McClelland, *q.v.*, 405.

Veysey, Laurence R. "Martha Carey Thomas." In *Notable American Women*, Edward T. James, ed. Cambridge, Mass.: Belknap Press, 1971, 446-450.

Vinacke, W. Edgar. "Sex Roles in a Three-Person Game." *Sociometry*, 22, 1959, 343-360.

______, and John R. Bond. "Coalitions in Mixed Set Trends." *Sociometry*, 24, 1961, 61-75.

______, and Thomas C. Uesugi. "Strategy in a Feminine Game." *Sociometry*, 26, 1963, 75-88.

Vincent, Carol. *Women in Prison*. New York: Popular Library, 1976.

______. "Female Songwriters: How They Relate to the Female World." 1978. Draft.

Vinyard, JoEllen McNergney. "Women and the City: Immigrants and Native Americans in Detroit, 1880." Paper presented at Berkshire Conference, 1974.

Vogel, Lise. "The Arts and Feminism: The Awakening Consciousness." *Feminist Studies*, 2, 1974, 3-37.

Waite, Linda D., and Glenna D. Spitze. "Female Work Orientation and Marital Events: The Transition to Marriage and Motherhood." Paper presented at American Sociological Association, San Francisco, 1978.

Walker, Kathryn E., and Margaret E. Woods. *Time Use: A Measure of Household Production of Family Goods and Services*. Washington, D.C.: American Home Economics Association Center for the Family, 1976.

Wallace, Jennifer. "The Honeymoon Is Over, and the Houseworker Gets Hired." *Moving Mountains*, A Feminist Quarterly, 2, Winter, 1977, 4-5.

Wallace, Michele. "Black Macho and the Myth of Superwoman." *Ms.*, Jan. 1979, 45 ff.

Walshok, Mary Lindenstein. "Occupational Values and Family Roles: A Descriptive Study of Women Working in Blue-Collar and Service Occupations." Paper presented at a seminar at the National Institute of Mental Health. Feb., 1977.

Warner, W. Lloyd, and Paul S. Lunt. *The Social Life of a Modern Community*. New Haven: Yale University Press, 1941.

______. *The Status System of a Modern Community*. New Haven: Yale University Press, 1942.

Warren, Michelle Barcus. "The Work Role and Problem Coping: Sex Differentials in the Use of Helping Systems in Urban Communities." Paper at American Sociological Association, San Francisco, 1975.

Warrior, Betsy, and Lisa Leghorn. *Houseworker's Handbook*. Cambridge, Mass.: Leghorn and Warrior Woman's Center, 1975.

The Washington Post, editorial, April 16, 1979.

WATKINS, MARILYN (courtesy Lynne R. Dobrofsky). 1978. Draft.

WATT, IAN. *The Rise of the Novel.* Berkeley: University of California Press, 1963. Present citation from R. L. Coser, ed., *The Family: Its Structure and Functions.* New York: St. Martin's Press, 1964.

WEEKES, CLAIR. *Simple, Effective Treatment of Agoraphobia.* New York: Hawthorn Books, 1976.

WEISSMAN, MYRNA M., and EUGENE S. PAYKEL. *The Depressed Woman: A Study of Social Relationships.* Chicago: University of Chicago Press, 1974.

WEISSTEIN, NAOMI, and HEATHER BOOTH. "Will the Women's Movement Survive?" *Sister*, 4, no. 12, n.d., 1-6.

WEITZMAN, LENORE. "Legal Regulation of Marriage: Tradition and Change." *California Law Review*, 62, 1974, 1169-1288.

WEKERLE, GERDA. "Vertical Village: Social Contacts in a Singles Highrise Complex." Paper presented at American Sociological Association, San Francisco, 1975.

______, REBECCA PETERSON, and DAVID MORLEY. *New Space for Women.* Boulder, Colo.: Westview Press, 1980.

WELTER, BARBARA. "The Cult of True Womanhood." In Wendy Martin, ed., *The American Sisterhood.* New York: Harper & Row, 1972, 243-256.

WERTZ, RICHARD W., and DOROTHY C. WERTZ. *Lying-In: A History of Childbirth in America.* New York: Free Press, 1977.

WEST, CANDACE, and DON H. ZIMMERMAN. "Women's Place in Everyday Talk: Reflections of Parent-Child Interaction." Paper presented at American Sociological Association, San Francisco, 1975.

WEST, HOLLIE I. "Michelle Wallace: Point, Counterpoint." *The Washington Post*, Feb. 7, 1979.

WEST, UTA. "Friends and Females." *Viva*, 2, 1975, 37-38, 106-108.

WESTLEY, WILLIAM A., and NATHAN B. EPSTEIN. *The Silent Majority.* San Francisco: Jossey-Bass, 1969.

WHYTE, WILLIAM E. *The Organization Man.* New York: Simon and Schuster, 1956.

WIEBE, ROBERT. *The Search for Order, 1877-1920.* New York: Hill & Wang, 1967.

WIKLER, NORMA JULIET. "Coming in and Moving Up: Women in the Health Professions." Keynote address at the Program for Women in Health Sciences, San Francisco, June, 1977.

WILLIAMSON, NANCY E. "Sex Preferences, Sex Control, and the Status of Women." *Signs*, 1, 1976, 847-862.

WILSON, E. O. *Sociobiology: The New Synthesis.* Cambridge: Belknap-Harvard, 1975.

WILSON, LOGAN. "The Sociography of Groups." In Georges Gurvich and W. E. Moore, eds., *20th Century Sociology.* New York: Philosophical Library, 1945.

WINTER, DAVID. Participant in Radcliffe College Centennial Symposium on Women and Power, an Exploratory View, 1979, Washington, D.C. Present citation from *Proceedings*, p. vii.

WIREMAN, PEGGY. "The Functions of Intimate Secondary Relationships." Paper presented at International Sociological Association. Uppsala. 1978.

WISEMAN, JACQUELINE. *The Social Psychology of Sex*. New York: Harper & Row, 1976.

WOLF, DEBORAH. *The Lesbian Community*. Berkeley: University of California Press, 1979.

WOLF, MARGERY. "Chinese Women: Old Skills in a New Context." In Rosaldo and Lamphere, eds., *Woman, Culture, and Society*. Stanford: Stanford University Press, 1974, 157-172.

WOLIN, SHELDON S. "Political Theory." *International Encyclopedia of the Social Sciences*, vol. 12. New York: Macmillan, 1968, 307-318.

WOLLSTONECRAFT, MARY. *A Vindication of the Rights of Women*. New York: Norton, 1967.

WOMEN'S ACTION ALLIANCE. *Women's Agenda*, vol. 1, no. 1, Feb. 1976.

WOMEN'S BUREAU. *Handbook of Women Workers*. Washington, D.C.: Government Printing Office, 1975.

WOOD, ANN DOUGLAS. "The Literature of Impoverishment: The Women Local Colorists in America 1865-1914." *Women's Studies*, 1, 1972, 3-46.

WOOD, MARY I. *The History of the General Federation of Women's Clubs*. Farmingdale, N.Y.: Dabor Services, Inc., 1979.

WRIGLEY, E. A., *Population and History*. London: University Library, 1969.

WRIGHT, QUINCY. "The Study of War." In *International Encyclopedia of the Social Sciences*, vol. 16. New York: Macmillan, 1968, 453-468.

YANKELOVICH, DANIEL, INC. *Generations Apart*. New York: Columbia Broadcasting System, 1969.

YOUNG, MICHAEL, and PETER WILLMOTT. *Family and Kinship in East London*. Baltimore: Penguin, 1962.

ZBOROWSKI, MARK, and ELIZABETH HERZOG. *Life Is with People: The Culture of the Shtetl*. New York: Schocken, 1952.

ZELDITCH, MORRIS. "Social Status." *International Encyclopedia of the Social Sciences*, vol. 15. New York: Macmillan, 1968, 251-256.

ZELLMAN, GAIL L. "The Role of Structural Factors in the Maintenance of the Sexual Status Quo." N.d. Draft.

ZIHLMAN, ADRIENNE L. "Motherhood in Transition: From Ape to Human." In Miller and Newman, eds., *The First Child and Family Formation*. Chapel Hill, N. C.: Carolina Population Center, 1978, 35-50.

———, and NANCY TURNER. "Women in Evolution: Part I: Innovation and Selection in Human Origins." *Signs*, 1, 1976, 585-608.

ZURCHER, LOUIS A., JR. *The Mutable Self: A Self-Concept for Social Change*. Beverly Hills, Calif.: Sage Publications, 1977.

Name Index

Subject Index

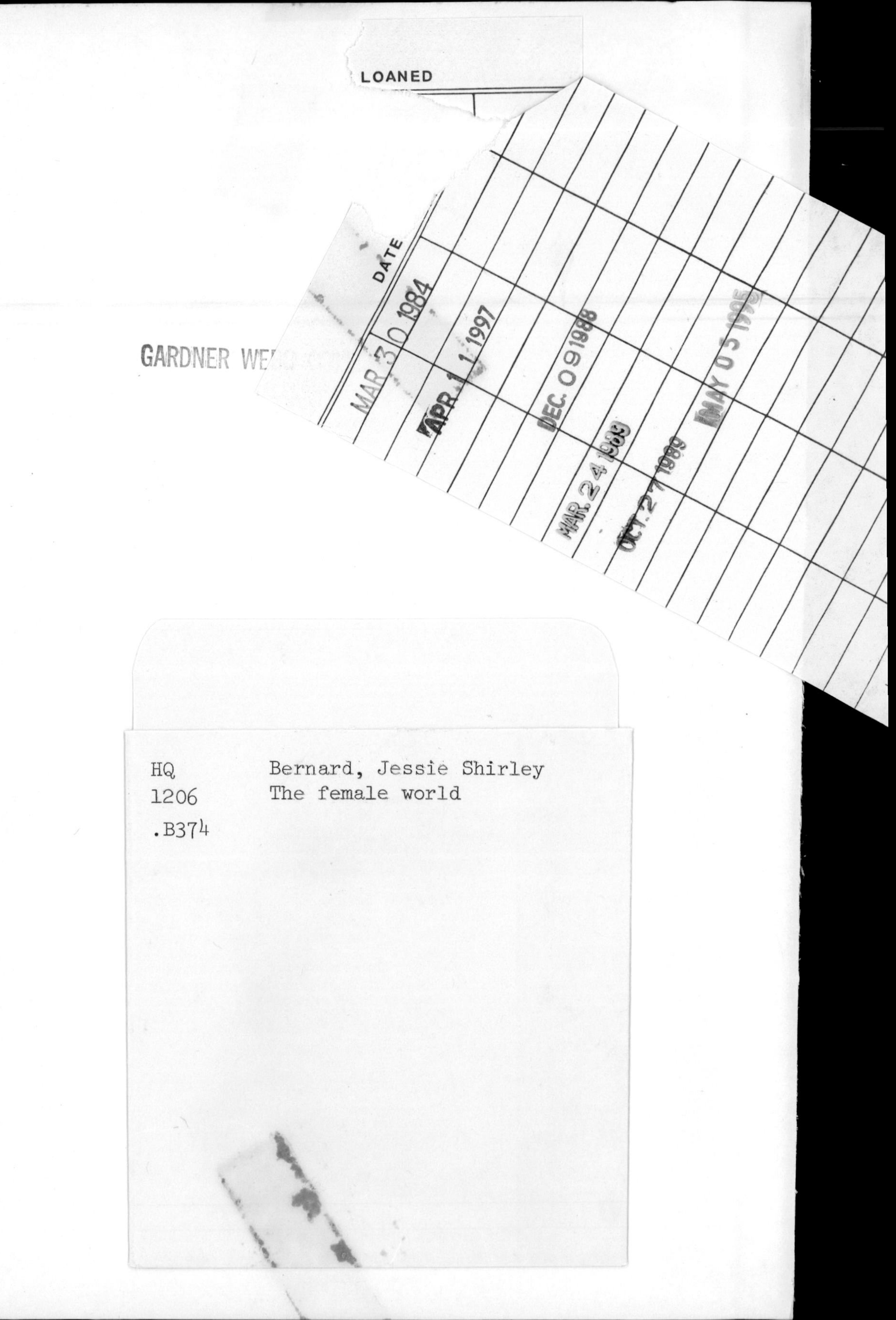

LOANED
DATE
MAR 30 1984
APR 11 1997
DEC 09 1988
MAR 24 1989
OCT 27 1989
MAY 05 1995
GARDNER WE